PUBLIC HUMAN RESOURCE MANAGEMENT

SIXTH EDITION

This book is dedicated to
Steven W. Hays
Scholar, mentor, and friend.

—R.C.K., J.D.C.

SAGE was founded in 1965 by Sara Miller McCune to support the dissemination of usable knowledge by publishing innovative and high-quality research and teaching content. Today, we publish more than 850 journals, including those of more than 300 learned societies, more than 800 new books per year, and a growing range of library products including archives, data, case studies, reports, and video. SAGE remains majority-owned by our founder, and after Sara's lifetime will become owned by a charitable trust that secures our continued independence.

Los Angeles | London | New Delhi | Singapore | Washington DC

PUBLIC HUMAN RESOURCE MANAGEMENT

PROBLEMS AND PROSPECTS

SIXTH EDITION

Richard C. Kearney
North Carolina State University

Jerrell D. Coggburn
North Carolina State University

Editors

Los Angeles | London | New Delhi
Singapore | Washington DC

Los Angeles | London | New Delhi
Singapore | Washington DC

FOR INFORMATION:

CQ Press

An Imprint of SAGE Publications, Inc.

2455 Teller Road

Thousand Oaks, California 91320

E-mail: order@sagepub.com

SAGE Publications Ltd.

1 Oliver's Yard

55 City Road

London EC1Y 1SP

United Kingdom

SAGE Publications India Pvt. Ltd.

B 1/I 1 Mohan Cooperative Industrial Area

Mathura Road, New Delhi 110 044

India

SAGE Publications Asia-Pacific Pte. Ltd.

3 Church Street

#10-04 Samsung Hub

Singapore 049483

Acquisitions Editor: Sarah Calabi

Editorial Assistant: Katie Lowry

Production Editor: Laura Barrett

Copy Editor: Lynn Weber

Typesetter: C&M Digitals (P) Ltd.

Proofreader: Eleni Georgiou

Indexer: Michael Ferreira

Cover Designer: Anupama Krishan

Marketing Manager: Amy Whitaker

This book was previously published by Pearson Education, Inc.

Printed in the United States of America

ISBN 978-1-4833-9345-2

This book is printed on acid-free paper.

15 16 17 18 19 10 9 8 7 6 5 4 3 2 1

TABLE OF CONTENTS

PREFACE

The first edition of this volume was published in 1983. When that book appeared, the Civil Service Reform Act of 1978 was just five years old, and words such as *managerialism, reinvention, outsourcing,* and the *new public management* had not yet been coined, at least in the context of public sector human resource management (HRM). Subsequent editions of the anthology have attempted to keep students apprised of the massive changes that have occurred in this field over the years. As such, the tables of contents from the previous five editions mirror shifting emphases, values, techniques, and—consistent with our enduring focus—differing *problems and prospects.*

In attempting to characterize the unstable ground upon which this discipline sits, we have used many different adjectives, including such hyperbolic expressions as *paradigm shift* (perhaps the least original of all choices) and *technical revolution.* However phrased, the central message that we have tried to convey—and which we continue to address in this version of the book—is that of rapid transformation and adjustment to diverse environmental stimuli. Today's students would not recognize the merit systems that typically existed in 1983, nor would practitioners of that era have been able to anticipate or appreciate many of the topics that are now central to this field. For that matter, the name of the field itself has been changing: from public personnel management (PPM) to public personnel administration (PPA), to human resource management (HRM) to strategic human resource management (SRHM) to human capital management (HCM). Such

evolution (confusion?) of nomenclature is partly placing old wine in new bottles, but it is also reflective of the field's dynamic qualities and its shifting values. We continue to believe that *Public Human Resource Management: Problems and Prospects* best captures the breadth of topics contained in this edition and, arguably, earlier ones.

We begin this anthology with a recommendation to readers that they take a moment to contemplate just how different the field is compared with that of thirty years ago. Already one of the original editors, Steve Hays, has retired to his lake house in South Carolina. From such an historical perch one marvels at the accomplishments (and, perhaps, recoils at the mistakes) that have occurred during a long and especially critical period in the evolution of public administration. Readers would be well served to familiarize themselves with the historical context that helped to spawn the changes documented in the twenty-seven original chapters contained in this volume. We think you will find the differences in contemporary HRM to be both extraordinary and profound.

As has been our intent since the beginning, the basic purpose of this anthology is to provide readers with a concise overview of the challenges (problems) and adjustments (prospects) of modern public HRM. To keep pace with developments in real-world HRM, this means that major alterations have been made in the content of this volume. Past editions of the book invested perhaps inordinate amounts of space on such topics as workplace diversity, affirmative action and equal employment opportunity (AA/EEO), merit system operation, and the like. While these traditional topics have become less salient, new topics have emerged. We hope that we have captured the essence of these shifting priorities in the readings that follow. Although the traditional challenges and techniques retain much of their significance, no contemporary work on HRM would be complete without paying attention to such topics as nonprofit management, postemployment benefits, emotional labor, benchmarking, and social media. Not one of these topics was contained in the previous edition of this book, but all now merit a complete chapter.

Consistent with past practice, this volume consists of originally authored manuscripts that represent a cross-section of the timeliest and best-informed scholarship in the area of public HRM. The book contains a mix of thought pieces, descriptive analyses, overviews of HRM in various settings, and theoretical essays. To be true to our promise of providing a solid overview of both problems and prospects, the selections summarize the biggest challenges confronting HRM practitioners and offer substantive suggestions for improving the practice of HRM. Obviously, then, the chapters focus more on the *future* of the field than its past (which provides one more incentive to the reader to examine the precursors of contemporary HRM reform). We are more concerned with providing the reader with a sense of where the discipline is headed, rather than where it has been.

Each chapter was prepared specifically for inclusion in this volume. The authors are established figures in public sector HRM; many of them practice and consult in the field as well. They were selected on the basis of their recognized competence in, and past contributions to, the topical areas that are addressed in their essays. The present volume is almost completely different from its immediate predecessor. Of the twenty-seven chapters (seven more than in the last edition), ten are authored by individuals who were not included in previous editions of the book. Only a few of the chapters might be considered updated versions of previous writings (and even these are each significantly updated). The number of new authors and topics provide clear evidence

of the changing nature of HRM, the expanding ranks of scholars, and the inherent value found in the "new scholarship" of HRM (a promise that was made in the first edition). We confess to being quite pleased with the group that has been assembled to share their perspectives and hope that you will agree that their insights are worthy of recognition.

The contributions are organized into four broad sections: The Setting, The Techniques, The Issues, and Prospects/Conclusion. Section One provides a thorough treatment of the political, legal, institutional, and managerial trends that serve as catalysts in the transformation of HRM. These chapters also contain sufficient contextual background to help contemporary students understand the significance of current developments across this panoramic field.

Section Two summarizes developments in the practice of HRM, with special emphasis on emerging personnel techniques and the ways that traditional approaches to the staffing function are being revised. Selections within Section Two address what are perhaps the most troublesome technical challenges of the age, including strategic HRM, performance appraisal, compensation dilemmas, benchmarking, and employee rights.

Section Three provides incisive discussions of eight critical issues in the field, including AA/EEO, gender issues, ethics, disability issues, veterans preference, labor relations, social media in the workplace, and HRM contracting.

Section Four—the conclusion—contains two chapters that offer both a prospective and retrospective capstone treatment of the field. Despite previous efforts to forecast the future that have humbled us, we venture once again fearlessly into the murky unknown.

As in the case with all four previous editions, a prime consideration in the design, preparation, and organization of the book was that it be sufficiently readable for both graduate and undergraduate students. For this reason, the authors were asked to provide enough background information so that both beginning and advanced students could understand and benefit from the content. Additionally, the authors were requested to furnish concrete examples and practical information to enhance the volume's applicability to practitioners wishing to broaden their perspectives in the field. We are satisfied that these objectives have been met in every respect.

Our principal debt in assembling this anthology is to our contributing authors. They richly deserve our sincere thanks, for their efforts are obviously the heart and soul of what follows. Because there are so many luminaries and emerging scholars in the area of public sector HRM, it was very difficult to decide which ones to ask for contributions. One of our continuing objectives is to bring new perspectives to this work. In so doing, we sincerely hope that anyone not included in this particular volume is not offended. With luck, there will be a seventh edition within a few years, thereby enabling us to call upon the talents of other leading scholars.

The contributors to the sixth edition of *Public Human Resource Management: Problems and Prospects* produced quality manuscripts and exhibited remarkable patience with our repeated requests for revision, clarification, and elaboration. We hope that all of the contributors are aware of the depth and sincerity of our appreciation.

Finally, we wish to thank those kind academic souls who have adopted previous editions or their courses in public HRM. This book has proven to have remarkably long legs in the profession, a reality that could only be made possible by the support and thoughtfulness of our fellow HRM faculty colleagues. Should any of you wish to communicate with us about this volume, or to propose future amendments or clarifications, please do not hesitate to do so.

The first five editions were coedited by Steve Hays of the University of South Carolina. Steve is content to allow HRM to move on without him, but he has left an indelible mark not only on this book, but on research and teaching in the field. We dedicate this sixth edition to Steve and his legacy in public HRM.

Richard C. Kearney
Jerrell D. Coggburn

PART I

THE SETTING

CHAPTER 1

COMPETING PERSPECTIVES ON PUBLIC PERSONNEL ADMINISTRATION: CIVIL SERVICE, NONSTANDARD WORK ARRANGEMENTS, PRIVATIZATION, AND PARTNERSHIPS

Donald E. Klingner
University of Colorado at Colorado Springs

ABSTRACT

This chapter (1) presents a historical perspective on public human resource management; (2) examines the effect of privatization and partnerships on traditional HRM values and systems; (3) discusses how privatization, partnerships and nonstandard work arrangements affect productivity, and (4) explores how the structure of HRM and the role of managers and HR managers changes under these alternative values, systems, and strategies.

A HISTORICAL PERSPECTIVE ON PUBLIC HUMAN RESOURCE MANAGEMENT

Public human resource management (HRM) in the United States can be viewed from at least four perspectives (Klingner, Nalbandian, and Llorens 2010). First, it is the functions (planning, acquisition, development, and discipline) needed to manage HR in public agencies. Second, it is the processes by which public jobs, as scarce resources, are allocated. Third, it is the interaction

among fundamental societal values that often conflict. These values are responsiveness, efficiency, employee rights, and social equity. Responsiveness means a budget process that allocates positions and therefore sets priorities and an appointment process that considers political or personal loyalty along with education and experience as indicators of merit. Efficiency means staffing decisions based on ability and performance rather than political loyalty. Employee rights mean selection and promotion based on merit, as defined by objective measures of ability and performance, and employees who are free to apply their knowledge, skills, and abilities without partisan political interference. Social equity means public jobs allocated proportionately based on gender, race, and other designated criteria. Fourth, public human resource management is the embodiment of human resource systems: the laws, rules, organizations, and procedures used to fulfill personnel functions in ways that express the abstract values.

Historically, U.S. public HRM systems developed in evolutionary stages or eras, analytically separate but, in practice, overlapping (see Table 1.1). As discussed in more detail below, in the *patrician* era (1789–1828), the small group of upper-class property owners who had won independence and established the national government held most public jobs. As this generation passed, an era of *patronage* emerged (1829–1882) during which public jobs were awarded according to political loyalty or party affiliation. Next, the increased size and complexity of public activities led to an era of *professionalism* (1883–1932) that defined public HRM as a neutral administrative function so as to emphasize modernization through efficiency and democratization by allocating public jobs, at least at the federal level, on merit (Heclo 1977). The unprecedented demands of a global

Table 1.1 The Evolution of Public HRM Systems and Values in the United States

Stage of Evolution	Dominant Value(s)	Dominant System(s)	Pressures for Change
Patrician Era (1789–1828)	Responsiveness	"Government by elites"	Political parties + Patronage
Patronage (1829–1882)	Responsiveness	Patronage	Modernization + Democratization
Professionalism (1883–1932)	Efficiency + Individual rights	Civil service	Responsiveness + Effective government
Performance (1933–1964)	Responsiveness + Efficiency + Individual rights	Patronage + Civil service	Individual rights + Social equity
People (1965–1979)	Responsiveness + Efficiency + Individual rights + Social equity	Patronage + Civil service + Collective bargaining + Affirmative action	Dynamic equilibrium among four competing values and systems
Privatization (1980–present)	Responsiveness + Efficiency + Individual accountability + Limited government + Community responsibility	Patronage + Civil service + Collective bargaining + Affirmative action + Alternative mechanisms + Flexible employment relationships	Dynamic equilibrium among four progovernmental values and systems, and three antigovernmental values and systems
Partnerships (2002—present)	Responsiveness + Efficiency + Individual accountability + Limited government + Community responsibility + Collaboration	Patronage + Civil service + Collective bargaining + Affirmative action + Alternative mechanisms + Flexible employment relationships	Dynamic equilibrium among four progovernmental values and systems, and three antigovernmental values and systems

depression and World War II led to the emergence of a hybrid *performance* model (1933–1964) that combined the political leadership of patronage systems and the merit principles of civil service systems. Next, social upheavals (1965–1979) presaged the emergence of the *people* era in which collective bargaining emerged to represent collective employee rights (the equitable treatment of members by management through negotiated work rules for wages, benefits, and working conditions), and affirmative action emerged to represent social equity (through voluntary or court-mandated recruitment and selection practices to help ameliorate the underrepresentation of minorities and women in the workforce). Thus, by 1980 U.S. public HRM could be described as a dynamic equilibrium among four competing values, each championed by a particular system, for allocating scarce public jobs.

THE EMERGENT PARADIGMS: PRIVATIZATION AND PARTNERSHIPS

The *privatization* paradigm emerged at the end of the 1970s when President Carter campaigned by running against the national government as a Washington "outsider." Following his election, he proposed the 1978 Civil Service Reform Act on grounds that included poor performance in the public service and difficulty in controlling and directing bureaucrats. Beginning in 1981, the Reagan administration, though starting from fundamentally different values and policy objectives, continued to cast government as part of the problem. Consequently, this paradigm shift was marked by increasing reliance on market-based forces, rather than program implementation by government agencies and employees, as the most efficacious tools of public policy. The emphasis on economic perspectives and administrative efficiency reflected the intense pressures on the public sector to "do more with less." This caused governments to become more accountable through such techniques as program budgeting, management by objectives, program evaluation, and management information systems. It also caused efforts to lower expenditures through tax and expenditure ceilings, deficit reduction, deferred expenditures, accelerated tax collection, service fees and user charges, and a range of legislative and judicial efforts to shift program responsibilities and costs away from each affected government.

The 1990s and 2000s brought continued efforts to reduce government—either by increasing its responsiveness and effectiveness or by "shrinking the beast" and putting more resources in the hands of individuals and businesses. These were exemplified by Vice President Gore's National Performance Review (National Performance Review 1993a, 1993b), aimed at creating a government that "works better and costs less" through fundamental changes in organizational structure and accountability, epitomized by the terms "reinventing government" or "new public management" (Osborne and Gaebler 1992). The Republican Party swept into control of Congress in 1994, 2002, and 2010 as a result of a shift toward three emergent nongovernmental values: personal accountability, limited and decentralized government, and community responsibility for social services. Proponents of personal accountability expect people to make individual choices consistent with their own goals and accept responsibility for the consequences of these choices, rather than passing responsibility for their actions on to society. Proponents of limited and decentralized government believe that government is to be feared for its power to arbitrarily or capriciously deprive individuals of their rights. They also believe that public policy, service delivery, and revenue generation can be controlled efficiently in a smaller unit of government in a way not possible in a larger one. And for some, a reduction in government size and scope is justified by perceived government ineffectiveness; by a high value accorded to individual freedom, responsibility, and accountability; and finally, by a desire to devote a smaller share of personal income to taxes. The most significant consequence of the emergence of the third value (community responsibility), at least as far as public HRM is concerned, has the delivery of local governments social services through NGOs funded by taxes, user fees, and charitable contributions.

Third-party social service provision has become more complex with an ideologically driven emphasis that directs contracting strategies towards faith-based organizations (FBOs). With the passage of the "charitable choice" component of the 1996 Personal Responsibility and Work Opportunity Reconciliation Act, charitable choice has expanded to include a range of federal programs, such as Temporary Assistance to Needy Families (1996); Welfare to Work Formula Grants (1997); Community Services Block Grants (1998); and drug abuse treatment programs (2000). The White House Center for Faith-Based and Communities Initiatives (CFBCI) and five similar offices in the Departments of Education, Justice, Health and Human Services, Labor and Housing and Urban Development were established to contract with faith-based agencies nationwide. According to a study conducted by the Rockefeller Institute of Government (2003), thirty-two states had also contracted with FBOs to provide some social services, and eight states had enacted legislation requiring the inclusion of FBOs in contracting. More recently, state departments of labor received directives from the U.S. Department of Labor (DOL) CFBCI requiring the development of state DOL strategic plans specifically aimed at increasing the number of faith-based grantees by providing training and technical assistance to these organizations as they competed for service provision contracts.

This emerging *partnerships* paradigm rests on the same values of personal accountability, limited and decentralized government, and community responsibility for social services that characterized the *privatization* paradigm, with an added strategic emphasis on cooperative service delivery among governments, businesses, and NGOs. The strategic element of this paradigm is undergirded by the belief that concrete results in public service delivery can only be achieved by the skilled deployment of human assets regardless of the framework within which it occurs. This new framework's advocates also argue that the skilled deployment of human assets is best accomplished outside of the traditional civil service model. This has combined with anti-union sentiment,

due also to public and legislative pressure to reduce the negative impacts of health care costs and defined benefit pension systems on state and local governments. These pressures increased dramatically due to the ideological effects of "Tea Party" Republicans in the 2010 midterm congressional elections. Because state and local governments depend heavily on property taxes, the collapse of real estate markets beginning in 2008 stressed their budgets. At the same time, the "Great Recession" of 2008–2011 resulted in decreased equity prices and returns and thus posed a long-term threat to the financial solvency of public employee pension systems.

As a result of combined financial pressures and anti-union sentiment, many states are rethinking and reinventing their public personnel systems, from far-reaching efforts in Georgia and Florida, the abolition of public sector collective bargaining in Wisconsin, and other more nuanced efforts to enhance third-party service delivery options (Selden 2006; Cayer and Kime 2006; Naff 2006; Hays, Byrd, and Wilkins 2006; Fox and Lavigna 2006; Nigro and Kellough 2006; Bowman, West, and Gertz 2006; Coggburn 2006; Battaglio and Condrey 2006).

Privatization and partnerships both rely upon the same two basic HRM strategies: using alternative organizations and mechanisms to deliver public services, and increasing the flexibility of employment relationships for the remaining public employees through a variety of nonstandard work arrangements (NSWAs).

Alternative Organizations and Mechanisms

These alternatives include purchase-of-service agreements, privatization, franchise agreements, subsidy arrangements, vouchers, volunteerism, and regulatory and tax incentives (International City Management Association 1989). These are not new. But they are increasingly common, and they supplant traditional service delivery by civil service employees hired through appropriated funding of public agencies.

Purchase-of-service agreements with other governmental agencies and NGOs have become commonplace. They enable cities and counties to offer services within a given geographic area, utilizing economies of scale. They offer smaller municipalities a way of reducing or avoiding capital expenses, personnel costs, and political issues associated with collective bargaining, and legal liability risks. In addition, the use of consultants (individuals or businesses hired under fee-for-service arrangements on an as-needed basis) increases available expertise and managerial flexibility by reducing the range of qualified technical and professional employees that the agency must otherwise hire.

Privatization, as the term is generally used in the United States, means that while a public agency provides a particular service, the service is produced and delivered by a private contractor (Savas 2000). It may result in the abolition of the agency (at times an intended ideological goal). Privatization offers all the advantages of service purchase agreements but holds down labor and construction costs on a larger scale. It has become commonplace in areas like solid waste disposal where there is an easily identifiable "benchmark" (standard cost and service comparison with the private sector) and where public agency costs tend to be higher because of higher pay and benefits (Kosar 2006; Siegel 1999; O'Looney 1998; Martin 1999).

Franchise agreements often allow businesses to monopolize a previously public function (e.g., cable TV and jitneys as a public transit option) within a geographic area, charge competitive rates for it, and then pay the appropriate government a fee for the privilege. Cities encourage franchising because it reduces their own costs, provides some revenue in return, and results in continuation of a desirable public service.

Subsidy arrangements enable private businesses to provide public services funded by either user fees to clients or cost reimbursement from public agencies. Examples are emergency medical services provided by private hospitals and reimbursed by public health systems, and rent subsidies to enable low-income residents to live in private apartments as an alternative to public housing projects.

Vouchers enable individuals to purchase public goods or services from competing providers on the open market. For example, educational voucher systems allow parents to apply a voucher to defray the cost of education for their children at competing public or private institutions, as an alternative to public school monopolies.

Volunteers contribute services otherwise performed by paid employees, or not at all. These include community crime watch programs in cooperation with local police departments, classroom teachers' aides who provide tutoring and individual assistance in many public schools, and community residents who volunteer services as individuals or through churches, and other nonprofit service agencies. Frequently, such contributions are required to "leverage" a federal or state grant of appropriated funds. Though they would probably not consider themselves volunteers (and still less as public agency "clients"), prison inmates are often responsible for laundry, food service, and facilities maintenance.

Regulatory and tax incentives encourage the private sector to perform functions that might otherwise be performed by public agencies with public funds. These include the zoning variances for roads, parking, and waste disposal granted to condominium associations. In return, the association provides services normally performed by local government (e.g., security, waste disposal, and maintenance of common areas).

Nonstandard Work Arrangements

All these alternative mechanisms provide public services without using public employees and in many cases without using appropriated funds. Yet even in those cases where public services continue to be provided by public employees working in public agencies funded by appropriations, massive changes have occurred in employment practices. Chief among these are increased use of temporary, part-time, and seasonal employment and increased hiring of exempt employees (those outside the classified civil service) through employment contracts. Increasingly, public employers reduce costs and enhance flexibility by meeting minimal staffing requirements through career civil service employees and hiring other employees "at will" into temporary or part-time positions (Mastracci and Thompson 2005).

These temps usually receive lower salaries and benefits than their career counterparts and are certainly unprotected by due process entitlements or collective bargaining agreements. Alternatively, where commitment and high skills are required on a temporary basis, employers may seek to save money or maintain flexibility by using contract or leased employees in exempt positions. While contracts may be routinely renewed with mutual approval, such "employees" may also be discharged at will in the event of a personality conflict, a change in managerial objectives, or a budget shortfall. These professional and technical workers usually receive higher salaries and benefits than can be offered to even highly qualified civil servants, and they enable management to cut personnel costs quickly if necessary without having to resort to seniority-based layoffs and the bureaucratic chaos precipitated by the exercise of civil service "bumping rights."

As this trend continues, the workforce of the future will include multiple work arrangements for workers hired under different terms and conditions. At a minimum, these include traditional employees hired to "permanent" full-time or part-time positions to civil service positions that may also be covered by collective bargaining agreements. They also include other workers hired to NSWAs—temporary workers (neither unionized nor covered by civil service), contract workers (hired through temp agencies, individual performance contracts, or contracts with their private employers), and volunteers.

Recalling that the first definition of HRM is the policies and procedures that determine how employees are managed, these multiple systems have developed because of the advantages they offer employers. We see a shift toward NSWAs because of their presumed greater flexibility, efficiency, and ideological conformance with market values. In practice, this means less concern for traditional hiring, training, and performance evaluation practices and more concern for contract-based employment. Contract workers are expected to have current competencies. Because their work is time-limited by the terms of a contract, counseling and performance appraisal are less vital than under collective bargaining

or civil service systems. Given the lack of career emphasis or protection, sanctions increasingly involve nothing more than the nonrenewal of a contract with individuals or with a firm.

The new strategies diminish employee rights. It is more likely that employees hired at will into temporary and part-time positions will receive lower pay and benefits and will be unprotected by civil service regulations or collective bargaining agreements. Whether or not the political neutrality of public employees suffers in this environment is unknown presently, but it seems logical to assume that as the criteria for success become more arbitrary or capricious, civil service employees—particularly those in mid-management positions—will begin to behave more like the political appointees whose jobs depend on political or personal loyalty to elected officials (Brewer and Maranto 2000).

The new strategies also threaten social equity (Wilson 2006). Pay comparisons over the past twenty years have uniformly concluded that minorities and women in public agencies are closer to equal pay for equal work than are their private sector counterparts. Managerial consultants are overwhelmingly white and male. Many part-time and temporary positions are exempt from laws prohibiting discrimination against persons with disabilities or family medical responsibilities.

These complex systems create conflicting expectations and accountability based on political, administrative, and market perspectives. An organization that primarily manages contracts may not be able to adequately manage performance. When an organization's workforce includes both NSWA workers and traditional employees, the result is always complexity and often confusion and uncertainty over the psychological contract (terms of employment) between the organization and its employees.

THE EFFECTS OF PRIVATIZATION, PARTNERSHIPS, AND NSWAS ON PERFORMANCE

The impact of the new strategies on efficiency has been mixed. On the plus side, the change in public agency culture toward identifying customers and providing market-based services increases productivity. And the threat of privatization or layoffs has forced unions to agree to pay cuts, to reduced employer-funded benefits, and to changes in work rules (Cohen and Eimicke 1994). But the personnel techniques that have become more common under these emergent systems may actually increase some personnel costs, particularly those connected with employment of independent contractors, reemployed annuitants, and temporary employees (Peters and Savoie 1994). Downsizing may eventually lead to higher recruitment, orientation, and training costs and loss of the organizational memory and "core expertise" necessary to effectively manage contracting or privatization initiatives (Milward 1996). Minimum staffing usually results in increased payment of overtime and higher rates of employee accidents and injuries. As the civil service workforce shrinks, it is also aging. This means increases in pension payouts, disability retirements, workers' compensation claims, and healthcare costs.

What is emerging, then, is a human resource framework that paradoxically embraces both collaborative and control-oriented managerial styles, exposing the underlying tensions inherent in the values of monitoring (compliance) and empowerment (outcomes). The tensions are evidenced by the debates over the desire to maintain control mechanisms associated with traditional civil service systems (risk adversity) and the strategic attractiveness of responsiveness and managerial empowerment (stewardship). Yet rising levels of ambiguity and turbulence at the national and state levels of government demand understandings that move beyond *either/or* thinking (Kisfalvi 2000).

Opposing and interwoven elements are evident throughout government as citizens and public officials struggle with the coexistence of authority and democracy, efficiency and creativity, freedom and control (Lewis 2000). The new HRM paradigm may be increasingly about the management of both control and collaboration and, more critically, about developing understandings and practices that accept, accommodate, and even

encourage these tensions. As an example, increasingly state government agencies are using a model of collaborative social service provision and approaches to addressing social problems. These often involve overlapping partnerships with various public sector organizations, a recognition that the complexity of social issues is in part due to its residence within an interorganizational framework, and a recognition that these problems cannot be tackled by any one organization acting alone. These new and often confusing organizational relationships suggest that HR managers will not only need to manage control and collaboration simultaneously but also become much more sophisticated in the competencies needed to work across organizational boundaries (Klingner 2008).

However, collaboration brings its own sets of problems in that contract compliance, rather than traditional supervisory practices, becomes the primary quality control mechanism. This creates a real possibility of fraud and abuse (Moe 1987). In this regard, state and local governments' experience suggests that privatization and service contracting outcomes are most likely to be successful when governments:

- Pick a service with clear objectives that can be measured and monitored
- Use in-house or external competition and avoid sole source contracting
- Develop adequate cost accounting systems to compare service alternatives and monitor contractor performance
- Consider negative externalities such as impacts on an existing workforce, impacts on the local economy, other governments or functions, governmental policies, or certain societal groups (Siegel 1999)

The impact of contemporary HRM strategies on the last traditional value (political responsiveness) is also problematic. Public-private partnerships raise fundamental accountability and performance issues for elected officials and public managers (Klingner, Nalbandian, and Romzek 2002). The emergent values and systems alter the fundamental role of government by placing greater emphasis on individuals and by shifting the focus of governmental social service delivery from a national to a state and local level. Continual budget cuts and pressures can result in a budget-driven rather than mission-driven agency. Budget-driven agencies that address public problems with short-term solutions designed to meet short-term legislative objectives are not likely to be effective. Long-range planning, or indeed any planning beyond the current budget cycle, is likely to become less important. Agencies will not be able to prepare effective capital budgets or to adequately maintain capital assets (human or infrastructure).

The conflict between traditional and emergent paradigms represents a fundamental conflict over the appropriate role of government in society. Supporters of privatization and partnerships see them as an opportunity to reduce the size of government ("downsizing") and reaffirm the basic competitive advantage of market-based models and the legitimacy of individual accountability and community responsibility. Critics see them as a retreat from hard-won historical advances in health, education, and welfare, and the acceptance— implicit or explicit—of increased income inequality and lack of opportunity for our country's poorest and most disadvantaged citizens. For them, the elected and appointed officials who preside over the dismantling of social and public infrastructure for the sake of short-term political gain are abdicating their responsibility to the public welfare. Realistic budget and policy analysis requires that Republicans agree to raise at least some taxes and simplify the tax code by reducing loopholes and that Democrats agree to reduce some entitlement programs (e.g., Social Security and Medicare) by tying them to income or life expectancy. The alternative is an increased national debt that increasingly undermines economic growth and represents a profoundly inequitably transfer of wealth from future generations to current ones. Our current national political stalemate (2010–?), based on Republican control of the House and Democratic control of the Senate and presidency, represents the failure of both parties to engage in the fundamental legislative process of rational decision making based on common acceptance of facts and compromise among competing values.

THE CHANGING STRUCTURE AND ROLE OF PUBLIC HUMAN RESOURCE MANAGEMENT

Three main groups share responsibility for public HRM. Political leaders are responsible for authorizing personnel systems and for establishing their objectives and funding levels. Personnel directors and specialists design and implement personnel systems or direct and help those who do. In civil service systems, they usually work within a personnel department that functions as a staff support service for managers and supervisors. Their main responsibility is achieving agency goals within a prescribed budget and a limited number of positions. HR directors and specialists both help line managers to use human resources effectively and constrain their personnel actions within the limits imposed by political leaders, laws, and regulations. Managers and supervisors are responsible for implementing the rules, policies, and procedures that constitute personnel systems, as they work with employees on a day-to-day basis.

While the basic HRM functions remain the same, the relative emphasis among functions and how they are performed differ depending on the system. HR under a patronage system heavily emphasizes recruitment and selection of applicants based on personal or political loyalty. Once hired, political appointees are subject to the whims of the elected official. Few rules govern their job duties, pay, or rights, and they are usually fired at will. Nor is development a priority.

In a civil service system, HR is a department or office that functions as an administrative support service to the city manager, school superintendent, hospital director, or other agency administrator. Because civil service is a complete system, HR has a balanced emphasis on each of the four major personnel functions—planning, acquisition, development, and sanction. HR is responsible for maintaining the classification system of positions that have been categorized according to type of work and level of responsibility. The pay system is usually tied to the classification system, with jobs involving similar degrees of difficulty being compensated equally. HR is also responsible for developing and updating the agency's retirement and benefits programs. It also handles eligibility and processing of personnel action requests (retirements and other related changes in job status). HR is responsible for advertising vacant or new positions, reviewing job applications, administering written tests, and providing a ranked list of eligible applicants to managers in units where vacancies actually exist. After the manager conducts interviews and selects one applicant, HR then processes the paperwork required to employ and pay the person. HR is responsible for orienting new employees to the organization, its work rules, and the benefits it provides. It may conduct training itself or contract for it. HR implements employee grievance and appeals procedures, advises supervisors throughout the organization of appropriate codes of conduct for employees, establishes the steps necessary to discipline an employee for violations of these rules, and develops procedures to follow in the event the employee appeals this disciplinary action or files a grievance. If employees are covered by a collective bargaining agreement, HR is usually responsible for negotiating the agreement (or hiring an outside negotiator who performs this function), bringing pay and benefit provisions into accord with contract provisions, orienting supervisors on how to comply with the contract, and representing the agency in internal grievance resolution or outside arbitration procedures.

HR is responsible primarily for implementing HR acquisition rules emphasizing social equity for minorities, women, and persons with disabilities. Thus, it most heavily affects recruitment, selection, and promotion policies and procedures. The affirmative action director shares responsibility with the personnel director in this area. Once members of these protected classes are hired, other personnel systems (civil service or collective bargaining) influence the ways planning, development, and discipline occur.

In general, reliance on NGOs reduces the absolute number of public employees, thereby reducing the HR department's functions. But it also increases the importance of planning and oversight because these are necessary to estimate the type and number of contract employees needed to provide a desired level of service, develop requests for proposals to outside contractors, evaluate responses to proposals by comparing costs and services, and overseeing contract administration. HR directors, staff, and managers work increasingly with citizen volunteers and community-based organizations to supplement paid staff. In these cases, public managers need to become more skilled in recruiting, selecting, training, and motivating volunteer workers (Pynes 2009).

Flexibility in employment relationships is achieved primarily by the increased use of temporary, part-time, and seasonal employment and by increased hiring of exempt employees (those outside the classified civil service) through employment contracts. Employee development is largely irrelevant: Most contingent workers are hired with the skills needed to perform the job immediately. Objective performance evaluation may still be required to maintain effectiveness, but not to maintain equity or discipline. Because at-will employees have no job retention rights, it's easy for employers to control the terms of the relationship. If employees do their jobs adequately, they get paid; if not, they are simply released at the end of their contract and not called back when workload once again increases.

The evolution of public personnel management in the United States adds emergent systems without replacing their predecessors. Instead, new and emergent systems interact and conflict in ways that reflect the dynamic interaction of laws, conditions, and policies. But regardless of the particular system or combination of systems that control HR policy and practice within a particular agency, the organizational structure and relationships within which public HR functions are carried out are established and regulated by law. Usually, the organization of public HRM follows a pattern that is tied closely to the evolution of personnel systems themselves. In the United States nationally, this process was represented by passage of the Pendleton Act (1883) and creation of the U.S. Civil Service Commission. This in some cases followed and in other cases encouraged the establishment of similar state and local civil service agencies. As public personnel management tried to unify the opposing roles of civil service protection and management effectiveness, the organizational location and mission of the central personnel agency became increasingly significant. In some cases it remained an independent commission. In others, it split into two agencies like the U.S. Merit Systems Protection Board and the U.S. Office of Personnel Management, one responsible for protecting employees against political interference under civil service rules, and the other responsible for administering and enforcing the chief executive's HRM policies and practices in other executive branch agencies. As collective bargaining and affirmative action emerged as separate personnel systems, separate agencies were often created at all levels of government to focus on these responsibilities. Other agencies like a Department of Labor (federal, state, or local) may have additional personnel responsibilities for regulating public employee pay, benefits, and working conditions. Often, these agencies have conflicting or overlapping roles in particular HRM functions.

Over time, the role of HR in public agencies has evolved with changes in the political and administrative context. The primary roles have been watchdogs against the spoils systems, collaboration with legislative restrictions, cooperation with management, and compliance with legislative mandates. During the *professionalism era* (1883–1932), HR professionals championed merit system principles because public HRM was generally viewed as a conflict between two systems, one evil and the other good. Public HR managers were considered responsible for guarding employees, applicants, and the public from the spoils system. This required knowledge of civil service policies and procedures and the courage to apply them in the face of political pressure.

During the *performance era* (1933–1964), HR sought to maintain efficiency and accountability, and legislators and chief executives sought to maintain bureaucratic compliance through budgetary controls and position management. Through such devices as personnel ceilings and average grade-level restrictions, it became the role of public personnel management to control the behavior of public managers and to help assure compliance with legislative authority. In effect, it was the responsibility of HR to synthesize two distinct values (bureaucratic compliance as the operational definition of organizational efficiency, and civil service protection as the embodiment of employee rights). There was tension between them because they were both symbiotic and conflicting. And together with the value of bureaucratic neutrality, they supported the concept of political responsiveness.

During the *people era* (1965–1979) the focus of public HRM shifted to *consultation* as HR managers demanded flexibility and equitable reward allocation through such alterations to classification and pay systems as rank-in-person personnel systems, broad pay banding, and group performance evaluation and reward systems. This trend coincided with employee needs for utilization, development, and recognition.

In the *privatization era* (1980–present), public HR still works consultatively with agency managers and employees and with compliance agencies. But its role and objectives are more contradictory. First, HR is required, more than ever, to manage government employees and programs in compliance with legislative and public mandates for cost control. Given the common public and legislative presumption that the public bureaucracy is an enemy to be controlled rather than a tool to be used to accomplish public policy objectives, its authority may be diminished by legislative micromanagement, or the value of cost control may be so dominant as to preclude concern for employee rights, organizational efficiency, or social equity. Second, HR may work increasingly with volunteers and NGOs (particularly FBOs). Because many public employees (particularly school teachers and administrators, police, and firefighters) are still covered by union contracts and collective bargaining agreements, civil service and collective bargaining are still important. But as risk management, cost control, and management of other types of employment contracts become more important, a calculating perspective of the joint possibilities for organizational productivity and individual growth tends to supplant a uniform and idealistic view of public services motivations. This represents a narrowing of the public HR perspective.

Third, and somewhat paradoxically, even as this minimalist view of personnel management emerges, there are countervailing pressures to develop an employment relationship characterized by commitment, teamwork, and innovation. Productivity is prized, risk taking is espoused, and variable pay systems that reward individual and group performance are touted. Perhaps the key to the paradox is the emerging distinction between "core employees" (those regarded as essential assets) and "contingent workers" (those regarded as replaceable costs). It is likely that public HR success will continue to require the ability to develop two divergent personnel systems, one for each type of worker within a dual labor

market system and to maintain both at the same time despite their conflicting objectives and assumptions.

With the emergence of the *partnership era* (2002–present), public HR is increasingly expected to operate within a framework of structures, process, and people that are to a large extent outside of immediate control yet are part of the collective enterprise. The ability to manage tensions will be the defining characteristic in shaping and managing collaborative agendas. Managing these tensions will be even more difficult as frequent changes in government policy and in partner organizations impact the roles of and job changes for public sector employees. Recognizing the effects of emerging structures and processes on employment systems, mobilizing and capacity building will be the benchmarks of collaborative success.

The impact of changing values and systems can be seen in Table 1.2.

Table 1.2 The Role of Public Human Resource Management in the United States

Stage of Evolution	Dominant Value(s)	Dominant System(s)	HRM Role
Patrician Era (1789–1828)	Responsiveness	"Government by elites"	None
Patronage Era (1829–1882)	Responsiveness	Patronage	Recruitment and political clearance
Professional Era (1883–1932)	Efficiency + Individual rights	Civil service	"Watchdog" over agency managers and elected officials to ensure merit system compliance
Performance Era (1933–1964)	Responsiveness + Efficiency + Individual rights	Patronage + Civil service	Collaboration with legislative limits
People Era (1965–1979)	Responsiveness + Efficiency + Individual rights + Social equity	Patronage + Civil service + Collective bargaining + Affirmative action	Compliance + Policy implementation + Consultation

Stage of Evolution	Dominant Value(s)	Dominant System(s)	HRM Role
Privatization Era (1980–present)	Responsiveness + Efficiency + Individual accountability + Limited government + Community responsibility	Patronage + Civil service + Collective bargaining + Affirmative action + Alternative mechanisms + Flexible employment relationships	Compliance + Policy implementation + Consultation + Contract compliance + Strategic thinking about HRM
Partnerships (2002—present)	Responsiveness + Efficiency + Individual accountability + Limited government + Community responsibility + Collaboration	Patronage + Civil service + Collective bargaining + Affirmative action + Alternative mechanisms + Flexible employment relationships	Compliance + Policy implementation + Consultation + Contract compliance + Strategic thinking about HRM + Tension management + Boundary spanning

CONCLUSION

Public HRM can be viewed from several perspectives. First, it is the planning, acquisition, development, and discipline functions needed to manage human resources in public agencies. Second, it is the process by which public jobs are allocated as scarce resources. Third, it reflects the influence of seven symbiotic and competing values (political responsiveness, efficiency, individual rights, and social equity under the traditional pro-governmental paradigm; and individual accountability, downsizing and decentralization, and community responsibility under the emergent privatization and partnerships paradigms) over how public jobs should be allocated. Fourth, it is the personnel *systems* (i.e., laws, rules, and procedures) used to express these abstract values—political appointments, civil service, collective bargaining, and affirmative action under the traditional model; and alternative mechanisms and flexible employment relationships under the emergent privatization and partnerships paradigms.

Conceptually, U.S. public HRM can be understood as a historical process through which new systems emerge to champion emergent values, integrate with the mix, and in turn supplement—but not supplant or replace—their predecessors. From a practical perspective, this means that the field of public HRM is laden with contradictions in policy and practice resulting from often unwieldy and unstable combinations of values and systems and fraught with the inherent difficulties of utilizing competitive and collaborative systems to achieve diverse goals. Civil service is the predominant public HRM system because it has articulated rules and procedures for performing the whole range of HRM functions. Other systems, though incomplete, are nonetheless legitimate and effective influences over one or more HRM functions. While HR functions remain the same across different systems, their organizational location and method of performance differ depending upon the system and on the values that underlie it.

REFERENCES

Battaglio, R. P., and S. Condrey. 2006. Civil Service Reform: Examining State and Local Government Cases. *Review of Public Personnel Administration, 26*(2), 118–138.

Bowman, J., J. West, and S. Gertz. 2006. Radical Reform in the Sunshine State. In J. E. Kellough and L. Nigro (Eds.), *Civil*

Service Reform in the States: Personnel Policies and Politics at the Subnational Level. Albany, NY: SUNY Press, pp. 145–170.

Brewer, G., and R. Maranto. 2000. Comparing the Roles of Political Appointees and Career Executives in the U.S. Federal Executive Branch. American Review of Public Administration, 30(1), 69–86.

Cayer, J., and C. Kime. 2006. Human Resources Reform in Arizona—A Mixed Picture. In J. E. Kellough and L. Nigro (Eds.), Civil Service Reform in the States: Personnel Policies and Politics at the Subnational Level. Albany, NY: SUNY Press, pp. 239–257.

Coggburn, J. 2006. At-Will Employment in Government: Insights from the State of Texas. Review of Public Personnel Administration, 26(2), 158–177.

Cohen, S., and W. Eimicke. 1994. The Overregulated Civil Service. Review of Public Personnel Administration, 15(2), 11–27.

Fox, P., and R. Lavigna. 2006. Wisconsin State Government: Reforming Human Resources Management While Retaining Merit Principles and Cooperative Labor Relations. In J. E. Kellough and L. Nigro (Eds.), Civil Service Reform in the States: Personnel Policies and Politics at the Subnational Level. Albany, NY: SUNY Press, pp. 279–302.

Hays, S., C. Byrd, and S. Wilkins. 2006. South Carolina's Human Resource Management System: The Model for States with Decentralized Personnel Systems. In J. E. Kellough and L. Nigro (Eds.), Civil Service Reform in the States: Personnel Policies and Politics at the Subnational Level. Albany, NY: SUNY Press, pp. 171–201.

Heclo, H. 1977. A Government of Strangers. Washington, DC: Brookings Institution.

International City Management Association. 1989. Service Delivery in the '90s: Alternative Approaches for Local Governments. Washington, DC: ICMA.

Kisfalvi, V. 2000. The Threat of Failure, the Perils of Success and CEO Character: Sources of Strategic Persistence. Organization Studies, 21, 611–639.

Klingner, D. 2008. Toward a New ASPA: Building Global Governance Capacity through Networked Professional Associations. In Ronald Stupak (Ed.). International Journal of Organization Theory and Behavior, 11 3: 355-372.

Klingner, D., J. Nalbandian, and J. Llorens. 2010. Public Personnel Management: Contexts and Strategies, 6th ed. Upper Saddle River, NJ: Prentice Hall.

Klingner, D., J. Nalbandian, and B. Romzek. 2002. Politics, Administration and Markets: Competing Expectations and Accountability. American Review of Public Administration, 32(2), 117–144.

Kosar, D. 2006. Privatization and the Federal Government: An Introduction. Washington, DC: Congressional Research Service.

Lewis, M. 2000. Exploring Paradox: Toward a More Comprehensive Guide. Academy of Management Review, 25, 760–776.

Martin, L. 1999. Contracting for Service Delivery: Local Government Choices. Washington, DC: International City/County Management Association.

Mastracci, S., and J. Thompson (2005). Nonstandard Work Arrangements in the Public Sector: Trends and Issues. Review of Public Personnel Administration, 25(4), 299–324.

Milward, H. B. 1996. Introduction: Symposium on the Hollow State: Capacity, Control, and Performance in Interorganizational Settings. Journal of Public Administration Research and Theory, 6(4), 193–197.

Moe, R. 1987. Exploring the Limits of Privatization. Public Administration Review, 47(6), 453–460.

Naff, K. 2006. Prospects for Civil Service Reform in California: A Triumph of Technique over Purpose? In J. E. Kellough and L. Nigro (Eds.), Civil Service Reform in the States: Personnel Policies and Politics at the Subnational Level. Albany, NY: SUNY Press, pp. 259–278.

National Performance Review. 1993a. From Red Tape to Results: Creating a Government That Works Better and Costs Less. Executive Summary. Washington, DC: U.S. GPO.

———. 1993b. Reinventing Human Resource Management: Accompanying Report of the National Performance Review. Washington, DC: U.S. GPO.

Nigro, L., and J. E. Kellough. 2006. Civil Service Reform in Georgia: A View from the Trenches. In J. E. Kellough and L. Nigro (Eds.), Civil Service Reform in the States: Personnel Policies and Politics at the Subnational Level. Albany, NY: SUNY Press, pp. 117–144.

O'Looney, J. 1998. Outsourcing State and Local Government Services: Decision Making Strategies and Management Methods. Westport, CT: Greenwood.

Osborne, D., and T. Gaebler. 1992. Reinventing Government: How the Entrepreneurial Spirit Is Transforming the Public Sector. Reading, MA: Addison Wesley Longman.

Peters, B., and D. Savoie. 1994. Civil Service Reform: Misdiagnosing the Patient. Public Administration Review, 54(6), 418–425.

Pynes, J. 2009. Human Resources Management for Public and Nonprofit Organizations (3rd ed.). San Francisco: Jossey-Bass.

Riccucci, N. 2006. Civil Service Reform in New York: A Quiet Revolution. In J. E. Kellough and L. Nigro (Eds.), *Civil Service Reform in the States: Personnel Policies and Politics at the Subnational Level.* Albany, NY: SUNY Press, pp. 303–313.

Rockefeller Institute of Government. 2003. *The Public Benefit of Private Faith: Religious Organizations and the Delivery of Social Services*: Albany, NY: Rockefeller IOG.

Savas, E. S. 2000. *Privatization and Public–Private Partnerships.* New York: Chatham House.

Selden, S. 2006. Classifying and Exploring Trends in State Personnel Systems. In J. E. Kellough and L. Nigro (Eds.), *Civil Service Reform in the States: Personnel Policies and Politics at the Subnational Level.* Albany, NY: State University of New York Press, pp. 59–76.

Siegel, G. 1999. Where Are We on Local Government Service Contracting? *Public Productivity and Management Review, 22*(3), 365–388.

U.S. Merit Systems Protection Board. 1994. *Temporary Federal Employment: In Search of Flexibility and Fairness.* Washington, DC: U.S. MSPB.

Wilson, G. 2006. The Rise of At-Will Employment and Racial Inequality in the Public Sector. *Review of Public Personnel Administration, 26*(2), 178–188.

CHAPTER 2

WHAT EVERY PUBLIC SECTOR HUMAN RESOURCE MANAGER SHOULD KNOW ABOUT THE CONSTITUTION

David H. Rosenbloom
American University

Joshua Chanin
San Diego State University

Constitutional law is central to public human resource management (PHRM) at all levels of American government. Judicial branch interpretation of constitutional law regulates in one way or another merit examinations, recruitment, selection, training, promotions, affirmative action and diversity efforts, drug testing, and disciplinary procedures. These court decisions are not just another concern to be balanced among the many competing pressures that public managers face; they form the basis of our public administration and are central to its operation. Because public administrators take an oath to support the Constitution, the values embodied in constitutional law decisions are ethical and normative guides for the exercise of administrative discretion (Rohr 1978, 1986). If individual administrators or local governmental agencies violate the constitutional rights of applicants or employees, they are subject to legal action and may be held liable for monetary damages. Consequently, public human resource managers are expected to maintain a sophisticated knowledge of constitutional law. This chapter explains the basic structure underlying current constitutional doctrine and reviews the leading cases in the areas of greatest concern to today's PHRM. The following eight sections will rely on an up-to-date survey of relevant case law to familiarize those interested in PHRM with the application of the U.S. Constitution's First, Fourth, Fifth, and Fourteenth Amendments to public employment; as well as with the structure of public administrators' potential liability for constitutional torts arising out of breaches of their subordinates' or others' constitutional rights. The chapter concludes with a brief summary of these constitutional concepts and a few examples of the critical role constitutional law plays in maintaining the integrity of our public administration.

CONSTITUTIONAL DOCTRINE

Constitutional law has not always been central to the operation of our public administrative agencies. As surprising as it may seem, prior to the 1950s public employees in the United States had very few federally protected constitutional rights, and even less of an ability to assert these rights effectively within the framework of their employment. These public positions were governed by the "doctrine of privilege," a constitutional reasoning that held that because public employment was a privilege rather than a right, it could be offered on almost any terms the governmental employer saw fit, no matter how arbitrary. Not having a right to a position in the public service, the employee, upon dismissal, lost nothing to which he or she was entitled. As Justice Oliver Wendell Holmes made clear in an early case establishing the constitutionality of disciplining public employees for the content of their speech, "The petitioner may have a constitutional right to talk politics, but he has no constitutional right to be a policeman" (*McAuliffe v. New Bedford* 1892: 220). Under this approach, the Constitution failed to provide public employees and applicants with the very basic protections enjoyed by private citizens.

Although the doctrine of privilege had a certain logic, it also ignored the realities of citizens' interactions with government in the modern administrative state. If the Constitution did not protect public employees and applicants fired or denied jobs for virtually any reason, would not the same principle apply to other kinds of privileges, such as welfare benefits, government contracts, passports, public housing, drivers' licenses, and so forth? Could those be denied, as public employment sometimes was, partly because the individual favored racial integration, read Tom Paine or *The New York Times*, failed to attend church services, or engaged in a host of nonconformist and unconventional activities (Rosenbloom 2014: 119–122)? To the extent that "big government" creates a dependency of the people on government benefits, which were considered privileges, strict adherence to the doctrine of privilege would enable government to attach conditions to their receipt that could undermine recipients' constitutional rights. For instance, eligibility for unemployment benefits could require one to be willing to work on Saturday in violation of her constitutional right to free exercise of religion (*Sherbert v. Verner* 1963).

Notwithstanding a variety of twists and turns in the development of case law since the 1950s, the courts eventually developed an alternative method for analyzing the constitutional rights of public employees. The fundamental underlying premise is that "the government's interest in achieving its goals as effectively and efficiently as possible is elevated from a relatively subordinate interest when it acts as sovereign [dealing with citizens] to a significant one when it acts as employer. The government cannot restrict the speech of the public at large just in the name of efficiency. But where the government is employing someone for the very purpose of effectively achieving its goals, such restrictions may well be appropriate" (*Waters v. Churchill* 1994: 675). The contemporary approach, generally termed the "public service model," calls on judges to balance four often competing concerns: (1) the public employee's or applicant's interests as a member of the political community in exercising constitutional rights and enjoying constitutional protection from arbitrary, discriminatory, or repressive treatment by the governmental employer; (2) the government's interest as an employer in having an efficient and effective workforce; (3) the public's interest in the operation of public administration and government more generally; and (4) the judiciary's interest in avoiding undue involvement in day-to-day PHRM decisions (*Harvard Law Review* 1984; *Garcetti v. Ceballos* 2006; Rosenbloom 2014: 149–152).

Importantly, depending on the specific circumstances, the public's interest can coincide with either that of the employee or the government. For instance, the public shares a strong interest in robust First Amendment protection of whistle-blowers who alert the media to gross governmental mismanagement or government-created or -abetted dangers to the community's health or safety. Conversely, the government and the public share an interest in having very limited constitutional constraints on the dismissal of inefficient, dishonest, or unreliable civil servants. It is important to note that under the public service model all public employees can assert some of the rights they have as citizens or legal residents against their governmental employers. Consequently, the term *at-will employment* is a misnomer in the public sector. It refers to employees who lack a property right or interest in their positions (e.g., those who lack civil service protections against arbitrary treatment). Such employees have no constitutional procedural due process protections against dismissals or other adverse actions for ordinary work-related causes, such as inefficiency or insubordination. However, due process also applies to liberty interests and public employees retain First, Fourth, Fifth, and Fourteenth Amendment rights to some degree of freedom of speech, association, and exercise of religion, privacy, and equal protection of the laws.

Despite its imperfections, the public service model is certainly an advance over less complicated approaches such as the doctrine of privilege. However, because this approach requires a subjective and often elaborate balancing of the interest of employees, government, and the public, reasonable judges and human resource managers will often disagree on what the Constitution requires in specific circumstances. Judicial decision making under the public service model not only has the potential to cause disagreement; it can also generate constitutional decisions that are difficult to follow and apply to specific personnel decisions. As then Supreme Court Justice, and later Chief Justice, William Rehnquist noted:

> This customary "balancing" inquiry conducted by the Court . . . reaches a result that is quite unobjectionable, but it seems to me that it is devoid of any principles which will either instruct or endure. The balance is simply an ad hoc weighing which depends to a great extent upon how the Court subjectively views the underlying interests at stake. (*Cleveland Board of Education v. Loudermill* 1985: 562)

Rehnquist was specifically addressing procedural due process issues involved in the dismissal of a municipal employee. Much the same can be said of judicial decision making regarding free speech and other areas under the public service model, as is demonstrated by the following review of the contemporary constitutional law of public personnel.

FREEDOM OF SPEECH

Rankin v. McPherson (1987) outlines the current approach for analyzing public employees' constitutional rights to nonpartisan free speech. Ardith McPherson was a nineteen-year-old probationary clerk in the office of Constable Rankin in Texas. While talking with a coworker (who was apparently also her boyfriend) shortly after the assassination attempt on President Ronald Reagan, she remarked, "Shoot, if they go for him again, I hope they get him" (322). Another office employee overheard her remark and reported it to Constable Rankin, who fired McPherson after she admitted making the comment. Believing that the dismissal violated her right to free speech under the First and Fourteenth Amendments,[1] McPherson sued for reinstatement, back pay, and other relief. In analyzing the case, the Supreme Court's majority noted that "even though McPherson was merely a probationary employee, and even if she could have been discharged for any reason or for no reason at all, she may nonetheless be entitled to reinstatement if she was discharged for exercising her constitutional right to freedom of expression" (324). This is an example of why so-called at-will employment is an inapt term in contemporary PHRM.

The Court went on to explain the logical structure of public employees' right to free speech, beginning with whether the employee's remark touched on a matter of public concern (that is, of potential interest to the public). If a remark relates to a matter of public concern, it is considered of value to the public's informed discussion of government and public policy. Such comments are part of the free marketplace of ideas that is vital to the operation of our constitutional democracy. By contrast, statements of purely private concern, such as what one employee thinks of another's personality, intelligence, or clothes, are afforded minimal (if any) protection when they interfere with the proper functioning of government offices.

In *Rankin*, a 5–4 majority concluded that McPherson's remark touched upon a matter of public concern. It had been made in the context of a discussion of Reagan's policies, and McPherson, an African American, apparently offered it as a way of punctuating her disdain for the administration's approach to minorities.[2] Next, upon determining that McPherson's comment touched on a matter of public concern, the Court proceeded with the balancing required by the public service model. When weighing the government's interest in discharging an employee for statements that somehow undermine the mission of the public employer, courts must consider the responsibilities of the employee within the agency. An employee's burden of caution and responsibility for the words he or she speaks will vary with the extent of authority and interaction with and accountability to the public that the employee's role entails. Where, as in McPherson's case, "an employee serves no confidential, policymaking, or public contact role," the potential harm to the public office due to that employee's private speech is minimal and is outweighed by the employee's First Amendment rights (328).

Public employees' free speech protections include a right to "whistle-blow," which generally involves alerting elected officials or the public to gross waste, fraud, abuse, mismanagement, or specific government-created or abetted dangers to the health, security, or safety of the community. The Supreme Court has reasoned that due to their positions inside government, public employees are sometimes uniquely able to contribute to the "free and open debate, which is vital to informed decision-making by the electorate" and "accordingly it is essential that they be able to speak out freely without fear of retaliatory dismissal" (*Pickering v. Board of Education* 1968: 571–572).

A public employee's First Amendment protection for whistle-blowing and speaking out about their agencies' decision making and performance was narrowed by the Court's decision in *Garcetti v. Ceballos* (2006). There, the Court held that the First Amendment does not protect public employees' speech made pursuant to their professional duties, regardless of whether the content of the remarks is deemed a matter of public concern. In the 5–4 *Garcetti* holding, the Court's conservative majority

conjured up the doctrine of privilege in determining that "Restricting speech that owes its existence to a public employee's professional responsibilities does not infringe any liberties the employee might have enjoyed as a private citizen. It simply reflects the exercise of employer control over what the employer itself has commissioned or created" (*Garcetti v. Ceballos* 2006: 421–422). In short, a public employee's expression as part of his or her *work product* does not enjoy First Amendment protection.[3]

The Court's majority opinion in *Garcetti* drew a confusing distinction between the rights of individuals as public employees and as citizens: "refusing to recognize First Amendment claims based on government employees' work product does not prevent them from participating in public debate. The employees retain the prospect of constitutional protection for their contributions to the civic discourse. This prospect of protection, however, does not invest them with a right to perform their jobs however they see fit" (*Garcetti v. Ceballos* 2006: 422). This seems to suggest that whistle-blowers have more constitutional protection in their role as private citizens than they do as public employees. In other words, an employee garners more First Amendment protection if he or she raises a concern through external channels such as the media rather than through the professional chain of command or other internal channels established to protect whistle-blowers. Furthermore, rather than relying on the First Amendment to shield them from retaliatory action, the Court urged public employees who whistle-blow to familiarize themselves with and rely on protective statutes, such as the federal Civil Service Reform Act of 1978, as well as relevant state and local statutory provisions. If a statement is covered by the terms of such statutes, it is automatically considered a matter of public concern and the government is prohibited from retaliating, regardless of how disruptive the comments may be.

In *Lane v. Franks* (2014: 2), the Court attempted to further clarify the *Garcetti* holding by drawing a distinction between work product speech and "speech [on a matter of public concern] that simply relates to public employment or concerns information learned in the course of public employment," which continues to enjoy constitutional protection. In practice, however, distinguishing between speech that is part of a work assignment and speech resulting from something learned on the job is sometimes likely to be difficult. Consequently, public sector human resource managers should be cautious in applying the *Garcetti* and *Franks* rulings.

Public employees' constitutional right to free speech does not extend to partisan management or campaigning. In the Supreme Court's view, the governmental interests in workplace efficiency and the appearance of partisan neutrality outweigh the damage that governmental restrictions on political activity do to public employees' rights. Such measures also protect civil servants from being coerced by elected and politically appointed officials to support parties and candidates (*United Public Workers v. Mitchell* 1947; *Civil Service Commission v. National Association of Letter Carriers* 1973). The Court has given wide berth to governmental employers in this policy area by allowing considerable flexibility in the drafting of restrictions (*Broadrick v. Oklahoma* 1973).

Of course, the fact that political neutrality regulations are apt to be constitutional does not mean that governments will choose to impose them. The trend has been away from comprehensive restrictions on public employees' participation in partisan activities. For example, the 1993 Federal Hatch Act reform modified a variety of restrictions, some of which reached back to the early 1900s (see Rosenbloom 1971: 94–110). The Hatch Act reforms allow most federal employees to distribute partisan campaign literature, make speeches, hold offices in political organizations, stuff envelopes with campaign literature, make phone calls as part of a partisan political campaign, and solicit votes (though not funds). The amended law does not extend to members of the Senior Executive Service, however, and exempts some agencies, including the Merit Systems Protection Board, and positions, such as Administrative Law Judge, on grounds that overt partisanship would undermine their missions or functions. The Hatch Act Modernization Act of 2012 reduced restrictions on state and local employees' right to run for partisan office

and exempted District of Columbia employees from many of the Hatch Act restrictions previously applying to them. The federal Office of Special Counsel receives complaints of violations of the Hatch Act and provides advisory opinions on its application.

Can whistle-blowing and related speech on matters of public concern always be distinguished from partisan expression? The answer is clearly no, but the Supreme Court has yet to be confronted with the need to create a legal distinction between them. In terms of PHRM, therefore, some uncertainty remains in this area, especially during electoral campaign periods.

Applying the public service model to employees' speech can sometimes be further complicated by disputes over the exact content of the remarks at issue. In cases where the interpretations of speakers and bystanders differ, the public employer is permitted to act on what it reasonably believes was said, even in the absence of substantial evidence. The Supreme Court case law requires merely that the employer take reasonable steps to find out what the employee may actually have said. However, the Court's guidance in this area has been exceptionally vague: "only procedures outside the range of what a reasonable manager would use may be condemned as unreasonable" (*Waters v. Churchill* 1994: 678).

It is clear that the Supreme Court has given public human resource administrators much to think about regarding the scope of public employees' constitutionally protected speech. In sum, the following must be considered: What did the employee actually say? Were the remarks on a matter of public concern? Were they made pursuant to an employee's official duties as opposed to being based on something that he or she may have learned on the job? What was the specific context in which they were uttered? What is the nature of the employee's position with reference to confidentiality, policy making, and public contact? What is the relative value of the remarks to the public discourse? How great are the remarks' potential for disruption? To these factors must be added others from earlier case law, including whether the speech involves prohibited political partisanship, suggests disloyalty to the United

States, or is so without foundation that the employee's basic competence is called into question. Under the circumstances, it is not surprising that the Supreme Court admits, "competent decision-makers may reasonably disagree about the merits of a public employee's First Amendment claim" (*Bush v. Lucas* 1983: note 7).

FREEDOM OF ASSOCIATION

The contemporary constitutional law regarding public employees' First Amendment right of freedom of association is also central to some aspects of PHRM. In general, public employees' right to join organizations voluntarily (including political parties, labor unions, and even extremist racist and other antisocial groups) is well established, as is their right to refrain from associating with or supporting organizations (*AFSCME v. Woodward* 1969; *Elfbrandt v. Russell* 1966; *Shelton v. Tucker* 1960; *Elrod v. Burns* 1976; *Abood v. Detroit Board of Education* 1977). However, two areas of PHRM that have been specifically "constitutionalized" in this context should be noted.

First, it is possible for union security agreements to violate public employees' constitutionally protected freedom not to associate; no public employee can be required to join a union as a condition of holding his or her job. However, an agency shop is permitted: This arrangement requires nonunion members to pay a "counterpart" or "fair share" fee to the union that represents their collective bargaining unit. In *Abood v. Detroit Board of Education* (1977) the Supreme Court "rejected the claim that it was unconstitutional for a public employer to designate a union as the exclusive collective-bargaining representative of its employees, and to require nonunion employees . . . to pay a fair share of the union's cost of negotiating and administering a collective bargaining agreement" (*Chicago Teachers Union v. Hudson* 1986: 243–244). But the Court also held that "nonunion employees do have a constitutional right to 'prevent the Union's spending a part of their required service fees to contribute to political candidates and to express political views unrelated to its duties as an exclusive bargaining representative'" (*Chicago Teachers Union v. Hudson* 1986: 244).

Certain procedural safeguards accompany a public employee's First Amendment protection against being compelled to underwrite a union's political agenda. In the Supreme Court's words, "the constitutional requirements for the Union's collection of agency fees include an adequate explanation of the basis for the fee, a reasonably prompt opportunity to challenge the amount of the fee before an impartial decision maker, and an escrow account for the amounts reasonably in dispute while such challenges are pending" (*Chicago Teachers Union v. Hudson* 1986: 249). In *Knox v. Service Employees International Union* (2012), the Supreme Court added the requirement that "when a public-sector union imposes a special assessment or dues increase," as opposed to annual dues, "the union must provide a fresh . . . notice [to nonmembers in the bargaining unit] and may not exact any funds from nonmembers without affirmative consent" (*Knox v. Service Employees International Union* 2012: 22). In other words, with special assessments and increases, the nonmember employees must have the opportunity to *opt in* before the union can deduct funds from their paychecks rather than to opt out afterward. *Knox* strengthens public employees' First Amendment right not to be compelled to support causes that they oppose. Undoubtedly, though, it will make it more difficult for unions to raise funds to oppose unforeseen political initiatives, such as efforts to reduce public employees' compensation to limit state or local governmental budgetary shortfalls.

Second, beginning with its holding in *Elrod v. Burns* (1976), the Court began to establish substantial constitutional barriers to the use of political partisanship in public personnel decisions. *Elrod* was triggered when the newly elected sheriff of Cook County, Illinois, fired or threatened to dismiss sheriff's office employees who were not members of or sponsored by the Democratic Party. The employees bringing the suit were all Republicans holding non-civil service positions and had no statutory or administrative protection against arbitrary discharge. The Court held for the first time that patronage dismissals could violate public employees' freedom of association and belief. However, it was divided and unable to form a majority opinion on the standard that the government must meet when dismissing someone based on partisan affiliation.

Four years later, in *Branti v. Finkel* (1980), the Court revisited the issue of patronage dismissals. Two employees of the Rockland County, New York, Public Defenders Office were dismissed solely due to their affiliation with the Republican Party. The Court's majority now agreed that "the ultimate inquiry is not whether the label 'policy maker' or 'confidential' fits a particular position; rather, the question is whether hiring authority can demonstrate that party affiliation is an appropriate requirement for the effective performance of the public office involved" (518). This standard places a heavy burden of persuasion on elected officials and political appointees who would dismiss employees based on their partisan affiliation.

The next patronage case to reach the Supreme Court was *Rutan v. Republican Party of Illinois* (1990). The governor of Illinois ordered a hiring freeze prohibiting state officials from filling vacancies, creating new positions, or recalling furloughed employees without his "express permission." About 5,000 positions became open annually and several employees who were denied promotions, transfers, or recalls charged that the governor was "operating a political patronage system" by granting permission to fill openings only with employees having "Republican credentials" (62, 67). The Court held that "the rule of *Elrod* and *Branti* extends to promotion, transfer, recall, and hiring decisions based on party affiliation and support" (79). Accordingly, for most intents and purposes, partisanship is an unconstitutional justification for taking public personnel actions.

In reaching these decisions regarding public employees' freedom of association, the Supreme Court considered the various claims that union security arrangements strengthen labor-management relations and that patronage promotes democracy and loyalty to elected officials, as well as governmental efficiency. However, using the public service model, the Court concluded that these interests could be secured by means that were less invasive of public employees' First Amendment rights.

The patronage cases illustrate that constitutional law is forever changing and that even "a practice as old as the Republic" may eventually succumb to new constitutional thinking (*Elrod v. Burns* 1976: 376).

PRIVACY

The Fourth Amendment affords protection to private individuals against "unreasonable" government searches and seizures. Traditionally, courts have addressed Fourth Amendment issues in the criminal justice context. During the 1980s, however, as drug testing became common practice, the scope of the amendment's application to public employees emerged as an important issue in PHRM. In law enforcement cases, the amendment requires that searches and seizures be pursuant to warrants, or, where these are impracticable, probable cause (reasonable suspicion that an individual is engaged in criminal wrongdoing). In applying the public service model, courts have construed the Fourth Amendment to permit government employers to meet a much lower standard to justify administrative (non-law enforcement) searches. Consistent with the public service model, this lower threshold both manifests and facilitates the government's significant interest in the performance of its employees and the efficiency of its agencies.

In *O'Connor v. Ortega* (1987), a divided Supreme Court held that "individuals do not lose Fourth Amendment rights [against unreasonable government searches and seizures] merely because they work for the government instead of a private employer" (723). The justices also agreed that the relevant threshold question is whether the employee has a reasonable expectation of privacy in the workplace. Such an expectation is defined as one that, according to the courts, society is prepared to share. If there is no reasonable expectation of privacy, then the search will not violate the Fourth Amendment. If there is such an expectation, then the search must be reasonable in its inception and scope. In practice, this approach often requires that judges analyze cases individually on their own merits rather than according to broad principles. *O'Connor* requires that workplace searches of offices, desks, files, and so forth be based on a reasonable suspicion that an employee may have engaged in behavior for which discipline would be appropriate.

In *City of Ontario v. Quon* (2010), the Supreme Court extended *O'Connor*'s logic to the "electronic sphere" (760). The extent to which a governmental employer can obviate its employees' Fourth Amendment protections against administrative searches through policy statements regarding expectations of privacy remains uncertain. In *Quon*, Ontario's "Computer Policy stated that '[u]sers should have no expectation of privacy or confidentiality when using' City computers" (758). Whether that policy extended to Quon's text messaging was in dispute. However, the Court held that even if Quon had a reasonable expectation in his texting, the City's search of his messages was reasonable in its inception and scope because "a reasonable employee would be aware that sound management principles might require the audit of messages to determine whether . . . pager[s] [were] being appropriately used" (762). While ruling against *Quon* based on the specific facts of the case, the Court left open the issue of when, if ever, public employees might have a reasonable expectation of privacy in their use of government owned computers, pagers, and other electronic devices because "[a] broad holding concerning employees' privacy expectations vis-à-vis employer-provided technological equipment might have implications for future cases that cannot be predicted" (760).

The Supreme Court has also held that in certain cases where the "special needs" of the government outweigh the privacy rights of individuals, public employers may conduct warrantless searches, even in the absence of a reasonable suspicion that an employee has engaged in wrongdoing. In most of these situations, the government's interests (as well as the public's) are asserted through suspicionless drug-testing programs, which randomly test certain public employees, regardless of whether there is a reasonable basis for believing that any of these employees use illegal drugs. For example, in *Skinner v. Railway Labor Executives Association* (1989), the Court held that the Federal Railroad Administration (FRA) may subject certain railroad employees, although

working for private corporations, to random, suspicionless blood and urine tests for the presence of drugs or alcohol. The Court reasoned that the government's legitimate interest in protecting its citizens from railroad employees under the influence of alcohol or drugs significantly outweighed the Fourth Amendment privacy interests of the employees. In *National Treasury Employees Union v. Von Raab* (1989), the Court extended this rationale to those public employees who carry firearms or are engaged in drug interdiction. Accordingly, the Court noted that such employees have a reduced expectation of privacy "by virtue of the special, and obvious, physical and ethical demands of those positions" (711). HIV and other health-related testing programs present similar legal issues. In this context, blood- and urine-testing regimes must be reasonable in terms of purpose and procedure. However, as such practices become more common it is increasingly difficult for employees and applicants to claim that they violate a reasonable expectation of privacy (see, e.g., *Fowler v. New York* 1989).

Further, anyone engaged in law enforcement, public safety, and national security positions can be subjected to a reasonably designed suspicionless drug-testing program. Public human resource managers should remember that such testing programs are only for administrative objectives, such as greater cost-effectiveness, safety, health, and productivity. Searches for potential criminal punishment require warrants or probable cause, without which evidence generated by them usually may not be used as a basis for prosecution.

LIBERTY

The broad issue of public employees' constitutional liberty has also been the subject of significant litigation. This area of jurisprudence, called *substantive due process*, focuses on the meaning of the word *liberty* in the Fifth and Fourteenth Amendments, which respectively prohibit the federal government and states (and their political subunits) from depriving anyone within their jurisdictions of life, liberty, or property without due process of law. Courts have interpreted the due process clause to include those fundamental rights that are "implicit in ordered liberty" and are "deeply rooted" in our society's history and traditions. Many of these rights, including, for example, the right to use contraception or the right to travel, are not mentioned explicitly in the text of the Constitution.

It is common, even natural, for government employers to exercise control over public employees, particularly where matters of public policy, workplace efficiency, and employee morale are concerned. To this end, Senator Sam Ervin found that in the 1960s public employees were requested "to lobby in local city councils for fair housing ordinances, to go out and make speeches on any number of subjects, to supply flower and grass seed for beautification projects, and to paint other people's houses" (United States Senate 1967: 9). Today, it is more common for federal employers to pressure employees to participate in blood drives, charitable campaigns, and similar programs. A court will deem such conditions unconstitutional only if they are found to violate an employee's fundamental rights, or if the court determines the conditions to be nothing more than tenuously connected to the interests of the government (see *United States v. National Treasury Employees Union* 1995). The liberty interests of public employees have the potential to affect government employment practices, but to date have not done so significantly. Public employees' reproductive decisions are an exception; their grooming preferences and residency requirements illustrate the general tendency.

Cleveland Board of Education v. LaFleur (1974) focused on the constitutionality of a policy requiring mandatory, unpaid maternity leave for public school teachers. The Court found the mandatory leave policy unconstitutionally restrictive, but used language broad enough to provide protection for public employees' reproductive choices. The Court stated that it "has long recognized that freedom of personal choice in matters of marriage and family life is one of the liberties protected by the Due Process Clause of the Fourteenth Amendment" and that "there is a right 'to be free from unwarranted governmental intrusion into matters so fundamentally affecting a person as the decision whether to bear or beget a child'" (639).

In the Court's view, the liberty to bear children must remain free of undue or purposeless governmental interference. Choices with regard to grooming and residence have been given lesser protection. In *Kelley v. Johnson* (1976) the Court found no constitutional barrier to grooming regulations applying to male police officers. Although a lower court held that "choice of personal appearance is an ingredient of an individual's personal liberty" (241), the Supreme Court placed the burden of persuasion on the employee challenging the regulation to "demonstrate that there is no rational connection between the regulation . . . and the promotion of safety of persons and property" (247). The challengers were unable to do this despite the government's questionable rationale: The government claimed that the grooming standards would make the police more readily identifiable to the public (ignoring, apparently, that police officers wear uniforms) and that they would promote esprit de corps, despite the police union's vehement opposition to them.

Finally, in *McCarthy v. Philadelphia Civil Service Commission* (1976), the Court upheld the constitutionality of residency requirements for firefighters. It did so without much discussion and in the face of petitioner McCarthy's rather compelling concern for the wellbeing of his family. The decision remains good law and, consequently, public employees can be required to live within the jurisdictions in which they work or a specified distance from it. Though these issues are not frequently litigated and are no longer capturing headlines, the principles are still very much alive in current constitutional jurisprudence; public sector human resource managers should understand and follow the law established in this line of cases.

EQUAL PROTECTION

Contemporary equal protection analysis under the Fourteenth and Fifth Amendments is of critical importance to PHRM. Equal protection doctrine regulates government affirmative action policies, procedures having a disparate impact on different social groups, and overt discrimination against individuals based on race, ethnicity, citizenship, gender, age, and other factors. The threshold question in an equal protection inquiry is whether a law, policy, decision, custom, or practice classifies individuals according to some characteristic such as race, gender, wealth, residency, or education. Such categorizations—either explicit or implicit—must be present in order to justify an equal protection challenge.

What distinguishes an actual classification, such as one created by law, from practices that are ostensibly neutral but have a disparate impact on different categories of people, such as racial groups or males and females? The Court addressed that difference in *Washington v. Davis* (1976), a case in which unsuccessful candidates for the Washington, DC, police academy sued on grounds that the department's use of an exam testing verbal skills, which African Americans failed disproportionally, amounted to a racially discriminatory hiring practice. In finding for the police department, the Supreme Court made clear that public human resource practices that appear neutral on their face but bear more harshly on one racial group than another, as has often been the case with merit examinations, will not be unconstitutional simply because of their disparate impact. To violate the equal protection clause, public practices must manifest a discriminatory purpose of some kind. The Court emphasized that such a purpose need not be "express or appear on the face of the statute" and made clear that it could be "inferred from the totality of the relevant facts" (*Washington v. Davis* 1976: 241–242). Such implicit classifications are treated identically to explicit ones. Once they have determined that a classification exists, courts rely on a three-tiered structure to determine its constitutionality. What follows is a brief description of this framework, with a particular focus on the application of each tier in the context of PHRM.

Suspect Classifications

Courts consider legal classifications based on race or ethnicity as "suspect," or highly likely to violate equal protection principles. These suspect classifications, historically employed to disadvantage members of minority groups, can be very difficult for governments to justify. Reviewing courts subject laws that create suspect classifications to "strict scrutiny," the most intense and exacting form of judicial review. In these cases, the government will bear a heavy burden of persuasion and receive little if any deference. Courts deem suspect classifications constitutional only if they are found to serve a compelling governmental interest and are "narrowly tailored" to achieve that purpose. To date, workforce diversity has not been considered a compelling governmental interest by the Supreme Court.[4] Affirmative action for members of minority groups may be viable if its purpose is to remedy past, proven discrimination against racial or ethnic groups. The leading case in this area is *United States v. Paradise* (1987), in which a federal judge imposed hiring and promotion quotas for African Americans in the Alabama Department of Public Safety. The case so divided the Supreme Court that it was unable to form a majority opinion. Nevertheless, most of the justices agreed that the remedy was a constitutional means to overcoming decades of discrimination and resistance to equal protection in the Alabama state patrol. A majority also agreed that the relief was adequately narrowly tailored.

In the public personnel context, narrow tailoring requires that five conditions be met:

1. Less drastic and equally efficacious remedies, such as fines, are impractical or unavailable.
2. There must be a fixed stopping point at which use of the classification ends. This may be based on time, for example, three to five years, or successful remediation of the previous violation of equal protection, such as minorities having gained 25 % of the positions the governmental workforce involved.
3. The quotas, goals, or targets must be proportionate to the racial and/or ethnic composition of the relevant population or workforce base. For example, a 25 % quota for African Americans would be disproportionate in Vermont, but not in Alabama.

4. Waivers must be available so that if the agency is unable to find qualified candidates then it will not be forced to hire or promote incompetents, on the one hand, or remain understaffed, on the other.

5. The approach cannot place a harsh burden on "innocent third parties." The general principle is that those employees to whom the classification does not apply (e.g., non-minorities) should not be made objectively worse off by the government's efforts to promote inclusion and diversity, as in affirmative action. Consequently, firing or furloughing nonminorities to free up positions for minorities is considered a harsh burden, whereas not providing training to nonminorities, which reduces their opportunities for advancement but does change their rank, pay, or other working conditions, is not (see *Wygant v. Jackson Board of Education* 1986; *United Steel Workers of America v. Weber* 1979).

In *Grutter v. Bollinger* (2003), dealing with affirmative action for applicants to the University of Michigan Law School, the Court added a sixth condition that logically applies in the public personnel context as well: that each candidate be afforded an individualized assessment of his or her qualifications.

It is important to note that racial and ethnic classifications are considered suspect even if their purpose is to enhance minority employment opportunities. At various times since the 1970s, when the Supreme Court began hearing affirmative action cases, efforts have been made to distinguish between classifications based on "invidious discrimination" and those that are deemed "benign," or intended to promote the employment interests of minorities and women. In *Adarand Constructors v. Pena* (1995), a 5–4 majority of the Supreme Court deviated from previous Court jurisprudence and defied considerable academic and pundit commentary suggesting that benign racial or ethnic classifications pose little threat to equal protection because they lack a discriminatory purpose. The Court held that "all racial classifications, imposed by whatever

federal, state, or local governmental actor, must be analyzed by a reviewing court under strict scrutiny" (227). In the majority's view, requiring such scrutiny is the only way to ensure that there is no intent to discriminate, or if there is one, it is somehow justified by a compelling governmental interest and is narrowly tailored.[5] In a concurring opinion, Justice Clarence Thomas took pains to explain that, in his view, the entire distinction between invidious and benign was untenable and irrelevant: "government-sponsored racial discrimination based on benign prejudice is just as noxious as discrimination inspired by malicious prejudice. In each instance, it is racial discrimination, plain and simple" (241). In *Johnson v. California* (2005), a case involving prison administration, the Supreme Court held that racial classifications purported to be neutral rather than invidious or benign are also subject to strict scrutiny.

Quasi-Suspect Classifications

Classifications based on biological sex are "quasi-suspect" and subject to an intermediate level of scrutiny. In these cases, the burden of proof is on the government to show that the classification is substantially related to the achievement of important governmental objectives. Originally, courts considered these classifications nonsuspect and evaluated them using a much less rigorous standard of review. As society and the judiciary became more conscious of the discriminatory effects of efforts to "protect" women from long working hours, physically demanding jobs, participating on juries in cases involving depravity, and so on, these classifications were raised to an intermediate level. In practice, courts evaluate sex-based classifications using a standard comparable to that of a strict scrutiny review, requiring governments to provide an "exceedingly persuasive justification" for their use (*United States v. Virginia* 1996: 533). Intermediate scrutiny poses a challenge to government employment practices based on traditional thinking about "male" and "female" jobs, workplace behavior, physical strength, and other capacities. Practices based on outdated perceptions of gender roles may be vulnerable to constitutional challenge. Although it is currently easier in a technical sense to justify affirmative action for women than for racial or ethnic minorities because classifications based on biological sex do not receive strict scrutiny, public sector human resource managers should be alert to the likelihood that such programs will be unconstitutional in the absence of a very strong governmental interest.

Nonsuspect Classifications

The federal courts consider classifications based on residency, wealth, age, education, and similar factors to be nonsuspect. Public policies use such classifications frequently and for a variety of reasons—eligibility for benefits of some kind such as social security, voting, drivers' licenses, and so forth. Judges subject these classifications to a lower level of scrutiny through what has become known as the "rational basis" test. The burden of persuasion is generally on the challenger to show that such classifications are not rationally related to the achievement of a legitimate governmental purpose. Courts typically grant a great amount of deference to the judgment of lawmakers and governmental employers in such cases. For instance, the Supreme Court found a rational connection between the state's interest in public safety and its policy requiring police officers to retire at age fifty. No equal protection violation was found, despite the fact that many officers would be physically and mentally fit to continue in their jobs well beyond age fifty (*Massachusetts Board of Retirement v. Murgia* 1976). At present, classifications based on sexual orientation are nonsuspect. However, as with other nonsuspect classifications, they must serve a legitimate governmental purpose.

PROCEDURAL DUE PROCESS

In addition to their substantive aspects, the due process clauses of the Fifth and Fourteenth Amendments guarantee certain procedural rights to individuals being deprived of life, liberty, or property by the federal or a state or local government. In determining the extent of procedural due process to be afforded in administrative matters, courts balance three factors: (1) the individual's interests at stake; (2) the risk that the procedures used, if any, will result in an erroneous decision, and the probable value of additional procedures in reducing the likelihood of error; and (3) the government's interests, including administrative burdens and financial costs, in using the procedures in place. The underlying assumption in this formula is that although additional procedures will generally reduce mistakes, they also add costs. For example, the high cost of guaranteeing a full-fledged adjudicatory hearing, which includes the right to witness confrontation, cross-examination, and legal representation, might be considered necessary in cases where the interest at stake is substantial enough to require a very low error rate. Conversely, where an individual's interest is minimal, the government may be required to provide nothing more than notice of the decision-maker's rationale and an opportunity to challenge the decision in writing. Cases involving the rights of public employees illustrate that procedural due process balancing takes place within the framework of the public service model.

In *Board of Regents v. Roth* (1972), the Supreme Court identified four individual interests that would give public employees a right to a full hearing in dismissals: (1) where the dismissal was in retaliation for the exercise of constitutionally protected rights, such as freedom of speech; (2) "where a person's good name, reputation, honor or integrity is at stake because of what the government is doing to him" (573); (3) where the dismissal diminishes a public employee's future employability; and (4) where the employee has a property right or property interest in the position, such as tenure or a contract.

The public service model is important in determining both the timing and the nature of the hearing. In *Cleveland Board of Education v. Loudermill* (1985), the Supreme Court held that a security guard who allegedly lied on his application was entitled to notice of the allegations, an explanation of the employer's evidence, and an opportunity to respond—all prior to being terminated. The Court noted that *Loudermill* had a property right in his job by virtue of being a "classified civil servant." The pretermination requirement is an "initial check against mistaken decisions—essentially, a determination of whether there are reasonable grounds to believe that the charges against the employee are true and support the proposed action" (545–546). This serves the interests of the employee as well as those of the public and the government. In cases involving employment terminations, such as those at issue in *Roth* and *Loudermill*, a pretermination hearing frequently helps the state avoid additional personnel costs caused by unnecessary turnover and complex posttermination litigation.

A court's procedural due process balancing changes when employee suspensions are at issue. In *Gilbert v. Homar* (1997), the Supreme Court reasoned that no due process was required prior to suspending a law enforcement officer who had been charged with a felony. In this case, the governmental and public interests in an effective workforce outweighed those of the employee. As the Court explained, "So long as a suspended employee receives a sufficiently prompt post-suspension hearing, the lost income is relatively insubstantial, and fringe benefits such as health and life insurance are often not affected at all" (932). The Court also noted that the government has reasonable grounds for suspending an employee who has been formally charged with criminal behavior.

An adverse action triggering procedural due process protections may be based on a mix of factors, some of which involve constitutional rights and others that do not. For instance, an employer may also consider an employee who has engaged in controversial speech to be incompetent or disruptive for reasons unrelated to his or her remarks. In such a case, the employer will have the opportunity to demonstrate "by a preponderance of the evidence that it would have reached the same decision . . . even in the absence of the protected conduct" (*Mount Healthy School District Board of Education v. Doyle* 1977: 287).

Because procedural due process analysis considers the probability that the government is acting in error, the public employer will often investigate an employee before taking disciplinary action. In *LaChance v. Erickson* (1998), the Supreme Court held that employees suspected of lying to or attempting to mislead investigators in an effort to defend themselves may be disciplined

for their falsehoods without any violation of their due process rights. Courts have determined that the due process "right to be heard" does not protect an employee from sanctions resulting from lying. However, where an investigation may lead to criminal charges, the public employee does maintain the right to remain silent under the Fifth Amendment.

As in other areas, the public service model's balancing approach in procedural due process cases provides public sector human resource managers with a rough set of guidelines, but it may not prove sufficient to inform particular administrative decisions. Individual facts and circumstances may ultimately determine close legal questions. For example, it is difficult in the abstract to know how quickly after suspending an employee an employer must provide a hearing in order to meet the current "prompt post-suspension hearing" requirement. As always, the best way to keep track of answers to such questions is to follow the case law in one's jurisdiction, including rulings by the federal district courts and courts of appeals in one's judicial circuit.

LIABILITY

It cannot be overemphasized that a public manager's need for knowledge and understanding of relevant constitutional doctrine is much more than academic. As a result of several Supreme Court decisions over the past three decades, such knowledge has become a positive job requirement (Rosenbloom, O'Leary, and Chanin 2010: 271–287). Today, a public sector manager occupying a position at any level of government may well be personally liable for compensatory and even punitive damages, if found to have violated "clearly established . . . constitutional rights of which a reasonable person would have known" (*Harlow v. Fitzgerald* 1982: 818; see also *Smith v. Wade* 1983; *Hafer v. Melo* 1991). "Clearly established" in this context itself is not altogether clearly established. In *Hope v. Pelzer* (2002) the Court held that "clearly established" does not require a judicial precedent in a case with materially similar facts, only that the public employee has "fair warning" from constitutional law and values that his or her behavior will violate someone's rights. However, in *Reichle v. Howards* (2012), "clearly established" was defined as such "that every 'reasonable official would [have understood] that what he is doing violates'" a right (*Reichle v. Howards* 2012: 2093; brackets in the original text). The Supreme Court essentially reiterated this standard with reference to police in *Plumhoff v. Rickard* (2014): "a defendant cannot be said to have violated a clearly established right unless the right's contours were sufficiently definite that any reasonable official in the defendant's shoes would have understood that he was violating it" (2023).

An exception to personal liability exists for federal personnel in some cases where the individual whose rights have been violated is able to obtain a remedy in alternative fashion established by legislation or, presumably, executive order, such as through appeal to the Merit Systems Protection Board (*Bush v. Lucas* 1983). Moreover, public employees have absolute immunity from civil suits for damages for violations of individuals' constitutional rights when they are performing adjudicatory functions, such as hearing examiners or "prosecuting" adverse actions (*Butz v. Economou* 1978; *Forrester v. White* 1988; *Burns v. Reed* 1991). Nevertheless, it must be emphasized that absolute immunity attaches to the specific function rather than the job title. Thus, a hearing examiner has absolute immunity when engaged in adjudication, but not when hiring or firing his or her secretary.

In addition to the federal constitutional principles outlined in this chapter, public sector human resource experts must be aware of state constitutional law, which may also affect public sector human resource matters. Where a state's protection of public employees' rights such as privacy or substantive due process exceeds that of the federal Constitution, state and local governments must meet the higher state standard. Public managers at all levels of government may avoid liability by exercising their constitutional "right to disobey" any order requesting implementation of an unconstitutional law or policy so as to prevent infringement of others' protected rights (*Harley v. Schuylkill County* 1979). This ability, of course, is premised on an understanding of the constitutional rights at issue and a facility with the public service model

for balancing all the interests at stake. Gaining reasonable knowledge of the constitutional law—both state and federal—that governs one's actions is the best way to avoid violating rights. Public managers need not be lawyers, but they must develop the ability to recognize if and when decisions, actions, procedures, or policies run afoul of the law.

CONCLUSION

Contemporary efforts to improve public sector performance serve two components of the public service model—the governmental and public interests. However, the interests and rights of employees may receive limited attention. The tools of contemporary public administration—downsizing, performance measurement and management, newer electronic communication technologies and social media, outsourcing, competitive sourcing, and collaborative governance arrangements—can increase the immediacy of the Constitution in dealing with human resources. For instance, downsizing and competitive sourcing can bump up against procedural due process and equal protection rights. Where civil service status or other property interests in employment are involved, dismissals cannot constitutionally be arbitrary, capricious, discriminatory, or unauthorized by law. If individual employees are picked as targets for reductions in force, they will almost certainly have substantial due process rights. Depending on the circumstances, and especially in cases where agencies have been under court order to increase diversity (as in *United States v. Paradise*), downsizing that has a harmful impact on the employment interests of minorities or women will be subject to challenge under the equal protection clause.

In an age in which employers can monitor employees' computer usage, including key strokes, email, and use of pagers and other communication devices, new Fourth Amendment privacy questions are certain to arise, as in *Quon*.

Outsourcing and collaborative governance present a special set of constitutional issues when they involve a public function (such as incarceration) or so entwine the government and a private organization that it is impossible to tell where one begins and the other ends (e.g., public-private partnerships). In those circumstances, under current "state (i.e., governmental) action" doctrine, at the state and local levels, the private organization and its employees may well become liable for violating individuals' constitutional rights. A private individual working directly for a state or local government is likely to have the same qualified immunity as public employees (*Filarsky v. Delia* 2012). Yet one working for a private organization under contract with a government may not. For example, in *Richardson v. McKnight* (1997), a prison guard employed by a private prison management firm was held to a higher liability standard. Unlike a public employee, he was subject to liability for violating prisoners' constitutional rights regardless of whether they were clearly established or a reasonable person would have known of them. Private organizations that become state actors by virtue of their contractual or other cooperative arrangements with the federal government are not liable for money damages in constitutional tort suits (*Correctional Services Corporation v. Malesko* 2001). Neither are their employees, at least in so far as state tort law offers an alternative through which the injured party may be compensated (*Minneci v. Pollard* 2012).

A human resource expert aware of constitutional principles and current doctrine could bring this constitutional dimension to bear on organizational decisions concerning outsourcing and collaborating with private entities. Will the private organizations, whether for profit or nonprofit, seeking government contracts be working in policy or program areas in which constitutional rights are relevant? Will their organizational cultures and staffing levels ensure that such rights will be protected? Could they and their employees withstand liability suits? Would it be better public policy to keep the function within a government agency in order to make sure that the employees are properly trained with respect to their constitutional responsibilities?

By taking a proactive role in alerting decision-makers to constitutional issues, particularly those presented in First, Fourth, Fifth, and Fourteenth Amendment jurisprudence, public sector human resource experts will not only protect individual rights but also reduce susceptibility to lawsuits. Incorporating a constitutional dimension into public administration will give managers better and more consistent information and skills to protect employees' rights as well as to achieve organizational goals within the framework of our democratic-constitutional government.

NOTES

1. The first ten amendments to the Constitution, known as the Bill of Rights, apply directly to the federal government. The Fourteenth Amendment, which was ratified in 1868, prohibits the states (and their political subunits) from violating many of these rights as well. The due process clause of the Fourteenth Amendment protects individuals from the deprivation of life, liberty, or property by sub-national governments. Over the years, the term *liberty* has been read by the Supreme Court to "incorporate" much of the Bill of Rights, including the First and Fourth Amendments, which are of particular importance to PHRM. This is why McPherson can argue that her First Amendment rights, which are incorporated into the Fourteenth Amendment, have been violated. Because the Fourteenth Amendment is what applies the First Amendment to state and local governments, she argues that it has been violated as well. As is discussed later in the chapter, the Fourteenth Amendment also prohibits the states and their subunits from depriving any person within their jurisdiction "equal protection of the laws." Known as the equal protection clause, this provision is interpreted to apply to the federal government through the word *liberty* in the Fifth Amendment, a process called "reverse incorporation."

2. *Connick v. Myers*, 461 U.S. 138 (1983), establishes that courts must consider a public employee's comment in its original context when evaluating whether the comment touches on a matter of public concern.

3. The Court noted that an exception might be made for faculty at public universities and colleges, whose work product involves teaching and writing.

4. In *Grutter v. Bollinger* (2003), the Supreme Court held that diversity in higher education can constitute a compelling governmental interest. The Court's reasoning would seem to apply to diversity in public sector human resource management as well: "In order to cultivate a set of leaders with legitimacy in the eyes of the citizenry, it is necessary that

the path to leadership be visibly open to talented and qualified individuals of every race and ethnicity" (332).

5. As an interesting and relevant aside, courts may also hold local governments and agencies liable for monetary damages when their policies are closely connected to violations of individuals' constitutional rights, regardless of whether those rights can be said to be clearly established or should be reasonably known (*Monell v. New York City Department of Social Services* 1978; *Pembaur v. Cincinnati* 1986).

REFERENCES

Abood v. Detroit Board of Education, 431 U.S. 209 (1977).

Adarand Constructors v. Pena, 515 U.S. 200 (1995).

AFSCME v. Woodward, 406 F.2d 137 (8th Cir. 1969).

Board of Regents v. Roth, 408 U.S. 564 (1972).

Branti v. Finkel, 445 U.S. 507 (1980).

Broadrick v. Oklahoma, 413 U.S. 601 (1973).

Burns v. Reed, 500 U.S. 478 (1991).

Bush v. Lucas, 462 U.S. 367 (1983).

Butz v. Economou, 438 U.S. 478 (1978).

Chicago Teachers Union v. Hudson, 475 U.S. 292 (1986).

City of Ontario v. Quon, 560 U.S. 746 (2010).

Civil Service Commission v. National Association of Letter Carriers, 413 U.S. 548 (1973).

Cleveland Board of Education v. LaFleur, 414 U.S. 632 (1974).

Cleveland Board of Education v. Loudermill, 470 U.S. 532 (1985).

Connick v. Myers, 461 U.S. 138 (1983).

Correctional Services Corporation v. Malesko, 534 U.S. 61 (2001).

Developments in the Law—Public Employment. 1984. *Harvard Law Review, 97*(7), 1611–1800.

Elfbrandt v. Russell, 384 U.S. 11 (1966).

Elrod v. Burns, 427 U.S. 347 (1976).

Filarsky v. Delia, 132 S.Ct. 1657 (2012).

Forrester v. White, 484 U.S. 219 (1988).

Fowler v. New York, 704 F. Supp. 1264 (S.D.N.Y. 1989).

Garcetti v. Ceballos, 547 U.S. 410 (2006).

Gilbert v. Homar, 520 U.S. 924 (1997).

Grutter v. Bollinger, 539 U.S. 306 (2003).

Hafer v. Melo, 502 U.S. 21 (1991).

Harley v. Schuylkill County, 476 F. Supp. 191 (E.D. Penn 1979).

Harlow v. Fitzgerald, 457 U.S. 800 (1982).

Hope v. Pelzer, 536 U.S. 730 (2002).

Johnson v. California, 543 U.S. 499 (2005).

Kelley v. Johnson, 425 U.S. 238 (1976).

Knox v. Service Employees International Union Local 1000, 132 S.Ct. 2277 (2012).

LaChance v. Erickson, 522 U.S. 262 (1998).

Lane v. Franks, U.S. 134 S.Ct. 2369 (2014).

Massachusetts Board of Retirement v. Murgia, 427 U.S. 304 (1976).

McAuliffe v. New Bedford, 155 Mass. 216 (1892).

McCarthy v. Philadelphia Civil Service Commission, 424 U.S. 645 (1976).

Minneci v. Pollard, 132 S.Ct. 617 (2012).

Monell v. New York City Department of Social Services, 436 U.S. 658 (1978).

Mount Healthy School District Board of Education v. Doyle, 429 U.S. 274 (1977).

National Treasury Employees Union v. Von Raab, 489 U.S. 656 (1989).

O'Connor v. Ortega, 480 U.S. 709 (1987).

Pembaur v. Cincinnati, 475 U.S. 469 (1986).

Pickering v. Board of Education, 391 U.S. 563 (1968).

Plumhoff v. Rickard, 134 S. Ct. 2012 (2014).

Rankin v. McPherson, 483 U.S. 378 (1987).

Reichle v. Howards, 132 S.Ct. 2088 (2012).

Richardson v. McKnight, 521 U.S. 399 (1997).

Rohr, John. 1978. *Ethics for Bureaucrats*. New York, NY: Marcel Dekker.

Rosenbloom, David H. 1971. *Federal Service and the Constitution*. Ithaca, NY: Cornell University Press.

———. 2014. *Federal Service and the Constitution* (2nd ed.). Washington, DC: Georgetown University Press.

Rosenbloom, David H., Rosemary O'Leary, and Joshua Chanin. 2010. *Public Administration and Law* (3rd ed.). Boca Raton, FL: CRC/Taylor & Francis.

Rutan v. Republican Party of Illinois, 497 U.S. 62 (1990).

Shelton v. Tucker, 364 U.S. 479 (1960).

Sherbert v. Verner, 374 U.S. 398 (1963).

Skinner v. Railway Labor Executives Association, 489 U.S. 602 (1989).

Smith v. Wade, 461 U.S. 30 (1983).

United Public Workers v. Mitchell, 330 U.S. 75 (1947).

United Steel Workers of America v. Weber, 443 U.S. 193 (1979).

United States Senate. 1967. "Protecting Privacy and the Rights of Federal Employees" S. Rept. 519. 90th Cong., 1st Sess. August 21.

United States v. National Treasury Employees Union, 513 U.S. 454 (1995).

United States v. Paradise, 480 U.S. 149 (1987).

United States v. Virginia, 518 U.S. 515 (1996).

Washington v. Davis, 426 U.S. 229 (1976).

Waters v. Churchill, 511 U.S. 661 (1994).

Wygant v. Jackson Board of Education, 476 U.S. 267 (1986).

CHAPTER 3

THE DEATH AND LIFE OF PRODUCTIVITY MANAGEMENT IN GOVERNMENT

Albert Hyde
San Francisco State University

Frederik Uys
University of Stellenbosch, South Africa

INTRODUCTION: WHY DOESN'T PRODUCTIVITY MATTER TO PUBLIC SECTOR HUMAN RESOURCE MANAGEMENT?

"As society makes demands beyond the private sector's ability to fulfill, government responds with two tools—regulation or money. But both approaches are incurring greater frustrations. We are coming to realize that we have a more finite resource base than previously suspected. Public expenditure may simply bid up the price rather than improve the results.

Thus we understand why it is that as government grows more expensive, not only public sector, but also total national productivity may decline. This effect is not inevitable; government is not necessarily less productive than other sectors of the economy. In fact, government often plays a catalytic role, enhancing the productivity of business. But unless government incorporates a productivity consciousness in all of its activity, it will tend to grow stagnant as it grows larger."

—George Gilder,
National Commission on Productivity and
Work Quality, 1975, *Public Productivity Review, 1*(1), 6.

Writing for the inaugural issue of a new public sector journal in 1975 devoted to government productivity management, George Gilder warned of an impending era where the economy of the United States could be significantly threatened in terms of its competitiveness, growth, and ultimately its standard of living. Gilder was greatly concerned, as were many economists, business executives, and political leaders at that time, with the emergence of a new period of stagnation in productivity in the U.S. Coming out of the Second World War with minimal damages to its industrial infrastructure, the U.S. would become the dominant economy of the world. This was fueled by average annual rates of national productivity growth of 2.8% from the late 1940s to early 1970s. So when productivity rates fell by more than half to 1.1% in the 1970s (and, more significantly, the U.S. lagged behind emerging reindustrialized competitors Japan and Germany), and despite much national consternation could still improve to only 1.4% in the 1980s, various commissions were formed to find solutions to the "productivity crises."

In the center of all this was the public sector. The post–World War II period in the United States is historically regarded as a new plateau for the public sector because government was bigger at all levels. Federal, state, and local governments would account for 25% of national gross domestic product and government organizations were larger; employing some 2.4 million federal, 1.5 million state, and 4.8 million government workers[1] (Shafritz and Hyde 2012: 80). Those levels beginning in the 1970s were now being seen in the context of larger U.S. economic change and global competiveness.

Victor Fuchs in his definitive economic assessment of the post–World War II era noted that this period marked the emergence of the world's first service economy. U.S. employment would increase from 57 million jobs to nearly 75 million jobs by 1967, and the vast majority of the new jobs added to the economy would be in the service industry. Government's now nearly 9 million workers were a significant part of a now larger American workforce where more than half provided services as opposed to producing things. Among many implications, Fuchs noted two other key points: First, he noted that unlike the industrial production sector where quality of labor inputs was at best stable or declining, the quality of the labor inputs (education and skill levels) was increasing. Second, he pointed to several service industry examples and noted that while overall productivity levels showed modest annual increases, measurements of productivity, quality, and technology demanded more analysis to understand service sector differences and would require more robust measurement techniques (Fuchs 1968: 3–4). In a truly classic case, he compared beauty shops to barbershops (sorry, that is what they were called in the 1960s) and found beauty shops a benchmark of service growth, high quality and variety of services offered, and high productivity (and low idle time) while the barbershop was at best a hold-over place of stable technology, minimal range of service, and low productivity (Fuchs 1968: 6).

The student of public sector human resource management (HRM) in the modern era may well wonder what this old historical crisis about economic growth and productivity, barbershops, and the rising services industry has to do with current HRM theory and practice.

After all, not many HRM books devote much attention to productivity or how it is defined and measured, much less how it can be applied to sustain performance or drive innovation. But the larger point is that for over 25 years—from 1967 to 1994—productivity was systematically measured in most of the federal government agencies and test measured across a good sample of state and local governments. Public management in the last third of the 20th century expended some credible effort in gauging labor inputs, output, and costs while grappling with how to measure the quality and value of government effort.

An understanding of the basics of productivity management (i.e., goals, objectives, metrics, and applications), why productivity programs were abandoned, and how productivity management integrates technology and information resources goes beyond simple lessons learned. This chapter has three learning objectives for public sector human resource managers and students:

- First, how government organizations work is still important. In a current era where high performance and outcomes-focus dominate, the tendency is to just look at results and ignore the means. But government agencies and their partners and contractors need to focus on the means *and* the ends—in part because they are also high-reliability organizations and because resources are going to be more limited as government budgets tighten to meet rising debt limitations. If government is to be "competitive" in an all but certain era of growing resource scarcity and chronic fiscal stress, it must be able to demonstrate some sense of "productivity consciousness." Further, if government expenditure is going to come under increased scrutiny and fiscal pressure, it would help to have "productivity growth" re-established in public management so that it can demonstrate the return on investment for both its workforce and the intermediate outputs it uses through contractors and suppliers.
- Second, in this new century an increasingly loud and polarizing political debate about the role,

size, debt levels, and effectiveness of government programs now includes questions and challenges about the compensation levels, work value, and performance levels of public sector workers. The latter is the essence of productivity, which might contribute essential information and objective analysis to balance the often overheated rhetoric dominating current discussions.

- Third, the development of much more sophisticated productivity methodologies that include capital intensity, labor composition, R&D levels, and multifactor productivity that show the effects of technology, efficiency, resource reallocation, and other capital-labor interactions. This offers public sector human resource managers new perspectives on innovations, quality, and service growth. A better understanding and potential application of current productivity metrics offer an opportunity to reassess the value proposition of government effort and its service work ethic. They also can shed light on the value of different strategies for workforce composition and work disposition; for example, are part-time or contract employees as productive as full-time employees, and are employees who telework as productive as employees who come to offices every day?

For a beginning, this chapter returns to the 1960s, a period in the United States where confidence in government was high and government agencies were expanding their roles and tackling a range of new social and economic problems. Overlapping interests of congressional members and political and business leaders about slowing national productivity rates and economic anxieties over rising inflation and unemployment rates would ultimately result in the establishment of a productivity measurement program for the federal government. By the early 1970s the newly reformed Office of Management Budget would take the lead in establishing a statistical reporting system that began with data that would cover about half of the federal civilian workforce for a base year in 1967

and reach almost nearly 70% by 1994 (Fisk and Forte 1997: 19–20).

HOW TO MEASURE PRODUCTIVITY IN GOVERNMENT AND WHY?

Measuring productivity is essential to any serious economy. Any nation that desires to be competitive, provide an adequate standard of living for its citizens, and generate some level of wealth transfer for its future generations begins with a goal of meeting a level of productivity growth that will cover its birth and immigration rates and provide for its elderly citizens—conventionally about 2%. Productivity growth is also traditionally correlated with compensation and employment. Throughout most of the 20th century, rates of productivity change were "procyclical"—meaning productivity rates increased during periods of economic growth and expansion but tended to contract during business downturns (McGratten and Prescott 2012).

Following the Second World War, productivity growth in the U.S. was solid and substantial, outstripping most of the international competition. When the great productivity slowdown hit the U.S. in the 1970s, the discussion of what government should do to foster productivity largely focused on what were perceived failings in government economic and regulatory policies that were seen as hampering private sector productivity growth. Critics of government pointed to deficit spending, byzantine tax systems, regulatory interventions in markets, and lack of effective public investment in research & development (R&D) and education. Some of these criticisms—or "unnecessary burdens" as they were called in a 1984 White House Conference—are "the usual suspects," so to speak (White House Conference 1984: 4). However, underlying this reexamination of private and public sector poor performance was the recognition that the United States was in the midst of a major transition to a new economy—one based primarily on services and information—and that the old industrial management and workforce control systems and strategies were no longer adequate.

In the early 1970s, congressional interest led directly to creating a formal productivity measurement program in the federal government (Fisk and Forte 1997: 19). While the politics and institutional arrangements that surrounded the program to be launched by the Office of Management Budget, the Office of Personnel Management (then the Civil Service Commission), and the Government Accountability Office (then named the General Accounting Office) with measurement via the Bureau of Labor Statistics is interesting, the focus here is on the who, what, and how of measurement.

Once baselines were created with the measurement system, the program (usually acronymed FPMP for the Federal Productivity Measurement Program) would include about half of the civilian federal workforce at the start and reach about two-thirds of the workforce by the mid-1970s (Fisk and Forte 1997: 20). There were some major missing agencies, such as the intelligence agencies, the State Department, and large portions of the Defense Department. But even among these excepted agencies, some support functions were included for measurement (logistics and administrative support for Defense, contractors for NASA, etc.).

Determining what would be measured was seen as the real challenge. Agencies had to designate some form of final output. The primary focus was on some form of physical count—such as volume of mail for the Post Office, or number of inspections, claims or invoices paid, student days taught, licenses processed, health care visits, and so on. To be fair, this challenge to identify outputs was neither a formidable nor a new phenomenon for government. The prevailing budgeting system for the federal (and many state governments) coming out of the midcentury was performance budgeting, which included extensive program work output measurements both as efficiency indicators and the basis for using work measurement to establish staffing levels for programs. Performance budgeting was a precursor for productivity management; as one early budgeting textbook noted, "The contentions for the new productivity field in the 1970s are very reminiscent of the earlier claims for performance budgeting. Performance budgeting sought to establish management's right and responsibility to ascertain how much work was being accomplished, at what cost, and for what results as measured against specified performance standards. In the 1970s the questions are still the same, only it seems they are being asked by different people" (Hyde 1978: 78).

Under the FPMP, agencies established different program output measurements and integrated them into a final organizational output index. Box 3.1 outlines the calculation elements that are part of conventional productivity measurement.

Traditional Productivity Measurement	Output Metrics	Input Metrics
$Y= f(L, C, IX)t$ Where, $Y = Output$ $L = Labor$ $C = Capital$ $IX = Intermediate Products$	Output per employee year Final Output (Tangible) Examples: • Post Office: Mail Volumes • Social Services: Claims Paid • Forest Service: Fire Acres Or Intermediate Activities (Contracts, Personnel, Supply, Maintenance, Investigations, etc.)	Number of employee years Compensation per Employee Unit Labor Costs No estimates of capital or computing included

Source: Federal Productivity Measurement Program (FPMP) (1972–1994).

Labor was measured by counting the total number of employee years, compensation levels for each employee year, and a unit labor cost. The resulting calculation is then indexed at 100 for the first measurement year for the FPMP, as illustrated in Figure 3.1 which shows changing rates of federal productivity versus the private sector over the period. Federal productivity actually rose by a respectable rate of 1.5% annually from 1967 to 1982 before slowing to a .6% annual rate during the "productivity slowdown" era from 1982 to 1994. The 1.5% rate slightly exceeded private sector productivity of 1.4% but trailed the private sector rate of 1.3% in the next period.

In commenting on what this quarter century of productivity output data shows, some major qualifications must be noted. First, the labor input in the federal productivity calculation (shown in Table 3.1) was an aggregate workforce input number. It did not include submeasures of capital, equipment, technology, or other factors that could affect outputs. Second, while the cost of labor input numbers did include full wage numbers (salary, benefits, incentives, etc.), qualitative submeasures of skill levels or qualifications were not included. Third, labor functions were measured in the FPMP but with an aim of showing productivity comparisons across different functions. FPMP provided average annual productivity rates for 24 federal occupational groups, with two functions showing negative productivity index rates: electric power utility personnel and medical services. These are also the two functions with the highest unit labor costs compared with the function (Finance)

Figure 3.1 FPMP Annual Rates of Change—Labor Productivity in Federal Government vs. U.S. Private Sector Rates, 1967–1994

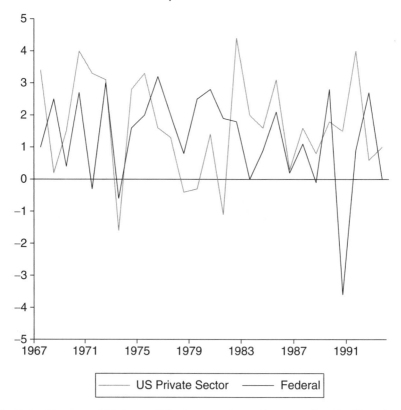

Source: U.S. Monthly Labor Review, May 1997, and U.S. Bureau of Labor Statistics, Labor Productivity Database (data.bls.gov/time series/PRS85006092).

with the highest productivity, which had the lowest unit labor costs; this points to the sensitivity of the FPMP to wage factors.

In productivity management terms, this effort by the FPMP certainly qualified as a good start. It demonstrated that federal productivity levels were certainly in line with the national experience and in the same league as the private sector. While the data qualifications weren't trivial, there was a decent foundation to make assessments about federal productivity contributions in macroeconomic terms and solid trend data for agencies to review unit productivity performance levels.

However, in 1994, the FPMP was a victim of a major round of federal budget cuts and the Bureau of Labor Statistics suspended the measurement side of the program. Thereafter, no systematic productivity measurement would be undertaken at the federal level except for the U.S. Postal Service. It is certainly safe to say that few managerial tears were shed on the loss of the federal productivity program. And, as will be noted, the dismantling of the FPMP did not leave a vacuum. Following the National Performance Review at the outset of the Clinton-Gore administration in 1993, total quality management[2] was essentially the successor to productivity management. Quality management was a better or perhaps more comfortable fit for most federal agencies, with its blend of participatory management groups and measurement methodologies that appealed to a predominantly white collar workforce and to labor groups that championed labor-management partnerships.

Before assessing the federal productivity management effort, productivity efforts at the state and local level should also be mentioned. While no systematic effort was made to report on subnational public productivity levels, there was interest in testing measurement strategies and methodologies. BLS—as their exemplary 1998 final study attests—selected ten different state and local services to develop and report productivity statistics on. While the big three (police, fire, and education) were excluded from the study—the range of services studied made quite clear that calculating productivity was both feasible and methodologically defensible. These early investigations grappled with how to determine output measurements for services ranging from more blue collar–oriented activities in enterprises (utilities and transit services) to mostly white collar (parole and corrections to employment and social services). BLS also chose three services where numerous private sector systems existed for comparison. Table 3.1—taken from the 1998 study—highlights the comparisons.

In the three state and local services in which public and private sector comparisons were made, public sector productivity tracked and compared favorably. But it should be noted that these three services were among the least personnel intensive. The service area with the lowest productivity rates was local jails, although the longer-term counterpart of state prisons had better productivity rates even though labor inputs were about the same. BLS's assessment of the corrections area (jails and prisons) is all the more interesting because it developed means to account for overcrowding. Further they pointed to the recidivism issue—which they weren't able to factor in a meaningful way—which would clearly alter the output measurement. Another interesting distinction drawn in this productivity study was how mass transit productivity rates showed improvement when the output metric was vehicle revenue miles as opposed to number of trips.

One final contribution—worth further reflection—was BLS's estimates of rates of labor intensity for government services. Although this was soon to change with the full arrival of the computer and Internet technology era starting around 1995, Figure 3.2 (which calculated for one baseline year, 1992) shows labor compensation as the percentage of total operating expenditures for different government functions. Human resource managers, of course, would appropriately point to functions like police, fire, and education and conclude that when over 80% of the operating budget is human resources, the quality and skill levels of those resources are paramount. Productivity management advocates would certainly concur but add that tracking the labor productivity rates of these invaluable assets is also critical.

Table 3.1 Annual Labor Productivity—State & Local Governments—10 Functions over Select Years

Service (Years Measured)	Output	Labor Input	Labor Productivity (Government)	Comparison Labor Productivity (Private Sector Counterparts)
Electric power (1967–1992)	3.6%	1.5%	2.1%	2.3%
Natural gas (1974–1992)	−0.7%	0.9%	−1.6%	−2.2%
Water supply (1967–1992)	1.8%	1.2%	.6%	
Mass transit (passenger trips) 1967–1992	.5%	2.6%	−2.1%	
Mass transit (vehicle revenue miles) 1967–1992	2.2%	2.6%	−.5%	
Alcohol beverage sales (1967–1992)	−.1%	−1.2%	0.9%	0.9%
State prisons (1973–1992)	7.8%	7.8%	.1%	
Local jails (1970–1992)	4.7%	7.3%	−2.4%	
Juvenile institutions (1971–1992)	.3%	1.4%	−1.1%	
Unemployment insurance (1967–1992)	3.7%	2.3%	1.3%	
Employment services (1972–1987)	0%	−.9%	1.0%	

Source: U.S. Bureau of Labor Statistics, 1998, Measuring State and Local Government Productivity: 9.

While the agency productivity output and labor costs measurements were the primary quantitative emphasis, BLS also attempted more qualitative evaluations. Agency managers were surveyed about their explanation for shifts in productivity that perhaps foretold of the perceived value of FPMP as an important human resources

Figure 3.2 Personnel Compensation as Percentage of Total Operating Expenditures for Select State and Local Government Functions, 1991–1992

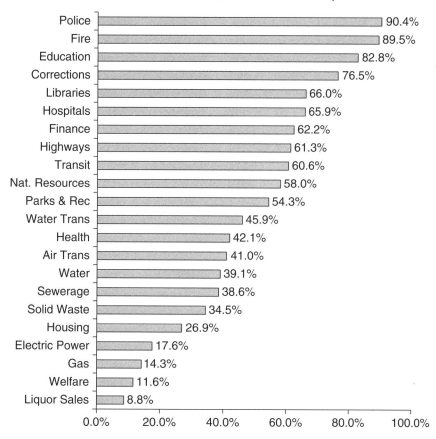

Source: U.S. Bureau of Labor Statistics, 1998, Measuring State and Local Government Productivity: 23.

managerial tool. Fisk and Forte in their closing assessment of the FPMP note that most agencies explained major shifts in productivity levels as driven by workload volatility and technology. In the 1970s unforeseen political, financial, or environmental events were identified as the primary driving forces that would cause an agency to ramp up or scale down work efforts and staffing levels, which would then shifted productivity levels. Later, in the 1980s agency comments pointed to major changes in office automation and computing as major driving forces (Fisk and Forte 1997: 27). In other words, productivity measurement wasn't seen as having much of an effect other than to register the impacts of external factors.

Another political development may have also shaped this managerial disinclination toward productivity measurement. In 1985 the Reagan administration promulgated an executive order as part of his newly re-elected administration's federal management improvement program. Entitled the President's Productivity Improvement Program, the 23 designated primary federal agencies under OMB's direct purview were to institute formal programs that would establish a productivity office and publish a productivity improvement plan with a formal measurement system. On the first page on the executive order draft, OMB announced that a 20% improvement goal by 1992 for all agencies would be set. Further in the document, OMB proclaimed that these implemented productivity goals would "be translated into projected cost savings" (Wright 1984).

Federal agency managers certainly understood and both resented and resisted this type of "productivity math"—where productivity gains were "pre-ordered" to be used to decrease agency budgets as opposed to increasing service quality, investing in agency capabilities, or supporting innovation efforts. NASA, having launched a major contractor and agency effort around productivity improvement a year earlier, was typical of agency response—notifying OMB that under this program they were essentially being penalized for their efforts and therefore were disinclined to participate (NASA-JSC 1985). As the Reagan administration's political capital was diverted to other more pressing matters (the Iran-Contra affair, etc.), the OMB initiative was set aside and quietly left to expire at the end of Reagan's second term.

There is a long history of "lapsed" public sector management efforts driven by executive mandate to reduce agency budget levels whether at the federal or state government level. Politically, programs launched from auspices of one executive are almost always let go when a new administration takes over. However, this instance entails the additional peril of using productivity measurement primarily as a budget tool for cost-cutting as opposed to a management reinvestment tool for service quality improvement, upgrading infrastructure or technology, or enhancing public service commitment. The latter is what makes productivity management an important management tool—its use in ensuring that economies and industries innovate and grow, and don't stagnate.

OLD LESSONS LEARNED— NEW QUESTIONS NEEDED

As mentioned, budget cutbacks in the first two years of the Clinton administration would result in termination of the federal productivity measurement effort. In addition to changing budget priorities, new management initiatives (some call them fads) like total quality management, and lack of political support from agency managers with long memories about the ill-fated OMB 1985 productivity program, the productivity environment itself was changing. For the student of human resources management to make sense out of the change in the 1990s and in order to draw appropriate lessons for the future, five factors need to be examined.

First and foremost, national productivity improved dramatically, emerging out of its two-decade slumber. Driven primarily by new technology and capital investment, private sector productivity annual growth rates reached 2.1% in the mid-1990s and over 2.5% by 2000, as Figure 3.3 illustrates. Debates among economists about Robert Solow's famous query in 1987—"You can see the computer age everywhere but in the productivity statistics"—now shifted from what the problem was to what was now driving the solution and whether it would last (Brynjolfsson 1993). In the late 1990s, after productivity soared nationally and federal government budgets reached surplus levels for the first time in seemingly decades, interest in productivity plummeted.

It also should be noted that productivity measurement also changed in an effort to capture the increasing complexity of the now ascendant digital revolution. Coming out of the productivity slowdown period, there remained great concern that a services-dominated economy would hamper productivity and economic growth (Baumol, Batey Blackman, and Wolff 1989). Remarkably, economists looking at productivity trends in a so-called stagnant sector found—as a Brookings symposium of leading economists noted—"services now lead the way." The consensus estimate was that service industries contributed over 73% of labor productivity growth in the 1990–2000 period and 76% of U.S. total productivity growth (Triplett and Bosworth 2004: 2).

Obviously U.S. productivity growth improved dramatically, as Figure 3.2 shows. Not quite as obvious was why, given the new domination of services in the U.S. economy. During the 1990s the American economy added more than 19 million jobs while manufacturing goods production sectors were basically flat. This doesn't mean that manufacturing productivity

Figure 3.3 U.S. National Rates of Average Productivity Growth, 1947–2011, Private Sector Nonfarm business (excludes all levels of government)

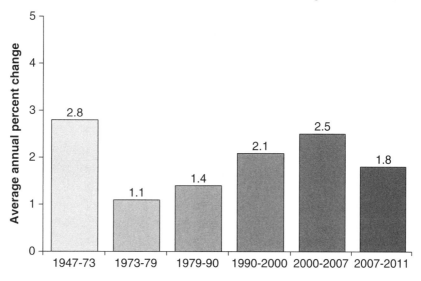

Source: Bureau of Labor Statistics (2011).

decreased. Quite the opposite: Since 2000, U.S. manufacturing jobs have declined by over 30% while manufacturing output has increased by almost 50% (de Rugy 2011). Basically, the U.S. manufacturing labor force has dropped to under 12 million workers who are now producing the equivalent total output as the previous 17 million workforce.

U.S. MANUFACTURING: OUTPUT VS. JOBS SINCE 1975

To many economists and management analysts, it was clear that something else was in play. It became increasingly obvious that the impact of "other dimensions" of productivity had not been adequately measured before. To be fair, organizational purchases of capital—even computers and other technology investments—were part of the productivity equation that included the total costs of labor and capital equipment. As economists debated both if and when the investments made by the U.S. in both the private and public sector would materialize up to the mid-1990s productivity turnaround, pressure mounted to augment the methodology for

measuring productivity. The resulting metric called *multi-factor productivity* still produced an output ratio per labor hour, but it was expanded to include labor-capital interactions to estimate what contributions were made by technology, other efficiency actions, and resource reallocations.

Currently—if one looks at the 2011 multifactor productivity trends from the U.S. Bureau of Labor Statistics of U.S. national averages (excluding government services)—the following larger view is possible (Figure 3.4). The introduction of multifactor productivity not only enlarged the organization view of capital and labor resources, it also provided a means for assessing different strategies for human resource investments. Capital intensity also included a separate breakout for the contribution of information processing equipment and software. So, for example, a state government's motor vehicle registration and licensing department could reassess how to align its technology support, capital equipment ratios, workforce mix of service employees and contractors, and Internet services provision to achieve the most optimal productivity levels.

Figure 3.4 National Productivity Growth Rates for Private Nonfarm Business Sector, 1987–2011

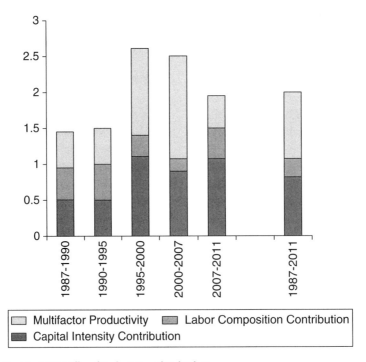

Source: Bureau of Labor Statistics, May 9, 2012 Office of Productivity and Technology.

A second factor entailed internal shifts in public sector workforces. The movement towards a super-majority white collar workforce had been underway for some time. Government agencies at all levels contracted out support functions and blue collar jobs, accelerating this trend. By the mid-1990s, the federal workforce was below 15% blue-collar positions; by 2010 the percentage went below 10%. But much more importantly, government workforces were becoming more highly compensated as average grade levels increased. Productivity measurements capture this of course when labor costs are attached to labor hours. So when viewing the FPMP statistics in Table 3.1, both the effects of annual salary increases given across the board to the workforce and rising costs from promotions and labor compositions are in play.

Figure 3.5 shows a 50-year decadal perspective of how the federal workforce has shifted from a 50%–25% split

between the lowest six grades and the highest five grades, By the end of the FPMP, the split was 30% for lowest grades and 45% for the top five for white collar workers. In 2014, the top five grades accounted for just under 62% of the federal workforce. Of course, those grade increases reflect higher education levels, greater skill qualifications, longer tenure, and an older force. But similarly, productivity measurement using today's methodologies are capable of measuring impacts of labor composition and if in place might have been useful in assessing the impacts of these shifts. For example, one factor often mentioned in looking at current workforce dynamics in government is contract management. Instead of framing the question in terms of staffing—that is, aligning employee grade levels with the level and award amounts of contracting—the productivity question might produce a different assessment of the optimal mix of organizational and contractual staffing.

Figure 3.5 Grade Level Change in the Federal Government in the Civilian White Collar Workforce by Decade, 1962–2014

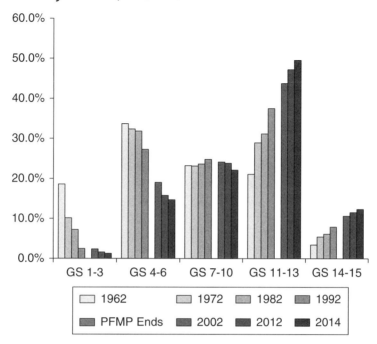

Source: Compiled by the authors using federal employment data from www.fedscope.opm (2002, 2012, 2014), the 1962, 1972 Civil Service Commission Federal Civilian Workforce Statistics Report, and the 1982 and1992 Office of Personnel Management Federal Civilian Workforce Statistics Reports.

So externally the national productivity picture brightened, and internally the labor structure of many government organizations shifted toward a high quality in terms of human factors workforce. Two other factors emerged in the 1990s that pushed the demise of productivity management. The advent of quality management, already mentioned, in effect superseded productivity. Quality management in the public sector also got some help from a major effort in the American service industry to embrace the principles of quality management. Telecommunications, banking, insurance, and even health care organizations began to develop their own versions of quality with a distinct service focus. These industries all had major counterparts in the public sector at federal, state, and local levels (along with being suppliers, contractors, and partners), and they strongly encouraged benchmarking and sharing of best practices

with government agencies. Many of these service industry corporations helped fund studies on quality practices among state and local governments and set up advisory committees to help launch government-wide efforts.

At the federal level, when the September 1993 National Performance Review report was issued, quality management was not a primary reference point. However the report's second chapter—"Putting Customers First"—was quality management 101 from top to bottom. The administration issued Executive Order 12862 embedding all of these quality expectations into agency management requirements. All federal agencies dealing with the public were required to identify their customers, set quality standards for service, survey their customers, and act to make government services "equal to the best in business." Unlike the aforementioned formal productivity programs where improvements might be translated into cost savings and staffing reductions, quality improvements were reinvestments in the agency's performance.

Quality management also was highly compatible with the aims and natural interests of a highly skilled workforce. Quality management called for very high levels of workforce participation or what was generally called "empowerment." Workers at all levels were expected (and trained) to join together in any number of variations of quality groups or project efforts to analyze quality problems (improvement teams) or to devise new solutions (process redesign teams). Most of these teams operated outside of the classic formal hierarchical and representation structures of government bureaucracy. Many of the efforts included contractors, partners, and even client and customer groups.

Essentially, the core dimensions of quality management—internal process measurements, external customer focus, employee participation, and contractor involvement—were all highly compatible with the public management premises and goals embodied in the Reinventing Government movement. For much of the decade, quality management was seen as a preferred framework for organizational change that emphasizes work groups and processes with a customer focus that was superior to more formal organizations focused on work through functional specializations. But formal quality management would face a similar fate as productivity with the presidential election change in 2000. One of the first acts of the Bush administration was to issue an executive order ending labor-management partnerships. While the executive order neither prevented government agencies from labor consultations nor promoting quality program aspects, the management emphasis at the federal level shifted to competitive government, technology innovations, new personnel systems, and new budget priorities.

A fourth factor—the emergence of performance results management—also played a pivotal role in productivity's demise as both management change strategy and methodology for assessing performance. Following passage of the Government Performance Results Act in 1993, federal agencies went through a five-year trial period putting in a budgeting system that asked agencies to prepare five-year strategic plans with performance goals based on outcomes. Indeed, reliance on outputs— the core numerator in productivity metrics—was seen as a problem with underperformance. Both the Office of Management and Budget and the GAO (then the General Accounting Office—soon to be renamed the Government Accountability Office) championed this new direction.

There were few dissenters. It was difficult to argue with the strong current of performance management— or, as an assessment of the demise of FPMN by the research staff at the Minneapolis Federal Reserve Bank quoted one Beltway expert, "I don't care how fast a government worker goes through a pile of paper until I know whether the pile of paper needs going through in the first place . . . . productivity numbers tell me nothing until I have a measure of the benefit" (Wirtz 2000: 6). So the federal emphasis (and many state governments likewise pursued performance results budgeting variations) was on measuring the effects—or social outcomes—of government programs. Productivity was equated with more simplistic efficiency while performance was to be best understood in terms of measuring effectiveness.

This is a pivotal issue that productivity management has always recognized but been unable to reconcile. One of the most influential early management theorists in productivity—Michael Packer[3]—addressed this in an MIT white paper in 1982 aptly titled "What's Wrong with Organizational Productivity Analysis?" Packer sorted through the different measurement issues highlighting the degrees of difficulty and reliability in various service industry and government organizations, especially those with substantial R&D efforts, intelligence roles, or those that produce more intangible outputs. He also noted all the objections that managers would have about measurement and data analysis methods, especially if the numbers were going to be used to make comparisons to other private sector entities. But his point was that managers weren't going to be impressed by simply knowing how the organization's current productivity rates were trending. Packer urged that organizational productivity data be used to interpret the range management flexibilities and potential scale of improvement and innovation in the same vein that business enterprises use market research and economics (Packer 1982: 9–10).

Packer's concerns are still valid today. If human resource managers want to understand how much progress is being made in pursuit of organizational goals and concurrently how effective the use of human, capital, technology, and information resources is, they will need analytical tools for measuring productivity. Productivity analytical tools go beyond simply adopting a vocabulary of management efficiency used to proclaim that new initiatives (the movement to cloud computing in government comes readily to mind) will make the workforce more productive.

But perhaps a case example is needed to illustrate this point. Federal agencies today are striving to comply with requirements to allow teleworking in their agencies. Most use surveys of workers in their teleworking programs that show higher job satisfaction, more time spent doing task work, and less time doing administrative work. A study at the Patent and Trademarks Office found teleworking employees processed more patent applications per year than their in-office counterparts, according to the Commerce Department Office of Inspector General. That makes them more or equally productive, except that the Inspector General noted that teleworkers didn't process applications at a greater rate; they simply reviewed patents for more hours than their office-bound counterparts (U.S. Dept. of Commerce 2012). Of course, the program is successful on a number of other fronts, but in terms of Packer's organizational productivity analysis framework challenge, the questions still remain: How productive is teleworking and how do you know?

This basic human resource management question deserves more than subjective answers. In another detailed assessment of teleworking using national government employee survey data, Mahler provides a sterling examination of the benefits of teleworking programs and questions whether there may be a rift between those who are and those who are not allowed to participate. The survey results point to strong agreement that those who telework report higher levels of job satisfaction and improved personnel productivity (Mahler 2012: 413). But how do they know, since there are no basic quantitative measurements of organizational, unit, or much less individual productivity in place? No disparagement of teleworking or any other form of flexible work arrangements using new technologies is intended; the point is simply to reinforce the need for organizational productivity measurement, especially in government services.

There remains an unranked fifth factor that, despite a great amount of activity that occurred and continues to be made, is of less certain significance. This would include organizational change management strategies based on participatory management in the workplace. When these "change strategies" have been charted in the private sector, results in terms of productivity management are mixed.

Some change management strategies have pursued linking compensation to productivity. Results here have generally followed Blinder's conclusion that changing the way workers are treated increases productivity more than changing compensation practices (Blinder 1990: 13). A 1999 NBER–MIT metastudy on productivity improvement concluded that progressive human resource policies and practices produced little net organizational productivity benefits, as increased labor costs tended to offset increases in productivity improvements, where they were measured (Lester 1999) or even resulted in lower performance and diminished organizational reputation (Keating et al. 1999).

Other multiple organizational case reviews are more positive, as Black and Lynch have noted in a 2004 Federal Reserve Bank of San Francisco research note. They found that those organizations supporting workplace innovations—specifically work teams, more flexible job definitions, and up-skilling of the workforce—tended to be more productive than traditional organizations (Black and Lynch 2004: 2), These efforts also have multiple objectives—to support workforce retention, enhance morale, and promote engagement and commitment to organizational values. Of course, in government agencies where productivity is no longer measured, these are the only managerial objectives that remain.

A Concluding Note and a Postscript

This chapter, despite its odd title, began with three objectives and a hope. The objectives were to recast productivity measurement methods and management strategies to promote better understanding of several key debates about whether governments are competitive, workforces are compensated appropriately, and organizations are using their resources optimally.

It's already clear that the national debate about the size and role of government is most likely to be argued on political grounds. Whatever the shape of the 2016 federal budget, discretionary program spending or the remaining programs after entitlements and interest requirements are destined to be further crowded in the coming decade. This was apparent back in 2006 when McKinsey published a study calling for a renewal of the federal productivity program so that federal productivity could be part of what they called "performance transparency" (Danker et al. 2006). That the study was basically ignored, even by the largely pro-business Bush administration, proves once again that sector productivity comparisons are neither compelling nor convincing.

However, the organizational productivity challenge is going to be of increasing interest. As the public-private pay comparability debate continues, human resource managers are going to face increasing pressure (and media scrutiny) to explain how staffing, productivity, and compensation levels are linked. Debates about the necessary numbers of police, teachers, nurses, and other public work functions are going to go deeper than arguing trends in crime rates, test scores, and health care outcomes. Many government functions are already on the defensive about why well-intentioned efforts are not always translating into improved outcomes. Governments may find that to obtain additional resources to achieve better results, they will have to demonstrate that their good intentions are matched by

high productivity levels and optimal use of resources. This will become even more apparent as technology alters every aspect of work from content to methods to work skill competencies.

Public managers may well want to revisit the current quality of performance paradigm in which being responsive and delivering services that meet citizen preferences seems to be all that matters. The means (i.e., productivity) in which organizations determine that the right things are being done using the right mix of resources most efficiently is also essential. Again, this is going to be even more critical as technology and connectivity transform the production and service processes. Public services, especially those that are human interaction intensive, are not going away. However, productivity measurement can provide human resource managers with critical information about how to use technology shifts in support of the next stages of public service innovation. Hopefully, the need for organizational productivity metrics and opportunity for using multifactor productivity analysis in the public sector will bring productivity management back to the forefront of human resources management.

Finally, it is altogether fitting and indeed ironic, that there is a renewed debate about national productivity levels. In this new decade since 2010, U.S. productivity growth rates have slumped dramatically, to dismal levels, even below the terrible 1970s (Blinder 2014):

1870–2013	2.3%
1948–1973	2.8%
1973–1995	1.4%
1995–2010	2.6%
2010–2013	0.7%

While economists have been somewhat surprised by this and there is disagreement about the causes, this time there is consensus about the long-term consequences and potential negative effects. Governments will also find that they are part of the debate about what to do.

Robert Solow, of the "computers and productivity" linkage mentioned earlier, noted in a recent interview that what is most different now is the recognition that what drives productivity growth most is management differences. Paraphrasing Solow, it's not how capital intensive or technological advances that matter most. It's "failure in management decisions"—the inability or unwillingness to rethink and reallocate tasks within organizations to compete successfully (Solow 2014). Of course, that reallocation of tasks to an organization's workforce is the essence of human resources management and a reminder of why productivity measurement matters.

NOTES

1. The 9 million total government workers in the 1970s compares with 14 million total full-time government workers (there are also over 5 million part-time employees) according to the last available census of government in 2012. About 90% of that growth has been in state and local government (U.S. Census 2014).
2. Although the literature on quality management in the public sector is extensive—beginning with quality circles in the 1980s merging into full blown total quality management programs in the 1990s, an Executive Order mandating customer service quality standards and reviews—that goes beyond the scope and space allotted for this review.
3. Michael Packer died in the World Trade Center in New York City during the September 11 terrorist attacks; he was delivering a keynote address at a conference there.

REFERENCES

Baumol, William J., Sue Anne Batey Blackman, and Edward Wolff. 1989. *Productivity and American Leadership.* Cambridge, MA: MIT Press.

Black, Sandra A., and Lisa M. Lynch. 2004. Workplace Practices and the New Economy. Federal Reserve Bank of San Francisco, CSIP Notes Number 2-4-10, April.

Blinder, Alan S. 1990. *Paying for Productivity.* Washington, DC: Brookings Institution Press, 13.

Blinder, Alan S. 2014. The Unsettling Mystery of Productivity. *Wall Street Journal*, November 24.

Brynjolfsson, Erik. 1993. The Productivity Paradox of Information Technology: Review and Assessment. *Communications of the ACM*, December.

Danker, Tony, Thomas Dohrmann, Nancy Killefer, and Lenny Mendonca, L. 2006. How Can American Government Meet Its Productivity Challenge? McKinsey & Company, July.

Dertouzos, Michael L., Richard K. Lester, and Robert M. Solow. 1989. *Made in America: Regaining the Productive Edge* (MIT Commission on Industrial Economy). Cambridge, MA: MIT Press.

De Rugy, Veronique. 2011. U.S. Manufacturing: Outputs vs. Jobs since 1975. Mercatus Center White Paper, George Mason University, January.

Fisk, Donald M. 1985. The Federal Productivity Measurement System: The Process and Selected Statistics. *Management Science and Policy Analysis Journal-Letter, 2*(3).

Fisk, Donald, and Darlene Forte. 1997. The Federal Productivity Measurement Program: Final Results. *Monthly Labor Review*, May, 19–28.

Fuchs, Victor. 1968. *The Service Economy.* New York: National Bureau of Economic Research/Columbia University Press, 1968.

Gilder, George. 1975. Public Sector Productivity National Commission on Productivity and Work Quality. *Public Productivity Review, 1*(1), 4–8, 6.

Hyde, Albert C. 1978. Performance Budgeting. In *Government Budgeting: Theory, Process, Politics.* Oak Park, IL: Moore Publishing, 77–81.

Keating, Elizabeth K., et al. 1999. Overcoming the Improvement Paradox." *European Management Journal, 17*(2), 120–134.

Lester, Richard K. 1999. *The Productive Edge.* New York: Norton.

Mahler, Julianne. 2012. The Telework Divide: Managerial and Personnel Challenges of Telework. *Review of Public Personnel Administration, 32*(4), 407–418.

McGratten, Ellen R., and Edward C. Prescott. 2012. The Labor Productivity Puzzle. Federal Reserve Bank of Minneapolis, Working Paper 694, May.

NASA-JSC. 1985. An Assessment of NASA's Productivity Management Program—Johnson Space Center. University of Houston Clear City Consulting Report, ed. Albert C. Hyde, July.

National Academy of Sciences. 1979. *Measurement and Interpretation of Productivity.* Washington, DC: NAS.

Packer, Michael B. 1982. What's Wrong with Organizational Productivity Analysis? MIT Laboratory for Manufacturing and Productivity, Paper LMP-MRP-81–15, July.

Shafritz, Jay M., and Albert C. Hyde. 2012. *Classics of public administration*, 7th ed. Boston: Wadsworth.

Solow, Robert. 2014. Prospects for Growth: An Interview. *McKinsey Quarterly*, September.

Triplett, Jack E., and Barry Bosworth (Eds.). 2004. *Productivity in the U.S. Services Sector: New Sources of Economic Growth.* Washington, DC: Brookings Institution Press.

U.S. Census. 2014. 2012 Census of Governments: Employment Summary Report, G12-CG-EMP, edited by Lisa Jessie and Mary Tarleton, March 6.

U.S. Department of Commerce, Office of Inspector General. 2012. The Patent Hoteling Program Is Succeeding as a Business Strategy. Report OIG-12-018-A. February.

U.S. Department of Labor, Bureau of Labor Statistics. Measuring State and Local Government Productivity: Examples from Eleven Studies. Bulletin 2495. June.

White House Conference on Productivity. *Productivity Growth: A Better Life for America.* April.

Wirtz, Ronald. 2000. Icebergs and Government Productivity. Minneapolis Federal Reserve Bank. June. Available at https://www.minneapolisfed.org/publications/the-region/icebergs-and-government-productivity. Accessed on November 7, 2012.

Wright, Joseph R. Jr. 1984. Memorandum on Productivity Improvement Program. Office of Management and Budget, September 27.

CHAPTER 4

HUMAN RESOURCE MANAGEMENT IN THE FEDERAL GOVERNMENT DURING A TIME OF INSTABILITY

James R. Thompson
University of Illinois–Chicago

Robert Seidner
U.S. Office of Management and Budget

The period 2006–2014 can be characterized as one of instability in federal human resource management (HRM) practices and policies. The most significant reforms of the preceding period, the creation of separate personnel systems at the Departments of Homeland Security and Defense, were repealed. The substantial immunity that the federal workforce had enjoyed from the effects of the economic recession that began in 2008 ended when employee pay was frozen and pension contributions for new employees increased in 2011. A showdown between President Obama and congressional Republicans over an increase in the federal debt ceiling in the summer of 2011 forced agencies to develop contingency plans for a government shut-down; and although a shut-down was avoided at that time, the compromise that was reached simply postponed the showdown. Throughout 2013, hundreds of thousands of federal employees were furloughed without pay. The culmination occurred on October 1, 2013, when the lack of a budget forced much of the government to shut down for 16 days. These conditions contributed to the onset of the long-awaited "tsunami" of retirements by

federal employees as members of the baby boom generation headed for the exits.

This discussion of recent HRM developments in the federal government is organized into three sections. The section on "Discontinuities" includes a discussion of those HRM developments that represent a departure by the Obama administration from the policies of its predecessor while the section on "Continuities" highlights programs where linkages between the Obama and Bush administrations can be identified. The section on "New Initiatives" reviews those areas of activity in which the Obama administration has left its own distinctive mark.

Discontinuities

Repeal of MaxHR and the National Security Personnel System

The exemption of the Departments of Homeland Security and Defense from key provisions of Title 5 of the United States Code in 2002–2003 was among the most radical changes to the civil service system in decades.[1] The civil service has long been characterized by a relatively consistent set of employment rules across agencies.[2] The intent was to create a sense of cohesion within the workforce and to counteract centrifugal tendencies. Although there had been occasional, small-scale exemptions to this policy over the decades, the creation of the MaxHR system at the Department of Homeland Security (DHS) in 2002 and the National Security Personnel System at the Department of Defense (DoD) in 2003 represented exemptions of such magnitude as to represent a change in the system itself.

DHS and DoD include a combined 46% of all civilian federal employees (Congressional Research Service 2011). Thus, when these agencies were exempted from portions of the Title 5 rules relating to compensation, performance management, and labor-management relations, it appeared to signal the demise of the traditional civil service model and the triumph of a "strategic" approach to HRM in which each agency would be allowed to customize HRM policies to the agency's specific mission and strategy (Thompson 2006). However, such predictions proved to be premature. A coalition of federal employee unions successfully challenged both programs in court, and Congress subsequently withdrew authorization, leaving the pre-2002 status quo substantially in place.

Union opposition to the National Security Personnel System (NSPS) and MaxHR was provoked primarily by the proposed labor-management relations provisions, which would have narrowed the scope of issues subject to collective bargaining and provided for agency-specific and management-controlled labor-relations boards to resolve collective bargaining disputes (Thompson 2007a). A coalition of federal employee unions sued to stop implementation of MaxHR on the grounds that those rules would deny employees their statutory right to bargain over working conditions. The courts sided with the unions and forced DHS back to the drawing board. By the time the court case was resolved in 2006, the political landscape had shifted. Members of both parties in Congress called upon the department to consult with the unions on the terms of a new system. The department instead decided to put the entire initiative on hold while retaining the traditional Title 5 personnel rules. The few

HRM changes that have been made at DHS since have been incremental rather than radical in nature.

Early developments at the Department of Defense paralleled those at DHS: Rules with provisions similar to those proposed by DHS were challenged by the unions in court on the grounds that they violated the right of employees to bargain collectively. Although a District Court decision favored the unions, a panel of judges of the U.S. Court of Appeals for the District of Columbia ruled in 2007 that the proposed rules were in compliance with the law and allowed NSPS implementation to go forward. After Congress intervened to suspend authority for the proposed labor-management relations provisions, the department determined that only non-bargaining unit personnel would be included in NSPS. By late 2008, over 200,000 such employees had been transitioned to NSPS. However, after President Obama took office in 2009, the federal employee unions prevailed upon their congressional allies to repeal NSPS entirely. In October 2009, President Obama signed the 2010 National Defense Authorization Act repealing NSPS and directing that all DoD employees who had transitioned to NSPS be converted back to the traditional Title 5 rules.

Compensation and Classification

Although the demise of both NSPS and MaxHR represent a setback for those who regard the provisions of Title 5 as out of date, pressures for reform of the civil service system have persisted. The General Schedule system of compensation and classification has been subject to particular criticism. The General Schedule (GS) is widely regarded as outdated, overly rigid, not compatible with the needs of an increasingly professional workforce, and insufficiently sensitive to performance in matters of pay setting (Office of Personnel Management 2002).

In a 2012 report entitled "Bracing for Change: Chief Human Capital Officers Rethink Business as Usual," the Partnership for Public Service (PPS) reported that "nearly all CHCOs [chief human capital officers] agreed that the current 1949-era GS pay and classification system is outdated and doesn't meet the needs of a dynamic and changing 21st century workforce" (Partnership for Public Service 2012a: 16). The chief human capital officers expressed preference instead for a system of "paybanding." With paybanding the narrow grades that characterize the General Schedule would be replaced with broad salary bands and managers would be permitted more discretion in setting the pay of their subordinates (Thompson 2007b). Under this approach there is less need for classification experts from the personnel office to make fine distinctions between the relative responsibilities of positions at different grade levels. Instead, a supervisor or manager equipped with some technical support can decide the band to which a position is assigned. Paybanding was first introduced to the federal sector in 1980 at a naval research facility in California and has subsequently been implemented in a number of additional agencies and units with generally positive results (Thompson and Seidner 2008).

The Renewal of Labor-Management Partnerships

In no area has the contrast between the Bush and Obama administrations been greater than in the area of labor-management relations. The Bush administration took a generally hostile stance toward the federal employee unions as exemplified by the proposed MaxHR and NSPS personnel rules, which would have significantly compromised the collective bargaining rights of employees in those two agencies. In 2001, soon after taking office, President Bush issued Executive Order 13203 repealing an executive order issued by his predecessor that mandated the creation of labor-management partnership councils throughout the government.[3] In 2002, the Bush administration denied collective bargaining rights to employees in the newly created Transportation Security Administration.

As an early indicator of the Bush administration's general demeanor on labor-management matters, the repeal of President Clinton's executive order on partnerships took on special importance. Labor-management relations in the federal government have traditionally been adversarial in character. In 1993, as part of his effort to "reinvent" the federal government, President Clinton issued Executive Order 12871 creating a National Partnership Council and directing that similar councils be created within each of the major departments and agencies.[4] The intent was to encourage an attitude of collaboration between labor and management in addressing workplace issues. A 2001 evaluation of the program found that the partnership initiative had improved the labor-management climate in many agencies and had resulted in a reduced number of grievances and unfair labor practice charges (Office of Personnel Management 2001). However, President Bush's 2001 executive order dissolved the National Partnership Council and rescinded any "orders, rules, regulations, guidelines, or policies implementing or enforcing" EO 12871.

The partnership concept proved resilient, however. During his first year in office, President Obama issued Executive Order 13522 directing the creation of a new National Council on Federal Labor-Management Relations to include both union and management representatives and led by the director of the Office of Personnel Management (OPM) and the deputy director of OMB. With more than 60% of the Executive Branch unionized, a significant proportion of all federal employees are represented on the Council. Similar to the Clinton program, Obama's executive order directed the creation of agency-level "forums" to "promote partnership efforts between labor and management in the executive branch."[5] Also similar to the Clinton program, attention has been directed to section 7106(b) of Title 5, which lists matters on which agencies may choose to bargain but on which they are not required to bargain. When President Clinton directed that bargaining take place on these "permissive" subjects of bargaining as part of EO 12871 he met with resistance from agencies. President Obama took a different approach, creating a set of eight "pilots" "to evaluate the impact of bargaining over permissive subjects under 5 U.S.C. 7106(b) (1)." Performance management practices (discussed further below) have also been a subject of discussion within the Council, with several unions partnering with their respective agencies to improve employee engagement and organizational effectiveness.

In another labor relations matter, the Obama administration reversed the decision by the Bush administration to deny collective bargaining rights to the 40,000-plus airport screeners employed by the Transportation Security Administration. In November 2012, those employees approved a contract negotiated by the American Federation of Government Employees, which the employees had selected as their bargaining agent (Davidson 2012).

The "Deprivileging" of Federal Employees

Until 2011, federal employees had experienced only limited repercussions from the effects of the Great Recession of 2008–2010. Government data shows that whereas the number of state and local government employees dropped by over 500,000 between July 2008 and July 2011, federal government employment actually increased by 86,000 jobs during this same period.[6] This disparity could be attributed to the fact that unlike state and local governments, the federal government can run budget deficits. In fact, the Obama administration made deficit funding a part of its strategy for counteracting the effects of the recession. However, by 2011, political pressure to reduce the size of the deficit grew and as part of deficit reduction negotiations between Congress and the president, the pay of federal employees was frozen effective January 1, 2011. The pay freeze was subsequently extended for three years, ending when federal employees were granted a 1% increase in 2014. Also as a consequence of the deficit reduction negotiations, federal employees hired after December 31, 2012, will contribute 3.1% of their pay to the cost of their pensions, up from .8% for employees hired before that date (Lunney 2012a).

Proponents of the pay freeze have contended that federal employees are overpaid relative to their private sector counterparts. A 2010 study by the Heritage Foundation concluded that the total compensation of federal employees with health and retirement benefits included is 30%–40% higher than that of their private sector counterparts (Heritage Foundation 2010). A subsequent report by the Congressional Budget Office

found that while employees at *lower* pay levels were *overpaid* relative to their private sector counterparts by approximately 15%, employees at *higher* levels were *underpaid* by as much as 25% (Congressional Budget Office 2010).

The debate over federal pay and the imposition of a freeze on federal pay signifies a sharp departure from past practices. In the past, with the federal workforce widely distributed geographically, political considerations had mitigated in favor of an attitude of accommodation between the two parties with regard to federal pay. The change symbolized by the 2011 pay freeze and subsequent pronouncements critical of federal employees was driven in part by the aggressive antigovernment ideology espoused by members of Congress associated with the Tea Party movement.[7] For federal employees the shift in attitudes has meant that positive aspects of the federal work environment once taken for granted are increasingly at risk.

Workforce Planning and Management

A central element of President Bush's "President's Management Agenda" was the "strategic management of human capital," to which workforce planning was central (Office Management and Budget 2002). Although such planning remains a priority, its execution has proved problematic in light of the turbulent political environment. Congress did not pass a single timely budget during the first six years of the Obama administration. Instead, each year saw "continuing resolutions" that simply pushed decisions forward for several months. Further, each such resolution kept funding at the same level as the previous period, thus equating to cuts in agency budgets because of the failure to reflect increased costs built into contracts, inflation, and unforeseen costs.

Between 2009 and 2013 the federal government was within hours of shutting down three different times because of budget disputes with the threat finally becoming a reality in October 2013. Occasional furloughs have occurred at agencies such as at the Federal Aviation Administration where more than 3,000 employees were sent home after their 26th temporary budget failed to pass in Congress. The most notorious of the budget scuffles started with the 2011 debate over the debt-ceiling limit. What is normally a procedural move to approve an increase in the debt ceiling morphed into an epic political debate over the size of government. Agencies were left to plan for a possible government shut-down. The settlement, dubbed "sequestration," called for $109 billion in automatic, across-the-board spending cuts on January 2, 2013, that would translate to a cut of approximately 8.5% for most departments. Instead of thinking 5–10 years ahead as rational planning would dictate, agencies have been left in constant crisis mode with decisions required about each project and employee. Senior leadership in each agency has had to divert their attention to this effort, and employee morale has plummeted.

The Retirement "Tsunami"

The continuing crisis over the federal budget may have been a factor in the decision of many retirement-age feds to finally pull the plug. The so-called retirement "tsunami" had been anticipated since the early 2000s as large numbers of baby-boom generation employees approached retirement age. Little evidence of such a tsunami emerged until 2011, however, when 105,000 retirement applications were filed by federal employees, a 24% increase over 2010 levels. From January 1–September 30, 2012, OPM processed more than 93,000 retirement applications, 10,000 more than they had in a comparable period the year before (Lunney 2012b). With retirements continuing at an annual rate of approximately 100,000, the federal government is losing about 5% of its workforce each year.

The retirements have left some agencies stretched thin. Agencies generally aren't allowed to hire until the incumbent has officially left the payroll, meaning there is no chance to train a replacement in the interim. Further, agencies have been reluctant to hire in light of continuing uncertainty over the budget.

Continuities

Notwithstanding these "discontinuities," in some areas of activity the Obama administration has built on the work

of its predecessor including those of workforce engagement and the "blended" or "multisector" workforce.

Workforce Engagement

The issue of worker engagement has gained prominence in the federal HRM community in recent years largely as a consequence of the efforts of the Partnership for Public Service (PPS), a nonprofit organization that promotes government service. Beginning in the mid-2000s, PPS has issued an annual report entitled *Best Places to Work in the Federal Government*.[8] The report compiles data from the Office of Personnel Management's Federal Employee Viewpoint Survey (FEVS) to calculate a Best Places to Work "score" for each federal agency based on an index that measures employees' agreement or disagreement with three statements included in the survey:

- I recommend my organization as a good place to work.
- Considering everything, how satisfied are you with your job?
- Considering everything, how satisfied are you with your organization?

The PPS describes its index as one of "employee satisfaction and commitment" rather than as one of "engagement." However, the job attitudes assessed correspond to those used in other studies where worker engagement is a focus. For example, the Merit Systems Protection Board (MSPB) issued a 2008 report entitled "The Power of Federal Employee Engagement" in which it devised a measure of engagement based on "pride in one's work or workplace," "satisfaction with leadership," "opportunity to perform well at work," "satisfaction with the recognition received," "prospects for future personal and professional growth," and "a positive work environment with some focus on teamwork" (Merit Systems Protection Board 2008).[9] According to the MSPB, "engaged employees are absorbed intellectually and emotionally in their work and vigorously invest their best efforts in producing the outcomes needed for the organization to achieve its goals" (Merit Systems Protection Board 2009: i).

The Best Places to Work report has garnered attention in part as a consequence of the rankings generated. Separate rankings are generated for large agencies, medium agencies, small agencies, and agency "subcomponents." The media have picked up on the results to highlight those agencies at both the top and bottom of the rankings. Particular prestige is accorded those agencies that score well.

The rankings have also served to stimulate some agencies to make improving engagement a priority. For example, the U.S. Department of Transportation (DOT) ranked near the bottom of the rankings in 2009. Then-Secretary LaHood set as a priority the goal that the department be among the top-rated large agencies. A constant focus on improvement led to programs such as IdeaHub, a portal where any employee can make a suggestion on which other employees are then allowed to vote. If enough employees agree, the secretary's Innovation Council explores implementation. DOT implemented more than 40 suggestions in three years. Also, SES members were required to adopt new employee communication tactics, including hosting listening sessions to hear feedback. Since DOT started to focus on engagement, it has become one of the top ten places to work in government.

In part as a consequence of the continued attention being directed at working conditions, employee engagement was made one of the metrics in the President's Management Agenda. Also, whereas results of the FEVS were only available at the agency level, OPM now releases FEVS results for more than 20,000 organizational units, along with trend data and index scores for employee engagement and global satisfaction. Agencies are increasingly able to use the data to link to mission outcome and target specific areas for improvement.

The Blended Workforce and "Nonstandard" Work Arrangements

During the 2000s, attention within the federal HRM community was directed at what was labeled the "blended" or "multisector" workforce (Thompson and Mastracci 2005). The focus was on how federal agencies

could balance the use of full-time employees with workers in alternative arrangements including part-time workers, seasonal workers, and contract workers. As an example, agencies such as the Internal Revenue Service and the National Park Service that experience seasonal fluctuations in workload have found it advantageous to make extensive use of seasonal employees. The Naval Research Laboratory enters into contracts with staffing firms whereby individuals with specialized skills are brought in on a temporary basis to work alongside regular employees on a research project. Once the project is complete, the contract worker can be reassigned or simply released.

From the agency perspective, the use of contract workers in place of permanent employees offers significant advantages. First, staffing firms are not bound by federal hiring and pay restrictions and thus have recruitment advantages over the agencies. Second, permanent employees cannot be let go at the end of a project without going through lengthy reduction-in-force procedures. After the September 11 terrorist incident, the intelligence community relied heavily on contract employees in responding to congressional and executive branch demands that it ramp up its counterterrorism activities. By 2007, it was estimated that contract employees made up a third of the CIA's workforce (Pincus 2007). Although the Bush administration was generally sympathetic to the use of contract employees, subsequent to 2006 when the Democrats took control of the House of Representatives, pressure was exerted to reduce the proportion of contract employees in favor of hiring more federal employees. In 2010, the Office of Federal Procurement Policy issued a policy memo instructing agencies to "avoid an overreliance on contractors for functions 'closely associated with inherently government' or that are 'critical' for the agency's mission" (Brodsky 2010).

The Obama administration added a new element to the blended workforce discussion when a new policy facilitating the use of phased retirement was approved in 2012. Phased retirement is when a full-time employee retires but continues to work on a part-time basis. The new law permits agencies to allow select employees to retire but to remain employed on a half-time basis. These employees collect half their full-time salary as well as a corresponding proportion of their retirement annuities. The advantage of phased retirement from the perspective of the agency is that it is able to retain the knowledge and experience that long-time employees bring to the workplace. For example, some agencies use the part-time retirees to train or mentor new employees. Many older employees in turn prefer to remain active while working less than a full-time schedule.

The Obama administration has also promoted the use of telework by federal employees and in 2010 Congress passed the Telework Enhancement Act. Telework arrangements allow employees to work from their homes or from a remote location. Studies have shown that telework can assist with employee retention and recruitment, for example by reducing commuting time. Telework can also facilitate continuity of operations in case of an emergency or natural disaster. OPM has updated its procedures to direct employees with a telework agreement to work from home when the government closes an office for weather or as a consequence of other emergency conditions. Previously employees were provided administrative time off for those days. By the end of 2013, about half of federal employees were eligible to telework (Office of Personnel Management 2013).

New Directions

Hiring Reform

One area of activity where the Obama administration has left its mark is that of hiring reform. Hiring reform was a natural issue in which to get involved in light of the president's appeal to members of the millennial generation and because of his interest in promoting public service. The slow and opaque nature of the federal government's hiring process has long been identified as a deterrent to government service for newer workforce entrants. In 2006, the Merit System Protection Board issued a report in which it reported that "promising candidates interested in public service turn away from careers with the Federal Government because they cannot decipher the application process, cannot wait 6

to 9 months for a hiring decision, or cannot find a job offer that is competitive with other employees" (Merit Systems Protection Board 2006: 1).

In May 2010, President Obama issued a memorandum on "Improving the Federal Recruitment and Hiring Process."[10] The primary goal was to improve the notoriously complex hiring process while simultaneously making working for the government "cool again." The president's mandate made explicit demands that agencies overhaul the technical and structural aspects of hiring. Specifically, it mandated "plain language" and shorter job announcements, resume-only applications, expanded assessment and applicant referral (known as "category rating"), and significantly reduced time-to-hire periods. From a cultural standpoint, hiring reform requires that managers be held accountable for their role in the hiring process as part of their performance evaluation. Within a year, OPM announced that the average time-to-hire had dropped from 160 days to 105 days and that nearly 90 % of job announcements were five or fewer pages long.

Hiring the Next Generation

Consistent with its intent to make government service attractive to students and newer workforce entrants, the Obama administration overhauled the federal government's internship programs. Prior to the new Pathways program, students interested in government employment were confronted with a confusing array of internship programs, each designed for a separate purpose. For example, under the Federal Career Intern Program (FCIP), students were hired for two-year internships that could be converted to permanent positions upon completing the program without having to compete with other applicants. The Student Temporary Experience Program (STEP) was intended to help students pay for college, while the work performed under the Student Career Employment Program (SCEP) had to relate to the academic and career goals of the student. Under STEP, the work did not have to relate to the student's academic or career interests, and STEP participants were not eligible for noncompetitive conversion to permanent employment.

The FCIP and SCEP programs in particular were popular with agencies because of the flexibility they afforded in recruiting, assessing, and selecting job candidates. However, in 2010, the Merit Systems Protection Board found that FCIP violated provisions of Title 5 governing veterans' preference and fair competition for jobs. Rather than revamp FCIP, President Obama determined to scrap the program along with SCEP and STEP in favor of a new set of Pathways student employment programs.

In December 2010, President Obama issued Executive Order (EO) 13562 entitled "Recruiting and Hiring Students and Recent Graduates." The EO cites the benefits to the federal government from hiring students and recent graduates "who infuse the workplace with their enthusiasm, talents, and unique perspectives."[11] The executive order created three Pathways programs each targeting a different audience:

- Internship Program: The Internship Program is targeted at current undergraduates as well as at high school and trade school students with targeted skills sets. The primary purpose is to provide students with a means of financial support during their years in school.
- Recent Graduates Program: The purpose of the Recent Graduates Program is to promote careers in the federal government. Individuals within two years of graduation from qualifying educational institutions are eligible to apply.
- Presidential Management Fellows Program: According to the executive order, the Presidential Management Fellows Program "aims to attract to the Federal service outstanding men and women from a variety of academic disciplines at the graduate level who have a clear interest in, and commitment to, the leadership and management of public policies and programs." To qualify, an individual must have received an advanced degree within the preceding two years. The goal is to appoint each fellow to a career-ladder position upon completion of the program. PMF graduates can generally enter the federal workforce at a level

higher than others with similar qualifications and receive special recognition as prospective organizational leaders.

Unfortunately, as a consequence of continuing fiscal pressures faced by agencies, the number of internships and recent graduate hiring has plummeted, from a high of about 46,000 in 2010 to about 6,000 in 2013.

Workforce Diversity

A second area in which the Obama administration has left its mark is that of workforce diversity. Separate executive orders have been issued requiring agencies to improve the hiring of individuals with disabilities,[12] Hispanics,[13] Asian and Pacific Islanders,[14] Native Americans,[15] African-Americans,[16] and women.[17] In the 2013 Federal Equal Opportunity Recruitment Program Report, the Office of Personnel Management reported that the federal workforce was 17.9 % Black, 8.2 % Hispanic, 5.8 % Asian/Pacific, and 1.7 % Native American. Overall minorities constituted 34.6 % of the federal workforce while women constituted 43.5 %. Figure 4.1 shows the percentage of the federal workforce represented by each group compared with the percentage each group represents in the civilian labor force as a whole. The figure shows that with the exception of Hispanics, the government's record in hiring women and minorities is relatively strong (Office of Personnel Management 2013).

The Obama administration has extended diversity to include the hiring of veterans. Although veterans' preference has existed since the Civil War, President Obama has placed additional demands on agencies to increase the number of veterans hired. Executive Order 13518, Employment of Veterans in the Federal Government, directed each agency to establish a Veterans Employment Program Office, to develop an operational plan for promoting veteran employment, and to provide annual training to human resource personnel on veterans' preference.[18] In 2012, OPM reported that the number of veterans employed by the federal government grew from 512,000 in 2009 (25.8% of the workforce) to 567,000

Figure 4.1 Comparison of Permanent Federal Workforce and Total Civilian Labor Force (September 2012)

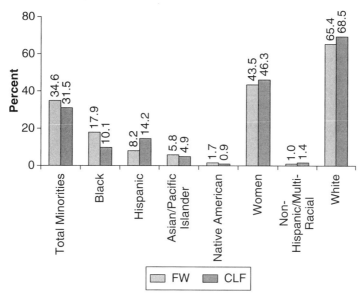

Source: OPM (2013).

(28.3% of the workforce) in 2011.[19] Additionally, a new focus has centered on hiring the spouses of military members.

Performance Management

Performance management has long been an area of concern within the federal government. One problem has been a reluctance on the part of supervisors to make meaningful distinctions in employee performance. In a 2011 speech, then-OPM director John Berry commented that "Employees may be getting useful feedback from their manager, but the formal review process seems to take place in Garrison Keillor's Lake Wobegon where everyone is above average" (Davidson 2011). Berry offered a "blueprint for changing the way we manage personnel performance" to include performance standards that are, detailed, objective, aligned to agency mission and goals and had employee buy-in."

The National Council on Federal Labor-Management Relations subsequently approved a package of reforms to overhaul performance management practices in the government. The Council agreed to pilot the new program, called GEAR (Goals, Engagement, Accountability, and Results) at six agencies. The changes, more evolutionary than revolutionary, provide for quarterly reviews of employee performance and improvements to "the assessment, selection, development, and training of supervisors."[20] In a departure from the recommendations of other reform groups, under GEAR, performance ratings would not be linked to pay.

Senior Executive Service Reforms

The Senior Executive Service, consisting of the top tier of career civil servants as well as a small percentage of political appointees, was created by the Civil Service Reform Act of 1978. The intent was that SES members serve as a corps of generalist executives whose careers would traverse agency lines and who would thereby promote interagency collaboration and cooperation. In a 2012 report, the Partnership for Public Service (PPS) and McKinsey & Company cited the benefits of this model: "Executive mobility increases the government's ability to fulfill cross-agency missions. It also allows individual agencies to build executive managerial skills, fill vacancies strategically and infuse new thinking into the organization" (Partnership for Public Service 2012b: 1). However, in concluding that "The original vision for the SES as a mobile corps of leaders has never come to fruition," PPS and McKinsey & Co. cited data showing that only 8% of SES members have worked at more than one agency during their careers. Options for increasing mobility and listed in the report include (1) requiring SES candidates to demonstrate "multisector, multiagency or multifunctional experience," (2) allowing agencies to pilot a variety of mobility programs, (3) having agencies report on cross-agency mobility and (4) centralizing management of SES mobility. To date, OPM has not acted on these recommendations. However, in 2012, OPM did act to create a new SES performance management system centered on the same five "core qualifications" used for selection into the SES: leading people, leading change, results driven, business acumen, and building coalition.

Perhaps the most dramatic change for the SES was the passage of the Department of Veterans Affairs Management Accountability Act of 2014 in response to scandals where leaders manipulated the wait times of veterans seeking medical care from one of the Veterans Health Administration hospitals. For the first time, an SES member could be fired with their appeal process curtailed. Previously, SES would be placed on paid administrative leave and could appeal their termination to the Merit System Protection Board (MSPB). The new law allows the secretary to immediately fire a member of the SES, and MSPB must adjudicate the appeal within 21 days.

CONCLUSION

As of early 2015, it was unclear whether and to what extent reform of the civil service and of HRM practices in general would be a priority during the remaining years of the Obama administration. In November 2014, Republicans won a majority of seats in the U.S. Senate giving them control of both houses of Congress. The incoming chair of the Senate Homeland Security and Government Affairs Committee expressed his support for reforms that would give agency heads "the tools and flexibility to discipline the workforce to effectively manage" (Clark 2014). Similarly, the incoming chair of the House Oversight and Government Reform Committee said in an interview that the government needs to make it easier "to root out the bad apples" in the federal workforce (Davidson 2014). He further expressed support for a measure that would extend to other agencies the authority granted the Department of Veterans Affairs to expedite the removal of senior executives. Any such changes, however, would have to secure the approval of President Obama, whose term of office extends to January 2017.

NOTES

The views expressed in this paper are those of Mr. Seidner personally and not those of either the Office of Management and Budget or the federal government.

1. Title 5 of the United States Code includes those laws relating to federal personnel matters.
2. Various groups of federal employees including those in the Department of Veterans Affairs, the intelligence community, and the Foreign Service have been exempted from provisions of Title 5 over the decades, but a large proportion of federal employees remain under traditional Title 5 rules.
3. Executive Order 13203 of 2001, Revocation of Executive Order and Presidential Memorandum Concerning Labor-Management Partnerships.
4. Executive Order 12871 of 1993, Labor-Management Partnerships.
5. See Executive Order 13522, at http://www.whitehouse.gov/the-press-office/executive-order-creating-labor-management-forums-improve-delivery-government-servic. Accessed December 8, 2014.
6. Data retrieved from Bureau of Labor Statistics, www.bls.gov.
7. See http://en.wikipedia.org/wiki/Tea_Party_movement. Accessed December 8, 2014.
8. See www.bestplacestowork.org. Accessed December 8, 2014
9. Categories assessed include employee skills/mission match, strategic management, teamwork, effective leadership, performance-based rewards and advancement, training and development, support for diversity, family friendly culture and benefits, pay, and work/life balance (http://www.bestplacestowork.org).

10. See Presidential Memorandum—Improving the Federal Recruitment and Hiring Process, http://www.whitehouse.gov/the-press-office/presidential-memorandum-improving-federal-recruitment-and-hiring-process.

11. See Executive Order 13562, Recruiting and Hiring Students and Recent Graduates, http://www.whitehouse.gov/the-press-office/2010/12/27/executive-order-recruiting-and-hiring-students-and-recent-graduates.

12. Executive Order 13548, "Expanding Federal Employment for Individuals with Disabilities."

13. Executive Order 13555, White House Initiative on Educational Excellence for Hispanics.

14. Executive Order 13515, White House Initiative on Asian Americans and Pacific Islanders.

15. Executive Order 13592, American Indian and Alaska Native Educational Opportunities.

16. Executive Order 13621, White House Initiative on Educational Excellence for African Americans.

17. Executive Order 13506, White House Council on Women and Girls.

18. Executive Order 13518, Expansion of Employment Opportunities in the Federal Government for Veterans, http://www.gpo.gov/fdsys/pkg/FR-2009-11-13/pdf/E9-27441.pdf. Accessed November 9, 2012.

19. Feds@Work: Initiative Grows Government Employment for Veterans. AOL Government, August 31, 2012, http://gov.aol.com/2012/08/31/opm-initiative-grows-number-of-federally-employed-veterans/. Accessed November 14, 2012.

20. "Update on GEAR Pilots," presented January 18, 2012, to the National Council and Federal Labor-Management Relations, http://www.lmrcouncil.gov/meetings/handouts/GEAR%20Update%20January%2018-2.pdf. Accessed November 10, 2012.

REFERENCES

Brodsky, R. 2010. Administrative puts its stamp on "inherently governmental." Nextgov.com, March 31. http://www.nextgov.com/defense/2010/03/administration-puts-its-stamp-on-inherently-governmental/46345/. Accessed December 8, 2014.

Clark, C. 2014. Sen. Johnson speaks on aligning public-private sector pay, keeping hearings polite. www.govexec.com, November 10. http://www.govexec.com/oversight/2014/11/sen-johnson-speaks-aligning-federal-private-sector-pay-keeping-hearings-polite/98630/. Accessed December 8, 2014.

Congressional Research Service. 2010. Federal Employees: Pay and Pension Increases since 1969. http://assets.opencrs.com/rpts/94-971_20100120.pdf. Accessed December 8, 2014.

———. 2011. The Federal Workforce: Characteristics and Trends. http://assets.opencrs.com/rpts/RL34685_20110419.pdf. Accessed December 8, 2014.

Davidson, J. 2011. Federal HR Boss Calls for New Employee Evaluation System. www.washingtonpost.com, March 16. http://www.washingtonpost.com/blogs/federal-eye/post/federal-hr-boss-calls-for-new-employee-evaluation-system/2011/03/15/ABBQ7hZ_blog.html. Accessed December 8, 2014.

———. 2012. TSA Contract Proposal Calls for New Performance Management System, Higher Clothing Allowance. www.washingtonpost.com, August 2. http://www.washingtonpost.com/blogs/federal-eye/post/tsa-contract-proposal-calls-for-new-performance-management-system-higher-clothing-allowance/2012/08/02/gJQALwbUSX_blog.html. Accessed December 8, 2014.

———. 2014. Chaffetz, Incoming Committee Chair, Seeks to Fire "Bad Apples" in Federal Workforce. *Washington Post*, November 20. http://www.washingtonpost.com/politics/federal_government/chaffetz-incoming-committee-chair-seeks-to-fire-bad-apples-in-federal-workforce/2014/11/20/e6034640-70ed-11e4-ad12-3734c461eab6_story.html. Accessed December 8, 2014.

Heritage Foundation. 2010. *Inflated Federal Pay: How Americans Are Overtaxed to Overpay the Civil Service.* Rep. No. CDA 10-05. Washington, DC: Heritage Foundation.

Lunney, K. 2012a. Protecting Federal Pay and Benefits Remains Top Priority for Union. www.govexec.com, November 7. http://www.govexec.com/pay-benefits/2012/11/protecting-federal-pay-and-benefits-remains-top-priority-union/59346/. Accessed November 9, 2012.

———. 2012b. Retirement Claims Surge in September. www.govexec.com, October 5. http://www.govexec.com/pay-benefits/2012/10/retirement-claims-spike-September/58627/?oref=workforce_week_nl. Accessed December 8, 2014.

Merit Systems Protection Board. 2006. *Reforming Federal Hiring: Beyond Faster and Cheaper.* Washington, DC: Government Printing Office.

———. 2008. *The Power of Federal Employee Engagement.* Washington, DC: U.S. Government Printing Office.

———. 2009. *Managing for Engagement—Communication, Connection, and Courage.* Washington, DC: U.S. Government Printing Office.

Office of Management and Budget 2002. *The President's Management Agenda.* Washington, DC: U.S. Office of Management and Budget.

Office of Personnel Management. 2001. *A Final Report to the National Partnership Council on Evaluating Progress and Improvements in Agencies' Organizational Performance Resulting From Labor-Management Partnerships.* Washington, DC: Office of Personnel Management.

———. 2002. *A Fresh Start for Federal Pay: The Case for Modernization.* Washington, DC: Office of Personnel Management.

———. 2012. *Federal Equal Opportunity Recruitment Program Report.* http://www.opm.gov/policy-data-oversight/diversity-and-inclusion/reports/feorp-2012.pdf. Accessed April 15, 2015.

———. 2013. *Telework Report to Congress.* http://www.telework.gov/Reports_and_Studies/Annual_Reports/2013teleworkreport.pdf. Accessed December 8, 2014.

Partnership for Public Service. 2012a. *Bracing for Change: Chief Human Capital Officers Rethink Business as Usual.* Washington, DC: Partnership for Public Service.

———. 2012b. *Mission-Driven Mobility: Strengthening our Government Through a Mobile Leadership Corps.* Washington, DC: Partnership for Public Service.

Pincus, W. 2007. Hayden Works to Absorb New Hires at CIA—After Almost a Year as Director He Calls Huge Personnel Surge His "Biggest Challenge." *Washington Post*, April 15, p. A9.

Thompson, J. R. 2006. The Federal Civil Service: The Demise of an Institution. *Public Administration Review, 66,* 496–503.

———. 2007a. Federal Labor-Management Relations Reforms under Bush: Enlightened Management or Quest for Control? *Review of Public Personnel Administration, 27,* 105–124.

———. 2007b. *Designing and Implementing Performance-Oriented Payband Systems* Washington, DC: IBM Center for the Business of Government.

Thompson, J., and S. Mastracci. 2005. *The Blended Workforce: Maximizing Agility through Nonstandard Work Arrangements* Washington, DC: IBM Center for the Business of Government.

Thompson, J. R., and R. Seidner. 2008. A New Look at Pay-banding and Pay for Performance: The Views of Those Participating in Federal Demonstration Projects. In H. S. Sistare, M. H. Shiplett, and T. F. Buss (Eds.), *Innovations in Human Resource Management: Getting the Public's Work Done in the 21st Century*. Armonk, NY: M.E. Sharpe, pp. 147–169.

CHAPTER 5

AFTER THE RECESSION: STATE HUMAN RESOURCE MANAGEMENT[1]

Sally Coleman Selden
Lynchburg College

INTRODUCTION

For the past five years, human resource management (HRM) professionals in state government have helped implement changes needed to adapt to the recession and to respond to fiscal constraints within their states. Changes have included making workforce reductions, reducing budgets, and reforming state civil service systems and procedures to be more efficient (Galinsky and Bond 2009). Although government jobs are typically considered among the most stable, states have implemented employee layoffs or reductions-in-force, pay freezes, furloughs, and pay cuts, resulting in slightly smaller state workforces (Duggan, Lewis, and Milluzzi, 2010). For example, rather than cutting pay directly, Nevada's legislators had state employees take off one unpaid day each month, reducing their salaries by 4.6% for a savings of $333 million. As an experiment, employees in Utah moved to a four-day work week to save the state money in 2008 (Galinsky and Bond 2009). In 2011, the state abandoned the practice after determining that cost savings were not realized (Loftin 2011). Some states have seen a drop in full-time equivalent (FTE) positions. Georgia, for example, saw its number of FTEs decline by 3% from 2010 to 2011 and then another 8.33% between 2011 and 2012.

Pennsylvania implemented workforce reductions in fiscal years 2008–2009 and 2009–2010 due to a significant reduction in revenues. A statewide hiring freeze began in September 2008 and continued throughout 2010. The state also closed multiple facilities, including state hospitals, schools, and regional state government offices. Overall in a two-year period, Pennsylvania realized a workforce reduction of over 1,200 employees and an additional 2,200 unfilled vacancies. These actions represented an estimated monthly savings of $19.2 million to the Commonwealth. When implementing these workforce cost-cutting strategies, the state attempted to be sensitive to the adverse impact on staff laid off by enacting measures intended to ease state workers' transition from Commonwealth employment. A testimony to the success of this initiative has been reflected in the fact that the challenges to the workforce reduction have been successfully defended in multiple employee appeal forums since its implementation.[2]

Even as the economy continues its recovery, state human resource (HR) professionals will continue to grapple with improving efficiency. During the recessionary period, the state of Washington's Department of Personnel (DOP) focused on improving efficiency with three key initiatives. First, the DOP implemented a centralized security and monitoring for the Human Resource Management System (HRMS), which released 243 DOP personnel from security administration duties and helped standardize how HRMS roles were used across agencies (survey of Washington in 2012). Second, DOP implemented a "no print option" for payroll and gave employees 24/7 secure access to view their earnings statements via the on-line Employee Self Service (ESS) portal. From 2008 through 2011, 79% of employees were converted to "no print option," which saved about 4.6 cents printing cost per statement (survey of Washington in 2012). Considering that the state of Washington employs about 58,932 persons, this represents a little over $2,000 per pay period. Third, DOP implemented a system that allowed employees to request and supervisors to approve leave electronically, through the online ESS portal. This reduced the handling time required of time/attendance keepers and HR staff and minimized leave reporting error rates (survey of Washington in 2012). One agency found a 67% decrease in payroll staff time after implementing the online leave program.[3]

Much has been written in recent years regarding changes that are taking place within the field of public personnel management (human resource management). Scholars have focused on civil service reforms with studies examining the erosion of civil service protections and the effects of those changes (e.g., Bowman and West 2006; Coggburn et al. 2010; Crowell and Guy 2010; French and Goodman 2012; Green et al. 2006; Kellough and Nigro 2006; Nigro and Kellough 2008; Williams and Bowman 2007). Scholars and practitioners have emphasized the role human resource management played as a strategic partner within state government organizations (e.g., Effron, Grandossy, and Goldsmith 2003; Selden 2006). HR in the public sector continues to change, but it is difficult to discern whether this is merely the evolution of the field or a by-product of the recession (Herring 2013). Many of the changes have been related to technology. Across states, HRM departments have been leveraging technology systems and processes to do things with fewer people (Herring 2013).

This chapter draws upon the experience of state governments as documented by surveys and interviews of state human resource management directors in 2000, 2007, and 2012.[4] Over the past 12 years, the field has witnessed many changes in state civil service systems, and the most recent results indicate that the political pressures on civil service systems are increasing. First, this chapter discusses the concept of civil service in state governments. Second, it explores characteristics of state human resource management systems, highlighting the complexity and differences that exist across states. Third, it describes broad change strategies witnessed in states during the recession, including workforce cost-cutting. Fourth, it discusses employee retention within state governments and highlights practices associated with lower voluntary turnover. Fifth, the chapter discusses recruiting and hiring state government employees. Sixth, it highlights state efforts to train and develop their workforce. Finally, the chapter explores the impact of the recession on state government employees.

CIVIL SERVICE IN STATE GOVERNMENTS

The origins of state merit systems are inextricably linked to the depoliticization of the civil service (Aronson 1974; Conover 1925). Over 125 years ago, the Pendleton Act provided the blueprint for a modern, unified, and politically impartial civil service. The hallmarks of a "merit" system include relative security of tenure in office, the use of written, competitive examinations, and neutral administration (Sylvia and Meyer 2001). New York enacted the first civil service system in 1883—the same year Congress passed the Pendleton Act (Conover 1925). The following year, Massachusetts implemented its civil service (Conover 1925). It took more than twenty years before another state, Wisconsin, established a merit system for its state government (Aronson 1974; Conover 1925). In the 1920s and 1930s, technical developments in the field of personnel, including testing and classification, laid the groundwork for a more scientific approach to HRM. Despite the advances, many states did not adopt civil service legislation until the passage of the Social Security Act in 1935, which included a provision for grants to states. The act stipulated that states must be "federally approved," which meant that states needed to guarantee proper and efficient administration to receive funding. Leonard White proclaimed in a 1945 article in the *Public Personnel Review*, "the importance of this amendment to the steady improvement of personnel standards in the State and county government cannot be exaggerated" (Aronson 1974: 136). The legacy of the type of civil service system established by the Pendleton Act is evident. Today, some states have a civil service system characterized by an elaborate, and sometimes fragmented, web of laws, rules, regulations, and techniques embracing the merit principle. For example, New York's structure governing its civil service system is, according to Riccucci (2006: 305), "fragmented and overlapping. This is statutorily driven. For managers and human resources specialists, it engenders a good deal of frustration and tension." States, however, vary in terms of the percentage of employees covered by their classified civil service system.

Employees covered by civil service systems are often referred to as classified or merit system employees. As shown in Table 5.1, the percentage of classified employees across states did not change significantly between 1999, 2007, and 2012. In the mid- to late 1990s, a few states, such as Florida and Georgia, shifted a significant amount of their workforces from the classified service to the nonclassified service or an employment-at-will system. Today, more than 88% of Georgia's workforce is in the nonclassified service, up from 80% in 2007 (Kerrigan 2012b).

Most civil service systems provide employees certain administrative and legal due process rights before discharging them for cause, although the rights vary across classified merit systems (Lindquist and Condrey 2006). The rationale for providing such protections is to protect public sector employees from partisan pressure and removal. "Employment at will" typically connotes an employer's right to terminate an employee without a reason and an employee's right to leave when she or he elects. Both federal legislation and state laws provide exceptions to the doctrine of employment at will, including, but limited to, participation in union activities, whistleblowing, public policy, employer motivation, race, ethnicity, religion, national origin, sex, and disabilities. Montana, for example, is the only state that has passed legislation that prohibits employers from discharging employees without "good cause."

States take different approaches to managing their nonclassified employees. Employees in the nonclassified service in some states, such as Alabama and Connecticut, are subject to the same rules and regulations of employment that apply to employees in the classified service regarding appointment and dismissal. In other states, such as Nebraska and New Hampshire, the central HR department does not have any authority over nonclassified employees and therefore they do not maintain records in the central HR department on those employees. In Virginia, state agencies with nonclassified employees are responsible for establishing their own set of HR policies for those employees.

Table 5.1 State Government Workforce Characteristics

	1999	2007	2012
Percent of state workforce classified	87%	87%	85%
Percent of state workforce that are political appointees	n/a	3.8%	3.5%
Percent of state workforce that is covered by labor agreements	46.3%	47.3%	38.6%
Percent of state workforce that is temporary	6.3%	7.1%	4.5%

Source: Survey of states by author in 1999, 2007, and 2012.

In recent years, civil service reformers have sought to remove civil service protections from a critical mass of state employees (e.g., Crowell and Guy 2010; Goodman and Mann 2010; Kellough and Nigro 2006). These reforms sought to redefine the relationship between public employees and their employers by allowing for at-will termination without the protection of procedural due process (Kellough and Nigro 2006). In practice, although some states have implemented system-wide civil service reforms, the percentage of employees covered by the civil service system has fluctuated over time as administrations have changed (Goodman and Mann 2010). Some administrations may grant employees in the nonclassified service civil service protections before leaving office. Other states may exempt particular departments, employee classes, or agencies either permanently or temporarily to create more personnel flexibility (Goodman and Mann 2010). Many civil service reformers and opponents of civil service contend that states will have more flexibility to manage their workforces if state employees serve "at-will" and, therefore, do hold a property interest in their positions.

However, the nature and form of civil service protections, including due process protections, can vary from state to state. Moreover, due process procedures may vary across nonclassified personnel systems. The underlying assumption of reformers is that employees serving in nonclassified personnel systems have few, if any, due process protections. Since reformers often focus on how difficult it is to terminate tenured state employees serving in the classified service, it is instructive to examine variations in due process procedures for disciplinary actions adopted by states for both their classified and nonclassified employees.

Based upon the recommendations of a focus group of state personnel directors, a set of five questions were developed and included on the 2007 and 2012 surveys. States were asked "for employees in the classified system, does your state: allow employees to appeal disciplinary actions; require pre-termination hearings; have an external review of all termination requests; have an external source review termination requests when appealed by the employee; and require notification of termination." States responded: yes, no, or varies by agency. These

Table 5.2 Employment Security Classified and Nonclassified Systems

	2007		2012	
	Classified Service	Nonclassified Service	Classified Service	Nonclassified Service
Employment Security Index (additive index of the following five measures)	3.7	1.4	2.6	.8
Allow employees to appeal disciplinary actions?	98%	43%	93%	29%
Require pre-termination hearings?	74%	14%	43%	7%
Have an external source review all termination requests?	21%	10%	7%	7%
Have an external source review termination requests when appealed by the employee?	83%	26%	62%	0%
Require notification of termination?	93%	45%	93%	50%

Source: Survey of states by author in 2007 and 2012.

same questions were posed to state personnel executives for the nonclassified service.

The analysis focused on states which provided protections to all persons serving in either the classified or nonclassified service, since it is not possible to discern what share of agencies provided each of the aforementioned protections when the response was "varies by agency." The five items were summed to create an index from 0 to 5. As shown in Table 5.2, employees serving in the classified service in 2012, on average, had more procedural due process protections (2.6) than employees serving in the nonclassified service (.8). However, across both the classified and nonclassified services, the data indicated that states were providing fewer procedural due process protections to all employees than they were in 2007.

CHARACTERISTICS OF STATE HUMAN RESOURCE MANAGEMENT SYSTEMS

Historically, in a traditional classified civil service system, the authority to administer HR activities belonged to a central personnel or HR department. The purported benefits of this approach included equitable treatment of employees, consistency in the delivery of services, efficiency gains through economies of scale, and clearly delineated roles between central HR department and state agencies. In the 1990s, many scholars and practitioners pushed for state central HR departments to decentralize their authority over some HR practices and provide more flexibility to public agencies and their managers (for a discussion, see Kellough and Nigro 2006).

States have reduced their human resource management staff over the past five years. As shown in Table 5.3, states' HR departments on average employ approximately .71 human resource management staff (both agency and central HRM) per 100 state employees. In 2007, states had approximately 1.21 HRM staff per 100 employees. Between 2005 and 2012, the percentage of employees doing HR work declined by 66% (Hackler 2012).

The majority of HRM employees are housed in state line agencies but some states, such as Alabama, Iowa, Indiana, and Michigan, have over 30% of their HRM staff located centrally. In July of 2006, Utah's Department of Human Resource Management grew from 38 to 182 staff members; but in 2012, the number of HRM professionals in the central office dropped to 16, with a total of 142 statewide (central and departments). On the other end of the spectrum of centralization is Florida, which has approximately 3% of its HRM staff in its central office.

HRM REFORM AND RESTRUCTURING INITIATIVES IN THE STATES

Over the past 12 years, state civil service systems have undergone considerable changes. The underlying philosophy that has driven public dialogue emerged as part of the new public management philosophy (NPM) (Condrey and Battaglio 2007). Advocates for reform have pushed for HRM systems that reduce civil service rules and emulate private sector HR practices.

Table 5.3 Characteristics of Central HRM Department

	2007	2012
Total HRM staff per 100 state employees	1.2	.71
Central HRM staff per 100 state employees	0.25	.12
Percent of HRM staff working in central HRM office	23.19%	13.04%

Source: Survey of states by author in 2007 and 2012.

SYSTEM CHANGE: CIVIL SERVICE REFORM

In the late 1990s and early 2000s, Georgia and Florida implemented radical system-wide civil service reforms that changed the nature of civil service within those states. In 2002, Washington adopted system-wide changes to its personnel system but without abolishing its civil service system. After more than a decade and much public dialogue on reducing civil service protections and increasing at-will employment for public sector employees, civil service reforms are on the rise again. In the past two years, Arizona, Indiana, and Tennessee adopted sweeping civil service reform. Colorado is continuing to pursue similar reforms.

In 2011, Indiana enacted civil service reform. The changes weakened seniority in its personnel system and reduced the number of employees in the civil service or merit system (Kerrigan 2012b). Prior to the change, approximately 80% of Indiana's state workforce was classified. The percentage of classified state employees had fallen to approximately 13% as of December 2012 (Hackler 2012).

In 2012, two states—Arizona and Tennessee—adopted sweeping reforms to their civil service systems, which impacted selection and termination policies and grievance procedures. Arizona's governor, Jan Brewer, made civil service reform a platform issue for the 2012 legislative session. Over time, Arizona's system will shift away from a traditional civil service structure towards an at-will structure that more closely approximates the approach used by private sector organizations. New hires in Arizona state government are no longer part of the civil service system. Similar to the approach used in Georgia in 1996, current Arizona state government employees, who have civil service protections, who are promoted, transferred, or receive a raise will convert to an at-will status (Maynard 2012).

In April of 2012, Tennessee's governor, Bill Haslam, signed the Tennessee Excellence, Accountability, and Management (T.E.A.M.) Act, which ushered in significant civil service reform in the state that is consistent with reforms passed in Georgia, Florida, and Indiana (Kerrigan 2012a). According to the state,[5]

> The T.E.A.M. Act established a system of personnel administration to help attract, select, retain and promote the best employees based on merit and equal opportunity, free from coercive political influence. . . . The T.E.A.M. Act removed requirements for testing, scoring and rank ordering applicants, allowing applicants to be approved based only on minimum qualifications. Rather than interviewing only those with a score that falls into the top 5 on a list, agencies may interview any qualified applicant who possesses the knowledge, skills, abilities and competencies identified for the position. Veterans' preference in hiring is included. Reductions in force are no longer based strictly on seniority, and bumping and retreating have been eliminated. Job performance plans that are specific, measurable, achievable, and relevant to the strategic goals of the agency are required for all employees. The opportunity for merit pay is included in the Act. A cumbersome five-step grievance process which included a pre-termination due process hearing has been replaced with a streamlined three-step appeal process.

The state expects that the changes will provide more flexibility in Tennessee's hiring process, streamline the appeals process, and revamp the performance evaluation system, linking it to pay increases and layoff decisions (Kerrigan 2012a).

The concerns about the constraints of state civil service systems became a rallying point for reformers in states since the economic recession began in late 2007, and it has intensified recently and resulted in significant changes in three states. Efforts to roll back state civil service systems and eliminate employee job protections in Arizona, Indiana, and Tennessee, and efforts to repeal collective bargaining rights for public employees in Wisconsin and several other states, are direct results of this trend. The political impetus is being provided by activist governors, the reform movement is fueled by fiscal stress and the need for increased budget austerity, and it is changing the face of state governments (Bowman et al. 2003; Goodman and Mann 2010; Hays and Sowa 2006; Kellough and Nigro 2006; Nigro and Kellough 2000).

HRM Restructuring Initiatives

While not as sweeping as civil service reform, states have also implemented structural changes within their personnel systems (see Table 5.4). Between 2007 and 2012, states have implemented an array of HRM restructuring initiatives that are consistent with Hal Rainey's observation that "the continuing complaints about the rigidity of the civil service personnel systems" have motivated governments to pursue flexibility using many different paths (Rainey 2006: 36). A review of state efforts shows that efforts targeted toward shared services have continued, while states have decreased efforts at improving specific HRM processes (see Table 5.4).

In the past few years, some states have implemented a service delivery model that balances centralized and decentralized delivery of human resources—shared services—which had diffused through the private sector in the mid-2000s (Ulrich, Younger, and Brockbank 2008; Selden and Wooters 2011). A shared services model of human resource management creates a centralized service function that considers employees and agency-based HRM professionals as internal customers. This approach is designed to enable a state to better leverage existing resources, to reduce duplication of human resource management activities across state agencies, and to provide more consistent, higher-quality services to internal customers by concentrating existing resources and streamlining processes (Selden and Wooters 2011). Idaho, for example, took a two-fold approach to HR in the state. Large state agencies in Idaho maintained their HR office. HR units and professionals within smaller agencies were consolidated into a "shared services" HR unit that provided HR services to all small agencies within the state.

Utah also has implemented a consolidated decentralized model of human resource management. In 2005, the governor consolidated HRM but did not fully centralize it. Transactional HR activities, such as payroll processing and retirement calculations, were centralized in the Employee Resource Information Center, a shared services call center. Service delivery was decentralized to HR within the agencies so that strategic decisions would be executed at the agency level, but the central HR department supported agency HR through its shared consultant services.

Table 5.4 Percentage of States Implementing HRM Restructuring Initiatives in 2007–2011 compared with 2004–2006

	2004–2006 (%)	2007–2011 (%)
Process improvement	65.9	28.1
Shared services	39.0	37.5
Consolidation	26.8	28.1
Centralization	24.4	31.3
Decentralization	24.4	15.6
Outsourcing	19.5	12.5

Source: Survey of states by author in 2007 and 2012.

Pennsylvania also implemented an HR Service Center to unify high-volume HR transactions into a single, state-wide organization. According to the state,[2]

The center provides state-wide customer service to 80,000 employees, 43 agency HR offices and executive leadership. The center is supported by a complex array of technology, including the commonwealth's ERP system; a hybrid cloud HR knowledge base that plugs into our ERP employee self service functionality; call center telephony, management and metric packages; third-party provided customer relationship management applications; document management applications and more.

The Commonwealth has also achieved one of the most highly integrated shared service centers, providing enterprise-wide support for employees, personnel/position transactions, application/ERP operational support and HR data reporting. By answering routine HR inquiries and processing common HR transactions centrally, agency HR staff is freed up to pursue more strategic work, such as safety initiatives, succession planning, recruitment and training and development.

Today, approximately 66 % of employee HR needs are met by employee self service and 28 % are met at the HR Service Center level, leaving only 6 % that require the input or involvement of a program or policy expert. With an implementation cost of $1.4 million and an annual delivery cost of just $78 per employee, the center is a cost-effective shared services initiative. The implementation of the center also has improved HR service to agencies and employees of the commonwealth by providing efficient transactions processing and consistent communications across agencies. The HR Service Center is expected to save approximately $3.5 million each year by reducing the overall number of HR staff statewide; eliminating many costly errors; and reducing benefits appeals.

The Commonwealth of Pennsylvania is a leader in shared services within the public administration sector.

Due to the scope of change, the implementation of the HR Service Center had wide internal impacts for both employees and agencies.

The examples illustrate how states are changing their delivery of HRM services, with an effort to provide better, more efficient services to internal customers. Under the shared services model, central HRM works in partnership with agency HRM professionals to determine what services they need. Adopting shared services is not as radical as reforms that remove civil service protections of public employees. Instead, the shared services model seeks to modernize state human resource management systems by utilizing new technologies and partnerships and by better supporting services to agencies and departments (Selden and Wooters 2011).

WORKFORCE COST-CUTTING STRATEGIES

As noted in the beginning of the chapter, states have adopted different strategies to reduce their labor costs due to fiscal challenges. We asked state HR directors which workforce cost-cutting strategies the state had implemented during FY 2009, FY 2010, FY 2011, and FY 2012. The results of the 2012 survey showed that states have adopted varied approaches when planning their workforce cost-cutting strategies. After four years, states have continued to adopt one or more of the cost-cutting strategies highlighted in Table 5.5. In FY 2012, layoffs were still being implemented in 80% of states to help balance budgets. The long-term impact of continued layoffs is unknown. Research documents that survivors of layoffs may find that their jobs have changed; they may have more responsibilities and report to different managers; their colleagues may have changed; or they may have new rules, policies, and procedures to follow (Allen et al. 2001; Datta et al. 2010). All of which creates stress for the employee, decreases commitment, lowers job satisfaction, and decreases morale (e.g., Armstrong-Strassen 2002; Ashford, Lee, and Bobko 1989 Datta et al. 2010).

Furloughs function like "temporary layoffs" and result in a reduction in pay for employees during that fiscal year. Furloughs were used by almost half of the states in FY 2010, but their use has decreased the past two years. When furloughed, state employees suffer real wage losses for the fiscal year, which impacts their standard of living. Over the past four years, states have utilized hiring and pay freezes to reduce expenditures. More than 30% of states maintained hiring freezes in 2012. States with hiring freezes were not able to replace employees that left, which may have increased the level of stress within the state workforce. Like survivors of layoffs, employees working in environments with hiring freezes may find they are asked to take on additional responsibilities without additional compensation or recognition, until the hiring freeze is lifted. States were much less likely to use early retirement buy-outs, pay cuts, and benefit reductions to reduce their workforce costs.

When implementing its cost-cutting strategies, Utah relied heavily upon the leadership of state agencies and the Department of Human Resource Management (DRHM) to guide its effort:[6]

The overarching strategy used by Utah's governor was to focus on finding operational efficiencies. This included allowing each agency head to determine how and where budget cuts would be implemented. Agency heads were able to consult with their management teams and employees to determine where they could find efficiencies while minimizing the negative impact on their employees and customer service. This approach resulted in each agency tailoring its own strategy(s) to best meet its needs including better utilization of technology, elimination of unnecessary programs and processes, redesign of processes, as well as reductions in staff. DRHM overhauled the State's reduction-in-force (RIF) rules, policies, and procedures. This overhaul shifted the focus of RIFs from seniority to proficiency. Emphasizing proficiency over seniority allowed agency managers to reduce staff while retaining key skill sets necessary to accomplish their agency missions and to maintain customer service levels.

In evaluating its options in 2010, Pennsylvania decided to reduce costs by restructuring the health plans offered throughout the state. The Commonwealth selected one national Medicare PPO and three regional Medicare HMOs. The selected health plans provided similar coverage and minimal disruption to members and greatly simplified administrative processes. In addition, the Commonwealth was able to cut its 2010 expenditures for this coverage by 16% or approximately $16 million annually.[2]

Table 5.5 Workforce Cost-Cutting Strategies Implemented by States FY2009–FY 2012

	FY 2012 (%)	FY 2011 (%)	FY 2010 (%)	FY 2009 (%)
Hiring freezes	31.3	43.8	56.3	68.8
Pay freezes	31.3	56.3	62.5	43.8
Layoffs	81.3	87.5	87.5	62.5
Furloughs	18.8	31.3	50.0	37.5
Early retirement incentives	12.5	25.0	31.3	18.8
Pay cuts	6.3	6.3	0	0
Benefits cuts	12.5	18.8	6.3	6.3

Source: Survey of states by author in 2012.

RETENTION OF STATE EMPLOYEES

Nearly all states worry about their workforces, especially given the workforce reduction strategies that have been implemented during the recessionary period and the large percentage of state employees who remain eligible to retire. The good news is that voluntary turnover fell during the recession; however, this trend is expected since there were fewer alternative employment opportunities in the market. On average, the percentage of the state workforce leaving voluntarily fell from about 7% in FY 2007 to 6.3% in FY 2012. The recession did not seem to impact turnover patterns of new hires, however. On average, about 22% of new hires quit or were fired in FY 2012, which was consistent with the percentage in FY 2007.

For example, Washington's total turnover was 8.6% in FY 2008 and fell to 7.7% in FY 2009.[3] Even though the turnover reduction was perceived as positive, the state recognized that the economic downturn created risks associated with retention in the workforce such as disengaged employees remaining in jobs, losing key talent and top performers, bad job fit for employees landing in new roles as a result of layoff process, delayed retirements, and discouraged managers. To mitigate these risks, Washington focused on employee engagement. The state compared and analyzed data from the Washington State Employee Survey between November 2007 and October 2009 with the Gallup Q12 survey to determine if there was an issue of employee disengagement in the workforce. Based on the results, the state's senior executives identified the following strategic roles for leadership in challenging times to engage staff: aligning and engaging (or re-engaging) middle and line managers; fostering open, honest communication with employees; articulating the organization's strategy, future, and job expectations; focusing on development—encouraging learning and growth; giving feedback and recognition; and communicating progress on the goals. Voluntary turnover in Washington did not vary significantly over the past three fiscal years: 3.5% in FY 2010, 4.1% in FY 2011, and 4% in FY 2012.[3]

When examining factors correlating with voluntary turnover across states, one trend stood out in the 2012 findings (analysis not shown): factors predicting voluntary turnover of state workers differed from factors predicting new hire voluntary turnover. Consistent with the 2007 findings, the data showed that total compensation, salary plus benefits, was the most important predictor of voluntary turnover of state employees, predicting over 56% of the variance in 2012 compared with 54% in 2007. Base pay and benefits contribute to a state's ability to attract and retain employees, while performance-based pay is argued to increase employee productivity. In 2012, 55% of states indicated that the state provided increased compensation to some extent for individual high performers. About 33% of states connected pay increases to group or team performance.

Table 5.6 presents the average cost of total compensation, which includes salary and benefits, as of June 30, 2003, June 30, 2007, and June 30, 2012. On average in 2012, states spent $64,877 on salary and benefits per

Table 5.6 Average Cost of Total Compensation for Classified State Employees (as of June 30, 2003, 2007, and 2012)

	25th percentile	Mean	Median	75th percentile
2003	$42,631	$49,471	$47,405	$53,493
2007	$48,843	$57,042	$56,611	$64,252
2012	$55,840	$64,877	$64,962	$76,008

Source: Survey of states by author in 2003, 2007, and 2012.

classified state employee, an increase of 14% since 2007 and 31% since 2003. As of June 30, 2012, on average, salary comprised 69.1% of total compensation, up from 64% in 2008. In 2012, expenditures on benefits account for the remaining 30.9% of total compensation.

An analysis of factors expected to impact new hire turnover revealed that employee referrals in the hiring process, formal on-the-job training by experienced supervisors or employees, self-managed teams, externally competitive salaries, and pay increases tied to team performance were associated significantly with lower new hire turnover. These factors accounted for 80% of the variance in 2012 new hire voluntary turnover.

As the economy improves, states are concerned about whether or not they will be able to retain employees, especially in particular fields when there is significant competition with the private sector. In Alabama, the HR director is worried about the retention of engineers. The state has been successful in recruiting and retaining engineers during the recession because fewer alternative employment opportunities existed. In 2013, the state implemented changes to its retirement system that will make state employment less attractive to job candidates. With the new plan, people working for Alabama will no longer be eligible to retire after 25 years of service, and their benefits are reduced slightly.

RECRUITING AND HIRING NEW STATE GOVERNMENT EMPLOYEES

Despite the adoption of hiring freezes in some states, the overall hiring patterns across states were similar between 2007 and 2012. On average, states hired 2,181 new employees in 2007 or 1.1 new hires per 10 state employees, compared with a slight increase in 2012 of 2,310 new employees or 1.2 new hires per 10 state employees. Similarly, the average age of new hires in state government in 2012 was 37.4 years, which was consistent with the average age of hires in 2007. However, in 2012 states received more job applications per job opening. On average, states received 74.8 applications per job opening in 2012, which was 19% higher than the number of applications received in 2007. As this suggests, the demand

for state government jobs appeared to increase during the recessionary period. Alabama's HR director noted that the state has been able to recruit people in high-level positions such as chief information officers and chief operating officers who were working in the private sector and who would never have considered state government prior to the recession. Applications in Alabama were up the past few years, and the perception is that people are interested in working for the state because of job security. The majority of positions in Alabama are civil service, which offers certain job protections that are attractive in the labor market (Graham 2013).

As shown in Table 5.7, states have not focused their recruiting efforts on strategies that would attract recent college graduates to state service. Job fairs were the most commonly used recruitment strategies with more than 70% of states using them to some extent. Less than one-third of states operated a centralized college recruiting program or offered paid internships at least to some extent. Even fewer states utilized a recent graduates program or management fellow programs. The use of social media as a recruiting tool had not diffused across states as illustrated by the percentages of states using Facebook, Twitter, and LinkedIn to connect to prospective employees. Maine is particularly concerned about the age of its workforce. The state has developed new protocols for internships and is in the process of conducting focus groups with individuals under 28. The objective is to develop recruiting and retention plans that target younger members of the labor force (Oreskovich 2013).

During the 2007–2012 period, some states, such as Montana and Louisiana, implemented online recruitment systems to improve the efficiency of their hiring systems. Louisiana's LA Careers allows applicants to apply online for state employment opportunities and then the system automatically tracks job announcements and hiring processes.[6] Even though the state implemented a centralized system, hiring remains a decentralized function. The online system affords agencies the capability to attract highly qualified applicants with an easy-to-use online job posting and application system. LA Careers provides prospective employees with a direct application method that, in turn, provides agencies with a potentially shorter time-to-hire. LA Careers also provides HR with a means to easily screen electronic applications for minimum qualifications by effectively utilizing supplemental questions and offers reporting tools to find, track, and measure critical data. The state also migrated from written exam grade records to the online system in order to provide agencies with one efficient and comprehensive system to review electronic applications and exam scores. Prospective job candidates may walk in and take the civil service exam. Once a candidate tests, grade notices are sent out within 24 hours in most cases unless testing occurs over the weekend. Since going live with LA Careers in February of 2012, the system has received and tracked more than 286,000 applications, with 97% of applications being submitted online versus in paper format.[7] Another feature of the online system is its Job Interest Card service. Job applicants can elect to receive an email notification each time a position opens with the State of Louisiana whose job category matches one of the categories the applicant has entered on their Job Interest Card. In a six-month period, over 171,000 Job Interest Cards were submitted to the state.[7]

TRAINING AND DEVELOPING STATE EMPLOYEES

Training and development programs contribute to state government performance by ensuring that employees

Table 5.7 Recruiting Practices in States, 2012

To what extent do you use the following practices:	Not at all (%)	To a very small extent (%)	To some extent (%)	To a great extent (%)	To a very great extent (%)
A centralized recruitment program	20.0	13.3	26.7	6.7	33.3
A centralized college recruitment program	53.3	13.3	20.0	0.0	13.3
Paid college internships	26.7	40.0	33.3	0.0	0.0
A recent graduates program	66.7	20.0	13.3	0.0	0.0
Management fellows program	86.7	6.7	6.7	0.0	0.0
Employee referral program	40.0	26.7	33.3	0.0	0.0
Monster.com	46.7	40.0	13.3	0.0	0.0
Jobster	93.3	6.7	0.0	0.0	0.0
Twitter	60.0	20.0	6.7	13.3	0.0
Facebook	47.7	26.7	13.3	13.3	0.0
LinkedIn	66.7	26.7	0.0	0.0	6.7
Other social networking sites	73.3	26.7	0.0	0.0	0.0
Job fairs	0.0	26.7	46.7	13.3	13.3

Source: Survey of states by author in 2012.

have the knowledge, skills, and competencies they need to meet the current demands of their jobs and to advance their careers with the organization. Training is a direct means of helping people acquire capabilities to perform their present jobs whereas development focuses on building employees' capabilities beyond those needed to perform in their current job. States noted that during the fiscal challenges, they were forced to revise their approach to training. Some states, such as Alabama and Louisiana, used in-house training more frequently during the recession rather than supporting outside training. To bridge the gap in resources, Oklahoma relied upon state workers to volunteer to train other state workers. Other states, such as Pennsylvania, New Mexico, North Carolina, and South Carolina, increased their use of online training.

Statutorily, Florida requires each state agency with Career Service (civil service) employees to implement and evaluate training programs that encompass modern management principles, that foster employee development, and that improve the quality of services. For FY 2011–2012, Florida agencies expended $27,821,092 on training, representing a 12.5% decrease from the $31,806,434 expended during FY 2010–2011.[8] Examples of training provided by the agencies included sexual harassment awareness, professional development, ethics, public records, civil rights, leadership, diversity, performance management, customer service, information security awareness, presentation skills, and safety.

While expenditures related to training have decreased, as shown in Table 5.8, some states continue to support training and development. For example, Utah's central HR office responded to the decrease in agency funding of training by developing and delivering "short courses" focused on critical issues of interest such as liability and other management-related topics. These courses are shorter in duration and cost significantly less than external courses. More than 50% of states provided leadership

Table 5.8 Training and Development in States, 2012

To what extent do you use the following practices:	Not at all (%)	To a very small extent (%)	To some extent (%)	To a great extent (%)	To a very great extent (%)
Job assignments and rotations as a career development tool	13.3	40.0	40.0	6.7	0.0
Formal investments in leadership development	6.7	20.0	53.3	20.0	0.0
Formal assessment of training needs	13.3	20.0	53.3	0.0	13.3
Formal program of on-the-job training conducted by experienced workers and/or supervisors	13.3	13.3	53.3	20.0	0.0
Personal development program for employees	13.3	33.3	33.3	6.7	13.3
Employee leadership potential evaluations	33.3	60.0	0.0	0.0	6.7

Source: Survey of states by author in 2012.

development and formal on-the-job training to some extent. Few states have implemented formal evaluation processes to identify employees with leadership potential. Job assignments and rotations were used to some extent by almost 47% of states.

THE IMPACT OF THE RECESSION ON STATE EMPLOYEES: KEY HRM WORKFORCE INDICATORS

Research indicates that when agencies implement workforce-cutting strategies, employees may become anxious about their job security, which may impact their morale, job satisfaction, and engagement with work (Green and Medlin 2010). Green and Medlin found that stressed and disengaged employees negatively impact an organization. HRM state directors were asked to assess the impact of the recession on key workforce indicators. As shown in Table 5.9, some states perceived that the recession had negatively impacted their ability to recruit and retain workers, but, surprisingly, most did not believe the state was worse off during the recession. However, on other workforce indicators, more than 50% of states perceived that employee morale, employee motivation, job satisfaction, employee stress, employee engagement, and the public's perception of state workers was worse than before the recession—an issue that may result in future recruitment and retention problems when the economy fully recovers. Of particular note was that almost 86% of states perceived workforce morale as worse than before the recession and almost 79% believed that employee stress was higher than before the recession. These findings are consistent with the research cited in the workforce-cutting section (e.g., Armstrong-Strassen 2002; Ashford, Lee, and Bobko 1989; Datta et al. 2010). In Alabama, morale is a concern as state government workers have not received merit or cost of living increases in over four years. At the same time, they have had to increase their contributions to the state retirement system and to pay more for health insurance.[9]

WHAT THE FUTURE HOLDS

As the economy continues to recover, states have both opportunities and challenges ahead. States will continue to grapple with the exit of the baby boomers' impact on the overall labor participation (Toossi 2005). While job applications were up in 2012, states have not adopted programs to recruit younger workers, which may be a key untapped labor pool. The average age of new hires remains high, and younger members of the labor force may not view state government employment as a viable option. States should continue to engage in succession planning, invest in training and development benefits, and position themselves—in terms of total compensation and employee development—to recruit and retain a diversity of workers. Factors that predict turnover of new hires were different than those of veteran employees. New hires were more likely to stay when they were receiving formal job-appropriate training and development. Such strategies provide guideposts for state HR departments.

The biggest potential challenge facing state governments is the long-term impact of the array of cost-cutting strategies employed for the past four fiscal years on the remaining state workers. HR directors indicated that employee stress, morale, satisfaction, and engagement have been negatively impacted during the recession. Given the constrained resources, most states have not adopted programs explicitly to address the consequences of workforce cost-cutting on their workforce. When unemployment decreases and more job opportunities open, states, like the federal government, may find that employees, especially the ones they wish to retain, may choose to leave for new positions.

Finally, given the groundswell of activity related to civil service reform, the field is likely to see civil service reforms implemented in other states. As a whole, "state employees have fewer civil service protections than they did a decade ago." One director of HR noted concerns about the movement toward fewer job protections for employees. Under the state's reformed system, an employee can be let go for any reason as long as the release does not violate a state policy. While the state has trained managers that HR will only approve terminating employees for merit, the question remains whether managers will start to exercise their new power by releasing people for nonmerit reasons.

Table 5.9 After the Recession: Government Performance in States, 2012

Compared with the period prior to the recession, rate your state government's performance on the following:	A lot worse than before the recession (%)	Worse than before the recession (%)	About the same as before the recession (%)	Better than before the recession (%)	A lot better than before the recession (%)
Ability to attract essential employees	0.0	0.0	50.0	50.0	0.0
Ability to retain essential employees	7.1	28.6	21.4	42.9	0.0
Relations among management and employees	0.0	28.6	64.3	7.1	0.0
Relations among employees	0.0	23.1	69.2	7.7	0.0
Workplace bullying	0.0	7.1	85.7	7.1	0.0
Employee morale	21.4	64.3	7.1	7.1	0.0
Employee motivation	7.7	53.8	30.8	7.7	0.0
Job satisfaction	0.0	57.1	35.7	7.1	0.0
Employee stress	28.6	50.0	14.3	7.1	0.0
Employee engagement	0.0	57.6	28.6	14.3	0.0
The public's perception of your state workers	7.1	42.9	42.9	7.1	0.0

Source: Survey of states by author in 2012.

These and other changes will continue in state HRM systems as the field evolves. State will continue to utilize technology to create efficiencies within the HRM function and to provide better services to internal and external customers.

NOTES

1. Produced by Sally Selden in partnership with the Pew Center on the States. The views expressed are those of the author and do not necessarily reflect the views of the Pew Center on the States.
2. Pennsylvania survey response, 2012.
3. Washington survey response, 2012.
4. The Government Performance Project collected data from state government human resource management professionals between the months of June and December in 1998, 2000, 2003, and 2007. The GPP administered a survey and collected over twenty-five documents from the central HRM departments. In 2003 and 2007, the GPP surveyed two state agencies about their HR practices. In addition, the GPP interviewed HRM professionals in the central HR department and selected state agencies. In 2012, the author surveyed states with support of the Pew Center on the States. As of February 1, 2012, half of the states had completed the online survey and preliminary interviews. In 2007, forty-one states completed the survey.
5. Tennessee survey response, 2012.
6. Utah survey response, 2012.
7. Louisiana survey response, 2012.
8. Florida survey response, 2012.
9. Alabama interview, 2012.

REFERENCES

Allen, Tammy D., Deena M. Freeman, Joyce E. A. Russell, Richard C. Reizenstein, and Joseph O. Rentz. 2001. Survivor Reactions to Organizational Downsizing: Does Time Ease the Pain? *Journal of Occupational and Organizational Psychology, 74*, 145–164.

Armstrong-Strassen, Marjorie. 2002. Designated Redundant but Escaping Lay-off: A Special Group of Lay-off Survivors. *Journal of Occupational and Organizational Psychology, 75*, 1–13.

Aronson, Albert H. 1974. State and Local Personnel Administration. In Frank J. Thompson (Ed.), *Classics of Public Personnel Policy*, 2nd ed. Pacific Grove, CA: Brooks/Cole Publishing Company, pp. 133–142.

Ashford, Susan J., Cynthia Lee, and Phillip Bobko. 1989. Content, Causes, and Consequences of Job Insecurity: A Theory-based Measure and Substantive Test. *Academy of Management Journal, 4*, 803–829.

Bowman, James, Marc G. Gertz, Sally C. Gertz, and Russell L. Williams. 2003. Civil Service Reform in Florida State Government: Employee Attitudes 1 Year Later. *Review of Public Personnel Administration, 23*(4), 286–304.

Bowman, James S., and Jonathan P. West. 2006. Civil service reform today: Symposium introduction. *Review of Public Personnel Administration, 26*(2), 99-101.

Coggburn, Jerrell D. 2006. The Decentralized and Deregulated Approach to State Human Resource Management in Texas. In J. Edward Kellough and Lloyd Nigro (Eds.), *Civil Service Reform in the States: Personnel Policy and Politics at the Subnational Level.* Albany, NY: State University of New York, pp. 203–237.

Coggburn, Jerrell D., R. Paul Battaglio Jr., James S. Bowman, Stephen Condrey, and Doug Goodman. 2010. State Human Resource Professionals' Commitment to Employment At Will. *Review of Public Personnel Administration, 40*(2), 189–208.

Condrey, Steve E., and R. Paul Battaglio Jr. 2007. A Return to Spoils? Revisiting Radical Civil Service Reform in the United States. *Public Administration Review, 67*(3), 424–436.

Conover, Milton. 1925. Merit Systems of Civil Service in the States. *The American Political Science Review, 19*(3), 544–560.

Crowell, Elsie, and Mary Ellen Guy. 2010. Florida's HR Reforms: Service First, Service Worst, or Something in Between? *Public Personnel Management, 39*(1), 15–46.

Datta, Deepak K, James P. Gutherie, Dynah Basuil, and Alankrita Pandey. 2010. Causes and Effects of Employee Downsizing: A Review and Synthesis. *Journal of Management, 36*, 281–348.

Duggan, Mike, Julie Lewis, and Mallory Milluzzi. 2010. Labor Relations in Hard Times. *Illinois Public Employee Relations Report, 27*(2), 1–8.

Effron, Marc, Robert Grandossy, and Marshall Goldsmith (Eds.). 2003. *Human Resources in the 21st Century.* Hoboken, NJ: Wiley.

Elazar, Daniel J. 1984. *American Federalism: A View from States* (3rd ed.). New York: Harper and Row.

Fox, Peter D., and Robert J. Lavigna. 2006. Wisconsin State Government: Reforming Human Resource Management While Retaining Merit Principles and Cooperative Labor

Relations. In J. Edward Kellough and Lloyd Nigro (Eds.), *Civil Service Reform in the States: Personnel Policy and Politics at the Subnational Level.* Albany, NY: State University of New York, pp. 279–302.

French, P. Edward, and Doug Goodman. 2012. An Assessment of the Current and Future State of Human Resource Management at the Local Government Level. *Review of Public Personnel Administration, 32*(1). 62–74.

Galinsky, Ellen, and James Bond. 2009. The Impact of the Recession on Employees. Families and Work Institute. http://familiesandwork.org/site/research/reports/Recession2009.pdf. Accessed on March 26, 2012.

Goodman, Doug, and Stacy Mann. 2010. Reorganization or Political Smokescreen: The Incremental and Temporary Use of At-Will Employment in Mississippi State Government. *Public Personnel Management, 39*(3), 183–209.

Graham, Jackie. 2013. Interview with the director of the Alabama State Personnel Department, February 17, 2013.

Green, Kenneth W., and Bobby Medlin. 2010. Impact of Recession-Based Workplace Anxiety. *International Journal of Management and Enterprise Development, 9*(3), 213–232.

Green, Richard, Robert Forbis, Anne Golden, Stephen L. Nelson, and Jennifer Robinson. (2006). On the Ethics of At-Will Employment Relations in the Public Sector. *Public Integrity, 8*(4), 305-327.

Hackler, Dan. 2012. Interview with director of Indiana State Personnel Department, December 13, 2012.

Hays, Steven W., and Jessica E. Sowa. 2006. A Broader Look at the "Accountability" Movement: Some Grim Realities in State Civil Service Systems. *Review of Public Personnel Administration, 26*(2), 102–117.

Herring, Jeff. 2013. Interview with the director of the Utah HRM Department, February 16, 2013.

Kaiser Family Foundation and Health Research and Educational Trust. 2005. Annual Employer Health Benefits Survey. http://www.kff.org/insurance/7315/upload/7315.pdf. Accessed on January 14, 2008.

Kearney, Richard. 2006. The Labor Perspective on Civil Service Reform in the States. In J. Edward Kellough and Lloyd Nigro (Eds.), *Civil Service Reform in the States: Personnel Policy and Politics at the Subnational Level.* Albany, NY: State University of New York, pp. 77–93.

Kellough, Edward J., and Lloyd Nigro (Eds.). 2006. *Civil Service Reform in the States: Personnel Policy and Politics at the Subnational Level.* Albany, NY: State University of New York.

Kellough, Edward J., and Sally Selden. 2003. The Reinvention of Public Personnel Administration: An Analysis of the Diffusion of Personnel Management Reform in the States. *Public Administration Review, 63*(2), 165–176.

Kerrigan, Heather. 2012a. Civil Service Reform Comes to Tennessee. http://www.governing.com/topics/public-workforce/col-civil-service-reform-tennessee.html. Accessed on January 21, 2013.

Kerrigan, Heather. 2012b. Civil Service Reform: Lessons from Georgia and Indiana. http://www.governing.com/topics/public-workforce/col-civil-service-reform-lessons-from-georgia-indiana.html. Accessed January 21, 2013.

Leonard, Bill. 1998. What Do HR Executives Want from CEOS? *HR Magazine, 43*(13), 92–98.

Lindquist, Stefanie A., and Stephen E. Condrey. 2006. Public Employment Reforms and Constitutional Due Process. In J. Edward Kellough and Lloyd Nigro (Eds.), *Civil Service Reform in the States: Personnel Policy and Politics at the Subnational Level.* Albany, NY: State University of New York, pp. 95–114.

Loftin, Josh. 2011. Utah Ends 4-day Workweek Experiment, Provo Says it Still Works for Them. *Deseret News,* http://www.deseretnews.com/article/705390321/Utah-ends-4-day-workweek-experiment-but-Provo-says-it-still-works-for-them.html?pg=all. Accessed February 16, 2013.

Maynard, Melissa. 2012. Civil Service Reform Passes in 3 States. http://www.governing.com/blogs/view/civil-service-reform-passes.html. Accessed January 21, 2013.

Nigro, Lloyd. G., and J. Edward Kellough. 2000. Civil Service Reform in Georgia. *Review of Public Personnel Administration, 20*(4), 41–54.

———. 2006. The States and Civil Service Reform: Lessons Learned and Future Prospects. In J. Edward Kellough and Lloyd Nigro (Eds.), *Civil Service Reform in the States: Personnel Policy and Politics at the Subnational Level.* Albany, NY: State University of New York, pp. 315–324.

———. 2008. Personnel reform in the states: A look at progress fifteen years after the Winter Commission. *Public Administration Review,* 68(s1), s50-s57.

Oreskovich, Joyce. 2013. Interview with the director of the Maine Bureau of Human Resources, February 17, 2013.

Rainey, Hal G. 2006. Reform Trends at the Federal Level with Implications for the States: The Pursuit of Flexibility and the Human Capital Movement. In J. Edward Kellough and Lloyd Nigro (Eds.), *Civil Service Reform in the States:*

Personnel Policy and Politics at the Subnational Level. Albany, NY: State University of New York, pp. 95–114.

Riccucci, Norma M. 2006. Civil Service Reform in New York State: A Quiet Revolution. In J. Edward Kellough and Lloyd Nigro (Eds.), *Civil Service Reform in the States: Personnel Policy and Politics at the Subnational Level*. Albany, NY: State University of New York, pp. 303–313.

Selden, Sally. 2006. Classifying and Exploring Reforms in State Personnel System. In J. Edward Kellough and Lloyd Nigro (Eds.), *Civil Service Reform in the States: Personnel Policy and Politics at the Subnational Level*. Albany, NY: State University of New York, pp. 59–76.

Selden, Sally, Patricia W. Ingraham, and Willow Jacobson. 2001. Human Resource Practices: Findings from a National Survey. *Public Administration Review, 61*(5), 598–607.

Selden, Sally, and Rob Wooters. 2011. Structures in Public Human Resource Management: Shared Services in State Governments. *Review of Public Personnel Administration, 31*(4), 349–368.

Sylvia, Ronald, and C. Kenneth Meyer. 2001. *Public Personnel Administration* (2nd ed.). New York: Wadsworth.

Texas Legislative Budget Board Staff. 2007. Texas State Government Effectiveness and Efficiency: Select Issues and Recommendations. January. http://www.canatx.org/CAN-Research/Reports/2007/TX_Govt_Effective_Efficiency_Report_80th_0107.pdf. Accessed January 14, 2008.

Toossi, Mitra. 2005. Labor Force Projections to 2014: Retiring Boomers. *Monthly Labor Review*, November. http://www.bls.gov/opub/mlr/2005/11/art3full.pdf. Accessed January 13, 2008.

Ulrich, Dave, Jon Younger, and Wayne Brockbank. 2008. The Twenty-First Century HR Organization. *Human Resource Management, 47*(4), 829–850.

White, Erin. 2006. The Best vs. the Rest. *The Wall Street Journal*, January 31. http://www.wsj.com/articles/SB113858499858359631. Accessed January 13, 2008.

Williams, Russell L., and James S. Bowman. 2007. Civil Service Reform, At-will Employment, and George Santayana: Are We Condemned to Repeat the Past? *Public Personnel Management, 36*, 65–77.

CHAPTER 6

STRATEGIC HUMAN RESOURCES MANAGEMENT AT THE LOCAL LEVEL: BALANCING ENDURING COMMITMENTS AND EMERGING NEEDS

Heather Getha-Taylor
University of Kansas

INTRODUCTION

Local government workforces are experiencing rapid and unprecedented change. Some of the most prominent challenges include managing reductions in force, succession planning for an increasingly aging workforce, addressing pressures for outsourcing, and responding to ever growing demands for services. Further, the gap between expected performance and available resources continues to grow. Local government employees are responsible for critical public service commitments, including public health and safety, and are at the same time dealt the deepest personnel management cuts. This chapter considers this stark situation by examining the need to strategically balance enduring commitments and emerging needs.

In 2012, Ann Arbor council member Christopher Taylor wrote about the difficulty of managing such challenges. While writing specifically about governance in Michigan, his statement could certainly be applied more broadly:

We live in an economically and politically challenged state. Michigan's political culture has for years now driven us to become a low-service state that cabins cities' ability to solve local problems and provide exemplary municipal services; systematically diminishes support of public and higher education; and deemphasizes and underresources long-standing infrastructure needs. (Taylor 2012)

Many local governments across the United States are facing similar circumstances. A key question is how to maintain a strong public workforce amid these constraints. Despite difficulties, trade-offs are not mandatory. For instance, the city of Albany, Oregon, has successfully balanced effective management with emerging local trends such as an unemployment rate that exceeds the national average and poverty rates (especially among disabled citizens) that exceed state averages. While service gaps may be expected in this context if growing needs outstrip public resources, the city's performance was recognized four years in a row by the International City/County Management Association (ICMA), and in 2011 and 2012, the city received the ICMA Certificate of Excellence Award. Albany's city manager, Wes Hare, cites strategic planning as key to the city's success during what has been an otherwise trying time.

> A well run city, in the end, is a place where people want to live. Albany's Strategic Plan calls for us to achieve that goal by maintaining safety, a healthy economy, great neighborhoods, and effective government services. By most measures, the community has been successful over the past decade, although many challenges remain. I believe we will overcome those challenges by maintaining a commitment to rigorously analyze our weaknesses, measure our performance, and take corrective action when we know there is a need to do so. (Hare 2012)

Scholarship and practice together advocate for strategic management approaches. When applied to workforce issues, strategic human resources management (HRM) moves an organization toward a specific vision via practices aimed to meet key objectives (Daley 2002). SHRM offers a road map to guide organizations from their current realities to expected end goals. Yet it is difficult to maintain a strategic map when boundaries shift. Understanding how to effectively manage the local government workforce when budgets shrink, demands increase, and goals change is a priority. Given the impact of external forces on internal planning practices, it is important to consider ways in which local governments can maintain a strategic focus during times of turbulence.

There are a number of key dimensions impacting the practice of strategic HRM, including planning, structure, process, values and culture, organizational context, leadership and management, labor-management relations, environmental elements, and technological considerations (Farazmand 2007). This chapter considers local government HRM from a systems perspective by examining the external and internal forces that together impact the ability to bridge organizational, employee, and societal expectations. This chapter presents illustrations of ways in which local governments have successfully sustained a strategic workforce management emphasis during turbulent times. Finally, while this chapter highlights some of the most pressing workforce management issues facing local government, it also provides recommendations for engaging in strategic practices at the local level.

LEARNING FROM THE PAST

Historical foundations shed light on current challenges and illustrate previous efforts to reform, reshape, or revitalize the public service. Emergent forces call attention to the ongoing value tensions between patronage and merit, neutrality and responsiveness, and efficiency and effectiveness (Ingraham 1995). These long-standing tensions are well rooted in the Jacksonian or spoils era, which was marked by political partisanship, regular turnover, and overt corruption. While originally framed as an opportunity to return government employment to "the common man," patronage hurt the image of public employment at all levels. Yet it served political purposes, including responsiveness and party loyalty (Loverd and Pavlak 1983). Freedman (1994) summarizes both sides of the coin: "While there have been periods when patronage achieved widespread acceptance and the practice has at all times had its defenders, for much of our history patronage has been considered undemocratic and unsavory if not downright corrupt and immoral" (pp. 8–9).

The patronage system thrived in the years leading up to the assassination of President Garfield by a disgruntled office seeker in 1881. Corruption and inefficiencies affected all levels of government. Kickbacks, overpayments, and work stoppages led to pushes for reform, but entrenched bosses didn't see the potential of politics without patronage and vocally criticized the "snivel service" reform efforts (Van Riper 1958: 62, in Freedman 1994). High-profile, publicized cases of opportunistic grift helped turn the tide, including examples like the New York County clerk who retained up to $80,000 in fees as part of his salary (Hoogenboom 1961: 256 in Freedman 1994).

The landmark Pendleton Act of 1883 ushered in merit reform at the federal level but did not include city provisions. It was not long, however, before local reforms were underway. The National Municipal League wrote the model legislation to introduce municipal merit provisions. The original draft served to counter mayoral power; the law was amended in 1916 to city manager form (Martin 1989). Civil service reform and the introduction of merit system tenets at the local level served to insulate personnel from political influence and also "rationalize" administration (Tolbert and Zucker 1983). The effort spread quickly: By 1935, merit legislation was enacted in over 450 U.S. cities (Van Riper 1951). Tolbert and Zucker (1983) summarized the local level reform efforts: "Local government structure became clearly patterned by the wider culture over time; civil service procedures became ubiquitous" (25).

The intervening years have witnessed an ebb and flow of reform initiatives aimed to enhance such aspects as responsiveness and performance in the bureaucracy. Yet, beginning with the effort to replace patronage in large scale, Martin (1989) notes: "Civil service and other reformers were destroying party power without replacing it with democratic alternatives. Once their reforms caused abuses, having no fresh ideas, they continued to call for even more unsuccessful reforms" (324). These reform efforts, however, focused on the extrinsic push for change without consideration of implementation or internal management factors. Freedman (1994) notes: "Many of the merit systems are incomplete and/or riddled with loopholes. Even when a civil service law looks good on paper, it is often evaded. . . . In the real world, there are no foolproof systems" (25).

According to Ingraham (1995), reform alone is not the answer. "All the management techniques in the world will falter in the public sector if the environment in which they are implemented is one of distrust and constant challenge" (13). It is difficult to learn the lesson that recognizes the interplay that exists among external forces, organizational performance, and individual investment. For instance, Arthur Proctor's 1921 text on public personnel administration (among the first of its kind) also complained of similar concerns, including resource constraints and high public employee turnover. Further, Fred Telford's pioneering 1927 and 1929 publications on the topic also identified underfunding and

external forces as major contributors to government's inability to meet personnel management goals. When we fast-forward to present day, we find that contemporary approaches to HRM still present difficulties in balancing external forces and internal needs. Dominant societal and political values determine the ways in which organizations set goals and conceptualize the role (and priority) of HRM now and for the future (Condrey 2012).

CURRENT CONTEXT

The challenge of balancing multiple expectations is exacerbated by contemporary economic forces, which reshaped the local government workforce in dramatic ways (Government Accountability Office 2010; Martin, Levey, and Cawley 2012). Namely, in the aftermath of the Great Recession of 2007–2008, local government employment was at its lowest level in over 30 years (Greenstone and Looney 2012), and all but nine states experienced reductions in their local government workforces (U.S. Census Bureau 2011). Cuts in local government jobs, including the critical areas of public safety and education, have both short-term and long-term implications for service delivery and societal outcomes. When the goal is saving money, personnel costs are generally considered first as they constitute the greatest portion of local government spending.

In addition to adding more part-time workers (Maciag 2012), some localities responded by suggesting solutions such as mass privatization in an effort to cut costs. Perhaps one of the most dramatic recent examples is the case of Costa Mesa, California. In March 2011, the city faced a projected $15 million deficit in the city's $114 million budget. The city council voted 4–1 to layoff nearly half of the city's 450 employees and outsource jobs in order to cut costs (Medina 2011). The ensuing battle made national headlines as it highlighted a variety of contentious issues that divided employees, citizens, and elected officials, including public employee collective bargaining provisions, growing retirement costs, and the potential of contracting out government services. Following the layoff announcement, 29-year-old Costa Mesa maintenance worker, Huy Pham, committed suicide at city hall (Marinucci 2011). Accounts indicate that Pham was affected by the "demonizing" of public employees, which may have contributed to taking his life (Washburn, Santana, and Elmahrek 2011).

Especially in times of economic strain, public employees, and their associated benefits, can become targets for attack (Befort 2012). Negative sentiment toward public workers generally, and public unions specifically, is a palpable force (McDermott 2011). Yet the reasons for such animosity, namely concerns surrounding unfair public pay plans, are largely unfounded (Buntin 2010; Keefe 2012). Dramatic reforms, then, must be considered carefully. In the case of Costa Mesa, in August 2012, a ruling by a panel of appellate court justices prevented the layoffs and outsourcing, but proponents of the actions planned to pursue charter city status. This change would allow them to privatize city services, thereby saving money on pensions and other employee benefits (Appellate Court: No Costa Mesa Layoffs 2012). The expected savings would support capital improvement projects, but the plan violated the city's collective bargaining agreement with employees (Dobruck and Zint 2014). At the time of this writing, the legal battle between Costa Mesa and the Costa Mesa Employees Association continues. In an interesting juxtaposition, the city has withdrawn the pink slips but remains committed to outsourcing. In this case and others, the challenges of balancing external forces, such as the need to meet revenue shortfalls, with internal forces, such as the need to protect employee rights, are painfully apparent.

The postrecession economic constraints were felt most strongly at the local government level. Local revenues dropped for six years in a row (Greenblatt 2012), and this was illustrated in a shrinking municipal and county workforce. The 2011 Annual Survey of Public Employment and Payroll reported a total of 10.7 million full-time employees working at the local government level and 3.3 million part-time employees, which represented an overall reduction of 3% from peak pre-recession local government employment levels (U.S. Census Bureau 2011). Pay and hiring freezes, layoffs, and furloughs were expected to constrain the local government workforce for years (Center for State and Local Government Excellence 2012). These practices are still occurring but are now accompanied by other promising trends, including the move to hire employees. Still, the size of the local workforce remains smaller than it was pre-recession (Center for State and Local Government Excellence 2014).

Further, in the most recent report of state and local government workforce trends, survey respondents indicated that recruiting and retaining qualified public servants is a top priority for the future (Center for State and Local Government Excellence 2014). And at the same time, managing the workload is a concern as well. Together, these factors can create a volatile mix. For example, a report revealed that some government staffing shortfalls resulted in caseload backlogs of over a year for teacher misconduct investigations in California, backlogs of over six months for child protective service visits in Arizona, and elevator inspections that may be nine years overdue in Iowa (Maynard 2011). Simply put, public safety can be seriously threatened as a result of HRM gaps at the local level.

EXTERNAL FOCUS: ALIGNING CONSTRAINTS AND EXPECTATIONS

Perlman and Benton (2012) consider the variety of adaptations taking place at the local government level in response to these "new normal" expectations. The authors conclude that cost-cutting measures that rely on staffing cuts alone illustrate a preference for addressing "low hanging fruit that can be snatched without great exertion" (10), but such decisions do not transform organizations and improve outcomes. Rather, the authors argue that instead of focusing only on labor costs/inputs, policy makers and reformers should broaden the focus to include the demand side of the equation. In such high-profile cases as teacher misconduct investigation, child protective services, and public safety, the demand side is clear. Yet it will take systematic change to address broader issues.

A systems perspective helps highlight the contemporary local government HRM challenges. Local governments are interconnected with (and dependent on) their external environment, including the variety of societal and political stakeholders that contribute resources and determine direction. As a result of this structure, external forces permeate internal processes and actions. This holistic perspective provides a framework for understanding complexity. Effective internal adaptation is difficult in systems marked by conflict, ambiguity, and uncertainty. This represents a chaotic reality in any system and especially for local government human resource managers.

Recent events demonstrate these tensions. Debates surrounding public employee rights, including merit systems protections and collective bargaining provisions, have been hotly contested across the United States and specifically in Wisconsin and Ohio in 2011. In the Wisconsin case, Governor Scott Walker worked to curb public employee unions, which spurred thousands of protestors to descend on the steps of the state capitol. It also led to a gubernatorial recall initiative. The recall was unsuccessful and Walker's restrictions on public unions were overturned in September 2012 as violations of union members' freedom of speech and association and equal protection of the laws (Greenhouse 2012). In 2013, a federal court ruling upheld Walker's initiative, known as Act 10, which restricts unions from bargaining about employee benefits and employment conditions aside from base pay. Union membership has withered as Wisconsin's public employees "have little reason to pay dues to a union that can no longer do much for them" (Greenhouse 2014). In Ohio, voters rejected Governor John Kasich's efforts to curb public employee unions. While most state-level civil service reforms do not apply to municipal workers, some local governments are also considering reforms that center on streamlining regulations and enhancing flexibility on such matters as dismissal (Cuda 2012).

Preserving employee protections during calls for more responsive and cost-effective processes can be daunting, especially when local governments must address looming, competing needs for the future. In addition to investments that will ensure a strong municipal workforce for the future, cities face imminent physical infrastructure investments as well (Abels 2012). This requires tough choices, especially given the confounding impact of a depressed labor market (Bivens 2014). The question, it seems, is whether employee protections and cost-effective public value creation are two mutually exclusive concepts. What we do know is the importance of the professional local government workforce in achieving outcomes of interest. Folz and Abdelrazek (2009) found that the presence of professional managers at the local level translates into higher levels of services and community value. Simply finding a cheaper alternative does not make it a better one in the short term or the long run.

These and other dilemmas challenge municipalities in their ability to recruit and retain their best employees. Specifically, external forces threaten the core underlying principles that characterized government work and the people who have chosen a public service career. For instance, Liff (2007) notes that government employees were traditionally drawn to the public workplace by better job security, developmental and advancement opportunities, and the chance to make a difference. Those and other expectations are tempered in the contemporary environment: Local governments risk both broken formal agreements and unsubstantiated psychological contracts (Berman et al. 2013). The latter, "unwritten understanding about mutual needs, goals, expectations and procedures" (228), are important motivational tools: They help managers understand employee interests and align individual expectations with organizational needs. In absence of resources to meet shared expectations, organizations risk alienating employees.

On the one hand, it seems that local employees and their organizations face external forces that present potentially insurmountable odds for success. Yet there are resources that may not be fully acknowledged. For instance, polls show that citizens attribute the highest level of trust to local government employees (Conley 2012). Local government employees represent the clearest link between the people and democracy. It is expected that mutual trust developed between local employees and citizens will contribute to social capital creation. It is also expected that trust will induce reciprocal capacity building that will help both citizens and employees jointly respond to shared challenges (Mathie and Cunningham 2002).

INTERNAL FOCUS: ENGAGING IN STRATEGIC INITIATIVES AMID CHANGE AND CONSTRAINTS

While the role of human resource managers could be reactionary and short-sighted in response to external forces, a focus on strategic management counters that risk. The contemporary strategic emphasis reflects the evolution of the role of HRM within public organizations. This process transformed human resource managers from a technical role to working alongside organizational leaders to jointly design a strategic focus that aligns human resources with organizational goals (Ban and Gossett 2010; Pynes 2013). Further, the contemporary public management values of performance and partnership undergird this transformation (Klingner 2012).

Given that external forces impact internal decisions, translating external pressures for performance into internal mechanisms that support performance can be a challenge. For instance, in absence of an environment that could provide sufficient financial incentives for performance, one particularly promising development is related to the developing work on *employee engagement*. High levels of individual-organizational engagement are expected to contribute to improved performance as well as employee motivation. A 2012 Governing Institute survey of state and local government workers revealed that while over half of public employees were actively engaged in their jobs, nearly 40% said they would be likely to leave if working conditions do not improve. This attitude is more prominent among those 34 years of age or younger (also known as Generation Y and the millennial generation). The survey revealed the value of engagement in employee retention, satisfaction, and the employees' willingness to recommend their workplace to others.

An important question follows: how to enhance engagement? Bilmes and Gould (2009) press this question further by highlighting the distance separating

typical government agencies from what they refer to as "people-focused" private companies. According to the authors, "people-focused" companies offer flexibility, promotions, and perks and align individual development with strategic goals. By comparison, typical government agencies are inflexible, focus more on mission than on people, and provide few meaningful avenues for recognition (63). Engagement is strained in contexts where people are not prioritized. Yet, a decade before Bilmes and Gould's work, Hays and Kearney (2001) surveyed HRM professionals who predicted that recognition, in the way of performance appraisals and merit pay, would be top concerns for the future. A follow-up study by French and Goodman (2012) offered additional support for those findings. Further, according to their study, French and Goodman found that the broader employee benefit of "employee recognition" is expected to take on even greater priority in the years ahead (69). Given expected retirements and the need for the next generation of public employees, it is important to give this benefit additional attention, even in an environment of constrained resources.

LEARNING FROM SUCCESSFUL EXAMPLES

Given the complexities of balancing external forces and internal needs, a question emerges: What can be learned from local governments that have effectively balanced enduring commitments and emergent needs in the era of the "new normal?" Examples of successful municipalities are presented using Selden's (2009) strategic human capital framework (see Figure 6.1). The framework includes the following five components: (1) strategic planning, (2) recruitment and selection, (3) retention, (4) training and development, and (5) performance management. Together, these elements contribute to alignment of mission and goals. Each component is presented via an award-winning local government example. Details for each example are publicly available and accessible online (see the award granting organizations' websites).

Coconino County, Arizona, illustrates the first component, *strategic human capital planning*, and was recognized by the International Public Management

Figure 6.1 Strategic Human Capital Management (Selden 2009)

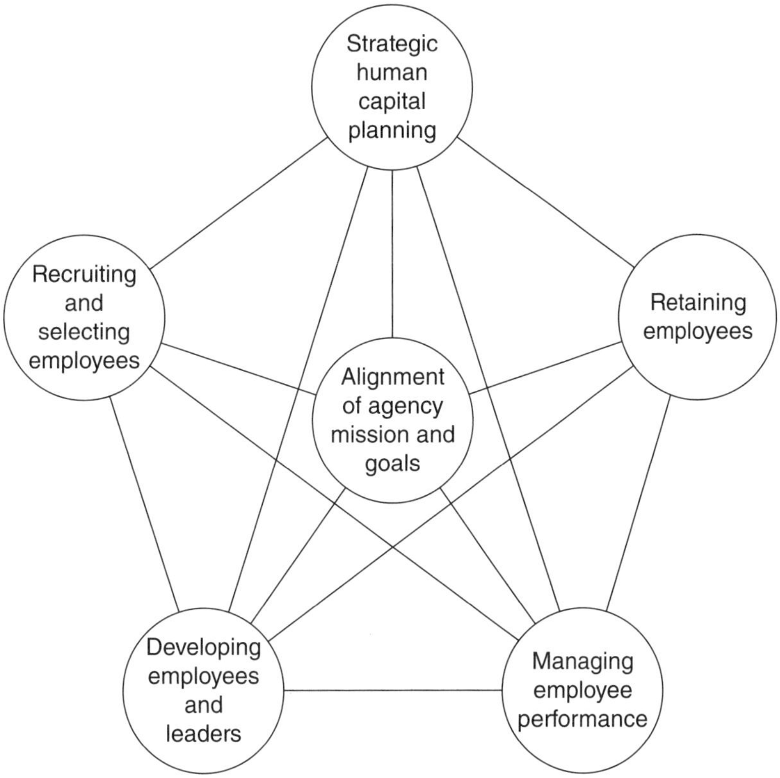

Source: Selden, Sally Coleman. 2009. *Human Capital: Tools and Strategies for the Public Sector*. Washington, DC: CQ Press.

Association for Human Resources (IPMA-HR) in 2011 when the county received the IPMA-HR Award for Excellence. The county's award application highlighted their Premier Employer Committee (PEC). This committee includes employees across the county that work together with the human resources department to brainstorm and develop innovative strategies and also elevate the organizational status of human resources. As a result of this initiative, a variety of new efforts were introduced, including a revised performance management system, cross-training strategies, a retention survey, a knowledge retention survey, and prioritization of employee programs during budget reductions to effectively prepare for and overcome obstacles in the future.

The second component of the framework is *strategic recruiting and selection*. To illustrate this component,

local governments in San Mateo and Santa Clara counties, California, are presented. These local governments together received honorable mention for the Center for State and Local Government Excellence's 2011 Local Government Workforce Excellence Award. This recognition highlighted their regional, multigovernment initiatives to recruit new employees. The governments work together and with local university career centers to provide an internship program, job shadow experiences, and an annual forum. Not only does this effort align with the goal of strategic hiring, but it also illustrates the contemporary public management value of partnership.

The next component of the framework centers on strategic efforts to *retain employees*. For this element, the example of the city of Beverly Hills is offered. In 2010, Beverly Hills received the IPMA-HR Award for

Excellence for its efforts to utilize technology to relieve human resource managers of some more standard processing tasks to allow them to engage in more strategic initiatives, including those intended to help retain employees. As a result of this change, human resource managers are now able to focus on designing and delivering programs focused on staff development, enhancing effectiveness, and improving morale. It is expected that this redirection of human resource staff will result in multiple positive outcomes, including improved overall productivity and city excellence.

Strategic training and development is the next component of the framework. In 2011, Coconino County, Arizona, received honorable mention for the Center for State and Local Government Excellence's Local Government Workforce Excellence Award. The award recognized the Coconino County's innovative strategies to balance the need to cut costs with the desire to continue to develop and retain employees. The county provides training and education opportunities to employees at every stage of their career, including planning classes for those phasing into retirement. In addition, it prioritizes succession planning and is supporting cost-effective cross-training activities. These investments help transfer valuable expertise from mentors to their successors and also prepare the next generation of leaders for additional responsibilities in the years to come.

The final component of the framework is *strategic performance management*. In 2011, the City and County of San Francisco was recognized by the Center for State and Local Government Excellence's for the Local Government Workforce Excellence Award. The award highlighted San Francisco's collective performance management efforts, including attention to employee feedback and utilizing the resulting information for continual improvement. For instance, supervisors and managers receive 360-degree feedback. Further, there is alignment between performance appraisals and subsequent annual performance expectations. Finally, organizational performance data is shared via cost-effective communication channels such as an organization newsletter and website.

Together, these examples illustrate the promise of applying strategic actions to achieve goals and mediate external turbulence. To meet the demands of the future, even more initiatives like these will be necessary. The goal of showcasing these prominent examples is to highlight success and inspire additional creativity, so it seems appropriate to conclude with two additional examples of local government ingenuity that spring from external necessity. In 2011, the County of Los Angeles was recognized by the IPMA-HR Award for Excellence for efforts to address increasing health care costs and also enhance employee engagement. The county partnered with a variety of public, private, and not-for-profit organizations to offer a "Countywide Fitness Challenge." The partnership revealed creative methods to improve employee health and also engage employees in sharing both the problem and the solution. Rising health costs are expected to affect government employers at all levels, so identifying cost-effective tools to meet this hurdle will be a priority in the years ahead.

Further, the City of Livermore, California, received the 2009 IPMA-HR Award for Excellence for its efforts to foster a diverse workforce and also cut costs. The city's "Support Our Staff" (SOS) program supports temporary workers with developmental disabilities who provide administrative support at no cost to the city. The participants receive on-the-job-training and have received high marks for their contributions to the city's operations. The SOS program allows employees to focus on other responsibilities and also work alongside individuals with disabilities. Livermore finds this accomplishes a variety of goals, including dispelling stereotypes and increasing overall productivity. The partnership has been effective in this context and indicates the value of finding other strategic solutions for the future.

CONCLUSION

While these examples serve to illustrate a variety of successful, strategic, contemporary innovations, it is clear that the resizing and reshaping of the local government workforce represents a "new normal" that will influence choices and capacity now and in the future. While responding to budget cuts is an important priority, it should not be the only one. Collectively, scholars, practitioners, and citizens need to think carefully about how to best balance current demands for a smaller, more efficient workforce with future aspirations. Short-term fixes may undercut long-term needs.

These examples show that the challenges facing local governments are daunting but not insurmountable. The solutions, however, rest with the men and women working in public service. It is important to note that it will be difficult to sustain a strong municipal workforce in light of increased demands for services, accompanying cuts in resources, and public sentiment that does not support public employees. These strong external forces must be balanced with an internal focus and investment in strategic HRM in order to continue to deliver high-quality services and produce public value.

Unfortunately, strategic approaches are often neglected in times of (real or perceived) crisis. For many local governments, the current context may present such a situation and perpetuate the "paradox of strategic planning" (Bryson and Roering 1988) where "it is most needed where it is least likely to work" (1002). Namely, the authors indicate that governmental strategic planning works best when a number of contextual factors are in place, including "enough slack to handle potentially disruptive crises." While external forces can certainly affect the ability to plan effectively, it is not the only reason that strategic human resource management fails. Rather, internal management issues such as resistance, poor communication, and lack of support/interest can also impact strategic efforts.

To avoid these pitfalls, organizations need to focus on developing individuals to confront the internal and external management challenges of the future. Bowman et al. (2004) identify three sets of competencies that are critical for public managers in the future. Those competency clusters include leadership competencies (including assessment, negotiation, and change management); ethical competencies (including moral reasoning, values management, and prudent decision making); and technical competencies (including program management, resource stewardship, and strategic planning).

To circle back to the start of this chapter, it is expected that Albany, Oregon's city manager, Wes Hare, would likely endorse this list, given his comments on the importance of strategic management. Hare considers this approach to be much more than just a tool to best utilize public resources amid changing conditions: He considers it an accountability issue as well. Comments from his professional blog illustrate this point: "The most important city asset is the trust of our citizens, and nothing will erode that trust more quickly than mismanagement of city funds" (July 20, 2012). At the same time, Hare seems quite ready to face the road ahead with confidence: "Resources will continue to be constrained, however, and that circumstance is unlikely to change anytime soon."

REFERENCES

Abels, Michael. 2012. Managing Through Collaborative Networks: A Twenty-First Century Mandate for Local Government. *State and Local Government Review, 44*(1), 29S–43S.

Appellate Court: No Costa Mesa Layoffs. 2012. *Orange County Register,* August 17. http://www.ocregister.com/articles/city-368886-officials-court.html

Ban, Carolyn, and Charles W. Gossett. 2010. The Changing Roles of the Human Resource Office. In Stephen Condrey (Ed.), *Handbook of Human Resource Management in Government* (3rd ed.). Thousand Oaks, CA: Sage, pp. 5–26.

Befort, Stephen. 2012. Public-Sector Employment Under Siege. *Indiana Law Journal, 87*(1), 231–238.

Berman, Evan, James S. Bowman, Jonathan P. West, and Montgomery Van Wart. 2013. *Human Resource Management in Public Service: Paradoxes, Processes, and Problems.* Thousand Oaks, CA: Sage.

Bilmes, Linda J., and W. Scott Gould. 2009. *The People Factor: Strengthening America by Investing in Public Service.* Washington, DC: Brookings Institution Press.

Bivens, J. 2014. *The Short- and Long-Term Impact of Infrastructure Investments on Employment and Economic Activity in the U.S. Economy.* Economic Policy Institute. Briefing Paper 374. http://www.epi.org/publication/impact-of-infrastructure-investments/.

Bowman, James S., Jonathan P. West, Evan M. Berman, and Montgomery Van Wart. 2004. *The Professional Edge: Competencies in Public Service.* Armonk, NY: M.E. Sharpe.

Bryson, John M., and William D. Roering 1988. Initiation of Strategic Planning by Governments. *Public Administration Review,* 48(6), 995–1004.

Buntin, John. 2010. Targeting Public Sector Unions. *Governing,* March 1. http://www.governing.com/topics/public-workforce/Targeting-Public-Sector-Unions.html

Center for State and Local Government Excellence. 2012. State and Local Government Workforce: 2012 Trends. http://slge.org/wp-content/uploads/2012/04/S-L-Govt-Workforce-2012_12-195_web.pdf.

———. 2014. State and Local Government Workforce: 2014 Trends. http://slge.org/wp-content/uploads/2014/05/Workforce_Trends_2014.pdf.

Condrey, Stephen E. 2012. Public Human Resource Management: How We Get to Where We Are Today. In Norma M. Riccucci (Ed.), *Public Personnel Management: Current Concerns, Future Challenges.* Boston: Longman, pp. 1–13.

Conley, Larry. 2012. Poll: People Trust Local Government. *American City & County,* June 18. http://americancityandcounty.com/health-amp-welfare/polls-people-trust-local-government

Cuda, Amanda. 2012. Civil Service Reform a Concern for Many. *HR News Magazine,* August.

Daley, Dennis M. 2002. *Strategic Human Resource Management: People and Performance Management in the Public Sector.* Upper Saddle River, NJ: Prentice Hall.

Dobruck, J., and Bradley Zint. 2014. Judge delays ruling on city layoffs. *Daily Pilot,* April 24. http://articles.dailypilot.com/2014-04-24/news/tn-dpt-me-0425-cmcea-lawsuit-20140424_1_city-layoffs-cmcea-city-services.

Farazmand, Ali. 2007. Strategic Public Personnel Administration: A Conceptual Framework for Building and Managing Human Capital in the 21st Century. In Ali Farazmand (Ed.), *Strategic Public Personnel Administration: Building and Managing Human Capital for the 21st Century.* Westport, CT: Praeger, pp. 3–21.

Folz, David H., and Reem Abdelrazek. 2009. Professional Management and Service Levels in Small U.S. Communities. *The American Review of Public Administration, 39,* 553–569.

Freedman, Anne. 1994. *Patronage: An American Tradition.* Chicago: Nelson-Hall.

French, P. Edward, and Doug Goodman. 2012. An Assessment of the Current and Future State of Human Resource Management at the Local Government Level. *Review of Public Personnel Administration, 32,* 62.

Governing Institute. 2012. Survey of 2,200 State and Local Government Workers Establishes Comparative Benchmark for Public Sector Organizations. *HR News Magazine,* October.

Government Accountability Office. 2010. *State and Local Government's Fiscal Outlook.* Washington, DC: GAO.

Greenblatt, Alan. 2012. When Will Governments Hire Again? *Governing,* December. http://www.governing.com/topics/economic-dev/gov-when-will-govt-hire-again.html.

Greenhouse, Steven. 2012. County Judge Strikes Down Some Restrictions on Public Unions in Wisconsin Law. *The New York Times,* September 14. http://www.nytimes.com/2012/09/15/us/judge-strikes-parts-of-wisconsin-union-law.html?_r=0.

———. 2014. Wisconsin's Legacy for Unions. *The New York Times,* February 22. http://www.nytimes.com/2014/02/23/business/wisconsins-legacy-for-unions.html.

Greenstone, Michael, and Adam Looney. 2012. A Record Decline in Government Jobs: Implications for the Economy and America's Workforce. Brookings on Job Numbers blog, www.brookings.edu, August 3.

Hare, Wes. 2012. The Well Run City. http://weshare.cityofalbany.net/, January 13.

Hays, Steven W., and Richard C. Kearney. 2001. Anticipated Changes in Human Resource Management: Views from the Field. *Public Administration Review, 61*(5), 585–597.

Ingraham, Patricia W. 1995. *The Foundation of Merit: Public Service in American Democracy.* Baltimore: Johns Hopkins University Press.

Keefe, J. 2012. Are Public Employees Overpaid? *Labor Studies Journal, 37*(1), 104–126.

Klingner, Donald E. 2012. Building Public HRM Capacity in Fragile and Transitional States. In Norma M. Riccucci (Ed.), *Public Personnel Management: Current Concerns, Future Challenges.* Boston: Longman, pp. 14–27.

Liff, Stewart. 2007. *Managing Government Employees.* New York: American Management Association.

Loverd, Richard A., and Thomas J. Pavlak. 1983. The Historical Development of the American Civil Service. In Jack Rabin, Thomas Vocino, W. Bartley Hildreth, and Gerald Miller

(Eds.), *Handbook on Public Personnel Administration and Labor Relations.* New York: Marcel Dekker, pp. 3–24.

Maciag, Mike. 2012. Full-Time Government Jobs Down, Part-Time Employment Up. *Governing,* August 23. http://www.governing.com/blogs/by-the-numbers/state-local-full-time-part-time-jobs-data.html.

Marinucci, Carla. 2011. Battle Over Public Employees Rocks Orange County. *San Francisco Chronicle,* September 3. http://www.sfgate.com/politics/article/Battle-over-public-employees-rocks-Orange-County-2311669.php.

Martin, Daniel. 1989. *The Guide to the Foundations of Public Administration.* New York: Marcel Dekker.

Martin, Lawrence L., Richard Levey, and Jenna Cawley. 2012. The "New Normal" for Local Government. *State and Local Government Review, 44,* 17–28.

Mathie, Alison, and Gord Cunningham. 2002. From Clients to Citizens: Asset-Based Community Development as a Strategy for Community-Driven Development. Coady International Institute. http://www.communityrestorationtrust.com/PDF/communitydevelopment.pdf.

Maynard, Melissa. 2011. Short-staffed and budget-bare, overwhelmed state agencies unable to keep up. The Pew Charitable Trust's *Stateline,* December 14.

McDermott, Kevin. 2011. Public Workers Feel Targeted. *St. Louis Post Dispatch,* September 5. http://www.stltoday.com/news/local/govt-and-politics/public-workers-feel-targeted/article_c0db3101-7519-528b-b401-fe1890d4f630.html.

Medina, Jennifer. 2011. Short on Funds, but Long on Pink Slips. *The New York Times,* March 24.

Perlman, Bruce J., and J. Edwin Benton. 2012. Going it Alone: New Survey Data on Economic Recovery Strategies in Local Government. *State and Local Government Review, 44,* 5–16.

Proctor, Arthur W. 1921. *Principles of Public Personnel Administration.* New York: Appleton.

Pynes, Joan. 2013. *Human Resources Management for Public and Nonprofit Organizations.* Fourth Edition. Thousand Oaks, CA: Sage.

Selden, Sally Coleman. 2009. *Human Capital: Tools and Strategies for the Public Sector.* Washington, DC: CQ Press.

Taylor, Christopher. 2012. This I Believe: Ann Arbor's Future is Bright. www.annarbornews.com, December 30. http://www.annarbor.com/news/opinion/this-i-believe-ann-arbors-future-is-bright/.

Telford, Fred. 1927. Needed Personnel Legislation, Federal and Local. *Public Personnel Studies, 5,* 106–110.

———. 1929. Some Trends in Public Personnel Administration. *Public Personnel Studies, 7,* 150–158.

Tolbert, Pamela S., and Lynn G. Zucker. 1983. Institutional Sources of Change in the Formal Structure of Organizations: The Diffusion of Civil Service Reform, 1880–1935. *Administrative Science Quarterly, 28,* 22–39.

United States Census Bureau. 2011. *Annual Survey of Public Employment and Payroll.* Washington, DC: U.S. Census Bureau.

Van Riper, Paul. 1951. *History of the United States Civil Service.* Evanston, IL: Peterson.

Washburn, David, Norberto Santana Jr., and Adam Elmahrek. 2011. Costa Mesa Employee Commits Suicide at City Hall. *Voice of OC,* March 17. http://voiceofoc.org/2011/03/costa-mesa-employee-commits-suicide-at-city-hall/.

CHAPTER 7

THE NONPROFIT SECTOR LABOR FORCE

Beth Gazley
Indiana University–Bloomington

INTRODUCTION

Approximately 1.6 million organizations are recognized under the federal tax code as "nonprofits": exempt entities organized for public or mutual benefit purposes. Two-thirds of these organizations are private foundations, public charities, or religious congregations recognized jointly as 501(c)(3) organizations.[1] The remainder are recognized under one of 29 other tax codes depending on the nature of their mission, including 501(c)(4) social welfare organizations (6% of all nonprofit organizations), 501(c)(5) labor unions (3%), 501(c)(6) business leagues (4%), 501(c)(7) social clubs (3%), and 501(c)(8) fraternal societies (3%) (Roeger et al. 2012).

About 13.7 million paid employees and an estimated 49 million or more volunteers comprise the nonprofit labor force (Roeger et al. 2012; Leete 2006). This figure represents nearly as many people employed in the business retail sector and twice the number of people employed in construction, finance, or transportation (Salamon, Sokolowski, and Geller 2012). By comparison, all levels of government employ 22.5 million persons and involve an estimated 16 million or more volunteers (U.S. BLS 2011, 2012).[2]

As Table 7.1 illustrates, the nonprofit labor force is also growing, representing 10.6% of the U.S. labor force in 2010, up from 8.8% one decade earlier. This increase outpaces both the government and business sectors in terms of total jobs added (Roeger et al. 2012). Not included but bound to increase this figure considerably is the indirect nonprofit labor force, the commercial entities that support the nonprofit sector as providers of insurance, banking, information technology, philanthropic advising, and other services.

NONPROFIT EMPLOYMENT DATA: DIVERSE AND ELUSIVE

Despite this strong contribution to the nation's economy, employment data on the nonprofit sector are hard to capture. Some observe that employment information is the largest missing piece in nonprofit data needs overall (Roeger et al. 2012: 44). The challenge lies in the fact that the U.S. Department of Labor does not record annual employment data separately for private nonprofit and private for-profit organizations. The Urban Institute's National Center for Charitable Statistics is a primary source of current data, and this chapter also presents some estimated data (in Table 7.2) from the American Community Survey.

Another challenge in understanding nonprofit employment lies in the enormous diversity of the sector. Its scope of activities encompasses large portions of the arts and cultural, health care, educational, environmental, recreational, human and social services, philanthropic, political, and civic subsectors. Within each

Table 7.1 Nonprofit Employment (in thousands) and Wages (in billions of current dollars) as Share of Total U.S. Employment[a]

Year	Business		Nonprofits		Government		Total U.S. Workers[b]	Nonprofit Share of Total Workers	Total Annual Wages	Nonprofit Share of Total Wages
	Workers	Wages	Workers[b]	Wages[c]	Workers	Wages				
2000	99,336	3,760	11,659	359	20,790	700	131,785	8.8%	4,832	7.4%
2001	98,737	3,823	11,971	382	21,118	740	131,826	9.1	4,958	7.7
2002	96,480	3,795	12,348	408	21,513	788	130,341	9.5	5,003	8.2
2003	95,878	3,890	12,538	430	21,583	826	129,999	9.6	5,160	8.3
2004	97,154	4,090	12,660	451	21,621	861	131,435	9.6	5,417	8.3
2005	99,176	4,331	12,723	468	21,804	899	133,703	9.5	5,712	8.2
2006	101,212	4,626	12,900	496	21,974	939	136,086	9.5	6,077	8.2
2007	102,216	4,891	13,164	525	22,218	989	137,598	9.6	6,423	8.2
2008	101,009	4,941	13,272	555	22,509	1,042	136,790	9.7	6,557	8.5
2009	94,834	4,620	13,418	574	22,555	1,074	130,807	10.3	6,284	9.1
2010	93,637	4,725	13,699	588	22,482	1,090	129,818	10.6	6,418	9.2

[a]Adapted from Roeger et al. (2012: Table 2.5).

[b]Calculations by Roeger et al. (2012), based on U.S. Department of Labor, Bureau of Labor Statistics, Current Employment Statistics (2000–2010); U.S. Census Bureau, Economic Census (1997, 2002, 2007); and Urban Institute, National Center for Charitable Statistics, Core Files (Public Charities, 2000–2010).

[c]Wages from nonprofit institutions serving households (NPISH) only, and not adjusted for inflation. For a detailed discussion on what is omitted from NPISH calculations, please consult the Urban Institute.

of these subsectors, the mix of volunteer and paid labor varies, from fields such as religion that are dominated by voluntary labor to fields such as health care reliant mainly on paid professional staff. The nonprofit workforce is also shaped by the norms and expectations of each industry. Some industries such as education and health care are dominated by nonprofit organizations, while others such as the arts have a much stronger influence from for-profit activities (Salamon et al. 2012).

The sector's diversity also creates enormous imbalances in size and wealth. Two employment fields dominate: health[3] and education. Representing 22% of all reporting organizations, these entities were responsible for 72% of the sector's wages in 2010 and controlled 47% of its assets (Roeger et al. 2012). By contrast, religious organizations, labor unions, and grant-making foundations capture approximately 1% each of total nonprofit wages.

Finally, the nonprofit workforce is also shaped by the diversity in revenue sources. The most common pattern finds nonprofit employees engaged in programmatic activities that are reimbursed wholly or in part through earned income, such as through public or private health insurance, tuition, ticket sales, dues, and other fees for services rendered. This portrait of a large, paid, professional workforce focused on client and member services challenges the stereotype of a largely unpaid or undercompensated amateur workforce reliant on philanthropic revenue.

This chapter's discussion of personnel challenges and opportunities in the nonprofit sector is set against this broad and diverse landscape of civil society organizations. It discusses the demographic changes that influence nonprofit employment and service provision in the U.S. and the economic forces that challenge effective human resource management in the nonprofit sector. In this chapter, I focus on recruitment and retention as particular challenges facing nonprofit human resource managers at both the executive and staff level, and I offer the most recent research on effective personnel management. A separate chapter in this volume by Jeffrey L. Brudney focuses on the recruitment, retention, and management of volunteers.

ECONOMIC AND DEMOGRAPHIC CHALLENGES

The United States is "simultaneously aging and growing more diverse" (Halpern 2006: 4). Observers also describe a "growing and unhealthy gap between the haves and the have-nots" (Walker 2006). Even before the most recent economic recession, increases in health care costs, welfare reform, and fiscal constraints on federal, state and local governments placed new demands on public and private services.

These trends pose both workforce and workplace challenges for the nonprofit sector. As service providers, nonprofit organizations assisting disadvantaged populations report higher demands for their help (Bishop 2006; Salamon and O'Sullivan 2004). And as employers, securing and retaining a workforce with the right combination of knowledge, skills, and abilities has been a longstanding challenge for nonprofit organizations both within and without the charitable subsector. Increased competition from other sectors for highly skilled employees, high executive management turnover, the labor intensity of some portions of the sector, and limited success in the ability to recruit and retain skilled volunteers all combine to make 21st-century human resource management in the nonprofit sector an enormously demanding activity.

THE NONPROFIT LABOR FORCE

The employee profile of the nonprofit sector reflects the strong representation of service industries (compared, for example, with heavy industry such as manufacturing and transportation in the for-profit sector). Table 7.2 offers a recent demographic snapshot of the sector, with two points of comparison: the present nonprofit sector is compared to the 1989 nonprofit workforce and also to the for-profit and government labor forces. These figures suggest that, both 24 years ago and in the 2006–2010 time period, substantially more nonprofit employees were female (66% of the nonprofit workforce then and now) when compared with business (45%) or state, local, and federal governments (55%). The nonprofit sector

Table 7.2 Characteristics of U.S. Nonprofit, For-Profit, and Public Sector Workers

Characteristics	1989 Nonprofit[a]	2006–2010 ACS 5-Year Estimates[b]			
		Nonprofit	For-Profit/ Self-Employed	Government	Total U.S. Workforce
Sex					
Male	33.4	33.9	54.9	44.7	49.1
Female	66.6	66.1	45.1	55.3	50.9
Race or ethnicity					
White	83.8	77.7	76.0	74.4	75.9
Hispanic	2.5	9.0	13.3	10.0	12.5
African American	9.5	12.2	10.8	15.2	11.6
Asian	2.4	4.5	4.9	4.0	4.8
Native American[c]		.8	.8	1.3	.9
Other/Multiple	1.9	4.8	7.4	5.0	6.8
Education level					
Less than HS diploma	9.2	7.4	14.8	4.8	12.7
High school or GED	21.7	17.7	29.7	19.8	27.3
Some college	17.6	21.2	24.5	22.8	24.0
Associate's degree	9.4	9.5	7.7	8.3	7.9
Bachelor's degree	22.6	24.6	16.4	23.4	18.1
Graduate degree	19.4	19.6	7.0	20.8	10.0

[a]1989 comparison figures appeared in the 5th edition of this book and were reprinted by permission of Yale University Press from W. W. Powell and R. Steinberg (Eds.), *The Nonprofit Sector: A Research Handbook*, 2nd ed. (New Haven, CT: Yale University Press). Copyright 2006 Yale University Press.

[b]Five-year population estimates from the American Community Survey Public Use Microdata Sample, U.S. Census Bureau. Figures are weighted, based on self-reported answers, and exclude individuals who are unemployed or working without pay. Note that "Race" and "Hispanic" are separate ACS questions, so figures will not total 100%. Comparisons between 1989 and 2006–2010 nonprofit employment data should be made with caution due to changes in sampling methods.

[c]"Native American" also includes Alaskan and Pacific Islander/Hawaiian.

has also become more racially and ethnically diverse, although in select categories still not as diverse as the business or government sectors. The nonprofit sector at present is also substantially more educated than the U.S. workforce at large, on par with the government sector, with nearly 45% holding a bachelor's or graduate degree.

Nonprofit wages vary widely according to geography, occupation, and employee qualifications. Controlling for these factors, organizational size and funding mix are the strongest predictors of salary difference within particular nonprofit industries. Across sectors, nonprofit wages on average are slightly lower than those in the government and for-profit sectors (Leete 2006; Ruhm and Borkoski 2003). Executive compensation in the nonprofit sector is substantially lower than that of for-profits (Twombly and Gantz 2001). Governmental comparisons are not readily available, but they tend to suggest that nonprofits compare favorably to government agencies on the basis of wages but that public sector employees have the advantage when it comes to benefits (Roeger et al. 2012).

Selective controlled occupational or industry studies often erase these disparities, and nonprofit salaries often surpass for-profit compensation. Similar wages are most likely to be found in industries where both sectors are active, such as child care, home health care, and teaching (Salamon 2002). These industries must compete for the same labor force, and this labor force has the advantage of being able to cross all sectors in search of employment. Take the example of a registered nurse seeking employment. In larger communities, this trained professional is likely to find for-profit, nonprofit, and public health care facilities competing for the best talent. In other words, wage disparities between the sectors do crop up, but they tend to be associated with circumstances particular to an industry rather than to the nonprofit sector as a whole (Salamon 2002: 61).

Scholars have wrestled over both the nature and extent of these pay disparities and over their causes. A combination of internal and external circumstances—particularly market pressures, government regulation, differences in employer behavior caused by presence/absence of a profit motive, and employee self-selection—explain many of the observable differences. In other words, our registered nurse may find the mission-oriented culture of a nonprofit health care institution more attractive, although the compensation is smaller. The great diversity within the sector makes generalizations difficult, but many individual economic studies find evidence of "sorting" behaviors and a complicated matching process that involves both employer and employee choice (Leete 2006: 162). Understanding what attracts employees and volunteers to the nonprofit labor market therefore becomes a principal area of exploration in this chapter.

A CHALLENGING RECRUITMENT ENVIRONMENT

A 2007 report in the Johns Hopkins University Center for Civil Society Studies series was published under the title "The Nonprofit Workforce Crisis: Real or Imagined?" (Salamon and Geller 2007). This provocative title alludes to an apparent disconnect between perception and reality when it comes to the sector's ability to recruit a viable labor force. Selective studies find nonprofits to be fairly resilient in their ability to meet workforce challenges such as job growth, including during the most recent recession (Salamon and Geller 2007; Salamon et al. 2012).

The optimism is reinforced by an understanding that many nonprofit jobs are countercyclical to the economy, meaning many organizations were actively recruiting employees during the most recent recession to fill greater demands in education, social and human services, health care, and other industries. Figure 7.1 reflects a snapshot of employment trends up to the current recession (Irons and Bass 2004). Here, the countercyclical and robust growth in nonprofit employment during the 2001 recession can clearly be seen. Although not shown here, Salamon et al. (2012) report similar results for the current recession, where nonprofit employment increased 1.9% between 2007 and 2009 while for-profit employment decreased by 3.7%.

However, Figure 7.1 and the recent Johns Hopkins research both also illustrate the greater volatility of nonprofit employment, where peaks and troughs respond not only to direct labor trends but also to policy initiatives, local or national events that spur an interest in public service, and indirect economic conditions such as philanthropic discretionary income. Salamon et al. (2012) found that the rates of nonprofit recessionary job growth

Figure 7.1 Growth in Employment

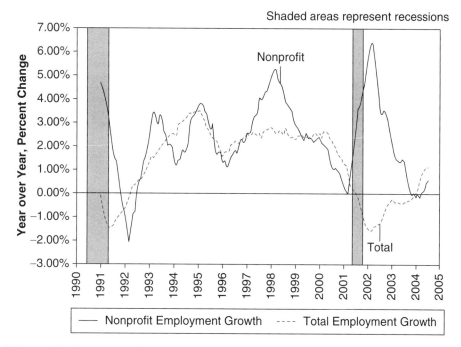

Source: Reprinted with permission from Recent Trends in Nonprofit Employment and Earnings: *1990–2004*, Washington, DC: OMB Watch (August 2004).

varied by as much as 100% from region to region and from one subsector to another. Even in fields presumed to be more vulnerable to limits on disposable income, such as the arts, employment growth surpassed the for-profit sector considerably during the 2007–2009 period.

Because of or possibly in spite of this growth, many nonprofit organizations report a challenging recruitment environment. And although this is not a phenomenon unique to one sector, nonprofits have higher annual turnover rates than government and business (3.1%, compared with 2.7% in the business sector and 1% in government) (Cappelli 2005; Weitzman et al. 2002). Some extrapolated analyses project a "leadership deficit" in the tens of thousands based on current growth of the sector, anticipated retirements, and employee transitions to other sectors (Tierney 2006).

The most pressing ongoing workforce challenges appear to rest on the sector's ability to offer competitive salaries and to recruit qualified staff, particularly in smaller organizations (Ban, Drahnak, and Towers 2002; Salamon and Geller 2007). The extent of the labor deficit varies widely according to geography and organizational characteristics. In one statewide study, larger nonprofits and those dependent on government funding report the greatest recruitment challenges (Grønbjerg and Clerkin 2004).

To the extent that they occur, recruitment challenges experienced by individual organizations have important repercussions. An organization's inability to find the right staff will make the jobs of other staff more challenging. An inability to find staff who reflect the demographic characteristics of clients will make it more difficult to serve particular client populations. In one employment survey examining managerial responses to vacancies or turnover, 26% of nonprofit organizations reported responding to labor shortages by retaining underperforming staff, and 22% postponed or cancelled new programs (Peters et al. 2002).

The cost of an unfilled position should always be acknowledged and, in fact, can be calculated monetarily. Based on an assumption that each current employee produces labor with a positive revenue impact, the formula to calculate the daily revenue value for an employee is the following: $(R/E)/365$, where R = annual organizational revenue and E = number of employees. Assuming an organization with $1 million in annual revenues and 16 employees, each staffperson has a daily value of $171. Therefore, a position left unfilled for two months would cost this organization more than $10,200.

EFFECTIVE EMPLOYEE RECRUITMENT AND RETENTION

Turnover, defined as a permanent departure, also has its costs, including staff time or other resources to manage both the separation and replacement processes. Turnover rates for an organization can be calculated by the following formula: $T/W \times 100\%$, where T = number of staff departures within a specified time period and W = the average size of the workforce in that time period. If our hypothetical $1 million organization lost or replaced two of its 16 staff in the past year, the turnover rate would be 12.5%. All turnover rates should be compared periodically, both internally over time and to organizations in similar communities and industries, to understand whether more attention should be paid to employee retention.

Since staff turnover compromises organizational performance, learning the practices of effective recruitment and retention becomes an organizational imperative. Competitive salaries, benefits, and advancement opportunities represent the principal organizational factors that support nonprofit staff recruitment, while retention rests on additional organizational practices such as effective orientation and training (Preston 2002; Salamon and Geller 2007). With respect to compensation, two widespread pieces of conventional wisdom about nonprofit compensation challenge human resource managers. The first is that nonprofit employers will have difficulty finding employees because they cannot compete for labor on the basis of salary alone. The second,

somewhat competing assumption is that nonprofit workers "are motivated by mission, not money" (Bacon 2004: 1). This second assumption is based on a theory of donative labor that posits that nonprofit employees "derive utility from the nature of the good produced and are thus willing to accept a lower (compensating) wage" (Leete 2001: 137).

MISSION AND MONEY

Both of these assumptions hold a kernel of truth. Indeed, as noted earlier, nonprofit employers must work hard to find and keep those skilled professionals who can easily cross sectoral boundaries. Nonprofits have lagged behind the business sector particularly when it comes to performance-based compensation, thus making it more difficult to retain the high performers attracted to this kind of incentive. And although the research is slim in this area, some evidence from public service motivation research suggests that nonprofit employees engage in sector-switching more frequently than both public and commercial sector employees (Piatak 2012).

But the problem with these assumptions lies in the suggestion that individuals are motivated by only one or the other of these employment features, either by mission *or* money. In reality, most individuals make job choices based on a combination of motivating factors, including salary but also including an expectation of other, possibly nonmonetary benefits. Theuvsen (2004: 125) observes that "most [employee] actions are in fact extrinsically as well as intrinsically motivated." What this means is that employees are motivated to perform their work to achieve both psychological or self-determined needs and also for instrumental reasons or needs that are dependent on their employer. Table 7.3 offers some examples of how this mix of intrinsic and extrinsic benefits can be realized in a nonprofit environment.

An overemphasis in recruitment or job design on the extrinsic rewards of a position, such as pay, can cause an employer to overlook important personal benefits inherent to nonprofit work, such as the ability to produce work of social value, to serve others, and to effect change. The value in understanding how to help employees achieve

Table 7.3 Intrinsic and Extrinsic Motivations

	Intrinsic Motivations	Extrinsic Motivations
Definitions (Ryan and Deci 2000)	To be motivated to perform a task for psychological or self-determined needs, in which the reward is in the task itself.	To be motivated for an instrumental reason, in which the outcome is separable from the individual, i.e., the rewards depend on action external to the employee.
Workplace examples	Work that is interesting, builds competencies or self-efficacy, offers autonomy, allows employee to achieve new knowledge or satisfy curiosity, provides spiritual benefits (such as faith-based employment), offers aesthetic rewards (such as work on behalf of arts organizations), fulfills self-realized altruistic goals (such as work on behalf of disadvantaged persons).	Material rewards such as pay and benefits, praise, recognition, emotional support, training.
Supportive nonprofit personnel practices	Communication with staff about the community impact of their work, career ladders, mentoring, reverse mentoring, training and professional development, flex-time, job design (e.g., to create jobs with greater responsibility, challenges, variety).	Professional development opportunities, family-friendly job benefits (e.g., flex-time, telecommuting, and family leave time), transportation subsidies, health benefits, child care and elder care subsidies, recognition of exceptional performance, rewards for longevity.

these benefits cannot be overstated, given that this is an area where nonprofit organizations may enjoy an enormous competitive advantage. Nonprofit organizations should begin by understanding the intrinsic motivations of prospective employees. They achieve this objective by engaging in the foundational activities of effective recruitment: job design, screening, and interviewing, where a purposeful discussion of employee goals can be achieved.

Nonprofits will also perform well at recruitment when they are able to communicate the extrinsic rewards of a position in terms of both monetary and nonmonetary benefits. Salient monetary strategies include employee benefits, salary adjustments, and pay for performance policies (Ban et al. 2002). Nonmonetary retention strategies focus on job enrichment and advancement opportunities (Day 2004).

Research suggests that employees do behave differently with respect to the mix of motivators. Data from the National Administrative Studies Project III finds a positive relationship between nonprofit employment and an individual's desire for more responsibility and also for family-friendly policies. The study does not find a relationship between salary preference and sector of employment (Lee and Wilkins 2011).

RETENTION STRATEGIES

Organizations must also practice managerial techniques that encourage new employees to stay. Studies suggest that many employees join the nonprofit sector for reasons that are distinct from those that keep them in their jobs. Over time, the salience of mission may become a less important driver of employee job satisfaction than pay, workplace culture, and opportunities for advancement (Ban et al. 2002; Brown and Yoshioka 2003). In other words, an organization must understand employee motivations both in terms of what attracts them to nonprofit work (such as mission, workplace culture, or an opportunity to realize public benefit goals) and also in terms of what keeps them from leaving (such as benefits, advancement opportunities, supervisor quality, and workplace culture). Returning to our earlier example,

our registered nurse may find over time that the charitable mission of an employing hospital chain is not a sufficient motivator to keep this individual from pursuing a better benefits package at a hospital in the commercial or public sector.

Small- to mid-sized nonprofit organizations may find themselves particularly challenged in their ability to retain staff on the basis of pay. Many low-cost strategies are available for them. Retention strategies with a potentially high impact and low cost include professional development opportunities, family-friendly job benefits such as flex-time, telecommuting, and family leave time, transportation subsidies, health benefits, career ladders, and child care and elder care subsidies. Supervisors can be supported with professional development and supervisor support programs. Managers can recognize exceptional performance through public recognition and reverse-mentoring and can reward longevity through anniversary gifts. Nonprofits can ensure employees continue to understand their contributions to the organizational mission by performing outcome evaluations and communicating the results to staff (Brown and Yoshioka 2003). In all cases, compensation strategies consistent with organizational goals, culture, and strategy—and those that can be defended from an equity basis—will be most easily accepted by staff.

Information on the impact of such policies is scarce. It is difficult to assess the influence of organizational human resource strategies on employee retention in isolation from other external factors that attract individuals to nonprofit work (such as personality) or cause them to leave (such as family needs). One study of nonprofit executives suggests that many senior staff, at least, are willing to accept a greater emphasis on nonsalary benefits. Half of those surveyed preferred a salary increase to improve their compensation packages; the remainder suggested retirement contributions, vacation time, and other monetary and nonmonetary benefits (Bell, Moyers, and Wolfred 2006). Fewer than half feel they are making a high financial sacrifice to work where they do—yet the same number believe the next CEO will expect to earn at least 10% more than they do. These figures suggest that nonprofit executives are aware of their market value but willing to negotiate with their boards to create benefits packages that meet their needs. Similar research for other staff levels would be useful.

WORK AND PAY EQUITY

An additional retention challenge lies in improving work and pay equity. Although the overall amount of discriminatory employer behavior appears to be smaller in the nonprofit sector when compared with the for-profit sector (Leete 2006), pay discrimination according to gender and other demographic characteristics has been found in many studies of the nonprofit sector (Bell et al. 2006; Grey and Benson 2003; Lipman 2002). Selective occupational analyses (e.g., fundraising) find some patterns indicative of gender discrimination in advancement opportunities, salaries, and performance bonuses (Gibelman 2000; Mesch and Rooney 2008). Although more cross-sectoral comparisons (e.g., non-profit/government comparisons) would be helpful, nonprofits are no more immune to discriminatory practices than any other sector. And many nonprofit employees have minimal legal protection if their employer's small size restricts their coverage under federal labor laws. Managers should understand that a mission with social value does not substitute for a thorough understanding of employment law.

EXECUTIVE RETENTION: CAN COMPENSATION REDUCE TURNOVER?

Across the nonprofit sector, studies also find a high rate of turnover at the executive director level. According to two national studies by the Bridgespan Group and CompassPoint, three-quarters of nonprofit CEOs reported plans to leave their job within five years, creating a potential leadership deficit that may limit the ability of many nonprofits to meet their organizational objectives (Bell et al. 2006; Tierney 2006). The annual survey of executive compensation and benefits produced by the Chronicle of Philanthropy found that nearly one-third of surveyed nonprofits replaced a top executive in 2006 (Barton and Panepento 2007). Compounding

the problem is an absence of succession planning at the majority of surveyed nonprofits (Hrywna 2007).

It is important to mention that executive turnover has benign features: Few CEOs plan to leave the sector entirely—many intend to transition to other nonprofit positions that offer new opportunities or to related fields such as consulting (Tierney 2006). Thus, the turnover in executive staff may not represent a heavy loss of institutional knowledge for the sector overall and may in fact help to disseminate knowledge through and between sectors.

However, the two most commonly cited reasons for leaving are troubling. We first observe that the turnover is only partially due to an aging workforce and planned retirements (DRG 2006; Teegarden 2004). Rather, the majority of executive directors point specifically to dissatisfaction with their boards of directors or their compensation package as the factors that will drive them out of their current positions (Bell et al. 2006). Although it is typical for professional staff in any sector to move on to larger organizations in search of better pay or new challenges, even at the largest nonprofit organizations a substantial minority (41%) of executive directors plan to leave within the next three to five years.

Nearly half of those intending to leave report frustration with unsupportive boards (Bell et al. 2006). The dynamic between board and CEO has been addressed widely in the nonprofit management literature, with strong opinions but little general agreement about the best balance of roles and responsibilities between the staff and the governing members of the organization (see, for example, Carver 2007; Harris 1993). As a result, both boards and executive staff can impose unreasonable or unacceptable expectations on one another. In no other sector do we find a group of part-time, uncompensated individuals with varying levels of expertise and organizational allegiance who are legally in charge of an organization. Even as the regulatory environment has grown more complex and the amount of information board members are required to understand has increased, it is not at all clear that board members are receiving the training and incentives they need to do their jobs well. Executive turnover may reflect this situation.

Second, fundraising pressures place a heavy burden on nonprofit CEOs. The nonprofit fundraising environment has generally grown more challenging over time, fueled by greater donor expectations, heavier regulatory burdens, and increased competition from within and without the sector. Nonprofit CEOs have more to know and more to do to secure organizational resources, and they consequently cite financial stability as their chief internal organizational challenge (Bell et al. 2006).

Both of these causes for executive turnover reflect fundamental characteristics of the sector that may be difficult to address, particularly when understood in the context of legal restrictions on nonprofit executive compensation. It is a common misunderstanding that nonprofit executive pay levels are capped in some way. In reality, boards of directors enjoy great discretion in setting pay levels provided they can justify their decisions with comparable market data and evidence that the decision was made in a way that avoids conflicts of interest. However, the public nature of these salaries (disclosure is required in the 990 tax return since passage of the Taxpayer Bill of Rights) and the amount of press that has been generated about "unreasonable" nonprofit executive pay have made many boards conservative in their approach to compensation.

Recent years have seen a slight loosening of the regulations and increased realization by boards of the need to create competitive compensation packages to attract executive talent. The change has been supported by the entry of more business executives into nonprofit employment and board service. Nonetheless, public and donor pressure, legal restrictions that reflect the nondistribution constraint, and other features of the regulatory environment provide strong incentives to boards of directors to minimize risk in setting executive compensation packages.

Although salary and benefits, particularly pension payments and bonuses, are likely to continue to improve in the nonprofit sector, they can be expected to do so in a highly stratified way, with the largest organizations initiating the greatest pay increases. Although the nation's largest nonprofits are currently increasing executive salaries faster than their for-profit counterparts, average sectoral salaries for other positions are barely keeping pace with inflation (Barton, Di Mento, and Sanoff 2007; Barton and Panepento 2007; Hrywna 2007; Schwinn and Wilhelm 2003). It remains to be seen how small- to mid-sized nonprofit organizations address executive turnover, how the salary push at the executive level translates to mid-level professionals, and what tools and strategies are found to be most helpful.

CONCLUSION: IMPROVING NONPROFIT HUMAN RESOURCE MANAGEMENT CAPACITY

The first years of the 21st century present nonprofits with a challenging human capital environment. Competition with other sectors for labor, greater demands for nonprofit services, an aging workforce, and pressures of the executive position are creating higher staff turnover than in other sectors, particularly at the executive levels. Many nonprofits are more successful at attracting volunteers than in keeping them. High turnover affects organizational efficiency and service quality. This chapter suggests that the solution lies in great part in finding personnel with the right mix of interests, skills, and motivation to be attracted to the nonprofit sector and then employing the right human resource practices and strategies to retain them.

This environment demands a strategic outlook from human resources managers and a strong set of management skills. On the first count, nonprofits can benefit from a holistic approach to human resource management embodied in the concept of *strategic human resources management* (Pynes 2013). SHRM practices are integrated with organizational mission. They are aligned with organizational priorities and attuned to workplace culture and external dynamics. Strategic human resource practices occur at the center of the organization rather than the periphery, and they are embraced by all supervisors rather than a single HR department. They are proactive in anticipating the impact of market forces and in designing strategies to take advantage of internal or external strengths and opportunities.

The strategic human resource manager must be supported in these activities with adequate resources and knowledge. Beginning at the board level, nonprofit executives must understand the process of employee recruitment, motivation, and retention as interrelated activities dependent on all staff for success. The HR function in many nonprofits is understaffed and under-resourced; boards might profit with a review of their internal functions and an assignment of greater organizational resources to staff and volunteer management. Furthermore, nonprofit jobs are increasingly professionalized, and the rapid increase in graduate programs in nonprofit management offers HR managers new opportunities to broaden their skills and knowledge about employee expectations (Pynes 2013). As educational levels increase, more nonprofit managers can be expected to implement the managerial tools and strategies that support effective personnel recruitment and retention.

To the extent that each organization applies a more strategic approach to human resource management functions, the results are bound to support both mission achievement and organizational efficiencies. Effective recruitment, for example, could be supported by disseminating organizational information through websites, including employees and board members in recruiting, and being prepared to demonstrate organizational successes to job candidates (Dicke and Ott 2003). Younger workers can be attracted through internship programs and attention to professional advancement. Careful screening of job candidates and volunteers to understand their expectations and level of interest can assign them appropriately and support retention of both paid and unpaid staff. Career ladders should be developed for both paid and key unpaid staff. Staff and executive compensation strategies can take advantage of—and be justified by—the market research that is now widely available. These strategies require a certain mindset from nonprofit managers and board members, one that embraces rather than retreats from the challenges this sector faces. Above all, they require nonprofit managers to understand and be able to capitalize on the powerful attraction of nonprofit work.

NOTES

1. Based on 2010 figures from Internal Revenue Service and Urban Institute National Center for Charitable Statistics. Note that many charitable organizations do not file for recognition with the IRS, so that IRS and NCCS figures are always a partial representation of the sector. Employment figures should also be considered incomplete.

2. The distribution of volunteers between the nonprofit and government sectors is an estimate, since national volunteer statistics have not captured this information since 1992. In that year, approximately one in four Americans volunteered in the public sector (in libraries, fire departments, schools, parks and recreation departments, advisory boards, etc.) (Brudney 1999). To extrapolate a current figure, I use the Bureau of Labor Statistics' 2011 estimate of 65 million adult volunteers to arrive at a ratio of 1:3, or approximately 16 million government volunteers and 49 million nonprofit volunteers. These figures should be considered rough estimates given lack of current data. Moreover, the number of volunteers is most likely underestimated, given reliance on data measuring only "formal" (institutional) volunteering and on inconsistent definitions of volunteering.

3. This figure includes health care, mental health, disease-related, and medical research organizations.

REFERENCES

Bacon, Su. 2004. Workers are Motivated by Mission, Not Money. *The Kansas City Star*, May 18.

Ban, Carolyn, Alexis Drahnak, and Marcia Towers. 2002. *Human Resource Challenges of Human Service and Community Development Organizations: Recruitment and Retention of Professional Staff in the Not-for-Profit Sector*. Pittsburgh, PA: The Forbes Fund.

Barton, Noelle, Maria Di Mento, and Alvin P. Sanoff. 2007. Top Nonprofit Executives See Healthy Pay Raises. *Chronicle of Philanthropy*, September 28. http://www.philanthropy.com/free/articles/v18/i24/24003901.htm.

Barton, Noelle, and Peter Panepento. 2007. Executive Pay Rises 4.6%. *Chronicle of Philanthropy*, September 20, 2006. http://www.philanthropy.com/free/articles/v19/i23/23003401.htm.

Bell, Jeanne, Richard Moyers, and Timothy Wolfred. 2006. *Daring to Lead 2006: A National Study of Nonprofit Executive Leadership*. Washington, DC: CompassPoint Nonprofit Services and Eugene and Agnes E. Meyer Foundation.

Bishop, Sheilah Watson. 2006. Nonprofit Federalism and the CSBG Program: Serving the Needs of the Working Poor in the Post-TANF Era. *Administration & Society*, 37(6), 695–718.

Brown, William A., and Carlton F. Yoshioka. 2003. Mission Attachment and Satisfaction as Factors in Employee Retention. *Nonprofit Management & Leadership*, 14(1), 5–18

Cappelli, Peter. 2005. Will There Really be a Labor Shortage? *Human Resource Management*, 44(2), 143–149.

Carver, John. 2007. *The Policy Governance Model*. http://carver governance.com/model.htm.

Day, Nancy. 2004. Total Rewards Programs in Nonprofit Organizations. In R. Herman (Ed.), *The Jossey-Bass Handbook of Nonprofit Leadership & Management* (2nd ed.). San Francisco: Jossey-Bass, pp. 660–702.

Dicke, Lisa A., and J. Steven Ott. 2003. Post-September 11 Human Resource Management in Nonprofit Organizations. *Review of Public Personnel Administration*, 23(2), 97–113.

DRG. 2006. *2006 Nonprofit CEO Survey Results*. New York: The Development Resource Group. http://www.drgnyc .com/2006_Survey/Index.htm.

Gibelman, Margaret. 2000. The nonprofit sector and gender discrimination: A preliminary investigation into the glass ceiling. *Nonprofit Management & Leadership*, 10(2), 251–269.

Grey, Samuel R., and Philip G. Benson. 2003. Determinants of Executive Compensation in Small Business Development Centers. *Nonprofit Management & Leadership*, 13(3), 213–222.

Grønbjerg, Kirsten A., and Richard M. Clerkin. 2004. *Indiana Nonprofits: Managing Financial and Human Resources*. Bloomington: Indiana University School of Public and Environmental Affairs.

Halpern, R. Patrick. 2006. *Workforce Issues in the Nonprofit Sector*. Kansas City, MO: American Humanics.

Harris, Margaret. 1993. Exploring the Role of the Boards using Total Activities Analysis. *Nonprofit Management & Leadership*, 3(3), 269–281.

Hrywna, Mark. 2007. Nonprofit Times 2007 Salary Survey. *The Nonprofit Times,* February 1. http://www.nptimes .com/07feb/special%20report.pdf.

Irons, John S., and Gary Bass. 2004. *Recent Trends in Nonprofit Employment and Earnings: 1990–2004*. OMB Watch. http://www.ombwatch.org/article/articleview/ 2347/1/101?TopicID=3.

Lee, Young-joo, and Vicky M. Wilkins. 2011. More Similarities or More Differences? Comparing Public and Nonprofit Managers' Job Motivations. *Public Administration Review*, 71(1), 45–56.

Leete, Laura. 2001. Whither the Nonprofit Wage Differential? Estimates from the 1990 Census. *Journal of Labor Economics*, 19(1), 136–170.

————. 2006. Work in the Nonprofit Sector. In Walter W. Powell and Richard Steinberg (Eds.), *The Nonprofit Sector: A Research Handbook* (2nd ed.). New Haven, CT: Yale University Press, pp. 159–179.

Lipman, Harvey. 2002. Charities Pay Women Less Than Men, Study Finds. *Chronicle of Philanthropy*. http://philanthropy .com/premium/articlas/v14/i19/19004001.htm.

Mesch, Debra J., and Patrick M. Rooney. 2008. Determinants of Compensation for Fundraising Professionals: A Study of Pay, Performance, and Gender Differences. *Nonprofit Management & Leadership,*18(4), 435–463.

Peters, Jeanne, Anushka Fernandopulle, Jan Masaoka, Christine Chan, and Timothy Wolfred. 2002. *Help Wanted: Turnover and Vacancy in Nonprofits*. San Francisco: CompassPoint Nonprofit Services.

Piatak, Jaclyn Schede. 2012. Sector Switching in Good Times and Bad: Are Public Sector Employees Less Likely to Change Sectors? Paper prepared for the 2012 Annual Meeting of the American Political Science Association, August 29–September 2, New Orleans, LA.

Preston, Anne E. 2002. *Task Force Report: Compensation in Nonprofit Organizations*. Alexandria, VA: National Center on Nonprofit Enterprise.

Pynes, Joan E. 2013. *Human Resources Management for Public and Nonprofit Organizations* (4th ed.) San Francisco: Jossey-Bass.

Roeger, Katie L., Amy S. Blackwood, and Sarah L. Pettijohn. 2012. *The Nonprofit Almanac 2012*. Washington, DC: The Urban Institute Press.

Ruhm, Christopher J., and Cary Borkoski. 2003. Compensation in the Nonprofit Sector. *Journal of Human Resources*, 38(4), 992–1021.

Ryan, Richard M., and Edward L. Deci. 2000. Intrinsic and Extrinsic Motivations: Classic Definitions and New Directions. *Contemporary Educational Psychology,* 25(1), 54–67.

Salamon, Lester M. 2002. What Nonprofit Wage Deficit? *The Nonprofit Quarterly*, Winter, 61–62.

Salamon, Lester M., and Stephanie Lessans Geller. 2007. *The Nonprofit Workforce Crisis: Real or Imagined?* Baltimore: Johns Hopkins University Center for Civil Society Studies and Institute for Policy Studies.

Salamon, Lester M., and Richard O'Sullivan. 2004. *Stressed but Coping: Nonprofit Organizations and the Current Fiscal Crisis.* Baltimore: Johns Hopkins University Center for Civil Society Studies and Institute for Policy Studies.

Salamon, Lester M., S. Wojciech Sokolowski, and Stephanie Lessans Geller. 2012. *Holding the Fort: Nonprofit Employment during a Decade of Turmoil.* Nonprofit Employment Bulletin No. 39. Baltimore: Johns Hopkins University Institute for Policy Studies.

Schwinn, Elizabeth, and Ian Wilhelm. 2003. Nonprofit CEOs See Salaries Rise: Pay Raises Beat Inflation Rate Despite Economic Squeeze. *Chronicle of Philanthropy, 15*(24). Available at http://www.philanthropy.com/free/articles/v15/i24/24002701.htm.

Teegarden, Paige Hull. 2004. *Change Ahead: Nonprofit Executive Leadership and Transitions Survey.* Baltimore: Annie E. Casey Foundation.

Theuvsen, Ludwig. 2004. Doing Better While Doing Good: Motivational Aspects of Pay-for-Performance Effectiveness in Nonprofit Organizations. *Voluntas: International Journal of Voluntary and Nonprofit Organizations, 15*(2), 117–136.

Tierney, Thomas J. 2006. *The Nonprofit Sector's Leadership Deficit.* The Bridgespan Group. http://www.bridgespangroup.org/kno_articles_leadershipdeficit.html.

Twombly, Eric C., and Marie Gantz. 2001. *Executive Compensation in the Nonprofit Sector: New Findings and Policy Implications.* Washington, DC: The Urban Institute. http://www.urban.org/url.cfm?ID=310372.

U.S. Bureau of Labor Statistics (BLS). 2007. *The Employment Situation: August 2007.* http://www.bls.gov/news.release/empsit.nr0.htm.

———. 2011. *Volunteering in the United States: 2011.* http://www.bls.gov/news.release/volun.nr0.htm.

———. 2012. *Economic News Release: Employment Situation 12/07/2012.* http://www.bls.gov/news.release/empsit.t17.htm.

Walker, David M. 2006. *America at a Crossroads.* Speech given at Independent Sector's CEO Summit, Minneapolis, Minnesota, October 23, 2006.

Weitzman, Murray S., Nadine T. Jaladoni, Linda M. Lampkin, and Thomas H. Pollak (Eds.). 2002. *The New Nonprofit Almanac and Desk Reference: The Essential Facts and Figures for Managers, Researchers, and Volunteers.* San Francisco: Jossey-Bass.

PART II

TECHNIQUES

CHAPTER 8

STRATEGIC HUMAN CAPITAL

Joan E. Pynes
University of South Florida

Recently published articles in *State and Local Government Review* (Frederickson 2010; Perlman 2010; Reeves 2012; Perlman and Benton 2012) and articles published in the *Federal Time*s (Losey 2011, 2012a, 2012b, 2012c), *Government Executive* (Lunney 2012), the *Washington Post* (Davidson 2012), Federal News Radio (O'Connell 2012), and reports by the National Governors Association, the National Association of State Budget Officers, and the Center for State and Local Government Excellence indicate that public sector workforces are shrinking. The study "State and Local Government Workforce 2012 Trends" found that a majority of state and local governments laid off employees due to the Great Recession of 2007–2009. Pension reforms in many states such as Illinois, Oregon, Michigan, and others provoked other public employees to retire sooner than they may have planned (Bass 2012; Davis 2010; Dewan and Rich 2012; Maciag 2012; Looming Pension Reform 2012; Thompson 2011). A report by HIS Global Insights predicts that local government jobs will not recover until 2017 (Russ 2012). More recently, a report by the Partnership for Public Service notes that 114,000 people left the federal government in 2013 (Partnership for Public Service 2014). Despite the economy starting to recover and some local governments adding positions, a review of the 2012 Current Populations Survey shows that public sector

employees tend to be older than the rest of the labor force (Maciag 2013).

Federal agencies have been hit by budget reductions as well as retirements, and it is likely to continue. Some 63,000 federal jobs were shed between May 2014 and May 2014 (Lunney 2014). Many federal agencies have offered buy-outs or early retirement options to their employees. The agencies reducing their workforces include the Department of Agriculture, United States Air Force, Bureau of Alcohol, Tobacco, Firearms and Explosives, Department of Commerce, Department of Education, Federal Trade Commission, Government Accountability Office, Government Printing Office, Department of Health and Human Services, Department of Housing and Urban Development, Department of Justice, Library of Congress, Nuclear Regulatory Commission, Postal Service, Smithsonian Institution, and Social Security Administration (Buyout Watch 2011; Pavgi 2012).

The report *Bracing for Change: Chief Human Resource Officers Rethink Business as Usual* issued by the Partnership for Public Service and Grant Thornton LLP (2012) noted the continuing challenges affecting the public sector. The challenges are declining budgets, higher employee turnover, inadequate succession planning, a lack of key human resource management competencies, and voids in agency leadership skills. While agency leaders may not be able to influence declining budgets, they can support efforts to reduce employee turnover, support the development of key staff competencies, and provide training for agency leadership skills. Efforts can also be made to develop succession planning programs. Given the rapidly changing environments, organizations need to plan for their future needs and be engaged in strategic human capital planning.

Strategic human capital planning (SHCP) is the process of analyzing and identifying the need for and availability of human resources to meet the organization's objectives. Organizational leaders need to understand how their workplaces will be affected by impending changes and prepare for the changes accordingly. To be competitive, organizations must be able to manage the forces that impact their ability to remain effective. They need to match their human resources requirements with the demands of the external environment and the needs of the organization. Strategic human capital planning refers to the implementation of human resource activities, policies, and practices to make the necessary ongoing changes to support or improve the agency's operational and strategic objectives.

This chapter will begin by discussing traditional methods of human resources planning (HRP) and succession planning, and the importance of training and development activities. It will also provide alternative perspectives in addressing the staffing needs organizations may have and the required competencies for human resource management staff. It will conclude with a discussion of the problems and prospects of strategic human capital planning.

TRADITIONAL HUMAN RESOURCE PLANNING

Traditional human resource planning depends on forecasting to assess past trends, evaluate the present situation, and project future events. Forecasting human resource requirements involves determining the number and types of employees needed by skill and competency level. First, organizations or departments audit the skills of incumbent employees and determine their capabilities and weaknesses. Positions are also audited. In most

organizations there are jobs that have become vulnerable due to technology or reengineering. Some employers have cut noncore business lines and created new revenue-producing lines. Job analyses must be conducted to provide information on what skills and competencies are now needed. The basic requirements of a job should be defined and converted to job specifications that specify the minimum knowledge, skills, abilities, and other characteristics (KSAOC's) necessary for effective performance. The skill requirements of positions do change, so any changes that occur must be monitored and reflected in the job specifications. Organizations must also keep abreast of the skills that their employees possess. Human resource planning uses data inventories to integrate the planning and utilization functions. Data inventories compile summary information, such as the characteristics of employees, the distribution of employees by position, employees' performance, and career objectives. Specific data that are typically catalogued are age, education, career path, current work skills, work experience, aspirations, performance evaluations, years with the organization, and jobs for which one is qualified. Expected vacancies due to retirement, promotion, transfer, sick leave, relocation, or termination are also tracked. Using a computerized human resource information system (HRIS) to compile these data makes the retrieval of information readily available for forecasting workforce needs (Pynes 2009a, 2009b).

While the external environment is uncertain, attempts must be made to anticipate expansions or reductions in products and services or other changes that may affect the organization. Based on these analyses, plans can be made for the recruitment and selection of new employees, the shifting of employees to different units, or the retraining of incumbent employees.

A demand forecast anticipates the workforce that will be needed to accomplish future functional requirements. The result is a forecast of the type of competencies and the numbers and locations of employees needed in the future. An important part of the demand forecast is examining not only what work the organization or units will perform in the future but how that work will be performed.

How will jobs and workload change as a result of technological advancements, economic, social, and political conditions?

What are the consequences or results of these changes?

How will divisions, work units, and jobs be designed?

How will work flow into each part of the organization? What will be done with it?

Once the above questions have been answered, the next step is to identify the competencies employees will need to carry out that work. The set of competencies provides management and staff with a common understanding of the skills and behaviors that are important for the future (Pynes 2009a, 2009b).

Human resource planning is an attempt to match the available supply of labor with the forecasted demand. The process of comparing the workforce demand forecast with the workforce supply projection is referred to as a gap analysis. The purpose is to identify any gaps and surpluses in staffing levels and competencies that will be needed to carry out the functional requirements of the organization. A gap occurs when the projected supply is less than the forecasted demand. It indicates a future shortage of needed employees. Strategies such as recruitment, training, and succession planning will need to be developed and implemented. A recent article in *Government Technology* noted that in some regions of the United States, information technology (IT) departments are seeking skilled workers. To address the ability to compete with the private sector the states of Delaware and Utah made some structural changes such as removing the IT departments from civil service systems and increasing salaries (Towns 2012).

A surplus is when the projected supply is greater than forecasted demand. This indicates future excess in some categories of employees that may also require action to be taken. The surplus data may represent occupations or skill sets that will no longer be needed in the future or at least not to the same degree. Downsizing, retraining, transfers, or separation incentives may need to be implemented to address surplus situations.

A private sector organization that anticipated future changes in its workforce was BMW, the German automobile maker. Looking ahead, BMW realized that the age of its plant workers was expected to rise. With an aging manufacturing workforce, there is greater absenteeism because employees are often out of work for longer periods of time and output is harder to maintain. BMW was concerned about its productivity and remaining competitive. Additional concerns were that the health care costs for a person over 65 are roughly three times the costs for those between the ages of 30 and 50. To avert productivity setbacks down the road, BMW staffed a production line of employees with a mixture of ages to mimic the average age of its production workers in 2017. Together, management and the employees developed productivity improvement changes such as managing health care, enhancing workers' skills and the workplace environment, and instituting part-time policies and made changes to management processes. Workers were encouraged to describe their aches and pains and what they would change in the production line. They were encouraged to write down their suggestions and management implemented their ideas. There were many ergonomic changes such as vertically adjustable tables that could be adjusted to each worker's height to reduce back strain. New chairs that were more comfortable were developed, and flexible magnifying lenses helped workers distinguish among small parts. Job rotation was instituted to balance the strain on the workers' bodies. A physiotherapist developed strength and stretching exercises. The production line achieved a 7% productivity improvement in one year, bringing productivity up to be on par with lines in which the workers were younger. The line's target output kept increasing and absenteeism dropped to below the plant average (Loch et al. 2010).

SUCCESSION PLANNING

Despite the aging of baby boomers and their anticipated retirements once their retirement funds bounce back, succession planning has not become a priority for most organizations. A report on succession planning published by the Society for Human Resource Management

(SHRM) in 2010 found with few expectations that there are critical lapses in CEO succession planning in North American public and private companies. Likewise a survey conducted by the American Management Association (AMA) of 1,098 senior managers also found that their companies are not prepared in the sudden loss of a key member of the senior management team (Light 2011a). The public sector is also not prepared. Recent reports such as *Building the Leadership Bench: Developing a Talent Pipeline for the Senior Executive Service* (Partnership for Public Service 2013) and the report *Bracing for Change: Chief Human Resource Officers Rethink Business as Usual* (Partnership for Public Service and Grant Thornton LLP 2012) recognized the need for federal agencies to update and improve their succession plans and the Government Finance Officers Association (GFOA 2011) made the following recommendations in regard to succession planning:

Develop an integrated approach to succession management.

Continually assess potential employee turnover.

Provide a formal written succession plan as a framework for succession initiatives.

Develop written policies and procedures to facilitate knowledge transfer.

Development of leadership skills should be a key component of any succession planning initiative.

Encouragement of personal professional development activities should be a key part of the succession planning effort.

Design of better recruitment and retention practices may aid in the succession process.

Consideration must be given to collective bargaining agreements and how those agreements fit in with the overall succession plan.

Consider nontraditional hiring strategies.

Many managers and executives are near retirement age. In some instances, there will be leadership challenges.

SHCP would follow these trends and anticipate how they may affect their organizations. An emphasis needs to be made to arrange for knowledge transfer and the continuity of operations. In the public sector, the majority of professional work is knowledge intensive, involving analysis, the exercise of judgment, and problem solving. Employees are knowledge workers and their expertise is important. Preparing employees to move into new positions requires coaching, mentoring, and new skills training. Knowledge management is the deliberate coordination of an agency's staff, processes, and structures to improving organizational effectiveness. Preparing employees for leadership positions minimizes workplace disruption. Some agencies encourage knowledge sharing by developing communities of practice, where workers who have particular activities or tasks in common share their experiences. Formal mentoring programs have been used in a number of organizations to prepare public employees for new positions. New York State Mentoring Workgroup found that formal mentoring programs can achieve results in succession planning, the retention of valuable employees, improving the representation of women and minorities in management positions, enhancing morale and productivity, and facilitating knowledge transfer (cited in Reeves 2010: 63).

Organizations need to be prepared. A succession analysis should be prepared that forecasts the supply of people for specific positions. Succession plans should be used to identify potential personnel changes, to select backup candidates, and to keep track of attrition. The external supply of candidates is also influenced by a variety of factors, including developments in technology, the actions of competing employers, geographic location, and government regulations.

TRAINING AND DEVELOPMENT

When forecasting the availability of human resources, organizations need to consider the internal and external supply of qualified candidates. The internal supply of candidates is influenced by training and development and by transfer, promotion, and retirement policies. Assessing incumbent staff competencies is critical. An assessment of employees' competency levels should be undertaken. This will provide information for determining the number of those available and capable of fulfilling future functional requirements. It will provide important information as to what recruitment, training, and other strategies need to be deployed to address workforce gaps and surpluses. If necessary skills do not exist in the present workforce, employees will need to be trained in the new skills or external recruitment must be used to bring those skills to the organization. The employer must identify where employees with those skills are likely to be found and recruitment strategies must be developed.

Strategic human capital planning would follow these trends and anticipate how they may affect their organizations. For organizations facing a worker shortage, is it possible to postpone the retirement of or recruit older workers? Can training opportunities and technology be improved to impart different skills? Can full-time positions be divided into part-time work? Is it possible to permit phased retirements to allow workers to reduce their hours or responsibilities in order to ease into retirement? Understanding that experienced workers often possess valuable knowledge and understand the cultural nuances existing in organizations, phased retirement provides an opportunity for experienced workers to mentor younger employees and transfer institutional knowledge. Unless an organization has a mechanism in place to preserve worker knowledge, its loss can negatively affect the organization.

If staffs are going to be promoted to leadership positions or redeployed in new areas, they are going to need training and development. Regardless of an employee's skill set, new positions require information on department or unit standard operating procedures and responsibilities, and possibly the equipment and technology used by that unit. In other cases, employees may be required to assume more challenging responsibilities. For example, the downsizing of managerial staff in many organizations has required that first-level supervisors possess conceptual and communication skills in addition to their technical and applied skills. Higher-level managers must develop skills that will enable them to scan the external environment and develop organizational strategies. Training and development are used by organizations to improve the skills of employees and enhance their capacity to cope with the constantly changing demands of the work environment. Leaders of today's organizations need to master a range of skills. They need to be strategic thinkers yet also be tactical. They need to be conceptual thinkers but also action-oriented. And they need to be able to anticipate but also react to change, master new skills, and know how to develop their teams (Schaefer 2014).

Change has become an inevitable part of organizational life and organizations, and employees must learn how to manage change. Employees are often working in teams to deliver services and are often using new technology. Problem-solving skills, initiative, the ability to function as a team player, interpersonal skills, and the creativity to seize opportunities are some of the critical skills needed in organizations. Technical experience and competence is no longer enough.

An example of a local government that saw the need for succession planning was Plano, Texas. Plano is a municipality in Texas with a population of 261,350 in 2011. Looking forward, it recognized the need to prepare its workforce for the future. Like many public sector workforces, much of its management team was eligible to retire in a few years: 46% in 2006 and 70% in 2010. To prepare for the impending retirements in 2002 it developed a Management Preparation Program of Plano, referred to as MP3, which is still in operation. The Plano Institute of Excellence, developed as an outgrowth of MP3, is used across the city to promote continuous learning and professional development. The curriculum has expanded to include courses and development opportunities for lower-level individual employees, supervisors, managers, and executives. At each level there are required courses, acknowledged organizational competencies, functional competencies, and development opportunities. What began more than one decade ago as a blueprint for succession planning has evolved into a training and development institute for interested and eligible employees.

Is There a Different Way?

In *Talent on Demand: Managing Talent in an Age of Uncertainty*, Peter Cappelli (2008) argues for a new way of managing talent, looking at the strategies used in supply chain management and portfolio diversification. He believes that successful planning requires understanding that the future is uncertain. He faults succession planning as an attempt to find the right person today to fill a particular job five years from now and then grooming this person accordingly. However, an organization does not necessarily know what the job will be like in the future, and there is no guarantee that the person will still be around. Some jobs change, some may no longer be needed, and the person being groomed may go elsewhere. This is similar to supply chain management, when the firm is trying to match supply to an uncertain and changing demand.

Instead of targeting a specific person for a particular job down the road, Cappelli recommends creating a diversified pool of talent. He borrows concepts from portfolio management theories, an approach whereby the risks of certain investment falling in value are ideally offset by different investments that will rise in value. Rather than have each division in a decentralized organization predict the number of staff it will need and then run the risk of too many staff or too few, organizations should pool the divisions with respect to hiring so these variations are cancelled out. The organization can then move people around to fill posts where needed. Groups of individuals with diverse skill sets should be identified. They should be trained and developed and then deployed where they are needed. If an organization ends up with fewer employees with the skills it requires, it can procure individuals with those skills from an employment agency or it can outsource the service. It is a more flexible method of securing talent. Cappelli (2008) refers to it as the "make-versus-buy-decision." Is the "make-versus-buy decision" consistent with the values of public sector human resources management/personnel? Related to this is the use of a temporary workforce or contingent workers.

Temporary Workforce

As public employers are terminating employees, part-time employment in state and local government rose 4% in 2011 (McCann 2011) and governments are using more contract workers. These workers work for public agencies, but they are procured through a staffing agency or other third party. These work arrangements, as well as seasonal, part-time, on-call, and temporary agency work, are referred to as *nonstandard work arrangements*. Many previously employed full-time workers are now filling short-term openings as contractors, consultants, freelancers, and temps (Grossman 2012; Thompson and Mastracci 2005; Surge in Temp Jobs 2012). While relying on part-time public employees is fairly recent (except for parks and recreation summer programs), temporary and part-time workers have always been part of the labor force. In fact, during the 1990–2008 period, employment in the temporary help services industry grew from 1.1 million to 2.3 million (Luo, Mann, and Holden 2010: 3). According to Luo et al. (2010) the growth of temporary workers can be attributed to a variety of factors including business emphasis on specialization and the opportunity to be flexible in response to changes in consumer demand. Staffing firms also introduced new technologies for matching employees to jobs and expanded the services offered to clients to include more training. In recent years the fastest growing occupational groups have been legal, business and financial operations, computer and mathematical, education, training and library, and community and social services occupations (Luo et al. 2010: 3–5).

The technology company Oracle produced a white paper in 2010 titled *Successfully Executing and Managing a Contingent Workforce Strategy* (Richey and Bannon 2010: 5–6). The analysis provided eight benefits of using a contingent workforce and identified seven risks of using a contingent workforce.

The benefits of using a contingent workforce include:

Allowing the organization to move quicker, as contingent workers already have many skills and experience required.

Reducing the costs associated with recruiting and training new employees due to their prior experience and reduced ramp-up time.

Providing diverse sources of interaction for the knowledge workers on a team, which helps keep knowledge workers' perspectives fresh.

Strengthening an organization's succession planning efforts by increasing the likelihood that staffing can be conducted on a "just-in-time" basis while competitors face shortages.

Increasing an organization's ability to attract, retain, and motivate high-performing individuals who may not otherwise work in a full-time position.

Enabling an organization to proactively plan for the economic impact on expected talent shortages.

Lowering benefit costs, since many contingent workers do not qualify for employer benefits.

Lowering employer/payroll taxes.

The risks of using a contingent workforce include:

The possibility that workers' misclassification, either through negligence or deliberate means, may lead to legal action.

Legal questions about employer-offered benefits and workers' compensation, depending on the type of worker hired.

Noncompliance with governmental taxes, such as payroll taxes.

Inadequately executed contracts between either the contracting vendor or the individual worker (independent contractor).

The possibility that knowledge management contract workers may be less willing to share their knowledge in order to maintain their contract status.

Workers working for multiple organizations, which may create legal conflicts.

Animosity from the regular employees who view the contingent worker as possibly getting better work or working conditions.

The white paper notes that it is important to recruit the correct workers, making sure that the procurement systems are integrated with the HR/talent systems in place and that once hired they are trained and engaged to increase their effectiveness. As governments are expected to collaborate more, share services, and lower their pension and health care obligations, it can be expected that the public sector employers will increase their use of contingent workers. Some workers with family obligations prefer contract work because it gives them more flexibility. Others prefer it because it allows them to work on a variety of projects with different individuals and different agencies. However, there are some workers employed as contract workers because they do not have a choice. They have only been offered contract work. In regard to public employers, one needs to evaluate the wisdom of relying on part-time workers to perform important government functions.

THE NEED FOR NEW HR COMPETENCIES

The demands placed on organizations are changing, and with those changes is the recognition that the skills and competencies of human resource management professionals must change as well.

The Society for Human Resource Management (SHRM) has made public its revised HR Competency Model. The model consists of nine primary competencies (www.shrm.org/competencies):

HR Expertise and Practice

Relationship Management

Consultation

Organizational Leadership and Navigation

Communication

Global and Cultural Effectiveness

Ethical Practice

Business Acumen

Critical Evaluation

The International Public Management Association for Human Resources (IPMA-HR) identified four important roles that HR leaders contribute to an organization. Twenty competencies fall within the primary roles (www.ipma-hr.org/professional-development/certfication/competencies). The four roles are:

Business Partner

Change Agent

Leader

HR Expert

IPMA-HR recognizes that many of the 20 competencies are shared across more than one role.

A recent advertisement in *HR News Magazine,* advertised for a human resources talent director to lead a municipally owned utilities department. The advertisement called for applicants to provide strategic leadership over talent acquisition, workforce development, apprenticeship, and employee services units. Other HR positions require skills in HR system analytics. Workers in such positions would evaluate HR systems and processes, provide advisory services on HR information system needs, provide internal technical support and liaison activities, work with HR staff on the future devlopment of systems, and create, update, and manage web content.

PROBLEMS AND PROSPECTS OF STRATEGIC HUMAN CAPITAL PLANNING

In less progressive organizations, human resource management (HRM) departments are often relegated as a secondary support function rather than a driver of an organization's future. Many departments spend their time ensuring compliance with rules and regulations rather than acting as strategic partners. There are also financial costs associated with SHCP. Some public organizations may be reluctant to spend additional resources on employees fearing a backlash from its elected officials and citizens. In some instances, leaders may want a greater integration of the HRM function with organizational strategy but often do not understand just what that means. HRM professionals may not have the flexibility to initiate new programs or to suggest new organizational structures. There may be a reluctance to invest in new technology. This is especially true when organizational change issues may challenge existing rules and regulations as well as embedded standard operating procedures.

Another reason why SHCP is neglected is because very often HRM professionals lack the capabilities and skills necessary to move HRM to a more proactive role. To be strategic partners, HRM departments must possess high levels of professional and business knowledge. HRM must establish links to enhancing organizational performance and be able to demonstrate on a continuing basis how HRM activities contribute to the success and effectiveness of the organization. Sometimes the political realities of public organizations undermine change. Very often elected officials and appointed officials have a short-term perspective regarding how they want agencies to operate. Changes in policies and procedures take time to implement and are often not immediately apparent. Elected officials may also be predisposed to favor short-term budget considerations over long-term planning.

To be ready to change, an integrated and strategic approach is needed. Critical components identified as being necessary include the following (Boudreau and Ramstead 2007; Cappelli 2008; Cascio and Boudreau 2011; Fitz-Enz 2009, 2010; Krell 2011; Partnership for Public Service 2011):

Leadership: Are leaders actively engaged with and supportive of the agency's HR activities?

Culture: Does the culture support talent development and the sharing of talent?

Strategic alignment: Are talent management strategies and initiatives aligned to the broader strategic plans and objectives of the organizations? Workforce planning and future skills need to be identified and a leadership framework needs to be in place.

Talent assessment: Does the organization have objective, standardized mechanisms for assessing the most important skills and behavior of incumbents and external candidates? Are competencies tracked at the individual, unit, and agency level and are gaps recognized?

Learning and development: Are learning and development processes and tools used to support the growth of employees? Are development activities targeted to eliminating competency gaps?

Performance management: Does the performance management process effectively measure and provide useful feedback on the right behaviors and skills in the workforce?

Human resource capability: Is the HR function viewed as a values partner relative to talent acquisition, assessment, development, coaching, and deployment?

HR analytics: Do HR analytics exist to measure and link HR tasks and responsibilities to business outcomes?

As expectations continue to change for HR strategy responsibilities, HR staff need to develop new skills if they do not already possess them (Pynes 2013).

CONCLUSION

Regardless of whether an organization chooses to purchase the talent it needs rather than develop it, human resource planning is still important because organizations or units still need to know what skill demands are required and whether or not they reside in the organization.

Strategic human capital planning determines the staffing needs of the organization and ensures that qualified personnel are recruited and developed to meet organizational needs. Should there be a shift in demand

for services, organizations must know whether there are potential employees with the requisite skills available to provide these services or whether they have to develop the skills or purchase them. Forecasting an agency's human resource supply reveals the characteristics of its internal supply of labor; it also helps to assess the productivity of incumbent employees, implement succession planning, and identify areas where external recruitment or training and development are necessary.

Turnover, including retirements, must be anticipated and planned for. Human resource planning must track the skills of incumbent employees and keep skill inventories. If incumbent employees do not possess required skills then they must be developed or procured from outside of the firm. The availability and stability of financial support; the advancement of technological changes, legal regulations, and social and cultural changes; and the evolution of human resource requirements must be considered when developing strategic plans.

The SHCP process, once established, can anticipate and prepare for major changes affecting the workplace. It serves as the foundation of any serious organization initiative. It can guide management in identifying and implementing the appropriate human resource learning activities for resolving organizational problems or adapting to meet new opportunities.

REFERENCES

Bass, Frank. 2012. Number of governments shrinks for first time since '70s. *Bloomberg*, September 7. http://www.bloomberg.com/news/2012-08-31/number-of-governments-shrinks-for-first-time-since-70s.html.

Boudreau, John W. 2010. *Retooling HR: Using Proven Business Tools to Make Better Decisions about Talent*. Boston: Harvard Business Press.

Boudreau, John W., and P. M. Ramstad. 2007. *Beyond HR: The New Science of Human Capital*. Cambridge, MA: Harvard Business School Press.

Buyout Watch. 2011. Government Executive. www.govexec.com, August 30. http://www.govexec.com/pay-benefits/2012/08/buyout-watch/34645/.

Cappelli, Peter. 2008. *Talent on Demand: Managing Talent in an Age of Uncertainty*. Cambridge, MA: Harvard Business School Press.

Cascio, Wayne F. 2009. Employment outsourcing and its alternatives: Strategies for long-term success. Alexandria, VA: SHRM Foundation. www.shrm.org.

Cascio, Wayne F., and John W. Boudreau. 2011. *Investing in People: The Financial Impact of Human Resource Initiatives* (2nd ed.). London: FT Press.

Cuda, Amanda. 2012. An Eye on the Future: The Importance of Succession Planning in the Public Sector. *HRNews, 78*(9), 6–7, 13.

David, Scott. 2010. 4,755 Take Retirement Deal in Michigan. *Lansing State Journal,* http://www.lansingstatejournal.com/fdcp/?1289403245468.

Davidson, Joe. 2012. Federal Agencies Tighten Belt with Buyouts, Early Retirements. The Washington Post, January 12. http://www.washingtonpost.com/politics/federal-agencies-tighten-belts-with-buyouts-early-retirements/2012/01/11/gIQAIBg0rP_story.html.

Davis, Scott. 2010. 4,755 Take Retirement Deal in Michigan. *Lansing State Journal,* November 10. www.lansingstatejournal.com.

Dewan, Shaila, and Motoko Rich. 2012. Public Workers Face New Rash of Layoffs, Hurting Recovery. *The New York Times,* June 19. http://www.nytimes.com/2012/06/20/business/public-workers-face-continued-layoffs-and-recovery-is-hurt.html?pagewanted=all.

Fitz-Enz, Jac. 2009. *The ROI of Human Capital: Measuring the Economic Value of Employee Performance* (2nd ed.). New York: AMACOM.

———. 2010. *The New HR Analytics: Predicting the Economic Value of Your Company's Human Capital.* New York: AMACOM.

Fredrickson, Elizabeth. 2010. When the Music Stops: Succession Is More Than Filling Seats. *State and Local Government Review, 42*(1), 50–60.

Government Finance Officers Association (GFOA). 2010. Generational Change Task Force Report. http://www.gfoa.org/downloads/GFOA_GenChangeReportFINAL.pdf.

Government Finance Officers Association (GFOA). 2011. *Key Issues in Succession Planning.* http://www.gfoa.org/index.php?option=com_content&task=view&id=1765.

Grossman, Robert J. 2012. Strategic Temp-tations: Don't Just Rent Workers; Plan Every Facet of Your Relationship with Staffing Companies. *HR Magazine, 57*(3), 24, 26–32.

Hanson, Wayne. 2013. Rethinking Your IT Workforce. *Government Technology,* http://www.govtech.com/management/Rethinking-Your-IT-WorkForce.html.

Krell, Eric. 2011. Change Within: Align Your HR Team's Goals with Corporate Strategy. Here's How. *HRMagazine, 56*(8), 43–44, 46, 48–49.

Lawler, Edward. E., and John W. Boudreau. 2009. *Achieving Excellence in Human Resources Management: An Assessment of Human Resource Functions.* Stanford, CA: Stanford University Press.

Lawler, Edward E., and John W. Boudreau. 2012. *Effective Human Resources Management: A Global Analysis.* Stanford: CA: Stanford University Press.

Lawler, Edward. E., Jay Jamrog, and John Boudreau. 2011. Shining Light on the HR Profession. *HRMagazine, 56*(2), 38–41.

Light, Joe. 2011a. Sudden Leader Loss Leaves Firms in Limbo. *The Wall Street Journal,* January 24. http://online.wsj.com/article/SB10001424052748704754304576096110473597184.html.

———. 2011b. Labor Shortage Persists in Some Fields. *The Wall Street Journal,* February 7. http://online.wsj.com/article/SB1000142405274870437610457612581603676882.html.

Loch, Christoph. H., Fabian J. Sting, Nikolaus Bauer, and Helmut Mauermann. 2010. How BMW Is Defusing the Demographic Time Bomb. *The Harvard Business Review,* March, 99–102.

Looming Pension Reform Leads to Rush to Retire in Illinois. 2012, August 13. *McClatchy Newspapers.* http://www.governing.com/news/state/mct-looming-pension-reform-leads-to-rush-to-retire-in-Illinois.html.

Losey, Stephen. 2011. Retirements Surge 24% Over Last Year. *The Federal Times,* December 12. http://www.federaltimes.com/article/20111212/PERSONNEL02/112120301/Retirements-surge 24-over-last-year

———. 2012a. Shrinking Staffs Imperil Mission at Key Agencies. *The Federal Times,* June 18. http://www.federaltimes.com/article/20120618/PERSONNEL02/306180001/Shrinking-staffs imperil-missions-key-agencies.

———. 2012b. October 5. Retirements Spike in September. *The Federal Times,* October 5. http://www.federaltimes.com/article/20121005/BENEFITS02/310050001/Retirements-spike- September.

———. 2012c. September 5. Retirement Applications Increase in August. *The Federal Times,* September 5. http://www.federaltimes.com/article/20120905/BENEFITS/120905001/Retirement-applications-increase-August.

Lunney, Kellie. 2014. Federal Government Continues to Shed Jobs. *Government Executive*, June 6. http://www.govexec.com/pay-benefits/2014/06/federal-government-continues-shed-jobs/86017/.

Lunney, Kellie. 2012. Spending Cuts Likely to Trigger Furloughs. *Government Executive*, September 6. http://www.govexec.com/pay-benefits/2012/09/spending-cuts-likely-trigger-furloughs/57920/.

Luo, Tian, Amar Mann, and Richard Holden. 2010. The Expanding Role of Temporary Help Services from 1990 to 2008. *Monthly Labor Review*, *133*(8), 3–16.

Maciag, Mike. 2012. Local Government Employment Declines for 12th Month. *Governing*, September 12. www.governing.com.

———. 2013. Public Sector Has Some of Oldest Workers Set to Retire. *Governing*, August 26. www.governing.com.

ManpowerGroup. 2010. ManpowerGroup Annual Survey Shows More Than Half of U.S. Employers Cannot Find the Right Talent for Open Positions. May 19. www.manpowergroup.com.

McCann, Bailey. 2011. Part-Time Workers Closing the Gap for State Government. Civic Source, October 2. CivSourceonline.com.

McKinsey Quarterly (2011, May). The Growing US Jobs Challenge. *McKinsey Quarterly*. https://www.mckinseyquarterly.com.

Murray, S. (2011). Job Engine Shifts to Higher Gear: U.S. Payrolls Grow at Swiftest Rate in Five Years Despite Rise in Unemployment Rate to 9.0%. *The Wall Street Journal*, May 7, 1–2.

Nelson, Kimberly L. 2012. Municipal Choices During a Recession: Bounded Rationality and Innovation. *State and Local Government Review*, *44*(1S), 44S–63S.

O'Connell, Michael. 2012. Has the Long-Anticipated Retirement Tsunami Finally Started? FederalNewsRadio.com, April 30.

Partnership for Public Service. 2011. Preparing the People Pipeline: A Federal Succession Planning Primer. http://ourpublicservice.org.

Partnership for Public Service. 2013. Building the Leadership Bench: Developing a Talent Pipeline for the Senior Executive Service. http://ourpublicservice.org.

Partnership for Public Service. 2014. Federal Departures. http://ourpublicservice.org.

Partnership for Public Service and Grant Thornton LLP. 2012. *Bracing for Change: Chief Human Resource Officers Rethink Business as Usual*. Washington, DC: Author. http://ourpublicservice.org.

Partnership for Public Service and IBM Center for The Business of Government. 2011. *From Data to Decision: The Power of Analytics*. Washington, DC: Author. http://ourpublicservice.org.

Pavgi, Kedar. 2012. Social Security Offers Thousands of Employees Early Retirement. *Government Executive*. www.govexec.com, August 8. http://www.govexec.com/management/2012/08/social-security-offers-thousands-employees-early-retirement/57295/.

Perlman, Bruce J. 2010. Introduction: New Rules and Approaches for Succession Planning. *State and Local Government Review*, *42* (1), 48–49.

Perlman, Bruce J., and J. E. Benton. 2012. Going It Alone: New Survey Data on Economic Recovery Strategies in Local Government. *State and Local Government Review*, *44*(1S), 5S–16S.

Pynes, Joan E. 2009a. *Human Resources Management for Public and Nonprofit Organizations: A Strategic Approach* (3rd ed.). San Francisco: Jossey-Bass.

———. 2009b. Strategic Human Resources Management. In S. Hays, R. Kearney, and J. Coggburn (Eds.), *Public Personnel Administration: Problems and Prospects* (5th ed.). Englewood Cliffs: Prentice-Hall, pp. 95–106.

———. 2013. *Human Resources Management for Public and Nonprofit Organizations: A Strategic Approach* (4th ed.). San Francisco: Jossey-Bass.

Rampell, C. 2011. Companies Spend on Equipment, Not Workers. *The New York Times*, June 9, A1.

Reeves, T. Zane. 2010. Mentoring Program in Succession Planning. *State and Local Government Review*, *42*(1), 61–66.

Richey, Jay, and Race Bannon. 2010. *Successfully Executing and Managing a Contingent Workforce Strategy*. An Oracle White Paper. April. http://www.ihrimpublications.com/white_papers/Managing_Contingent_Workforce-White_Paper.pdf.

Ritz, A., and C. Waldner. 2011. Competing for Future Leaders: A Study of Attractiveness of Public Sector Organizations to Potential Job Applicants. *Review of Public Personnel Administration*, *31*(3), 291–316.

Russ, Hilary. 2012. State, Local Government Jobs Won't Recover until 2017: Report. September 24. Thomson Reuters. http://www.reuters.com/assets/print?aid=USBRE88N0SF20120924.

Schaefer, Ruediger. 2014. Shifting the Talent Curve: Organizations Need to Rethink How They Manage Talent and Develop the Next Generation of Leaders. *HRO Today Magazine,* September, 72–74.

Society for Human Resource Management. 2010a. *Succession Planning.* Workplace Visions, 6. Alexandria, VA: SHRM. www.shrm.org.

———. 2010b. *What Senior HR Leaders Need to Know: Perspectives from the United States, Canada, India, the Middle East and North Africa.* Arlington, VA: SHRM. www.shrm.org.

———. 2011. *Staff Levels and the Use of Contingent and Part-Time Workers.* Arlington, VA: SHRM. www.shrm.org.

Southern, Craig. 2012. An Eye on the Future: The Importance of Succession Planning in the Public Sector. *HRNews, 78*(9), 10–11, 14–15, 22.

Stafford, Diane. 2011a. Some Changes Are Permanent. *McClatchy-Tribune Newspapers*, printed in *The St. Petersburg Times*, February 8, 10F.

———. 2011b. Job Market Shifts toward Ad Hoc Work. *Kansas City Star*, printed in *The St. Petersburg Times*, March 6, 3D.

Staley, O., D. MacMillan, and C. Vannucci. 2011. Where the New Jobs Are. *Bloomberg News*, printed in *The St. Petersburg Times*, May 1, B1, B2.

Surge in Temps Jobs Alters Work Dynamic. 2012. *The Washington Post,* February 19; *The Tampa Bay Times*, February 19, 15A.

Thompson Jr., Dennis. 2011. More than 8,000 in PERS Retire in 2011. *The Statesman Journal*, December 21. http://www.statesmanjournal.com/article/20111221?NEWS/112210391/More-than-8-000.

Thompson, J. R., and S. Mastracci. 2005. Nonstandard Work Arrangements in the Public Sector. *Review of Public Personnel Administration*, *25*(4), 299–324.

Towers Watson. (2012). Perspectives: To Drive Strategic Alignment and Workforce Agility, Successful Organizations Embrace Change. towerswatson.com.

Towns, Steve. 2012. The Battle for Skills. *Government Technology, 25*(2), 6.

U.S. Merit Systems Protection Board. 2008. *Attracting the Next Generation: A Look at Federal Entry-Level New Hires.* Washington, DC: Government Printing Office.

CHAPTER 9

SUPPLANTING COMMON MYTHS WITH UNCOMMON MANAGEMENT: THE EFFECTIVE INVOLVEMENT OF VOLUNTEERS IN DELIVERING PUBLIC SERVICES

Jeffrey L. Brudney

University of North Carolina, Wilmington

Volunteer service has long held the imagination of elected leaders, public and nonprofit organization officials, and the general public in the United States. A series of annual, national surveys conducted by the U.S. Bureau of Labor Statistics (2015) beginning in 2002 documents an impressive record of interest and participation in volunteering. Based on a very large representative sample of about 60,000 eligible households conducted by the U.S. Census Bureau for the Bureau of Labor Statistics (the same sample that is used to estimate employment and unemployment among the nation's civilian noninstitutional population age 16 and over), 25.4% of Americans volunteered in the year ending in September 2013.

An earlier series of biennial surveys conducted in 1988–1999 by the Gallup Organization on behalf of the Independent Sector organization shows even higher rates of volunteering among Americans, approaching half the population (Weitzman et al. 2002: 69–75).

These statistics suggest that the U.S. can boast an army of volunteers. Indeed, about 62.6 million people volunteered through or for an organization at least once between September 2012 and September 2013 (Bureau of Labor Statistics 2015).

Over the 12-year period for which comparable survey data are available, the percentage of volunteering in the U.S. has surpassed one-quarter of the population in each year, with a low of 25.4% (2013) and a high of 28.8% (in 2003, 2004, and 2005). The American Time Use Survey (ATUS), which asks respondents how they spent the past 24 hours, places these statistics in a more immediate light for practicing public (and nonprofit) human resource managers: According to the ATUS, on an "average day" these officials can expect to work with 16.6 million volunteers, amounting to 6.8% of the adult population (in 2010), who spend an average of about two and a half (2.46) hours volunteering (Roeger, Blackwood, and Pettijohn 2012: 119). Converted to an annual basis, the dimensions of the "volunteer army" dramatically emerge: *The Nonprofit Almanac 2012* (Roeger et al. 2012: 120–121) estimates that Americans volunteered 14.9 billion hours in 2010, the equivalent of 8.8 million full-time employees (an FTE works 1,700 hours a year), with an assigned monetary value of volunteer time of $283.8 billion (based on an assigned hourly wage of $19.07, the average private nonfarm hourly wage).

An army of volunteer labor cannot—and should not—be overlooked, lest this productive capacity be lost to the myriad organizations, and their clients, that might benefit from it. Thus, volunteer management merits the attention of human resource managers. This chapter provides the foundation for how public sector human resource managers can work effectively with volunteers. It does so by exploring and correcting popular myths about volunteers and volunteer management that can otherwise stymie effective collaboration.

A TRADITION OF VOLUNTEER INVOLVEMENT IN GOVERNMENT

The roots of volunteerism in the United States extend as far back as the 1830s, if not before, when the prescient French visitor to these shores, Alexis de Tocqueville, characterized the young republic as a nation of "joiners"—of causes, endeavors, and associations of seemingly endless variety. Governments at the local, state, and federal levels have actively sought and involved volunteers (Brudney 1990b). Over the past half-century U.S. presidents of both political parties have celebrated and expanded this venerable tradition by creating and strengthening volunteer opportunities.

Perhaps the best-known service program for Americans, the Peace Corps, originated in the administration of President John F. Kennedy; its domestic counterpart, the VISTA program (Volunteers in Service to America), began under President Johnson; and the founding of the ACTION agency, intended to consolidate all federal volunteer programs, occurred under President Nixon (Brudney 1990b). President Carter is the most famous volunteer to the Habitat for Humanity organization, as well as the father of the Atlanta Project, a massive grassroots effort to revitalize that city. In his two terms in office, President Reagan frequently extolled the virtues of volunteering. His successor, George H. W. Bush, promoted Points of Light, a vision that survives his presidential administration in a foundation that bears that name. President Bush also created a White House Office of National Service, the first office ever established in the White House devoted to promoting volunteerism (Brudney 2000: 44). President Clinton, too, endorsed volunteer service. In 1993 he signed into law the National and Community Service Trust Act, which authorized the AmeriCorps program that has attracted hundreds of thousands of Americans into service. More recently, President George W. Bush launched the USA Freedom Corps, a program aimed at promoting and coordinating volunteer opportunities within the United States and abroad and connecting Americans to opportunities to serve in federal volunteer programs such as AmeriCorps, Peace Corps, and Senior Corps. One of the first legislative accomplishments of President Barack Obama on April 21, 2009, was passage of the Edward M. Kennedy Serve America Act, named in memory of the Massachusetts senator. The Serve America Act dramatically expanded the Corporation for National and Community Service by tripling the number of AmeriCorps placements; the Act was intended to enlist volunteers in helping to address critical national problems, diversify the volunteer base, stimulate social innovation, and support the nonprofit sector to work effectively with volunteers (Nesbit and Brudney 2013a).

The historical roots of volunteerism in the U.S. and the high-level political support accorded to this activity are not the sole reasons that students of public personnel administration need to develop an appreciation and understanding of volunteer involvement. More often than they might expect, students who choose a career in government may find themselves working with volunteers either directly or indirectly to accomplish the public's business. Volunteers are prevalent in the delivery of many government services, for example, health care, education, social services, recreation, environmental preservation, fire protection, public safety, and culture and the arts (Nesbit and Brudney 2013b). Although the statistics elude precise calculation, governments in the U.S. are responsible for at least 20–30% of all volunteer activity, programs, and support services. In addition, government agencies are very frequently interconnected with nonprofit organizations—the chief employers of volunteer labor—in complicated, service-delivery networks. As Lester M. Salamon (1999: 55) observed, "a complex 'mixed economy' of welfare exists in the United States, with nonprofit, for-profit and government institutions all deeply involved, sometimes on their own, but increasingly in collaboration with each other" (see also Salamon 2003). Thus, even if their agency does not use volunteers directly, public personnel administrators may well find that their job requires them to work with nonprofit organizations that do and to handle all attendant personnel matters.

Despite the high profile of volunteerism in the U.S., the everyday issues and challenges of involving non-paid workers in the delivery of public services have had comparatively little exposure. This topic is not a standard feature in the formal education of administrators employed in either the public or the nonprofit sector (Brudney and Stringer 1998). As a result, several myths have arisen regarding volunteer involvement. Like most myths, the ones in this domain have a germ of reality, but they have been exaggerated to the point that they are no longer useful and, in fact, impede successful management of a vital human resource. Accordingly, this chapter critically examines—and debunks—five primary myths regarding the participation of service volunteers in public and nonprofit organizations.

THE VOLUNTEER AVAILABILITY MYTH:
If You Build It, They Will Come

This reassuring adage may well apply to and gratify the ownership of professional sports franchises, who typically find that adoring fans will seek out the action on their own and support the team even when the franchise relocates to a new city. Unfortunately, public and nonprofit organizations that rely on volunteers for their important work encounter a much different reality: The only situations for which any evidence exists that large numbers of volunteers will come forward spontaneously to lend their time and talents are natural and human-made emergencies, crises, or disasters. Evidently, the

glare of publicity and the manifest needs of the victims are overpowering lures to many volunteers. These situations are transient, however, and do not produce lasting assistance from volunteers. As emergencies fade from view or are tamed, the energy, zeal, and helping instinct of citizens recede with them.

The purposes and circumstances for which leaders of government and nonprofit agencies seek volunteers are far different. Most often, they want volunteer participation to assist their organizations with the ordinary, nonspectacular, though no less essential, tasks of providing services to clients. Normally, these activities must be performed on a continuous rather than episodic basis (as in emergencies) and occur well outside the public (and media) eye. Conducting tours of the local museum, providing emergency medical services, counseling youthful offenders, handling clerical and receptionist duties, visiting the home-bound elderly, officiating and coaching in youth leagues, advising small businesses, offering adult literacy classes, staffing a telephone bank, preparing meals at a homeless shelter, and helping citizens to fill out income tax forms are examples of the tasks that government and nonprofit organizations routinely need and ask volunteers to perform. (For listings of many other ways in which governments involve volunteer workers, including detailed descriptions of programs, see Nesbit and Brudney 2013b; Ulrich 1999; Manchester and Bogart 1988: 73–82, 139–216.)

To find and enlist citizens willing to lend a hand to such endeavors, recruitment is a key managerial function in volunteer programs. But if as documented above, one-quarter or more of the U.S. population belongs to the "volunteer army"—that is, performs "activities for which people are not paid, except perhaps expenses . . . through or for an organization" (Bureau of Labor Statistics 2015)—how great an obstacle can recruitment pose? The answer is that attracting citizens for volunteer roles may well be the single most difficult task confronting the use of this service option. Surveys of those whose job it is to manage volunteers bear out this contention (Hager and Brudney 2011; Brudney 1993; Duncombe 1985). In some service domains such as fire protection, potential volunteers have proven sufficiently scarce or resistant to calls for assistance that it can actually prove cost-effective to hire paid personnel instead (Brudney and Duncombe 1992).

The source of the recruitment problem is two-fold. First, from the perspective of organizations that seek volunteers, survey estimates of the gross rate of volunteering are markedly inflated. The percentages derived from national surveys (such as those undertaken by the Bureau of Labor Statistics and the Gallup Organization described above) that include any type of volunteering to an organization ("formal volunteering"), whether regular (on a continuous basis) or sporadic (one-time only or episodic), to all types of institutions (secular, religious, nonprofit, public, for-profit), over a calendar year (irrespective of the number of times and the amount of time the individual volunteers during the year). The BLS survey, for example, advises respondents "to include volunteer activities that you did through or for an organization, even if you only did them once in a while." By this inclusive definition, a person who volunteers four hours every week to the humane society and a person who volunteers one time over a 12-month period to staff a walk-a-thon fund-raiser are equally "volunteers." Correcting for these factors, Brudney (1990a) estimates that the effective pool of volunteers available to government agencies is far less than the size suggested by most survey research.

The second source of the recruitment problem is that although the volunteer population remains substantial after these corrections, it is highly prized by huge numbers of government agencies as well as nonprofit organizations, and even an increasing number of for-profit businesses through corporate social responsibility (CSR) activities. To borrow an apt analogy from the world of paid work, the interest of several potential "employers" in this labor drives up its "price," making it more valuable in the marketplace for volunteers. As a result, volunteers can afford to be quite "choosy" or selective in their choice of (unpaid) opportunities.

To intensify the recruitment problem still further, nonprofit organizations and governmental agencies need volunteers not only to assist in their day-to-day operations but also to serve in a policy-making or governance capacity. Almost all nonprofit organizations and many public agencies have governing boards, commissions, review panels, advisory committees, or other oversight bodies that must be staffed by citizen volunteers. The involvement of volunteers in policy making is crucial not only to ensure citizen input and representation to the organization but also to provide long-term guidance, strategic direction, and community legitimacy (Carver 2006).

As a result of these factors, organizations must compete for the services of volunteers. Fortunately, a variety of sound methods can assist them in recruitment battles:

- *Job design strategies* that focus on meeting volunteers' needs and motivations through the content and variety, as well as progression in responsibility, of the tasks and positions made available.
- *Human capital strategies*, which enable participants to acquire contacts, training, and references on the volunteer job that increase their market value for paid employment.
- *Organizational change and development strategies* that center on building an agency culture receptive to volunteers.
- *Facilitation strategies* that make it easier or more convenient for people to volunteer, such as extending the opportunity to volunteer beyond traditional work hours (evening and weekends), or reimbursing all out-of-pocket expenses incurred by volunteers (for example, mileage, parking, meals, and child care).
- *Flexibility strategies*, such as establishing volunteer jobs that can be performed outside the agency (for example, in the home or automobile) or tasks and assignments that are conducive to group-based volunteering (for example, by the family, religious congregation, or work department or organization).
- *Outreach strategies*, which include publicizing the volunteer program at the workplace, school,

church, synagogue, neighborhood group, civic and other associations, and so forth.

- *Policy strategies*, such as service on agency boards, commissions, panels, and committees, which afford volunteers the opportunity to take an active role in organizational governance (and that may require or recommend prior service as a volunteer in agency operations).
- *Ceremonial strategies*, which allow volunteers the chance to affiliate with important groups and organizations, meet elected officials or other dignitaries, and receive public recognition for service.

If administrators in public and nonprofit organizations build worthwhile programs—*and* develop and implement coherent strategies for recruitment—then, indeed, volunteers are likely to come.

THE VOLUNTEER (NON)MANAGEMENT MYTH:
You Can't Fire (or Discipline) a Volunteer

This chestnut has long been a favorite of administrators and employees who reject volunteer involvement reflexively. The myth holds that volunteers cannot be managed, presumably because without the leverage of pay or compensation to keep them in line, nonpaid workers cannot be controlled.

The grain of truth sustaining this myth is that it *is* more difficult to manage a nonpaid than a paid workforce. Service provider volunteers are less dependent on the organization than are paid staff, both because they do not have to take their livelihood from it, and they almost always enjoy many more options (organizations) willing to "employ" them, that is, to engage their services (since they are offered to the agency at very low cost). This greater dependence of paid personnel on the organization generally translates into increased compliance among this group than among volunteers with traditional means of agency control, such as rules, procedures, directives, and hierarchical superiors, as well as heightened sensitivity to the threat (and imposition) of

disciplinary action. Justifiably, paid workers must also be more concerned with the material rewards offered by the organization, so that they are highly attuned and usually responsive to organizational values, means, and procedures. With regard to policy volunteers, despite the manifest need for them, governing boards, commissions, panels, and committees staffed by citizen volunteers can sometimes be ill-informed, impatient, intrusive, and even inept.

Yet, as scholars and practitioners have discovered, pay and perquisites are not the only tools of the manager; moreover, for some purposes, such as motivating employees to better performance, their potency is subject to considerable dispute (see, e.g., Rainey 2014). In dealing with policy volunteers, too, some experts hold the organization and those in authority, rather than members of the governing board, responsible for lapses in governance and policy making (see, e.g., Carver 2006); academic and practitioner consultants insist that appropriate board training and development can address problems related to effective board leadership and discipline (see, e.g., Brudney and Murray 1998). To manage nonpaid workers, textbooks in the field of volunteer administration (see, e.g., Connors 2012; Seel 2010; McCurley and Lynch 2011; Ellis 2010; Fisher and Cole 1993) suggest a variety of useful techniques for public (and nonprofit) personnel managers:

- *Concise organizational mission statements*, to emphasize and explain the vital and complementary roles of volunteers and paid staff in achieving agency goals.
- *Job descriptions for volunteer positions*, to elucidate the duties and responsibilities of nonpaid jobs and attendant lines of supervision.
- *Screening procedures*, such as interviews and application forms, to make sure that prospective volunteers have an appropriate background and interest in the agency positions available.
- *Volunteer probationary periods and "contracts,"* to communicate the importance of service to the individual and the agency.

- *Orientation sessions*, to acquaint volunteers with the mission and goals of the agency, its norms and values, and work environment and procedures and to allow citizens a chance to reevaluate their decision to donate time.
- *Volunteer policy manuals*, to elaborate further the expectations of the agency regarding the behavior and performance of volunteers, as well as the attendant privileges, rights, and protections enjoyed by nonpaid staff.
- *Training classes and other learning opportunities*, to build competence and confidence on the part of volunteers.
- *Nonpaid "career ladders,"* to build volunteer commitment and motivation through jobs that offer increased responsibility.
- *Evaluation procedures*, to ascertain the level and quality of volunteer performance; identify and remedy any problems, whether emanating from the organization or the volunteer; and renegotiate volunteer roles as circumstances warrant.
- *Recognition techniques and ceremonies*, to celebrate and honor meritorious achievement, lengthy service, or special commitment on the part of volunteers.

Even with these mechanisms in place, however, it can prove necessary, albeit dispiriting, for the personnel manager to fire or otherwise discipline a volunteer (most managers of employees do not relish this prospect either). Still, the alternative—countenancing repeated transgressions or poor performance, thus sending the wrong message to employees, other volunteers, and agency clients that staff (nonpaid or paid) are free from organizational direction and oversight—is much worse. One purpose of the policy manual for volunteers highlighted above is to explain these (and other important) provisions of the workplace. The eminent management authority Peter F. Drucker (1990: 183) counsels that in cases of egregious misconduct, volunteers "must be asked to leave."

Should a problem arise with a volunteer worker, a responsible course for the manager to follow is as follows:

- *Ascertain the facts*: If the problem concerns an employee-volunteer relationship, for example, do not assume that the volunteer is at fault. Investigate the complaint.
- *Be firm*: If the investigation warrants, point out the seriousness of the problem to the volunteer. Make sure that she or he understands the seriousness of the breach, and the consequences of further violation.
- *Follow through and document*: If the problem persists, apply sanctions consistent with agency policy. Just as in other matters of agency personnel management, prepare and retain a written record of the complaint and its resolution.

In order to motivate and guide work behaviors toward agency goals, the management of volunteers does call for the application of complimentary techniques to the hierarchical control procedures commonly used in business firms. For example, managers who strive to build a climate of trust, cooperation, teamwork, challenge, growth, achievement, and commitment among volunteers are more likely to be rewarded with successful performance (see Brudney 1990b; Walter 1987). In their international bestseller, *In Search of Excellence*, Peters and Waterman (1982) found that "America's best-run companies" use this approach for managing paid employees—with enviable bottom-line results. Perhaps in this domain, the field of volunteer administration has important insights to offer the world of paid personnel administration, especially at a time when organizational material rewards are so seriously constrained as in the public sector. Smith and Green (1993) make this connection explicit: Their article recommends "Managing Employees As If They Were Volunteers."

THE VOLUNTEER COST-SAVINGS MYTH:
Think of All the Money We'll Save

In the movement to involve volunteers in the delivery of public services, no rationale is mentioned more often, or given greater credibility, than the cost savings that will presumably follow. Implicitly or explicitly, most discussions of volunteers in service to government or nonprofit organizations allude to this possibility, or even certainty. In an environment of scarce resources, it makes sense for public personnel administrations to think about labor economies. Yet, more often than not, the potential for volunteer assistance to generate cost savings has been assumed rather than demonstrated. Since volunteer labor is donated or "free," how could the conclusion be otherwise?

At least two factors jeopardize this presumption. The first might be evident from the earlier discussions of recruitment and managerial issues: Organizations must invest resources in the volunteer program and its effective management. Based on a major study of a large, representative sample of nonprofit organizations, Hager and Brudney (2004a, 2004b) outline the requisites of an effective volunteer program and associated best practices. Writing in an earlier era, Haeuser and Schwartz (1984: 28) attested to the prevalence of the cost-savings myth: "Many professionals, like the general public, believe that the use of volunteers costs nothing, but, in fact, an effective volunteer program is not necessarily cheap." This effort imposes costs, including those incurred for the following program elements:

- A paid volunteer coordinator.
- Liability insurance protection for nonpaid workers.
- Reimbursement of the work-related expenses of volunteers.
- Volunteer recruitment, screening, orientation, training, placement, and evaluation activities.
- Training for employees in working with volunteers.
- Policy manuals and other informational materials.
- Office space, furnishings, utilities, equipment, supplies, postage, and so forth.

Other program elements (and costs) might well be appended to this list, including volunteer recognition awards and events, a volunteer newsletter, and identification badges and uniforms as needed.

Even if volunteers were a truly free resource, a second factor would dispute the presumption of cost savings to be realized by public and nonprofit organizations from citizen involvement in the delivery of services. Stated simply, introducing volunteers will not save any money unless cutbacks are exacted elsewhere in agency budgets. Given the substantial difference in labor costs between volunteers and employees, some government and nonprofit officials (and members of the general public) have no doubt eyed paid positions as the target for budget reductions, with the idea that volunteers might step into them. No matter how attractive this policy might seem from a fiscal perspective, it is most ill advised, for several reasons.

First, public law and contracts with employee unions prohibit many government organizations from substituting volunteers for paid staff. Second, the effects on employees of such labor substitution (or its anticipation) are highly demoralizing. The apprehensions and antagonisms that arise impair the ability of both paid staff and volunteers to perform their jobs and distract attention and resources from organizational missions. Third, a strong ethic pervades the field of volunteerism that volunteers should not be utilized to the detriment of paid staff. In its Code of Ethics and Standards, the Association for Volunteer Administration subscribed to the principle that volunteer administration exists "to enhance and extend the work of professional and other employed persons in certain service fields," not to displace them (quoted in Fisher and Cole 1993: 177). Fourth, the technical nature of the services provided by many government and nonprofit agencies, and the qualifications personnel must have to participate in various aspects of the service process, impose a final constraint on the potential for labor substitution. In an overtime analysis of volunteer involvement in local government service delivery since the 1980s, Nesbit and Brudney (2013b) found that volunteers consistently participate in a relatively modest array of service domains, encompassing cultural and arts programs, public safety, and health and human services.

Although achieving cost savings is a legitimate priority in both the nonprofit and public sectors, the legal, ethical, and practical dilemmas raised by possible displacement of paid staff for volunteers offer convincing evidence that the strategy would undermine the very effectiveness of volunteer participation (For a complete discussion of these issues, see Brudney 1990b: 32–36). Even when agency officials have effected cutbacks and subsequently endeavored to recruit volunteers to bolster performance (in opposition to such prescriptions), assertive leadership, rather than volunteers per se, is the source of whatever budgetary savings may have been realized. That is, the savings would have been achieved quite apart from having volunteers. For volunteers to "save money," budget cuts had to be enacted through some other means.

Nevertheless, the involvement of volunteers does offer important economic and productivity benefits to government and nonprofit organizations. First and foremost, volunteers can help these entities to increase cost-effectiveness—that is, to hold costs down in achieving a given level of service or to boost service quality or amount for a fixed level of expenditure. The reason is not hard to find: From an economic perspective, the definitive characteristic of the approach is that it spares the expense of compensating monetarily citizens whose donations of time and talents can dramatically expand organizational capability. Since pay and benefits account for a significant proportion of agency budgets, a volunteer program holds the promise of a healthy economic return to sponsoring organizations. In area after area of activity—law enforcement, economic development, parks and recreation, libraries, health care, human services, natural resources, recreation, programs for the elderly, counseling services, education, homelessness, culture and the arts, and so forth—volunteers have greatly assisted organizations in extending the reach and scope of services at minimal cost. The typical experience of most agencies that enlist volunteers is that the amount of funding necessary to support them is relatively insignificant, especially when compared with the number of hours donated, the market price for this labor, and the activities that would otherwise not be performed. Nevertheless, funding for the volunteer program can finance services valued at several multiples

of actual dollar outlays (Brudney and Nezhina 2012). For example, the National Park Service boasts some 77,000 volunteers and estimates that it derives $32 worth of service for each dollar invested in recruiting and training.

Second, in addition to raising the level of organizational productivity directly through donating their time and talents, volunteers can also increase the productivity of paid staff. By assuming a portion of agency work responsibilities, volunteers relieve pressures on beleaguered employees. When volunteer involvement allows these staff to devote greater care and attention to the tasks for which professional training and expertise qualify them, and less to mundane duties that would otherwise occupy their time, human resources are allocated more efficiently, with consequent improvements in agency performance. In law enforcement, for example, police officers typically work in criminal investigation and apprehension, while citizen volunteers (and neighborhood groups) assist them with routine surveillance and reporting. Conversely, volunteers might assume technical duties, such as legal, computer, accounting, or strategic planning, in an agency in which employees lack these skills or requisite experience.

Third, volunteers contribute to the resource base necessary for innovation in government and nonprofit organizations. By allocating the labor and skills of its volunteers to a new project, an agency can experiment quickly and inexpensively with a policy initiative, without first having to obtain start-up funding for a demonstration or pilot program. The speed and dispatch with which a volunteer effort can be up and operating are inspiring. For instance, within a few short weeks of a court order in Alabama amending traditional practices for training election poll workers, volunteers were in the field carrying out the judicial mandate (Montjoy and Brudney 1991). Such an option is not "free," of course, but it does allow an organization to test promising changes and alternatives in policies, procedures, or services without great delay or generous funding. Particularly in a climate of fiscal austerity, the resource flexibility presented by a volunteer program should not be overlooked.

One further economic benefit merits consideration. Although experts caution that volunteering should not be treated as a credentialing process for paid employment, trained volunteers are an attractive and convenient source of proven recruits for regular positions. The federal government as well as several state and local personnel systems accept relevant volunteer work as experience for paid jobs. President Clinton maintained that his national and community service initiatives would create a huge new corps of police officer and teacher trainees with the experience and skills to enter the paid labor force.

As these points illustrate, a more accurate and persuasive frame than cost savings for interpreting the economic value of volunteer involvement is the gains in productive capability the approach offers to public and nonprofit organizations. As the director of the department of human resources in a Florida county commented (Lotz 1982: 10),

> During the last fiscal year, volunteers provided over $930,000 worth of services. True, we didn't save that amount in taxes, but financially strapped programs used volunteers creatively to enhance objectives and to get more bang for the buck. Volunteers in several programs meant the difference between a caretaker program and a program able to provide quality care.

THE VOLUNTEER LIABILITY MYTH:
But We Can't Afford the Risk

More than a few agency leaders have seized on liability issues as a reason for not introducing volunteer workers into their organizations. Because volunteers can put themselves, clients, and the organization at risk—and the organization is responsible for the actions of its employees and volunteers (Vargo 1995b: 329)—these matters deserve attention at the highest levels. Groble and Brudney (2015) reviewed all court cases and case law following in the wake of the federal Volunteer Protection Act; Congress passed the VPA in 1997 to encourage volunteerism by providing legal safeguards for volunteers. Their analysis demonstrates that although

volunteers can avail themselves of the VPA's protection, their success in invoking this defense is mixed. Anxiety should not preclude action, however: Well-developed procedures exist for dealing with the risks occasioned by volunteer involvement. Moreover, a comprehensive plan for risk management carries many organizational benefits, including encouraging safe actions, protecting agency assets, conserving resources, increasing employee loyalty and productivity, and reducing insurance costs (Vargo 1995b: 322).

Because the risk management plan requires considerable research and preparation and can affect many areas of organizational operations, a good practice is to form a management committee representing the various departments to design and implement it. Developing a risk management plan for volunteers comprises four steps (Kahn 1993: 912–913):

- Identify, evaluate, and prioritize the potential risks encountered in the volunteer program.
- Devise strategies for reducing, or possibly avoiding, the risks identified.
- Implement and periodically reassess the risk management plan.
- Provide liability insurance protection for volunteers as needed.

The first step consists of identifying and evaluating potential risks that may be encountered in the volunteer program. The risk management committee should examine the activities of each volunteer position and enumerate the ways that the volunteer could cause injury to others and the ways in which the volunteer could be personally injured. The committee should prioritize the risks by evaluating which can be expected to occur most often, which might cause greatest damage or harm, and which are most likely to result in liability for the organization. At this stage of plan development, group decision-making techniques such as brainstorming can be especially useful.

The second step in the risk management process consists of devising strategies for reducing, or possibly avoiding, the risks identified. The risk management committee may conclude that in certain areas the risks are too great and recommend that agency leadership make a policy decision to terminate these activities (consider, for example, a sterile needle exchange program for drug users). In other areas, however, the committee may determine that the organization can and should continue the activity but must impose safeguards to limit risk to an acceptable level.

For these latter activities, formulating and implementing agency policy is an effective risk management response. Vargo (1995a: 317) recommends adoption of the following policies to guide the volunteer program:

- Volunteers should complete an application with the organization that solicits work and volunteer experience, education, and references.
- Qualifications should be listed for each volunteer job.
- All volunteer applicants should be interviewed.
- The references of volunteers selected for the organization should be contacted and this information documented.
- A criminal background check should be conducted for volunteers who will be working with vulnerable populations such as children or the elderly.
- Volunteers should have a job description and understand the requirements and limits of the job.
- Volunteer activities should be monitored and reviewed on a regular basis.
- Volunteers should receive job training as necessary.

Well-designed policies in the context of risk management not only limit the probability that accidents will occur but also help ensure that volunteer jobs are staffed and functions are performed as effectively as possible (Kahn 1993: 912–913). In short, they are good volunteer administration practice.

The third step in the risk management process is implementation and periodic reassessment of the plan. Because agencies, services, activities, personnel, and information all change with the passage of time—possibly raising new or unforeseen hazards and risks as well as offering novel solutions to address existing or emerging problems—periodic reevaluation of the risk management plan is highly recommended. Even when the organization has invested substantial time, effort, and care in formulating and implementing a risk management plan, accidents involving volunteers (or employees or clients) as well as lawsuits can still occur. These occasions afford an opportunity to reevaluate the risk management plan to see what changes might be warranted to prevent reoccurrence in the future. They also point up the need to provide liability insurance protection for volunteer workers.

The risk management plan incorporates a sensible series of steps to identify, evaluate, and limit the risks and hazards associated with volunteer service in the organization. It is a complement, not a substitute, for insurance coverage for volunteers. It cannot eliminate risk altogether, but it does offer a realistic approach to the problem. After the plan has been formulated and implemented, the agency will continue to perform some activities that entail (reasonable) risk; in these areas, organizational leadership will have determined that the risk must be accepted in order to maintain the integrity of the agency mission. For those risks it has judged reasonable and necessary for the effective performance of the agency, leadership needs to make certain that the agency's liability insurance coverage embraces volunteers as well as employees. The purchase of insurance protection is the last technique used in developing the risk management plan; all other methods should be evaluated and considered prior to seeking liability insurance (Vargo 1995b: 327).

To determine the type and amount of liability coverage an agency may require for its volunteer workers, organizational leadership will need to consult an industry professional. Myths to the contrary, well-established practices for risk management exist for volunteers, and liability insurance coverage as part of the risk management plan is available (Vargo 1995a, 1995b; Ellis 2010; McCurley and Lynch 2011; Graff 1995: 130–135).

In fact, Vargo (1995b: 337) counsels that a secondary liability insurance policy for bodily injury and property damage accidents caused by volunteers while working for an organization is "very economical." Just as for paid employees, good personnel management practice for volunteers calls for good risk management practice.

THE VOLUNTEER ADVERSARY MYTH:
How Can We Be Friends?

One impediment to the involvement of volunteers known for exasperating program leadership and citizen participants alike is the often indifferent or antagonistic reception by paid staff (see, e.g., Graff 1984; Wilson 1981). When paid workers must share the workplace and environment with nonpaid counterparts, especially in a climate of fiscal austerity, they may come to view volunteers as competitors—for organizational resources, clients, and positions—rather than as collaborators in attaining agency goals. Although discord may be understandable, it is enervating and must be alleviated. Part of the answer to this problem is adoption of the managerial methods discussed above for governing the volunteer program and clarifying its purpose and parameters, for both employees and volunteers. Part of the answer, too, lies in airing the myth that volunteers are the adversary of paid staff.

Not only does the volunteer community reject the idea of labor substitution as a goal for involvement, but also volunteer activity appears to breed respect and approbation, rather than complaints or ridicule, for the public sector. Despite the oft-noted apprehension of employees regarding their participation, volunteers make effective advocates of agency interests who help to further organizational missions, achieve increased appropriations, and thereby preserve government budgets and paid positions (see, e.g., Marando 1986). No evidence exists that volunteers are motivated by a desire to cut agency budgets or paid staff or taxes. In national surveys conducted by the Gallup organization in the 1980s, just 2–5% of those volunteering gave as a reason to "help keep taxes down" (Gallup 1986: 37–41). On the contrary, they are much more likely to press for monetary increases in the policy domains where they have chosen to give their time and attention. Typically, they focus on these domains precisely because they believe that more resources ought to be allocated to them. Much as people vote for preferred candidates at the ballot box, volunteers "vote" for favored policy or service arenas through donating their time to specific organizations or becoming program advocates.

As residents and members of the community, volunteers can aid an organization in promoting good public relations, including creating awareness of the constraints that frequently plague employees in pursuing agency missions. They can also engage in crucial support activities with external constituencies normally precluded to government employees, such as fund-raising and lobbying. Partly as a result of the independence and credibility that the public attributes to them, volunteers have earned the distinction of premier fund-raisers. They are just as adept at mobilizing popular support and petitioning centers of power. Lobbying campaigns by volunteers helped to shield the California public library system from the property tax limitations incorporated in Proposition 13 (Walter 1987) and to protect the U.S. Small Business Administration from repeated attacks by President Reagan and his appointees (Brudney 1990b).

Volunteers are not interested in replacing paid staff members. Instead, they lend their support to agency missions and, in general, act as effective proponents. Additional ways in which volunteers assist employees include the following:

- Sparing employees from mundane duties that nevertheless must be performed, and affording them greater latitude to focus on the tasks for which they have professional training or expertise.
- Giving employees access to specialized skills and abilities that they do not currently possess and that can assist them on the job.
- Presenting employees with the opportunity to gain valuable experience as managers and supervisors.
- Offering empathy and emotional support to employees, who may labor in psychologically

draining and volatile service environments, such as those related to AIDS, homelessness, child welfare, and substance abuse.

- Providing employees with constructive feedback and advice, not generated through normal channels, that may be a source of productive innovation and change.
- Increasing the ability of employees to learn first-hand about community needs, conditions, and expectations, and evaluations of agency services.

In sum, volunteers offer advantages to paid staff members, in addition to those reaped by their organizations. In an era in which many political leaders, as well as a large segment of the population, have embraced initiatives to privatize government operations, public employees should be aware of the allies they have in volunteers.

CONCLUSION

Directly or indirectly, students and administrators in the public personnel field are likely to encounter volunteer workers on the job. Volunteers already assist myriad organizations at all levels of government, and their use is accelerating. In addition, through contracting and participation in complex service delivery networks, nonprofit organizations provide a huge and growing proportion of all publicly financed human and social services. They rely heavily on volunteers to do so.

This chapter has elaborated five key issues concerning the involvement of volunteers in service delivery in public and nonprofit organizations. The discussion was intended to expose and dispel popular myths regarding volunteers that can impair the constructive utilization of this vital human resource. First, while a substantial proportion of Americans volunteer, they are not poised to come to the aid of any particular agency; they must be recruited to service in a sharply competitive market for their time and talents. Second, although volunteers pose a genuine challenge for effective management, a set of useful techniques has been developed and refined for this purpose. Third, volunteer involvement may not

directly yield monetary savings to stressed agency budgets, but this option can assist officials in maintaining, or even enhancing, service quality and amount and in making the most cost-effective use of all organizational resources. Fourth, introducing volunteers may entail the risk of liability and exposure to sponsoring organizations, but risk management procedures can accommodate the risk and yield stronger overall management as well. Finally, despite the difficulties that have sometimes marred their successful participation, volunteers are not adversaries of employees. Volunteers can and do assist paid staff, their agencies, and—perhaps most important of all—the clients and constituencies who are the chief beneficiaries of their services.

REFERENCES

Brudney, J. L. 1990a. The Availability of Volunteers: Implications for Local Governments. *Administration and Society, 21*(February), 413–424.

———. 1990b. *Fostering Volunteer Programs in the Public Sector: Planning, Initiating, and Managing Voluntary Activities.* San Francisco: Jossey-Bass.

———. 1993. Volunteer Involvement in the Delivery of Public Services: Advantages and Disadvantages. *Public Productivity and Management Review, 16*(3), 283–297.

———. 2000. Points of Light: Building Social Capital? In Dale McConkey and Peter A. Lawler (Eds.), *Social Structures, Social Capital, and Personal Freedom.* Westport, CT: Praeger, pp. 43–59.

Brudney, J. L., and W. D. Duncombe. 1992. An Economic Evaluation of Paid, Volunteer, and Mixed Staffing Options for Public Services. *Public Administration Review, 52*(September/October), 474–481.

Brudney, J. L., and V. Murray. 1998. Do Intentional Efforts to Improve Boards Really Work? The Views of Nonprofit CEOs. *Nonprofit Management and Leadership, 8*(Summer), 333–348.

Brudney, J. L., and T. G. Nezhina. 2012. Evaluating Volunteer Programs. In Tracy Daniel Connors (Ed.), *The Volunteer Management Handbook: Leadership Strategies for Success* (2nd ed.). Hoboken, NJ: Wiley, pp. 363–387.

Brudney, J. L., and G. E. Stringer. 1998. Higher Education in Volunteer Administration: Exploring—and Critiquing—the State of the Art. In Michael O'Neill and Kathleen

Fletcher (Eds.), *Nonprofit Management Education: U.S. and World Perspectives*. Westport, CT: Greenwood/Praeger, pp. 95–109.

Bureau of Labor Statistics. 2015. *Volunteering in the United States, 2013*. http://www.bls.gov/news.release/volun.nr0.htm.

Carver, J. 2006. *Boards That Make a Difference: A New Design for Leadership in Nonprofit and Public Organizations* (3rd ed.). San Francisco: Jossey-Bass.

Connors, T. D. (Ed.) 2012. *The Volunteer Management Handbook: Leadership Strategies for Success* (2nd ed.). Hoboken, NJ: Wiley.

Duncombe, S. 1985. Volunteers in City Government: Advantages, Disadvantages and Uses. *National Civic Review, 74*(9), 356–364.

Drucker, P. F. 1990. *Managing the Non-Profit Organization: Practices and Principles*. New York: HarperCollins.

Ellis, S. J. 2010. *From the Top Down: The Executive Role in Successful Volunteer Involvement* (3rd ed.). Philadelphia: Energize.

Fisher, J. C., and K. M. Cole. 1993. *Leadership and Management of Volunteer Programs: A Guide for Volunteer Administrators*. San Francisco: Jossey-Bass.

Gallup, Inc. 1986. *Americans Volunteer, 1985*. Princeton, NJ: Gallup Organization.

Graff, L. L. 1984. Considering the Many Facets of Volunteer/Union Relations. *Voluntary Action Leadership*, Summer, 16–20.

———. 1995. Policies for Volunteer Programs. In T. D. Connors (Ed.), *The Volunteer Management Handbook*. New York: Wiley, pp. 125–155.

Groble, P. A., and J. L. Brudney. (2015). When Good Intentions Go Wrong: Immunity under the Volunteer Protection Act. *Nonprofit Policy Forum, 6*(1), 3–24.

Haeuser, A. A., and F. S. Schwartz. 1984. Developing Social Work Skills for Work with Volunteers. In F. S. Schwartz (Ed.), *Voluntarism and Social Work Practice: A Growing Collaboration*. Lanham, MD: University Press of America, pp. 23–34.

Hager, M. A, and J. L. Brudney. 2011. Problems Recruiting Volunteers: Nature versus Nurture. *Nonprofit Management and Leadership, 22*(2), 137–157.

———. 2004a. *Balancing Act: The Challenges and Benefits of Volunteers*. Washington, DC: Urban Institute, December.

———. 2004b. *Volunteer Management Practices and Retention of Volunteers*. Washington, DC: Urban Institute, June.

Hodgkinson, V. A., and M. S. Weitzman. 1996. *Giving and Volunteering in the United States: Findings from a National Survey*. Washington, DC: Independent Sector.

Independent Sector. 1999. Giving and Volunteering in the United States, 1999: Findings from a National Survey. http: //www.indepsec.org/GandV/s_keyf.htm. Accessed May 15, 2000.

Kahn, J. D. 1993. Legal Issues in the Involvement of Volunteers. In T. D. Connors (Ed.), *The Nonprofit Management Handbook: Operating Policies and Procedures*. New York: Wiley, pp. 907–919.

Lotz, A. R. 1982. Alternatives in Health and Human Services. *Public Management, 64*(10), 10–12.

Manchester, L. D., and G. S. Bogart. 1988. *Contracting and Volunteerism in Local Government: A Self-Help Guide*. Washington, DC: International City Management Association.

Marando, V. L. 1986. Local Service Delivery: Volunteers and Recreation Councils. *Journal of Volunteer Administration, 4*(4), 16–24.

McCurley, S., and R. Lynch. 2011. *Volunteer Management: Mobilizing all the Resources of the Community* (3rd ed.). New York: Interpub Group.

Montjoy, R. S., and J. L. Brudney. 1991. Volunteers in the Delivery of Public Services: Hidden Costs . . . and Benefits. *American Review of Public Administration, 21*(December), 327–344.

Nesbit, R., and J. L. Brudney. 2013a. Projections and Policies for Volunteer Programs: The Implications of the Serve America Act for Volunteer Diversity and Management. *Nonprofit Management and Leadership, 24*(1), 3–21.

———. 2013b. Volunteer Use in Local Government Service Delivery. In *The Municipal Year Book 2013*. Washington, DC: International City County Management Association, pp. 79–88.

Peters, T. J., and Waterman, R. H., Jr. 1982. *In Search of Excellence*. New York: Harper & Row, 1982.

Rainey, H. G. 2014. *Understanding and Managing Public Organizations* (5th ed.). San Francisco: Jossey-Bass.

Roeger, K. L., Amy S. Blackwood, and Sarah L. Pettijohn. 2012. *The Nonprofit Almanac 2012*. Washington, DC: Urban Institute.

Salamon, L. M. 1999. *America's Nonprofit Sector: A Primer* (2nd ed.). New York: Foundation Center.

———. 2003. *The Resilient Sector: The State of Nonprofit America*. Washington, DC: Brookings Institution Press.

Seel, Keith (Ed.). 2010. *Volunteer Administration: Professional Practice*. Dayton, OH: LexisNexis.

Smith, A. C., and F. B. Green. 1993. Managing Employees As If They Were Volunteers. *SAM Advanced Management Journal, 58*(3), 42–46.

Ulrich, C. 1999. *Volunteer Programs in Cities and Counties*. International City/County Management Association IQ Service Report, 31(8), August.

Vargo, K. S. 1995a. Board Member Liability and Responsibility. In T. D. Connors (Ed.), *The Volunteer Management Handbook*. New York: Wiley, pp. 309–321.

———. 1995b. Risk Management Strategies. In T. D. Connors (Ed.), *The Volunteer Management Handbook*. New York: Wiley, pp. 322–338.

Walter, V. 1987. Volunteers and Bureaucrats: Clarifying Roles and Creating Meaning. *Journal of Voluntary Action Research, 16*(3), 22–32.

Weitzman, M. S., N. T. Jalandoni, L. M. Lampkin, and T. H. Pollak. 2002. *The New Nonprofit Almanac and Desk Reference*. San Francisco: Jossey-Bass.

Wilson, M. 1981. Reversing the Resistance of Staff to Volunteers. *Voluntary Action Leadership,* Spring, 21.

CHAPTER 10

PERSONNEL APPRAISAL NO MATTER WHAT: DYSFUNCTIONAL, DETRIMENTAL, DANGEROUS, SELF-DEFEATING

James S. Bowman
Florida State University

"Appraisal is given by someone who does not want to give it to someone who does not want to get it."

—*Anon.*

Evaluating employees is the keystone of orthodox human resource administration: It can provide feedback on the effectiveness of recruitment, position management, training, compensation, and adverse actions. Textbooks discuss the strengths and weaknesses of various assessment techniques and the rating errors that typically accompany them. Despite some misgivings, their authors generally find that personnel reviews are essential and assume they are, or can be, feasible and desirable. The supposed objective is employee development, and the stated aim is scoring accuracy. Yet appraisals can also be illusionary and insidious. Development is often overshadowed by punishment, and precision discounted in light of more compelling goals. Stated differently, the law of unintended consequences operates in this human resource management function. It is "no wonder," writes Grote, that "performance appraisal is such an easy target for *Dilbert* cartoons" (2011: 175).

This chapter challenges the means-focused functional rationality inherent in the traditional approach to individual assessment. Instead of emphasizing "how to," it examines goal-oriented substantive rationality—the purpose and end of appraisal itself. The initial section takes a capsule look at the requirement. The second section analyzes the result of personnel evaluation and rejects honesty as the prime objective. The root problem with assessments is identified in the third section, and the section that follows suggests ways the process may be reformed. The fifth section discusses the ramifications of compromised evaluation systems on performance pay and workforce discipline. The penultimate section explores competing future prospects for appraisal: re-entrenchment or revelation. The conclusion offers closing reflections on this flawed human resource practice.[1]

THE REQUIREMENT: THE PROBLEM

Because many management decisions may hinge on evaluation outcomes, the function can be pivotal in managing employees. An emotional, inexact, human process, it is a difficult task—one that is problematic in most organizations. Creating, implementing, and maintaining such a system is not easy, as programs serving multiple purposes may serve none of them particularly well. In business, for instance, one survey found that 87% of managers and employees believed that performance appraisals were neither useful nor effective (Williams 2012). A meta-analysis of over 600 studies, in addition, found that at least 30% of evaluations *decreased* employee performance (Kluger and DeNisi 1996). There is no reason to believe, as demonstrated below, that the situation is different in government. Only 20% of federal employees, for instance, indicate that the process motivates them to do a better job (United States Merit Systems Protection Board [USMSPB] 2003).

Personnel ratings, then, are one of an administrator's most onerous and odious issues precisely because they are both important and imprudent. Few managerial responsibilities have attracted more attention and so successfully resisted solution than employee assessment (Halachmi 1995: 322). What these widely used and reviled systems reveal is that instead of being a solution, they are often part of the problem. In point of fact, many authorities agree that appraisal contributes not only to poor morale and turnover but also to organizational corruption and workplace violence (Kelloway, Barling, and Harrel 2006; USMSPB 2012).

The reason is that there are few jobs with clear and comprehensive output measures that eliminate the need for discretion. Accordingly, evaluation methods—such as trait rating, critical incident technique, behaviorally anchored rating scales, management by objectives— typically are judgmental in nature. It is neither necessary nor useful to discuss all these instruments here; not only are they routinely described in textbooks but to do so would encourage the belief that the issue of performance measurement is merely one of technique. What should be recognized is that all appraisal strategies, albeit in differing degrees, are deficient (in that pertinent factors are not considered) and contaminated (in that irrelevant factors are included).[2]

Indeed, available research does not support a clear choice among methods. Each has its own advantages and disadvantages, and selecting one to address a concern likely will cause a new problem. There is no foolproof approach. Notice too that the systems are backward looking because there is no systematic, built-in continuous improvement process. Thus, appraisals tend to be self-defeating because they perpetuate the organizational status quo. The search for the perfect instrument— a goal that has eluded researchers for generations— may be futile, but it continues unabated. Psychologically, supervisors form broad opinions that affect evaluation of actual performance. Precisely because these decisions rely on rater cognitive abilities—which are notoriously prone to error—adulterated evaluations are common. The technique used, in short, is decidedly not the essential issue in personnel appraisal because the type of tool does not seem to make much difference.

This seems intuitively sensible because human beings often make evaluations about others in daily life. And people commonly make judgments about someone's personal traits because they can be a powerful way to describe an individual; these features are so salient that recalling something about a person usually elicits a personal characteristic. Indeed, vivid personal qualities are important on the job; employees can hardly perform without them. Such characteristics are often a shorthand way of describing an individual's behavior and performance. This may explain why some experts contend not only that personal rating scales are reasonably valid and reliable but also that they are more acceptable to both employers and employees (Cascio 2009; Gomez-Mejia, Balkin, and Cardy 2011). And the use of informal (if not formal) subjective criteria seems inevitable especially for ambiguous white-collar and managerial jobs. Not surprisingly, then, "courts do not reject subjectivity" (Barrett and Kerman 1987: 486) so long as raters focus on behavior and support judgments with facts. If they are consistent in their subjectivity, a defensible judgment has been rendered.

This deference by the courts to employers has been stated as the *business judgment rule* and has been acknowledged by the courts plainly: 'We do not assume the role of a 'super-personnel department,' assessing the merits or even rationality of employers' nondiscriminatory business decisions.' . . . The appraisal is a record of a manager's opinion. If the employee and the manager disagree about that opinion, the manager wins. (Grote 2011: 10; original emphasis)

If personal attributes are a more natural way to think about other people (Gomez-Mejia et al. 2011), then requiring supervisors to use nontrait techniques—as most organizations do—is a sleight of hand that introduces well-known psychometric mistakes (e.g., halo effect, leniency error, recency bias). Most employees tend to believe that their supervisor's liking of them influences evaluations, and to the extent that managers like good workers, such compatibility can represent true performance levels. Attempting to minimize or remove subjectivity may not improve accuracy (Hauenstein 1998).

In the light of the difficulties with various evaluation schemes, much skepticism, a sense of despair, and even doubts about the possibility of performance appraisal exist (Nigro, Nigro, and Kellough 2007: 169–170). Investing heavily in these systems, then, does not make a lot of sense. The daily press of business makes them a peripheral, not central, responsibility; they are often isolated from getting the job done. There are few incentives—and sometimes genuine disincentives—to use appraisal as a management tool. Appraisal systems, which have been liken to a kind of organizational *kabuki*, are typically elaborate, stylized, baffling—and yet predictably ineffectual (McGregor 2013). Employee reviews are frequently done for the sake of evaluation: an irrelevant, once-a-year formality to complain about, complete, and forget. Many managers do not perceive a need to do assessments and, as noted below, do not want to produce them. Appraisal programs quickly become "organizational wallpaper" that exist in the background but are not expected to add value.

THE RESULT: DISCRETION RULES

For all the reasons mentioned, the evaluation requirement commonly results in tainted reviews. Ratings may be as much a reflection of raters as they are of those being rated. In many organizations, appraisals are adroitly seen as political; they are not necessarily a rational

exercise because results can be deliberately manipulated in a strategically prudent manner. The goal is not measurement precision but rather management discretion, interpersonal fairness, and institutional effectiveness. There are numerous situations—to foster retention, to acknowledge increased workloads, to be competitive with other organizations—in which providing inaccurate, but politically expedient, employee reviews is sound management.

Leniency error, for example, is the consequence of a desire to maintain good working relationships, encourage a marginal employee, show empathy for someone with personal problems, maximize the size of a merit raise, or avoid confrontations. Useful appraisals, in other words, are not necessarily true. Gaming and fudging the system can be critical for workgroup cohesion, beneficial employer-employee relations, and overall good management. Candid evaluations are remarkably ill-suited to achieve that purpose. Indeed, most workers think they are doing a good job. The default assessment, then, is generally inflated: Why convert an acceptable employee into a hostile one when it can be reported that he meets expectations? An effective evaluation, in short, is not necessarily an accurate one.

THE ROOT: HUMAN NATURE

The questionable character of the appraisal requirement, and the resulting emphasis on managerial discretion, suggests something fundamental lies at the root of personnel assessments: human nature. It is natural, for instance, for raters to reduce risk by avoiding, delaying, or distorting negative information. Further, implicit personality theory submits that people generally judge the "whole person" based on initial impressions and stereotyping; ratings, at the expense of accuracy, tend to justify these global opinions. Clashing role expectations, in addition, are inherent in the process as supervisors must reconcile being a helpful coach with acting as a critical umpire. This conflict of interest is a powerful political reason to emphasize leniency (the "Santa Claus" effect). Better-than-deserved ratings also occur because one's own managerial skills may be questioned if employees receive poor evaluations. Thus, when subordinate reviews are exaggerated, the supervisor may look like a capable administrator. Finally, most people have an understandable distaste for formally evaluating others; they are as reluctant to judge others as they are to be judged themselves.

To summarize, because many jobs are not amenable to objective assessment, ratings typically incorporate nonperformance trait factors. When this occurs, of course, it leads to a breach of the most revered principle of human resource management: that appraisals evaluate performance, not the person. In the misguided belief that objective criteria are possible, necessary, and desirable, appraisal is notably vulnerable to the illusion of manageability. If only employees would try harder, then the personnel system might be validated. Verisimilitude trumps veracity; performance evaluation seldom improves performance. All of these issues are exacerbated when, as discussed later, reviews are tied to performance pay plans and employee disciplinary programs—thereby raising the stakes in appraisal and making the already existing problems more severe. The pervasiveness of this concern accounts for the use of the term "personnel appraisal," not "performance appraisal," as a more useful—and meaningful—way to characterize this management function.

REFORM: LIMITING THE DAMAGE, ENHANCING PERFORMANCE

Service ratings, then, remain as one of the most criticized areas in management and seem to be endured only because more productive alternatives are not currently in wide use. Because evaluation is a matter of judgment, the challenge is how assessment and the information it generates is used. The issue is to decide what to evaluate in a manner that meets the needs of the organization and the individual. Recognize, however, that in appraisal there no "objective reality," or ways to measure it, that everyone agrees to. Ironically, the "problem supervisors encounter is not *knowing* who are the best performers, but rather *measuring* and *documenting* performance differentials" (Perry 2003: 147; emphasis original).

The goal is not to create a perfect system but rather to minimize the abundant problems with evaluation.[3] Bersin (2007) identified seven elements that should constitute assessment (goal setting, alignment of individual and organizational goals, self-assessment, 360 reviews, managerial appraisal, competency assessment, development planning)—six of which emphasize coaching and development and only one (managerial appraisal) that does not. The job of the decision maker is to identify strengths in people and move them into the right position. This coaching-based, organization-centric, employee-engaged approach can change the way one thinks about performance and the role of evaluation.

Samuel Culbert (2010), for instance, recommends performance *previews:* instead of top-down reviews, the administrator and subordinate together are held responsible for establishing objectives and achieving results:

> The boss or manager engages in a dialogue with an employee about how a specific task or project will be completed before action is taken. This places onus on the employee to specify the how and what action will be taken, but also places onus on the boss to discuss what supportive actions are necessary, creating a two-sided, reciprocally accountable performance system. The boss's job then, is to guide, coach, tutor and assist the employee rather than judge, evaluate and find fault. (Williams 2012)

Supervisors truly manage in an effort to ensure that everyone can succeed because it is their job to produce desired outcomes. The emphasis is on the future and what supervisors and their employees need from each other to accomplish what they both want—what should be started, stopped, and kept in order to effect organizational accomplishment.

Typical barriers to worthwhile evaluation include the absence of several key factors: trust in the organization, supervisory training and top management support, rater accountability, and overall evaluation of the system itself (Roberts 2003). Ways to overcome such obstacles are providing constructive, nonthreatening feedback and coaching; avoiding numeric rating scales that pigeon-hole employees and pit them against each other; employing multiple data sources through use of peer reviews; and utilizing group evaluations. It might be argued, though, that if employees are given an important mission, provided training, and offered competitive salaries, then appraisal becomes epiphenomenal and redundant.

Indeed, a landmark book (Coens and Jenkins 2000) offers 12 documented cases—including government, nonprofit, health care, retail, educational, manufacturing, and industrial organizations—that benchmark how orthodox appraisal can be successfully abolished. While each case had its own unique characteristics, there were important similarities shared by these diverse workplaces that did away with evaluations:

- They had traditional, scaled performance review practices linked to pay and disciplinary systems.
- Their multiple-purpose appraisal function did not meet objectives and was seen as counterproductive.
- The basic assumptions about employees were changed—people wanted to work and contribute—thereby empowering them to reinvent the nature of evaluations and take responsibility for their own growth.
- The focus of change was from individual appraisal to systems and processes in the organization—improvement did not come from mandatory annual personal assessment but from educating employees to develop better work procedures.
- Formal feedback or annual meetings were not required as personnel were helped "just in time" when needed; the emphasis is not on evaluation, but excellence.
- Individual incentive pay was dropped and raises were based on skill advancement, teamwork, market increases, and cost of living adjustments.
- Disciplinary processes were rarely used.

This organization-focused approach resulted in increased productivity and morale, a decline in grievances and turnover, as well as an overwhelming desire to never return to antiquated performance appraisals.

RAMIFICATIONS: PERFORMANCE PAY AND EMPLOYEE DISCIPLINE

While organizations conduct traditional evaluations for many reasons, the most fundamental one is to improve individual performance. In an effort to achieve that objective, pay and discipline plans are commonly used. It should be evident that attempts to tie compensation to an already execrable appraisal process are dubious at best. The same is true for widely used, but seldom questioned, discipline programs. It follows that these two management functions invite further employee alienation—the precise opposite of what advocates claim. Alfie Kohn (1993: 58–59) explains, "Rewards have a punishment effect because they, like outright punishment, are manipulative. 'Do this and you'll get that' is not really very different from 'Do this or here's what will happen to you.' . . . Relying on incentives [positive or negative] to boost productivity does nothing to address possible underlying problems and bring about meaningful change." The assumption behind incentive pay and disciplinary programs seems to be that employees need to be either bribed or brow-beaten, rewarded or reprimanded, at work.

Pay for Performance

The specious nature of performance pay becomes evident when examining causation issues, motivation implications, and institutional problems (Bowman 2010). First, incentive remuneration works well if the following conditions are met: employees have to complete well-defined tasks, the output is clearly measurable, and the result can be attributed to one person's efforts (Bohnet and Eaton 2003). These factors confound causation because most white-collar employees are faced with multifaceted problems, hard-to-measure work products, and team-oriented work environments—none of which fit well with individual incentives.

Second, assumptions about motivation are central to pay-for-performance plans. These programs may be effective provided that employees work primarily for cash and care about pay levels. Yet people are interested not only in money but also in job satisfaction and challenge—something not subject to performance pay. Indeed, most research suggests that humans do not want to believe that they work only for money, a finding that is especially true for public servants. Employees can even be offended when treated as if they can be manipulated by transparent pecuniary incentives; such payments create the idea that work is all about reward, not service.

"People who do exceptional work may be glad to be paid and even more glad to be well paid," writes Kohn (1993: 62), "but they do not work to collect a paycheck. They work because they love what they do." Thus, performance compensation is apt to be ineffective with the largest and most productive group of employees (Oh and Lewis 2009). Personnel, furthermore, are less interested in absolute pay than in comparisons relative to some reference point such as others' salaries, the jurisdiction's resources, or the state of the economy—considerations not germane to pay for performance. In fact, although everyone wants to be a winner, incentive plans—coupled with tight budgets—mean that this is not possible. A system that manages for failure, by guaranteeing that most will be losers, is not a useful motivational tool.

Third, institutional factors also affect performance pay systems. These programs operate best when employees know what to do and whom to serve. Knowledge of an organization's objectives, however, is not a given for the rank-and-file; the absence of clear goals is a result of multiple or changing leaders with different objectives. This "multiagency" problem is especially evident in government where staff serve many masters: chief executives, legislators, political appointees, career managers, judges, and the public. Frey and Osterloh (2005) provide a summary critique of variable pay plans, arguing that social-psychological relationships at work metastasize into transactional contracts wherein doing one's duty and engaging in prosocial organizational citizenship behavior—without extra incentives—is, at best, obtuse. Importantly, performance pay further undercuts the neutrality of raters, thereby eroding

procedural fairness and opening the door to self-serving managerial bias.

Incentives can be relevant under the right conditions but "ideal conditions are rarely met in empirical reality" (Bohnet and Eaton 2003: 251). A meta-study of 39 empirical research projects in the private sector found that financial rewards were not related to performance quality (Jenkins et al. 1998). As might be expected, then, among the many techniques used by national Alfred P. Sloan workplace excellence award winners,[4] performance pay is not one of them; recent books on civil service reform also reject incentive compensation (Bilmes and Gould 2009; Donahue 2008). "There is," wrote Larry Lane and colleagues (2003: 138), "an utter lack of empirical evidence in the private and public sectors that pay for performance has any positive effect on either morale or productivity."

In brief, while money matters, it matters in complicated ways. Managers often have little in-depth appreciation of compensation complexities (Ariely 2010: 37). Careful investigation—not intuitive reasoning, "common sense," and misguided confidence—is needed to understand how incentive pay operates. Performance-contingent rewards can subvert the meaning of work itself and encourage the retention of the wrong type of employees. The U.S. Merit Systems Protection Board (2006) stipulated that pay-for-performance systems can only be effective if there is a supportive organizational culture, fair-minded and well-trained supervisors, a system of checks and balances, an ongoing program evaluation effort, and a rigorous performance appraisal system. The circular logic of bureaucratic reform is perhaps best expressed this way: "The reality is that pay-for-performance is likely to be of little benefit to organizations with serious performance problems and may actually be harmful" (Perry 2003: 150).

Instead of a performance pay system, the goal should be that the work itself is the source of motivation and the pay schedule should not be a demotivator. A basic compensation policy, designed to be wage-competitive by paying "at market," neutralizes money as a factor in management. A wage-lead approach, while perhaps desirable, is not practical for most of public employment, and a wage-lag plan, while possibly tempting, is counterproductive in most white-collar occupations. The competitive, wage-match strategy works well when complemented by across-the-board adjustments to address cost-of-living increases, skill pay to credit employee development, and special modifications if rare cases reveal that the policy is not consistent with the market (see also Joiner 1994).

Employee Discipline

The second common ramification of personnel appraisal is the link to employee discipline. Like managing incentive monies, adverse action against a staff member can be awkward and difficult. Indeed, second only to the appraisal function itself, administrators dislike using disciplinary sanctions, generally for many of the same reasons. Poor performers, alas, may be tolerated if officials lack familiarity with detailed personnel rules, need extensive documentation, require management support, or wish to avoid onerous employee grievances (USMSPB 1995). Supervisors, accordingly, may sidestep discipline procedures and write acceptable personnel reviews for marginal employees to avoid unpleasantness (something that may haunt them if there is a subsequent attempt to discharge someone for inadequate performance).

Given the nature of the issues involved, taking constructive action nonetheless is indispensable to ensure a productive workforce. Yet the typical agency has a progressive discipline system characterized by the application of increasing severe coercive measures: informal counseling, verbal warning or reprimand, written warning or reprimand, minor suspension, major suspension, and separation. Because this approach can be autocratic, adversarial, and intimidating, some jurisdictions have replaced it with positive, nonpunishment strategy based on the premise that adults must assume responsibility for their own conduct (see also USMSPB 2008).

Rather than treating people "worse and worse and expecting them to get better and better," this affirmative strategy uses reminders instead of reprimands. More participative than punitive, the technique utilizes three steps. First, there is a conference to find a solution to the problem, with an oral agreement to improve. This is followed by a subsequent meeting, if reform is not accomplished, to determine why the agreed-upon solution did not work (with a written reminder that the solution is the responsibility of the individual as a condition of employment). Finally, if change is not forthcoming, a day of paid leave is provided wherein the worker is expected to return the next day either with a "last chance" written commitment or a decision to resign. In brief, the employee, not the employer, is the decision maker.

Employee discipline, in any case, is part of a manager's job. As unpleasant as termination may be, "it's not the people you fire who make your life miserable, it's the ones you don't" (Grote 2011: 191). Performing this task well is an opportunity to learn how to improve other human resource management functions—including appraisal. Failing to demand even minimal competence implies that performance does not matter, which encourages the wrong kinds of behavior, affects the morale of contributing employees, and damages the reputation of the agency as a whole.

RE-ENTRENCHMENT OR REVELATION?

Despite the appraisal requirement—with its typical results, root problem, reform attempts, and damaging pay and punishment ramifications—the melancholy search for the best "genuine fake" technique continues relentlessly no matter what. "Symptom solving" is seductive and easier than genuine problem solving. Beliefs about traditional evaluation are so deeply held that when repeatedly refuted, they paradoxically become stronger. Bad ideas persist because people become comfortable with them, and they prefer the certainty of misery to the misery of uncertainty. Peering into the years ahead, personnel evaluations are apt to become more complex through re-entrenchment—although they might become less complex should a revelation occur.

Re-entrenchment

Should the long-standing preference for person-centered evaluations persist, then ongoing trends such as organizational downsizing, workforce changes, and electronic monitoring will likely complicate appraisals. Personnel offices have shrunk, placing more responsibilities on line managers. At the same time, downsizing has reduced the number of supervisors, requiring the remaining ones to evaluate more subordinates. The potential for both system design and implementation problems, as a consequence, has increased.

Changes in workforce composition also imply a more vexing climate for appraisals. Employees are becoming increasingly diverse, and evaluating people of all colors and cultures is more arduous than assessing a homogenous staff. In addition, the fastest-growing part of the working population is contingent employees—temporaries, short-term contract workers, volunteers—who, by definition, present evaluation challenges. Finally, the virtual workplace—unbound by time and space—is likely to exacerbate assessment issues. It not only alters the nature of interpersonal relationships to only those behaviors that can be tracked electronically but also affects the quality of workplace superior-subordinate relations by questioning employee rights to privacy, autonomy, and respect.

Undaunted, reformers are encouraged, not dissuaded, by these formidable developments and are seldom deterred by past appraisal failures. After all both employers and employees tend to support the idea of appraisals at least in the abstract when human beings are not involved. Increased emphasis on evaluations is the result, resting on the belief that the employee is the primary factor in productivity. Ratings can become a control mechanism to force conformance to the status quo, as beleaguered managers find appraisals to be a convenient, if technically problematic, ideological tool. "When they sign off on them, their job is done; the responsibility for quality and productivity is returned to where, in their view, it belongs—the subordinate" (Bowman 1994: 132).

Revelation

Alternatively, should institutions begin to shift away from person-centered and toward organization-centered appraisals, individual evaluations may

be less complex in the years ahead—or perhaps abolished altogether (Coens and Jenkins 2000). The premise of organization-focused evaluation is that quality services are a function of the processes and the system in which they are produced. Systems consist of people, policies, technology, supplies, and a sociopolitical environment within which all operate. Note that these parameters are beyond appraisee control; indeed, the employees themselves are hired, tasked, and trained by the organization. Problems generally do not originate with employees but from the organization's lack of understanding of work processes. If shoddy services are delivered, the problem rests with management practices, which individual performance appraisal only serves to reinforce.

A person-only assessment, stated differently, is deficient if the goal is to comprehend all factors affecting performance. In a well-designed management system, virtually all staff will perform properly; a weak system will frustrate even the finest people. Traditional, person-centered appraisal methods are based on a faulty, unrealistic assumption: that individual employees are responsible for outcomes derived from a multidimensional system. Because an organization is a group of people working to achieve a common goal, the managerial role is to foster that collaboration. If the result is inadequate, then it is management's responsibility—and no one else's.

From this perspective, the causes of good or bad performance are spread throughout the organization and its processes. If there is a problem, it is systemic. Many results in the workplace are outside the power of employees who are usually made responsible for those outcomes. When more than 90% of performance problems are the consequence of the management-designed system (Deming 1992), holding low-level minions accountable is a way of evading responsibility; the cause of most performance problems lies not within the employee but within the organization as created by its leaders.

Because employees have little authority over organizational systems, relevant appraisals should provide two kinds of feedback: system performance data automatically generated from process controls (in which evaluation is built into the work process itself) and individual performance data—used for personal developmental purposes—derived from anonymous multi-rater 360-degree evaluations (focusing on attributes such as teamwork, employee satisfaction, timeliness, communication skills, and attendance).

The key is to listen to customers of the process and emphasize constant process improvement. By making the system as transparent as possible, the focus can be kept on nonthreatening analyses of work processes and people's contributions to those processes. Such an approach would be organizationally valid, socially acceptable, and administratively convenient—critical criteria for any appraisal method. Importantly, it would change the evaluative function from an adversarial one to a constructive collaborative effort.

Yet the field of human resource management—reflecting American individualism as well as "learned helplessness"—emphasizes people rather than systems. With unquestioned faith in meritocracy, federal agencies, for example, are required to conduct individual evaluations; appraising subordinates is such a prominent part of an administrator's role that abolishing evaluations could make supervisors seem unnecessary. Most reforms, accordingly, aim to change the worker (the most difficult kind of change), despite the fact that the individual is usually not the best object of appraisal. Instead, the work and the workplace must be altered to improve performance. While better methods of providing feedback to individuals in the context of the system are certainly available, the basic issue is how to change the organization, not employees, through continuous improvement. As Clark (2012) observed, "Actions are accomplished through a process. A system is a collection of processes with a common aim. Systems determine over 90% of the result." Work processes, in other words, should be analyzed to resolve workplace problems and enhance performance.

The federal government's Baldrige Performance Excellence Program (2011) criteria—leadership; strategic planning; customer focus; measurement, analysis, and knowledge management; workforce focus; operations, and results—furnish a proven method for assessing organizational performance. A number of agencies (National Oceanic and Atmospheric Administration, Internal Revenue Service, Social Security Administration) and private companies (Motorola, Merrill Lynch, Procter & Gamble), accordingly have modified their approach to appraisals. To better reflect a systems perspective, they have incorporated teamwork (in addition to individual achievements), citizen/customer feedback (in addition to supervisory opinions), and process improvement (in addition to results) dimensions into their evaluations.

A more complete reform would be to clearly state a performance standard and then assume that most employees will do the job for which they were hired. A manager at the National Rural Electric Cooperative argues that for the small number who do not do their jobs, "Investigate why. Some will need further training or management counseling. Some may be an actual problem. But deal with those problems on a case-by-case, and not through a generic, faulty performance appraisal system" (Boudreaux 1994: 24; see also Eckes 1994).

At first glance, the approach described here may be seen partly consistent with the most recent appraisal fad: performance management (see, e.g., Moynihan 2008). This strategy emphasizes that managing performance (not merely appraisal but also planning, accountability, compensation, training) is essential to institutional goal setting. Thus, it is said to be a continuing cycle of goal setting, coaching, development, and assessment—as if this was irrelevant in earlier reform attempts. From a systems perspective, in any event, the name change from performance appraisal to performance management exemplifies the "wrong-problem problem"—it tries to solve the "wrong problem precisely," by emphasizing the individual instead of the organization. It should come as no surprise, then, that just 5% of managers are "very satisfied" with their performance management process (Grote 2011: 158).

CONCLUSION

In theory, personnel appraisal can provide feedback on management functions such as selection, position management, training, and compensation. Given the many problems with evaluation, however, it often does not supply this information. Even when done with great care, individual-focused assessments can be devastating to people and destructive to organizations. A major recent survey that revealed that 98% of managers and employees believed that performance reviews were unnecessary. Edward Lawler, a senior leading researcher on evaluation, reacted to this finding saying, "Performance appraisals are dead" (quoted in Jozwiak 2012).

This discussion has focused on the appraisal requirement, result, root, reform, and its ramifications for pay and discipline. As the chapter subtitle suggests, this human resource process is dysfunctional, detrimental, dangerous, and self-defeating. For the future, instead of re-entrenchment, revelations exist about how organizational-level reviews can be—and are—done. Still, management practices are seldom discarded simply because they do not work. Whether the appraisal function becomes more or less difficult in the years ahead, it is worth doing only if it is an integral part of the management system and if it helps both the institution and the individual develop to full potential.

NOTES

1. Parts of this chapter are derived, expanded, and updated from Bowman (1999).
2. Thus, while the intuitive appeal of trait rating is considerable, it is susceptible to both contamination and deficiency errors. Alternatively, systems based on employee behavior may hold promise because they are job related, but they are vulnerable to deficiency errors and require high technical demands coupled with limited applicability. Results-derived approaches, like the others, may have face validity but often suffer from a host of deficiency and implementation problems (e.g., prosocial behaviors and gaming issues, respectively).
3. It is, of course, possible to marginalize formal requirements entirely. In one major unit of a large hospital, a charismatic manager decided that whatever the hospital administration did, he was going to run his department on the basis of quality management techniques. Well in advance of the hospital's tedious annual performance appraisal drill, he gathered his employees together, reviewed the hospital's form, and told them that what it represented was the starting point for them to continuously improve. "What do we need to do, given the fact that this basic form is mandated, in order to complete it well enough to keep the personnel monkeys off our backs but also get some good out of the process for ourselves?" he asked his team. He funded a series of weekly pizza meetings for a task force of employees who were charged with developing an answer to his question that everyone supported enthusiastically (Grote 1996: 351).
4. The Sloan excellence awards recognize employers whose programs and practices create effective and flexible workplaces.

REFERENCES

Ambrose, M. L., G. S. Alder, and T. W. Noel. 1998. Electronic performance monitoring: A consideration of rights. In M. Schminke (Ed.), *Managerial ethics: Moral management of people and processes* (pp. 61–80). Mahwah, NJ: Lawrence Erlbaum.

Ariely, D. 2010. *The upside of irrationality.* New York: Harper.

Baldrige Performance Excellence Program. 2011. *2011–2012 Criteria for performance excellence.* Gaithersburg, MD: National Institute for Standards and Technology.

Barrett, G., and M. Kerman. 1987. Performance appraisals and terminations: A review of court decisions since *Brito vs. Zia* with implications for personnel practices. *Personnel Psychology, 40*(3), 489–503.

Bersin, J. 2007. *Performance management: Taking aim at performance appraisal.* http://www.talentmgt.com/performance_management/2007/December. Accessed February 2, 2008.

Bilmes, L., and W. Gould. 2009. *The people factor.* Washington, DC: Brookings Institution Press.

Bohnet, I., and S. Eaton. 2003. Does performance pay perform? Conditions for success in the public sector. In J. Donahue and J. Nye, Jr. (Eds.), *For the people: Can we fix the public service?* (pp. 238–254). Washington, DC: Brookings Institution Press.

Bowman, J. 1994. At last, an alternative to performance appraisal: Total quality management. *Public Administration Review, 54*(2), 129–136.

———. 1999. Performance appraisal: Verisimilitude trumps veracity. *Public Personnel Management, 28,* 557–576.

———. 2010. The success of failure: The paradox of performance pay. *Review of Public Personnel Administration, 30*(1), 70–88.

Boudreaux, G. 1994. What TQM says about performance appraisal. *Compensation and Benefits Review,* May/June, 20–24.

Cardy, R. L., and G. H. Dobbins. 1994. *Performance appraisal: Alternative perspectives.* Cincinnati, OH: South-Western.

Cascio, W. 2009. *Managing human resources* (8th ed.). Boston: Irwin.

Cascio, W., and H. Aguinis. 2010. *Applied psychology in human resource management* (7th ed.). Upper Saddle River, NJ: Prentice Hall.

Clark, T. 2012. Halftime in America: Part 3. *FedSmith,* July 2. www.fedsmith.com. Accessed October 15, 2002.

Coens, T., and M. Jenkins. 2000. *Abolishing performance appraisals: Why they backfire and what to do instead.* San Francisco: Berrett-Koehler.

Culbert, S., with L. Rout. 2010. *Get rid of performance review!* New York: Business Plus.

Deming, W. E. 1992. *The new economics.* Cambridge: MIT/CAES.

Donahue, J. 2008. *The warping of government work.* Cambridge, MA: Harvard University Press.

Eckes, G. 1994. Practical alternatives to performance appraisal. *Quality Progress,* November, 57–60.

Frey, B., and M. Osterloh. 2005. Yes, managers should be paid like bureaucrats. *Journal of Management Inquiry, 14*(1), 96–111.

Gomez-Mejia, L. R., D. B. Balkin, and R. L. Cardy. 2011. *Managing human resources* (7th ed.). Upper Saddle River, NJ: Prentice Hall.

Gresing-Pophal, L. 2001. Motivate managers to review performance. *HRMagazine,* March, pp. 44–48.

Grote, D. 1996. *The complete guide to performance appraisal.* New York: AMACOM.

———. 2011. *How to be good at performance appraisals.* Boston: Harvard Business Review Press.

Halachmi, A. 1995. The practice of performance appraisal. In J. Rabin, T. Vocino, W. Hildreth, and G. Miller (Eds.), *Handbook of public personnel administration* (pp. 321–355). New York: Marcel Dekker.

Hauenstein, N. 1998. Training raters to increase accuracy and usefulness of appraisals. In J. W. Smither (Ed.), *Performance appraisal: State of the art in practice* (pp. 404–442). San Francisco: Jossey-Bass.

Hauser, J. D., and C. H. Fay. 1997. *Managing and assessing employee performance.* In H. Risher and C. H. Fay (Eds.),

New strategies for public pay (pp. 185–206). San Francisco: Jossey-Bass.

Jenkins, C., Jr., A. Mitra, N. Gupta, and J. Shaw. 1998. Are financial incentives related to performance? A meta-analytic review of empirical research. *Journal of Applied Psychology, 83,* 777–778.

Joiner, B. 1994. *Fourth generation management: The new business consciousness.* New York: McGraw-Hill.

Jozwiak, G. 2012. Is it time to give up on performance appraisals? *HRMagazine,* October 22. www.hrmagazine.co.uk. Accessed January 30, 2013.

Kelloway, E., J. Barling, and J. Harrel. 2006. *Handbook on workplace violence.* Thousand Oaks, CA: Sage.

Kluger, A.N., and A. DeNisi. 1996. The effects of feedback interventions on performance: A historical review, a meta-analysis, and a preliminary feedback intervention theory. *Psychological Bulletin, 119*(2), 254–284.

Kohn, A. 1993. Why incentive programs cannot work. *Harvard Business Review,* September/October, 54–63.

Lane, L., J. Wolf, and C. Woodward. 2003. Reassessing the human resource management crisis in the public service. *American Review of Public Administration, 33*(2): 123–145.

McGregor, J. 2013. The corporate kabuki of performance reviews. *Washington Post,* February 14.

Moynihan, D. 2008. *The dynamics of performance management.* Washington, DC: Georgetown University Press.

Murphy, K. R., and J. N. Cleveland. 1995. *Understanding performance appraisal: Social, organizational and goal-based perspectives.* Thousand Oaks, CA: Sage.

National Performance Review. 1993. *From red tape to results: Creating a government that works better and costs less.* Washington, DC: Government Printing Office.

Nigro, L., F. Nigro, and J. Kellough. 2007. *The new public personnel administration* (6th ed.). Belmont, CA: Thomson Wadsworth.

Oh, S., and G. Lewis. 2009. Can performance appraisal systems inspire intrinsically motivated employees? *Review of Public Personnel Administration, 29*(2), 158–167.

Palguta, J. 2001. Go beyond performance appraisal for good performance. *Federal Times,* October 1, p. 15.

Perry, J. 2003. Compensation, merit pay, and motivation. In S. Hays and R. Kearney (Eds.), *Public personnel administration: Problems and prospects* (pp. 143–153). Englewood Cliffs, NJ: Prentice Hall.

Roberts, G. 2003. Employee performance system participation: A technique that works. *Public Personnel Management, 32*(2), 89–97.

U.S. Merit Systems Protection Board. 1995. *Removing poor performers in the federal service.* Washington, DC: U.S. Merit Systems Protection Board.

———. 2003. *Federal workforce for the 21st century.* Washington, DC: U.S. Merit Systems Protection Board.

———. 2006. *Designing an effective pay for performance compensation system.* Washington, DC: U.S. Merit Systems Protection Board.

———. 2008. *Alternative Discipline: Creative solutions for agencies to effectively address employee misconduct.* Washington, DC: U.S. Merit Systems Protection Board.

———. 2012. *Employee perceptions of workplace violence.* Washington, DC: U.S. Merit Systems Protection Board.

Williams, R. 2012. Constructive criticism is an oxymoron we should do away with. *Financial Post,* November 13. http://business.FinancialPost.com. Accessed November 13, 2012.

CHAPTER 11

TRENDS IN PUBLIC SECTOR COMPENSATION—PAY ADMINISTRATION

Jared J. Llorens
Louisiana State University

INTRODUCTION

Establishing and maintaining an effective compensation system is one of the most critical challenges for contemporary public organizations. At their heart, compensation systems and associated practices communicate both how an organization views its employees as well as its goals for the future. However, meeting the challenge of effective compensation is made more difficult in the public sector due to a host of political, managerial, and economic constraints. While for-profit organizations in the private sector may tailor and adjust their compensation systems within the broader context of applicable federal, state, and local laws, public sector organizations must operate within the additional constraints of fluctuating public revenues, changing political contexts, and shifts in public opinion. To shed light on this topic of critical importance to public sector human resource management, this chapter provides a brief overview of public sector compensation practice and highlights some of the contemporary trends impacting the field today. In particular, the chapter focuses on continued pay reform efforts, the increasingly controversial topic of public sector pay comparability, and how public sector pay administration will most likely be affected by developing trends in the provision of public sector retirement benefits.

THE COMPONENTS AND GOALS OF PUBLIC SECTOR COMPENSATION SYSTEMS

Compensation systems, whether they operate in the public or nonprofit sectors, are typically composed of two primary components: pay and benefits. In its most basic form, pay takes the form of wages and salaries and can be viewed simultaneously as a tool for rewarding work, placing value on particular occupations within an organization and as a means of increasing employee productivity. Benefits, both employment and postemployment, refer to the nonwage components of total compensation and typically include retirement benefits, health care benefits, and related benefits such as paid leave.

For most organizations, the overriding goal in the area of compensation is to provide a total compensation portfolio that includes an optimal combination of both wage and nonwage benefits in order to ensure the presence of a qualified and high-performing workforce. For example, an organization in the rapidly evolving high-tech industry must develop and do a great job of maintaining a compensation portfolio that is attractive to an in-demand labor force commonly characterized by its youth and geographic mobility. It is for this reason that companies such as Google and Facebook provide extremely attractive wage rates, generous employee stock options, and work-life benefits thought to be necessary to recruit and retain tech-savvy job candidates. In the case of Google, the need to offer competitive compensation packages has also led to very creative nonwage benefits such as gourmet food cafeterias and employee massages (Google 2012). Additionally, Facebook has received a great deal of attention in the past year for the number of its employees who have become millionaires due to the value of their employee stock options following Facebook's initial public offering (Fowler and Raice 2012). In contrast, those organizations employing seasonal or low-skilled workers would probably not offer such generous benefits since they would not be essential to filling their positions. For example, a community swimming pool might limit its compensation package to hourly wages for lifeguards who will only be employed through the summer months, and a municipality would probably not provide perks such as employer-funded cafeterias for its rank-and-file employees.

Although the broader goals of compensation might overlap between the public and private sectors, the flexibility inherent in private sector compensation systems is generally not present in the public sector since the latter is substantially limited by both statutory restrictions on public sector pay and broader public perceptions of appropriate wage and nonwage benefits for public sector employees. In contrast to private sector companies, public organizations seeking to recruit in-demand job candidates, such as those in the area of information technology, are simply, by their very nature, unable to offer any type of stock options to potential employees, and similarly, the court of public opinion would most likely not support any attempt by the public sector to provide innovative nonwage benefits like those provided by Google. As a result, most public organizations are forced to emphasize alternative aspects of total compensation (such as generous retirement benefits, increased job security, or the opportunity to serve the public interest) in their effort to recruit and retain a qualified workforce.

In light of the supplemental chapters addressing the topics of employment and postemployment benefits, this chapter will focus primarily on major trends in the pay component of public sector compensation and how

these trends might also be influenced by broader trends impacting total compensation.

KEY TRENDS AND CRITICAL CHALLENGES IN PUBLIC SECTOR PAY

Pay Reform

Though it may appear to be a simple process to the uninformed observer, the act of establishing pay administration systems for public sector employees has been a critical issue since the founding of modern civil service systems, with the defining challenge being the ability of public employers to compensate individuals in a fair and equitable manner while also operating within the fiscal and political constraints referenced earlier. While private organizations can set their wage rates in accordance with their individual profit margins and growth potential, public organizations must rely upon the will of elected representatives to determine wage rates that meet both the needs of hiring organizations and broader public sentiment on the worth of public services. In many respects, this key difference has been the primary driver of the ongoing debate surrounding public sector pay administration and can be readily seen in decisions concerning the manner in which public sector employees are paid as well as their relative pay rates in the broader labor market.

In terms of common approaches to public sector pay administration, there are essentially two types of pay systems in operation in most modern U.S. civil service systems. First, traditional pay systems tend to be the most common and are characterized by their foundation in formal job classification processes. In a traditional system, jobs are formally defined and assigned a rank on the basis of their relative worth within the organization. Pay rates are then assigned to individual rank levels based upon comparable pay rates in the broader labor market. Given their emphasis on how a particular job is valued relative to others within an organization, these traditional systems tend to prioritize internal pay equity over individual or external pay equity with the private sector, and they have been credited with making public sector employers models in terms of fairness and equity in the workplace (Llorens 2008).

Table 11.1 Federal General Schedule Base Annual Pay Rates—2015

Grade	Step 1	Step 2	Step 3	Step 4	Step 5	Step 6	Step 7	Step 8	Step 9	Step 10
1	18,161	18,768	19,372	19,973	20,577	20,931	21,528	22,130	22,153	22,712
2	20,419	20,905	21,581	22,153	22,403	23,062	23,721	24,380	25,039	25,698
3	22,279	23,022	23,765	24,508	25,251	25,994	26,737	27,480	28,223	28,966
4	25,011	25,845	26,679	27,513	28,347	29,181	30,015	30,849	31,683	32,517
5	27,982	28,915	29,848	30,781	31,714	32,647	33,580	34,513	35,446	36,379
6	31,192	32,232	33,272	34,312	35,352	36,392	37,432	38,472	39,512	40,552
7	34,662	35,817	36,972	38,127	39,282	40,437	41,592	42,747	43,902	45,057
8	38,387	39,667	40,947	42,227	43,507	44,787	46,067	47,347	48,627	49,907
9	42,399	43,812	45,225	46,638	48,051	49,464	50,877	52,290	53,703	55,116
10	46,691	48,247	49,803	51,359	52,915	54,471	56,027	57,583	59,139	60,695
11	51,298	53,008	54,718	56,428	58,138	59,848	61,558	63,268	64,978	66,688
12	61,486	63,536	65,586	67,636	69,686	71,736	73,786	75,836	77,886	79,936
13	73,115	75,552	77,989	80,426	82,863	85,300	87,737	90,174	92,611	95,048
14	86,399	89,279	92,159	95,039	97,919	100,799	103,679	106,559	109,439	112,319
15	101,630	105,018	108,406	111,794	115,182	118,570	121,958	125,346	128,734	132,122

Source: http://www.opm.gov/policy-data-oversight/pay-leave/salaries-wages/2015/general-schedule/.

The U.S. federal government's General Schedule (GS) compensation system functions as a classic example of this traditional approach to pay administration.

As can be seen in Table 11.1, the GS system, which covers most federal civilian employees, consists of 15 grade levels with 10 incremental steps within each grade (U.S. Office of Personnel Management [OPM] 2015). Annual pay rates increase by grade and step level, and federal occupations are assigned to a particular grade level based upon a formal job analysis and ranking process. Typical of most traditional compensation systems, the federal GS system is highly structured in that employee pay increases only occur in those instances in which an employee either moves into a higher occupational grade (i.e., a promotion) or is rewarded for seniority through a step (within-grade) increase. Although external pay equity is sought by benchmarking grade-level pay rates to the private sector, traditional compensation systems such as the federal GS system tend to be less sensitive to fluctuations in market pay rates and place a strong emphasis on stability and consistency.

Though traditional systems perform quite well in ensuring equal pay for work of equal value, scholars and reformers have continually noted their inherent weakness in rewarding high-performing employees and adapting to a rapidly evolving labor market (see, e.g., OPM 2002). For instance, most traditional pay plans restrict pay rates for employees based upon the formal duties of their position, and, as a result, high-performing employees within these pay plans generally receive pay comparable to average- or low-performing employees in those cases in which employees have identical job duties. Theory and conventional wisdom suggest that this performance/reward disparity holds the potential to lower employee productivity by reducing the incentive for high performance in those cases where employees may be primarily motivated by pay (Adams 1963). As a result, there have been two major pay reform trends—merit pay and pay-banding—that have maintained their momentum over the past 30-plus years to address this inherent weakness in traditional public sector compensation practices.

The first reform, merit pay (or pay for performance) is arguably the most popular and controversial of modern pay reform trends. Merit pay reforms typically seek to emphasize individual equity by tying pay rates or increases to the results of employee performance evaluations or particular performance metrics. The second common reform, pay-banding (or broad-banding), attempts to provide greater pay flexibility within traditional compensation plans by providing ranges (i.e., bands) for individual pay rates that can be set at the discretion of managers or pay administrators. Though different in approach, the common goal of both reforms has been to provide greater managerial flexibility in the pay-setting process to more adequately reward high-performing employees or high-quality job candidates.

To illustrate the mechanics of merit pay systems, the State of Louisiana recently attempted to implement a merit pay plan for its classified state employees that would have ended annual across-the-board pay increases for employees with satisfactory performance evaluations and instead would link pay increases to three distinct performance appraisal ratings. Those employees with a rating of *Satisfactory* would have received a 3% pay increase, those with a rating of *Excellent* would have received a 4% increase, and those with a rating of *Outstanding* would have received a 6% increase (Anderson 2011). Interestingly enough, the proposal was ultimately vetoed by Louisiana's governor on the grounds that it did not grant sufficient managerial flexibility in linking pay increases to employee performance.

To illustrate the mechanics of pay-banding reforms, Table 11.2 highlights a pay-banding system currently in place for attorneys working in the U.S. Government Accountability Office (GAO) (2012).

Unlike the traditional GS compensation system, which links pay progression to seniority or increased occupational duties, managers in a pay-banding system may set individual employee pay rates anywhere within an established pay range. In the GAO example above, the annual pay rates for new attorneys assigned to Band I range from $75,259 to $108,669, and hiring managers are able to use their discretion in setting appropriate rates depending upon the qualifications and characteristics of the selected job candidate. For example, if a manager is interested in hiring a recent law school graduate

Table 11.2 U.S. Government Accountability Office—Attorney Salary Rates

Band Level	2012 Salary Ranges	Eligibility for Promotion Consideration
I	$75,259–$108,669	After two years, eligible for promotion to Band II
II	$103,206–$144,443	After two years at Band II, eligible for promotion to Band III
III	$128,623–$155,500	

Source: http://www.gao.gov/careers/legal_benefits.html.

from a top university who has received a competing salary offer of $85,000, then he or she can choose to match or go higher than that salary offer since it is within the range specified by the pay-banding system. However, it should also be noted that GAO's plan retains a key characteristic of traditional compensation plans by placing a tenure requirement upon employees moving from band level I to II and II to III.[1]

Both merit pay and pay-banding reforms are conceptually appealing for their potential to address the weaknesses inherent in traditional pay systems, but there is a substantial body of research highlighting the difficulties of implementing and effectively administering such pay plans in the public sector (see, e.g., Perry, Engbers, and Jun 2009). As many scholars have pointed out, the effective implementation of merit pay plans relies heavily upon the ability of public organizations to develop effective and accurate performance management systems as well as the capacity to provide performance pay increases that are substantial enough to encourage increased employee performance. However, meeting the goal of effective performance management is a continual challenge for many public sector organizations since establishing clear performance metrics can be difficult for those occupations that may have complex duties coupled with ambiguous outcomes (e.g., a federal management analyst). Further, most public sector organizations are substantially limited in the amount of pay that can be used to reward high-performing employees in the form of bonuses or performance awards. Unlike private sector organizations that may be able to offer commissions on profits attributed to an employee's individual contribution to the organization, public organizations must

allocate performance rewards from limited and often dwindling tax-generated revenue pools. Combined, these challenges represent some of the major roadblocks to the successful implementation of merit pay systems in the public sector, but, to date, there has been no substantial drawback in the efforts of public sector organizations to implement these types of plans.

Even though pay-banding may circumvent some of the issues associated with merit pay plans, this reform is not without its own challenges. As previously stated, one of the key benefits of traditional pay systems has been their ability to defend the principal of equal pay for work of equal value by substantially minimizing the ability of managers to allow their personal biases to enter into the pay-setting process. As a result, research has consistently shown that women and minorities, two groups that have historically experienced substantial labor market discrimination, have experienced significantly less wage discrimination in the public sector as opposed to the private sector, where there is typically much greater latitude in setting individual pay rates (see, e.g., Llorens et al. 2008). While beneficial for aligning pay rates with performance-related factors, pay-banding systems also create the potential for bias and discrimination in the pay administration process in those instances in which individuals with identical job duties are paid at different rates on the basis on nonperformance related factors (e.g., race, gender, or personal appearance) (Friel 2001).

Pay Comparability

Although designing public sector pay systems that protect equity and reward individual performance has often proved challenging, one developing topic in the area of pay administration centers on the extent to which public sector pay rates are or should be comparable to those offered in the private sector. This topic has always been of importance to the practice of public sector pay setting, and it has enjoyed renewed attention in recent years with the broader downturn in the private sector labor market resulting from the economic crisis beginning in 2008. At the heart of the matter are two competing viewpoints on both how public sector employees should be paid relative to their private sector counterparts and what methods should be used to measure pay comparability.

Since the founding of the earliest civil service systems, conventional wisdom in the field of public administration has held that public employees should be adequately compensated for their work contributions but that there should be no expectation of extreme wealth or riches—especially given public sector job security and the belief that public employees are motivated by the ability to serve the public good (Smith 1977; Langbein and Lewis 1998; Berman et al. 2010). In practice this has meant that public sector employers have consistently embraced the de facto policy of paying wages that typically fall below those afforded to private sector employees, where there is considerably less job security but a greater potential for higher wage rates.

While the prevailing paradigm of public sector pay comparability assumes the continual presence of qualified employees willing to work for public employers at below-market wage rates, the persistent underpayment of public sector employees was cited as a major recruitment and retention barrier during the relatively strong economic period of the 1990s and early 2000s. Many public managers simply held that they were at a competitive disadvantage when attempting to hire talented job candidates, particularly in the science and technology fields, because their pay rates fell too far below those available in the private sector (see, e.g., Bureau of Labor Statistics [BLS] 2009). This viewpoint was one of the primary drivers of calls to increase public wage rates and can be seen, at the federal level, in the passage of the Federal Employees Pay Comparability Act of 1990 (FEPCA). Given the presence of federal employees in every major metropolitan area in the U.S., FEPCA first sought to ensure greater wage equity across federal employment by providing locality pay adjustments based upon the cost of labor in metropolitan areas. For example, labor costs in San Francisco are much higher than labor costs in Jackson, Mississippi, and, as a result, federal employees in San Francisco receive higher locality pay adjustments.

To address the broader issue of pay comparability, FEPCA also established a goal of setting federal pay rates within 5% of comparable private sector wage rates based upon annual salary surveys conducted by the BLS. This component of the statute also highlights how public sector pay administration differs substantially from similar processes in the private sector. Since the passage of FEPCA, BLS salary comparisons have consistently found that federal employees are, on average, substantially underpaid when compared to their private sector counterparts; but no presidential administration since the passage of FEPCA has proposed a corresponding federal pay increase to bring overall pay rates within the 5% goal originally set forth in the Act. Further, efforts to achieve pay comparability at the federal level are also hindered by the Act's mandate that increases to the GS pay system be applied equally across all grade levels, even in light of BLS findings that only employees in higher-grade levels are underpaid relative to their private sector counterparts.[2]

This second aspect of FEPCA has also been the impetus for a broader discussion on the appropriate methodology for comparing the wages of workers in the public sector with those in the private sector; and as prior research has pointed out, one's choice of methodology can oftentimes lead to contradictory conclusions concerning overall pay comparability (Miller 1996). For example, one methodological approach commonly applied in the popular press is to simply compare the average wages of all public and private sector workers. Figure 11.1, below, highlights the results of average wage comparisons using data from the National Compensation Survey conducted by the BLS (Federal Salary Council 2010; BLS 2011).

Figure 11.1 Mean Annual Wage Estimate for Full-Time Employees, 2010

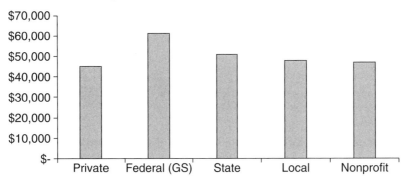

Source: Federal Salary Council (2010); BLS (2011).

As can be seen in Figure 11.1, simply comparing average wages shows that public sector and nonprofit employees earn considerably more than their private sector counterparts, with federal employees enjoying the highest pay rates. However, such a conclusion is highly misleading because of differences in the occupational composition of each of the employment sectors. Unlike the public and nonprofit sectors, the private sector labor market contains a large percentage of low-wage, service sector occupations, which have the effect of driving down average wage rates for private sector employees.

To address this methodological shortcoming, compensation experts across government and the private sector have commonly sought to compare the wage rates of similar jobs in the public and private sectors. For instance, comparing the salary of a first-year accountant in the public sector with a first-year accountant in the private sector would yield a much more accurate assessment of wage comparability between the two sectors. Using this approach at the federal level, BLS estimates have shown that, contrary to results derived from average pay comparisons, federal employees are actually underpaid by approximately 15% but that this underpayment exists primarily at the higher GS grade levels, with employees in grade levels 9 through 15 experiencing pay gaps ranging from 9.2% to 25.9% (Federal Salary Council 2010).

In contrast to both of the approaches described above, compensation researchers have asserted that a more accurate assessment of public/private pay comparability should compare the wages of individuals with comparable human capital characteristics while also controlling for other wage-determining factors. Commonly referred to as the human capital approach, this method entails estimating the difference in wages between public and private sector employees, typically using a formal wage regression model, while controlling for such characteristics as education, age, marital status, and occupation. Comparability estimates derived using this methodological approach are standard in the academic literature and have consistently shown that certain segments of the public sector enjoy wage premiums whereas others experience wage penalties. Further, results have also shown that wage differentials vary considerably by level of government and even within each level of government depending upon such factors as gender, union influence, and taxable resources available to public employers (see, e.g., Borjas 2002; Llorens 2008; Sherk 2010). Additionally, research using this approach has consistently shown that women and minorities in the public sector tend to earn more than their private sector counterparts, most likely as the result of more formalized and restrictive compensation practices in the public sector (Llorens et al. 2008).

Retirement Benefit Trends and Public Sector Pay

Although the debate concerning public sector wages shows no sign of waning in the coming years, a complete assessment of public sector compensation must also take into account the role of public sector benefits. As previously mentioned, benefits typically comprise retirement, health care, and related provisions such as child care and paid leave. However, recent trends in public sector benefits have almost exclusively centered on the provision of retirement benefits for public employees and the ability of public employers to meet their long-term, postemployment benefit obligations (Coggburn and Kearney 2010; Pew 2010). At the heart of recent trends in public sector benefits is the question of what type of retirement benefit plans should be offered to public sector employees and the impact of benefit plan choices on broader goals related to public sector compensation. As will be highlighted in the following discussion, this question is of critical importance to public sector pay administration given the role that generous public sector benefit plans have played in offsetting the effect of perceived pay rate disparities in the public sector.

Overall, there are two primary retirement benefit plan options utilized by both public and private sector employers—defined benefit and defined contribution plans. Defined benefit plans (i.e., pensions) have been the traditional option provided by public employers and have been recognized for their ability to bolster the attractiveness of total compensation plans in light of low wage rates. Employees under these plans typically contribute a percentage of their annual pay during their employment, along with a set employer contribution, and upon retirement, retirees are promised a fixed percentage of their salary (typically based upon age and tenure) for life. These plans have historically been considered quite generous since the burden of investing employee and employer retirement contributions rests entirely upon the employer, thus eliminating all employee risk and responsibility in managing retirement investments.

In contrast, defined contribution plans (i.e., 401(k)-style plans) allow employees to control the investment of their retirement contributions, along with employer matching contributions, and their entire retirement portfolio is portable should they switch employers throughout their work career. The most substantial

differences between the two plans, however, are that employees, not employers, bear all of the investment risk in a defined contribution plan, and upon retirement, benefits in a defined contribution plan are limited to the value of an employee's individual retirement portfolio. For example, if an employee's retirement portfolio is worth $650,000 at retirement, his benefits will be limited to that amount, regardless of his lifespan after retirement. In contrast, a retiree in a defined benefit plan would be guaranteed a fixed annual retirement benefit for life, regardless of how her investments performed during their employment.

While defined benefit plans were the norm for private and public sector employees for much of the 20th century, the past 25 years have witnessed a dramatic shift from defined benefits to defined contribution plans in the private sector due to the latter's relatively low employer cost. Unlike defined benefit plans, in which employers pay lifetime benefits, defined contribution plans only require employer matching contributions prior to an employee's retirement. As a whole, the public sector has continued to provide defined benefit plans although they are rarely offered in the private sector. As of March 2014, 83% of state and local government employees had access to defined benefit plans (75% participation rate), but only 19% of their private sector counterparts had access to such plans (16% participation rate).[3] In contrast, 60% of private sector workers had access to a defined contribution plan (42% participation rate) and only 33% of state and local government employees had access to such plans (16% participation rate) (BLS 2014).

Although this issue is addressed in greater detail in an accompanying chapter, there is a growing concern that public sector defined benefit plans are not sustainable in the long-term due to the growing inability of public employers to meet the financial responsibility of paying their retirees (Pew 2010). As noted above, one of the key characteristics of a defined benefit plan is that the risks associated with investing employer and employee retirement contributions rest entirely upon the employer. As a direct result of the economic downturn in 2008, many public employers have acknowledged that the value of their retirement investments has dropped to levels that have made it virtually impossible for them to meet their long-term pension obligations without significant increases in employer or employee contributions. In extreme cases, investment losses have even caused some public employers to default on their payments to current retirees, triggering a wave of lawsuits which will have major implications for the long-term viability of public sector retirement benefits (Corkery 2012). As a result, there is a growing trend in public employers seeking to develop alternative retirement benefit plans that are less costly to maintain and increase employee control of their retirement benefits.

As the Pew Center on the States has pointed out, some of the major options for employers seeking to address unfunded pension liabilities include transitioning employees to defined contribution plans or increasing the percentage of employee salaries contributed to their pension plans prior to retirement (Pew 2010). However, the provision of relatively generous defined benefit plans has allowed total compensation in the public sector to remain competitive, even when wage rates have fallen below those available in the private sector. Reform efforts such as those listed above will inevitably increase the importance of competitive wage rates since the longevity of an employee's postretirement income will be more closely related to their wage rates during their working years. This increased emphasis on wage rates presents a very real culture shift for public sector pay administration, which has traditionally focused less on external wage equity and more on internal wage equity and job stability. Perhaps more important, this shift will also place a greater emphasis on processes for assessing the competitiveness of public sector wage rates, a topic currently affected by considerable methodological inconsistency.

CONCLUSION

This chapter has sought to highlight some of the major trends in public sector compensation related to pay system reform and public/private pay comparability.

Although the public sector has traditionally maintained highly structured pay systems that have prioritized internal equity over external and individual equity, there continues to be calls for an increased connection between employee pay and individual performance. Likewise, the recent economic downturn has served as the impetus for a renewed focus on public sector wage rates and their comparability to private sector rates. While there continues to be considerable debate over the appropriate means of comparing public and private sector wages, increasing calls for retirement benefit reform will only heighten the importance of ensuring that public sector employees are paid in a manner that promotes the presence of a high-performing workforce.

NOTES

1. While the GS compensation system is the standard for federal civilian employees, agencies can request permission to implement reformed systems when it is deemed necessary for recruiting and retaining a qualified workforce.

2. For a comprehensive discussion of this issue, please see Condrey, Facer, and Llorens (2012).

3. Retirement plan options for federal, nonpostal employees are similar to those for state and local government employees with a major distinction based upon an employee's entry into federal service. Employees hired before 1987 contribute 7–8% of their wages to the Civil Service Retirement System (CSRS), which operates as a defined benefit plan. CSRS-covered employees do not contribute to Social Security and upon retirement, those employees with 30 or more years of service receive approximately 55% of the average of their three highest paid years of service (OPM 1998). Employees hired since 1987 participate in the Federal Employees Retirement System (FERS), which is a hybrid plan consisting of Social Security, a defined benefit annuity, and a defined contribution plan, the Thrift Savings Plan, which is invested in the market according to each employee's risk tolerance.

REFERENCES

Adams, J. Stacy. 1963. Toward an Understanding of Inequity. *Journal of Abnormal Social Psychology, 67,* 422–436.

Anderson, Ed. 2011. State Civil Service Panel Denies 4 Percent State Employee Raises for 2011–12. *Times Picayune,* March 2. http://www.nola.com/politics/index.ssf/

2011/03/state_civil_service_panel_will.html. Accessed November 29, 2012.

Berman, Evan M., James S. Bowman, Jonathan P. West, and Montgomery Van Wart. 2010. *Human Resource Management in Public Service* (3rd ed.). Thousand Oaks, CA: Sage.

Borjas, George J. 2002. *The Wage Structure and the Sorting of Workers into the Public Sector.* Working Paper 9313. Cambridge, MA: National Bureau of Economic Research.

Coggburn, Jerrell, and Richard C. Kearney. 2010. Trouble Keeping Promises? An Analysis of Underfunding in State Retiree Benefits. *Public Administration Review, 70,* 97–108.

Condrey, Stephen, Rex Facer, and Jared Llorens. 2012. *Moving towards a More Strategic Federal Pay Comparability Policy.* A joint publication of the National Academy of Public Administration and the American Society for Public Administration. http://www.memostoleaders.org/sites/default/files/MEMO1_0.pdf. Accessed November 30, 2012.

Corkery, Michael. 2012. Pension Crisis Looms Despite Cuts. *Wall Street Journal,* September 21. http://online.wsj.com/article/SB10000872396390443890304578010752828935688.html. Accessed November 29, 2012.

Fowler, Geoffrey A., and Shayndi Raice. 2012. Winners, Losers and the Start-Up Road Not Taken. *Wall Street Journal,* May 18. http://online.wsj.com/article/SB10001424052702303360504577412031389480536.html. Accessed November 28, 2012.

Friel, Brian. 2001. Pay-banding Pros and Cons. *Government Executive,* October 18. http://www.govexec.com/pay-benefits/pay-benefits-watch/2001/10/pay-banding-pros-and-cons/10247/. Accessed November 29, 2012.

Google. 2012. Working at Google. http://www.google.com/about/jobs/lifeatgoogle/working-at-google.html. Accessed November 28, 2012.

Langbein, Laura I., and Gregory B. Lewis. 1998. Pay, Productivity and the Public Sector: The Case of Electrical Engineers. *Journal of Public Administration Research and Theory, 8,* 391–412.

Llorens, Jared. 2008. Uncovering the Determinants of Competitive State Government Wages. *Review of Public Personnel Administration, 28,* 308–326.

Llorens, Jared, Jeffrey Wenger, and J. Edward Kellough. 2008. Choosing Public Sector Employment: The Impact of Wages on the Representation of Women and Minorities in State Bureaucracies. *Journal of Public Administration Research and Theory, 18,* 397–413.

Miller, Michael. 1996. The Public Private Pay Debate: What Do the Data Show? *Monthly Labor Review, 119,* 18–29.

Perry, James L., Trent A. Engbers, and So Yun Jun. 2009. Back to the Future? Performance-related Pay, Empirical Research, and the Perils of Persistence. *Public Administration Review, 69,* 39–51.

Pew Center on the States. 2010. *The Trillion Dollar Gap. Underfunded State Retirement Systems and the Roads to Reform.* http://www.pewstates.org/uploadedFiles/PCS_Assets/2010/Trillion_Dollar_Gap_Underfunded_State_Retirement_Systems_and_the_Roads_to_Reform.pdf. Accessed November 30, 2012.

Sherk, James. 2010. *Inflated Federal Pay: How Americans Are Overtaxed to Overpay the Civil Service.* A Report of the Heritage Center for Data Analysis. Washington, DC: The Heritage Foundation. http://www.heritage.org/research/reports/2010/07/inflated-federal-pay-how-americans-are-overtaxed-to-overpay-the-civil-service. Accessed November 30, 2012.

Smith, Sharon P. 1977. *Equal Pay in the Public Sector: Fact or Fantasy.* Research Report Series No. 122. Princeton, NJ: Industrial Relations Section, Princeton University.

U.S. Bureau of Labor Statistics (BLS). 2009. Fifty years of BLS surveys on federal employees' pay. *Monthly Labor Review,* September.

———. 2011. Occupational Earnings Tables: United States, December 2009–January 2011, National Compensation Survey. http://bls.gov/ncs/ncswage2010.htm#Wage_Tables. Accessed August 20, 2011.

———. 2014. Retirement Benefits, March 2014. http://www.bls.gov/ncs/ebs/benefits/2014/benefits_retirement.htm. Accessed January 8, 2015.

U.S. Federal Salary Council (FSC). 2010. Data for the 2010 pay agent's report to the President for the RUS locality pay area. Provided at the October 29, 2010, Federal Salary Council meeting in Washington, DC.

U.S. Government Accountability Office (GAO). 2012. Benefits for GAO Attorneys. Accessed November 28th, 2012. http://www.gao.gov/careers/legal_benefits.html.

U.S. Office of Personnel Management (OPM). 1998. *CSRS and FERS Handbook.* http://www.opm.gov/retire/pubs/handbook/hod.htm. Accessed November 30, 2012.

———. 2002. *A Fresh Start for Federal Pay: The Case for Modernization.* http://www.opm.gov/strategiccomp/whtpaper.pdf. Accessed November 30, 2012.

———. 2015. 2015 Salary Tables and Related Information. http://www.opm.gov/policy-data-oversight/pay-leave/salaries-wages/salary-tables/15Tables/html/GS.aspx. Accessed January 8, 2015.

CHAPTER 12

EMPLOYEE BENEFITS: PATTERNS AND CHALLENGES FOR PUBLIC ORGANIZATIONS

Rex L. Facer II
Brigham Young University

Lori L. Wadsworth
Brigham Young University

INTRODUCTION

Historically, benefits have been seen as a way to make up for lower compensation in the public sector. Additionally, benefits, in part due to their long-term impact, have often been seen as a way to increase favor with employees without having to incur a dramatic cost increase in the short term. Essentially, benefit costs often occur in the future. However, that is all changing. For one, the rapid cost increases in some benefits, such as health care, has placed a significant strain on public sector budgets. Additionally, even though benefits like sick leave and retirement frequently had small short-term costs, the long-term costs were high; accounting and other management practices are pushing for the cost of these and other benefits to be planned for and borne by the organization when it incurs the liability, instead of when it has to pay for the benefit (see Calabrese and Marlowe's chapter on postemployment benefits for a thorough discussion of this issue).

Additionally, public sector pay and benefits have been in the news on a regular basis over the last few years (see, e.g., Biggs and Richwine 2012; Cauchon 2010a, 2010b, 2011; Davidson 2010; Katz 2014; Korte 2014). In part this is driven by reports by the Cato Institute (Edwards 2006), the Heritage Foundation (Sherk 2010), and the American Enterprise Institute (Biggs and Richwine 2011) criticizing public pay and benefit practices. These reports have focused on public sector compensation practices, often including benefits in their analysis. In their analysis, these authors frequently use alternative analytical strategies that are different from those typically used by HR professionals in managing pay and benefits. One of the conclusions from these studies is that when benefits are figured into compensation, public employees are overcompensated, especially as a result of generous benefits. Biggs and Richwine's analysis notes that "our measures do show that benefits play a significantly larger role for federal employees than for private sector employees" (2011: 22). Further they "estimate a federal benefits premium of approximately 63 % relative to benefits paid by large private employers" (23). While there are significant concerns about their methodological approach, their analysis has significantly shaped the perception that public employees, specifically federal employees, receive far more generous benefits than their private sector counterparts.

An important part of the argument of Biggs and Richwine (2011) and others is that when making comparisons between compensation in employment sectors, both direct compensation (salary or wages) and benefits should be included. From an economic perspective this approach is analytically reasonable; this does, however, assume that employees make decisions based on the total compensation package available. That includes direct compensation (salary or wages, and bonuses) plus benefits. However, the scholarship, practice, and experience of HR professionals suggest an alternative strategy for thinking about benefits. Berger and Berger (2008), for example, argue that there should be separate surveys for compensation, benefits, and the work experience. Compensation would target salaries and wages and any variable pay, benefits surveys examine either the availability, cost, or value of the benefits provided, and the work experience surveys look at acknowledgement, work-life balance, culture, development, and environment. Specifically addressing the importance of examining benefits separately from compensation, they note "employee benefit programs are complex and multifaceted. Comparison of programs typically requires specific expertise and is difficult to complete without a single common denominator on which all programs are measured" (Berger and Berger 2008: 129–130).

While we believe that employers should strategically think from a total compensation model—pay, benefits, and work experience—we also believe that employers should address each of those areas using different, but appropriate, strategies.

In this chapter we recognize that not all benefits are the same. Some benefits are readily available to the employee for use now, while other benefits are not available until after employment is complete (e.g., pension or retirement benefits). This chapter focuses on understanding current benefit practices in modern organizations, with a special emphasis on public sector organizations. We do not address retirement-related

benefits; a discussion of those benefits is available in Marlowe's chapter.

In this chapter we first focus on "mandatory" benefits. These are benefits all organizations must provide for their employees. These include workers compensation, social security, and unemployment insurance. Next we review commonly provided benefits, including health care benefits (health insurance, dental insurance, vision insurance, and long-term care); time-off benefits, and life insurance. Finally we review a set of other benefits that are offered less frequently. We conclude the chapter with a discussion of strategies for managing the costs of benefits.

MANDATORY BENEFITS

Workers Compensation

Workers compensation is a required benefit, mandated by state law in all 50 states. It is designed to provide financial protection for employees who are injured on the job or while performing a job-related activity. Compensation is provided for (1) medical expenses, (2) cost of any necessary rehabilitation treatment, (3) lost wages due to the injury, and (4) death benefits for surviving family members, similar to life insurance (Phillips and Gully 2014).

The employee does not have to prove that they are not at fault for the accident or injury, although the organization can withhold coverage if it is proven that the employee intentionally caused the accident in order to receive workers compensation coverage (Lussier and Hendon 2013).

Workers compensation coverage can come from three possible sources, dependent on the state requirements. First, it can be purchased through the state workers compensation fund; second, the organization might purchase workers compensation coverage through a private insurance company; and third, large organizations might choose to self-insure.

The rate for workers compensation is based on the type of job for each employee. Those jobs that are more dangerous, or more likely to be associated with an accident or injury, will be assessed higher premiums. Also, if the organization has a history of employee accidents or injuries, higher premiums will be assessed.

Social Security

There are four types of benefits provided under the Federal Old Age, Survivors, Disability, and Health Insurance Program (most employed individuals are familiar with the acronym OASDHI, which appears on their paycheck stub) created by the Social Security Act of 1935. As described in the title, these four benefits are retirement income ("old age"), survivor income (for surviving dependent family members of employees who have contributed into Social Security), disability income, and health care benefits (Medicare). These Social Security programs are financed by contributions made by the employee and matched by the employer. Current taxes collected pay for current recipients—any surplus is invested in federal government bonds that are held in the Social Security Trust Fund and guaranteed by the U.S. government (Social Security Administration, n.d.).

The retirement income comes in the form of monthly benefits to retired workers and is computed as a percentage of the employee's previous earnings. In order to be eligible for Social Security retirement benefits, the employee must receive a minimum of 40 credits. Generally, an individual can receive up to four credits per year, based on a minimum salary requirement (Lussier and Hendon 2013). Individuals born before 1938 must be at least 65 years old prior to retirement to receive full retirement benefits. More recently, this age requirement has been changed so that individuals born after 1959 are not eligible for full benefits until age 67 (WorldatWork 2007).

The health insurance program, otherwise known as Medicare, is the most expensive part of the Social Security program (WorldatWork 2007). Medicare is available for individuals age 65 and over who qualify for the Social Security retirement income program. In addition, individuals with disabilities are eligible for Medicare 24 months after they start receiving Social Security Disability Insurance (Healthcare.gov). Medicare is similar to other health insurance plans in that it covers a portion of the cost of health care, while the individual is responsible for the rest.

Unemployment Insurance

Unemployment insurance was created as part of the Social Security Act of 1935. Although it is a federal program, it is administered through the states (Lussier and Hendon 2013). Each employer is required to pay into the state's unemployment insurance fund as a tax. This benefit provides a temporary income for employees during periods of involuntary unemployment. Employees generally receive weekly stipends to assist them as they continue to look for work. Individuals can be denied unemployment coverage if they were discharged for misconduct or fraud, if they quit voluntarily, or if they refuse to look for work while receiving unemployment. In addition, if the recipient refuses suitable work while unemployed, they can be disqualified from receiving benefits (Lussier and Hendon 2013).

COMMONLY PROVIDED BENEFITS

Health Care

Health care benefits are offered by many employers in all sectors of the workplace (see Table 12.1). This is especially true of large organizations. In 2012, private firms with more than 500 employees offered medical coverage to 89% of employees, while state and local government employers with more than 500 employees offered medical coverage to 90% of employees. However, not all employees choose to participate in an employer's offered coverage. For large private firms, there is a take-up rate of 76%, while for large state and local government organizations the take-up rate is 83%. There are many factors that affect employees' participation in the available medical coverage. For example, employees may have access to a better plan through their spouses' employment. Alternatively, employees may choose to not participate because they perceive the cost as too high. Nevertheless, medical coverage is perhaps the most widely available benefit. However, medical coverage comes in several varieties. There is a wide

Table 12.1 Health Insurance Coverage by Size of Organization

	Private Employers			State and Local Government Employers		
	1–99	100–499	500+	1–99	100–499	500+
Percent of employees with access to health coverage	57%	82%	89%	73%	85%	90%
Percent of employees participating in health coverage	41%	59%	68%	63%	72%	75%
Take-up rate	72%	72%	76%	86%	85%	83%

Source: Bureau of Labor Statistics, National Compensation Survey, March 2012.

range of plans and coverage under health care benefits; these plans generally fall into four main categories—traditional plans, health maintenance organizations (HMOs), preferred provider organizations (PPOs), and health savings accounts (HSAs).

Traditional Health Care Plans

Traditional health care plans are based on individuals covering a certain percentage of health care costs, while the insurance company covers the rest (e.g., the employee pays 20% and the insurance company pays 80% of the medical costs). A traditional plan generally allows the employee the freedom to select their own health care professionals.

Health Maintenance Organizations

As defined by HealthCare.gov, HMOs limit individuals' selection of health care professionals to those "who work for or contract with the HMO." If you seek services through the HMO, the copayments are small and there are few or no deductibles (Kiplinger Washington Editors 2010). In those instances where individuals choose to see a health care professional not on the approved list or seek treatment at a noncovered facility, they might be required to cover the full cost of their services. The focus of HMOs is on preventative health care and wellness through routine check-ups.

Preferred Provider Organizations

Under a preferred provider organization (PPO) plan, individuals receive health care coverage through a network of providers, similar to an HMO (California Department of Managed Health Care 2012). The costs are covered by the PPO at a higher rate if the individual receives care from health care providers on the PPO's approved list. The PPO is able to keep costs down by negotiating agreements with the preferred providers to accept a lower amount of payment for services received. A PPO generally provides greater flexibility than an HMO, because individuals can receive care from a non-preferred provider, but they do so by paying a higher percentage of the costs.

Health Savings Accounts

A health savings account (HSA) is basically a savings account to pay for your portion of medical expenses. According to the Society for Human Resource Management (SHRM 2012), HSAs are offered by 43% of organizations. In an HSA, the individual establishes an account using their own money from which they can withdraw funds to pay for qualified health care expenses. The funds are set aside pre-tax, so there is a tax savings to the individual. In order to qualify for a health savings account, the individual must be in a high-deductible, low-premium health care plan (Internal Revenue Service

[IRS] 2012). A high-deductible plan kicks in after you have reached your deductible. For example, the IRS requires that HSA plans have an individual deductible of $1,200 or higher, and a deductible on a family plan of $2,400 or higher (IRS 2012). The employee is responsible for the payment of most fees up to that deductible. But once the deductible is hit, the plan will generally pay for all expenses.

The IRS establishes a maximum contribution that employees can make to an HSA per calendar year (for 2013, the maximum contribution is $3,250 for individuals and $6,450 for family coverage). In addition, the IRS has set a limit on the out-of-pocket expenses for individual coverage at $6,050 and for family coverage at $12,000 (IRS 2012).

Other Health Care Insurance Benefits

Dental Insurance

According to recent data from the International Public Management Association for Human Resources (IPMA-HR 2011), 97% of public organizations offer dental insurance. Dental plans frequently cover four types of services: preventative and diagnostic services, basic services, major services, and orthodontics (WorldatWork 2007). Plans vary significantly in the amount of benefit provided for each type of service. Most dental plans cover a large share of the costs of preventative and diagnostic services. This encourages participants to receive regular dental care and hopefully minimize the long-term cost to the insurance plan. Dental plans often pay a smaller portion of the costs for other services. Orthodontic treatments generally have a lifetime maximum. These plans may be separate from or part of the general health insurance offered by the organization.

Vision Insurance

Vision insurance is offered less frequently than health insurance and dental insurance. IPMA-HR (2011) reports that 82% of public organizations offer vision insurance. Vision insurance also varies dramatically based on the plan. These plans cover some or all of the costs for annual eye exams and eyeglasses. For vision plans that do not include eyeglass coverage, organizations may provide separate benefits through a preferred provider who agrees to offer employees of the organization a known discount. These plans may be separate from or part of the general health insurance offered by the organization.

Long-Term Care Insurance

As the population continues to age, long-term care becomes more important to employees (Dell 2010). Long-term care insurance is a benefit that is sometimes offered as an optional benefit to health care coverage. It is designed to help provide for the care of individuals when they need assistance with daily living due to illness or disability. This might be full-time care in a nursing home or assisted living facility, or it might be received through home health care. According to a 2012 survey of U.S. companies, it was reported that 51% of large companies provide long-term care insurance (SHRM 2012a). Of the organizations that offer this insurance, 71% of the insurance programs were through a group plan, while the other 29% offered long-term care insurance as an individual policy (SHRM 2012b). The premiums are generally paid entirely by the employee, but in some cases employers subsidize the premiums. Because long-term care insurance is considered a health care benefit, organizations can receive tax benefits for any premiums they pay, similar to health care premiums (SHRM 2012c).

Health Care Costs

Paying for health care is a significant challenge. Health care spending has grown dramatically over the last two decades. From 1990 to 2010, spending on health care increased by 231%, while the rest of the economy, excluding health care grew by 142% (Bureau of Economic Analysis, GDP data, bea.gov). Organizations have had to grapple with this strong growth while at the same time, at least for the last several years, facing increasing fiscal pressure.

As discussed above, the general model employed by most organizations is to offer medical insurance to the employee. If the employee elects to accept the

Figure 12.1 Worker and Employer Annual Health Insurance Premium Costs Family Coverage 2012 by Sector

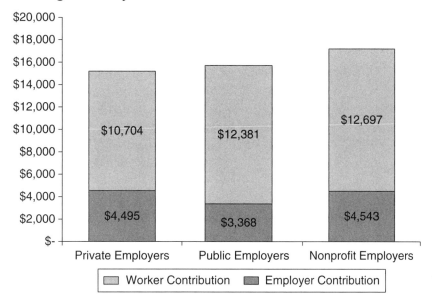

Source: Kaiser/HRET Survey of Employer Sponsored Health Benefits (2012).

coverage, the employee is expected to pay a share of the insurance cost, in addition to any deductible or copay which may be required. The following figures highlight the patterns across public, private, and nonprofit organizations. Figure 12.1 presents the cost borne by the employee and the employer for family health insurance. The average total annual cost for family health insurance for private firms ($15,199) is the lowest, while nonprofit organizations have the highest family coverage cost ($17,240). Public employers ask employees to pay $3,368 of the total annual cost for family coverage of $15,749. Therefore, public employees, on average, are paying $281 per month for their share of family health insurance coverage.

The pattern is similar for single coverage health insurance. The average total annual cost for single coverage health insurance for private firms ($5,297) is the lowest, while nonprofit organizations have the highest family coverage cost ($6,203). Public employers ask employees to pay $698 of the total cost for single coverage of $5,997. Therefore, public employees, on average, are paying

$58 per month for their share of their individual health insurance coverage.

There is a difference in the cost of insurance and the share employees are asked to pay when we look at all organizations. However, when we exclude smaller organizations (i.e., those with fewer than 200 employees) the differences between the insurance costs for public and private organizations are much smaller. The total cost of family coverage for large private firms is $15,544, while for large public organizations the total cost of family coverage is $15,673, a difference of less than 1%. The primary difference is in the share of the costs employees are asked to pay. Large private firms ask employees to pay $4,113, while public organizations on average ask employees to pay $3,462.

Applicable Legislation

Consolidated Omnibus Budget Reconciliation Act of 1985 (COBRA)

COBRA provides continuation of health insurance coverage for employees after leaving employment at the

Figure 12.2 Worker and Employer Annual Health Insurance Premium Costs Single Coverage 2012 by Sector

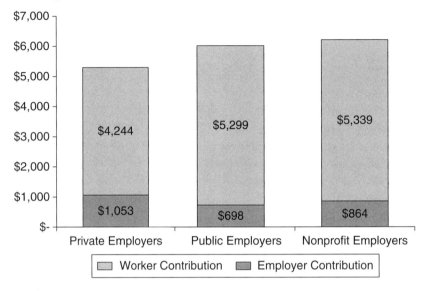

Source: Kaiser/HRET Survey of Employer Sponsored Health Benefits (2012).

Figure 12.3 Worker and Employer Annual Health Insurance Premium Costs Family Coverage 2012 by Sector for Large Organizations (200 or more employees)

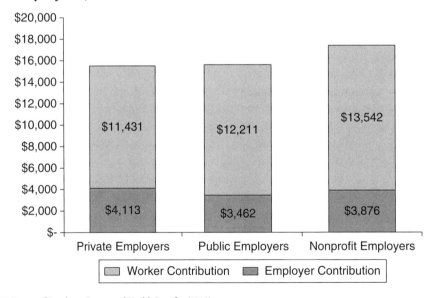

Source: Kaiser/HRET Survey of Employer Sponsored Health Benefits (2012).

organization (U.S. Department of Labor 2012a). The law does not apply to organizations with fewer than 20 employees. Generally, the organization is required to allow employees to continue health care coverage for 18 months, but in some cases, the time period can be extended to 36 months. The benefit to the employee is that during a period of unemployment, they can still continue health care coverage. The cost to the employee can be quite high, as the employee is responsible for paying the full health care premium during this time. If desired, the organization is allowed by the Department of Labor to charge employees a 2% administrative fee (U.S. Department of Labor 2012a).

The American Recovery and Reinvestment Act (ARRA) was a short-term program providing assistance for health care premium costs during the economic downturn. This program applied to those who lost their jobs on or before May 31, 2010. Eligible employees paid 35% of the health care premiums while the remaining 65% was reimbursed to the health care provider through tax credits (U.S. Department of Labor 2012a).

Patient Protection and
Affordable Care Act of 2010 ("Obamacare")

This law provides broad-sweeping changes to health care. To allow organizations time to ease into these new requirements, the Act has mandated a graduated implementation schedule. For example, the first changes to the health care system became effective in 2010, with additional changes becoming effective in successive years with the final changes becoming effective in 2016. Some of these changes include coverage of dependents up to age 26 whether or not the dependent is a full-time student, disabled, or married; prohibiting insurance companies from rescinding health care coverage unless the individual has engaged in fraud or intentional misrepresentation of information; requiring coverage of preexisting conditions in most situations; automatic enrollment for organizations with more than 200 full-time employees; coverage of preventive care services; and finally, in 2015, organizations with more than 50 full-time employees will be required to provide health insurance coverage

that is both affordable and adequate to their employees or pay the "Employer Shared Responsibility" payment (IRS 2014). With these changes, health care coverage will become a mandatory benefit for most organizations. This will create large-scale changes across the benefits landscape, as organizations that previously may not have provided health care benefits will need to ensure that employer-provided health insurance is available to their employees.

TIME-OFF BENEFITS

Generally, time-off benefits include vacation and sick leave as well as paid holidays. Organizations provide paid sick leave to encourage those who are sick to stay at home and recuperate, in the hopes of preventing the spreading of illness, thus keeping the workplace healthier. A recent study (SHRM 2013) reported that 86% of organizations provide some form of paid sick leave to their employees. IPMA-HR (2011) reported that 94% of public organizations responding to their survey provided paid sick leave for full-time employees and 54% offer paid sick leave for part-time employees. IPMA-HR's respondents indicated that sick days averaged between 11 and 15 days each year.

Recently, several states and cities have considered legislation requiring employers to provide paid sick leave to their employees. For example, beginning in 2012, the state of Connecticut now requires employers to provide at least five sick days per year. This Connecticut law also prohibits retaliation against employees who request or use sick leave.

Paid vacation days are not a required benefit in the United States, although according to one survey (SHRM 2013), 93% of organizations provide some form of paid vacation days to their full-time employees. The benefit to the organization is that employees can take the time off work to refresh and renew and step back from workplace stresses. Generally, vacation days can be accumulated, although there is often a limit on the number of vacation days allowed to carry over, as well as limitations on the number of vacation days employees can take at a given time.

Some organizations pool together vacation and sick leave into "paid time off" or PTO accounts. In these instances, employees accrue a certain amount of days or hours per month and then are allowed discretion over how to use that time. According to a recent study, 52% of organizations use PTO plans, up from 29% in 2004 (SHRM 2013).

According to a recent study conducted by the Society for Human Resource Management, most organizations (97%) provide paid holidays to their full-time employees (SHRM 2013). These employees receive an average of nine paid holidays each year. A recent trend is for organizations to provide a certain number of standard paid holidays plus some additional floating holidays each year. In this way, employees can take time off for holidays significant to them, while still providing workplace coverage for the other holidays.

Applicable Legislation

Family and Medical Leave Act of 1993 (FMLA) was created to provide opportunities for employees to better balance their work and family life. FMLA allows 12 weeks of unpaid leave in any 12-month period for care of self or dependent (child, parent, spouse, or guardian) with a serious health condition or for the birth, adoption, or placement of a child within the first 12 months after the child's birth (U.S. Department of Labor 2012b). In a June 22, 2010, news release, the Department of Labor clarified that FMLA could be applied to employees who care for children for whom the employee stand *in loco parentis*, regardless of the legal or biological relationship (U.S. Department of Labor 2010). In addition, employees can use FMLA to care for an individual who stood *in loco parentis* for them as a child.

FMLA applies to private sector organizations with 50 or more employees and to all public sector agencies. For employees to be eligible for FMLA, they must have been employed for at least one year and have actually worked at least 1,250 hours during the past 12 months (U.S. Department of Labor 2012b).

The National Defense Authorization Act of 2008 was the first expansion of FMLA. Under this Act, employees can take up to 12 weeks per year due to a spouse, child, or parent being on active duty. This allows the employee to take care of the home and family responsibilities normally covered by the family member now on active duty. In addition, employees can take up to 26 weeks of unpaid leave to act as a caregiver for a family member injured as a result of military service (U.S. Department of Labor 2013).

LIFE INSURANCE

Life insurance is an important benefit for employees and employers alike. Approximately 86% of organizations offer some kind of life insurance to their employees (SHRM 2013). However, for state and local governments with more than 100 employees, 82% offer life insurance compared with 77% of private firms with more than 100 employees (Bureau of Labor Statistics 2012). Premiums for basic life insurance coverage are usually paid by the employer; additional coverage is generally offered to employees (supplemental life insurance); however, the employee must pay the cost of the supplemental insurance. Because of the general coverage, about 97% of eligible employees receive life insurance benefits (Bureau of Labor Statistics 2012). Supplemental life insurance allows employees the opportunity to expand their coverage at a lower rate than they might find in their own personal life insurance policy. Organizations can take advantage of the market economies of scale by essentially "buying in bulk," making life insurance one of the most cost-effective benefits for organizations to offer. Recent studies suggest that younger employees (Prudential Insurance 2010) and women (Miller 2008) are less likely to have adequate life insurance plans in place and are less likely to purchase supplemental life insurance policies.

OTHER BENEFITS
Education Benefits

According to an IPMA-HR 2007 survey, approximately 89% of respondents reported that they offer tuition assistance. However, by 2012, this had dropped to 62% of respondents. Even for those programs not eliminated, many decreased the amount of benefits offered to employees (IPMA-HR 2011). The most common amount of assistance is between $1,000 and $2,000 per year. In most cases (85%), employees must provide proof of completion with an adequate performance to receive the tuition reimbursement; this is usually demonstrated by receiving a grade at or above the established minimum (IPMA-HR 2007).

Flexible Spending Accounts

Flexible spending accounts are available for employees to set aside pre-tax dollars for the use of medical and dental care accounts or child care. The money is established as a "trust fund" to be used throughout the year. Any unspent funds are returned to the plan at the end of the designated time period. Recent data suggest that 72% of organizations offer medical FSAs, and 71% offer dependent care FSAs for their employees (SHRM 2013).

Employee Assistance Programs (EAPs)

Many organizations (77% according to SHRM 2013) offer employee assistance programs (EAPs) to provide assistance for employees in resolving personal problems. EAPs found early success with alcohol treatment programs and smoking cessation programs. More recently, programs are offered in a wide variety of areas, for example, financial planning, legal assistance, family counseling, adoption assistance, child care assistance, and drug and alcohol treatment programs. Organizations can provide these programs in-house or they might outsource specialty services (Daniel 2012).

Wellness Programs

Recent research found that organizations have seen a decrease in health care costs due to the use of wellness programs (Miller 2012b). Nearly two-thirds of organizations offer wellness programs (SHRM 2013). However, for public organizations, just over 70% offer wellness programs (IPMA-HR 2011). These programs are instituted to promote healthy behaviors for employees. Some organizations provide on-site gyms, while others might subsidize gym memberships. According to one study,

73% of the organizations surveyed provided financial incentives to encourage employee participation in wellness programs (Miller 2012a). These incentives range from reductions in health insurance costs to bonuses for completing specific aspects of the wellness program (SHRM 2012a).

Child Care Assistance

Recent research from SHRM (2013) illustrates that organizations provide child care assistance in many forms, such as providing access to subsidized or non-subsidized child care (11%), allowing employees to bring children to work when they experience a child care emergency (26%), or providing referral information (12%). Kossek and Distelberg (2009) suggest other forms of child care assistance available in organizations are also available. One such program is the use of FSAs (flexible spending accounts), as mentioned above, to pay for child care costs using pre-tax dollars, thereby creating a cost savings for the employee. In addition, their research reported that 34% of the responding organizations provided some form of child care resources and referrals (Kossek and Distelberg 2009). One study looked at the incidence of "parenting in the workplace," meaning that employees bring their children with them to work and cared for them during the work day while also completing their work assignments (Secret 2005). The research suggests there are very few downsides to such an arrangement and some significant benefits.

What are the benefits of providing child care assistance? Research suggests that these benefits include decreased turnover (Baughman, DiNardi, and Holtz-Eakin 2003; S. Lee 2004), probably due to the low likelihood of finding another employer with similar benefits. In addition, there is some research suggesting increased job satisfaction as a result of child care assistance in the workplace (Barton 1992).

Elder Care Assistance

With an ever-increasing older population, more employees are called on to provide care for elderly parents and other relatives. This care generally takes the form of information about resources and referrals (Kossek and Distelberg 2009). Another way that organizations can assist is by providing time off (either paid or unpaid) to help employees care for elderly family members.

Recent research looked at the benefits of elder care assistance (Dembe et al. 2011). They surveyed individuals who had used employee sponsored elder care programs. The respondents reported that the use of such programs helped them continue to work productively, decrease absences from work, and maintain a more balanced home life (Dembe et al. 2011).

Alternative Work Arrangements

Working arrangements (the schedule and location where employees work) have received significant attention in the last several years. Employees often see alternative work arrangements as a benefit since it provides for more contiguous time off by allowing the employee to work outside of a traditional eight-hour-per-day, 40-hour-per-week schedule in the office. Alternative work arrangements come in many different formats such as the compressed work week, flextime, job sharing, and telecommuting. Each alternative work arrangement has its own advantages and disadvantages (see Arbon, Facer, and Wadsworth [2012] for a discussion on implementing compressed work schedules).

Compressed work weeks have employees working longer shifts for fewer days of the week. Extending work hours limits free time available on working days, but workers benefit by saving on time and travel, along with having extra time off during the traditional work week to accomplish nonwork tasks. There are three common forms of compressed workweeks: 4/10s (working 10-hour shifts for four days with three days off each week), 9/80 (a two-week schedule of eight 9-hour work days Monday through Thursday, one 8-hour Friday, and one Friday off every other week), and 3/36 (working 12-hour shifts for three days with four days off each week).

Flextime scheduling allows employees to start and finish work at times other than the traditional 8:00 am to 5:00 pm time period. Most flextime schedules have constraints on acceptable stop and start times. Additionally, most organizations using flextime require all employees to be at work for the core hours of the work day (e.g., the organization might require all employees to be working between 10:00 am and 2:00 pm). Flextime is typically offered as a work-life balance option, but it often helps save employees commute time and gas consumption.

Job sharing is an alternative that splits one job position between two or more workers. This is also often used as a work-life balance option for valued employees who prefer to change to part-time work. The trade-off in some organizations is reduced benefits (medical, vacation time, sick leave, 401k, etc.) for employees working fewer than 40 hours a week.

Telecommuting allows an employee to work from a remote location. This schedule gives workers autonomy to more efficiently balance their work and life priorities. In addition, the organization might realize cost savings as a result of lower overhead at the work site. There are some potential concerns about employee productivity and decreased sense of camaraderie at work because of decreased face-time with employer and coworkers.

CONCLUSION

There is a wide array of employee benefits available for organizations to consider; some of these are mandatory benefits, while others are optional. Previous research (Casper and Harris 2008; Muse and Wadsworth 2012) shows the importance of benefits in the employment relationship, suggesting that employees consider these benefits a "signal" of their value to their employer. Specifically, Dell (2010) reports that over 75% of employees list benefits as one of their top concerns when selecting an employer, and 30% of employees report that they have made a job-related decision based on the benefits package. Employees are asking and expecting to receive certain benefits from their employers (Cayer 2003), and that trend doesn't appear to be diminishing.

Add to that the changes that have and will occur as a result of the Patient Protection and Affordable Care Act of 2010, and organizations need to strategically consider the set of benefits they will provide for their employees while also considering the cost of those benefit programs for the organization. Coupling the recent fiscal challenges facing government and nonprofit organizations with the continuing escalation of healthcare benefits, organizations have sought to control costs. In some cases this has meant eliminating or suspending specific benefits. However, many organizations have sought other strategies to bring costs under control. Below we outline several strategies organizations are using.

Increasing Deductibles and Copayments

Employers can require employees to be responsible for a larger share of the insurance costs. This may occur in the payment of the premium or in the payment of the copay at the time of service. This strategy seeks to increase employees' awareness of the cost of the benefit, thereby encouraging them to use the benefit more wisely.

Focusing on Prevention and Wellness

As noted above, many organizations offer wellness plans. By offering benefits like on-site fitness centers or discounted gym memberships, free exercise classes, and health monitoring programs, employers hope to increase their employees' health and reduce their own health care costs. For example, employees of Maricopa County who do not use tobacco products receive an annual insurance-premium discount of $480 (M. Lee 2012).

Providing Financial Incentives

Many employers offer incentives for behaviors that directly improve health or help the employee better understand their current health status. This includes programs that provide a financial bonus to employees who complete health risk assessments and participate in wellness programs. Alternatively, some organizations give employees a fixed amount of money each year to spend on medical or health improvement–related expenses. Depending on the program, employees may be eligible to keep the unspent money at the end of the year as regular income.

Increasing Safety

Safe work environments reduce costs associated with injuries and associated issues. A common strategy is to establish an incentive for complying and creating safe work places. One area of savings as a result of these kinds of efforts is the decrease in workers' compensation costs. These incentives might be in the form of a reward to be split among all the employees for a specified number of days without an accident; the reward can be monetary or nonmonetary (e.g., food or a recreational activity). However, organizations need to be cautious that they don't encourage employees to not report workplace injuries simply to benefit from the reward.

Reviewing Benefit Package

Looking for cost savings provides organizations with a legitimate reason to review the benefit package available to employees. Benefits should be reviewed to identify those benefits that are not being utilized or which provide little value to employees. If organizations are paying for a benefit that no one is using or is of little value to the employees, they might be able to drop that benefit or switch it with another benefit that would be of more value to the employees, thereby getting more "bang for the buck."

While organizations need to carefully consider the benefits they provide to their employees, they would do well to recognize the value that these benefits can provide, both as a signal to their employees of their value and as a way to increase employee job satisfaction and organizational commitment (Breaugh and Frye 2007; Williams, Malos, and Palmer 2002).

REFERENCES

Arbon, Chyleen A., Rex L. Facer, and Lori L. Wadsworth. 2012. Compressed Workweeks: Strategies for Successful Implementation. *Public Personnel Management, 41*(3), 389–405.

Barton, Lawrence. 1992. Corporate Sponsored Child Care: A Benefit with High Satisfaction, Questionable Future. *International Journal of Manpower, 31*(1), 12–24.

Baughman, Reagan, Daniela DiNardi, and Douglas Holtz-Eakin. 2003. Productivity and Wage Effects of Family-Friendly Fringe Benefits. *International Journal of Manpower, 24*, 247–259.

Berger, Lance A., and Dorothy R. Berger. 2008. *The Compensation Handbook: A State-of-the-Art Guide to Compensation Strategy and Design*. New York: McGraw Hill.

Biggs, Andrew G., and Jason Richwine. 2011. *Comparing Federal and Private Sector Compensation. AEI Economic Policy.* Working Paper 2011-02, March 04, 2011. http://www.aei.org/files/2011/06/08/AEI-Working-Paper-on-Federal-Pay-May-2011.pdf. Accessed February 28, 2013.

———. 2012. The Truth about Federal Salary Numbers. *The Washington Post,* November 18. http://www.washingtonpost.com/opinions/the-truth-about-federal-salary-numbers/2012/11/18/08acd084-293e-11e2-bab2-eda299503684_story.html.

Breaugh, James A., and N. Kathleen Frye. 2007. An Examination of the Antecedents and Consequences of the Use of Family-Friendly Benefits. *Journal of Managerial Issues, 19*(1), 35–52.

Bureau of Labor Statistics. 2006. *National Compensation Survey: Employee Benefits in Private Industry in the United States, March 2006.* Washington, DC: U.S. Department of Labor. http://www.bls.gov/ncs/ebs/sp/ebsm0004.pdf. Accessed March 1, 2013.

———. 2012. National Compensation Survey: Employee Benefits in the United States, March 2012. Bulletin 2773. http://www.bls.gov/ncs/ebs/benefits/2012/.

California Department of Managed Health Care. 2012. PPO and POS Plans, State of California. http://www.dmhc.ca.gov/dmhc_consumer/hp/hp_ppos.aspx. Accessed February 25, 2013.

Casper, Wendy J., and Christopher M. Harris. 2008. Work-Life Benefits and Organizational Attachment: Self-interest Utility and Signaling Theory Models. *Journal of Vocational Behavior, 72*(1), 95–109.

Cauchon, Dennis. 2010a. Federal Pay Ahead of Private Industry. *USA Today,* April 8. http://usatoday30.usatoday.com/news/nation/2010-03-04-federal-pay_N.htm. Accessed February 28, 2013.

———. 2010b. Federal Workers Earning Double Their Private Counterparts. *USA Today,* August 13. http://usatoday30.usatoday.com/money/economy/income/2010-08-10-1Afedpay10_ST_N.htm. Accessed February 28, 2013.

———. 2011. Federal Workers Starting at Much Higher Pay Than in Past. www.usatoday.com, December 26. http://usatoday30.usatoday.com/news/washington/story/2011-12-26/federal-starting-salaries/52236360/1. Accessed February 28, 2013.

Cayer, N. Joseph. 2003. Public Employee Benefits and the Changing Nature of the Workforce. In Steven W. Hays and Richard C. Kearney (Eds.), *Public Personnel Administration: Problems and Prospects* (3rd ed.). Upper Saddle River, NJ: Prentice Hall, pp. 167–179.

Daniel, Teresa A. 2012. Managing Employee Assistance Programs. Society for Human Resource Management, October 3. http://www.shrm.org/TemplatesTools/Toolkits/Pages/ManagingEmployeeAssistancePrograms.aspx. Accessed February 12, 2013.

Davidson, Joe. 2010. Why Federal Workers Deserve What They're Paid. *Washington Post,* February 3. http://www.washingtonpost.com/wp-dyn/content/article/2010/02/02/AR2010020203722.html.

Dell, Torry. 2010. Making Benefits Matter. *Management Quarterly, 51*(2), 23–30.

Dembe, Allard E., Jamie S. Partridge, Elizabeth Dugan, and Diane S. Piktialis. 2011. Employees' satisfaction with employer-sponsored elder-care programs. *Journal of Workplace Health Management, 4*(3), 216–227.

Edwards, Chris. 2006. Federal Pay Outpaces Private-Sector Pay. *Tax & Budget Bulletin* (Cato Institute), May, No. 35.

HealthCare.gov. n.d. Health Maintenance Organizations. U.S. Department of Health and Human Services. http://www.healthcare.gov/glossary/h/healthmaintenanceorganization.html. Accessed February 21, 2013.

HealthCare.gov. n.d. Long-Term Care. U.S. Department of Health and Human Services. http://www.healthcare.gov/using-insurance/medicare-long-term-care/long-term-care/index.html. Accessed February 28, 2013.

HealthCare.gov. n.d. Medicare. U.S. Department of Health and Human Services. http://www.healthcare.gov/using-insurance/medicare-long-term-care/medicare/. Accessed February 28, 2013.

Internal Revenue Service (IRS). 2012. 2012 Instructions for Form 8889: Health Savings Accounts (HSAs). Department of the Treasury. http://www.irs.gov/pub/irs-pdf/i8889.pdf. Accessed February 21, 2013.

———. 2014. Questions and Answers on Employer Shared Responsibility Provisions Under the Affordable Care Act. http://www.irs.gov/Affordable-Care-Act/Employers/Questions-and-Answers-on-Employer-Shared-Responsibility-Provisions-Under-the-Affordable-Care-Act. Accessed December 15, 2014.

International Public Management Association for Human Resources (IPMA-HR). 2007. *Personnel Practices: Tuition Reimbursement Policies*. Alexandria, VA: IPMA-HR.

———. 2011. *Benefits in the New Economy: 2011 IPMA-HR Benchmarking Survey Report*. Alexandria, VA: IPMA-HR.

Katz, Eric. 2014. Federal Employees Really, Really Like Their Health Benefits. *Government Executive*, November 25. http://www.govexec.com/federal-news/fedblog/2014/11/federal-employees-really-really-their-health-benefits/99956/. Accessed December 15, 2014.

Kiplinger Washington Editors. 2010. Health Maintenance Organizations. June. http://www.kiplinger.com/article/insurance/T027-C000-S001-health-maintenance-organizations.html. Accessed February 21, 2013.

Korte, Gregory. 2014. For Christmas, Obama Gives Feds an Extra Day Off. *USA Today*, December 5. http://www.usatoday.com/story/news/politics/2014/12/05/obama-executive-order-christmas-holiday-december-26/19973733/.

Kossek, Ellen E., and Brian Distelberg. 2009. Work and Family Employment Policy for a Transformed Labor Force: Current Trends and Themes. In Ann C. Crouter and Alan Booth (Eds.), *Work-Life Policies*. Washington, DC: Urban Institute Press, pp. 3–49.

Lee, Michelle Ye Hee. 2012. Maricopa County Employees Who Fibbed about Smoking to See Hike in Premium. *The Republic*, April 5. http://www.azcentral.com/news/articles/20120402maricopa-county-workers-fibbed-smoking-premiums-hike.html. Accessed February 12, 2013.

Lee, Sunhwa. 2004. *Women's Work Supports, Job Retention and Job Mobility: Child Care and Employer Provided Health Insurance Help Women Stay on Jobs*. Washington, DC: Institute for Women's Policy Research.

Lussier, Robert N., and John Hendon. 2013. *Human Resource Management: Functions, Applications, Skill Development*. Los Angeles: Sage.

Miller, Stephen. 2008. Confronting the Gender Gap in Life Insurance Coverage. Society for Human Resource Management, September 15. http://www.shrm.org/hrdisciplines/benefits/articles/pages/gendergapinlifeinsurancecoverage.aspx. Accessed February 13, 2013.

———. 2012a. Companies Increase Wellness Incentive Dollars. Society for Human Resource Management, March 5. http://www.shrm.org/hrdisciplines/benefits/Articles/Pages/DollarValue.aspx. Accessed February 12, 2013.

———. 2012b. Study: Wellness Programs Saved $1 to $3 per Dollar Spent. Society for Human Resource Management, September 12. http://www.shrm.org/hrdisciplines/benefits/Articles/Pages/Wellness-Dollars-Saved.aspx. Accessed February 12, 2013.

Muse, Lori A., and Lori L. Wadsworth. 2012. An examination of traditional versus non-traditional benefits, *Journal of Managerial Psychology*, 27(2), 112–131.

Phillips, Jean M., and Stanley M. Gully. 2014. *Human Resource Management*. Mason, OH: South-Western Cengage Learning.

Prudential Insurance Research Report. 2010. *Reaching Gen Y—Easier Than You Think*. www.prudential.com, March. http://news.prudential.com/images/20026/GenYReportJune2010.pdf. Accessed February 13, 2013.

Secret, Mary. 2005. Parenting in the Workplace: Child Care Options for Consideration, *Journal of Applied Behavioral Science*, 41(3), 326–347.

Sherk, James. 2010. *Inflated Federal Pay: How Americans Are Overtaxed to Overpay the Civil Service*. Heritage Foundation Center for Data Analysis Report No. 10-05, July 7, 2010. http://www.heritage.org/research/reports/2010/07/inflated-federal-pay-how-americans-are-overtaxed-to-overpay-the-civil-service. Accessed February 28, 2013.

Social Security Administration (SSA). n.d. What Are the Trust Funds? http://www.ssa.gov/news/press/factsheets/WhatAreTheTrust.htm. Accessed December 15, 2014.

Society for Human Resource Management (SHRM). 2007. *Work/Life Balance Series Part I: Revisiting the Work/Life Balance Agenda*. Alexandria, VA: SHRM.

———. 2011. *2011 Employee Benefits: Examining Employee Benefits Amidst Uncertainty*. Alexandria, VA: SHRM.

———. 2012a. *2012 Employee Benefits: The Employee Benefits Landscape in a Recovering Economy*. Alexandria, VA: SHRM.

———. 2012b. Half of Biggest Employers Provide Long-Term Care Benefits. SHRM, March. http://www.shrm.org/hrdisciplines/benefits/Articles/Pages/LTC_update.aspx. Accessed February 28, 2013.

———. 2012c. Long Term Care: What Is Long-Term Care Insurance? SHRM, May. http://www.shrm.org/TemplatesTools/hrqa/Pages/Whatislong-termcareinsurance.aspx. Accessed February 28, 2013.

———. 2013. *2013 Employee Benefit Report*. Alexandria, VA: SHRM.

U.S. Department of Labor. 2010. US Department of Labor Clarifies FMLA Definition of 'Son and Daughter.' Release Number: 10-0877-NAT, U.S. Department of Labor, Wage and Hour Division, June 22.

U.S. Department of Labor. 2012a. An Employee's Guide to Health Benefits under COBRA. www.dol.gov/ebsa/publications/cobraemployee.html. Accessed February 14, 2013.

U.S. Department of Labor. 2012b. Need Time? The Employee's Guide to The Family and Medical Leave Act. U.S. Department of Labor, Wage and Hour Division.

U.S. Department of Labor. 2013. The Military Family Leave Provisions under the Family and Medical Leave Act, Fact Sheet #24M, February. U.S. Department of Labor, Wage and Hour Division.

Williams, Margaret L., Stanley B. Malos, and David K. Palmer. 2002. Benefit System and Benefit Level Satisfaction: An Expanded Model of Antecedents and Consequences, *Journal of Management*, 28(2), 195–215.

WorldatWork. 2007. *The WorldatWork Handbook of Compensation, Benefits and Total Rewards.* Hoboken, NJ: Wiley.

CHAPTER 13

POSTEMPLOYMENT BENEFITS: PENSIONS AND RETIREE HEALTH CARE

Thad Calabrese
New York University

Justin Marlowe
University of Washington

INTRODUCTION

The extension of average life expectancy is one of the great medical and economic success stories of the past century. With this success comes the need to arrange for financial security following one's working career. The two main components of that security are a pension—that is, a regular payment from an investment fund—and other postemployment benefits such as employer-subsidized health insurance and life insurance. In the public sector, these benefits are almost universally determined through contracts and negotiations with organized labor unions or the result of historical precedent that is difficult to alter except incrementally.

The objective of this chapter is to aid managers in understanding the various factors in determining retirement benefits, how those benefits are financed, how they affect government budgets, and how potential reform proposals are designed to alter future benefits. We believe this knowledge can help government HR managers better inform other policymakers' potential policy changes and how those changes might affect retiree benefits, employee morale, and HR strategy going forward.

We focus on retiree benefits for state governments, although local governments face many of the same basic challenges.

Human resource professionals should be aware of the importance of pensions and other fringe benefits to the total compensation package offered to public employees. Much of the existing empirical research analyzing the compensation of public employees compared with private employees finds that salaries and wages are in fact lower in the public sector.[1] The bulk of this same research also finds that these wage differentials largely disappear when total compensation—that is, when salaries and fringe benefits—between the sectors are compared. In other words, fringe benefits such as pensions and retiree health care effectively compensate public sector workers for lower average salaries. As such, changes to these existing fringe benefits may affect retention of current public workers, and future changes are almost certain to affect recruitment of public employees. These changes, then, are almost certain to influence public human resource management.

SCOPE OF THE ISSUE

According to the U.S. Census, nearly 20 million public employees belong to public pension systems. In 2010, pension systems covering state and local government employees held nearly $2.7 trillion in assets and paid out more than $200 billion in benefit payments to retirees. State-administered pension systems, however, reported nearly $3.3 trillion in total obligations that year, indicating a shortfall of more than $600 billion between assets needed to cover all promised benefits; this shortfall only refers to pension benefits and does not include other postemployment benefits (OPEB) such as retiree health insurance and life insurance.

From a budgetary perspective, public pension systems require significant public resources: in 2010, state and local governments made nearly $214 billion payments to pension systems; in 2001, these same governments had pension expenditures of $112 billion. In inflation-adjusted terms, pension spending by state and local governments has increased 57% in a single decade

Figure 13.1 Unfunded Pension and Other Postemployment Liabilities by State

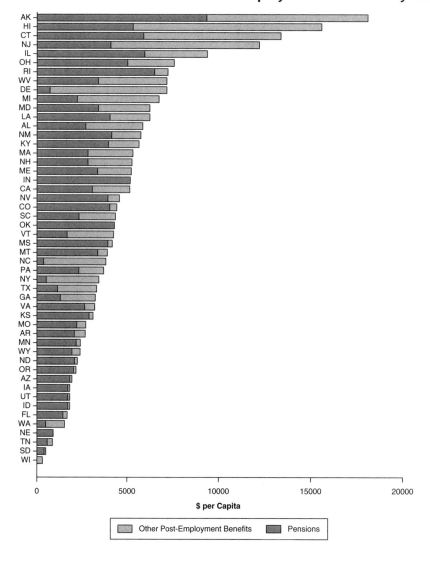

(Continued)

Figure 13.1 (Continued)

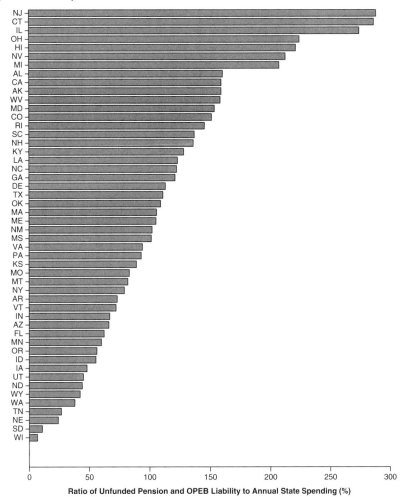

Ratio of Unfunded Pension and OPEB Liability to Annual State Spending (%)

Source: U.S. Census.

(Bureau of the Census 2011). Figure 13.1 shows the unfunded pension and retiree health care benefits for each state—individually and combined.

Figure 13.1, which is based on 2010 data, shows that unfunded retiree benefits vary widely across the states. Figure 13.1a shows the total per capita liability for each state, and how much of that liability is comprised of unfunded pension obligations and unfunded OPEB obligations. These total obligations range from $273/capita in Wisconsin to $18,089/capita in Alaska. Figure 13.1b shows each state's per capita accumulated unfunded liability as a percentage of per capita public total state expenditures. Those ratios range from 7% in Wisconsin

to 288% in New Jersey (Bureau of the Census 2010). Put differently, New Jersey's combined unfunded pension and OPEB liability is nearly three times its annual state spending. This figure suggests that some states would have little trouble in making their liabilities whole, while others would face significant stress.

Beyond just the sheer scope of public resources devoted to them, employee retirement benefits have consumed an increasing share of government operating budgets. Figure 13.2a shows the relative size of each state's pension and OPEB benefits in 2010. While the national average is below 7% for both combined, there is clear variation between the states. In some states annual spending on these benefits is less than 4% of total state spending. In others, retiree benefits consume more than 10% of state spending. As a point of comparison, not-for-profit organizations in 2010 devoted less than 2% of their total expenses to retirement benefits, which is significantly less than all states.[2]

One concern about benefit spending—especially among financial managers and budget decision makers—is that spending on these will crowd out current spending on other needed public goods and services. Figure 13.2a suggests that this concern is warranted in many states.

Some states choose to underfund their pension systems annually, and almost all do not pay the full annual costs of OPEB. This point is elaborated upon later in the chapter. Figure 13.2b shows the fraction of annual spending that would have to be devoted to retiree benefits in 2010 were the states to fully fund their annual

Figure 13.2 Current Annual Spending on Retiree Benefits by State

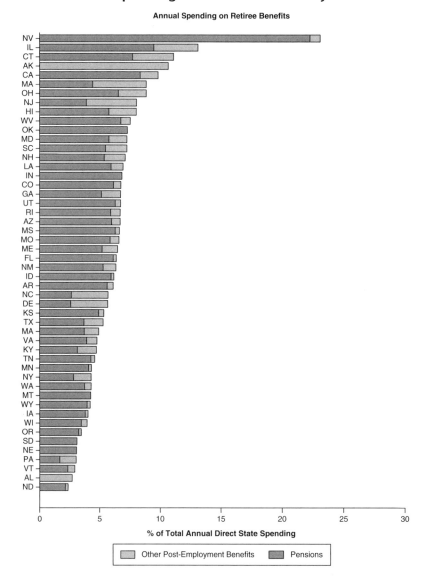

(Continued)

Figure 13.2 (Continued)

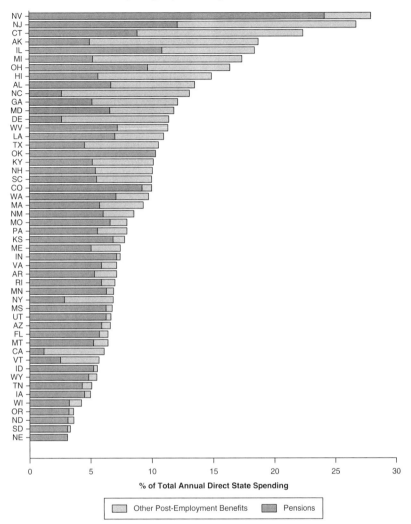

Annual Spending Required to Fully Fund Future Retiree Benefits

% of Total Annual Direct State Spending

Other Post-Employment Benefits   Pensions

Source: U.S. Census.

retiree benefit costs. Again, while there is great variation between the states, it is clear that a move toward fully funding retiree benefits would require states to increase annual spending out of operating budgets more than 3% on average. This may seem trivial, but consider that Figure 13.2a shows that the average state spends nearly 6.5% on retiree benefits currently; this average increase suggests that states would have to increase their funding of retiree benefits by over 50% from the current level to achieve full annual funding of these benefits. Given other

demands on public budgets, public officials are likely unwilling to devote the resources necessary to achieve full budget funding of retiree benefits. As these benefits continue to grow as a fraction of public spending, cities like Central Falls, Rhode Island, Vallejo, California, and Stockton, California—all of whom entered formal bankruptcy proceedings due in part to fiscal stress resulting from the financing of retiree benefits—serve as early warnings to public officials and managers of the potential dangers of maintaining the status quo.

TYPES OF RETIREMENT PLANS

Approximately 90% of all state and local employees have access to retirement benefits, and 95% of these workers actually participate in the benefit programs offered. By contrast, approximately 65% of all private employees have access to retirement benefits, and 75% of these workers participate in these systems (Bureau of Labor Statistics 2012). The importance of retirement benefits to budgetary and human resource matters should be evident to public managers, as they affect virtually all current and future employees.

Organizations that choose to offer retirement benefits have two primary options: defined contribution plans and defined benefit plans. Hybrid options that combine features of both these types of plans also exist but are not elaborated upon here. The defined contribution plan is the dominant type of plan offered by private companies, while public employers tend to offer defined benefit plans.

Defined Contribution Plans

Defined contribution plans offer participants accounts colloquially known as 401(k)s, named after the tax code subsection that established their tax-advantaged nature.[3] Defined contribution plan benefits are usually defined as a certain percentage of an employee's annual salary. For example, employers might contribute 5% of an employee's salary annually to the employee's 401(k) account. Importantly, individual employees typically own their 401(k)s and generally acquire the right to employer contributions to a retirement plan over a period of time—known as "vesting." Therefore, if an employee decides to change employers, any funds within the employee's 401(k) account remain with that employee—who may decide to either leave them in the former employer's defined contribution system or roll them over to another tax-advantaged retirement account.

When an individual retires, he or she may draw down funds from a defined contribution plan. However, if the retired employee outlives the account balance, the former employer will not supplement that individual's retirement income. As long as the employer made the required contributions to the employee's 401(k) account over time as promised, the employee's primary risk during retirement is that he or she will outlive the account balance. In a related vein, the employee's primary risk during his or her working career is that adequate funds are accumulated in the account and that the funds are invested in a manner that maximizes the individual's risk tolerance and expected investment returns.

Defined Benefit Plans

Defined benefit plans, on the other hand, are more complicated retirement vehicles. In a defined benefit plan, individuals do not have an individual account, do not own the funds accumulated in the pension fund, and do not guide pension investment decisions directly. Instead, all employer and employee contributions are deposited into the organization's pension fund for investing purposes. Benefits paid out to retirees also come from this combined fund.

One of the key considerations in a defined benefit plan is how long an employee must work to earn a pension. Most defined benefit plans set a minimum vesting time—typically five years of full-time service—before an employee has earned the right to draw benefits at retirement. Employees that switch employers and have not completed the minimum vesting requirement do not carry funds to the new employer; rather, any contributions made to the defined benefit pension fund—either by the employer or the employee—remain at the initial pension fund.

When an employee retires, benefits are typically guaranteed until the employee (and potentially dependents, such as a spouse) dies. Therefore, the risk of running out of retirement money—the primary risk facing a participant in a 401(k) retirement system—does not exist. If the pension fund were to exhaust all its resources, retirees would still be entitled to benefits earned during their working careers. The pension fund sponsor would be expected to provide additional funds to finance these benefits. This implicit guarantee is a main reason why private companies have moved away from defined benefit plans toward defined contribution plans. Approximately 83% of state and local government employees have access to a defined benefit pension plan, while in the private sector only 19% of employees have access to defined benefit plans.

An employee's defined benefit is usually calculated using three factors. First, benefits are based on an employee's final average salary (FAS), which is usually averaged over the final three to five years of the employee's working career. Second, the benefit is dependent upon the number of years of government employment. Third, the benefit is determined by the amount of benefit attributable to each year, also known as the "units of service." The units of service multiplied by the number of years of service is often referred to as the "replacement rate" because it represents how much preretirement income is replaced by the defined pension benefit.

To illustrate how employee benefits are calculated, suppose a worker is promised that each year of service will result in a pension benefit of 3% (the units of service), and she is expecting to work for 30 years total. According to the U.S. Census Bureau, the average state and local employee salary is approximately $51,000. Suppose the government expects employee salaries to increase 3% annually; this would indicate that the government could estimate this employee's final average salary of the last three years of her working career as approximately $120,220. Given this estimate, the worker's defined pension benefit annually would be $108,198 until the employee dies. The example should already reveal how dependent upon assumptions pension costs are. If, for example, salary growth were limited to 2% annually instead of 3%, the employee's estimated FAS would drop 25% to $90,580 and her annual benefits would also drop 25% to $81,522. On the other hand, if salary growth were 4% instead of 3%, the employee's estimated FAS would increase 32% to $159,133, resulting in an annual pension benefit of $143,220 until death.

A government's contribution to a defined benefit plan is usually based on an even more complex set of formulae requiring extensive assumptions based on statistical analysis performed by an actuary.[4] Governments do not know with certainty what the worker's FAS will be or the number of years she will ultimately work. Further, they do not know with certainty the longevity of the employee after she retires, nor do they know how much return these investments will earn in the future. All of these actuarial assumptions are forecast so that a required contribution to the pension system is determinable. The most important (and contentious) actuarial assumption is the assumed rate of return used to discount future benefits to present value liabilities. Beginning in 2015, government employers no longer use a simple assumed rate of return (averaging around 8% for most systems); rather, a new accounting rule change (Government Accounting Standards Board [GASB] Statement No. 68) requires pension systems to use a blended rate in which the funded portion of the liabilities is discounted by the assumed earnings on investments (as is currently done), but the unfunded portion is discounted by a significantly lower rate.

Once determined, a government's annual pension expenditure is generally composed of two parts. The first part is called the "normal cost" and refers to the cost incurred for the employee's current period of service. The second part is called the "supplemental cost" and refers to the portion of any unfunded accrued liability that the government chooses to pay over time. These supplemental costs can be from past failures to fully fund required pension costs or from actuarial assumptions being different from expectations. Importantly, past underfundings affect the current operating budget through this supplemental cost. Hence, the failure to adequately fund a pension system directly results in increased future public expenditures because future taxpayers by definition are financing this supplemental cost as a result of prior underfundings.

Risks of Pension Plans to Sponsoring Entity

The foregoing discussion should make a number of important aspects of organizational risk apparent. Most important, defined contribution plans minimize the sponsor's risk in providing open-ended retirement commitments to employees. Assuming that the sponsor makes the required contributions to individuals' accounts, it will not face future "catch-up" requirements—even if investment losses wipe out the retirement accounts of employees. As a result, what a sponsor owes to a retirement plan for budgeting purposes is absolutely certain and easy to forecast. For defined benefit plan sponsors, however, the exact opposite is the case. The sponsor must ensure that adequate funds exist to make benefit payments to retirees. This mean paying for the benefits earned not only in each year of an employee's working career but also during the employee's retirement. Therefore, if investment returns fail to meet expectations, or if demographic assumptions related to longevity during retirement, medical cost inflation, or other relevant factors vary from expectations, the sponsor is required to make up the difference. As a result, underfunding defined benefit systems frequently lead to increased expenditures financed through the operating budget to make up for these shortfalls.

Second, because defined contribution plans are generally funded as earned, the employee does not need to be concerned that the account balance will disappear if the employer ceases operations.[5] While such terminations are rare events in the public sector, governments seem to be facing long-term fiscal stress that may increase the probabilities that financing pension systems will remain an exceedingly difficult task for many sponsors. As such, while employees and beneficiaries participating in a defined benefit plan do not bear the investment risks of the pension plans—because benefits are guaranteed—they do bear the risk of a sponsor having a fiscal meltdown that makes it unable to finance the promised benefits.

A final risk bears stating as well. Nearly 25% of state and local employees are not covered by Social Security (Government Accountability Office 2005). When the 1935 Social Security Act became law, state and local employees were exempted because of concerns that the law effectively resulted in a federal tax imposed on other governments. The law has been amended over time to include an increasing amount of state and local employees, yet nearly 5 million workers remain outside the Social Security system—having their retirement benefits dependent upon defined benefit pension systems. For these employees, the risks of plan termination are obviously even greater as they do not have access to Social Security benefits.

PENSION FUND INSTITUTIONS

Having established that most public employees are covered by defined benefit pension plans, managers need to understand how these plans were established and function. Governments finance benefits and beneficiaries receive payments from a public employer retirement system (PERS), which is a fiduciary fund that is legally distinct from a sponsoring government—with its own board of directors or trustees. There are three distinct types of PERS.

The single employer PERS is the easiest to understand. In this case, a government has established a defined benefit pension plan as a separate trust distinct from routine operations of the sponsor. Only employees of the sponsor are eligible to participate in the PERS; benefits are financed through employee and employer contributions to the system. According to the Bureau of the Census (2011) there are more than 3,300 single employer PERS. Most are comprised of employees of individual cities or counties, and many are comprised of specialized employees within a city or county. For example, the City of El Paso, Texas, maintains two separate PERS: the El Paso Firemen & Policemen's Pension Fund for public safety workers, and the El Paso City Employees' Pension Fund for other city employees.

Because there are costs to administering a pension system as well as costs to investing assets to earn returns for paying benefits, some sponsors have opted to combine their pension systems into agent multiemployer systems to achieve cost savings. The idea behind the agent multiemployer PERS is that economies of scale can reduce the administrative and investment expenses incurred for plan sponsors by pooling together these tasks, leading to either increased resources for paying retirement benefits or lower pension expenditures for the plan sponsors. The agent multiemployer PERS keeps the asset and liability valuations of each sponsor separate;

in doing so, the PERS can determine the actuarially determined contributions for each participating sponsor.

Like the agent multiemployer PERS, a cost-sharing multiemployer PERS is a system with multiple plan sponsors. Whereas the agent multiemployer PERS maintains separate valuations and only provides shared administrative and investment services for sponsors, the cost-sharing multiemployer PERS has only one single actuarial valuation for those involved in the system. Because there is one common valuation, the cost-sharing multiemployer PERS determines a contribution rate required from participating sponsors, and the rate is the same for all employers. As an example, within one state, all local school districts might participate in one cost-sharing PERS that handles all the administrative and investment tasks for the districts; further, all districts face the same contribution rate because the assets and liabilities are valued as if all the school districts were actually one large statewide school district. The contribution required is usually expressed as a percentage of payroll.

The type of PERS matters because it dictates the budgetary discretion a manager has with respect to pension funding. Governments that participate in cost-sharing multi-employer PERS have little discretion in financing the full annual contribution to the PERS or in influencing actuarial recommendations. Typically, the PERS sends an annual bill to the government for the required contribution; failure to pay the bill results in penalties and interest—oftentimes at the assumed rate of investment return—making the government much more likely to pay the bill. Some states have systems in place in which state aid to local governments is actually diverted to the PERS if the local government fails to make the required contribution. Hence, managing a government involved in a cost-sharing multiemployer PERS results in having less budgetary discretion because the ability to defer pension expenditures is virtually nonexistent—especially for local governments involved in a state-run PERS (Fitch Ratings 2011). Governments in these cost-sharing PERS face tremendous pressure to finance the required contributions of the system.

On the other hand, a government with a single employer PERS has much wider latitude in its financing decision. A public manager in this case has increased budgetary discretion about whether the full bill is paid or not. Further, because the link between PERS and the government sponsor is more direct—because only one government is involved—the sponsor has more potential influence on what the actuary even recommends.

A manager of a government involved in an agent multiemployer PERS usually maintains a relatively high degree of budgetary flexibility; however, there may be increased pressure to fully fund an annual contribution. Due to the increased parties involved, an individual sponsor's ability to influence actuarial recommendations is potentially diminished in this case.

NOT JUST PENSIONS: OTHER POSTEMPLOYMENT EMPLOYEE BENEFITS

Up to this point, we have concentrated on employee defined pension benefits in our discussion. Most state and local governments also provide other postemployment employee benefits—referred to colloquially as OPEB—in the form of health care benefits, life insurance, long-term disability insurance, and other nonpension benefits.

Because some government employees—most notably public safety workers—are able to retire before they are eligible for federal Medicare health insurance benefits, many governments provide these retirees with either access to group health insurance plans—which are significantly cheaper than purchasing such plans as an individual—or actually pay for all or some of the health insurance premium of the retiree until he or she becomes eligible for Medicare. When these retirees do become Medicare eligible, some governments also reimburse retirees for their out-of-pocket Medicare Part B premiums.[6]

Although OPEB and pensions are conceptually similar, governments have financed them historically in very different ways. Public pensions—with some minor exceptions—have generally been prefunded during employees' working careers. That is, sponsors finance these benefits during employees' careers through annual contributions to a PERS. Certainly, some sponsors have done better or worse jobs than others, but prefunding pension benefits has generally been the accepted norm in how public pensions are financed. On the other hand, governments have financed OPEB almost exclusively on a pay-as-you-go basis. That is, governments have financed OPEB benefits only after an employee has retired, meaning these benefits for retirees are being made out of current budgetary resources exclusively.

In 2004, the GASB issued Statement No. 45—*Accounting and Financial Reporting by Employers for Postemployment Benefits Other than Pensions*—that required governments to begin reporting future OPEB expenses as employees earned them, and not simply what they were paying out annually for retirees. In effect, the GASB standard required governments to begin reporting OPEB more similarly to pensions.[7] As with pensions, OPEB expenses had to now be forecast using economic, actuarial, and demographic assumptions—including health care cost inflation assumptions, longevity after retirement, the timing of retirement prior to Medicare eligibility, and investment return assumptions, among others.

Like with defined benefit pensions, to calculate the actuarial present value of OPEB attributable to the current budget period—that is, the OPEB normal cost—a government had to have an actuarial cost method like its pension system. The unfunded liability for OPEB for prior years is amortized for up to 30 years.[8] Hence, most of the prior discussion about how pension benefits and normal costs are calculated is similar for a manager's understanding of OPEB. Importantly, the discount rate used for determining the actuarial present value of benefits is also a blended rate—with the funded portion using an assumed long-term rate of return and the unfunded portion using a more conservative (lower) rate. With recent changes in pension discount rates, these discount rate assumptions are more closely aligned than they were in the past.

Importantly, because OPEB is still essentially financed on a pay-as-you-go basis for most governments, the annual OPEB cost will usually include a normal cost for current employees and a significant supplemental cost for the accumulated unfunded liability for past employees who are currently retired. Further, because health care cost inflation is a key assumption of calculating the present value of OPEB, contemporary large increases in these costs above the normal rate of inflation obviously affect not just what governments pay for current employees' fringe benefits but also the value of OPEB benefits for current and future retirees.

REFORMING PENSIONS AND OPEB

In 2010 and 2011, 41 states implemented changes to employee retirement benefits, and nine states enacted some change during calendar year 2012 (National Conference of State Legislatures [NCSL] 2012). Many of these changes are designed to limit the share of annual budgets that pensions and OPEB will demand going forward. Managers who must propose or implement these changes need to have some understanding of what these alterations in benefits seek to accomplish. Here we do not discuss an exhaustive list of reform efforts; instead, we highlight how a manager's understanding of pension benefits and OPEB calculations from this chapter can be used to ascertain the outcome of some proposed change. Reform efforts generally seek to alter the funding of employee benefits, alter the calculation of employee benefits, or some combination of both.

Funding Changes

A common reform effort has sought to increase the amount of pension benefits and OPEB financed directly by employees rather than by the government sponsor. In 2010, 11 states implemented increased employee contributions for pensions, and 2011 saw 16 such enactments. In some cases, the increased employee contribution simply augments the current government contribution—resulting in increased funding to the pension system; in other cases, the government actually reduces its own contribution as a result of the employee increase. In both situations, the ultimate goal of this reform effort is to reduce the government sponsors' budgetary pressure to fund employee benefits; in the case where governments actually offset their own contributions, however, the budgetary effect is immediate. With respect to OPEB specifically, several states—including Connecticut, Michigan, and New Jersey, among others—now require employees to contribute a portion of their pay to cover retiree health care. A few governments have issued bonds to fund long-term pension and OPEB obligations. This strategy has had mixed results and in some cases has increased long-term pension obligations (Munnell et al. 2010).

Benefit Changes

Many governments have also increased the retirement age when an employee may draw full benefits. Between 2009 and 2011, governments increased the retirement age for state employees in 30 pension systems, teachers in 25 states, and public safety employees in 13 states (NCSL 2012). These changes provide budget relief over time because the jurisdiction supports the beneficiary through fewer years of retirement. That relief, however, is distant because most of these increases in retirement age requirements exempt current employees from the change, limiting the benefit change to future employees only.

One of the primary determinants of an employee's retirement benefits—and by extension, a government's expense—is the final average salary (FAS) calculation. Historically, the definition of "salary" has been generous and has included overtime and one-time bonuses. Therefore, in most situations, employees have an incentive to increase their salaries in the final years of employment through overtime—a practice known as "spiking." Significant overtime in the final years of employment can have significant long-term effects on benefits earned. As governments have increasingly sought ways to control growing pension costs, some pension plan sponsors have begun eliminating overtime in their calculations. Others have increased the number of years included in the FAS to include lower wage years in the calculation and to dissuade spiking.

Many governments provide cost of living adjustments (COLAs) for retirees. These COLAs are sometimes written into law, some are from contract negotiations with organized labor, and some require legislative action annually. COLAs can have significant implications for normal cost and reported liabilities and, as a result, for sponsor operating budgets. This is especially true if public officials grant COLAs when investment returns are strong, since this permanently increases costs even though the PERS may realize lower returns in the future.

Unlike many other benefit reforms, COLA reforms are relatively immediate. By limiting COLAs, sponsors limit unfunded liability growth and subsequent necessary increases in spending from current budgets. Limiting COLAs can take several forms. The most blunt is to simply not have any; for example, Florida state employees retirement system eliminated COLAs for employees between 2012 and 2016. Another option is to limit COLA increases to some predetermined level; for example, Rhode Island's state system now limits COLAs to the difference between a five-year smoothed investment return and 5.5%.

Other recent reform efforts have also sought to tweak the assumptions used in calculating benefits. For example, some pension systems have reduced the units of service. In doing so, each year of employment earns an employee a diminished level of retirement benefits—and reduces the amount the sponsor must finance through the normal cost. Others have implemented salary freezes—which also reduces the estimated value of the FAS. In both these examples, the potential savings to governments are relatively distant and may not be of much help in managing through short-term budgetary stress. Managers should be aware not only of how altering the assumptions used to determine benefits can produce budgetary savings but also when these savings are likely to appear.

Obviously, the most significant benefit change would be for a government to close a pension system and transition to a defined contribution plan. The transition from defined benefit to defined contribution plans—which occurred in the private sector several decades ago—has largely skipped the public sector. However, several governments—including the states of Michigan,

Texas, and Utah, among others—have implemented such a reform. Budgetary savings from these reforms are also mostly very distant, again because current retirees and employees are usually exempt from the transition. Therefore, moving to a defined contribution plan requires the plan sponsor to continue financing the annual required contributions of the existing defined benefit plan, which limits the immediate savings of these proposals. Because organized labor unions have vigorously fought this reform, public officials have rarely been willing to spend their political capital on an effort that yields minimal budgetary benefits in the short-term. However, the long-term budgetary savings and appeal should be clear to the manager. A defined contribution plan would eliminate pension underfundings by definition; without underfundings, current costs of pensions could not be shifted to future taxpayers. In addition, the risks of employee longevity and investment earnings would be shifted from the government to the employee.

PERS Changes

The preceding discussion assumes that governments can actually alter the benefits offered employees. This direct link between benefits and government might be accurate for single employer PERS, but it is not for multiemployer systems. Rather, in multiemployer systems, benefit changes might come from the PERS itself. For example, the California PERS—colloquially known as CalPERS—altered how it valued assets and liabilities in 2004 so that pension billings for member governments would be less volatile.

As another example, in 2012 the CalPERS board of directors reduced its assumed rate of return on investments from 7.75% to 7.5%. While this change may seem immaterial, the budgetary effect for plan sponsors is significant—this change by itself is expected to cost the state of California nearly $200 million more in pension contributions in 2013. This is a simple function of the time value calculations used in calculating pension benefits and required contributions: If these investment assumptions are reduced, pension plans are expected to earn less from investments and plan sponsors need

to fund the actuarial present value of employee benefits with increased current contributions instead. Given recent financial market returns, the pressure to reduce investment returns assumptions—which will have the effect of increasing reported liabilities and also increasing normal costs paid from current budgets—is unlikely to diminish.

CONCLUSION

Pensions and other postemployment benefits are two of the most crucial issues in contemporary public human resource management. How governments structure and fund these benefits matters a great deal to employee morale, to the tone of collective bargaining and labor relations, and to the heritage and culture of public sector employment. At the same time, as we have shown throughout this chapter, the traditional funding models for these benefits are not sustainable. As investment returns dwindle, health care cost inflation increases, and the pressure on annual budgets intensifies, governments have no choice but to rethink how to provide for the financial security of their retired employees. Human resource managers will need to carefully consider what these changes mean for recruitment, retention, and motivation of government workers in the future.

NOTES

1. See Chapter 6 in Munnell (2012) for a thorough review and analysis of the literatures on sector wage differentials and the role of fringe benefits in compensating employees for these differences.

2. Authors' calculation. Based on Form 990 information returns filed by 501(c)3 public charities with the Internal Revenue Service.

3. That is, subsection 401(k) established that employee contributions to these accounts would not be taxed until withdrawal, thereby lowering the annual amount of income taxes an individual owes to the federal government.

4. The illustration here assumes that governments fund their pension contributions in accordance with actuarial calculations. In reality, many governments follow statutory funding requirements that differ significantly from these actuarial calculations.

5. However, if the employee's retirement balance is invested largely in the employer's stocks or bonds—as is typical in many private firms—the value of the 401(k) plan will be largely wiped out by the sponsor's bankruptcy. This is not a necessary condition of defined contribution accounts, however, and reflects a suboptimal funding policy (from the employee's perspective) by private firms.

6. Medicare originally had two components—Part A for hospital insurance and Part B for medical insurance. Medicare Part B was structured so that beneficiaries would pay a monthly premium, similar to how active employees frequently finance their own health insurance. The monthly premium for Medicare Part B is approximately $100 per month.

7. Despite statements to the contrary by detractors, GASB Statement No. 45 does not require OPEB to be prefunded. Rather, it requires governments simply to report OPEB on an accrual basis rather than on a cash-funding basis.

8. The unfunded actuarial accrued liability for OPEB is reported on either the government-wide Statement of Net Position or in the notes, which uses full accrual financial accounting for reporting purposes. Importantly, this liability is not reported on the governmental funds Balance Sheet because it does not meet the definition of a liability using the modified accrual basis of financial reporting.

References

Bureau of the Census. 2010. *Census of Governments: State Government Finances*. Washington, DC: Bureau of the Census, 2010. http://www.census.gov/govs/state/historical_data_2010.html. Accessed October 18, 2012.

———. 2011. *Annual Survey of Public Pensions: State & Local Data*. Washington, DC: Bureau of the Census. http://www.census.gov/govs/retire/. Accessed October 18, 2012.

Bureau of Labor Statistics. 2012. *National Compensation Survey, Retirement Benefits: Access, Participation, and Take-Up Rates*. Washington, DC: Bureau of Labor Statistics. http://www.bls.gov/ncs/ebs/benefits/2012/benefits_retirement.htm. Accessed October 18, 2012.

Fitch Ratings. 2011. *Enhancing the Analysis of US State and Local Government Pension Obligations*. New York: Fitch Ratings. http://www.ncpers.org/Files/2011_enhancing_the_analysis_of_state_local_government_pension_obligations.pdf. Accessed October 18, 2012.

Government Accountability Office. 2005. *Social Security: Coverage of Public Employees and Implications for Reform*. Testimony before the Subcommittee on Social Security, Committee on Ways and Means, House of Representatives. Report GAO-05-786T. Washington, DC: Government Accountability Office. http://www.gao.gov/assets/120/111755.pdf. Accessed October 18, 2012.

Munnell, Alicia H. 2012. *State and Local Pensions: What Now?* Washington, DC: Brookings Institution Press.

Munnell, Alicia H., Thad Calabrese, Ashby Monk, and Jean-Pierre Aubry. 2010. Pension Obligation Bonds: Financial Crisis Exposes Risks. Issue Paper #9, January. Boston: Center for Retirement Research at Boston College. http://crr.bc.edu/wp-content/uploads/2010/01/SLP_9-508.pdf. Accessed October 18, 2012.

National Conference of State Legislatures. 2012. Pensions and Retirement State Legislation Database. Washington, DC: National Conference of State Legislatures. http://www.ncsl.org/issues-research/labor/pension-legislation-database.aspx. Accessed October 18, 2012.

CHAPTER 14

MOTIVATING PUBLIC SERVICE EMPLOYEES IN THE ERA OF THE "NEW NORMAL"

Gerald T. Gabris
Northern Illinois University

Trenton J. Davis
Georgia Southern University

INTRODUCTION

In 2008, when the authors wrote the previous edition of this chapter, the full impact of the recession on public service organizations was cloudy. At that time, the recession was parleyed as a nasty irritant likely to cycle into a robust economic recovery.

The unfortunate reality is that today's public service employee often serves as a convenient scapegoat for politicians and the news media alike when assigning blame for the high cost of government. This occurs even though the same politicians have often had a hand in perpetuating the wage and benefit systems they now deplore. For many years, for example, the Illinois state legislature routinely put off paying the state's share into its public employee pension system, resulting in Illinois having the worst funded state pension system in the country (Munnell 2012). To add fuel to the fire, politicians often allege that public sector unions have been overly influential in securing generous wage and benefit packages that are fiscally unsustainable. In 2012, Wisconsin, Indiana, and Michigan passed legislation severely restricting the scope of public employee collective bargaining rights. Thus, the Great Recession has given rise to draconian measures in how public organizations conduct their business.

PUBLIC SERVICE ORGANIZATION SURVIVAL TACTICS

Prior to the Great Recession, the public service was already adapting to changes in the role of government through increased privatization, public-private partnering, managed competition, strategic planning, and citizen engagement to name just a few (Denhardt and Denhardt 2011; Kettl 2005; Osborne and Gaebler 1992). To remain financially solvent, many have utilized one or more of the survival tactics shown in Table 14.1 (see Pagano, Hoene, and McFarland 2012: 7).

Many of these tactics have had severe consequences on employee motivation and morale. They have often been deployed in a blunt manner, where the value of minimizing pain has been overwhelmed by the need to just get it done. The use of these tactics has become so

Table 14.1 Public Service Organization Survival Tactics

1. Downsizing, reductions in force, layoffs.

2. Breaking collective bargaining agreements and contracts regarding pay raises.

3. Service reductions, fewer programs, closing facilities.

4. Pay and fringe benefit reductions, increasing employee contributions.

5. Elimination of employee training and development programs.

6. Emphasis on revenue enhancement, increased fees, and taxes.

7. Emphasis on alternative service delivery systems, off-loading services.

8. Greater emphasis on performance measurement and accountability.

pervasive that they constitute the core principles of the *new normal.*

While these tactics address short-term fiscal needs, they often generate long-term motivation problems. For example, acute downsizing has occurred in many public service organizations in order to balance their budgets. In the city of Elgin, Illinois, over 100 municipal workers lost their jobs during the period 2010–2012. Downsizing of this magnitude can create severe stress for the remaining employees, who are expected to absorb the work of their departed brethren. Early on in the recession, public employees were generally willing not just to accept added responsibilities but to operate in an environment in which no pay raises, reductions in fringe benefits, and the elimination of employee training and development initiatives were commonplace.

This brings us to the central focus of this chapter: We contend that how public organizations ultimately respond to this challenge will go a long way in determining how well they perform. A long-standing literature on public service motivation (PSM) argues that individuals who seek employment in and remain working for public service organizations are influenced by motive forces primarily grounded in public service work (Perry 1996, 2000; Perry and Wise 1990; Wright 2008). Yet much of PSM research is prerecession and was conducted prior to the widening of the political divide concerning the

role of government evident in the 2012 and early stages of the 2016 presidential races.

In the discussion to follow, we begin by considering several theories of motivation that may shed light on how public service organizations can motivate their workers in the face of these challenges. We then examine how the new normal might stimulate innovative strategies for using motivation models to benefit both the organization and the individual.

THEORIES OF MOTIVATION: RELEVANCE TO THE PUBLIC SERVICE

We define motivation as the drive individuals experience to satisfy perceived need deficiencies. When watching a television commercial for a juicy hamburger or refreshing soft drink, you may experience a pang of hunger or thirst. This is exactly what product providers hope for—that these nascent needs will lead you to purchase their products. If a need becomes intense enough, you will become restless until it is satisfied. This is a powerful idea because it shows how human behavior can be influenced in a manner preferred by management. By designing effective motivation strategies it becomes possible to tap into the motive forces driving employee behavior and have them achieve important organizational goals while also satisfying employees' personal needs. While some people choose work in the public service to satisfy their public service motivation needs, PSM theory does not provide clear guidance on how this can be practically applied on a large scale. Consequently, we need to consider the broader spectrum of motivation theories that might lead to practical strategies for moving employees toward the efficient completion of organizational goals.

Content Theories of Motivation

Content theories of motivation attempt to explain *what* drives individuals to engage in goal directed behavior (Hellriegel, Slocum, and Woodman 1986). For example, money constitutes an extrinsic motivator because it can be easily converted into tangible, externally useful things that drive motivation, whereas self-esteem serves as an intrinsic motivator that can satisfy individual internal needs for self-meaning. One of the best-known content motivation theories is the "hierarchy of needs" model developed by Abraham Maslow (1943). Maslow argues that humans must first satisfy basic physiological needs, such as hunger and thirst, before moving on to more complex needs, such as esteem and self-actualization. These latter needs involve higher psychological states that are more intrinsic than extrinsic.

Clayton Alderfer (1972) simplifies the Maslow construct with his practical ERG model. ERG theory proposes three broad categories of existence, relatedness, and growth needs. When a person can no longer grow in his or her job, growth ceases to function as a motivator. Instead of becoming demotivated, such individuals regress to lower-order need states as their primary motive focal point. For example, maintenance workers in a municipal garage might be motivated by growth if they think they can get promoted into first-level supervisory positions. Yet, once this avenue for growth closes, the workers would likely refocus their need for strong interpersonal relationships (Lazear 1995; Lazear and Rosen 1981). The benefits of becoming a respected in-group member outweigh potential promotions.

Other notable content motivation theories include the motivation-hygiene theory of Frederick Herzberg (with Mausner and Snyderman 1959) and the achievement theory of David McClelland (1961). Herzberg argued that two distinct factors separate extrinsic and intrinsic motive forces and that only intrinsic factors truly motivate people. Workers expect *hygiene factors* such as pay, equipment, and working conditions to be adequate for carrying out their jobs. If these factors fall below expectations, they serve to dissatisfy workers; however, once improved, they do not serve as primary motivators. Alternatively, intrinsic motivators such as achievement, recognition, autonomy, the work itself, and responsibility appeal to one's higher psychological needs.

McClelland's (1961) achievement theory takes a different tack. McClelland's research, which is based on the Thematic Apperception Test (TAT), found that individuals vary in their need for achievement, affiliation, and power (Stahl 1983). Achievement motivation is perhaps most crucial for job performance. Achievers prefer to set their own goals and tend to avoid extremes by taking on difficult but achievable tasks. Additionally, achievers prefer tasks that provide more rather than less feedback (Hellriegel et al. 1986). These behaviors parallel the more sophisticated thinking associated with goal-setting theory (Locke and Latham 1984) and provide important insights into how techniques such as "management by objectives" may lead to motivation.

One remaining content theory that posits an interesting, albeit controversial, approach to human motivation is Edward Deci and Richard Ryan's cognitive evaluation theory (1985). According to Deci and Ryan (1985), intrinsic motivation is related to an individual's need for self-determination (choice) and competence. Self-determination is maximized when individuals can choose among courses of action free from external constraints and receive positive yet noncontrolling feedback. Deci and Ryan's contention that monetary incentives may actually inhibit intrinsic motivation when the incentive is withdrawn, more so than if the incentive had never been given in the first place, is well known (Locke and Latham 1990). When monetary awards are used to reward high-performing individuals, they may feel that their capacity to be self-determining has been reduced (by external conforming expectations) and their competency called into question due to the absence of other, intrinsic-based motivators that drive feelings of self-determination. Although Deci and Ryan's propositions regarding how rewards adversely affect individual job performance have not been empirically validated by others (Gerhart and Rynes 2003), their ideas raise questions about the efficacy of merit pay systems.

Process Theories of Motivation

A more sophisticated approach to motivation involves process theories. Theories falling into this category include expectancy theory (Lawler 1973; Vroom 1964), goal-setting theory (Locke and Latham 1984), and the public service motivation (PSM) construct (Perry and Wise 1990). Process motivation theories explore *how* different motivational forces (both extrinsic and intrinsic) interact in ways that motivate individuals.

Expectancy theory is based on three primary assumptions (Lawler 1973; Vroom 1964). First, individuals must believe that their behavior is related or will lead to certain outcomes (rewards). This is known as the performance-outcome expectancy. Second, individuals place different values on outcomes. Third, individuals change or alter their behavior based on the perceived probability of success. This is known as the effort-performance expectancy. For example, an employee seeking a raise (outcome) may alter her work ethic (behavior). However, if the employee does not believe that a raise is obtainable or the employee is simply not very motivated by monetary rewards, then she is likely to remain unmotivated. Thus, the expectancy process would entail altering both the way an individual's performance is measured as well as the reward system itself. Such changes help ensure organizational members place an appropriate value on any rewards they receive and that the link between performance and outcomes is clearly defined (Burke 2002).

Locke and Latham (1990: 4) suggest, "Goal setting theory assumes that human action is directed by conscious goals and intentions [. . .] but does not assume that all human action is under direct conscious control." Goal-setting theory makes several important assumptions regarding how goals motivate people. First, goals should be difficult but achievable. If a goal is perceived

as too difficult, achieving it may be attributed more to luck than skill. Similarly, if a goal is seen as too easy, then skill is still not a factor. It is when goals balance skill with extraordinary effort that they convey a sense of genuine achievement. Second, goals should be proximate rather than distal. Individuals must perceive that by exerting effort a goal can be achieved quickly rather than 10 years later. Third, specific goals are more motivational than broad, abstract goals (Locke and Latham 1990).

A fourth and more controversial component of goal-setting theory involves the notion of participation. Some research supports the proposition that employee participation in goal setting helps motivate workers to exert more effort (Earley 1985; Erez 1986; Erez and Kanfer 1983; Latham and Saari 1979; Likert 1967). Goals are more likely to be accepted when not imposed by an external authority. Yet research by Latham and others indicates there is little difference in goal performance between assigned versus participative goals (Carroll and Tosi 1970; Dossett, Latham, and Mitchell 1979; Latham, Mitchell, and Dosset 1978; Latham and Yukl 1975). Goal-setting theory opens the door to many practical applications for public sector managers, which will be touched upon during our discussion of motivation strategies that follows.

In 1990, James Perry and Lois Wise coined the phrase "public service motivation" (PSM), defining PSM as "an individual's predisposition to respond to motives grounded primarily or uniquely in public institutions or organizations" (1990: 368). According to Perry and Wise, there are three motives primarily associated with an individual's decision to enter into public service: rational, normative, or affective. PSM theory has been sharpened over time by refining the conceptual components in Perry and Wise's study.

The key to formalizing a theory of PSM derives substantially from one's sociohistorical context or what Perry (2000: 480) calls *antecedents*. Here, an individual's family, schooling, religion, and professional training all combine to influence broader institutions. These institutions reinforce our quickening self-concept and provide a set of self-regulatory processes. It is our self-concept that strongly influences our individual behavior regarding what kinds of careers we choose, what kinds of rules we follow, and what kinds of obligations and commitments we have toward our vocations.[1]

There has been a substantial volume of research devoted to understanding PSM's derivations and what role it may play within public organizations. The empirical research focusing on public service motivation has been generally supportive; PSM appears to have at least prima facie value for helping us understand why some individuals are attracted to public service. A summary of the key themes drawn from this research is provided below.

In a study of federal employees using a large sample, Naff and Crum (1999) found evidence to support the proposition that public employees with high levels of PSM reported receiving higher performance ratings than their counterparts with lower PSM levels. Kim (2005) also found that PSM positively influenced organizational performance, confirming the findings of both Naff and Crum (1999) and Brewer and Selden (2000). However, when taking person-organization fit into account, Bright (2007) did not find a significant impact on employee performance. Bright (2007) argued that while PSM may, in fact, influence the performance of public employees to a degree, these influences are mediated by an employee's compatibility or fit with his or her organization. Camilleri (2009) noted, however, that the model fit depicting this argument is weak.

In another study of federal employees, Brewer and Selden (1998) found a linkage between whistle-blowing behavior and PSM scores. They averred that whistle-blowers behave in ways consistent with PSM theory and, therefore, are motivated strongly by the public interest, are high performers, and exhibit high job satisfaction (Brewer and Selden 1998). Bright (2005) examined attributes consistent with high PSM scores as well as how those attributes might influence other administrative issues, such as organizational role, rank, education, and monetary incentives. Bright (2005) found higher PSM scores to be associated with higher levels of education and gender, but not significantly associated with age or minority status. Importantly, he found that higher PSM scores were related to managerial status.

Using data drawn from the National Administrative Studies Project (NASP-II), Scott and Pandey (2005) examined whether PSM scores are associated with attitudes toward red tape. In general, they found PSM scores and perceptions of red tape to be negatively correlated. Scott and Pandey (2005) asserted that individuals with higher PSM scores are more likely to see rules as legitimate, rather than an impediment to their job. Another possibility, however, is that individuals scoring high on the PSM scale are likely to be higher-ranking managers (Bright 2005) and thus may simply be better situated to evade or game red tape obstacles in ways that lower-level employees are not.

Similar to Perry (2000), Moynihan and Pandey (2007) provide yet another glimpse on how organizational variables may associate with and influence PSM. They suggest that sociohistorical experiences, such as education, professional group membership, and group culture, influence a person's attitude toward public service motivation. Specifically, Moynihan and Pandey (2007) hypothesize that highly educated individuals who join professional management associations are more likely to develop self-concepts that embrace values consistent with PSM.

APPLIED MOTIVATION STRATEGIES FOR THE NEW NORMAL

To focus attention, this section will highlight motivation strategies intended to address the survival tactics employed by public organizations in response to the Great Recession (see Table 14.1). The motivation strategies that may offset the demotivational consequences of specific new normal survival tactics are summarized in Table 14.2.

It should be noted that these strategies derive largely from mainstream theories of motivation. While most of these strategies are not new, they have also never been subjected to widespread practice in the public sector. Given the lasting impact of the Great Recession, we contend that the timing for their broader application is

Table 14.2 Applied Strategies for Motivating Employees in the New Normal

Motivation Strategy	Survival Tactic							
	1	2	3	4	5	6	7	8
External equity	✓		✓	✓				
Job redesign	✓		✓			✓		✓
Semi-autonomous work teams	✓		✓			✓	✓	
Skill-based pay	✓	✓	✓	✓	✓			✓
Gainsharing	✓	✓	✓			✓	✓	✓
Nonmonetary incentives	✓	✓	✓	✓	✓	✓	✓	✓
Defined pension systems	✓							

ripe. With thoughtful and well-designed deployment, they can target anticipated negative consequences on employee morale associated with new normal survival tactics. However, before tackling the reasons why these strategies make sense for today's public service, we will first address two motivational techniques that may no longer be efficacious.

Merit pay as a strategy for motivating individual performance has become very difficult to implement effectively given current scarce resources. While many politicians espouse merit pay as a panacea for public service problems, few public service organizations have the resource capacity to meaningfully fund a merit pay initiative. Merit pay has never been easy to implement even during the best of times (Bowman 1994; Gabris and Mitchell 1986; Heneman 1992; Perry 1992; Thayer 1978), and in the present economic climate its chances for success are dismal. Second, in 2008, we made the case that public organizations might benefit from using an *efficiency wage* to motivate employees (Davis and Gabris 2008; Gerhart and Rynes 2003). An efficiency wage compensates employees with above average market rates, for the purpose of recruiting and retaining a better workforce. A broad literature (Yellen 1984; Gerhart and Rynes 2003) on efficiency wage models provides support for its effectiveness, and other research suggests it positively

associates with municipal service performance (Davis and Gabris 2008). Nonetheless, current economic conditions are too politically fragile for recommending the efficiency wage as a motivational tool for today's public service organizations.

External Pay Equity: Salary Does Matter

Near the heart of the current debate over the role of government is the question of what constitutes fair pay for public service employees. Wallace and Fay (1988) make the case that one of the most important beliefs an organization can inculcate in its workforce is that workers are receiving a fair wage in exchange for their labor, or *external equity*. When we provide our labor to produce a product for an organization we expect a fair return on investment (Becker 1975). While pay may not be the primary reason many individuals choose public service careers (Moynihan and Pandy 2007; Perry, Mesch, and Paarlberg 2006; Perry and Wise 1990), to assume that money plays no strategic role in influencing this choice would be folly (Lawler 1983). This issue is exacerbated by new normal assertions that public sector employees are often overpaid in relation to their private sector peers.

Therefore, public service organizations today, more than ever, may need to use monetary compensation as an extrinsic motivator for acknowledging the real value of their employees. This may also counteract the demotivational side effects connected with downsizing, increased workloads, and greater scrutiny of performance. So how can public service use external pay equity as a motivational strategy?

A postrecession belief avers that public employees are overpaid in relation to private sector workers. The latter may no longer have defined pensions, may lack health insurance, and may receive lower pay than prior to the recession. Thus, since private sector workers have taken so many hits, some politicians and the media claim that public sector employees also need to *sacrifice* by giving back what many perceive as overly generous pay and benefits that are not financially sustainable. Research exists that both confirms and denies their claims (Baker 2012; GAO 2012; Schumpeter 2011; Traub 2012). As a general principle we argue that public and private sector jobs, while similar in specific job content and requirement characteristics (Bemis, Belenky, and Soder 1983), derive from *qualitatively distinct labor markets*, where comparing the compensation patterns between the sectors does not address the practical compensation needs that public service organizations must answer. In other words, public and private sector wage markets are contextually separate because they operate on different assumptions.

Public service organizations need to attract qualified workers who can staff public service jobs at high proficiency levels over the course of a long career. Comparatively, private sector jobs involve more frequent turnover, where employees leave for better paying jobs as markets and the demand for labor shift. Public organizations hire employees for the long haul. This means that public service workers primarily receive internal pay raises that slowly increment their salaries upward over time. In good economic times, the odds are high that private sector workers can make substantially more income in contrast to public service employees, whose salary stability may look more attractive during economic downturns. Thus, private sector markets display much greater elasticity of demand (Wallace and Fay 1988) than the public sector equivalent.

Another feature distinguishing public sector jobs is that they have become more demanding since the recession. Hence, the market for establishing pay schedules adequate for meeting the external equity expectations of both current and future public employees is, by necessity, *similar public service organizations*, as these organizations are competing for the same talent pool (Thurow 1975; Lazear and Rosen 1981). To motivate candidates to apply for job openings, and to retain its trained workforce, public organizations must design entry-level and retention salaries on what the market will bear. The only efficient and effective way for public organizations to do this is by defining their market as comprising the comparable public service organizations competing for the same candidates. Consequently, the public sector must use wage markets that satisfy the compensation needs they require, rather than market models that appease a shorter-term political agenda.

Building on this argument, we contend that public service organizations need to emphasize the external market competitiveness of their starting salaries in order to attract qualified job applicants (Gerhart and Rynes 2003). Due to scarce financial resources, public organizations are unlikely to have sizeable pools of discretionary income available to fund viable merit pay programs. Thus, initial starting salaries should be more important because there will likely be fewer opportunities to increase pay once a person has been hired.

Job Redesign

Through downsizing and reductions in force, public service organizations now expect remaining employees to absorb many of the duties performed by departed coworkers. If this were only a short-term trend the great majority of public employees would pick up any slack without complaint. However, this rapid expansion of job duties in many public service jobs has long-term implications. Generally, public organizations want their employees to perform this new work as though nothing really has changed. So how might public managers use job redesign to acknowledge this increased workload and to further motivate the remaining lean workforce?

Hackman and Oldham (1980) argue that job motivation largely hinges on appealing to an employee's *intrinsic psychological needs* and that money is not a huge part of this equation. They further contend that three psychological states—meaningfulness of work, experienced responsibility, and knowledge of results—serve as moderators that can result in higher internal or intrinsic job satisfaction, while also addressing an employee's need for growth. To assess attitudes toward job satisfaction, Hackman and Oldham (1980) devised the job diagnostic survey (JDS), which measures such key job characteristics as skill variety, task identity, task significance, autonomy, and feedback, as well as growth need and various work context factors such as salary. When employees score their jobs on these indices, a measure called the motivational potential score (MPS) results. High MPS scores are interpreted as conveying high levels of job satisfaction.

The motivational opportunities for using job redesign are plentiful. First, employees want recognition for assuming new task responsibilities associated with leaner, smaller workforces. Employees will also likely want more autonomy coupled with better-developed feedback mechanisms associated with end users, supervisors, and the work itself. Thus, instead of acting as though nothing has changed, public organizations should take advantage of the current need to expand workloads as a means for increasing the motivational potential of the job itself. The initial cost to perform such job upgrades would be minimal. Public service organizations will likely need to increase the autonomy and range of discretion granted to their employees, if employees are to perceive their expanded roles as an authentic opportunity for growth. Public organizations that maintain very tight control over employees may result in employees' perceiving themselves as less in control of their jobs and becoming more disillusioned or burned out (Golembiewski, Munzenrider, and Stevenson 1986).

Semiautonomous Work Teams

Another challenge facing public service organizations in the new normal involves the silo mentality connected with the traditional bureaucratic model (Golembiewski 1977, 1995). Bureaucratic structure lends itself to dysfunctional processes and degenerative interpersonal relations patterns (Blake and Mouton 1984; Golembiewski 1985, 1995; Hammer and Champy 1993; Nadler and Tushman 1988). To improve workflow, however, employees doing different specialized jobs might serve on cross-functional teams that facilitate interunit collaboration necessary for solving problems. As public service organizations have downsized, the probability increases that specialized units have found themselves short-handed and unable to effectively accomplish their goals and missions. As bureaucratic units become leaner, they should utilize semiautonomous work teams more frequently as a tool for accomplishing unit goals.

Semiautonomous teams enable lean organizations to address intraunit goals and issues that transcend specialized unit boundaries. Semiautonomous work teams overcome this dilemma by providing the diverse expertise necessary for effectively dealing with both cross-disciplinary and intraunit goals and problems (Hackman and Oldham 1980; Lawler 1984, 1992). Participation on such teams can provide another valuable source of intrinsic motivation (Dyer 1987; Golembiewski and Kiepper 1988; Lawler 1992). Team-based structures downplay positional power and emphasize group problem solving where all members have a voice in decisional outcomes. Effective teams are characterized by high interpersonal trust, open and frequent communications, loyalty to the group cause, a sense of contributing to a larger purpose, an acceptance of common goals, and an expectation of high standards, all within a mutually supportive atmosphere (Blake and Mouton 1984; Golembiewski 1985; LaFasto and Larson 2001; Zacarro, Rittman, and Marks 2001).

Skill-Based Pay

As we have already suggested, competitive external market salaries may prove critical for generating external pay equity that is necessary for recruiting and retaining a quality public service workforce. But this may not be enough. As many public service organizations continue to struggle with funding a meaningful merit pay pool, they need more creative options for rewarding *individual* employee achievement. Skill-based pay represents one solution to this puzzle.

Skill-based pay is a compensation technique garnering renewed interest in the public sector as motivating tool (Gupta 1997; Gupta et al. 1992; Lawler 1994; Murray and Gerhart 1998; Thompson and Lehew 2000). Whereas most job-based pay derives from the compensatory value that a competitive market places on the job itself, skill-based pay rewards employees for acquiring new skills that provide value added after a person has been working in a job for a period of time. Skill-based pay addresses internal and individual pay equity needs by rewarding workers whose job performance adds value to the work organization (Wallace and Fay 1988). A maintenance worker, for instance, requires a basic set of job-related knowledge and skill to effectively carry out the requirements of the job. As work complexity increases, the mastery of new, more advanced competencies may be required. As the maintenance worker expands his skill set, he becomes more valuable to the organization. For most public organizations, recognizing skill-based pay requires a demonstration of advanced competencies with corresponding pay increments.[2]

Skill-based pay dovetails nicely with Herzberg's (1966) job enlargement strategy and Hackman and Oldham's (1980) concept of skill variety, where the responsibilities of an employee are expanded and rewarded in a way that leverages both intrinsic and extrinsic motivation. Edward Lawler (1983) makes a similar case regarding how pay can be used to motivate. Skill-based pay recognizes the expanded job duties many public service employees are experiencing due to downsizing. As public employees are increasingly expected to take on new tasks, to learn new skills, and to work in a leaner, less costly workforce, then it stands to reason they should be compensated for developing the requisite skill sets necessary for performing these expanded jobs. Skill-based pay can be precisely targeted, and once employees receive it, it does not require time-consuming annual performance evaluations. Moreover, it provides additional extrinsic monetary

motivation to offset increases in work-related stress that employees are experiencing from their expanded workloads. Finally, skill-based pay may be politically tenable because public workforces are providing more output with fewer employees.

Gainsharing

One technique showing promise as a motivational tool for intact work groups is gainsharing (Graham-Moore and Ross 1995; Hatcher and Ross 1991). Gainsharing can be defined as a monetary reward program connected with "collective" or intact work group performance. Assume that a forestry division within a city public works department has a budget of $10,000 for planting trees along city parkways. Through careful purchasing coupled with an improved planting technique, the forestry division completes this task by spending only $7,500—resulting in a $2,500 savings. Gainsharing would involve a formula for rewarding the efficiency of the work group by sharing a portion of the savings with them. In this way, the organization benefits by spending less to accomplish its stated goals, and individuals benefit by being rewarded for team efficiency and innovation. While gainsharing offers intriguing motivational possibilities, few public sector organizations utilize this technique (Graham-Moore and Ross 1995). Nevertheless, as public service organizations become more market driven, the use of gainsharing models may acquire more popularity for this sector over time.

By financially rewarding work group efficiency, gainsharing would appear to complement new normal expectations for public service organizations. Units that save money and reduce costs should be rewarded, thus incentivizing them to continue searching for cost containment strategies. A potential drawback is that political officials might attribute any cost savings to fat in the budget rather than to employee innovation.

Nonmonetary Incentives (NMIs)

For public service organizations facing the austerity of the new normal, nonmonetary incentives (NMIs) may offer an untapped source of motivational opportunity

(Allen and Helms 2002; Balantine et al. 2012; Gabris 2011; Gabris and Giles 1983). Before developing a non-monetary incentive process, we first need to clarify what the term means. The all-purpose *extrinsic* incentive is *money*. Money incentivizes behavior and, due to its efficiency, it can be converted into anything else of value. An NMI, therefore, provides something of value that appeals to both the extrinsic and intrinsic motive needs of a worker—extra time off for high performance could be an NMI under this definition.

Most public service organizations already utilize various NMIs to motivate their workers on an informal, ad hoc basis; however, few have developed formal, systemic NMI inventories for motivating their workforces in a consistent, predictable manner. One possible exception is the U.S. Department of Agriculture's Farm Service Agency (USDA 2012). Since not all employees are motivated by the same NMIs, a public service organization would need to construct an NMI inventory that would appeal to a large segment of its workforce.[3]

NMIs do have real dollar costs; they are not free and should not be conceived as a wholesale replacement for monetary rewards. What they provide is a lower-cost, partial supplement to organizational incentives when monetary incentives are fiscally tight. However, since most NMIs involve indirect costs and are flexible, they are easier to absorb on a tight budget. Additionally, part of the value of an NMI is the intrinsic and not just extrinsic value associated with it. Rewarding high performers with a cafeteria-style selection of NMIs is a type of formal recognition. It addresses the psychological need for recognition and also satisfies needs associated with individual equity. Still, comparably NMIs are relatively inexpensive. Paying for advanced training, awarding extra time off, or providing an employee with a flexible work schedule involve indirect costs that can be spread out over time and cost less than direct monetary rewards. In fact, NMI costs may not even appear in formal budgets because they are fungible.

Once sustainable funding for NMIs has been identified, public service organizations can use them as a formal tool for motivating employees. By having a menu of NMIs to choose from, employees can select the NMI that best satisfies an extrinsic need or has intrinsic personal value. NMIs should be based on merit and have enough consistency so that employees know they can rely on them if they meet performance expectations (Lawler 1973, 1990).

Defined Pension Benefits

While the new normal questions whether public organizations can afford existing defined pension benefits, we argue for the retention of defined pensions on the grounds that they play an integral role in recruiting, retaining, and motivating public service employees. Next to competitive salaries, defined pension benefits serve as a powerful extrinsic incentive that also conveys intrinsic appreciation for the work public service employees provide.[4]

With the exception of the recent recession, the rule of thumb has been that private sector jobs pay better than government or nonprofit sector work. It was largely accepted that individuals who pursued careers in teaching, municipal government, state service, nonprofits, or federal agencies would earn less money. The expectation was that public service employees would contribute to their pension systems (augmented by employer contributions) and, upon retirement, the defined payout would ensure a livable wage for the remainder of the retiree's life. For many public service employees, these pensions are their sole source of retirement income because they receive no Social Security. The fact that public service organizations have historically provided secure retirement is a major reason why many individuals choose to enter and remain in public service careers.

Beginning in the 1990s, many private sector firms began eliminating defined pension plans by switching over to defined contribution systems in the form of 401(k)s. By 2000, 66% of private sector pensions were in 401(k) plans, and only 10% remained in defined pension systems (*The Week* 2012). Essentially, the private sector has stopped providing retirement benefits for most of its workforce, and attention has now turned to whether the public service should do the same. To retain a corps of highly trained public service employees, who are doing more for less, without the promise of a decent retirement, is a recipe for disaster.

A pension guarantee is the incentive public sector employees rely on most when economic times get tough. It serves as the foundation stone around which other incentives are built. Without decent pensions, public sector work becomes less attractive because one could work in the private sector, earn more money over a career, and have a much heftier 401(k) to retire on.

RISING TO THE CHALLENGE: THE NEW PUBLIC SERVICE MOTIVATION

A central theme permeating this chapter suggests the role of government in providing public services is profoundly changing. No longer is government seen through the lens of interest group liberalism, as defined by Theodore Lowi (1969: 51). "It is liberalism because it is optimistic about government, expects to use government in a positive and expansive role, is motivated by the highest sentiments, and possesses a strong faith that what is good for government is good for society."

That view of government started to change substantially when Ronald Reagan began articulating a substantially diminished role for government in his first inaugural address in 1981 when he claimed, "Government is not the solution to our problem, government is the problem." This movement to deconstruct the administrative state became a focal point during the 1990s through the application of business practices and efforts to privatize and outsource government operations to the private sector. This eclectic cocktail of business techniques is called the new public management (NPM) (Boston et al. 1996; DiIulio 1994; Kaboolian 1998; Osborne and Gaebler 1992). A core NPM principle avers that the more we expose government to market competition, performance expectations, and market incentives, the more efficiently it will respond to market and customer demands. This trend of transferring government service functions to the private sector has been sharply accelerated by the Great Recession. Public organizations have adapted to these revenue losses by deploying the survival tactics we have labeled the new normal.

The puzzle facing today's public service organizations concerns how public sector employees can remain highly motivated given the paradigmatic shift in the core values of public administration. If PSM diminishes as a motive force driving individuals to enter or remain in the public service for primarily intrinsic reasons, the new normal may further necessitate reliance on extrinsic motivation strategies to secure the same ends. Table 14.3 summarizes a number of key trends associated with the new normal.

Table 14.3 Key Trends Associated with the New Normal

1. Individuals seeking public service careers today are motivated essentially by the same motive forces as their predecessors. PSM reflects a type of public philosophy embracing a positive, active role for government.

2. Public service organizations will continue to downsize when economic austerity demands. This will result in very lean government organizations.

3. Future government organizations will provide fewer direct services through in-house operations and instead rely much more on purchase of service contracts with private or nonprofit providers. Public managers will essentially become contract monitors rather than overseers of direct services through established governmental operations.

4. Even though the motive forces individuals experience for pursuing and continuing in public service careers today are similar to the prerecessionary era, the capacity of public service organizations to satisfy these motives while also utilizing to new normal survival tactics, may result in a disconnect between expectations and reality. Thus, public service organizations need to rely more on secondary, extrinsic motive forces to motivate their workforces.

Table 14.4 PSM Motivational Philosophies

1. PSM involves a helping attitude, a sense of compassion and self-sacrifice.

2. PSM flourishes in active-positive government/public service institutions.

3. PSM achieves fruition through some form of meaningful public service work or activity.

The dominant paradigm of public administration up until the mid-1990s emphasized the role of government as an active, positive force for addressing and resolving complex social problems. H. George Frederickson (2010) even makes the case that *social equity* is the third pillar of public administration. This meshes with Perry's contention (1996, 1997) that PSM consists of subscales: (1) attraction to public making, (2) commitment to the public interest/civic duty, (3) compassion, and (4) self-sacrifice. Moreover, PSM would appear to resonate well with the justice-as-fairness doctrine of John Rawls (1971) whose *difference principle* explains why the egalitarian distribution of public goods makes ethical sense. It would not be much of a stretch to suggest that the principles appearing in Table 14.4 underpin the motivation philosophy associated with conventional PSM theory (Perry and Vandenabeele 2008).

The difficult question becomes whether this kind of optimistic, positive, progovernment public philosophy that embraces social equity can realistically coexist with the survival tactics of the new normal and the shifting paradigm of public administration. This new paradigm appears to embrace a set of values that envision a more minimalist role for government in the provision and distribution of public goods and services. By adopting more business practices, and embracing market competition for the provision of services, public service organizations should become better at satisfying end user service needs at a lower cost. While not an explicit NPM principle, it would seem implicit that a smaller, leaner government that outsources most of its operations would have a lesser impact on social equity issues. This may help explain the rapid rise of the nonprofit sector as an alternative to government for addressing social equity issues.

In an email exchange with a Chicago area city manager on the topic of alternative service delivery, the manager related: "I am becoming more and more concerned that managers are really turning into maintainers, and losing the ability to connect with the new wave of elected officials." This manager is concerned that the new normal may be placing so much emphasis on alternative service delivery (ASD) that it is becoming more of a political ideology that elected officials see as an all-purpose panacea, rather than a carefully targeted strategy to use only where most appropriate. If taken to the extreme, reliance on ASD models could transform the traditional role of a public manager from an administrator responsible for the direct provision of public services delivered by a highly trained governmental workforce to that of a monitor of service contracts—where actual services are delivered by external providers.

Anecdotal evidence obtained from a conference on ASD found the elected official participants articulating a type of *new public service motivation* or NPSM that they would like their professional managers to espouse. The values associated with this NPSM are summarized in Table 14.5.

How might current and aspiring public service professionals, seeking to satisfy traditional PSM needs, adapt to the NPSM orientation? We believe that individuals entering or currently working in higher-level professional public service jobs will still find ample opportunities for satisfying traditional PSM drives. Yet, even at these higher professional levels, as public service organizations further utilize new normal survival tactics and techniques, employees may become gradually less motivated by the PSM drives that initially attracted them to the public service. Consequently, public service organizations will need to develop, and make available, *secondary motivation strategies* (or a Plan B, if you will) that rely more on extrinsic motivators for recruiting and retaining the best and the brightest. These secondary

Table 14.5 Values Associated with NPSM

1. Preference for minimalist, low-tax, lean government.

2. Belief in private sector efficiency and market competition as a core value.

3. Preference for distributive over redistributive (social equity) services.

4. Strong customer service satisfaction orientation.

5. Strong preference for public service choice.

6. Belief that in controlling government, one can limit unnecessary growth.

7. Preference for outsourcing governmental services whenever feasible.

motivation strategies will depend more on extrinsic motivators such as compensation based incentives and fringe benefits to offset the intrinsic motivation losses by diminishing PSM values. Over time, traditional PSM and NPSM may converge into an even newer synthesis regarding how public service motivates individuals. This futuristic PSM will likely incorporate motive forces that reflect an increasingly fuzzy public-private interface, where the primary strategies for motivating public sector employees will become eerily similar to those found in the private sector, and public service motivation becomes a secondary (intrinsic) motivational strategy.

NOTES

1. Consider the following situation: A student in the final stages of her undergraduate degree may rationally determine that securing a full-time job is the next logical step toward financial security. This individual strongly believes that nonprofit programs offer a great opportunity for helping people and for doing the normatively "right thing." So, our nascent public servant applies for a job with a human services agency. In this instance, the perceived need to help others may be influenced by her *antecedent* experiences that infuse her with a core set of values that she accepts as her own and also serve to define her "self-concept." The longer she works in the nonprofit sector, the more she identifies with its values and preferences. These are learned preferences that she internalizes and uses to define herself as a member of the nonprofit community. Ultimately, PSM is the result of a complex series of processes that

begin influencing an individual in childhood and continue throughout adult life.

2. For example, advancement from a clerical I (entry level position) to a clerical II job reflects this kind of increased competency. By allowing employees to grow horizontally in this manner, rewarded by corresponding increments in pay, public organizations can continue motivating employees without having to rely on infrequent vertical promotions or logistically complicated merit pay.

3. There are a number of nonmonetary incentives that may have broad appeal, including (1) extra time off, (2) flexible working hours, (3) advanced training programs, (4) educational tuition grants, and (5) special parking privileges, just to name a few.

4. While we realize that pension systems need reform to ensure long-term financial viability, an analysis of such reform is beyond the scope of this chapter. Our goal is to briefly explain why defined pension benefits remain so crucial for motivating today's public workforce.

REFERENCES

Alderfer, C. 1972. *Existence, Relatedness, and Growth: Human Needs in Organizational Settings*. New York: Free Press.
Baker, D. 2012. Everyone Agrees That the Decline in Private Sector Pay Has Been Understated. Huffington Post. http://www.huffingtonpost.com/dean-baker/everyone-agrees-that-the_b_1471489.html. Ballantine, A., N. McKenzie, A. Wysocki, and K. Kepner. 2012. The Role of Monetary and Non-Monetary Incentives in the Workplace as Influenced by Career Stage. University of Florida Extension Publication. http://edis.if.ufl.edu/pdffiles/HR/HR016.pdf.

Becker, G. 1975. *Human Capital: A Theoretical and Empirical analysis, with Special Reference to Education* (2nd ed.). Chicago: University of Chicago Press.

Bemis, S., A. Belenky, and D. Soder. 1983. *Job Analysis: An Effective Management Tool*. Washington, DC: Bureau of National Affairs.

Blake, R., and J. Mouton. 1984. *Solving Costly Organizational Conflicts*. San Francisco: Jossey-Bass.

Boston, J., J. Martin, J. Pallot, and P. Walsh. 1996. *Public Management: The New Zealand Model*. New York: Oxford University Press.

Bowman. J. 1994. At last, an Alternative to Performance Appraisal: Total Quality Management. *Public Administration Review, 54*, 129–136.

Brewer, G. A., and S. C. Selden. 1998. Whistle Blowers in the Federal Civil Service: New Evidence of the Public Service Ethic. *Journal of Public Administration Research and Theory, 8*, 413–439.

———. 2000. Why Elephants Gallop: Assessing and Predicting Organizational Performance in Federal Agencies. *Journal of Public Administration Research and Theory, 10*(4), 685–711.

Bright, L. 2005. Public Employees with High Levels of Public Service Motivation: Who Are They, Where Are They, and What Do They Want? *Review of Public Personnel Administration, 25*(2), 138–154.

———. 2007. Does Person-Organization Fit Mediate the Relationship between Public Service Motivation and the Job Performance of Public Employees? *Review of Public Personnel Administration, 27*(4), 361–379.

Burke, W. W. 2002. *Organizational Change: Theory and Practice*. Thousand Oaks, CA: Sage.

Camilleri, E. 2009. The Relationships between Personal Attributes, Organization Politics, Public Service Motivation and Public Employee Performance. *International Public Service Motivation Conference*. June, Bloomington, Indiana.

Carroll, S. J., and H. L. Tosi. 1970. Goal Characteristics and Personality Factors in a Management by Objectives Program. *Administrative Science Quarterly, 15*, 295–305.

Davis, T. J., and G. T. Gabris. 2008. Strategic Compensation: Utilizing Efficiency Wages in the Public Sector to Achieve Desirable Organizational Outcomes. *Review of Public Personnel Administration, 28*(4), 327–348.

Deci, E. L., and R. M. Ryan. 1985. *Intrinsic Motivation and Self-Determination in Human Behavior*. New York: Plenum Press.

Denhardt, J. V., and R. B. Denhardt. 2011. *The New Public Service* (3rd ed.). Armonk, NY: M.E. Sharpe.

DiIulio. J. (Ed.). 1994. *Deregulating the Public Service*. Washington, DC: Brookings.

Dossett, D. L., G. P. Latham, and T. R. Mitchell. 1979. Effects of Assigned vs. Participatively Set Goals, Knowledge of Results, and Individual Differences in Employee Behavior When Goal Difficulty Is Held Constant. *Journal of Applied Psychology, 64*, 291–298.

Dyer, W. G. 1987. *Team Building: Issues and Alternatives*. Reading, MA: Addison-Wesley.

Earley, P. C. 1985. *The Influence of Goal Setting Methods on Performance, Goal Acceptance, Self-Efficacy Expectations, and Expectancies Across Levels of Goal Difficulty*. Paper Presented at the American Psychological Association Meeting. August, Los Angeles, California.

Erez, M. 1986. The Congruence of Goal Setting Strategies with Socio-Cultural Values, and Its Effect on Performance. *Journal of Management, 12*, 585–592.

Erez, M., and F. H. Kanfer. 1983. The Role of Goal Acceptance in Goal Setting and Task Performance. *Academy of Management Review, 8*, 454–463.

Frederickson, H. G. 2010. *Social Equity and Public Administration*. Armonk, NY: M.E. Sharpe.

Gabris, G. T. 2011. What Alternatives Are Available When Downsizing Is No Longer an Option? Paper presented at the International City and County Managers Association Conference. September, Milwaukee, Wisconsin.

Gabris, G. T., and W. Giles. 1983. Improving Productivity and Performance Appraisal Through the Use of Non Economic Incentives. *Public Productivity Review, 7*(2), 173–191.

Gabris, G. T., and K. Mitchell. 1986. Personnel Reforms and Formal Group Participation Structure: The Case of the Biloxi Merit Councils. *Review of Public Personnel Administration, 6*(3), 94–115.

———. 1988. The Impact of Merit Raise Scores on Employee Attitudes: The Matthew Effect of Performance Appraisal. *Public Personnel Management, 17*(4), 369–387.

GAO. 2012. *Federal Workers: Results of Studies on Federal Pay Varied Due to Differing Methodologies*. GAO Report 12-564. Washington, DC: GAO.

Gerhart, B., and S. L. Rynes. 2003. *Compensation: Theory, Evidence, and Strategic Implications*. Thousand Oaks, CA: Sage.

Golembiewski, R. T. 1977. *Public Administration as a Developing Discipline: Volume I*. New York: Marcel-Dekker.

———. 1985. *Humanizing Public Organizations*. Mt. Airy, MD: Lomond Publishers.

———. 1995. *Practical Public Management*. New York: Marcel Dekker.

Golembiewski, R. T., and A. Kiepper. 1988. *High Performance and Human Costs*. New York: Praeger.

Golembiewski, R.T., R. F. Munzenrider, and J. G. Stevenson. 1986. *Stress in Organizations*. New York: Praeger.

Graham-Moore, B. E., and R. A. Ross. 1995. *Gainsharing and Employee Involvement*. Washington, DC: Bureau of National Affairs.

Gupta, N. 1997. Rewarding Skills and Competencies in the Public Sector. In H. Risher and C. Fay (Eds.), *Rewarding Public Employees: A Handbook for Rethinking Government Pay Programs*. San Francisco: Jossey-Bass, pp. 125–144.

Gupta, N., G. E. Ledford, G. D. Jenkins, and D. H. Doty. 1992. Survey-Based Prescriptions for Skill-Based Pay. *ACA Journal, 1*(1), 48–59.

Hackman, J. R., and G. R. Oldham. 1980. *Work Redesign*. Reading, MA: Addison-Wesley.

Hammer, M., and J. Champy. 1993. *Reengineering the Corporation*. New York: Harper/Business.

Hatcher, L., and T. L. Ross. 1991. From Individual Incentives to an Organization-Wide Gainsharing Plan: Effects on Teamwork and Product Quality. *Journal of Organizational Behavior, 12*, 169–183.

Hellriegel, D., J. W. Slocum, and R. W. Woodman. 1986. *Organizational Behavior*. New York: West.

Henneman, R. L. 1992. *Merit Pay: Linking Pay Increases to Performance Ratings*. Reading, MA: Addison-Wesley.

Herzberg, F. 1966. *Work and the Nature of Man*. Cleveland, OH: World Press.

Herzberg, F., B. Mausner, and B. Snyderman. 1959. *The Motivation to Work*. New York: Wiley.

Kaboolian, L. 1998. The New Public Management. *Public Administration Review, 58*(3), 189–193.

Kettl, D. F. 2005. *The Global Public Management Revolution*. Washington, DC: Brookings.

Kim, S. 2005. Individual-level Factors and Organizational Performance in Government Organizations. *Journal of Public Administration Research and Theory, 15*(2), 245–261.

LaFasto, M. J., and C. E. Larson. 2001. *When Teams Work Best: 6000 Team Leaders Tell What It Takes to Succeed*. Thousand Oaks, CA: Sage.

Latham, G. P., and L. M. Saari, 1979. The Effects of Holding Goal Difficulty Constant on Assigned and Participatively Set Goals. *Academy of Management Journal, 22*, 163–168.

Latham, G. P., T. R. Mitchell, and D. L. Dossett. 1978. Importance of Participative Goal Setting and Anticipated Rewards on Goal Difficulty and Job Performance. *Journal of Applied Psychology, 63*, 163–171.

Latham, G. P., and G. A. Yukl. 1975. Assigned Versus Participative Goal-Setting with Educated and Uneducated Woods Workers. *Journal of Applied Psychology, 60*, 299–302.

Lawler, E. E. 1973. *Motivation in Work Organizations*. Monterey, CA: Brooks-Cole.

———. 1983. *Pay and Organization Development*. Reading, MA: Addison-Wesley.

———. 1984. *High Involvement Management*. San Francisco: Jossey-Bass.

———. 1990. *Strategic Pay: Aligning Organizational Strategies and Pay Systems*. San Francisco: Jossey-Bass.

———. 1992. *The Ultimate Advantage: Creating the High Involvement Organization*. San Francisco: Jossey-Bass.

———. 1994. From Job-Based to Competency-Based Organizations. *Journal of Organizational Behavior, 15*, 3–15.

Lazear, E. P. 1995. *Personnel Economics*. Cambridge, MA: MIT Press.

Lazear, E. P., and S. Rosen. 1981. Rank Order Tournaments as an Optimum Labor Contract. *Journal of Labor Economics, 89*, 841–864.

Likert, R. 1967. *The Human Organization*. New York: McGraw-Hill.

Locke, E. A., and G. P. Latham. 1984. *Goal Setting: A Motivational Technique That Works!* Englewood Cliffs, NJ: Prentice Hall.

———. 1990. *A Theory of Goal Setting and Task Performance*. Englewood Cliffs, NJ: Prentice-Hall.

Lowi, T. J. 1969. *The End of Liberalism*. New York: Norton.

Maslow, A. A. 1943. A Theory of Human Motivation. *Psychological Review, 80*, 370–396.

McClelland, D. 1961. *The Achieving Society*. Princeton, NJ: Van Nostrand-Reinhold.

Moynihan, D. P., and S. K. Pandey. 2007. The Role of Organizations in Fostering Public Service Motivation. *Public Administration Review, 67*(1), 40–53.

Munnell, A. 2012. *State and Local Pensions: What Now?* Washington, DC: Brookings.

Murray, B., and B. Gerhart. 1998. An Empirical Analysis of a Skill-Based Pay Program and Plant Performance Outcomes. *Academy of Management Journal, 41*(1), 68–78.

Nadler, D., and M. Tushman. 1988. *Strategic Organization Design*. Glenview, IL: Scott-Foresman.

Naff, K. C., and J. Crum. 1999. Working for America: Does Public Service Motivation Make a Difference? *Review of Public Personnel Administration, 14*(4), 5–16.

Osborne, D., and T. Gaebler. 1992. *Reinventing Government*. Reading, MA: Addison-Wesley.

Pagano, M. A.,C. W. Hoene, and C. McFarland. 2012. *City Fiscal Conditions: 2012*. National League of Cities Research Brief on America's Cities. Washington, DC: National League of Cities, 1–12.

Paul, W. J., K. B. Robertson, and F. Herzberg. 1969. Job Enrichment Pays Off. *Harvard Business Review*, March-April, 61–78.

Perry, J. L. 1992. The Merit Pay Reforms. In Patricia W. Ingraham and David H. Rosenbloom (Eds.), *The Promise and Paradox of Civil Service Reform*. Pittsburgh: University of Pittsburgh Press, pp. 199–215.

———. 1996. Measuring Public Service Motivation: An Assessment of Construct Reliability and Validity. *Journal of Public Administration Research and Theory, 6*(1), 5–22.

———. 1997. Antecedents of Public Service Motivation. *Journal of Public Administration Research and Theory, 7*(2), 181–197.

———. 2000. Bring Society In: Toward a Theory of Public-Service Motivation. *Journal of Public Administration Research and Theory, 10*(2), 471–488.

Perry, J. L., D. Mesch, and L. Paarlberg. 2006. Motivating Employees in a New Governance Era: The Performance Paradigm Revisited. *Public Administration Review, 66*(4), 89–122.

Perry, J. L., and L. R. Wise. 1990. The Motivational Bases of Public Service. *Public Administration Review, 50*(3), 367–373.

Perry, J. L., and W. Vandenabeele. 2008. Behavioral Dynamics: Institutions, Identities, and Self-Regulation. In J. Perry and A. Hondeghem (Eds.), *Motivation in Public Management: The Call for Public Service*. New York: Oxford University Press, pp. 56–79.

Rawls, J. 1971. *A Theory of Justice*. Cambridge, MA: Harvard University Press.

Schumpeter. 2011. Are Public-Sector Workers Overpaid or Underpaid? *The Economist*. http://www.economist.com/blogs/schumpeter/2011/02/government_employees.

Scott, P. G., and S. K. Pandey. 2005. Red Tape and Public Service Motivation: Findings from a National Survey of Managers in State Health and Human Services Agencies. *Review of Public Personnel Administration, 25*(2), 155–180.

Stahl, M. J. 1983. Achievement, Power, and Managerial Motivation: Selecting Managerial Talent with the Job Choice Exercise. *Personnel Psychology, 36*(4), 775–789.

Thayer, F. C. 1978. The President's Management Reforms: Theory X Triumphant. *Public Administration Review, 38*(4), 309–314.

The Week Staff. 2012. How 401(k)s Are Failing Millions of Americans. theweek.com, April 20. http://theweek.com/article/index/226886/how-401ks-are-failing-millions-of-americans.

Thompson, J. R., and C. W. Lehew. 2000. Skill-Based Pay as an Organizational Intervention. *Review of Public Personnel Administration, 20*(1), 20–40.

Thurow, L. 1975. *Generating Inequality*. New York: Basic Books.

Traub, A. 2012. "Coddled" Public Employees Make Less Than Private Sector. Huffington Post, June 30. http://www.huffingtonpost.com/amy-traub/coddled-public-employees_b_558381.html.

Trivett, V. 2011. Public Sector Layoffs Add to Unemployment Rolls. CUNYontheEconomy, March 12. http://bizeconreporting.journalism.cuny.edu/2011/03/12/public-sector-Labor.

USDA. 2012. FSA Non-Monetary Awards Program. *FFAS Human Resources*. http://www.fsa.usda.gov/FSA/hrdapp?area=home&subject=erpm&topic.

Vroom, V. 1964. *Work and Motivation*. New York: Wiley.

Wallace, M. J., and C. F. Fay. 1988. *Compensation Theory and Practice*. Boston: PWS-Kent.

Wright. B. 2008. Methodological Challenges Associated with Public Service Motivation Research. In J. Perry and A. Hondeghem (Eds.), *Motivation in Public Management*. New York: Oxford University Press, pp. 80–90.

Yellen, J. L. 1984. Efficiency Wage Models of Unemployment. *American Economic Review, 74*, 200–205.

Zaccaro, S., A. Rittman, and M. Marks. 2001. Team Leadership. *Leadership Quarterly, 12*, 451–483.

CHAPTER 15

EMOTIONAL LABOR: THE RELATIONAL SIDE OF PUBLIC SERVICE

Mary Ellen Guy
University of Colorado Denver

Meredith A. Newman
Florida International University

We have to develop these relationships . . . in order to get our clients to . . . tell us the deepest and darkest, . . . I mean we see a variety of clients . . . severely sexually abused . . . I also knew that there was some alleged accusation that the mother may have been poisoning the kids when they went for visits . . . you have to establish a rapport—a connection. (Guy, Newman, and Mastracci 2008: 157)

The above quote captures the *human* side of governance, at the point where citizens and the state interact face to face or voice to voice—in this case in a social service agency. How does this caseworker manage her own emotions while attempting to manage the emotions of her young client in order to elicit trust and honesty? What does it take to "develop these relationships," to "establish a rapport—a connection" and maintain a professional edge without losing her balance? How does she perform this heart-wrenching work day in and day out and avoid burning out? These questions drive our discussion of emotional labor: the relational side of public service. Moving away from

"business as usual" and toward a service-oriented, citizen-centered model of public service delivery requires *new* skills in the public sector workforce. We live in a service economy—service with a smile. The private sector has long recognized the value of "customer service"—or, in our terms, emotion work and emotional labor. Public administration is in the process of catching up, and so emotional labor is an emerging issue in theory and practice.

The chapter is organized as follows: We begin with a discussion of what emotional labor is, and then we examine its centrality to the delivery of public services and describe its performance. Next we examine the problems that are associated with the omission of emotion work from the human resource functions of job analysis, recruitment and selection, training and development, performance appraisal, and compensation. We conclude with the prospects for incorporating emotion work and emotive skills into the human resource processes of public service agencies. Vignettes illustrate our points and reinforce the central principle of the chapter—that emotional labor is *real* work and should be acknowledged in human resource functions.

EMOTIONAL LABOR DEFINED

Emotional labor is well known to those who perform it, even if the term itself may be unfamiliar. Public servants *do* this work, but it is often viewed as peripheral to the *real work* of the organization. Emotion work is not well understood in human resource management, yet we know that those who employ relationship skills are all too familiar with the effort, knowledge, and skill that it takes to do this kind of work well. Here we give words to this work, to give its performance a name and shape—and in the process, to expose the missing links in human resource policies and practices. As one service manager put it in 2012, "to think about how much of my work is emotional labour that I've tended to downplay and think of it as time taken away from 'my real job.' Now I want my line manager to acknowledge its importance and that it takes time to perform emotional labour." (personal communication, June 26, 2012).

We know what physical labor is: It is tangible, compensable, and amenable to measurement and training. Emotional labor is more nuanced. It is mostly visible in the breech. Consider the case of a prison guard who shows fear toward offenders, a social worker who is cold and uncaring with clients, or a 911 operator who loses control during "hot calls." These workers fail to deliver public services effectively, that is, with *feeling*. The successful performance of emotional labor remains, for the most part, invisible and uncompensated and it belies easy measurement.

Emotional labor refers to the management of one's own feelings as well as those of the other in order to get the job done; it is emotion management. Emotional labor is a component of the dynamic relationship between two people: worker and citizen or worker and worker. It is confused with emotional intelligence due to the similarity of the words, but the two differ considerably. *Emotional intelligence* is a term that denotes the individual's *capacity* to recognize the emotional state of self or other, much as cognitive intelligence measures the capacity to perform analytic and verbal tasks

(Goleman 2006; Guy and Lee in press; Newman, Guy, and Mastracci 2009; Wong and Law 2002). Emotional intelligence is necessary to perform emotional labor. The fundamental difference between the two constructs is that emotional intelligence is located in the person while emotional labor is located in the job (Mastracci, Guy, and Newman 2012). In short, emotional labor is the *application* of emotional intelligence on the job.

Any definition of emotional labor begins with the seminal work of sociologist Arlie Hochschild (1983). Hochschild uses the term to mean the management of feeling in order to create an observable facial and bodily display for the purpose of producing a particular state of mind in others; because it is sold for a wage, it has exchange value. It is more than a facet of personality; it is a gesture in a social exchange (Hochschild 1979). Subsequently, it has been defined in a number of ways: as an invisible yet expected component of job performance (Karabanow 2000; Steinberg and Figart 1999a, 1999b); as the act of complying with organizationally mandated display rules (Ashforth and Humphrey 1993; Humphrey 2000); as the effort, planning, and control needed to express organizationally desired emotion during interpersonal transactions (Domagalski 1999; Morris and Feldman 1997); as artful affect (Guy, Newman, and Mastracci 2008: 97); and as work that requires the engagement, suppression, or evocation of the worker's emotions in order to get the job done (Guy et al. 2010). It is *relational* work that elicits behaviors and feelings from clients and citizens, but it also requires workers to manage their own emotions. In other words, the worker must perform the work in order to complete the job; it is a type of labor (see Guy and Newman 2004), and it is an invisible but necessary element in person-to-person transactions (Mastracci, Guy, and Newman 2012).

Emotional labor is both similar to and different from physical and cognitive labor. Compared to physical labor, both require skill and experience and are subject to external controls. Compared to cognitive labor, both are required for successful job performance. The former includes the application of factual knowledge to the intellectual analysis of problems and decision making. The latter is behavior performed for a wage and includes analysis and decision making in terms of the expression of emotion, whether actually felt or not, as well as its opposite: the suppression of emotions that are felt but not expressed. Emotional labor is performed during communication between worker and citizen and it requires the rapid-fire execution of several skills:

- Emotive sensing, which means detecting the affective state of the other and using that information to array one's own alternatives in terms of how to respond.
- Analyzing one's own affective state and comparing it with that of the other.
- Judging how alternative responses will affect the other, then selecting the best alternative.
- Suppressing or expressing emotions in order to elicit a desired response from the other.

Exchanges between worker and citizen require the worker to sense the right tone and medium for expressing a point or feeling and then to determine whether, when, and how to act on that analysis. To ignore this combination of analysis, affect, judgment, and communication is to ignore the social lubrication that enables rapport, elicits trust, and ensures that interpersonal transactions are constructive.

Emotional labor has multiple facets, ranging from authentic expression of the worker's emotional state to requiring workers to don masks and display an emotion they do not actually feel. The goal is to affect how the citizen feels. Successful job performance depends on it. For example, law enforcement needs citizens to be deferential and to trust their authority. Social services need citizens to feel that there is a constructive way to deal with their problems. Emergency responders need citizens to trust their expertise and be confident of their actions. In these terms, the jobs of a social worker and correctional officer can be viewed as opposite poles. One employs a smile and requires its incumbents to be "nicer than natural." The other employs toughness and

requires "tougher than natural" behavior. Acting in a neutral manner also demands emotion work as workers suppress their true feelings in order not to under- or overreact and in order to present an air of fairness and lack of bias.

Performing emotional labor is both proactive and reactive. For example, to maintain order, prison guards must create an air of authority, even if they are fearful of hostile prisoners. Social workers and investigators must build trust so that children who have been victims of abuse will confide in them and tell their stories. Operators at 911 call centers must create a sense of calm in order to obtain the information that they need to help callers who are near hysteria.

Now that we have presented *what* emotional labor is, we turn next to its place in public service.

THE CENTRALITY OF EMOTIONAL LABOR IN EFFECTIVE PUBLIC SERVICE DELIVERY

Over many years, as automation of systems-based work has increased and there has been a growing trend to customer self-service, the work of our frontline staff has become less of the clerical and more of the personal. This has led to the constant engagement of many of our staff with customers who are vulnerable and often subject to some degree of stress, and indeed at times, abusive and violent. (service leader, Australian Government Department of Human Services, Canberra, personal communication August 9, 2012)

Why are emotion work skills and emotional labor necessary in the delivery of public services? From multiple perspectives—employee wellness, quality of work life, performance, citizen trust, service outcomes—HR systems should reflect the *actual* work performed, including both the technical *and* emotive aspects of public service. *Cool heads, warm hearts* is what we want when workers meet citizens. To achieve this combination requires not only cognitive labor but also emotional labor. Consider a citizen's response when a public employee seems cold and uncaring. Such a perception causes the citizen to criticize the services being rendered, whether the job performance is technically correct or not. As the above quote illustrates, the work of service providers is becoming increasingly "personal."

Public service jobs require emotional labor because they involve relational exchanges and, more crucially, because they target vulnerable populations or people in vulnerable situations. This is especially the case in times of crisis. For example, first responders and emergency services personnel interact with citizens often on the worst days of their lives. They need to work smoothly in their squads and make good decisions under stressful circumstances, appearing calm and confident in order to calm teammates as well as victims. "First responders are the ones that run to danger, not away from it. In those situations . . . first responders have to function in an environment of emotional labor in order to properly carry out their jobs" (director of an emergency command post, Florida law enforcement, personal communication November 3, 2011).

Almost three-quarters of public sector jobs involve the performance of emotional labor. If the work involves person-to-person interactions (either face to face, or voice to voice in the case of call takers), between citizens and the state, or between coworkers, emotional labor will be required. Whether public servants come in contact with citizens over a reception desk, at the tax assessor's office, at a zoning hearing, at a traffic stop, or via a hotline, emotional labor will be required. Jobs that require emotional labor have three distinct characteristics in common (Hochschild 1983):

First, they require person-to-person contact.

Second, they require workers to manage the emotional state of another person.

Third, they allow the employer to exercise a degree of control over the emotional activities of employees.

These characteristics extend to routine frontline service work, to direct interaction with citizens in distress, and to coworkers in public agencies. People's perceptions of the quality of the public services they receive rest on this dynamic exchange between citizen and state. To engage in emotional labor is not simply to act with emotions at the forefront, but to recognize the way in which emotions influence outcomes in terms of service. It is not simply a matter of having feelings or emotions on the job, but about the need to bring emotive skill to bear in order to complete the job.

We have studied jobs that demand extraordinary compassion and caring as well as jobs that require enforcing discipline and authority. All demand emotional labor. Read the words of a warden characterizing his growing awareness of the centrality of emotion management:

My job is dealing with people every day . . . I think that it [emotional labor] does [relate] a lot with [my job]. I think it does a lot with everyone's . . . but . . . you don't come into a prison setting and think that. I don't think anyone does . . . I think that [I'm engaging in emotional labor] every single second of my day . . . I think the toughest part about my job is you have 1,900 inmates, and you have 400 staff. You know, you gotta go out and talk to those inmates. (Guy, Newman, and Mastracci 2008: 51)

For other workers, the emotive demands are immediately recognizable. Here a caseworker describes what it takes to develop rapport with children in her caseload:

There are some people you click with—you just have that connection. There are some you don't. A person can rub you the wrong way and be really hard to get to. I try to think what emotional string I can pull to get the person to relax, to calm down, to talk to me. It doesn't work to meet anger with anger. You have to stay professional, you have to stay calm, and to some degree you have to understand . . . You know, it's another face, another personality, another person with issues in front of me. (Guy, Newman, and Mastracci 2008: 65)

Whether the emotion management demands are unexpected or obvious, emotional labor is required.

Emerging research in this area underscores its importance. It is a "comes with" for all jobs where public servant meets citizen. Its absence is manifested in substandard job performance and its presence by exceptional service. The exercise of emotional labor is important because it results in heightened citizen satisfaction when they have had a good experience with a public official. It also results in heightened job satisfaction on the part of workers. Moreover, it reduces employee turnover and contributes to productivity because its performance can lead to job engagement. But emotion management has a downside—a propensity for worker stress and burnout. This discussion begs the question: If the concept is so pervasive, if emotional labor is inherent to public service, why do emotive skills remain outside the scope of human resource functions? What does its performance look like? It is to this that we now turn. Having sketched the parameters of emotional labor and discussed its centrality to the delivery of public services, we now fill in its center by examining *how* emotional labor is performed in service to the public.

THE PERFORMANCE OF EMOTIONAL LABOR

I've been in wars, I've been shot at, I've seen death, all that had never bothered me before, like Haiti. It's devastating to just think through it. I keep myself pretty busy just not to think about it. I'm under some medication to help me get through it. While I was doing it I didn't feel anything because I was focusing. (Member of the U.S. Southern Command, Doral, Florida, personal communication, April 2012)

This vignette illustrates one aspect of the performance of emotional labor—emotion suppression. A fire-rescue chief operates from a similar approach:

We had a news camera crew riding with us . . . we had a call where this car had crossed the center line and hit directly head on into another vehicle . . . It was a very bad accident. The mother that I was taking care of was in terrible shape and pinned in the car . . . we worked for probably forty-five minutes to cut her

out of the car to get her to the hospital, and after the call I look over and the camera man has his head in his hands, he had just thrown up . . . and he doesn't know how we even deal with that . . . We got back to the station and he put the video in to show us what he had shot . . . and it hit me. I realized it. I mean he was focusing in. I couldn't even tell you what that woman looked like. I never personalize it—I never put a face with the person. I think we just block everything out. (Mastracci, Guy, and Newman 2012: 92)

Emotional labor requires emotion regulation, which in this case means *suppression*. Emotion regulation extends to emotive *expression*, such as expressing care and compassion as the next vignette illustrates. The paramedic had treated a truck driver who had fallen asleep at the wheel, had crashed, and was trapped inside his cab:

The whole time I'm holding his hand . . . And then I can feel his hand getting colder and colder and he's getting more pale . . . He gave me a message and so I went and told his wife . . . I went to the wake . . . and then I pulled the wife aside and I introduced myself and I said I was with your husband holding his hand until the very end . . . he talked about how much he loves you and the kids and that's all he talked about and I just want you to know that . . . she was very thankful. (Mastracci, Guy, and Newman 2012: 4, 10).

There is little argument that public administration graduates should be proficient in management, analytic skills, and policy. These are essential cognitive skills. However, these skills are not enough. Those who work in emotionally intense jobs must manage their own emotions (suppression and expression) as well as the emotional state of the citizen. This requires skills that are missing from the usual list of knowledge, skills, and abilities (KSAs) that attach to the job.

Feedback from graduates often indicates that their training failed to adequately prepare them for the human processes (the relational work) involved in the administration and delivery of public services. Although they may already have cognitive skills, they are left on their own to acquire an appreciation for, and to develop skill in, nuanced emotive skills. A graphic illustration occurred July 2012 in a suburb of Denver, Colorado, when 12 moviegoers were murdered and 58 injured at the midnight premiere of *The Dark Knight Rises*. Medical responders and law enforcement officers had to address not only issues of safety, search and rescue, and medical aid but also had to exercise emotional management as they, in the dark of night, sought the shooter, located the wounded and dying, and transported victims to nearby hospitals (Guy, Newman, and Ganapati 2013). Responders drew upon their emotive skills as the crisis unfolded—they had to think on their feet when there were not enough ambulances to transport the wounded; they had to stay focused amid the screams of the terrorized moviegoers rushing to escape; and they had to suppress their own horror as they searched the blood-drenched theater for more victims. This is not to suggest that emotional labor comes into play only *in extremis*. As noted above, most public service jobs—those that involve working directly with citizens—require some form of emotional labor.

PROBLEMS SURROUNDING EMOTIONAL LABOR AND HUMAN RESOURCE FUNCTIONS

Emotional labor often remains invisible because job descriptions, performance appraisals, compensation schemes, and training programs barely recognize it. Those who are skilled at its performance are not rewarded. Their contributions are dismissed as "good interpersonal skills," and the time they spend doing what others cannot goes unacknowledged. Human resource functions need to capture *all* the skills required in the workplace. It is to this that we now turn.

Job Analysis

A traditional job analysis identifies the essential cognitive and physical tasks that are required and the proportion of effort that is dedicated to each. But job analyses often fail to acknowledge the emotional tasks that are important elements of a job. And this, in turn, leads to job descriptions that fail to mention an essential element of the job and a list of requisite KSAs that fail to mention emotive skills.

Job Description

A good job description is one that makes it possible for potential applicants to prescreen themselves. It should describe the tasks required to perform the work so that those considering the job can determine whether they possess the necessary skills. When a description fails to mention the emotive component or minimizes it to such a point that it seems to be peripheral to the work itself, newly hired trainees may be confronted with surprises for which they are unprepared when they learn that the job requires emotional labor every day. Take the example of emergency call takers. A typical job description treats the emotive aspect of the work as ancillary. In this example from the Orange County, California, Sheriff's Department, it is mentioned not among the skills but as a phrase included in the environmental conditions of the job, along with a requirement to work rotating shifts:

> Environmental Conditions: Incumbents must have the ability to work in an office environment with changing priorities, deadlines and multiple assignments concurrently; deal with emotional and/or hostile public on a daily basis and remain calm at the same time; and work rotating shifts, weekends and holidays. (Government Jobs 2012).

Although it is commendable that there is reference to the necessity to deal with "emotional and/or hostile public" while remaining calm (many descriptions do not even mention this), it minimizes this element of the job by placing mention of it as a contextual aspect of the job rather than as a central aspect of it. In fact, when their phones ring, emergency call takers never know whether they are going to encounter a call about a cat in a tree, a call in which someone is panicked and screaming into the phone about a horrific crime scene, or a call from someone who is about to commit suicide. In this type of job, emotional resilience and the ability to calm the caller is an absolute must and is as important as the ability to rapidly make dispatch decisions and operate communication equipment.

Recruitment and Selection

There is no one best way to screen and select for good emotion work skills. One first step for hiring authorities is to include interview questions that reveal the applicant's emotive competency. Hirers should listen astutely as job applicants respond to queries tailored to elicit information about their experience with prior emotionally intense situations. Of interest is the degree of self-awareness about their own emotional reaction and the emotional state of the other. For example, when asked what she looks for among job applicants, the executive director of the Denver Center for Crime Victims says:

> I'm looking for self-awareness, self-management. We ask what strategies do you use to cope with stress and the answers are amazing. Some people think the answer is to tell us that they don't have any stress. That that's it. 'Oh, I don't get stressed.' Impossible. Others think, Wow! That's a good question. Let me think about it. . . Self-awareness is huge. Self-management is huge. That's at the top of my list. (Mastracci, Guy, and Newman 2012: 47)

Self-awareness, other-awareness, and the ability to regulate one's own emotional state are elements of emotional intelligence. Based on the applicant's ability to articulate their own experience, supervisors make judgments about the applicant's emotive sensitivity and competency.

Training and Development

The training and development function often overlooks the development and enrichment of emotive skills. To the degree that workers learn to articulate the emotional demands of their jobs in as everyday a fashion as they articulate the cognitive demands, they are more likely to be able to constructively deal with emotionally intense experiences. Research into emotional labor demonstrates that the type of emotional labor most likely to lead to burnout is when the worker must "wear a mask," expressing one emotion while actually feeling another. To the degree that workers can be authentic in their emotive presentation, the more likely they are to have greater resilience when encountering intense situations.

Three procedures that have proven worthwhile for helping workers deal with the stresses of emotional labor are structured staff discussions, self-care plans, and critical incident debriefings. A description of each follows.

Staff Discussions

The biggest risks associated with emotionally intense work are lowered productivity and turnover, which is expensive for the employer, and burnout, which detracts from the worker's quality of personal life as well as work life. When workers trust one another enough to share their work-related emotional experiences, everyone benefits by sharing strategies for coping. Trust among coworkers, a willingness to talk about the experience and debrief, and a focus on learning from bad outcomes in order to improve performance the next time combine to help diminish burnout. Because emotional labor is performed in some venues that are not anticipated, dedicating time to open discussion of job stressors can serve an important function. Take the case of translators who work for victim assistance programs or in large general hospitals. When translating, interpreters speak in the voice of the citizen: "I was raped; I was beaten; I am in pain." The translator's job is also to mirror the emotive state of the speaker. This sort of work can result in vicarious trauma. Staff discussions that give voice to these experiences helps to develop trust among peers, teach coping strategies, and provide an outlet to discuss shared experiences.

Self-Care Plan

Another strategy that is effective in helping workers prevent burnout is called a *self-care plan*. The purpose of the plan is to remind workers of work/life balance and that personal growth proceeds apart from the work they perform. Used predominantly among victim assistance workers and domestic violence workers, a self-care plan requires the employee to set personal goals (such as physical, emotional, financial, intellectual, or spiritual) on an annual basis and report on their progress in conjunction with the annual performance appraisal.

The executive director of the Denver Center for Crime Victims is a strong advocate of self-care plans and credits them for lessening sick leave, absenteeism, and workers compensation claims at her agency. She explains, "we are the witness to horrible things that we have to be able to absorb and work with; you can't do that if you're not practicing self-care and if you don't have an environment that supports that practice" (personal interview, June 14, 2010). While self-care plans are used successfully in social services, another type of "release valve" is used more frequently in law enforcement and firefighting departments: critical incident debriefings.

Critical Incident Debriefing

A strategy used frequently by law enforcement, firefighters, and emergency rescue squads is called *critical incident debriefings*. These meetings serve a valuable function in dealing with vicarious trauma and posttraumatic stress by helping workers deal with intense emotions they had to suppress while the work was ongoing. Debriefings provide an opportunity to talk about experiences and emotions in a manner that suits the workplace culture. They usually involve meeting with a counselor to discuss the event and their feelings surrounding it. It may be required or it may be voluntary. The honest, forthright discussion of the incident provides a learning opportunity as well as an airing of the stresses. And often it helps workers realize that they did the best they could and that no action could have changed the outcome.

A conundrum arises when the organizational culture discourages the expression of vulnerability. This is often the case in police departments, many of which discourage expression of emotions that are other than tough and self-confident. Officers are reluctant to express doubts,

fears, or regrets because they fear ostracism by their peers. Critical incident debriefings are designed to overcome this block to an honest exchange of feelings, but they only succeed where the culture is supportive.

Performance Appraisal

Few performance appraisals acknowledge the emotional labor demands of a job. In a review of appraisal forms for state agencies, Mastracci, Newman, and Guy (2006) demonstrated that workers are rarely evaluated on the performance of emotive skills. The fact of the matter is, however, that in most public service jobs, these are essential skills. Those who are more skilled at the social "grease" necessary to expedite transactions with citizens are doing double duty compared with their less capable peers. A comprehensive evaluation should reward those who perform this work and make it obvious to those who are not as skilled that they should become more accomplished. This matters for agency performance as well as for individual rewards. Hsieh and Guy (2009) studied caseworkers who counseled delinquent youth. They correlated the youths' satisfaction scores with their caseworkers' proficiency at performing emotional labor and found a positive correlation between client satisfaction and caseworkers who were better at performing emotion work. In an era where performance matters, their results demonstrate the value that is added when workers have good emotion work skills.

Compensation

Merit pay is designed to reward the proficient exercise of skills. When the totality of skills required is not acknowledged, compensation rewards some but not all of the competencies that workers must exercise in order to do their job. To correct this shortcoming requires starting at the beginning of the loop that connects job analysis, job description, performance appraisal, and compensation. First, the emotion work requirements must be acknowledged. Then, at each step in the loop, they must be included.

In sum, the problems associated with emotional labor revolve around the fact that its performance is essential in most public service jobs but it is not acknowledged in traditional human resource processes. This oversight results in failure to identify and reward good performers, failure to address stresses that can lead to burnout, and failure to provide training and development to help workers enhance their skills. The prospects for when and how emotional labor will enter the lexicon of standard human resource processes are discussed next.

PROSPECTS FOR THE ACKNOWLEDGMENT OF EMOTIONAL LABOR

Imagine what it would be like if the emotive aspects of public service work were acknowledged and appreciated: Job descriptions would state not only the cognitive requirements of the job but also the emotive requirements. Workers who combine excellent cognitive skills with excellent emotive skills would be rated high and acknowledged for their performance. Their work would be compensated not only for their cognitive but also their emotive facility. Training and development programs would offer skill-building programs in emotive skills as well as technical skills. Those who work in emotionally intense settings would feel normal discussing their feelings rather than feeling like a weakling. Appreciation for the emotional ups and downs of work would be as normal as appreciation for the pressures of budget season and rushed deadlines. This is how incorporating a full appreciation of public service would affect the workforce.

Fortunately, we live in an era where there is growing appreciation for the affective side of experience. The human sciences are probing the subject in psychological, sociological, and neurological research. Some work settings, such as the victim assistance agency cited in this chapter, have already incorporated an appreciation of the emotion work skills required. Many first responders have already experienced multiple critical incident debriefing sessions. There is much more to do, however, before the subject is legitimated across the board. And the work of institutionalizing the issue will rest on the shoulders of human resource specialists working in concert with frontline supervisors.

CONCLUSION

Emotional labor is an important component of most public service jobs, but it remains invisible as long as job descriptions do not mention it, performance appraisals fail to rate its performance, training programs fail to provide skill development workshops, and compensation systems fail to reward those who are highly skilled in its performance. The current situation is that human resource systems are mostly silent on its performance. This deprives workers who are good at it from being rewarded. It also denies training and development for those who can improve their skills. And, it prevents service providers from capitalizing on citizen satisfaction as another measure of performance outcomes.

Public service is a relational enterprise. A citizen-centered approach to service delivery assumes a human touch. To this end, emotional labor is an emerging issue in human resource management that highlights the "cool heads and warm hearts" that citizens expect.

REFERENCES

Ashforth, B., and R. Humphrey. 1993. Emotional Labor in Service Roles: The Influence of Identity. *Academy of Management Review, 18,* 88–115.

Domagalski, Theresa A. 1999. Emotion in Organizations: Main Current. *Human Relations, 52*(6), 833–852.

Goleman, Daniel. 2006. *Emotional Intelligence: Why It Can Matter More Than IQ* (10th Anniversary Edition). New York: Bantam Books.

Government Jobs. 2012. 911 Call Taker. https://www.governmentjobs.com/view_job.cfm?JobID=95181&hit_count=Yes. Accessed November 1, 2014.

Guy, Mary E., and Hyun Jung Lee. In press. Emotional Intelligence and Emotional Labor: How Related Are They? *Review of Public Personnel Administration.* (First published on November 29, 2013. as doi:10.1177/0734371X13514095.)

Guy, Mary E., and Meredith A. Newman. 2004. Women's Jobs, Men's Jobs: Sex Segregation and Emotional Labor. *Public Administration Review, 64*(3), 262–271.

Guy, Mary E., Meredith A. Newman, and Nazife Ganapati. 2013. Managing Emotions While Managing Crises. *International Journal of Emergency Services, 2*(1), 6–20. DOI 10.1108/IJES-07-2012-0033.

Guy, Mary E., Meredith A. Newman, and Sharon H. Mastracci. 2008. *Emotional Labor: Putting the* Service *in Public Service*. Armonk, NY: M.E. Sharpe.

Guy, Mary E., Meredith A. Newman, Sharon H. Mastracci, and Steven Maynard-Moody. 2010. Emotional Labor in the Human Service Organization. In Yeheskel Hasenfeld (Ed.), *Human Services as Complex Organizations*. Thousand Oaks, CA: Sage, pp. 291–309.

Hochschild, Arlie. 1979. Emotion Work, Feeling Rules, and Social Structure. *American Journal of Sociology, 85*(3), 551–575.

———. 1983. *The Managed Heart: Commercialization of Human Feeling*. Berkeley: University of California Press.

Hsieh, Chih-Wei, and Mary E. Guy. 2009. Performance Outcomes: The Relationship Between Managing the "Heart" and Managing Client Satisfaction. *Review of Public Personnel Administration, 29*(1), 41–57.

Humphrey, R. H. 2000. The importance of job characteristics to emotional displays. In Neal M. Ashkanasy, Charmine E. J. Härtel, and Wilfred J. Zerbe (Eds.), *Emotions in the Workplace: Research, Theory, and Practice*. Westport, CT: Quorum, pp. 236–249.

Karabanow, J. 2000. The Organizational Culture of a Street Kid Agency: Understanding Employee Reactions to Pressures to Feel. In Neal M. Ashkanasy, Charmine E. J. Härtel, and Wilfred J. Zerbe (Eds.), *Emotions in the Workplace: Research, Theory, and Practice*. Westport, CT: Quorum, pp. 165–176.

Mastracci, Sharon H., Mary E. Guy, and Meredith A. Newman. 2012. *Emotional Labor and Crisis Response: Working on the Razor's Edge*. Armonk, NY: M.E. Sharpe.

Mastracci, Sharon H., Meredith A. Newman, and Mary E. Guy. 2006. Appraising Emotion Work: Determining Whether Emotional Labor Is Valued in Government Jobs. *American Review of Public Administration, 36*(2), 123–138.

Morris, J. Andrew, and Daniel C. Feldman. 1997. Managing Emotions in the Workplace. *Journal of Managerial Issues, IX*(3), 257–274.

Newman, Meredith A., Mary E. Guy, and Sharon H. Mastracci. 2009. Beyond Cognition: Affective Leadership and Emotional Labor. *Public Administration Review, 69*, 6–20.

Steinberg, Ronnie J., and Deborah M. Figart. 1999a. Emotional Demands at Work: A Job Content Analysis. *Annals of the American Academy of Political and Social Science, 561*(1), 177–191.

———. 1999b. Emotional Labor Since *The Managed Heart*. *Annals of the American Academy of Political and Social Science, 561*(1), 8–26.

Wong, C. S., and K. S. Law. 2002. The Effects of Leader and Follower Emotional Intelligence on Performance and Attitude: An Exploratory Study. *Leadership Quarterly, 13*, 243–274.

CHAPTER 16

MEASURING AND BENCHMARKING HUMAN RESOURCE MANAGEMENT

David N. Ammons
University of North Carolina at Chapel Hill

The collection and reporting of performance measures by public sector agencies has become so common that one prominent observer has written, only half-jokingly, "Everyone is measuring performance" (Behn 2003). Even if this declaration overstates the universality of performance measurement, it is indeed true that the practice is widespread. Furthermore, the movement toward performance management—the *use* of these measures to influence decisions and manage operations—has been called one of the major transformative trends in government in recent years (Abramson, Breul, and Kamensky 2006).

This chapter addresses performance measurement in public human resource management and identifies many of the common measures being reported. It also examines the practice of benchmarking HR performance as a means of assessing the adequacy of human capital management in a given organization.

MANAGING FOR RESULTS

Government agencies encumbered by rules and red tape often are criticized for being preoccupied with procedures and insufficiently focused on results. A performance management strategy attempts to shift the focus from "process-oriented and rule-driven management to performance-oriented and results-driven management"

(Behn 2002: 6). This shift is premised on doing four things: providing clear objectives aligned with the organization's mission and goals; allowing greater discretion at lower levels of the organization to enhance responsiveness, individual initiative, and creativity in pursuit of objectives; collecting relevant performance data and making it readily available; and insisting on accountability for results. This approach *lets managers manage* and also *makes managers manage* (Abramson et al. 2006: 5). It lets managers manage by giving them greater flexibility. It makes managers manage by holding them responsible for achieving and maintaining good performance.

Unlike broad and often ambiguous missions and goals, objectives in a performance management regime are specific and measurable. Aligned with the broader mission and goals, these objectives declare narrower and shorter-term targets. For instance, a goal of workforce diversity might produce narrower and more targeted objectives regarding underrepresented groups within specified time frames. The benefit of well-conceived objectives lies not only in their ability to focus the attention and efforts of work units on important priorities but also in their tendency to evoke innovative strategies for boosting performance. When coupled with devolved responsibilities for service managers, clear objectives and performance tracking can lead to earlier detection of performance gaps and quicker mid-course corrections for improved results. Evidence suggests that focusing on targets, strengthening performance information, and engaging in performance management often yields improved services and greater citizen satisfaction (Walker, Damanpour, and Devece 2011; Walker et al. 2011; Andrews and Moynihan 2002; Walker and Boyne 2006).

MEASUREMENT FOR ACCOUNTABILITY AND PERFORMANCE IMPROVEMENT

Many governments compile performance measures for external as well as internal reporting (Folz, Abdelrazek, and Chung 2009; de Lancer Julnes and Holzer 2001). These governments report performance measures to legislative bodies and citizens as a means of accountability. Their measures provide a record of what the government has done and, ideally, report the quality and efficiency of services and the extent to which a given program is achieving its objectives. This is the use of performance measures for *reporting* purposes. Governments engaged in performance management go beyond merely reporting their performance measures; they also use their measures to influence the strategic direction and operating decisions of the government—they use performance measures to manage for results.

Governments that use their measures to manage for results set the "measurement bar" much higher than those that use measures only for reporting. The measures needed for these two different purposes often are not the same (Charbonneau and Kim 2012; Halachmi 2005; Wisniewski and Stewart 2004). When governments collect measures only for reporting—and not for use in managing operations—they often focus on simple measures that demonstrate high volumes of agency activity. They hope that these output measures, which are easy to compile and report, will be sufficient to satisfy legislative and citizen audiences. Rarely, however, are simple output measures sufficient for managing performance. Measures that are most helpful for guiding operating decisions focus not simply on the quantity of outputs but also on service quality, efficiency, and effectiveness (Ammons 2002; Ammons and Rivenbark 2008; Folz et al. 2009).

STATUS OF PERFORMANCE MEASUREMENT IN PUBLIC HUMAN RESOURCE MANAGEMENT

A recent Pew Center report (2009) identified five aspects of human resource management that are especially important to public sector success: human capital planning, hiring skilled employees, retaining a competent workforce, training and developing the workforce, and managing employee performance. Many of the most common performance measures collected by HR agencies correspond to these vital functions. Especially common, according to a survey of the International Public Management Association for Human Resources (IPMA-HR 2010), are measures reflecting these basic HR statistics:

Employee headcounts

Length of service

Cost of benefits

Turnover rate

Time to fill vacancies

Service awards

Wellness program participation

Absenteeism

Wellness program costs

Number of employees per HR professional

IPMA-HR's case reviews revealed other measures collected by some agencies, though less commonly:

Workforce Diversity, Especially Examining the Percentage of Women and Persons of Color

Diversity in the organization's workforce compared to the relevant labor market

Diversity at the executive/supervisory level

Diversity on eligibility lists/pools of finalists

Diversity among hires

Ratio of supervisory to nonsupervisory employees

Basic HR Functions

Number of promotions

Resignations

Retirements

Terminations

Hires

Applications received

Candidates tested

Leave utilization

HR Efficiency/Effectiveness

Percentage of job descriptions that are up-to-date

Data entry error rate

Turnaround time for creating eligible list

Turnaround time for classification studies

Days to resolve employee relations issues

Satisfaction of hiring managers with staffing process (alternative: candidate quality rating)

Satisfaction of hiring managers with quality of hires

Wellness program: participation rate, progress rates of participants, health insurance costs

Employee Development

Percentage of employees with performance appraisal in past 12 months

Probationary separations, as a percentage of probationary employees

Disciplinary actions per 100 full-time equivalent (FTE) employees

Training hours per employee

Training hours as percentage of paid hours

Training costs as percentage of payroll

Percentage of employees with current individual development plans

Ratio of internal to external hires

Quality of Work Life

Employee morale, often gauged by employee satisfaction (obtained via survey) with employee recognition, supervisor, working environment, communication, empowerment, conflict resolution, organizational climate leadership and managerial effectiveness

Sick leave hours, as a percentage of paid hours

Overtime hours, as a percentage of regular hours

Grievances per 100 FTEs (disciplinary and non-disciplinary)

Appeals, as a percentage of all grievances (disciplinary and nondisciplinary)

Percentage of employees with up-to-date work plan, clear performance expectations

Rate of retention of high-performing employees

Percentage of employees indicating by survey that they would recommend this organization to a friend as a great place to work (reprinted by permission of IPMA-HR)

Individual human resource departments and agencies take many different approaches to reporting performance, as demonstrated by the sets of measures presented in this chapter. Some, like the cities of Santa Barbara, California (Table 16.1), and Sandy, Utah (Table 16.2), present a broad array of measures addressing a wide range of HR functions. Others, like Fairfax County, Virginia (Table 16.3), and the cities of Bellevue, Washington (Table 16.4), and Palo Alto, California (Table 16.5), report sets of measures addressing key objectives.

Some agencies are especially attentive to satisfying the needs of the departments and employees they serve and their role in nurturing positive employee morale. Their focus on customer satisfaction and favorable work relationships often is reflected in the measures they use to assess performance. For instance, the performance measures of the human resources department of the city of Coral Springs, Florida (Table 16.6), rely heavily on feedback from employees. Similarly, the human resources agency of the state of Washington uses employee survey responses to assess the work environment (Table 16.7).

Table 16.1 Performance Measures Reported for Human Resources: City of Santa Barbara, California

Performance Measures	Projected
Percent of employee performance evaluations completed on time	85%
Percent of classification recommendations to the requesting department within 45 working days of receipt of position description form from the department	95%
Days to complete internal (promotional) recruitments (average)	39
Days to complete external (open) recruitments (average)	49
Training updates with department representatives on pertinent issues related to human resources	2
Applications reviewed/processed	9,000
Recruitments conducted	75
Employees (regular and hourly) hired	400
Turnover of regular employees	7.5%
Percent of management positions filled by internal promotions	70%
Percent of supervisory positions filled by internal promotions	80%
Supervisor/manager requests for assistance regarding disciplinary issues	800
Employees who made benefit changes during open enrollment	500
Employee requests for assistance regarding benefits	9,000
Average number of LEAP training hours attended per employee	2

Source: City of Santa Barbara, California, *Adopted Two-Year Financial Plan for Fiscal Years 2014 and 2015*, pp. H-9 and H-10.

Table 16.2 Performance Measures Reported for Human Resources: City of Sandy, Utah

	2011	2012	2013
Take care of current employees			
Employee turnover rate	6.3%	5.6%	5.9%
Job audits	61	101	82
Provide cost-effective personnel service			
City employees (FTE)	576.19	574.6	582.5
Average time to fill a position (in days)	44	46	54

(Continued)

Table 16.2 (Continued)

	2011	2012	2013
HR cost per hire	$204	$220	$225
HR-staff-to-employee ratio (per 100 employees)	0.87	0.87	0.86
HR expense per FTE	$952	$976	$909
HR expense as percentage of operating expenses			
Consolidated Budget	0.87%	0.79%	0.70%
General Fund	1.41%	1.38%	1.22%
Percentage of payroll spent on health insurance benefits	13%	14%	14%
Health care expense per covered employee	$10,544	$11,409	$12,031
Maintain a highly qualified employee workforce			
Consultation (hours)	169	154	103
Recruitments	71	110	96
Employment applications	3,742	3,141	3,157

Source: City of Sandy, Utah, *Approved Budget: Fiscal Year 2014–2015*, p. 45.

Table 16.3 Performance Measures Reported for Human Resources: Fairfax County, VA

	Actual
Efficiency	
Number of resumes reviewed per employment analyst	22,821
Average centralized training expenditure per employee	$67.56
Outcomes	
Percent of employees who complete their probationary period	85%
Average gap between Fairfax County's pay range mid-points and comparable range mid-points in the market for core classes	5%
Employee satisfaction with the variety and quality of benefit programs offered	91% (est.)
Percent of employees who indicated DHR-sponsored training was beneficial in performing their jobs	95%

Source: Fairfax County, Virginia, *FY 2015 Adopted Budget Plan*, Volume 1, pp. 58–63.

Table 16.4 Performance Measures Reported for Human Resources: City of Bellevue, Washington

Performance Measure	FY 2013		2013 Target Met or Exceeded (✓) Not Met (−)
	Target	Actual	
Employee rating of statement "I feel the city offers good benefits"	3.75	4.19	✓
Turnover[a]	<5%	2.6%	✓
Percent of respondents who agree that the city works to attract, develop, and retain people with diverse backgrounds	70%	62%	−
Percentage of employees who complete their trial service period	90%	94.8%	✓
Percentage of employees who agree that training is made available to them to do their jobs better	80%	72%	−
Time to fill job requisitions (weeks)[a]	12	9	✓
Percentage of employee retirement plan contributions above 100% employer matched contributions	100%	60%	−

Source: City of Bellevue, Washington, *Annual Performance Report 2013*, p. 80.

[a] Calculated using the standard methodology of the International City/County Management Association (ICMA).

Table 16.5 Four Measures Designated as "Key" by the People Strategy and Operations Department of the City of Palo Alto, California

	Target	Actual
Percentage of key roles with succession plan in place	75%	75% (est.)
Days to fill a position	90	93
Employee attendance rate	98%	95.74%
Turnover of employees within first year	1%	8%

Source: City of Palo Alto, California, *Fiscal Year 2015 Adopted Operating Budget*, pp. 229–230.

Table 16.6 Performance Measures Reported for Human Resources: City of Coral Springs, Florida

Performance Measures	Goal	Actual
Percentage of employees who agree with the statement, "I would recommend working for the city to a friend"	90%	90%
Employee engagement index[a]	90%	84%
Percentage of employees who feel HR provides quality services	90%	96%
Percentage of employees who are satisfied with liaison services	90%	92%
Percentage of employees who are satisfied with wellness activities	90%	91%
Percentage of employees who believe that benefits are in line with needs	90%	80%
Quality of hire satisfaction[b]	90%	100%
Sick hours per employee	48	57.8
Percentage of minority applicants per recruitment	45%	63%
Percentage of employees who agree with the statement, "I am satisfied with the access to training resources to assist in my professional development"	90%	85%
Percentage of responses to customer requests within 48 hours	100%	95%
Percentage of service requests closed within 1 week	100%	96%

Sources: City of Coral Springs, Florida, *Proposed Fiscal Year 2015 Annual Budget*, p. 104, and personal communication with Dale Pazdra, director of human resources, December 1, 2014.

[a] The employee engagement index is based on respondent agreement with a set of five employee survey statements, including "I am asked for input on decisions affecting my work" and "My immediate supervisor supports me in achieving my developmental goals."

[b] Quality of hire satisfaction is an index based on hiring entity's agreement with a set of statements, including "Employee is pro-actively building rapport/ trust with co-workers" and "Employee is reliable and committed to working with the city."

Table 16.7 Assessing Employee Morale/Work Environment: State of Washington

The human resources agency of the State of Washington assesses employee morale and the state of the work environment by considering survey responses indicating agreement or disagreement with the statements below. Average ratings are reported as performance measures.

Q 1. I have an opportunity to give input on decisions affecting my work.

Q 2. I receive the information I need to do my job effectively.

Q 3. I know how my work contributes to the goals of my agency.

Q 4. I know what is expected of me at work.

Q 5. I have opportunities at work to learn and grow.

Q 6. I have the tools and resources I need to do my job effectively.

Q 7. My supervisor treats me with dignity and respect.

Q 8. My supervisor gives me ongoing feedback that helps me improve my performance.

Q 9. I receive recognition for a job well done.

Q10. We are making improvements to make things better for our customers.

Q11. A spirit of cooperation and teamwork exists in my workgroup.

Q12. I know how my agency measures its success.

Q13. My agency consistently demonstrates support for a diverse workforce.

Q14. I receive clear information about changes being made within the agency.

Q15. I am encouraged to come up with better ways of doing things.

Q16. We use customer feedback to improve our work processes.

Q17. In general, I'm satisfied with my job.

Source: State of Washington, *Human Resource Management Report: Performance Measure Parameters.* Washington State Human Resources. Last updated: August 2014. http://hr.wa.gov/WorkforceDataandPlanning/HRMPerformanceAccountability/Pages/default.aspx http://hr.wa.gov/SiteCollection Documents/Strategic HR/HRM Performance and accountability/HRM Performance Measure Parameters.doc. Accessed November 24, 2014.

The range of viable options for measuring various aspects of human resource management is broad. A portion of the measures recommended at the federal level is shown in Table 16.8.

Performance measures and benchmarks are not the same. Benchmarking places an organization's measures in the context of standards or the achievements of other organizations. That is where we turn our attention next.

Table 16.8 Sample of Recommended HR Performance Measures: U.S. Government

Retroactive payroll adjustments as a percentage of all payroll transactions (categorized by source)

Percentage of off-cycle payments made due to errors

Percentage of corrections required to correctly award pay and leave

Percentage of corrections required to correctly award bonuses

Percentage of employees that have pay and leave information available electronically

Percentage of work schedules submitted after the cut-off date

Percentage of employee time records submitted late

Percentage of time records amended or corrected in a time period

(Continued)

Table 16.8 (Continued)

Time it takes to send out W-2s

Percentage of corrections made to W-2s

Average time to respond to inquiries

Average time to resolve inquiries (from point of inquiry to resolution)

Percent of employees citing satisfaction with compensation (Human Capital Survey)

Job Satisfaction Index scores

Applicant satisfaction with application process, based on 10-point scale

Manager satisfaction with applicants, based on 10-point scale

Time to hire (average days from the time the hiring manager validates the need for the position to the time of entry on duty)

Retention rate of employees hired 2 years ago

Difference between competencies needed and competencies possessed by managers and leaders in each agency population/subgroup (e.g., bureaus/departments, headquarters/field, civilian/military)

Based on a statistically valid sample of training and employee development actions within a one-year period:
—% of training and employee development actions demonstrating severe transactional or programmatic problems or errors
—% of performance and awards actions demonstrating severe transactional or programmatic problems or errors
—% of staffing and compensation actions demonstrating severe transactional or programmatic problems or errors

Correlation between individual senior executives' performance appraisal ratings and their total compensation

Degree of linkage between all employees' performance appraisal plans and agency mission, goals, and outcomes

Difference between competencies needed and competencies possessed by employees in mission-critical occupations

Sources: Human Resources Line of Business: Performance Model Version 1, Report HRLOB-PM-200601 (Washington, DC: U.S. Office of Personnel Management, June 2006), pp. 33–39; *The Human Capital Assessment and Accountability Framework (HCAAF): Systems, Standards, and Metrics* (Washington, DC: U.S. Office of Personnel Management, March 2006); *Hire the Best Talent,* http://hr.performance.gov/initiative/hire-best/home, accessed October 24, 2012; and *Respect and Engage the Workforce,* http://hr.performance.gov/initiative/respect-engage-workforce/home, accessed October 24, 2012.

BENCHMARKING PERFORMANCE

Almost eight decades ago, future Nobel laureate Herbert Simon (1937) offered a preamble to modern benchmarking efforts. Simon called for comparative statistics that would reveal differences among governments in the efficiency and effectiveness of their services. He hoped that these statistics would allow governments to identify conditions and practices associated with greater efficiency and effectiveness.

Benchmarking can take different forms, but in the public sector it most often appears in the form, if not always the analytic spirit, envisioned by Simon—as the comparison of selected performance statistics of several governments (Askim, Johnsen, and Christophersen 2008).[1] Often such comparisons are compiled by an individual government, agency, or department on an unstructured, ad hoc basis. In these instances managers designing the comparison often instinctively include only other governments deemed similar to their own, hoping to gain the level playing field that would be important for a management report card but unintentionally denying their benchmarking project the variation among comparison units that is most conducive to interorganizational learning (Askim et al. 2008; Downe, Hartley, and Rashman 2004; Camp 1989). In other cases benchmarking projects are not the ad hoc initiatives of individual governments but instead are the cooperative undertaking of several units that share information and behave as a network (Askim et al. 2008).

Several cooperative benchmarking projects involving local governments have emerged at the national, state, and regional levels in recent decades.[2] Prominent benchmarking projects direct extensive preparatory efforts toward achieving uniformity in the measures being compared. They attempt to ensure to the extent possible that measurement terms have consistent meanings across participating governments and that efficiency measures are based on cost-accounting rules applied uniformly. This uniformity allows reliable government-to-government comparisons that put a spotlight on top performers and top performance marks. This sets the stage for further analysis and subsequent operating adjustments by governments wishing to pursue performance improvement. Performance marks achieved by others can become their targets. Furthermore, the operating procedures of performance leaders can serve as a blueprint for their own performance improvement.

Insights gained from comparisons of performance statistics have been credited with prompting changes in government operations, policies, and priorities (Walker et al. 2011; Ammons and Rivenbark 2008; Braadbaart 2007; De Witte and Marquez 2007; Williams 2005). However, not all participants in benchmarking projects take full advantage of the learning opportunity. Evidence suggests that few participants actually follow up with performance leaders (Longbottom 2000). Nevertheless, benefits may emerge by exercising other options revealed from insights derived by benchmarking. For instance, when governments perform above or near the group average they sometimes take reassurance from their good standing among counterparts and choose simply to maintain the status quo or even to divert resources from a service deemed to be in good shape to another

that is struggling or considered a higher priority (Askim et al. 2008).

HUMAN RESOURCE MANAGEMENT BENCHMARKS

Organizations focused on performance excellence and the achievement of desired results are rarely content with internal comparisons alone—for instance, comparisons that track improvement over time or reveal performance disparities among different offices or different neighborhoods. Such organizations wish to compare their performance with that of other service producers as a means of gauging performance adequacy in a broader context. They desire performance benchmarks.

Human resource benchmarks may be found in national or state performance statistics, performance standards, and in the performance marks of prominent organizations. For example, the Pew Center on the States recently reported these performance averages among state governments:

- 68 days to fill a classified position, with half of responding state governments falling in the range of 45 to 78 days.
- 23 applications per open classified position, with half reporting averages of 9 to 27 applicants per position.
- Voluntary turnover of 14% among new hires during their probationary period, with half of the states reporting rates between 8% and 18%.
- Involuntary turnover of 8%.
- Voluntary turnover of 7.4% among all nontemporary classified employees, excluding retirements, and 7.5% among nonclassified employees.
- 22.1 hours of training annually per employee, with a slightly higher average of 25.2 hours for managers.
- Training expenditures averaging 1.3% of total payroll dollars.
- 59.8% of state employees with career development plans in place, with half of the states reporting between 22% and 85% of their employees having career development plans.

- 87.3% of all classified employees having had a performance appraisal during the year and 58.2% of nonclassified employees.
- 28.6 days for "for-cause" terminations of classified employees and 6.6 days for nonclassified employees.
- 18.1 days for "behavioral issue" termination of classified employees compared to 6.9 days for nonclassified employees. (Pew Center 2009: 13–28; used by permission)

Public sector organizations may use these averages—or perhaps the upper bounds of the interquartile ranges—as their performance benchmarks.

Many HR agencies attempt to streamline their hiring processes to the extent possible in an effort to avoid losing top-flight applicants to competing employers. In the federal government such efforts yielded a time-to-hire average (i.e., average days from the time the hiring manager validated the need for the position to the time of entry on duty) of 93 days in 2011 (U.S. Office of

Table 16.9 Days Required for Various Steps in the Hiring Process: Survey Response Means

Hiring Step	Days (mean value of all responses)						
	Jobs in General	Professional	Adm./ Executive	Clerical	Public Safety	Labor	IT
HR asked to recruit	12	13	13	10	12	11	12
Vacancy announced	8	8	9	7	9	7	8
Application deadline	17	21	24	15	25	16	21
Testing evaluation begins	12	11	12	11	14	11	10
Testing evaluation complete	12	12	14	12	19	11	11
Hiring manager receives list	11	10	10	13	13	11	10
Hiring manager receives list (existing list)	5	5	5	5	6	4	4
Hiring manager receives list (no candidate list)	16	15	16	15	20	14	15
Time to begin interviews	9	9	9	8	10	8	8
Hiring manager offers job	8	8	9	7	13	7	8
New hire reports to work	15	18	29	14	18	14	16
Notification of vacancy until reports to work	49	51	54	45	57	44	48

N = 236 (mostly from cities and counties)

IT = information technology

Source: 2006 Recruitment and Selection Benchmarking. Research sponsored by NEOGOV. Alexandria, VA: International Public Management Association for Human Resources, 2006, p. 17. Used by permission.

Personnel Management [OPM] 2012). A quicker average of 49 days was reported for other levels of government in a 2006 IPMA-HR report (Table 16.9).

Organizations wishing to assess their own performance of routine HR functions—in terms of service quality, efficiency, or impact—may find it helpful to consider the performance records of other organizations regarding these functions. Tables 16.10 and 16.11 offer the performance marks of prominent municipal governments for several such functions. Using these as benchmarks, a government can assess its own performance and perhaps identify performance gaps that it can work to close.

Some organizations may choose to focus their benchmarking not simply on the quality and efficiency of HR services but also on the effectiveness of larger HR initiatives. For instance, organizations that direct a variety of efforts toward employee development and succession planning expect these efforts to pay off with a greater number of well-qualified internal candidates when vacancies present promotional opportunities. Such organizations may compare their own record of internal promotions with the records of other prominent public organizations (Table 16.12).

Many organizations attempt to gauge the efficiency of their HR operations by comparing their staffing ratio to the broadly accepted rule-of-thumb ratio of one human resource staff employee per 100 general employees. Surveys and benchmarking reports show this ratio to be near the average for public sector organizations (IPMA-HR 2010; ICMA 2010). However, small organizations tend to average a bit more than one HR employee per 100 general employees and large organizations tend to have slightly fewer than one per 100 employees.

Table 16.10 Prompt Position Audits for Reclassifications and Compensation Requests: Selected Cities

Juneau, AK

Average number of days from classification action initiation to resolution: 25 (2006); 9 (2007)

Austin, TX

Percentage of classification requests completed within 15 business days: 29.88% (2008)

Duncanville, TX

Time needed to reclassify an occupied position

    Average working days until HR recommendation: 4

    Average working days until final decision: 21 (2008)

Lubbock, TX

    Average number of days to classify filled positions: 26

    Average number of days to classify vacant positions: 9 (2007)

Honolulu, HI (city and county)

Percentage of classification requests completed within 30 days of receipt: 85% (2009)

Source: Excerpted from David N. Ammons, *Municipal Benchmarks: Assessing Local Performance and Establishing Community Standards*, 3d ed. (Armonk, NY: M.E. Sharpe, 2012), p. 185. Copyright © 2012 by M.E. Sharpe, Inc. Used by permission. All Rights Reserved. Not for reproduction.

Table 16.11 Benchmarks for Routine Functions in Human Resource Management: Selected Cities

Background Checks

Palm Bay, FL

Percentage of background checks completed quickly enough to allow hiring within 2 weeks of selection (excludes hiring of sworn officers): 99% (2008)

Benefits Administration

Springfield, MA

Percentage of health plan customer service encounters resolved within 1 day: 97% (2009)

Santa Ana, CA

Percentage of employees' benefits problems resolved within 1 day: 95% (2008)

Candidate Status Notification

Miramar, FL

Percentage of candidates notified within 3 weeks on status of application: 99% (2007)

Exit Interviews

Eugene, OR

Percentage of exit interviewees who say they would recommend the city as an employer: 92% (2008)

Boca Raton, FL

Percentage of separating employees who have exit interviews: 90% (2008)

Job Postings

Hurst, TX

Percentage of job announcements posted within 2 days of receiving employee requisition and accurate job description: 98% (2008)

Midland, TX

Percentage of jobs posted within 48 hours of receipt of authorized request: 98% (2008)

Orientation

Hurst, TX

Percentage of new employee orientations conducted within 3 days of employment: 90% (2008)

Boca Raton, FL

Percentage of new employees attending orientation within the first payroll of their employment: 100% (2008)

Miami-Dade County, FL

Percentage of new employees who completed orientation within 2 weeks of date of hire: 91% (2008)

Prompt Investigation of Discrimination Complaints

Hartford, CT

Percentage of discrimination complaints investigated within 180 days: 95% (2008); 70% (2009)
Percentage resolved within 180 days: 65% (2009)

Responsiveness

Juneau, AK

Percentage of questions about procedures and personnel rules answered within same business day: 99% (2006); 90% (2007)

Up-to-Date Personnel Files

Oklahoma City, OK

Percentage of employee record updates completed within 7 business days of receipt: 93% (2009)

Verification of Employment

Little Rock, AR

Percentage of "verification of employment" forms processed within 1 working day: 95% (2008)

Source: Excerpted from David N. Ammons, *Municipal Benchmarks: Assessing Local Performance and Establishing Community Standards,* 3d ed. (Armonk, NY: M.E. Sharpe, 2012), pp. 188–189. Copyright © 2012 by M.E. Sharpe, Inc. Used by permission. All Rights Reserved. Not for reproduction.

Table 16.12 Successful Employee Development/Succession Planning: Selected Cities

Santa Barbara, CA

Percentage of management positions filled by internal promotion: 76%
Percentage of supervisory positions filled by internal promotion: 92% (2009)

Santa Ana, CA

Percentage of appointments filled by promotion: 54.0% (2007); 35.0% (2008)

Olathe, KS

Percentage of positions filled from within: 48.4% (2008)

Tamarac, FL

Percentage of positions filled through internal promotions: 44% (2009)

Source: Excerpted from David N. Ammons, *Municipal Benchmarks: Assessing Local Performance and Establishing Community Standards,* 3d ed. (Armonk, NY: M.E. Sharpe, 2012), p. 185. Copyright © 2012 by M.E. Sharpe, Inc. Used by permission. All Rights Reserved. Not for reproduction.

CHALLENGES AND PROSPECTS

Performance measurement and benchmarking have much to offer the field of human resource management. Performance measurement, when properly done, can help HR professionals track progress toward strategic human capital management goals and more routine objectives, confirming when current operating strategies are working and sounding an alarm when they are not. Benchmarking can extend these benefits by examining an organization's performance in the context of what other organizations have achieved and setting the stage for subsequent steps toward performance improvement.

Despite favorable prospects for performance measurement and benchmarking, challenges to successful implementation are evident. For too many public sector organizations, performance measurement is an appendage to their work and not a tool they use to help them determine how to do their work or do it better (de Lancer Julnes and Holzer 2001). The measures compiled by many agencies remain anchored in the counting of activities and outputs rather than in tracking changes in outcomes (Perrin 2006). They use whatever is convenient or easy to collect, not what would be most pertinent to key objectives and would have greatest managerial value. This failing may have more serious ramifications than most HR professionals realize.

Many HR professionals strive to focus their work strategically and expect to have a place at the table in their organization's key discussions of strategy, much like their counterparts in budget and finance who bring financial data to these conversations. As one HR director noted, "We wonder why, when we are working with the largest asset in our organization, its people, we have been less effective than our finance counterparts in promoting our role in strategy discussions. I believe the answer is in data, specifically, data which aligns with the goals of the organization. . . . Selecting appropriate HR metrics that support business strategy, then using the data consistently to improve workforce performance and productivity is the next growth area for HR professionals" (IPMA-HR 2010: 20; reprinted by permission).

Benchmarking as a technique for spurring organizational learning holds considerable promise for public organizations in an environment that historically is reluctant to support research and development and perceives experimentation as risky. Benchmarking offers a low-cost option that emphasizes comparison and adaptation over pure experimentation. Yet challenges persist. Many officials are skeptical of interorganizational comparisons and exhibit little enthusiasm for the external reporting of comparisons unless they reflect favorably on their government (Hatry 2010). Some organizations claim to engage in benchmarking as a means of improving performance but grow defensive when some of their scores are lower than those of counterparts. At that point officials are prone to shift their focus from finding ways to improve their operations to finding reasons they should not be blamed for poor performance (Tillema 2007). Furthermore, many organizations that engage in benchmarking appear to focus their efforts not on matching top performers in a comparative set but instead merely toward achieving average performance (Bowerman et al. 2002; Llewellyn and Northcott 2005).

When Simon (1937) called for comparative statistics, he encouraged the use of these statistics not simply for praising performance leaders or "visiting judgment" on laggards but instead "as a means of pooling their experiences in arriving at factually based principles of administration" (Simon 1937: 527). Organizations have much to learn from one another. They can learn a great deal simply from the discovery of performance gaps and even more from exchanging information on practices and effective strategies that separate performance leaders from all others (National Performance Management Advisory Commission [NPMAC] 2010: 30).

Metzenbaum (2006) suggests that the overarching challenge is "to create a culture that encourages comparative measurement to illuminate solutions, detect problems, and positively motivate, while discouraging dysfunctional uses of and responses to measurement" (Metzenbaum 2006: 27). This challenge and the others articulated here remain not just for human resource professionals but also for the public sector as a whole.

NOTES

1. Variations that also claim the *benchmarking* label include the comparison of a government's performance statistics to prescribed performance standards; visioning initiatives that establish community, state, or agency targets called benchmarks; and best practice benchmarking, which focuses on adapting the practices of "best-in-class" performers.

2. Prominent among local government benchmarking projects are the national project sponsored by the International City/County Management Association (ICMA) and state-based projects in North Carolina, Florida, Michigan, Tennessee, and the Canadian province of Ontario (Coe 1999; Kopczynski and Lombardo 1999; NPMAC 2010).

ACKNOWLEDGMENT

The author gratefully acknowledges the research assistance of University of North Carolina graduate student Deepti Panjabi.

REFERENCES

Abramson, Mark A., Jonathan D. Breul, and John M. Kamensky. 2006. *Six Trends Transforming Government.* Washington, DC: IBM Center for the Business of Government.

Ammons, David N. 2002. Performance Measurement and Managerial Thinking. *Public Performance and Management Review, 25,* 344–347.

———. 2012. *Municipal Benchmarks: Assessing Local Performance and Establishing Community Standards* (3rd ed.). Armonk, NY: M.E. Sharpe.

Ammons, David N., and William C. Rivenbark. 2008. Factors Influencing the Use of Performance Data to Improve Municipal Services: Evidence from the North Carolina Benchmarking Project. *Public Administration Review, 68,* 304–318.

Andrews, Matthew, and Donald P. Moynihan. 2002. Why Reforms Do Not Always Have to 'Work' to Succeed: A Tale of Two Managed Competition Initiatives. *Public Performance and Management Review, 25,* 282–297.

Askim, Jostein, Age Johnsen, and Knut-Andreas Christophersen. 2008. Factors behind Organizational Learning from Benchmarking: Experiences from Norwegian Municipal Benchmarking Networks. *Journal of Public Administration Research and Theory, 18,* 297–320.

Behn, Robert D. 2002. The Psychological Barriers to Performance Management. *Public Performance and Management Review, 26,* 5–25.

———. 2003. Why Measure Performance? Different Purposes Require Different Measures. *Public Administration Review, 63,* 586–606.

Bowerman, Mary, Graham Francis, Amanda Ball, and Jackie Fry. 2002. The Evolution of Benchmarking in UK Local Authorities. *Benchmarking: An International Journal, 9,* 429–449.

Braadbaart, Okke. 2007. Collaborative Benchmarking, Transparency and Performance: Evidence from The Netherlands Water Supply Industry. *Benchmarking: An International Journal, 14,* 677–692.

Camp, R. C. 1989. *Benchmarking: The Search for Industry Best Practices That Lead to Superior Performance.* Milwaukee, WI: Quality Press.

Charbonneau, Etienne, and Younhee Kim. 2012. Reconfiguring Performance Information Linking with Accountability: Reporting and Internal Management. In Aroon Manoharan and Marc Holzer (Eds.), *Active Citizen Participation in E-Government: A Global Perspective.* Hershey, PA: IGI Global, pp. 1–19.

Coe, Charles. 1999. Local Government Benchmarking: Lessons from Two Major Multigovernment Efforts. *Public Administration Review, 59,* 110–123.

de Lancer Julnes, Patria, and Marc Holzer. 2001. Promoting the Utilization of Performance Measures in Public Organizations: An Empirical Study of Factors Affecting Adoption and Implementation. *Public Administration Review, 61,* 693–708.

De Witte, K., and R. Marquez. 2007. Designing Incentives in Local Public Utilities: An International Comparison of the Drinking Water Sector. Paper presented at European Group for Public Administration Conference. Madrid, Spain.

Downe, James, Jean Hartley, and Lyndsay Rashman. 2004. Evaluating the Extent of Inter-Organizational Learning and Change in Local Authorities through the English Beacon Council Scheme. *Public Management Review, 6,* 531–553.

Folz, David H., Reem Abdelrazek, and Yeonsoo Chung. 2009. The Adoption, Use, and Impacts of Performance Measures in Medium-Size Cities. *Public Performance and Management Review, 33,* 63–87.

Halachmi, Arie. 2005. Performance Measurement: Test the Water Before You Dive In. *International Review of Administrative Sciences, 71,* 255–266.

Hatry, Harry. 2010. Looking into the Crystal Ball: Performance Management over the Next Decade. *Public Administration Review, 70,* S208–S211.

International City/County Management Association (ICMA). 2010. *Comparative Performance Measurement: FY 2009 Data Report.* Washington, DC: ICMA.

International Public Management Association for Human Resources (IPMA-HR). 2006. *2006 Recruitment and Selection Benchmarking.* Research sponsored by NEOGOV. Alexandria, VA: IPMA-HR.

———. 2010. *Benchmarking Committee Report: HR Metrics.* Sponsored by the Washington State Department of Labor and Industries. Alexandria, VA: IPMA-HR. http://www.ipma-hr.org/sites/default/files/finalbenchreport.pdf.

Kopczynski, Mary, and Michael Lombardo. 1999. Comparative Performance Measurement: Insights and Lessons from a Consortium Effort. *Public Administration Review, 59,* 124–134.

Llewellyn, Sue, and Deryl Northcott. 2005. The Average Hospital. *Accounting, Organizations and Society, 30,* 555–583.

Longbottom, David. 2000. Benchmarking in the UK: An Empirical Study of Practitioners and Academics. *Benchmarking: An International Journal, 7,* 98–117.

Metzenbaum, Shelley H. 2006. *Performance Accountability: The Five Building Blocks and Six Essential Practices.* Managing for Performance and Results Series. Washington, DC: IBM Center for the Business of Government.

National Performance Management Advisory Commission (NPMAC). 2010. *A Performance Management Framework for State and Local Government.* Chicago: NPMAC.

Perrin, Burt. 2006. *Moving from Outputs to Outcomes: Practical Advice from Governments Around the World.* Washington, DC: IBM Center for the Business of Government.

Pew Center on the States. 2009. *People Forward: Human Capital Trends and Innovations.* Washington, DC: Pew Charitable Trusts. http://www.pewstates.org/uploadedFiles/PCS_Assets/2009/GPP_People_Forward_report_web.pdf.

Simon, Herbert. 1937. Comparative Statistics and the Measurement of Efficiency. *National Municipal Review, 26,* 524–527.

Tillema, Sandra. 2007. Public Sector Organizations' Use of Benchmarking Information for Performance Improvement: Theoretical Analysis and Explorative Case Studies in Dutch Water Boards. *Public Performance and Management Review, 30,* 496–520.

U.S. Office of Personnel Management (OPM). 2012. *Hire the Best Talent.* http://hr.performance.gov/initiative/hire-best/home. Accessed October 24, 2012.

Walker, Richard M., and George A. Boyne. 2006. Public Management Reform and Organizational Performance: An Empirical Assessment of the U.K. Labour Government's Public Service Improvement Strategy. *Journal of Policy Analysis and Management, 25,* 371–393.

Walker, Richard M., Gene A. Brewer, George A. Boyne, and Claudia N. Avellaneda. 2011. Market Orientation and Public Service Performance: New Public Management Gone Mad? *Public Administration Review, 71,* 707–717.

Walker, Richard M., Fariborz Damanpour, and Carlos A. Devece. 2011. Management Innovation and Organizational Performance: The Mediating Effect of Performance Management. *Journal of Public Administration Research and Theory, 21,* 367–386.

Williams, Mark C. 2005. *Can Local Government Comparative Benchmarking Improve Efficiency? Leveraging Multiple Analytical Techniques to Provide Definitive Answers and Guide Practical Action.* Dissertation. Virginia Commonwealth University, Richmond, Virginia.

Wisniewski, Mik, and Derek Stewart. 2004. Performance Measurement for Stakeholders: The Case of Scottish Local Authorities. *International Journal of Public Sector Management, 17,* 222–233.

CHAPTER 17

MANAGING EMPLOYEE PROBLEMS: STATE GOVERNMENT GRIEVANCE AND COMPLAINT RESOLUTION SYSTEMS AND PRACTICES

Jessica E. Sowa
University of Colorado Denver

INTRODUCTION

Conflict is a natural part of all workplaces. Conflict can arise from differences in concrete benefits or sanctions, when people feel they have been rewarded or punished differently in relation to their colleagues. Conflict can also arise around the nature of work itself, with employees holding different perspectives on how to address the fundamental tasks of the workplace (Litterer 1966; Jehn and Mannix 2001; Brewer and Lam 2009; Jehn, Rispens, and Thatcher 2010). In governments at all levels, conflict can be especially challenging, as political pressures can affect the nature of work, the nature of benefits, and the overall working environment facing government employees (Ingraham 1995; Elling and Thompson 2006; Crowell and Guy 2010). Civil service or merit systems were designed to protect or insulate employees from political or partisan intrusion, providing certain protections and affording them procedures or processes that would ensure that they were treated fairly if problems arose in the execution of their duties. However, administrative reforms across state governments in the United States have changed the structures and practices

governing public employees, prompting the need to examine the nature of the systems in place to address workplace complaints and conflicts (Coggburn 2000, 2001; Bowman and West 2006; Kellough and Nigro 2006; Hays and Sowa 2006; Crowell and Guy 2010).

Designing effective systems for resolving employee complaints can have significant tangible benefits in the workplace, including improved employee morale, reduced turnover, and increased employee loyalty. However, the challenge rests with designing systems that provide employees with sufficient procedures for seeking redress but also manage the costs of employee complaints for the employer, with these costs including time spent resolving the complaints (informally and formally) and reduced productivity associated with disgruntled employees.

This chapter examines the process of resolving employee complaints in state governments, with a focus on the rights of employees and how they are protected through the policies and practices of these governments and the ways in which state government as an employer can manage employee complaints in the most efficient and effective way possible. From the employee perspective, the critical question in addressing their complaints is the degree to which their employer has in place structured processes of grievance or complaint that will afford them due process. From the employer perspective, the critical question is how to help their managers reduce employee complaints overall, thereby hopefully avoiding the formal grievance process. From the employer perspective, effective management of employee complaints is not simply about the systems in place but also the development of managers who can address employee problems when they arise. This chapter will attempt to do the following:

- Define employee grievances and discuss the classic model of grievance procedures in government.
- Discuss the concept of organizational justice as applied to grievance policies and procedures.
- Explore the current practices of state governments with reference to their grievance or complaint procedures, highlighting different trends in grievance procedures.
- Explore how to handle employee problems when they arise, highlighting some alternative ways to resolve employee problems outside of the formal grievance process.

GRIEVANCE PROCEDURES: THEORY AND PRACTICE

Classic Model of Grievance Procedures

Labor relations provide a starting point for understanding how employee complaints are addressed in the workplace with a definition of and model for resolving grievances. Formally defined, an employee grievance is "an employee or union complaint (or, albeit infrequently, a management complaint) arising out of dissatisfaction with some aspect of the contract or work environment" (Kearney 2001: 298). In considering the employee/employer relationship, whether it is established through civil service procedures, union contracts, or state law, the power generally rests with management, with the structures and practices surrounding this relationship favoring the needs of management. Therefore,

in order to get employees to agree to this relationship, there needs to be a way to mediate this power imbalance—employees need to know that management will honor their side of the employment relationship and treat employees fairly. Grievance and other structured complaint procedures provide workers with a way to seek redress if management fails to uphold their agreement (Daley 2007).

In determining what aspects of the employee/employer relationship are subject to the grievance process, Richardson (1977: 162) states that the inclusion of actions in the grievance process is "limited only by the variety of circumstances that might arise in the employment relationship and by the real or imagined grievances arising therefrom." Theoretically, if an employee perceives a slight or wrong in any aspect of the employee relationship with management, they could formally complain about that wrong through the grievance process. Therefore, it is of particular importance that state governments carefully design their formal complaint and grievance systems for several reasons. Bounding what aspects of the employment relationship or contract fall within the formal grievance structure ensures that managers are not overwhelmed with capricious complaints that could threaten their autonomy and ability to direct and correct employee performance. In addition, for state governments, it is critical to recognize that certain components of the employment relationship, such as pay and benefits, have larger government-wide implications and therefore need to be guarded from individual employee complaints. While grievance procedures vary greatly across jurisdictions, some common personnel issues included under grievance procedures are job assignments, layoffs, reductions in force, reprimands, suspensions, and discharges (Mesch 1995; Kearney 2001).

While grievance and formal complaint resolution procedures vary across and within state governments, the traditional model of the grievance process generally involves three main steps, with the steps focused on addressing and resolving the grievance in the most expeditious way possible. The steps include the following:

1. The initial complaint: The process begins when an employee brings a complaint forward to a supervisor. The complaint is usually initiated orally, providing the supervisor a chance to resolve the complaint in an informal manner at this initial step.
2. Written complaint: If the complaint is not resolved informally between the supervisor and the employee, a formal grievance is then initiated. The grievance is detailed in written form, signed by the grievant (the employee), and forwarded up the management structure. Depending on the structure of the grievance process, the grievance may be handled by the next management level from the immediate supervisor of the employee filing the grievance. If the grievance is not resolved, the next step becomes necessary.
3. Higher management involvement: Depending on the structure of the grievance process, when the grievance is unresolved at the lower management level, the grievance then may be referred for resolution to a higher level of management, such as a department head or a labor relations manager. In addition, an external committee, such as an employee relations board, may also become involved in resolving the grievance (for examples of different forms of these steps, see Kearney 2001; Colorado 2015a).

If these steps fail to produce a resolution, many grievance procedures will include a final step for arbitration, involving a neutral third party (Mesch 1995). In most grievance procedures, specific time limits associated with each step are in place, thereby ensuring expeditious resolution of the complaint (Kearney 2001). Figure 17.1 provides a visual example of the classic model of grievance procedures.

As the classic grievance procedure model in some form is still used in many jurisdictions, it is important to understand the larger, underlying reason for having a structured complaint resolution process—the question of why state governments and state government employees should care about grievance procedures.

Figure 17.1 The Classic Model of Grievance Procedures

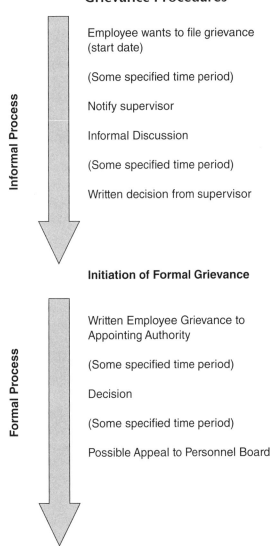

Informal Process

Employee wants to file grievance (start date)

(Some specified time period)

Notify supervisor

Informal Discussion

(Some specified time period)

Written decision from supervisor

Initiation of Formal Grievance

Formal Process

Written Employee Grievance to Appointing Authority

(Some specified time period)

Decision

(Some specified time period)

Possible Appeal to Personnel Board

Source: Adapted from the State of Colorado State Personnel Board Minimum Requirements for the Employee Grievance Process (Colorado 2015a).

Why Grievance Procedures Are Necessary

State governments need to have some form of grievance or complaint resolution process in place in order to create workplaces that foster an environment of organizational justice. Organizational justice is fundamentally about how employees construct meaning around their treatment in the workplace—whether they perceive themselves to have been treated fairly and how this perception impacts the nature of the employment relationship (Greenberg 1987; Moorman 1991; Nabatchi, Bingham, and Good 2007; Nesbit, Nabatchi, and Bingham 2012). Research has demonstrated that employees' perceptions of organizational justice have a significant impact on many aspects of the employment relationship, including performance, productivity, and overall employee morale (Folger and Konovsky 1989; Blader and Tyler 2003; Rubin 2009, 2011). In their research on organizational justice and mediation at the United States Postal Service, Nesbit, Nabatchi, and Bingham (2012: 262–263), summarize the research on organizational justice and differentiate between four different components of organizational justice:

1. Distributive justice: Fairness is associated with reward distribution—"whether an employee perceives the reward allocation decision of a supervisor or management to be fair (and favorable)" (262).
2. Procedural justice: Perceptions of fairness are structured by the nature of the process used to make decisions.
3. Informational justice: Fairness is associated with the transparency of the decision-making process— "the explanation of decision-making procedures and the extent to which those explanations provide the information necessary to evaluate the process and its enactment" (263).
4. Interpersonal justice: Fairness is related to how people are treated by management in a decision-making process.

In considering the design and operation of grievance processes, attention is generally placed on procedural and informational justice, how the grievance system creates a structured due process that allows employees to seek redress and makes explicit the steps involved in resolving the complaint. Employees are more likely to accept personnel decisions that are unfavorable to their interests as long as those decisions are made with a fair and transparent procedure (Rubin 2009). However, good grievance or complaint processes should foster procedural, informational, *and* interpersonal justice on the part of the participants in the resolution of complaints. The more that employees perceive that they have been afforded a fair process, one that is transparent to them, and have been treated with respect during this process, the more that they will accept the ultimate resolution of the complaint process, even if the decision is not in their favor. In addition, as grievance procedures generally include an emphasis on resolving the complaint at the earliest and lowest stage possible, creating a climate of interpersonal justice in state government agencies is equally important. The more that managers are able to instill a strong sense of interpersonal justice in relation to their employees, the more likely it is that grievances may be resolved before being put into writing and entering the formal system.

Therefore, state governments need to consider both the processes in place to resolve employee complaints and how managers in these governments are trained in their interpersonal interactions with employees. While grievance processes and other systems of complaint resolution can impose costs on management in terms of time and attention, the overall benefits associated with how employees perceive their treatment—the organizational justice benefits—may outweigh the costs. The following section explores the current processes in place in state governments in relation to how these governments address and process employee complaints.

STATE GOVERNMENT GRIEVANCE OR COMPLAINT RESOLUTION PROCEDURES

For this chapter, existing state laws, policies, and procedures were examined to determine current trends in the practices of state governments in handling employee complaints. Across the 50 states, there is significant variation in their grievance procedures, including who and what is covered, the structure of the grievance procedures, and the role of alternative dispute resolution and mediation for resolving complaints. Exploring practices across state governments in the United States highlights such trends as the relationship between union representation and grievance procedures, the decentralization of grievance procedures, the scope of grievances, and the growth of processes to resolve complaints before the formal grievance process, including mandated informal counseling and alternative dispute resolution processes.

Union Representation and Grievance Procedures

While the private sector has seen an overall decline in union representation, membership in public unions remains strong, even with recent right-to-work movements and challenges to unions in states such as Wisconsin and Michigan (Kearney 2010; Davis 2013). In state governments with significant union representation among state employees, the structure of grievance and complaint procedures is strongly influenced by collective bargaining agreements. As collective bargaining agreements structure the employee relationship—from leave and vacation policies to overtime to retirement practices—for many state employees, grievance procedures are focused on resolving complaints associated with the implementation of the collective bargaining agreements. If employees believe that there have been violations or misapplications of provisions of the collective bargaining agreements, they can seek redress through either state law or through the provisions in the contracts.

Kearney (2010) highlighted that many states still have high levels of public sector unionization, both in terms of representation and membership. In states with strong union representation in state government employment, state law governs the labor relations for state employees, addressing such issues as the right to union representation, recognition of employee organizations, and the manner in which disputes surrounding collective bargaining agreements can be addressed. As such, these laws usually include provisions concerning the establishment of and nature of grievance procedures for resolving conflicts with the agreements. For example, Title 5 of the Connecticut General Statutes addresses state employees, with Chapter 68 defining the collective bargaining

structure for state employees and establishing the role of the State Board of Mediation and Arbitration in addressing grievances (State of Connecticut 2012). Chapter 150E of the General Laws of the Commonwealth of Massachusetts allows for inclusion of formal grievance procedures in any collective bargaining agreement, with the grievance procedures designed for resolving differences in the interpretation of the collective bargaining agreement (Commonwealth of Massachusetts 2012). Chapter 89 of the Hawaii Revised Statutes governs collective bargaining in public employment, allowing public employees to enter into written agreements with representatives of public employee organizations to establish grievance procedures (Michie's Hawaii Revised Statutes Annotated 2010). Therefore, in states with significant union representation and/or strong collective bargaining agreements, state law specifies the role of the employee organizations in structuring the grievance process.

In these states, the grievance procedures generally follow the classic model, with multiple specified steps of increasing formality in the resolution of the grievance, as evidenced by the grievance procedure established in a current collective bargaining agreement between the State of Vermont and the Vermont State Employees' Association, Inc. In this collective bargaining agreement, the grievance procedure includes four steps of varying levels of formality (Step 1: Immediate Supervisor, Step 2: Department Head, Step 3: Department of Human Resources, and Step 4: Labor Relations Board; State of Vermont 2015). At the earlier levels, there are both informal and formal requirements (informal consultation to seek to resolve the conflict) with formal written detailing of the grievance. In addition, each step within the process has a clearly specified time period for fulfillment.

As stated, for states with strong union representation, collective bargaining agreements, while varying depending on the particular employee organization, generally allow for grievances surrounding the interpretation of the agreement. However, some states have established procedures alongside the contractual grievance procedures or have established provisions to protect those employees not included within collective bargaining agreements. For example, the state of California details multiple different ways to file an appeal, grievance, or complaint, differentiating between contract grievances, nonmerit statutory appeals, merit-based appeals (handled by the state personnel board), and discrimination complaints (State of California 2012). Delaware, under Section 18 of the State of Delaware Merit Rules, allows employees to file grievances concerning the application of state merit rules or law. The section states that employees covered by collective bargaining agreements should follow the grievance procedures outlined in the agreements, but allows for the use of merit grievance procedures if the subject being grieved is not covered under the negotiable issues in the collective bargaining agreement (State of Delaware 2012).

Therefore, states with significant union representation have collective bargaining agreements that provide comprehensive grievance procedures for those employees governed by the agreements. However, the challenge is for those employees not covered by collective bargaining agreements. As seen, states have taken to providing additional avenues for protection for noncovered employees through merit procedures or other avenues for appeal. Overall, one can conclude that state government employees covered by collective bargaining agreements generally have access to the most formal and structured grievance policies.

Decentralization of Grievance Procedures

Since the early 1990s, state governments have enacted a growing decentralization of personnel practices, moving away from a centralized personnel agency or civil service board and giving more responsibility to individual departments to set their human resource management policies and practices (see Hays and Sowa 2006). This decentralization also extends to the employee complaint process, with states decentralizing grievance procedures to the agency level. While many state governments provide language in their laws and personnel regulations concerning the minimum level of grievance procedures that should be afforded employees, these governments allow individual agencies to further specify the protections

and process that employees can use to address personnel actions taken against them. For example, Missouri, through the Code of State Regulations, has decentralized grievance procedures to the individual agency level, covering those personnel actions not subject to appeal to the personnel advisory board. Each agency is required to construct written procedures addressing certain minimum provisions, including time frames for each step in the process, provisions for prohibiting retaliation and discrimination surrounding the filing of a grievance, and a method for informing employees of the grievance procedures (State of Missouri 2012). Arkansas also provides for each agency to establish their own set of rules related to the resolution of disputes or to handle employee grievances that must be approved by the Office of Personnel Management and then given to each agency's employees (State of Arkansas 2015).

Similarly, South Carolina, with its State Employee Grievance Procedure Act, allows for each agency to establish grievance procedures, with these procedures to be approved by the state human resources director (State of South Carolina 2012). The Office of Human Resources provides a model grievance procedure policy for agencies to use. North Carolina also allows individual agencies to establish grievance procedures, emphasizing in the employee handbook that employees should carefully review their agency's grievance procedure to "identify issues that are grievable through the internal agency grievance process and those that may be appealed directly to the Office of Administrative Hearings without completing the internal agency grievance process" (State of North Carolina 2012: 26). Arizona recently passed major personnel reform (HB 2571), setting up a personnel system that will transform the majority of its workforce to at-will status (State of Arizona 2012a). However, even prior to this, Arizona had decentralized grievance practices to individual agencies. With the new reform, the Arizona Statewide Employee Handbook specifies that these agency level grievance procedures apply to covered employees only, with uncovered employees serving at the pleasure of their particular appointing authority (State of Arizona 2012b).

As states decentralize personnel authority across a wide variety of policies and practices, it is not surprising that grievance procedures would be included in this movement. This decentralization could be positive in some instances: Some agencies may deliver services that require significant discretion on the part of their employees and therefore may want to have in place more stringent protections. However, if states choose to go this route, they should ensure that agencies are provided with model policies that specify the minimum protections required and the central personnel office within state governments should periodically audit individual agencies to ensure that (1) the policy is in place, (2) the policy has been clearly explained to employees, and (3) that employees feel empowered to use the policy if needed. Otherwise, there could be an adverse impact on the overall perceptions of organizational justice in these governments and the perception that certain agencies are not the "best" in which to work or fail to provide adequate protection.

Scope of Grievances

When designing a grievance or complaint resolution process, states must carefully consider which personnel issues to include and how expansive the coverage of the grievance procedures will be. While states vary in terms of expansive coverage to restrictive lists of possible actions to grieve, states generally address certain issues.

First, in most states, even those with reformed personnel systems that emphasize deregulation of the personnel function and at-will status for most employees, there are provisions for a certain minimum level of coverage. For example, Georgia, one of the states most often discussed with reference to personnel reform and deregulation of the personnel function, still provides a certain level of protection for its employees. The State Personnel Board Rules clearly detail what is and is not open for complaint (State of Georgia 2015: 2–4; see Table 17.1).

States recognize that even when they are seeking to narrowly draw their grievance procedures, a certain base level of protection must be in place. This protection generally centers on ensuring that government employees (even those not covered by collective bargaining agreements or civil service structures) who experience an adverse personnel action tied to clear claims of discrimination are afforded an avenue of recourse. State governments recognize that while reducing the formal personnel rules governing public employment

Table 17.1 State of Georgia

Issues Eligible (and Not Eligible) For Employee Complaint Resolution Procedure
Eligible for Complaint
Allegations of unlawful discrimination
Allegations of sexual or other forms of unlawful harassment
Retaliation for filing or participating in the complaint process
Retaliation or intimidation for exercising rights under the Rules of the State Personnel Board or agency policies
Erroneous, arbitrary, or capricious interpretation or application of policies and procedures
Unsafe or unhealthy working conditions
Any matter specifically included as eligible in an agency's policies
For classified employees only: written reprimand or written confirmation of an oral reprimand

(Continued)

Table 17.1 (Continued)

Not Eligible for Complaint

Suspension, demotion, salary reduction, or separation from employment

Issues pending or adjudicated by the State Personnel Board, Georgia Commission on Equal Opportunity, or through other state or federal administrative or judicial procedure

Issues subject to appeal, review, or relief as provided for in other agency policies and procedures

Performance expectations and evaluations

Actions implementing a reduction in force or furlough plan

Selection of an individual to fill a position, unless an allegation is made that the selection is in violation of the State Personnel Board Rules, agency policy, or law

Permanent changes in work hours or duties and responsibilities, unless a change is unsafe or unlawful

Temporary work assignments that do not exceed 90 days

Budget and organizational structure

Relocation of employees unless the relocation qualifies for reimbursement

Internal security practices established by the agency

For unclassified employees only: written reprimand or written confirmation of an oral reprimand

Any matter that is not within the jurisdiction or control of the agency

Source: State of Georgia. 2015. State Personnel Board Rules: 478–1.20 Employee Complaint Resolution Procedure. Georgia Department of Administrative Services. http://doas.ga.gov/assets/Human%20Resources%20Administration/State%20Personnel%20Board%20Rules/478-1-.20%20Employee%20 Complaint%20Resolution%20Procedure.pdf. Accessed April 7, 2015.

may be desirable to enhance managerial flexibility, it is still necessary to offer clear procedures in the event of unfair or unlawful discrimination in the employer/ employee relationship, such as discrimination covered by the Americans with Disabilities Act, Title VII of the Civil Rights Act of 1964, and other equal employment opportunity laws.

When states seek to narrowly draw their grievance procedures, with the focus on ensuring that the government is not unduly subject to a large number of employee complaints, most grievance procedures exclude matters that are outside of the purview of individual government agencies or constitute central government actions. For example, many grievance procedures explicitly place retirement systems, health insurance, life insurance, the classification system, and reductions in force outside of the structured grievance process. The state of Wyoming defines a grievance broadly in terms of disputes in interpretation of or implementation of the various laws and rules governing personnel and working conditions. However, the Wyoming personnel rules clearly exempt disputes associated with dismissals or reductions in force from the grievance process and establish a separate process for appeals associated with personnel disputes arising from unsatisfactory performance assessments (State of Wyoming 2012). As decisions on state-wide policies and practices such as reductions in force, health insurance, and retirement systems cover a significant amount of employees, opening up these parts of the employment relationship to the grievance process could create an avalanche of complaints and grievances. For example, if a state government changed health care coverage in order to save money during a fiscal crisis, such as those experienced by states in the United States in the late 2000s, if employees were allowed to grieve such a change, employees could organize and barrage the government with a flurry of grievances, thereby frustrating any change and causing serious financial difficulties for the state.

In addition, in constructing grievance procedures, state governments are attentive to protecting the rights of their managers to make managerial decisions concerning their employees in carrying out the statutory goals of their agencies. Managers often have to make hard decisions concerning the assignment of employees to various tasks and evaluation of their performance, decisions that even the most rational employee may have a hard time accepting as just if these decisions conflict with an employee's opinion of his or her role or performance. States are attentive to protecting this discretion on the part of managers in the grievance process, as allowing grievances on fundamental managerial actions could result in a complete standstill between managers and employees.

Some particular management actions excluded from the grievance process in many states include directing employees in the operation of the agency's mandate and hiring, promoting, transferring, and retaining employees. The state of Wisconsin's Human Resource Handbook clearly affirms the rights of management to direct their employees and lists a set of management rights (State of Wisconsin 2012). However, this does not imply that managers can make capricious decisions, such as transferring employees that they do not like or penalizing particular employees on their performance reviews. While these managerial actions are exempt from the grievance process, many state grievance procedures do allow for complaints or grievances on the manner of these actions versus the substance of these actions. This places the burden on the employee to demonstrate that the performance appraisal process or disciplinary process was misapplied versus simply disagreeing with the assessment of performance or sanction taken against the employee. This provides for procedural justice if the employee is treated unfairly but allows managers to engage in the difficult work of assessing and correcting employee performance.

It is clear that many states have designed their grievance policies and procedures with specific attention toward ensuring a balance of employee protection with limits on employees' ability to undermine managerial action and discretion. Even states without detailed restrictions on the scope of grievances recognize that managers often must make difficult decisions and take actions that may create employee discontent, protecting managers from employee reactions to criticism or discipline associated with employee performance. In addition, state governments realize that government-wide policies and practices should be removed from grievance policies to ensure that employees cannot frustrate policies that may cause individual discomfort but are designed to promote the welfare of the government as a whole.

Working on Reducing Formal Grievances: Oral Discourse and Mediation

While recognizing the need to provide for employee protections, state governments acknowledge that the initiation of formal grievances can be a cumbersome and contentious process. The formal grievance process can require significant paperwork and time investment on the part of both the employee and employer and may prolong conflict between the two parties. Therefore, more states are exploring processes to reduce the need to use the formal grievance process. These processes include encouraging or mandating of oral discourse prior to filing the formal written grievance and the use of mediation and alternative dispute resolution processes to resolve employee complaints.

Conflicts arising between a manager and an employee can come from many different sources—differing information, differing beliefs about performance, differing opinions about the implementation of agency policy. While states should endeavor to protect employees and make them feel that they have formal recourse in the case of conflict, strongly encouraging or mandating employees to discuss the source of the conflict with a manager before initiating further steps is a common sense and practical way of reducing conflicts that may be based on miscommunication or other misunderstandings. For example, Arizona requires agency grievance procedures to include a provision for mandatory oral discourse prior to the filing of the grievance. Employees are required to inform their manager of their conflict and intent to file a grievance. The purpose of the oral discourse is to provide a final, informal opportunity for the manager and the employee to communicate before entering the formalized grievance process. The Arizona policy also states that employees cannot file the grievance unless they have completed this step (State of Arizona 2012c). North Carolina's handbook for state employees includes language that affirms the need to try to build a positive working relationship between management and employees and resolve conflicts informally. The handbook states (State of North Carolina 2012: 26):

A positive relationship between employees and supervisors is based on mutual trust, respect, and open communication. If you have a problem or grievance concerning your employment, you should first discuss the issue or concern with your immediate supervisor. In most cases, these discussions can clear up any misunderstanding or disagreement.

Numerous other state rules governing grievance procedures encourage resolving grievances at the lowest level possible in agencies. Therefore, if not already included, states should consider either strongly encouraging or mandating oral discourse between supervisors and employees. This initial dialogue may reduce the need to engage in the formal grievance process.

In addition to informal oral discourse prior to the filing of grievances, more states are adopting some form of alternative dispute resolution (Reeves 1995). Alternative dispute resolution (ADR) processes include a number of different techniques that are designed to help people in traditionally adversarial positions come to agreement. The U.S. Office of Personnel Management (OPM) provides a resource guide that includes over 10 different forms of ADR processes, including interest-based problem solving, facilitation, and mediation (OPM 2001). In particular, there has been a growing body of research on the use of workplace mediation in the public sector, with these scholars demonstrating that mediation can have significant positive benefits on the workplace in terms of dispute resolution and overall organizational justice (Bingham and Wise 1996; Nabatchi 2007, Nesbit, Nabatchi, and Bingham 2012). Nesbit, Nabatchi, and Bingham (2012: 264) define mediation as a "dispute resolution process in which a neutral third party (i.e. the mediator) assists the disputants in reaching a mutually agreeable solution to the issue at hand." When informal discussion has failed in reaching a resolution in a supervisor-employee disagreement, the use of mediation or other forms of ADR is another way of seeking to resolve conflict before entering the formal grievance process.

Including mediation in addition to or alongside formal grievance procedures can be a way of resolving employee complaints more efficiently, as mediation can contain the costs associated with execution of the full grievance processes and can reduce the level of adversarial conflict between the manager and employee (Bingham and Novac 2001; Jameson et al. 2012). Colorado provides a State Employee Mediation Program, established in 1986. This program is designed as an alternative to the grievance process or can be used in association with it. In the Colorado process, mediation can occur before a formal grievance, but either party involved in a formal grievance can request mediation, suspending the grievance process until the mediation is concluded (State of Colorado 2015b). Arkansas, Kentucky, Nevada, Ohio, North Carolina, Virginia, and Oregon are among the many states that have instituted such programs. In North Carolina, in 2005, the Office of State Personnel created a new employee mediation and grievance policy that allowed state agencies to include mediation as the first step in their grievance procedures (Jameson et al. 2012). In an examination of the costs and benefits of this policy change, Jameson and colleagues found that mediation had produced positive benefits for both the agencies using it and the employees involved in the mediation process.

While mediation and dispute resolution programs can help resolve conflict between employees and managers and perhaps reduce or eliminate the desire of the employee to file a formal grievance, these programs are generally voluntary and do not preclude employees from continuing in the grievance process. Mediation programs are generally designed to quickly and economically resolve disputes in the workplace; when employee complaints involve complex issues or claims of discrimination in a personnel action, mediation programs may not necessarily be appropriate. Both mediation and mandatory informal and formal discourse as part of the grievance process represent sound strategies to reduce the need to initiate formal grievances. However, in using such strategies, state governments should be careful to inform employees of their rights under the state policies. Employees should recognize that they still have recourse if a resolution is not achieved through these processes. If not, the organizational justice associated with the complaint and grievance procedures would be significantly reduced and employees could believe that management prefers expeditious resolutions at the expense of fair resolutions.

Dealing with Employee Problems: Problems and Prospects

In considering how state governments provide for resolving employee problems, it is clear that the trend is still toward putting in place formal systems of complaint that allow employees to seek redress. Even in states with significant deregulation of the personnel function, employees are provided with systems to ensure that they have recourse if faced with discrimination or unjust actions on the part of their supervisors. As stated, states are also moving toward encouraging practices that reduce the need to go through the formal grievance process, encouraging dialogue between supervisors and employees to resolve misunderstandings and providing for alternative dispute resolution processes. However, there are some additional actions that states could consider implementing to reduce the number of employee complaints that have to be resolved. The following are several recommendations for future research and future action to improve the overall organizational justice in state governments and address employee problems overall.

Management Training for Emotional Intelligence

One of the first steps toward reducing employee problems may be investing in better training of managers to recognize problems as they arise and engage in corrective action before the problem reaches an actionable stage (see the chapter by Guy in this volume). Research has demonstrated that the emotional intelligence of managers can have a significant impact on the climate of a workplace (Momeni 2009). While scholars have operationalized the concept in different ways, emotional intelligence is fundamentally about the ability to recognize emotions in oneself and others and manage those emotions (Goleman 2006). If managers are trained to better perceive and recognize emotions, their ability to understand when problems are brewing among their employees may allow for them to intercede and correct problems before they reach the level that necessitates a complaint. As countless studies have demonstrated since the advent of organizational theory, individuals promoted to the level of management are not always necessarily well trained in interpersonal skills. Investing in training for managers to improve their emotional intelligence may improve how they manage their employees, thereby improving the interpersonal justice perceptions of employees and overall organizational justice and reducing the number of problem employees and subsequent employee complaints that have to enter the grievance process.

Increased Investment in Conflict Resolution

As stated, research has demonstrated that investment in ADR systems can have a positive impact on workplaces, both in terms of morale and with the reduction of formal employee complaints. To reduce the number of problems arising in state government workplaces, more states should not only implement systems of ADR as described in this chapter but should also consider investing in the development of conflict resolution skills for employees. Reviewing training offerings on state government human resource department websites demonstrates that training is available for managers in conflict resolution. More research should be conducted on how prevalent this training is, how many managers avail themselves of this training, and the impact this training has on managers' performance. If managers are better trained in conflict resolution, they may be able to reframe problems with employees to come to a mutual understanding and thereby resolve the problem in a manner that serves all the interests involved.

Longitudinal Examination of Grievance and Complaint Patterns

Well-designed grievance procedures, especially those that encourage resolving conflicts at early stages or through mediation, should lead to a reduction in grievances over time. The question is the degree to which the resolution of conflicts through mediation and the grievance process produces information that can be brought back into agencies and used to foster organizational learning. If employee grievance and complaint resolution processes can be structured to provide lessons on how to avoid particular problems in the future, this could lead to an overall reduction in complaints. Future research that examines the incidence and patterns of complaints over time in individual agencies could determine whether complaint resolution procedures that encourage discussion and mediation can be used to instruct managers on their performance and improve their performance over time.

To create workplaces that recognize that conflict is a natural part of an engaged workforce and manage that conflict appropriately, the first step is establishing structured complaint and grievance procedures. The organizational justice, and in particular procedural justice, that these systems provide for employees is a valuable investment. For state governments seeking to reexamine their grievance procedures, the advice would be to seek a balance between the needs of management and the rights of employees to be treated in a fair and equitable manner. Providing employees with recourse to address adverse personnel actions, whatever the outcome, is inherently necessary for the well-being and satisfaction of these employees. Doing so will also contribute to the development of an overall climate of organizational justice within these agencies. Implementing policies and practices to reduce the need to use this recourse, whether through better training of managers in conflict resolution, requiring mandatory oral discourse, or implementing alternative dispute resolution processes, can add to the justice perceptions provided through the formal system and hopefully reduce the need to engage in the structured grievance process. The critical requirement is to make sure that employees feel that they have access to recourse in the case of complaints, as this contributes long term to the operating environment of government agencies, making grievance policies and procedures, with all the associated practices, a necessary part of personnel regulation in state government.

REFERENCES

Bingham, L. B., and M. C. Novac. 2001. Mediation's Impact on Formal Discrimination Complaint Filing: Before and After the REDRESS® Program at the U.S. Postal Service. *Review of Public Personnel Administration, 21,* 308–331.

Bingham, L. B., and C. R. Wise. 1996. The Administrative Dispute Resolution Act of 1990: How Do We Evaluate its Success? *Journal of Public Administration, Research and Theory, 6,* 383–414.

Blader, S. L., and T. R. Tyler. 2003. What Constitutes Fairness in Work Settings? A Four-Component Model of Procedural Justice. *Human Resource Management Review, 13,* 107–126.

Bowman, J. S., and J. P. West. 2006. Ending Civil Service Protections in Florida Government: Experiences in State Agencies. *Review of Public Personnel Administration, 26,* 139–157.

Brewer, B., and G. K. Y. Lam. 2009. Conflict Handling Preferences: A Public-Private Comparison. *Public Personnel Management, 38,* 1.

Coggburn, J. 2000. The Effects of Deregulation on State Government Personnel Administration. *Review of Public Personnel Administration, 20,* 24–39.

———. 2001. Personnel Deregulation: Exploring Differences in the American States. *Journal of Public Administration Research and Theory, 11,* 223–244.

Commonwealth of Massachusetts. 2012. General Laws: Chapter 150E: Labor Relations: Public Employees. http://www.malegislature.gov/Laws/GeneralLaws/PartI/TitleXXI/Chapter150E. Accessed November 1, 2012.

Crowell, E. B., and M. E. Guy. 2010. Florida's HR Reforms: Service First, Service Worst, or Something in Between? *Public Personnel Management, 39,* 15–46.

Daley, D. M. 2007. If a Tree Falls in the Forest: The Effects of Grievances on Employee Perceptions of Performance Appraisals, Efficacy, and Job Satisfaction. *Review of Public Personnel Administration, 27,* 281–296.

Davis, R. S. 2013. Union Commitment and Stakeholder Red Tape: How Union Values Shape Perceptions of Organizational Rules. *Review of Public Personnel Administration, 33*(4), 365–383.

Elling, R. C., and T. L. Thompson. 2006. Human Resource Problems and State Management Performance Across Two Decades: The Implications for Civil Service Reform. *Review of Public Personnel Administration, 26,* 302–334.

Folger, R., and M. A. Konovsky. 1989. Effects of Procedural and Distributive Justice on Reactions to Pay Raise Decisions. *Academy of Management Journal, 32,* 115–130.

Goleman, D. 2006. *Emotional Intelligence* (10th Anniversary Edition). New York: Bantam Dell.

Greenberg, J. 1987. Reactions to Procedural Injustice in Payment Distributions: Do the Means Justify the Ends? *Journal of Applied Psychology, 72,* 55–61.

Hays, S. W., and J. E. Sowa. 2006. A Broader Look at the 'Accountability Movement:' Some Grim Realities in State Civil Service Systems. *Review of Public Personnel Administration, 26,* 102–117.

Ingraham. P. W. 1995. *The Foundation of Merit: Public Service in American Democracy.* Baltimore: Johns Hopkins University Press.

Jameson, J. K., R. Berry-James, J. Coggburn, and D. Daley. 2012. North Carolina Office of State Personnel Mediation and Grievance Programs Cost/Benefit Analysis. http://www.osp.state.nc.us/Guide/ER/mediation/Mediation%20and%20Grievance%20Programs%20Cost%20Benefit%20Analysis%20%208_%202012.pdf. Accessed November 15, 2012.

Jehn, K. A., and E. A. Mannix. 2001. The Dynamic Nature of Conflict: A Longitudinal Study of Intragroup Conflict and Group Performance. *Academy of Management Journal, 44,* 238–251.

Jehn, K. A., S. Rispens, and S. M. B. Thatcher. 2010. The Effects of Conflict Asymmetry on Work Group and Individual Outcomes. *Academy of Management Journal, 53,* 596–616.

Kearney, R. C. 2001. *Labor Relations in the Public Service* (3rd ed.). New York: Marcel Dekker.

———. 2010. Public Sector Labor-Management Relations: Change or Status Quo? *Review of Public Personnel Administration, 30,* 89–111.

Kellough, J. E., and L. G. Nigro. 2006. Dramatic Reform in the Public Service: At-Will Employment and the Creation of the New Public Workforce. *Journal of Public Administration Research and Theory, 16,* 447–466.

Litterer, J. A. 1966. Conflict in Organization: A Re-Examination. *Academy of Management Journal, 9,* 178–186.

Mesch, D. J. 1995. Grievance Arbitration in the Public Sector: A Conceptual Framework and Empirical Analysis of Public and Private Sector Arbitration Cases. *Review of Public Personnel Administration, 15,* 22–36.

Michie's Hawaii Revised Statutes Annotated. 2010. Charlottesville, VA: Lexis Law Publishing.

Momeni, N. 2009. The Relation Between Managers' Emotional Intelligence and the Organizational Climate They Create. *Public Personnel Management, 38,* 35–48.

Moorman, R. H. 1991. Relationship between Organizational Justice and Organizational Citizenship Behaviors: Do Fairness Perceptions Influence Employee Citizenship? *Journal of Applied Psychology, 76,* 845–855.

Nabatchi, T. 2007. The Institutionalization of Alternative Dispute Resolution in the Federal Government. *Public Administration Review, 67,* 646–661.

Nabatchi, T., L. B. Bingham, and D. Good. 2007. Organizational Justice and Dispute Resolution: A Six-Factor Model for Workplace Mediation. *International Journal of Conflict Management, 18,* 148–176.

Nesbit, R., T. Nabatchi, and L. B. Bingham. 2012. Employees, Supervisors, and Workplace Mediation: Experiences of Justice and Settlement. *Review of Public Personnel Administration, 32,* 260–287.

Reeves, T. Z. 1995. The Use of Employee-Based Grievance Systems. *Review of Public Personnel Administration, 15,* 73–80.

Richardson, R. C. 1977. *Collective Bargaining by Objectives.* Englewood Cliffs, NJ: Prentice Hall.

Rubin, E. V. 2009. The Role of Procedural Justice in Public Personnel Management: Empirical Results from the

Department of Defense. *Journal of Public Administration Research and Theory, 19,* 125–143.

———. 2011. Exploring the Link between Procedural Fairness and Union Membership in the Federal Government. *Review of Public Personnel Administration, 31*(2), 128–142.

State of Arizona. 2012a. Personnel Reform: A Cornerstone of Productivity, Efficiency, and Accountability. http://hr.az .gov/PR/index.html. Accessed November 15, 2012.

State of Arizona. 2012b. State Personnel System Employee Handbook. http://www.hr.state.az.us/PDF/Statewide_ Employee_Handbook.pdf. Accessed November 15, 2012.

State of Arizona. 2012c. Final Rules: Title 2. Administration. Chapter 5. Department of Administration State Personnel System. http://www.hr.state.az.us/PDF/Personnel_Rules .pdf. Accessed November 20, 2012.

State of Arkansas. 2015. State Employee Dispute Resolution Policy Number 70.06. http://www.dfa.arkansas.gov/offices/ personnelManagement/policy/Documents/70_06State EmployeeDisputeResolution.pdf. Accessed January 13, 2015.

State of California. 2012. California Department of Human Resources: Appeals and Grievances. http://www.calhr .ca.gov/state-hr-professionals/Pages/appeals-and-grievances.aspx. Accessed November 15, 2012.

State of Colorado. 2015a. Colorado State Personnel Board Rule 8–8: Minimum Requirements of Employee Grievance Process. https://www.colorado.gov/pacific/sites/default/ files/Rules7-1-13.pdf. Accessed January 10, 2015.

State of Colorado. 2015b. Department of Personnel and Administration: State Employee Mediation Program. https://www.colorado.gov/pacific/c-seap/state-employee-mediation-program-semp. Accessed January 10, 2015.

State of Connecticut. 2012. Chapter 68: State Personnel Act. http://search.cga.state.ct.us/dtsearch_pub_statutes .html. Accessed December 1, 2012.

State of Delaware. 2012. State Employee Merit Rules. http:// delawarepersonnel.com/search/mrules.asp?page= Sections&ID=18.0. Accessed November 30, 2012.

State of Georgia. 2015. State Personnel Board Rules: 478-1.20 Employee Complaint Resolution Procedure. Georgia Department of Administrative Services. http://doas .ga.gov/assets/Human%20Resources%20Administration/ State%20Personnel%20Board%20Rules/478-1-.20%20 Employee%20Complaint%20Resolution%20Procedure .pdf. Accessed April 7, 2015.

State of Missouri. 2012. Rules of the Office of Administration. Division 20–Personnel Advisory Board and Division of Personnel. http://www.sos.mo.gov/adrules/csr/current/ 1csr/1c20-4.pdf. Accessed November 15, 2012.

State of North Carolina. 2012. NC Office of State Personnel: Inside State Government: A Handbook for State Employees. http://www.osp.state.nc.us/State%20Employee%20 Handbook%202012.pdf. Accessed November 15, 2012.

State of South Carolina. 2012. State Employee Grievance Procedure Act. http://www.ohr.sc.gov/OHR/OHR-employee .phtm#grievance. Accessed November 15, 2012.

State of Vermont. 2015. Agreements Between the State of Vermont and the Vermont State Employees' Association, Inc. Non-Management Bargaining Unit. Effective July 1, 2014—Expiring June 30, 2016. http://humanresources. vermont.gov/sites/dhr/files/Documents/CBA/DHR-Non-Management_Contract_14_16.pdf. Accessed January 11, 2015.

State of Wisconsin. 2012. Wisconsin Human Resources Handbook. Chapter 430: Employee Grievance Procedure. http://oser.state.wi.us/docview.asp?docid=7358. Accessed October 25, 2012.

State of Wyoming. 2012. State of Wyoming Personnel Rules, May 29, 2012. http://www.wyoming.gov/loc/06012011_1/ DOCS%20HR/Rules/PersonnelRules05-29-12.pdf. Accessed November 5, 2012.

U.S. Office of Personnel Management. 2001. Alternative Dispute Resolution: A Resource Guide. http://www.opm .gov/er/adrguide/adrguide2001.pdf. Accessed March 24, 2015.

PART III

THE ISSUES

COMBATING DISCRIMINATION AND ITS LEGACY: AFFIRMATIVE ACTION AND DIVERSITY IN THE PUBLIC SECTOR

J. Edward Kellough
University of Georgia

Discrimination directed against racial, ethnic, and other minorities and women has a long and distressing history. This chapter is about the ways in which government organizations in the United States have responded to historic patterns of discrimination in public personnel systems. Obviously, there are many reasons why government should be involved in combating discrimination in public employment. Fundamental notions of merit and justice, for example, require that the public service be free from prejudice. As Hays (1998) notes in a broad discussion of civil service selection procedures, "public jobs are public resources, to which everyone has a potential claim." The process by which those valuable resources are distributed must not be closed to specified groups of people identified by factors such as sex, race, or ethnicity. In addition, government has a responsibility, through its own employment practices, to provide an appropriate example for nongovernmental organizations (Krislov 1967). If government cannot protect women and minorities from discrimination within the ranks of its own workforce, how can we reasonably expect it to counter discrimination in private employment or other endeavors? Finally, government efforts to open the public employment

process to underrepresented groups are desirable also because we know that a governmental bureaucracy reflective of the public it serves, in terms of such characteristics as race, ethnicity, and sex, can help to ensure that all interests are appropriately considered in policy formulation and implementation processes. There is a growing body of empirical research to demonstrate that a more representative public bureaucracy promotes greater governmental responsiveness to a variety of public interests (see, e.g., Meier 1993; Meier and Stewart 1992; Selden 1997; Selden, Brudney, and Kellough 1998; Wilkins and Keiser 2006).

EARLY ACTION IN RESPONSE TO DISCRIMINATION

Despite strong arguments for equal employment opportunity, and notwithstanding constitutional guarantees of equal protection of the laws and merit system rules designed to ensure that applicants for public employment would be judged only on the basis of their abilities, discrimination in the public sector was extensive and openly practiced well into the twentieth century. Rosenbloom (1977) notes, for example, that during the administration of William Howard Taft, a policy of segregation of whites and African Americans was initiated within the Census Bureau, and African American appointments were reduced in areas of the country such as the South where whites objected to their employment. Under the subsequent administration of Woodrow Wilson, other discriminatory practices were encouraged or condoned, such as the segregation of offices, restrooms, and lunchrooms. It was also under Wilson that a photograph was for the first time required to accompany applications for federal employment. Although that requirement was eventually dropped, at the time, it was apparent that "the color of one's skin had become a test of fitness for federal employees" (Rosenbloom 1977: 54).

It was not until the 1940s that the most egregious discriminatory practices were confronted by the federal government, and then meaningful action was taken only after early civil rights advocates, led by A. Philip Randolph, threatened a mass rally in the nation's capital to protest discrimination by the government and defense industry contractors. The Roosevelt administration was decidedly cool to the idea of such a public expression of African American sentiment. Roosevelt feared that a massive protest rally in Washington, D.C., designed to call attention to racism within the United States, would divide the country along racial lines just as we were being forced to contemplate the possibility of war against Nazi Germany and its racist ideology. There was speculation that the march would turn violent, that social unrest would spread across the country, and that military discipline would be disrupted.

Nevertheless, efforts by Roosevelt to dissuade Randolph and other leaders of the March on Washington movement failed until the president agreed to establish, through issuance of a new executive order (EO 8802), an administrative organization with authority to investigate allegations of discrimination by defense contractors and federal agencies (Kellough 2006). This organization, known as the Fair Employment Practices Committee (FEPC), was the first federal government agency designed to protect minority interests since the period of reconstruction following the Civil War (Reed 1991: 15). Following the issuance of Roosevelt's

order creating the FEPC on June 25, 1941, the anticipated protest march was canceled, just days before it was scheduled to occur. The order rested on the president's ability to act independently of Congress to set the terms and conditions of executive agency contracts and to regulate the federal personnel system under existing civil service law. At this point in American history and politics, there was no chance that a substantive antidiscrimination program would come from Congress since numerous key leadership positions in that institution were filled by conservative Southern Democrats committed to racial segregation. Consequently, reliance on executive authority was essential if a policy of nondiscrimination was to be pursued. To avoid the need to ask Congress for funding to support the FEPC, money for the Committee's operations came from a presidential discretionary fund appropriated for the operation of agencies within the Executive Office of the President.

The FEPC soon established itself as a serious force in the struggle against discrimination. The Committee held highly publicized hearings to investigate alleged discriminatory practices and began a process of directing public attention to the plight of minorities in important segments of the labor market. But as might be expected, this work generated substantial opposition, especially from influential Southern Democrats whose support Roosevelt needed on a number of other issues, and as a result, the Committee placed the president in a politically difficult position. Congress eventually refused to appropriate money for operation of the Committee, and on June 28, 1946, the FEPC filed its final report and officially went out of business. During the years of its operation, however, the Committee achieved considerable success in documenting discriminatory practices by a number of defense contractors and federal agencies.

Following abolition of the FEPC, President Truman urged Congress to act, but when it became clear that congressional action would not be forthcoming, he issued another executive order (EO 9980) creating a Fair Employment Board (FEB) within the Civil Service Commission. The responsibilities of the FEB, which was established in 1948, were limited to the investigation of complaints of discrimination arising from within federal government agencies. Truman later created a second committee to perform similar work with regard to government contractors. That organization, known as the Committee on Government Contract Compliance, was established by Executive Order 10308 of December 1951.

In 1955 Eisenhower abolished Truman's FEB and established, by executive order, a new committee independent of the Civil Service Commission. Eisenhower's new organization was known as the President's Committee on Government Employment Policy (PCGEP). The PCGEP was set up as an agency-funded entity, so that direct appropriations from Congress for its operation were not needed. The Committee continued the work of investigating complaints of discriminatory practices within federal agencies—work that had been undertaken earlier by the FEPC and the FEB, and as was the case with its predecessors, it could not compel agencies to change employment decisions, even if it found convincing evidence of discrimination.

THE DEVELOPMENT OF A PROACTIVE APPROACH

During the Truman administration, staff members from the FEB realized that a policy resting primarily on the investigation of complaints might not be the most effective means of confronting discrimination. It was believed that the extent of discriminatory practices was much broader than what was suggested by the number of formal complaints filed. Many minority group members, it was found, were hesitant to register complaints because they feared retaliation or retribution if they spoke out. As a result, the FEB initiated a very limited and experimental program of "constructive action" to counter discrimination. This program consisted of "conferences with fair employment officers and outside organizations, periodic surveys and appraisals, and the adoption of some new recruitment techniques, better training programs, and steps toward further integration" (Rosenbloom 1977: 64). Eisenhower's PCGEP maintained this program, although it apparently did little to emphasize the approach.

Dramatic change was to occur, however, when John F. Kennedy entered the presidency. At the very beginning of the Kennedy administration, the president fundamentally reorganized the federal antidiscrimination effort. Executive Order 10925, issued on March 6, 1961, consolidated programs regarding government contract compliance and the federal civil service under a newly established authority known as the President's Committee on Equal Employment Opportunity (PCEEO). The committees that had operated during the Eisenhower years were dissolved. The PCEEO received and investigated complaints as the earlier committees had done, but Kennedy's order required substantially more than what had been mandated earlier. The new order required that the positive program of recruitment and outreach to the minority community, begun under Truman, be a primary and integral part of the federal effort. Under Kennedy, this approach became known as "affirmative action."

Kennedy's program placed a substantial new obligation on federal agencies. Earlier efforts were focused primarily on prohibiting federal employers from engaging in discriminatory behavior. That is, agencies were directed, for the most part, *not to do* certain things. They were not to disadvantage minority job applicants or employees because of race or ethnicity. Kennedy maintained these requirements, but in addition, he stressed that federal organizations were *to do* other things: they were to undertake and emphasize certain actions such as minority recruitment and the provision of training to promote greater equality of opportunity. The difference between the two approaches is that between a negative prohibition on the one hand and an affirmative requirement on the other.

Following Johnson's rise to the presidency in 1963, a number of additional developments occurred regarding the structure and operation of the federal program. First, Congress finally acted to prohibit discrimination by private employers and organizations receiving federal assistance through passage of the Civil Rights Act of 1964. That legislation marked a fundamental shift in the government's approach to the problem of discrimination, but, significantly, its provisions did not initially apply to the federal civil service. Also, there was no requirement under the law that employers engage in affirmative action. Consequently, the PCEEO, which was continuing its program of requiring affirmative action by federal agencies (and federal government contractors), came under strenuous attack by some members of Congress who argued that the Committee's work was no longer needed since the Civil Rights Act had established the Equal Employment Opportunity Commission (EEOC) to implement a policy of nondiscrimination, and contractors would fall under the jurisdiction of the EEOC (Graham 1990). Of course, that argument completely ignored the issue of discrimination within federal agencies. In order to save the federal affirmative action program, President Johnson, through Executive Order 11246 of 1965, transferred authority for the nondiscrimination effort within the federal civil service to the Civil Service Commission and gave the Department of Labor authority with respect to federal contractors. In 1967, through Executive Order 11375, Johnson added language prohibiting discrimination on the basis of sex to existing affirmative action programs.

Progress in the employment of minority group members was slow throughout the remainder of the 1960s, however, and the social unrest characteristic of much of that decade helped to persuade many people that additional action to strengthen the campaign against discrimination was needed. The Nixon administration pushed for a more aggressive approach, and in 1971 the U.S. Civil Service Commission authorized federal agencies to establish numerical goals and timetables for minority employment (Rosenbloom 1977: 107–110). Under this method, numerical goals were targets for the representation of women and minorities in an organization. Timetables were dates or timeframes within which specified goals were planned to be accomplished. Although goals and timetables required no organization to accept individuals who did not possess necessary qualifications, they did allow for the consideration of race, ethnicity, and sex in selection or placement decisions.

The policy decision to authorize goals and timetables marked another dramatic shift in the nature of the federal equal employment opportunity (EEO) program.

An employment goal, if it is meaningful, implies that a limited preference will be extended to minority group members or women when they possess requisite qualifications. That is to say, an employer who has established a goal for increasing the employment of minorities or women, who then subsequently locates qualified minority or female job applicants, will prefer those individuals over equally qualified nonminorities or men. To do otherwise would suggest that the goal is essentially meaningless. This situation indicates, however, that the use of goals and timetables transcends a strict or literal interpretation of nondiscrimination since selection policies are not purely neutral. This orientation to affirmative action, which eventually came into wide use, was authorized, however, only when minority group members or women were measurably underrepresented in an organization. Nevertheless, affirmative action in this form spawned substantial controversy and judicial activity. In fact, so much attention has been focused on numerical strategies for affirmative action in public employment and elsewhere, that goals and timetables, and the preferences they imply, now form the dominant paradigm of affirmative action policy in the minds of most people.

With the establishment of affirmative action goals and timetables, the federal government's EEO program rested on several distinct elements. The earliest initiatives, begun under Roosevelt, consisted of executive orders prohibiting discrimination and procedures for the investigation of complaints. The first affirmative action programs emerged later under Kennedy in the form of recruitment efforts, training programs, and other positive measures designed to promote the employment of minorities and women. Eventually, goals and timetables were authorized, which implied preferences for minority group members and women under specified circumstances. Table 18.1 illustrates these components of the program. In general, it should be clear that by the early 1970s, affirmative action could take many specific forms, and implications for the principle of nondiscrimination were different for different approaches. In all cases, however, affirmative action involved, and still involves, efforts to promote the employment of members of groups that have historically suffered discriminatory treatment.

As the nation was dealing with the social tumult of the 1960s, other important developments occurred with respect to equal employment opportunity. One of the more important of these was passage of the Age Discrimination in Employment Act (ADEA) of 1967. Congress had considered prohibiting discrimination on the basis of age earlier when it debated and passed Title VII of the Civil Rights Act of 1964, but it was decided that legislative action on that issue should wait until after the Department of Labor had investigated the problem and issued a report. The ADEA, which was passed three years later, prohibits employment discrimination against persons ages 40 years or older. When it was first enacted, protection was extended only through age 65,

but through subsequent amendments, that restriction was eliminated. More significantly for our purposes, the law was also amended in 1974 to cover all state, local, and federal government organizations.

In addition, the Equal Employment Opportunity Act of 1972 brought all state, local, and federal government agencies under coverage of Title VII of the Civil Rights Act of 1964. This legislation gave the EEOC direct responsibility for monitoring state and local government employment practices. Under EEOC guidelines, state and local governments were required to collect and report data on minority and female employment, and by the mid-1970s goals and timetables and the preferences they carry were well established as a part of the affirmative action process at these levels of government. With respect to the federal government, the 1972 law reaffirmed the program implemented by the Civil Service Commission, but a reorganization order by President Carter coinciding with the 1978 Civil Service Reform Act transferred authority for supervision of federal EEO and

Table 18.1 Equal Employment Opportunity and Affirmative Action Programs

Individual-Based Reactive Policies	Group-Based Proactive Policies (Affirmative Action)	
Approaches That Pre-Date Affirmative Action	**Early Approaches to Affirmative Action**	**Preferential Approaches to Affirmative Action**
Executive orders and other laws prohibiting discrimination	Workforce analysis	Voluntary goals and timetables for the selection of members of targeted groups
Procedures for the investigation and resolution of complaints	Removal of artificial barriers to minority and female selection	Consent decrees specifying selection goals and timetables
	Career development and upward mobility programs	Court-ordered selection goals and timetables
	Recruitment and outreach efforts	
Equal Employment Opportunity Programs Based on a Strict Interpretation of the Principle of Nondiscrimination		*Programs That Transcend Equality of Opportunity and Nondiscrimination in a Strict Sense by Permitting Preferences*

Source: Kellough 2006. Copyright 2006 by Georgetown University Press. "Table 1.1 Affirmative Action and Equal Opportunity". From *Understanding Affirmative Action: Politics, Discrimination, and the Search for Justice,* J. Edward Kellough, p. 11. Reprinted with permission. www.press.georgetown.edu

affirmative action practices to the EEOC (Kellough and Rosenbloom 1992). In issuing guidelines for the federal program, the EEOC initially placed great emphasis on numerical goals and timetables in agency affirmative action plans; but during the Reagan years (1981–1988), the agency backed away from that approach. Subsequent EEOC regulations permitted but did not require agencies to develop numerical goals for minority and female employment in instances where those groups were underrepresented.

An important Supreme Court case from 2009 provided additional guidance on questions of discrimination in public employment hiring procedures. In *Ricci v. DeStefano* (557 U.S. 557) a group of mostly white firefighters in New Haven, Connecticut, who had passed exams and were eligible for promotion filed a lawsuit alleging disparate treatment when the city discarded the examination results because no African American firefighters scored sufficiently high to be eligible for promotion. This was done despite the fact that the city had made substantial efforts during the development of the exams to ensure that they were valid, that is, that they accurately measured qualifications for promotion.

The city defended its action by arguing that had it certified the examination, it would have faced disparate impact litigation initiated by African American firefighters. The Supreme Court ruled that the decision to ignore the exam results amounted to disparate treatment (intentional racial discrimination against those who had passed the exams), and the Court reasoned that an employer cannot engage in disparate treatment simply to avoid a possible disparate impact law suit. In the words of Justice Kennedy, who delivered the majority opinion, "Fear of litigation alone cannot justify the City's reliance on race to the detriment of individuals who passed the examinations and qualified for promotions" (557 U.S. 557 at 33).

The federal government began to address the problem of discrimination against the disabled in the 1970s. The Rehabilitation Act of 1973, for example, prohibited discrimination against "otherwise qualified handicapped individuals" by any organization receiving federal financial assistance or by federal contractors or agencies. The purpose of the law was to ensure that no qualified individual who also happened to have a disability would be subject to discrimination under any program or activity supported by the federal government. The provision that recipients of federal funding be barred from discrimination essentially meant that all state and local governments would be covered by the law. Provisions prohibiting discrimination by federal contractors and federal agencies also required "affirmative action" involving recruitment, outreach, and training by those organizations.

In 1990, Congress again addressed the problem of discrimination against the disabled through passage of the Americans with Disabilities Act (ADA). This law was based on principles established by the Rehabilitation Act of 1973 and the regulations that had been issued to implement that earlier legislation (Kellough 2000). The ADA is comprehensive in that it extends prohibitions on discrimination against the disabled to private employers without federal contracts but it also applies directly to state and local governments, although affirmative action is not mandated. Federal agencies are not covered by the ADA, however, because it was reasoned that they are sufficiently governed by the Rehabilitation Act and its affirmative action requirements.

THE AFFIRMATIVE ACTION CONTROVERSY

As previously noted, affirmative action policies, especially those involving preferences for minorities and women, have engendered significant debate. The dispute over affirmative action is best understood, however, when we realize that such policies are intended to have the effect of redistributing opportunity from those who have been historically advantaged to groups that have suffered disadvantages because of race, ethnicity, sex, or other traits or circumstances (Edley 1996). In the context of government affirmative action, this redistribution of opportunity may involve highly valued jobs. Thus, the stakes are high, and the outcomes can be extremely important for people on both sides of the issue. Employment, after all, provides the means by which most individuals support themselves and their families financially. Beyond that, employment can be an avenue to self-fulfillment, a way of defining who we are and what we do. We should expect, therefore, that policies operating to alter the distribution of employment opportunities will very likely be opposed by individuals who prefer an earlier distribution.

We should realize also that affirmative action involving the use of limited preferences is more vulnerable to criticism than other approaches such as recruitment or outreach. This is true simply because the existence of preferences appears to contradict the concept of equality of opportunity. It is difficult for anyone to oppose efforts based firmly on the principle of nondiscrimination, such as broader recruitment or upward mobility programs, but numerical approaches including goals and timetables are more easily opposed by those who argue that a strict interpretation of equal opportunity should prevail. From the view point of those opposed to affirmative action, preferences amount to reverse discrimination; numerical goals, often referred to as "quotas" by opponents, have the effect, it is argued, of illegitimately discriminating against nonminority males and sometimes nonminority women. The key question is whether the racial, ethnic, and sex-based distinctions inherent in affirmative action goals and the accompanying preferences can be justified. Those who equate affirmative action with reverse discrimination argue that such distinctions cannot be defended. They suggest that selection decisions should be based solely on individual merit without consideration of factors such as race, ethnicity, or sex.

However, others remind us that precise measures of individual merit or qualifications are often beyond our reach. They argue that limited advantages for women and minorities in such personnel actions as selection, promotion, assignment, and transfers should be allowed to make up for past or current discrimination. Usually, this view rests on an idea known as compensatory justice, which is the notion that groups, such as minorities or women, who have suffered discrimination and have been denied opportunity as a result, should be given certain advantages to compensate for that injustice.

Proponents of affirmative action draw a distinction between discrimination motivated by racial or gender animus, on the one hand, and limited minority or female preferences, on the other, that are sometimes present in affirmative action programs intended to assist those who have historically been the victims of racism, ethnocentrism, or sexist attitudes. Opponents of affirmative action counter that while the compensatory argument may hold for identifiable victims of discrimination it should not be applied across-the-board to groups, since some group members may not have suffered discriminatory treatment. But it can be very difficult or impossible to determine if any particular individual has not been victimized by discrimination. It should also be remembered that affirmative action is not intended to benefit specified individuals; rather, it is a means of requiring employers or other institutions to ensure that their employment processes give consideration to all qualified people. Additionally, arguments for race-, ethnic-, and sex-based affirmative action are not limited to remedial justifications alone. Such programs are also often defended in more utilitarian terms in that they work to integrate society more rapidly than other approaches, reduce income inequalities, further distributive justice, and promote efficiency by ensuring that the talents of all individuals are used (Taylor 1991).

As the controversy over affirmative action grew in the 1990s, new programs emphasizing "diversity management" emerged (Kellough 2006: 67–71). Proponents of diversity management argued that such programs would be less controversial than affirmative action because they were based on the idea that we should welcome all individuals and value their differences. In contrast to the preferences associated with affirmative action, diversity management strategies focused on inclusiveness and suggested that we should work to ensure that all employees succeed to the fullest extent of their abilities. In practice, however, many diversity management efforts looked very much like older affirmative action programs. A study from 2004, for example, found that by the year 1999, 88% of federal agencies claimed to have a diversity management program, but 25% of those agencies had established their programs by simply changing the name on the door of the affirmative action office (Kellough and Naff 2004).

THE SUPREME COURT AND PREFERENTIAL AFFIRMATIVE ACTION: EXAMINING THE LIMITS OF LEGAL PERMISSIBILITY

From a legal perspective, preferential affirmative action arises in three ways. It may be the result of (1) a court order, (2) a consent decree sanctioned by a court to settle litigation, or (3) a voluntary decision by an organization. Affirmative action required by court order is authorized by Title VII of the 1964 Civil Rights Act when a federal court has found evidence of discrimination. Standards for the review of court ordered preferential affirmative action are articulated by the Supreme Court in *Firefighters Local v. Stotts*, 467 U.S. 561 (1984), and *United States v. Paradise*, 480 U.S. 149 (1987). Guidelines for permissible preferential affirmative action embodied in consent decrees are similar to those for voluntary affirmative action and are established in *Firefighters v. City of Cleveland*, 478 U.S. 501 (1986). Voluntary affirmative action, consisting of race- or sex-conscious practices established by an organization with no pressure arising out of litigation, includes preferential programs such as numerical goals and timetables set by a government agency for the employment of specified numbers of minorities or women (Selig 1987).

Because most affirmative action is voluntary, in the sense that the term is used here, a closer look at the legal parameters of such action is warranted. In general, preferential affirmative action programs voluntarily adopted by government organizations are limited by the prohibitions on discrimination contained in Title VII of the Civil Rights Act of 1964 (as amended) and constitutional guarantees of equal protection of the law. Section 703 of Title VII of the 1964 Civil Rights Act defines as unlawful any employment practice that discriminates against any individual on account of race, color, religion, sex, or national origin. Thus, race- or sex-based affirmative action implemented by public institutions must be reconciled with those Title VII prohibitions on

discrimination. Likewise, the equal protection clause of the Fourteenth Amendment forbids states to deny to any person within their jurisdictions the "equal protection of the laws," and distinctions established by states and their local subdivisions on the basis of race and gender incorporated into affirmative action plans must therefore be reconciled with that equal protection guarantee. Because the Fourteenth Amendment applies only to actions of the states, however, its restrictions do not limit the federal government. The due process clause of the Fifth Amendment, which applies to the federal action, has been interpreted by the Supreme Court as requiring equal protection of the laws (*Bolling v. Sharpe* 347 U.S. 497), and thus constitutional constraints are also imposed on federal affirmative action.

Statutory limitations on affirmative action established by Title VII have been interpreted by the Supreme Court in two important cases (Kellough 1991, 2006). The first was *United Steelworkers of America v. Weber* (443 U.S. 193, 1979). At issue was the legality of a plan negotiated as part of a collective bargaining agreement between Kaiser Aluminum and Chemical Corporation and the United Steelworkers of America, which reserved for African Americans 50% of the openings in an in-plant craft training program until the black proportion of craft workers in the plant approximated the proportion of blacks in the local labor force. The Supreme Court upheld the legality of the affirmative action plan, arguing that although Title VII, as indicated in section 703 G, cannot be interpreted as *requiring* preferential treatment to overcome a racial imbalance, it does not preclude voluntary efforts to overcome such an imbalance. In view of the legislative history and purposes of Title VII, the Court held that the prohibition on discrimination could not be read literally to proscribe all race-based affirmative action plans. Writing for a majority of the Court, Justice Brennan noted that if Congress had meant to prohibit all race-conscious affirmative action it easily could have done so "by providing that Title VII would not require or *permit* racially preferential integration efforts" (*Steelworkers v. Weber*: 205, emphasis in original).

Because *Weber* addressed the legality of voluntary affirmative action by a private employer, the question remained as to whether its outcome would guide the statutory review of similar programs undertaken by a public employer. This question was addressed in 1987 in *Johnson v. Transportation Agency, Santa Clara County, California* (480 U.S. 616). The Court applied the criteria outlined in *Weber* to a voluntary race- and sex-based affirmative action plan adopted by the Transportation Agency which provided that, in making employment decisions within traditionally segregated job classifications where women or minorities were significantly underrepresented, the agency could consider the sex or race of a job candidate along with the individual's qualifications. No specific number of positions was set aside for minorities or women, but the eventual objective was to have minorities and women employed in positions roughly in proportion to their representation in the relevant local labor force. Following the *Weber* precedent, the Court upheld the agency's affirmative action plan; and with the announcement of the *Johnson* decision, a relatively clear set of standards emerged for judging the statutory legality of voluntary preferential affirmative action programs by government employers. When challenged under Title VII, such programs must be designed to address a manifest racial or gender imbalance in traditionally segregated job categories. Further, when considering whether a manifest racial or gender imbalance exists, the employer must consider the proportion of minorities or women in traditionally segregated positions relative to their proportions with the requisite qualifications in the local labor force. Affirmative action must also be constructed as a temporary strategy, and race or sex may be only one of several factors included in the decision process.

Constitutional restrictions on voluntary affirmative action by government organizations evolved through a series of cases beginning in the 1980s and are considerably more rigorous than the constraints imposed by the Court in *Weber* and *Johnson*. Consequently, these restrictions establish the effective operational limits for governmental affirmative action. As was noted earlier, the issue turns on judicial interpretation of the concept of equal protection of the laws. In most circumstances, the courts apply one of two analytical standards when deciding whether government actions that create classifications among people violate the equal protection components of the Fifth or Fourteenth Amendments. The first standard simply requires that a rational relationship exists between the distinctions imposed and a legitimate governmental end. Under this standard, individuals challenging governmental policies bear the burden of showing that classifications or distinctions drawn by government between people are irrational. Few laws reviewed under this standard of scrutiny are found in violation of equal protection.

But when government classifications limit fundamental freedoms or rights or force distinctions based on race or national origin, the second major standard requiring a heightened level of scrutiny commonly known as *strict scrutiny* is usually applied. Under the application of strict scrutiny, the government must defend the validity of its actions by demonstrating that they serve a compelling governmental interest and are narrowly tailored to meet that interest in that there are no less intrusive or less drastic alternatives available to meet the government's end. This is the standard by which preferential affirmative action by government is judged. In 1986, in *Wygant v. Jackson Board of Education* (476 U.S. 267), a plurality of the Supreme Court endorsed the principle that strict scrutiny should be the basis for review of affirmative action by state or local government; later, in 1989, in *City of Richmond v. Croson* (488 U.S. 469) a majority endorsed the application of strict scrutiny to review affirmative action by subnational governments.

Strict scrutiny also became the appropriate level of review for federal government affirmative action programs as the result of the Supreme Court's ruling in 1995 in *Adarand v. Pena* (515 U.S. 200). Following that decision, any racial classifications incorporated into voluntary affirmative action programs by state, local, or federal employers must be shown to serve a compelling governmental interest in order to achieve constitutional legitimacy. Exactly what type of interest will be sufficiently compelling to permit such action by a public employer is unclear, but it is likely that the correction of past discrimination by the government employer involved may be one such interest. Once a compelling governmental interest is identified, the method used to achieve that interest must be narrowly tailored. This means that affirmative action should not impose any undue burden on innocent third parties; that is, the government must use the least intrusive means available to achieve its end. Affirmative action that compromises a bona fide seniority system during times of layoffs, for example, will not withstand constitutional scrutiny if it places an undue burden on nonminorities. Affirmative action in the form of hiring or promotion goals and timetables may be less intrusive than a program that violates seniority rights (see *Wygant*); and given evidence of past discrimination by government, such an approach could presumably be acceptable, although there is no way to know with certainty how the Court will respond to such a case.

In the mid-1990s, affirmative action programs reviewed under strict scrutiny were struck down by the Fifth and Eleventh Federal Circuit Courts of Appeal and upheld by the Sixth and Ninth Circuits (see *Hopwood v. State of Texas*, 78 F.3d 932, 5th Cir., 1996; *Johnson v. Board of Regents of the University System of Georgia*, 263 F.3d 1234, 11th Cir. 2001; *Smith v. University of Washington School of Law*, 233 F.3d 1188, 9th Cir. 2000; and *Grutter v. Bollinger* 288 F.3d 732, 6th Cir. 2002). All of those cases, however, involved challenges to affirmative action in public college or university admissions rather than public employment. The *Grutter* case involved a preferential affirmative action plan at the University of Michigan School of Law. The Supreme Court heard an appeal of *Grutter* along with a companion case (*Gratz v. Bollinger*), also from the University of Michigan, and decisions by the Court in those cases in 2003 helped to settle questions of the constitutionality of preferential affirmative action in university admissions. In *Grutter* (539 U.S. 306, 2003) and *Gratz* (539 U.S. 244, 2003), a majority of the Court held for the first time that student body diversity at a state university was a compelling interest of government. In

Grutter, the court found that the affirmative action program at the law school was also narrowly tailored and was therefore constitutional. In *Gratz,* the Court found that an undergraduate admissions program involving minority preferences was not narrowly tailored and consequently was not constitutional.

For proponents of affirmative action in the public employment context, these opinions were not directly helpful; but the reasoning underlying the Court's finding that student body diversity served a compelling state interest could be relevant. In essence, the Court found that diversity within a student body was compelling because it enhanced the ability of the university to do its job. That is, the Court was persuaded that diversity improves the learning environment within a university of college. To the extent that a similar rationale could be developed in support of affirmative action in public employment, the constitutionality of affirmative action in that context might also be strengthened. Such an argument could conceivably be built from the literature on representative bureaucracy and the fact, as noted at the beginning of this chapter, that a representative public workforce helps to ensure that all interests are reflected in policy-making and implementation processes. Of course, the composition of the Supreme Court has changed since 2003. Justice O'Connor, who was instrumental in the Court's decision in *Grutter*, was replaced by Samuel Alito in January of 2006. Since his appointment, Alito has voted regularly with conservatives on the Court including Scalia, Thomas, Kennedy, and Chief Justice Roberts, who replaced Rehnquist in 2005. Given his record, Alito is not likely to be as sympathetic to affirmative action as was Justice O'Connor, and that could prove to be important in future cases addressing this issue. Other changes in the Court that have subsequently occurred are not likely to tip the balance on this issue since Justices Souter and Stevens were replaced by generally liberal Justices Sotomayor and Kagan in 2009 and 2010, respectively.

As a consequence, many civil rights activists feared the new Court would overrule *Grutter* and effectively end affirmative action after it agreed to hear arguments in

Fisher v. University of Texas in 2012. Abigail Fisher, who was denied undergraduate admission to the University of Texas in the fall of 2008, brought the case. Another plaintiff, Rachel Michalewicz, joined Fisher initially but dropped out of the litigation before it reached the Supreme Court. At the time the original case was filed in District Court, as many as 75%–80% of the university's students were admitted under a program that guaranteed admission to students finishing in the top 10% of their high school classes. Fisher failed to qualify under the top 10% program and was forced to compete for admission under an alternative procedure used to fill remaining positions. That procedure, developed to be consistent with the Court's guidance in *Grutter*, involved a holistic look at applicant qualifications that were defined to include past academic performance, experience, and race/ethnicity. Under this process, Fisher was denied admission, and she filed suit in District Court claiming that other students who were less well qualified were admitted when race/ethnicity was considered. In short, Fisher claimed she was denied admission because of her race (she is white) in violation of the equal protection guarantees of the Fourteenth Amendment. The District upheld the university's admissions program, and the Fifth Circuit affirmed that decision (*Fisher v. State of Texas*, 631 F.3d 213, 5th Cir., 2011).

At the Supreme Court, Justice Kagan recused herself from the case because of work she did when she was solicitor general prior to her appointment to the Court. Kagan's recusal meant that there were only three justices remaining on the Court who had supported affirmative action in the past. Nevertheless, when the Court issued its ruling in June of 2013, it simply remanded the case back to the Fifth Circuit and directed that the Circuit Court be certain to apply strict scrutiny in its new decision (570 U.S. _____, 2013; 133 S. Ct. 2411, 2013). By doing so, the Court effectively upheld the *Grutter* decision. Subsequently, the Fifth Circuit, when taking the case on remand, ruled that the University of Texas program was constitutional when reviewed under strict scrutiny, and in doing so affirmed their earlier decision (Fifth Circuit, Case No. 09-50822, July 15, 2014). Fisher immediately petitioned the Court for a rehearing en banc, but the Fifth Circuit denied that petition on November 12, 2014. Fisher expressed an intention to appeal once more to the U.S. Supreme Court, but as of this writing there has been no further action on the case.

EQUAL EMPLOYMENT OPPORTUNITY AND AFFIRMATIVE ACTION IN THE FUTURE

Will affirmative action continue to survive as the twenty-first century progresses? If the employment of minorities and women continues to increase in areas where they are currently underrepresented, it will eventually become difficult to sustain political support for preferential forms of the policy. Ultimately, then, such practices may come to an end. But, of course, the debate will focus, and to a considerable extent has already focused, on the question of how much progress for minorities and women is sufficient. At this time, women and minorities remain underrepresented in higher-level positions in many government agencies, so we can expect the issue to remain on the agenda for some time to come provided there is no action by the Supreme Court to restrict current constitutional limitations imposed on preferential programs. Such a ruling by the Court could come, however, in the form of a very restrictive interpretation of the circumstances that would comprise a government interest sufficiently compelling to enable preferential affirmative action in public employment to survive strict scrutiny. Of course, preferential affirmative action by the federal government could be curtailed also through congressional action, and states may move to prohibit such policies, as has already been done by state constitutional amendments in California, Washington, and Michigan.

What will be left of affirmative action if goals and preferential policies are eliminated? In that situation, future programs might resemble affirmative action typical of the early 1960s, based largely on minority outreach or recruitment efforts. Employers, for example, could still work to attract minorities or women into their pool of applicants, but actual selection decisions would be required to be free from the consideration of race or sex. Whether such policies will be effective in overcoming discrimination against women and minority group members is open to question. One factor that may work to the advantage of minorities, however, is the ever-increasing racial and ethnic diversity in the United States. As minorities become a larger segment of the population nationally, many organizations may find increased advantages in drawing on the talents and abilities of all people, regardless of racial or ethnic background.

REFERENCES

Edley, Christopher, Jr. 1996. *Not All Black and White: Affirmative Action, Race, and American Values.* New York: Hill and Wang.

Graham, Hugh David. 1990. *The Civil Rights Era: Origins and Development of National Policy, 1960–1972.* New York: Oxford University Press.

Hays, Steven. 1998. Staffing the Bureaucracy: Employee Recruitment and Selection. In Stephen E. Condrey (Ed.), *Handbook of Human Resource Management in Government.* San Francisco: Jossey-Bass, pp. 298–321.

Kellough, J. Edward. 1991. The Supreme Court, Affirmative Action, and Public Management: Where Do We Stand Today? *The American Review of Public Administration, 21*(3), pp. 255–269.

———. 2000. The Americans with Disabilities Act: A Note on Personnel Policy Impacts in State Government. *Public Personnel Management, 29*(2), 211–224.

———. 2006. *Understanding Affirmative Action: Politics, Discrimination, and the Search for Justice.* Washington, DC: Georgetown University Press.

Kellough, J. Edward, and Katherine C. Naff. 2004. Responding to a Wake-Up Call: An Examination of Federal Agency Diversity Management Programs. *Administration and Society, 36*(1), 62–90.

Kellough, J. Edward, and David H. Rosenbloom. 1992. Representative Bureaucracy and the EEOC: Did Civil Service Reform Make a Difference? In Patricia W. Ingraham and David H. Rosenbloom (Eds.), *The Promise and Paradox of Civil Service Reform.* Pittsburgh: University of Pittsburgh Press, pp. 245–266.

Krislov, Samuel. 1967. *The Negro in Federal Employment: The Quest for Equal Opportunity.* New York: Praeger.

Meier, Kenneth J. 1993. Representative Bureaucracy: A Theoretical and Empirical Exposition. In James L. Perry (Ed.), *Research in Public Administration.* New Greenwich, CT: JAI Press, pp. 1–35.

Meier, Kenneth J., and Joseph Stewart Jr. 1992. The Impact of Representative Bureaucracies: Educational Systems and Public Policies. *The American Review of Public Administration, 22*(3), 157–171.

Reed, Merl E. 1991. *Seedtime for the Modern Civil Rights Movement: The President's Committee on Fair Employment Practice, 1941–1946.* Baton Rouge: Louisiana State University Press.

Rosenbloom, David H. 1977. *Federal Equal Employment Opportunity: Politics and Public Personnel Administration.* New York: Praeger.

Selden, Sally Coleman. 1997. *The Promise of Representative Bureaucracy: Diversity and Responsiveness in a Government Agency.* Armonk, NY: M.E. Sharpe.

Selden, Sally Coleman, Jeffrey L. Brudney, and J. Edward Kellough. 1998. Bureaucracy as a Representative Institution: Toward a Reconciliation of Bureaucratic Government and Democratic Theory. *American Journal of Political Science, 42*(3), 717–744.

Selig, Joel L. 1987. Affirmative Action in Employment: The Legacy of a Supreme Court Majority. *Indiana Law Journal, 63,* 301–368.

Taylor, Bron Raymond. 1991. *Affirmative Action at Work: Law, Politics, and Ethics.* Pittsburgh: University of Pittsburgh Press.

Wilkins, Vicky M., and Lael R. Keiser. 2006. Linking Passive and Active Representation by Gender: The Case of Child Support Agencies. *Journal of Public Administration Research and Theory, 16*(1), 87–102.

CHAPTER 19

GENDERED ORGANIZATIONS AND HUMAN RESOURCE MANAGEMENT PRACTICES THAT FOSTER AND SUSTAIN GENDERED NORMS

Sharon Mastracci
University of Utah

Lauren Bowman
University of Illinois at Chicago

In Western culture, sex segregation is conspicuous for its rarity. The acceptance of two female members to the infamously exclusive Augusta National Golf Club made headlines in 2012, as did the admission of female students to the historically male-only educational institutions Virginia Military Institute and the Citadel in the 1990s. Gender is an inescapable dimension of interpersonal interaction at the workplace because there remains a "very high rate of interaction between men and women, compared to, say, that between rich and poor or European- and African-Americans. Gender divides the population into two roughly equal-sized segments; it also cross cuts most kin and household groups, forcing some degree of regular cross-sex interaction in virtually everyone" (Ridgeway and Smith-Lovin 1996: 173). Informal rules have evolved to guide interactions between women and men where laws and traditions have either faded away or failed to reach (Ferguson 1983).

Gendered norms, or expectations of workplace behavior based on stereotypes of men and women, emerge via repeated interpersonal interactions. Organizations were not gender-free blank slates that became gendered once women entered in the workforce; they are not "gender-neutral organisms *infected* by the germs of workers' gender (and sexuality and race and class) identities but as sites in which these attributes are presumed and reproduced" (Britton 2000: 418). Organizations begin with the norms and values of their founders, and women and people of color stand out against these largely white, male backgrounds. Gender in organizations is revealed by the gendered norms and processes in workplaces that foster and sustain inequities between women and men. Stivers explains why public administration is best understood at the level of relationships, in *organizations,* not at the individual, atomized, reductionist level (2008: 1011, emphasis supplied):

> To study social reality, one cannot add up and then slice and dice individual responses to preconceived questions, such as in survey research. The approach

has to be capable of accessing a nonindividual form of reality, and it has to focus not on causal explanation but rather on explicating the meaning of the social situation for the people in it.

Why is this form of research important for public administration? *Because much of public administration goes on in social realities and intersubjective processes*: organizations, teams, networks, associations, bureaus, agencies, and so on. These are the realities so little accessed in public administration that we tend to refer to what goes on in them as "the black box". They are the taken-for-granted processes and understandings that all of us exist in, but that we often do not notice.

Theories of organizational norms and practices address precisely "a nonindividual form of reality" and "the meaning of the social situation for the people in it" (Stivers 2008: 1011). Stivers cites sociological research to illustrate how social reality through organizational norms and customs are studied, and we also take cues from research in sociology to illuminate what is possible in public administration research involving gender. Public administration is an important context in which to study gendered organizations. Lower rates of occupational segregation by gender exist in nonprofits and public sector organizations compared with private sector firms (Kmec 2005; Martin 2003). But inequality between men and women remains. Public and nonprofit organizations maintain gendered norms and practices, as all firms do, to a greater or lesser degree. Given the inescapability of gender interactions and the importance of interactions to understanding public administration, we draw heavily from the gender and organizations literature in sociology. But moving forward, it must be public administration scholars who accept the challenge to study gendered organizations in the public sector, for public organizations are unique. They symbolize the *polis*, they are responsive and accountable to the public, and public servants' decisions must take the perspective of the collective into account: "These elements together are what make government a

system, for in combination they comprise what we call a bureaucracy" (Appleby 1945: 159).

Much of the sociological literature examines private sector firms, but unlike government agencies and departments, private sector firms come and go. Public agencies can and do merge and reorganize, but they do not come and go, and they tend to be older than private sector firms (Mastracci and Herring 2010). Public agencies also seek efficiency and effectiveness, but they must uphold democratic ideals in their operations and pursue fairness and equity as well. Unlike private firms, "government is different because it must take account of all the desires, needs, actions, thoughts, and sentiments of [more than 300 million] people. Government is different because government is politics" (Appleby 1945: 164). Therefore, although the gendered nature of organizations has been established in sociology (Acker 1990, 1992; Britton 2000; Martin 2003), how *public* organizations are gendered must be taken up in public administration.

This chapter is divided into three sections. In the first section, Gender in Human Resource Management, we discuss why gender matters in the workplace: It is a significant dimension along which inequalities in pay and advancement opportunities arise and institutionalize. We review the literature on differential outcomes for women and men, including pay, advancement, and their professional networks. We also trace the evolution of feminist thought on gender and organizations. In the second section, Gendered Organizations: Dissecting the Processes and Practices That Produce Inequality, we address several questions: How is gender "socially constructed—talked about, acted on, used, denied, and ignored" (Martin 2003: 343) in the workplace? How can human resource management practices foster workplace equality? Several practices are examined: recruitment and hiring, performance evaluations and job descriptions, work/life balance programs, and language and imagery. In the third section, Problems and Prospects: Implications for Human Resource Management, we discuss the gendered organizations approach in public administration.

GENDER IN HUMAN RESOURCE MANAGEMENT

Gender matters in the workplace because it is a primary dimension along which inequalities in pay and disparities in opportunity arise and institutionalize. Furthermore, as Mary Ellen Guy and Susan Spice implore in the previous edition of this anthology: "an important function of the HR department is to monitor patterns of employment in the agency or jurisdiction and take note of those areas where job segregation is keen . . . *constant vigilance is required*" (Guy and Spice 2009: 251, emphasis supplied).

In her meta-analysis of research on gendered organizations, Dana Britton (2000) categorized articles according to their fundamental operating assumptions regarding the role of gender in creating and sustaining organizational norms. Her typology usefully organizes our discussion of gender in the workplace. In the first category, organizations and occupations are *inherently gendered*, which means that "they have been defined, conceptualized, and structured in terms of a distinction between masculinity and femininity, and . . . inequalities in status and material circumstances will be the result" (Britton 2000: 419).

In the second category, researchers assume that "organizations or occupations are gendered to the extent that they are male or female dominated" (2000: 420). This equates sex of the worker with the gendered expectations of the job. Britton refers to this as the *nominal approach* to applying the concept of gendering to organizational and occupational norms; it consists of counting the numbers of women and men in jobs and agencies and tracking changes in proportions over time. Nominalism assumes "that women and men are simply people, without gender identities, occupying the same cultural, historical, material, and political positions, subject to and participating in the same *neutral* organizational processes and *impartial* interpersonal interactions" (Ely and Meyerson 2000a: 604, emphasis original).

Another approach to studying gender in the workplace, which McCall (2005) calls structuralism, posits that gender inequities result from hierarchical positions held by women and men—where women and men are located on the organizational chart. In public administration, Alkadry and Tower's (2011) research would fall into this category; for they explain the gender pay gap among public sector procurement officers as a function of, in part, a respondent's number of direct reports. The more authority one has over others is predicted by sex, which in turn explains pay disparities between women and men. Structuralism underpins Rosabeth Moss Kanter's groundbreaking examination of *Men and Women of the Corporation* (1977), but as Britton observes, Kanter transcends nominalism and structuralism: "In her otherwise largely gender-neutral account, [she] may have been one of the first to characterize an occupation [as gendered], noting that the image of the top corporate manager relies on a 'masculine ethic' that 'elevates the traits assumed to belong to some met to necessities for effective management'" (Britton 2000: 420). Kanter's observation that effective management became conflated with the sex of the worker provides the bridge between the second and the third approaches.

The third approach—studying *gendered norms and practices*—decouples the sex of the worker and gendered expectations of the job, allowing the two to vary independently of one another (Britton 2000) so that a woman could hold a job with gendered-masculine expectations and vice versa. For instance, a female police officer may engage in highly masculinized work and be expected to perform her job according to masculine norms. Here, "occupations or organizations are gendered in that they are symbolically and ideologically described and conceived in terms of a discourse that draws on hegemonically-defined masculinities and femininities" (Britton 2000: 420). Discourse and images in the workplace define and reinforce gendered norms attached to an occupation or organization. Discourse is enacted over and over through social interactions, wherein gender norms are defined. In this third approach, gender is not sex, but rather "a complex social process enacted across a range of organizational phenomena, from formal policies and practices to informal patterns of everyday interaction, which appear to be gender neutral on their face, yet reflect and maintain a gendered order in which men and various forms of masculinity remain" (Ely and Meyerson 2000a: 590). Discourse—including words and reactions in interpersonal interactions—defines and reasserts gendered norms and practices, for "it is exactly in 'acting gender inappropriately' that women confront multiple problems in masculine work areas" (Kelan 2010: 183). Similarly, Ferguson concludes "our culture's definition of femininity is such that a woman cannot know if she is being successfully feminine unless she has a response from another person" (1983: 299).

In the paragraphs that follow, we review the literature along these three dimensions: First, organizations are inherently gendered; second, organizations are gendered to the extent that they are male or female dominated (nominalism); and third, organizations are gendered in the behaviors and practices that they value (Britton 2000).

Organizations Are Inherently Gendered

Research in this first category presume that organizations are inherently gendered, that "bureaucracy is male dominance in structural form" (DeHart-Davis 2009: 340) or "a structural expression of male dominance (Ashcraft 2001: 1301). No matter the sex of their inhabitants, bureaucracies are inherently male. Feminist public administration scholars, however, have been somewhat slower to impugn bureaucracy *in toto*, which "can both oppress and empower organizational women" (DeHart-Davis 2009: 360) and consider organizational structure in context: "Does the gender balance of an organization render its bureaucracy more or less empowering?" (DeHart-Davis 2009: 360). Indeed, as we discuss later in this chapter, bureaucratic processes can foster transparency and actually reduce bias (Baron et al. 2007; Kmec 2005). Such researchers ask whether gendered norms can change as the demographics of organizations change, which characterizes the second category.

Nominalism: Gauging and Tracking Proportions of Men and Women

Analyzing numbers of women and men in occupations or organizations over time is to see "work as gendered simply to the extent that men or women do it" (Britton 2000: 424). In public administration, G. B. Lewis (1994: 271) criticizes this approach to studying workplace inequality: "Simple cross-agency comparisons of the status of women, and excessive focus on women's share of total employment, give misleading pictures of agency efforts and success in promoting equality." The nominal approach underpins passive representative bureaucracy by gauging the extent to which public servants are employed in proportions similar to those of the population that they serve. Theories of active representation transcend nominalism to consider the extent to which public servants use administrative discretion to advocate on behalf of the constituency that they represent, as Naff (2001) found in her survey of public agency hiring managers.

In their meta-analysis of public administration scholarship, McGinn and Patterson (2005: 938) critique nominalism because "reporting survey respondents and organizational members by sex is frequently the end result . . . further interpretation of the implications of sex and gender is left to the speculation of individual readers." Trends over time are explored, but not meanings and implications of gender in organizations. Organizational-level norms are directly related to individual outcomes for working women. Women's lower pay, truncated advancement opportunities due to glass ceilings, and fewer employment benefits "arise primarily from the sex composition of jobs and firms rather than the sex of individual workers. The more similarly the sexes are distributed across positions within a firm and the more evenly they are distributed across firms, the more likely women and men are to enjoy equal opportunity and equal rewards" (Reskin and Bielby 2005: 83).

Gender matters at work because pay and career advancement opportunities consistently differ between women and men: less of both for the former, compared with the latter. Guy and Spice (2009: 244) reject the usual explanations for the gender pay gap: "The bottom line from these facts about women's educational levels and commitment to careers is that the wage disparity between women and men is not explained by a lack of either. The prevalence of men in higher ranks and women in lower ranks is also not explained by education or childcare responsibilities." Likewise, Naff (1994: 507) concludes that "differences in experience and education only partially account for the discrepancy" in promotions between women and men. Researchers have found organizational culture to play a role. G. B. Lewis (1994), studying federal-level white collar jobs, establishes a link between agency mission and the extent of occupational segregation by gender in an agency, where women are concentrated in clerical and technical positions with few opportunities for advancement. Sneed (2007) also finds a link between agency type—distributive, redistributive, regulatory, or general—and occupational segregation by gender and pay disparities by gender on the state level. Cornwell and Kellough (1994) find greater shares of female employment across the board in agencies with social equity functions, such as "education, public welfare, social insurance, housing and community development, and social security and Medicare" (1994: 269). Analyses linking agency mission and overrepresentation of women illustrate glass walls rather than glass ceilings. Glass walls segregate women into sex-typed agencies and departments, while glass ceilings restrict women to lower-paying jobs and limit opportunities for advancement.

Studies of professional networks indicate that "segregated voluntary associations help perpetuate a social world that is substantially ordered by gender" (Popielarz 1999: 234). Similarly, Ibarra (1997) found differences between male and female managers' professional networks owing to their differing statuses in organizational hierarchies, which yielded different career-related resources and information for women and men. McGuire (2002) teased out the material impacts of "shadow structures" or informal networks and processes "where employees build alliances, traded organizational resources, and managed their reputations . . . where unspoken rules of interaction make gender inequality possible and highly resistant to change" (2002: 303–304).

Informal, behind-the-scenes processes to allocate opportunities for advancement benefit insiders—usually men—and marginalize women and people of color. McGuire was told by employees that "only 'losers' went to human resources (i.e., used a formal procedure) to try to obtain promotions" (McGuire 2002: 318). She concluded, "women, in effect, face a double-edged sword; they obtain less instrumental help than men do from their informal network members, but if they turn to formal outlets to meet their instrumental needs, they risk being further marginalized" (2002: 318–319). Backlash arising from the use of formal outlets is akin to the "trap doors" analyzed by Guy and Spice, which "have a significant deleterious effect on a woman's career . . . [and] slows down what may have been . . . a rapid ascent up the chain of command" (2009: 245). These studies demonstrate that research can begin with a nominal approach, then move quickly to examining organizational culture.

Organizations Are Gendered in Their Norms, Practices, and Processes

The third approach "gained prominence with the move away from counting bodies in organizations, and emphasized instead how gender is socially constructed at work . . . gender is not a property of a person but a process that people enact in everyday situations" (Kelan 2010: 177). Gender at the individual level is evident in individual choices to follow behaviors expected of the sex group into which each person is categorized, from clothing and makeup choices, to hair styles, jewelry, and other personal appearance choices, to patterns of speech in a meeting, how to run a meeting, how to discipline an employee, even to what jobs to hold or careers are appropriate to pursue. These choices are informed by gender at the group level, which is evident in behaviors and choices that women and men tend to do in general. An individual woman or man may choose differently, but at the group level of analysis, certain tendencies arise and are gender coded/gender typed: Men engage in physical labor, employ competitive conversational styles (McCloskey 1999), engage in assertive or aggressive decision making, and serve as authority figures and disciplinarians. Women are supposed to care, engage in relationship building, support, and have the interests of the group in mind.

Gender at the organizational level is found in the organizational norms and practices that produce inequitable outcomes for women and men no matter the composition of the workforce; if the organization were to experience 100% turnover with replacement by random assignment of individuals, inequities between men and women would still emerge, based on accepted practices defined by the organization, which were established by its founders (Hannan 2005; Phillips 2005; Eisenhardt and Schoonhoven 1990; Stinchcombe 1965). Indeed, Hannan (2005: 59–60) asserts the intransigence of founding norms and practices: "core structures of organizations are subject to strong inertial pressures and efforts at changing such structures substantially increase the chances of failure . . . efforts to change raise fundamental questions about the nature of the organization." Organizational norms and practices are rooted in those of their founders, who in older public organizations were almost exclusively male, and those structures are resistant to change.

But what do gendered practices look like? How can we recognize whether one type of gendered behavior is rewarded while another is deemed unprofessional? One type of practice where such norms may be in play involves workplace reward structures: promotions and pay. Promotion criteria that reward the always-available worker with seemingly no obligations outside the workplace; that value forcefulness, competitiveness, and aggression toward others; and that value physical strength and stature, whether any of these things are related to the job, will likely favor men and result in men holding more positions of leadership and power. Historically male-dominated organizations that valorize tradition and consistency will remain male-dominated organizations. Even if not in terms of numbers, men will remain dominant in positions of leadership and power in the organization and valued work will be gendered masculine no matter the sex of the worker.

This defines the gendered organization. Stinchcombe (1965) "argued that new organizations incorporate practices that reflect the taken-for-granted assumptions of the time" (Hannan 2005: 59). What were the taken-for-granted assumptions of the time when public administration developed? Stivers traced the origins of public administration as a profession and observed (2000: 8):

During the time when public administration evolved, the link between masculinity and public power is clearly visible. In the early twentieth century . . . expectations about what was proper for women and men to do were perhaps more rigid and more divergent than they have ever been in American life . . . Public administration, like other social phenomena, emerged in this gendered context and was shaped by it in significant ways.

Among the most influential of those "significant ways" was the intense preoccupation with associating municipal reform with science rather than advocacy: "Science would show the one right way to manage government . . . Masculine images of command and control, centered in the chief executive and justified by scientific expertise, proved the final element in the bureau men's ideology" (Stivers 2000: 11). From these origins, public organizations were founded in gendered terms with masculinist norms. Acker generalizes this conclusion to all organizations: "The law, politics, religion, the academy, the state, and the economy . . . are institutions historically dominated by men, and symbolically interpreted from the standpoint of men in leading positions, both in the present and historically. These institutions have been defined by the absence of women" (1992: 567).

But, as women have entered public agencies and all types of organizations, those organizations evolve. Examining trends in men's and women's employment over time captures the extent to which occupational segregation by gender is a problem in an organization or industry. Trends over time allow one to determine the presence of glass ceilings or glass walls, which limit women's career advancement and pay. But rather than assume occupational segregation by gender indicates other aspects of sex typing in an organization or industry, as Britton (2000) warns: "Research should investigate whether and in what ways occupations dominated by one sex or the other (as most occupations are) are feminized or masculinized, rather than simply assuming that this is the case" (Britton 2000: 430). Likewise, Ely and Meyerson (2000a: 590) argue that gender is "a complex social process enacted across a range of organizational phenomena, from formal policies and practices to informal patterns of everyday interaction, which appear to be gender neutral on their face, yet reflect and maintain a gendered order in which men and various forms of masculinity predominate."

Studying gendered norms and practices transcends the nominal approach to define gendered expectations according to criteria for hiring and promoting workers—in other words, what is rewarded, as revealed by standard operating procedures as well as workplace symbols and discourse. Examining the gendered nature of workplace norms and practices is more nuanced than simply equating sex of the worker with gender of the occupation, or proportion of men or women in an organization with gendered norms of that organization. This section provided an overview of three approaches to studying gender in organizations: First, all organizations are inherently gendered; hierarchy and bureaucracy are equated with masculinity. Second, organizations are gender-typed according to the sex of the workers who nominally comprise the majority. Third, while masculinities and femininities generally coincide with the sex of the worker (Ferguson 1983) or the proportions of men and women in an organization (Kanter 1977/1993), the link is not determinative. This third approach allows researchers to examine practices separately from the demographics of the workplace. The second and third approaches are mutually reinforcing, but the third approach separates the sex of the worker from the gendered expectations of the job. The next section examines human resource management practices from this more nuanced approach.

GENDERED ORGANIZATIONS: THE PROCESSES AND PRACTICES THAT PRODUCE INEQUALITY

The concept of gendered organizations is an outgrowth of the movement toward understanding gender as socially constructed. While older research on organizations and gender viewed the two as separate, more recent work views gender as a major part of processes that structure the organization. Kanter (1977/1993) interpreted problems, such as barriers to women's advancement, as a result of where they were situated within the organization rather than inherent differences between men and women. Acker (1990) criticizes Kanter for viewing gender as existing outside the structure of the organization and failing to further investigate the dynamic of masculinity in organizations. Acker goes on to outline other approaches to gender and organizations (including the dual structure-bureaucracy and patriarchy-approach and the "feminization" approach that views bureaucracy as feminizing workers and clients), but finds these approaches wanting because they view organizations as gender neutral and fail to adequately explain gender structuring. Acker (1990: 146) instead views the term "gendered organizations" as meaning "that advantage and disadvantage, exploitation and control, action and emotion, meaning and identity are patterned through and in terms of a distinction between male and female, masculine and feminine." The idea of gendered organizations evolved alongside definitions of gender. As understandings of gender evolved from sex to social construction, understandings of gendered organizations also evolved to reflect that new definition, including organizations as social process.

Key aspects of gendered organizations manifest in human resource policies and practices. Guy and Spice (2009: 244) see gendered human resource practices as left over from decades past when the workforce was dominated by men: "The demographics of the workforce have changed faster than the HR practices that govern classification, compensation, and benefits." Clearly, the effects of being employed in such an organization can be felt even at the level of the individual employee (Acker 2000); but human resource management policies and programs can work to maintain inequalities between women and men. This is rooted in the tendency of organizations to develop processes and practices based on what Acker calls the "ideal worker." According to Ely and Meyerson (2000b: 109), this is problematic because, as Acker posited, the ideal worker is tacitly perceived as being masculine: "Women have been disadvantaged because organizations place a higher value on behaviors, styles, and forms of work traditionally associated with men, masculinity, and the public sphere of work, while devaluing, suppressing, or otherwise ignoring those traditionally associated with women, femininity, and the private sphere of home and family." Scholars often trace the gendering of an organization to aspects of its founding moments. Baron et al. (2007: 59) highlight the staying power of male and female roles: "The initial sexual division of labor within firms may represent one of the most influential organizational founding conditions and serve as a mechanism by which cultural blueprints and early structures and practices shape subsequent organizational development." This blueprint can guide future personnel decisions and shape organizational policy, guiding future action to maintain the gendering of the organization.

The importance of the founding moment lies not only in gender segregation but also in the gendered norms, processes, policies, and practices that shape organizations every day, though not necessarily in an overt sense. "Blatantly biased actions are viewed as illegitimate because western values frame them as wrong, but subtle forms of practicing gender . . . are not widely viewed as wrong" (Martin 2003: 361). The subtle forms of practicing gender produce the workplace processes and practices that produce and reproduce inequality. They can be found in human resource management activities such as recruitment and hiring, performance evaluation and job descriptions, implementing work/life balance programs, and workplace discourse.

Recruitment and Hiring

One way the gendering of organizations manifests and perpetuates is through recruitment and hiring.

From an increased likelihood of interviewing women for low-paying positions to hiring men more often for high-paying positions, gender can strongly impact who gets recruited and who gets overlooked (Fernandez and Mors 2008). Gender-stereotyped hiring criteria, emphasizing stereotypically masculine or feminine traits, can work to disadvantaging applicants that do not appear to fulfill those stereotypes (Pratto et al. 1997; Gorman 2005). However, the transparency generated by bureaucratized, formal processes for recruitment and hiring can work to decrease bias and increase women's opportunities to be hired in nontraditional occupations, mitigating occupational segregation and increasing women's potential for advancement.

Unfortunately, even with the presence of institutionalized hiring processes, informal paths for recruitment can provide an opportunity for biases to arise (Acker 2007). Kmec (2005: 326) explains how social networks introduce bias:

> Informal network recruitment, namely employer reliance on current employees to generate contacts, facilitates employer discretion and exposes the hiring process to the stereotyping and favoritism that tend to accompany discretion. . . . Although the reliance on current employees to generate referrals may benefit employers, this recruitment strategy can bias the hiring process against applications in nontraditional sex groups and maintain sex traditional employment.

Informal network recruitment is also important for ethnic and racial minorities, due to the significant role referrals play in structuring their job prospects (Elliott 2001). Acker (2007) highlights the rise of affirmative action as a turning point in hiring that spurred employers to use more open procedures, resulting in less segregation based on gender and race. Baron et al. (2007: 36) point to the positive impact of bureaucracy for general equality in the organization: "Bureaucratic rules and procedures governing recruitment, selection, and rewards improve opportunities and attainments for historically disadvantaged groups."

Acker (2007) faults the bureaucratic procedures used for recruitment and hiring, saying that even these supposedly transparent procedures cannot completely prevent bias. Hiring involves judging a candidate's competence, and this involves subjectivity to a certain degree, resulting in continued gender and race segregation in many organizations. Though formalized, transparent processes for recruitment, hiring, and promoting workers leave some room for personal biases, transparency remains a first line of defense against inequality in organizations. Studying promotion rates of women and men in the federal civil service, Naff (1994: 507) finds "assumptions about women's potential and career commitment remain in conflict with traditional criteria for evaluating employees' promotion potential." Both Burnier (2006) and DeHart-Davis (2009) argue that recent government reform efforts, including the National Performance Review, are gendered to the extent that dismantling formalized bureaucratic processes and introducing market-like principles potentially disrupts egalitarian efforts supported by transparent processes and can foster inequality.

Performance Evaluations and Job Descriptions

Organizations can reveal their gendered nature in other human resource functions, like performance evaluations and job descriptions. In her study of Florida state agencies, Newman (1995) found 40% of women working in what she calls "male-bastion agencies" felt they had been discriminated against in hiring or promotion, while only 4% of men felt the same. Performance evaluations play a central role in determining who moves up within an organization, who wields power in the organization, and who is permitted to shape procedures and processes in the organization, making them an extremely important component of gendering in organizations. Often, much like gendered hiring criteria, gendered promotion or reward criteria tend to emphasize gender stereotypes. Meyerson and Kolb (2000: 564) conclude that rewards and incentives can reveal gendering:

Anticipating or preventing problems and mediating small conflicts within and between groups . . .

invisible, relational work was typically associated with the feminine and done primarily by women, whereas visible, problem-solving work was typically associated with the masculine and done primarily by men. As a result, men's efforts were recognized and rewarded more often than women's.

Determining whether relational/emotional skills are valued similarly to more rational skills in Illinois state agency performance evaluations, Mastracci, Newman, and Guy (2006) did not find widespread recognition of emotional labor as a central element of work. Rather, emotional labor, when recognized, was markedly subordinate to rational skills in evaluation instruments. This failure to incorporate what is stereotypically thought of as behavior characteristic of women into performance evaluations is troubling because it implicitly prizes behaviors stereotypically associated with men over those associated with women. Transparency and formalized bureaucratic rules and procedures can, as in hiring, act to mitigate bias in performance appraisals, but as Mastracci et al. indicate, senior leadership in charge of creating performance evaluation instruments must be conscious of the potential for bias at play within the confines of formalized human resources practices. This confirms Ridgeway and Smith-Lovin (1996), who revealed how performance evaluation criteria reflect the behavior and actions of past successful jobholders and are applied to newcomers whether they fit the categories of the previous jobholders or not.

Like performance evaluation, job descriptions can harbor gendered language. Kanter (1977/1993) notes that high-level management positions are marked by descriptions that are utterly masculine, including words like "analytical" and "tough-minded." Obviously, a masculine job description most likely disadvantages women who, though they may be completely suitable for the job and even exhibit the characteristics outlined in the description, could be stereotyped as inherently feminine and therefore inappropriate for the position. Supervisory positions employ masculine archetypical behavior, emphasizing control, the ability to take charge of crisis situations, and availability to work long hours (Ely and Meyerson 2000a; Meyerson and Kolb 2000). Just as formal processes for recruitment and hiring can help to reduce sex-based biases (Baron et al. 2007; Kmec 2005; Meyerson and Kolb 2000), so can formalized performance evaluation processes reduce bias. Formalized processes can be instituted in any organization, but larger organizations tended to be more bureaucratic: "Establishment size (number of employees) is positively associated with formalization because large establishments are more likely than small ones to have a personnel system or full-time human resources department to enforce equitable hiring practices that support sex equity" (Kmec 2005: 329). Use of third-party entities to recruit and identify potential job candidates, or the use of impartial screening devices like the federal government's website USAJobs decreases sex-typing of candidates into jobs and thereby decreases occupational segregation by gender. "Research in the United States also suggests that gender segregation and wage inequality are often less marked in labor market sectors (such as government) . . . and organizations that use formal procedures governing hiring, evaluation, and promotion" (Britton 2000: 423).

Work/Life Balance Programs and Presenteeism

As women entered the workforce in greater numbers in the 1970s, many organizations responded by implementing work/life balance policies to facilitate women's ability to adequately address both work and home responsibilities. At that time, work/life balance policies were primarily aimed at women and often were referred to as family-friendly or work/family policies, tacitly connecting them to women's roles as caregivers to their families (Brannen et al. 1994; S. Lewis 2010). This became a gendered workplace norm that, though not visible in policy, exists in many organizations, fostering the perception by many workers that these policies are really intended for women (Smithson and Stokoe 2005; Scheibl and Dex 1998). Policies themselves, however, have changed. A variety of work/life balance policies exist for those with and without family care responsibilities,

including men. McDonald, Brown, and Bradley (2005) list four categories of policies: flexible work options (e.g., adjustable start/end times), specialized leave policies (e.g., work sabbaticals), dependent care benefits (primarily for family care such as maternity leave), and general services (e.g., health education programs). Formal work/life balance policies are now found in all sectors, with the federal government often acting as a model for the private and nonprofit sectors (Bruce and Reed 1994). While work/life balance policies are an attempt to reconcile the job with the reality that workers must attend to personal needs, the norms associated with the concept of the ideal worker can inhibit use of such policies or negatively impact the careers of those who decide to use them. Meyerson and Kolb (2000: 564) describe unintended outcomes of HR policies:

> Paid sick leave was formally available to all employees, but one had to discuss with one's supervisor the nature of one's illness in order to receive it. Young women, whose supervisor in every instance was a man, were often too embarrassed to discuss with him such illnesses as menstrual cramps. As a result, they received fewer authorized leaves. Unauthorized leaves were unpaid, and people who received too many of them risked being labeled "slackers."

Requiring employees to discuss the reason for leave creates an informal obstacle to use, especially when a gender dynamic such as the one in the previous example is present. Those who overcome such informal obstacles still face a variety of informal constraints based on organizational norms. Mahler (2012: 407) examines the "seldom-discussed costs of telework: the impact of those barred from telework." Telework and flexible working arrangements create a workplace that is not "organized on the assumption that reproduction takes place elsewhere and that responsibility for reproduction is also located elsewhere" (Acker 1992: 567). The old image of being chained to one's desk, given the existence of tools allowing one to work anywhere, may soon become an outmoded picture of productivity. Perhaps it already has. Constant physical presence at work, when not a requirement of the job as is the case for nurses, police officers, and security guards, is a deeply masculinist gendered practice, because it is premised on separate spheres of home and work, the demand for physical availability, and the value of so-called face time. The U.S. Office of Personnel Management (OPM) acknowledges the problematic potential of presenteeism, "the practice of sitting at one's desk without working, [which] can be just as problematic as absenteeism" (Berry 2011: para. 8). Presenteeism is a gendered workplace practice because it affects male and female workers differently, more often detrimentally to women, who retain primary responsibility for caregiving (Mastracci 2013).

Meyerson and Kolb (2000) note the effects that presenteeism has on the ability of women to advance in the organizational hierarchy: "The image of the 'ideal supervisor' was someone who was able to put work above all else in life [and] work overtime whenever necessary. . . . Because women carry a disproportionate share of responsibilities for home and family, it was difficult on a practical level for many women to work the overtime hours necessary to uphold this image" (565). Organizational logic defining the ideal worker to be physically available adversely affects female workers' ability to balance work and family demands as well as their promotion prospects. Ely and Meyerson (2000a: 602) also find that "the use of 'face time' at work as an indicator of 'commitment' [has] detrimental consequences for the careers of those, typically women, whose family responsibilities limit the amount of time they can spend at work." Formal policies intended to facilitate employee's ability to find a comfortable work/life balance are a step in the right direction, but organizations must look beyond formal policies at organizational logic and norms in order to actually make the policies useful and usable.

Workplace Discourse: Language and Imagery

To argue that organizations are gendered is not to imply that the buildings or bylaws are pink or blue. Gender is a concept whose meaning is upheld and reinforced through language and performative practices (Butler 1993). Whether used in casual conversation or spelled out in handbooks, gendered language can permeate many aspects of an organization. Acker (1990: 147) characterizes language as an area where dominance and submission are reproduced in organizations, as "men are actors, women the emotional support" during conversations. Whereas hiring, promotion, and work-life balance policies are controlled largely by senior leaders, language is unique in that workers themselves play a central role in perpetuating gendering through their interactions: "The gendering-through-discourse perspective has also proven useful in allowing us to see the ways in which workers themselves and culture as a whole perceive and construct occupations and organizations" (Britton 2000: 431). Like many aspects of gendering in organizations, language and performative practices are often thought of as neutral and completely lacking in gendered undercurrents by people working in organizations. Policies (as well as reports, evaluation instruments, recruitment notices, and many other documents central to daily organizational operations) are written in language that appears to lack any gendered connotations. However, gendering is insidious and cannot be adequately addressed by choosing to use inclusive pronouns alone: "Masking or minimizing gender differences within gender-neutral language does not, as a strategy, appear to be working as a means for advancing gender equality . . . Gender-neutral language of diversity and choice is not adequately addressing highly gendered patterns of living and working" (Smithson and Stokoe 2005: 164). And they also note that "Language change without corresponding culture change is bound to fail" (Smithson and Stokoe 2005: 157).

Beyond formal policies, the way men and women communicate, both verbally and nonverbally, can reproduce inequalities. Through interviews and observation conducted within multinational corporations, Patricia Yancey Martin (2003: 359) clarified how these interactions can affect women in professional positions: "Men at meetings acknowledge women's presence by nodding or saying hello, but they make extensive eye contact and talk mostly with other men. Such experiences give a message to women about their importance; that is, men's failure to treat women as if they are important tells women they are unimportant. This message is often debilitating even for highly educated professional women when it is given over and over again." Such interactions continually reaffirm the subordination of women and may work to disseminate gendered attitudes throughout other aspects of the organization, like hiring and promotions. On this account, Deirdre McCloskey possesses a unique perspective, having crossed from Donald to Deirdre. In her memoir, she describes in third person a situation where Donald conducts an informal experiment that illustrates gendered workplace practices (1999: 80):

> Without changing his tone, he adopted women's rules for conversation: Listen, do not interrupt, support the speaker, maintain eye contact, do not gratuitously change the subject. . . . within a few minutes, the other two men were treating Donald as a woman. They were going on with their ping-pong of competition, not looking, interrupting, not listening to him. . . . Later, he did the same thing in a group of women, and again, within minutes the women's rules led them to treat him as another woman.

Martin (2003) describes how a male manager's expectation that his female managerial counterpart would answer an unattended, ringing telephone when either person could have done so also betrays the presence of gendered workplace norms.

The public sector is often viewed as exceptionally active in terms of addressing equality issues, and gender has not played a large role in prominent scholarly work concerning government. Stivers (2002) challenges the gender neutral image of public administration in her book *Gender Images in Public Administration*. She examines the experience of working in the public sector, naming four prominent images of leadership present in the public context: the visionary, the symbol, the decision maker, and the definer of reality. Stivers notes

the conflict between these ideals, which are overtly masculine, and the feminine behavior expected of women. Language and imagery are harder to control with bureaucratic policies and rules, but efforts to consciously create written forms, handbooks, and policies in ways that exclude gendering can work to positively shape organizational discourse.

PROBLEMS AND PROSPECTS: IMPLICATIONS FOR HUMAN RESOURCE MANAGEMENT

Gender is an inescapable dimension of interpersonal interaction at the workplace, and informal rules and norms have evolved to establish expectations and guide behavior where laws and traditions have faded away or failed to reach. Gender in organizations is revealed not only by tracking numbers of women employed in different occupations over time but also by examining the gendered norms and processes in workplaces that bring about and sustain inequities between women and men. Public and nonprofit organizations maintain gendered norms and practices, as all firms do. Public administration scholars must accept the challenge to study how public organizations are gendered, for public organizations are unique.

What is more, to transcend the single dimension of gender and truly capture the complexity of organizational norms, public administration scholars must examine intersections of demographic categories on career outcomes. To establish that an organization is gendered also implies that it can be raced or race-typed (Yanow 2002). Further research in public administration should study norms and expectations related to race and ethnicity. Also, further research on active representative bureaucracy would investigate the motivations for advocating on behalf of a particular group; and research on the intersections of multiple demographic characteristics could study the groups with which representing public servants identify and whether they decide to advocate on behalf of one identity at the expense of another. Further research could also examine the gendered implications of bureaucratic workplace practices: "Informal procedures to hire, to evaluate, and to reward workers tends to advantage workers already in privileged positions. Formal work procedures that are consistently enforced, and for which managers are accountable, in contrast, could help to distribute organizational resources more equally" (McGuire 2002: 318).

Prospects for human resource management involve awareness of norms and overt actions to diminish their effects. Gender transcends the proportions of women and men in the workplace, the over- or underrepresentation of women or men in occupations, and concentrations of women and men across the organizational hierarchy. Gendered norms and practices are enacted through emotional labor—displaying tougher-than-tough or nicer-than-nice behavior for the purposes of doing one's job. A foundation for the more nuanced view of gendered organizations in the study of public administration has been laid by the research of Rita Mae Kelly and Meredith Newman on state agencies (2001), Raewyn Connell on local governments (2006), Camilla Stivers on the very genesis of public administration (1995, 2000), Helena Carreiras on the military and peacekeeping missions (2010), and by research on emotional labor in public service, which examines *how* the work is done as much as *who* is doing the work (Guy, Newman, and Mastracci 2008; Newman, Guy, and Mastracci 2009; Mastracci, Guy, and Newman 2012; Mastracci, Newman, and Guy 2006). Emotional labor is far from the only manner in which gender is produced and reproduced in the workplace. Human resource management practices, including hiring, evaluating, and rewarding workers, all have the capacity to produce and reproduce gendered norms and practices. What is the ideal organization, and what are the ideal practices? We are limited in our ability to envision them "because we ourselves are limited in our vision of a gender-equitable state by the gender relations of which we are currently a part, we resist anticipating in any detail what precisely a transformed end state looks like" (Ely and Meyerson 2000a: 592). We hope to have exposed the myth of gender neutrality assumed in many workplace processes and practices and to have given public managers and researchers reason to question assumptions of gender neutrality in the workplace.

REFERENCES

Acker. J. 1990. Hierarchies, jobs, bodies: A theory of gendered organizations. *Gender & Society, 4*(2), 139–158.

———. 1992. Gendered institutions: From sex roles to gendered institutions. *Contemporary Sociology, 21*(5), 565–569.

———. 2000. Revisiting class: Thinking from gender, race, and organizations. *Social Politics, 7*(2), 192–214.

———. 2007. Inequality regimes: Gender, class, and race in organizations. In Joan Z. Spade and Catherine G. Valentine (Eds.), *The Kaleidoscope of Gender: Prisms, Patterns, and Possibilities* (2nd ed.). Thousand Oaks, CA: Sage.

Alkadry, M. G., and L. E. Tower. 2011. Covert pay discrimination: How authority predicts pay differences between women and men. *Public Administration Review, 71*(5), 740–750.

Appleby, P. H. 1945. *Big Democracy*. New York: Knopf.

Ashcraft, K. L. 2001. Organized dissonance: Feminist bureaucracy as hybrid form. *Academy of Management Journal, 44*(6), 1301–1322.

Baron, J. N., M. T. Hannan, G. Hsu, and O. Kocak. 2007. In the company of women: Gender inequality and the logic of bureaucracy. *Work & Occupations, 34*(1), 35–66.

Berry, J. 2011. *Status of Telework in the Federal Government: Report to Congress*. Washington, DC: U.S. Office of Personnel Management.

Brannen, J., G. Meszaros, P. Moss, and G. Poland. 1994. *Employment and Family Life: A Review of Research in the UK (1980–1994)*. Sheffield, UK: Employment Department.

Britton, D. M. 2000. The epistemology of the gendered organization. *Gender & Society, 14*(3), 418–434.

Bruce, W., and Reed, C. 1994. Preparing supervisors for the future workforce: The dual-income couple and the work-family dichotomy. *Public Administration Review, 54*(1), 36–43.

Burnier, D. 2006. Masculine markets and feminine care: A gender analysis of the National Performance Review. *Public Administration Review, 66*(6), 861–872.

Butler, J. 1993. *Bodies That Matter: On the Discursive Limits of "Sex."* New York: Routledge.

Carreiras, H. 2010. Gendered culture in peacekeeping operations. *International Peacekeeping, 17*(4), 471–485.

Connell, R. 2006. Glass ceilings or gendered institutions? Mapping the gender regimes of public sector worksites. *Public Administration Review, 66*(6), 837–849.

Cornwell, C., and J. E. Kellough. 1994. Women and minorities in federal government agencies: Examining new evidence from panel data. *Public Administration Review, 54*(3), 265–270.

DeHart-Davis, L. 2009. Can bureaucracy benefit organizational women? *Administration & Society, 41*(3), 340–363.

Eisenhardt, K. M., and C. B. Schoonhoven. 1990. Organizational growth: Linking founding team strategy, environment, and growth. *Administrative Science Quarterly, 35*(4), 504–529.

Elliott, J. R. 2001. Referral hiring and ethnically homogenous jobs: How prevalent is the connection and for whom? *Social Science Research, 30*(3), 401–425.

Ely, R. J., and D. E. Meyerson. 2000a. Advancing gender equity in organizations: The challenge and importance of maintaining a gender narrative. *Organization, 7*(4), 589–608.

———. 2000b. Theories of gender in organizations. In B. M. Staw and R. I. Sutton (Eds.), *Research in Organizational Behavior,* 22, 103–151.

Ferguson, K. E. 1983. Bureaucracy and public life: The feminization of the polity. *Administration & Society, 15*(3), 295–322.

Fernandez, R. M., and M. L. Mors. 2008. Competing for jobs: Labor queues and gender sorting in the hiring process. *Social Science Research, 37*(4), 1061–1080.

Gorman, E. H. 2005. Gender stereotypes, same-gender preferences, and organization variation in the hiring of women, *American Sociological Review, 70*(4), 702–728.

Guy, M. E., M. A. Newman, and S. H. Mastracci. 2008. *Emotional Labor: Putting the* Service *in Public Service.* Armonk, NY: M.E. Sharpe.

Guy, M. E., and K. Schumacher. 2009. Gender and diversity. *Public Administration Review, 69*(1), 1–40.

Guy, M. E., and S. Spice. 2009. Gender and workplace issues. In Steven W. Hays, Richard D. Kearney, and Jerrell D. Coggburn (Eds.), *Public Human Resource Management: Problems and Prospects* (5th ed.). Upper Saddle River, NJ: Pearson.

Hannan, M. T. 2005. Ecologies of organizations: Diversity and identity. *Journal of Economic Perspectives, 19*(1), 51–70.

Ibarra, H. 1997. Paving an alternative route: Gender differences in managerial networks. *Social Psychology Quarterly, 60*(1), 91–102.

Jackson, R. A., and M. A. Newman. 2004. Sexual harassment in the federal workplace revisited: Influences by gender. *Public Administration Review, 64*(6), 705–717.

Kanter, R. M. 1977/1993. *Men and Women of the Corporation* (2nd ed.). New York: Basic Books.

Kelan, E. K. 2010. Gender logic and (un)doing gender at work. *Gender, Work, and Organization, 17*(2), 174–194.

Kelly, R. M., and M. A. Newman. 2001. The gendered bureaucracy: Agency mission, equality of opportunity, and representative bureaucracies. *Women & Politics, 22*(3), 1–33.

Kmec, J. A. 2005. Setting occupational sex segregation in motion: Demand-side explanations of sex-traditional employment. *Work & Occupations, 32*(3), 322–354.

Lewis, G. B. 1994. Women, occupations, and federal agencies: Occupational mix and interagency differences. *Public Administration Review, 54*(3), 271–276.

Lewis, S. 2010. Restructuring workplace cultures: The ultimate work-family challenge? *Gender in Management, 16*(1), 21–29.

Mahler, J. 2012. The telework divide: Managerial and personnel challenges of telework. *Review of Public Personnel Administration, 32*(4), 407–418.

Martin, P. Y. 2003. "Said and done" versus "saying and doing": Gendering practices, practicing gender at work. *Gender & Society, 17*(3), 342–366.

Mastracci, S. H. 2013. Time use on care giving activities: Comparing federal government and private sector workers. *Review of Public Personnel Administration, 33*(1): 3–27.

Mastracci, S. H., M. E. Guy, and M. A. Newman. 2012. *Emotional Labor in Crisis Response: Working on the Razor's Edge.* Armonk, NY: M.E. Sharpe.

Mastracci, S. H., and C. Herring. 2010. Nonprofit management practices and processes to promote gender diversity. *Nonprofit Management & Leadership, 21*(2), 153–173.

Mastracci, S. H., M. A. Newman, and M. E. Guy. 2006. Appraising emotion work. *American Review of Public Administration, 36*(2), 139–155.

McCall, L. 2005. The complexity of intersectionality. *Signs: A Journal of Women in Culture and Society, 30*(3), 1771–1800.

McCloskey, D. N. 1999. *Crossing: A Memoir.* Chicago: University of Chicago Press.

McDonald, P., K. Brown, and L. Bradley. 2005. Explanations for the provision-utilisation gap in work/life policy. *Women in Management Review*, *20*(1), 37–55.

McGinn, K., and P. M. Patterson. 2005. A long way toward what? Sex, gender, feminism, and public administration. *International Journal of Public Administration*, *28*(4), 929–942.

McGuire, G. M. 2002. Gender, race, and the shadow structure: A study of informal networks and inequality in a work organization. *Gender & Society*, *16*(3), 303–322.

Meyerson, D. E., and D. M. Kolb. 2000. Moving out of the 'armchair': Developing a framework to bridge the gap between feminist theory and practice. *Organization*, *7*(4), 553–571.

Naff, K. C. 1994. Through the glass ceiling: Prospects for the advancement of women in the federal civil service. *Public Administration Review*, *54*(6), 507–514.

———. 2001. *To Look Like America*. Boulder, CO: Westview Press.

Newman, M. A., M. E. Guy, and S. H. Mastracci. 2009. Beyond cognition: Affective leadership and emotional labor. *Public Administration Review*, *69*(1), 6–20.

Newman, M. A., R. A. Jackson, and D. B. Baker. (2003). Sexual harassment in the federal workplace. *Public Administration Review*, *63*(4), 472–483.

Phillips, D. J. 2005. Organizational genealogies and the persistence of gender inequality: The case of Silicon Valley law firms. *Administrative Science Quarterly*, *50*(3), 440–472.

Popielarz, P. A. 1999. (In)voluntary association: A multilevel analysis of gender segregation in voluntary associations. *Gender & Society*, *13*(2), 234–250.

Pratto, F., L. M. Stallworth, J. Sidanius, and B. Siers. 1997. The gender gap in occupational role attainment. *Journal of Personality and Social Psychology*, *72*(1), 37–53.

Reskin, B. F., and D. D. Bielby. 2005. A sociological perspective on gender and career outcomes. *Journal of Economic Perspectives*, *19*(1), 71–86.

Ridgeway, C. L., and L. Smith-Lovin. 1996. Gender and social interaction. *Social Psychology Quarterly*, *59*(3), 173–175.

Scheibl, F., and S. Dex. 1998. Should we have more family-friendly policies? *European Management Review*, *16*(5), 586–599.

Smithson, J., and E. H. Stokoe. 2005. Discourses of work/life balance: Negotiating 'gender blind' terms in organizations. *Gender, Work, and Organizations*, *12*(2), 147–168.

Sneed, B. G. 2007. Glass walls in state bureaucracies: Examining the difference departmental function can make. *Public Administration Review*, *67*(5), 880–891.

Stinchcombe, A. 1965. Organizations and social structure. In J. G. March (Ed.), *Handbook of Organizations*. Chicago: Rand McNally.

Stivers, C. 1995. Settlement women and bureau men: Constructing a usable past for public administration. *Public Administration Review*, *55*(6), 522–529.

———. 2000. *Bureau Men, Settlement Women: Constructing Public Administration in the Progressive Era*. Lawrence: University of Kansas Press.

———. 2002. *Gender Images in Public Administration* (2nd ed.). Thousand Oaks, CA: Sage.

———. 2008. Public administration's myth of Sisyphus. *Administration & Society*, *39*(8), 1008–1012.

Yanow, D. 2002. *Constructing Race and Ethnicity in America: Category-Making in Public Policy and Administration*. Armonk, NY: M.E. Sharpe.

CHAPTER 20

VETERANS' PREFERENCE AND THE FEDERAL SERVICE

Gregory B. Lewis
Georgia State University

In laying out the fundamental values underlying the federal service (e.g., neutral competence, representativeness, and executive leadership [Kaufman 1969] or responsiveness, efficiency, employee rights, and social equity [Klingner 2009]), scholars frequently overlook the goal of rewarding members of the military for their sacrifices in service to the country. Yet veterans' preference has been an important part of the federal personnel system at least since World War I, veterans composed half of the federal service from the end of World War II to the early 1970s, and veterans remain strongly overrepresented in the federal service today.

The strong preference for veterans in federal hiring creates potential trade-offs with other fundamental values. The challenge to social equity and representativeness may be strongest. The vast majority of members of the military are men, making veterans' preference an important impediment to federal employment of women. Past discriminatory practices in the military mean that whites and heterosexuals may disproportionately benefit from veterans' preference. Veterans' preference may also limit the representation of naturalized citizens, disproportionately hurting Hispanics and Asians, as people who immigrate to the U.S. as adults are unlikely to serve in the U.S. military. In addition, strong proponents of the merit system have long worried that

valuing military service above more direct measures of ability may lower the quality of the federal workforce, and federal managers have complained about the effects of veterans' preference on their discretion to choose the best person for the job.

This chapter begins with a history and description of veterans' preference in the federal service. It then uses data from the U.S. Census and federal personnel records to describe three patterns. First, being a veteran dramatically increases the probability that one works for the federal government. That increase holds for every subgroup examined and has grown strongly over the past 30 years. Second, eligibility for veterans' preference varies widely across subgroups. Men are far more likely than women to qualify, and blacks and whites are much more likely than Asians and Hispanics to do so. Gay men are less than half as likely as straight men to qualify, though lesbians are more than twice as likely as straight women to do so. Thus, veterans' preference has had a strong impact on the gender composition of the federal workforce and a weaker impact on the representation of Hispanics, Asians, and gay men. Third, veterans' preference might lower the quality of the federal service. Veterans' preference leads to a less educated (but more experienced) federal workforce. Veterans earn less than equally educated and experienced nonveterans of the same sex and race, and they do not advance as far as nonveterans hired into similar positions, suggesting that veterans have less potential than the nonveterans who would have been hired in the absence of preference. The conclusion then looks back at the trade-offs veterans' preference creates.

VETERANS' PREFERENCE IN THE FEDERAL SERVICE

Unofficial hiring preference for disabled veterans dates back to the Revolutionary War, but it became more formal when Congress passed a joint resolution in 1865 favoring the hiring of disabled Civil War veterans into the civil service (U.S. Civil Service Commission [CSC] 1955; Manela 1976). The preference was limited, however, because it only covered disabled veterans, because the attorney general ruled that it only applied *"other things being equal"* (italics in original), and because the lack of a uniform hiring process meant that the level of preference given depended on the appointing authority (CSC 1955: 2).

The Civil Service Act of 1883 (the Pendleton Act) created a more formal hiring process, making uniform application of veterans' preference possible; but it originally emphasized the principle that individual merit should determine whom the government hired and advanced, and it barely mentioned veterans' preference. It required competitive examinations for hiring in the lowest grades and the maintenance of a register of qualified candidates. The CSC forwarded only the top three names on the register for hiring officials to choose from (U.S. Merit Systems Protection Board [MSPB] 1995: 37); this "rule of three" largely persisted until 2010. In 1888, however, the CSC revised its rules to make 65 rather than 70 the passing score for disabled veterans and to put disabled veterans with passing scores at the top of the register; the attorney general strengthened preference by giving them absolute preference over others in hiring.

As World War I was ending, Congress passed the Veterans Preference Act of 1919, which extended hiring preference to honorably discharged, able-bodied veterans as well as to widows of deceased veterans and wives of severely disabled ones. It also expanded the number of positions in which preference would be considered. The CSC (1918, XVIII) initially argued against the legislation and in favor of "the principle that every citizen should have equal opportunity to compete for appointment in the public service, and that in each case the most efficient should be appointed." It quickly became more of a supporter, but it objected to giving absolute preference in hiring to veterans with passing scores, especially as covering nondisabled veterans meant that claims for preference ballooned from 600 to 60,000 per year (CSC 1955: 6). Instead, it proposed and President Warren G. Harding implemented a rule adding 10 points to the civil service exam scores of disabled veterans and 5 points to those of others eligible for preference. As World War II wound down, Congress codified that practice in the Veterans' Preference Act of 1944.[1]

Traditionally, all job applicants were rated on a 100-point scale, typically based on a written examination or an "unassembled" assessment of the applicants' qualifications conducted by the CSC or the department's personnel department, which then created a register of qualified applicants (those with scores of 70 or above). It ranked applicants by their scores, after adding 10 points for disabled veterans and 5 points for others eligible for veterans' preference. Veterans were placed ahead of nonveterans with the same scores, so that nonveterans with civil service exam scores of 100 ranked below disabled veterans with initial scores of 90 and other veterans with raw scores of 95. Under the Civil Service Reform Act of 1978, veterans with a compensable, service-connected disability of 10% or more "float" to the top of the register if they have passing scores. Until recently, the CSC (now U.S. Office of Personnel Management [OPM]) forwarded only the top three names on the register to hiring officials, the so-called rule of three mentioned earlier. A hiring official could not pass over a veteran to hire a nonveteran lower on the register without a written explanation approved by the CSC/OPM.

In 2010, following experimentation under other presidents, President Barack Obama eliminated the rule of three and replaced it with category rating.[2] An agency defines two or more categories of qualified applicants (e.g., highly qualified, well qualified, and qualified). Hiring officials can choose anyone in the top category, but veterans are listed first within each category, and hiring officials cannot pass over veterans to hire nonveterans in the same category without a written explanation approved by OPM. Whether the switch from the rule of three to category rating strengthens or weakens veterans' preference is not clear.

Preference does not apply in promotions, but veterans already employed by the federal government can receive preference in applying for other posted federal job openings. Veterans also receive preference in reductions in force. If an agency downsizes and eliminates positions, nonveterans lose their jobs before veterans in the same tenure group. In addition, veterans receive credit for their military service in pension calculations.

VETERANS' PREFERENCE AND THE PROBABILITY OF FEDERAL EMPLOYMENT

Veterans' share of federal employment rose rapidly after the Veterans Preference Acts of 1919 and 1944, though whether this was due to veterans' preference or the return of the troops is not clear. The veteran percentage of federal new hires jumped from 14% in 1920 to 29% in 1921. Only 15% of federal employees were veterans in 1944, but that rose to 41% in 1946 and 49% in 1949; about half of all federal employees were veterans until the early 1970s (Lewis and Emmert 1984: 330).

Veterans have continued to be dramatically more likely than nonveterans to hold federal jobs. The U.S. General Accounting Office (GAO 1977) found that 30% of federal employees but only 15% of the nonfederal workforce were veterans. Blank (1985) found that veterans were much more likely to work for government, especially the federal government, than nonveterans of the same sex, race, experience, and educational levels. Sanders (2007: 412) found that being a veteran raised the odds of a government job by about 40% for native-born citizens and nearly doubled the odds for immigrants, though he did not examine federal and state-local employment separately.

Based on data from the U.S. Census for 1 to 3 million full-time employees in each year (see the appendix for a description of the data and methods), the first line of Table 20.1 shows that veterans were about 20% more likely than nonveterans to work for the federal government in 1980 (8.8% of veterans and 7.0% of nonveterans worked for the federal service in 1980). That ratio rose from 1.2 in 1980 to 1.8 in 1990, 2.3 in 2000, and 4.0 in 2010. That is, by 2010, veterans were four times as likely as nonveterans to hold federal jobs. Between 1980 and 2010, the percentage of veterans who worked for the federal government nearly doubled, while the percentage of nonveterans who did so dropped by nearly half.

Veteran status markedly increased the probability of federal employment for every subgroup from 1990 on, even groups that tend to be underrepresented in the military. Its impact is strongest for women. Hispanic, Asian, and white women were all more than seven times as likely to be federal employees in 2010 if they were veterans than if they were not. (Groups in Table 20.1 are ranked based on the ratios for 2010.) Veterans' preference appears to have the least impact on white men's chances of federal employment in every year and to have a bigger impact on the probability of a federal job for those who did not complete high school than for better-educated Americans.[3]

VETERANS' PREFERENCE AND THE COMPOSITION OF FEDERAL WORKFORCE

The impact of veterans' preference on women's chances of federal employment raised political and legal controversy in the late 1970s. By law, women could make up no more than 2% of the military between 1948 and 1967, and the U.S. Army maintained the 2% cap until 1978 (Browne 1980: 1114). In 1976, a federal district court ruled that absolute veterans' preference in Massachusetts state government employment denied women equal protection of the law under the Fourteenth Amendment (*Feeney v. Commonwealth*, 366 N.E.2d 1262, 1977, reported in Browne 1980). GAO (1977)

Table 20.1 Ratio of Federal Employment of Veterans and Nonveterans, by Subgroup

	1980	1990	2000	2010
Percentage working for federal government				
Veterans	8.8	10.1	9.7	16.1
Nonveterans	7.0	5.5	4.2	4.1
Ratio (total)	1.2	1.8	2.3	4.0
Sex and race/ethnicity				
Hispanic women	2.6	4.7	4.9	9.5
Asian women	2.7	5.4	5.1	7.4
White women	2.9	4.9	4.5	7.2
Black women	2.0	2.8	2.8	5.4
Hispanic men	1.6	2.5	3.4	5.0
Asian men	1.4	2.7	3.7	4.9
Black men	1.4	1.8	2.2	3.4
White men	1.0	1.5	2.0	2.9
Educational attainment				
No high school	1.8	2.6	1.7	7.4
High school but no diploma	1.8	2.3	2.8	4.1
Some college	1.3	1.8	2.3	3.8
College graduate	1.2	1.8	2.6	3.8
Master's degree	1.1[a]	1.6	2.2	3.8
High school graduate	1.2	1.7	2.2	3.3
Professional degree	1.1[a]	2.0	2.4	2.6
PhD	1.1[a]	1.3	1.7	2.1
Relationship status				
Married women	[b]	5.2	4.4	5.2
Women with male partners	[b]	4.8	4.5	4.6
Unpartnered women	[b]	4.0	4.0	4.6
Women with female partners	[b]	2.6	2.4	4.2
Men with female partners	[b]	2.0	2.6	3.8
Married men	[b]	1.7	2.2	3.7
Unpartnered men	[b]	1.5	2.1	3.7
Men with male partners	[b]	1.6	3.1	2.8

Source: Calculated by author from 1980, 1990, and 2000 Public Use Microdata Samples of the U.S. Census and from the combined 2009, 2010, and 2011 American Community Surveys, also conducted by the U.S. Census Bureau. See appendix for details.

[a] The 1980 Census did not distinguish among master's, professional, and doctoral degrees.

[b] The 1980 Census did not identify unmarried partners, making this categorization impossible.

reported that federal hiring officials could not consider large numbers of highly qualified women because, even with perfect scores on civil service examinations, they ranked lower than less educated and experienced veterans with lower test scores. Arguing that veterans' preference discriminated against women and minorities, Congresswoman Patricia Schroeder (D-CO) led an effort to amend the Civil Service Reform Act (CSRA) of 1978 to allow veterans to use their preference only once, within 15 years of leaving military service (Newland 1993: 73). In testimony before Congress, CSC Chairman Alan Campbell argued that "the present limitations favoring preferential hiring from a labor pool which is 98% male and 92% nonminority places an inordinate burden on Federal agencies trying to implement affirmative action" (quoted in Lewis and Emmert 1984: 329).

Both the legal and political efforts to limit veterans' preference failed, however. The U.S. Supreme Court ruled that, despite its disparate impact on women, the Massachusetts statute was constitutional because it did not have a discriminatory intent (*Personnel Administrator of Massachusetts v. Feeney*, 442 U.S. 256, 1979, discussed in Browne 1980). Veterans' groups lobbied effectively against the effort to weaken veterans' preference, and the CSRA ended up adding near-absolute preference to veterans with compensable, service-connected disabilities of 10% or more (Newland 1993: 74).

Whatever its intention, however, veterans' preference clearly benefits far more men than women. Although 14% of the U.S. military are now women, men still outnumber women by 6-to-1 (Clemmitt 2009). The imbalance is even clearer in the civilian workforce. Despite the dramatic decline in the percentage of men in the full-time civilian labor force who have served in the military (from 44% in 1980 to 14% in 2010; see Table 20.2), men were still 8 times as likely as women to be veterans in 2010, down from nearly 30 times as likely in 1980. A similar gender disparity exists within each race/ethnicity.

Despite discrimination against African Americans and Asian Americans in World War II, the military has become a far more diverse and meritocratic institution, where race matters less than in many other parts

of society (Lundquist 2008). By 2000, 20% of active duty military were black, though Latinos and Asians remained underrepresented relative to their shares of the military-age population (Lutz 2008: 177). Table 20.2 confirms that blacks in the workforce have been more likely to be veterans than whites of the same sex since 2000, but Latinos and Asians are much less likely than non-Hispanic whites of the same sex to be veterans. These figures exclude noncitizens, but naturalized citizens may also be less likely than native-born citizens to have U.S. military service (Sanders 2007).

"Don't Ask, Don't Tell" ended in 2011, but the military had long prohibited the service of homosexuals (Berube 1990; Shilts 1993) and only partially loosened the restriction in 1993 (Rimmerman 1996). Virelli (2004) argues that, because the military explicitly prohibited service by gays, the case that veterans' preference unconstitutionally denies them equal protection of the law is even stronger for lesbians and gay men than it is for women. Table 20.2 confirms that men who live with male partners are only half as likely as married men to be veterans. In contrast, women who live with female partners are markedly more likely than other women to be veterans. Gates (2004) similarly finds that lesbians are overrepresented in the military, relative to other women, and that gay men are underrepresented. Further, some of those gay men and lesbians did not receive honorable discharges due to their sexual orientation and therefore do not qualify for veterans' preference; this may explain why veteran status increases the probability of federal employment less for gay men and lesbians than for married people of the same sex (Table 20.1). This may also help explain why partnered gay men are less likely than comparable married men to hold federal jobs; the over-representation of lesbians in the military may balance out their lower probability of receiving honorable discharges, leaving partnered lesbians reasonably equitably represented in the federal service (Lewis and Pitts 2011).

In sum, women and Hispanic, Asian, and gay men are all less likely to have military service and to qualify for veterans' preference. On the other hand, being a veteran appears to increase the probability of federal

Table 20.2 Percentage of Group with Military Service

	1980	1990	2000	2010
Sex				
Men	44.2	34.1	21.6	14.0
Women	1.6	1.7	1.9	1.8
Sex and race/ethnicity				
Black men	34.8	31.4	24.9	18.3
White men	45.8	35.3	22.2	14.5
Hispanic men	31.7	24.4	15.1	9.6
Asian men	29.9	18.3	9.4	5.6
Black women	1.6	2.4	3.1	3.2
White women	1.7	1.6	1.7	1.6
Hispanic women	1.4	1.6	1.5	1.4
Asian women	1.1	1.1	0.9	0.8
Relationship status				
Married men	[a]	37.7	24.7	15.6
Men with female partners	[a]	27.5	19.3	11.5
Unpartnered men	[a]	33.1	20.6	13.6
Men with male partners	[a]	17.2	10.7	6.4
Women with female partners	[a]	6.5	7.3	5.2
Unpartnered women	[a]	1.8	2.0	1.8
Married women	[a]	1.5	1.7	1.8
Women with male partners	[a]	1.8	1.8	1.6
Educational attainment				
Some college	30.0	23.0	16.1	11.1
High school graduate	28.9	22.1	14.3	8.9
Master's degree	30.5[b]	21.2	12.1	7.4
College graduate	30.8	18.9	10.3	6.4
Professional degree	30.5[b]	21.1	11.2	6.6
PhD	30.5[b]	21.5	10.4	5.3
High school but no diploma	30.1	18.5	8.8	3.3
No high school	15.0	11.2	5.8	3.6

Source: Calculated by author from 1980, 1990, and 2000 Public Use Microdata Samples of the U.S. Census and from the combined 2009, 2010, and 2011 American Community Surveys, also conducted by the U.S. Census Bureau. See appendix for details.

[a] The 1980 Census did not identify unmarried partners, making this categorization impossible.

[b] The 1980 Census did not distinguish among master's, professional, and doctoral degrees.

employment more for women, Hispanics, Asians, and blacks than for white men. Elsewhere, I estimate that, in the absence of veterans' preference, the male-female split in the federal service would be 50–50 rather than its current 57–43 (Lewis 2013), and the employment of Latinos, Asians, and gay men would probably all increase by 20%.

MANAGERIAL DISCRETION AND THE QUALITY OF FEDERAL EMPLOYEES

Veterans' preference also raises concerns about merit principles and managerial hiring discretion. The CSC initially opposed expansion of veterans' preference after World War I on merit grounds (Emmert and Lewis 1982: 48). The U.S. Merit Systems Protection Board (MSPB 1994: xii) argued that managers viewed veterans' preference "as an impediment to good hiring practices" and sometimes tried to get around it. GAO (1992) reported that agencies frequently sent back registers headed by veterans and relied increasingly on hiring mechanisms (e.g., the Outstanding Scholar program [OSP]) that allowed them to ignore veterans' preference. The percentage of entry-level professional and administrative positions filled through OSP rose from 1% in 1984 (MSPB 1994) to 30% to 40% in the mid- to late 1990s (Tsugawa 2011).

After MSPB ruled in 2006 that OSP violated the rights of veterans, federal hiring of entry-level professionals and administrators switched increasingly to the Federal Career Intern Program (FCIP), which President Bill Clinton had created in 2000. FCIP allowed agencies to recruit and hire on college campuses and at job fairs without posting job openings competitively and without awarding veterans' preference (MSPB 2008: 15). By 2007, about 70% of entry-level professional and administrative new hires entered under FCIP (Tsugawa 2011). A federal court ruled in 2008, however, that FCIP hiring had violated a particular veteran's rights (Rosenberg 2009); MSPB broadened the ruling in 2010 (Losey 2010); and President Obama dismantled FCIP shortly thereafter (Executive Order [EO] 13562, December 2010). OPM is currently implementing the Obama administration's new "Pathways for Students & Recent Graduates to Federal Careers" program, which includes internship programs and hiring routes for recent college graduates and which explicitly applies veterans' preference.

Federal hiring officials' avoidance strategies suggest that they believe that veterans' preference hampers their ability to hire the most qualified job applicants. Measuring the quality of federal employees is notoriously difficult, of course, so any conclusions about the impact of preference on quality are tentative. Labor economists typically use both education and work experience as proxies for employee productivity, as earnings increase with both. (Their argument is that, in a perfectly functioning labor market, pay equals the marginal productivity of workers, so any factor that increases pay implicitly signals increased productivity.) The use of OSP and FCIP suggests that veterans' preference decreases federal employment of college graduates, but a priori expectations about its impact on prior work experience are less clear.

The data show that newly hired veterans are less educated but more experienced than nonveteran new hires. In 1981–2009, veteran new hires had 0.5 fewer years of education, on average, than nonveteran new hires, but they were 7.8 years older, suggesting substantially more work experience (Table 20.3). The pattern is more extreme in professional and administrative positions: The veteran new hires had 1.1 fewer years of education and were 8.5 years older. The educational gap is narrower and the experience gap wider at GS-5 and GS-7, typical entry-level professional and administrative positions. Those two grades account for less than half of professional and administrative new hires, however. More professionals and administrators entered at GS-9 or GS-11 than at GS-5, and comparable numbers entered at GS-12 as at GS-5. In these grades, the educational disparity was larger, but the age gap was narrower.

A number of researchers have tested the hypothesis that veterans' preference leads to veterans being paid more than comparably educated and experienced nonveterans of the same race and sex (Taylor 1979; Grandjean 1981; Johnson and Libecap 1989; Lewis

Table 20.3 Mean Characteristic of New Hires, 1980–2009

| | Educational Attainment (Years) | | Age | |
	Nonveterans	Veteran–Nonveteran	Nonveterans	Veteran–Nonveteran
All new hires	14.5	-0.5	31.7	+7.8
Professionals and administrators				
All	16.4	−1.1	32.8	+8.5
GS-5	15.3	−0.5	27.9	+9.6
GS-7	15.9	−0.6	28.1	+9.8
GS-9	16.2	−1.5	31.5	+9.2
GS-11	17.0	−2.1	35.7	+6.6
GS-12	16.9	−1.6	37.8	+5.3
GS-13	17.3	−0.9	40.5	+3.7

Source: Calculated by author from U.S. Office of Personnel Management, 1% sample, Central Personnel Data File, 1980–2009.

All veteran-nonveteran differences are significant at .0001 level.

and Emmert 1984; Lewis 1988). The research has consistently shown, however, that veterans earn less than comparable nonveterans—leading to some speculation that preference causes veterans to enter federal service at higher levels than comparable nonveterans but that they fall behind as nonveterans receive more promotions (e.g., Taylor 1979: 473). My own analysis, using a better measure of federal civilian experience and running the regression separately for each year, confirms that veterans typically earn less than comparable nonveterans. The pay gap was 2% to 5% in 1992 through 1999 but has typically been 6% or 7% since 2000. On the other hand, separate analyses by year of federal service do not show a pattern of higher salaries for veterans when they first enter and then falling behind. Instead, over the 1990–2009 period, the pay gap was 1.6% to 3.2% throughout the first 10 years of the career, with no tendency toward the gap widening as the career progressed.

From the perspective of the quality of the civil service, however, the real question is not whether veterans earn more or less than comparable nonveterans, but whether they perform better than the nonveterans who would have been hired in the absence of veterans' preference. (On average, those nonveterans would have been younger, better educated, and more likely to be women, and the regression models remove all those differences.) I used two measures of performance. First, I have supervisors' ratings for 1981 through 2003. During this period, veterans and nonveterans who started in the same grade in the same agency in the same year got the same ratings for the first five years of their careers. After that, nonveterans got significantly higher ratings for the next 10 years. (The pattern is weaker but similar if I restrict the analysis to professionals and administrators.)

Second, I examined advancement patterns over the first decade of the federal civilian career for all new hires and for professional and administrative new hires (the first two columns of Table 20.4). Veterans fall behind by about one-sixth grade by the end of their first year, nearly one-third grade by the end of their second year, and by one-half grade by the end of their fifth year. The veteran-nonveteran gap appears to plateau among professionals and administrators but to continue to widen among other new hires. Patterns differ a little by entry grade, but even among those entering at GS-13, in middle-management positions, the veterans fall significantly behind the nonveterans they came in with by the end of year 6.[4]

In sum, veterans' preference brings in a more experienced but less educated federal workforce. The analysis suggests that nonveterans advance faster than veterans hired into the same grades in their first five years. After that, the pace of advancement is similar for both groups, but the nonveterans are getting higher performance ratings. The higher age and lower educational levels of veteran new hires probably explain this divergence—advancement differences are not significant once age, education, race, and sex are controlled. Veterans appear to be closer to their career peaks when they are hired, however, suggesting that the federal service would tend to hire applicants with more potential into the same positions, in the absence of veterans' preference.

CONCLUSION

Veterans' preference has a powerful impact on who gets federal jobs. Americans who have served in the military are currently four times as likely to hold federal jobs as Americans who have not. Serving in the military strikingly improves the chances of federal employment for men and women, whites and minorities, heterosexuals and gay/lesbians of every age and education level. These groups differ dramatically in their probabilities of qualifying for veterans' preference, however. Men still outnumber women 6-to-1 in the U.S. military, despite repeal of most laws that explicitly discriminate against women's service. The ban on gays in the military was only lifted in 2011, and immigration patterns probably limit the percentages of Hispanics and Asians who qualify for preference. The federal workforce would be more diverse in the absence of veterans' preference.

Table 20.4 Difference in Advancement Patterns between Veterans and Nonveterans

| Year | All | Professional and Administrative Only | | | | | | |
		All	Grade 5	Grade 7	Grade 9	Grade 11	Grade 12	Grade 13
1	−.17	−.17	−.07[a]	−.14[c]	−.35	−.14	−.12[c]	−.14[a]
2	−.30	−.30	−.11[a]	−.46	−.50	−.24	−.18	−.07[a]
3	−.44	−.44	−.44[c]	−.58	−.64	−.36	−.25	−.13[a]
4	−.47	−.49	−.55	−.67	−.69	−.43	−.26	−.21[b]
5	−.51	−.54	−.71	−.73	−.72	−.51	−.20[a]	−.21
6	−.52	−.54	−.70	−.74	−.70	−.49	−.19[a]	−.31[b]
7	−.51	−.52	−.64	−.69	−.66	−.51	−.38	−.37[c]
8	−.56	−.54	−.48[c]	−.79	−.65	−.48	−.54	−.34[b]
9	−.63	−.52	−.61	−.67	−.61	−.46	−.53	−.35[b]
10	−.69	−.55	−.48[b]	−.72	−.65	−.51	−.62	−.38[b]

Source: Calculated by author from U.S. Office of Personnel Management, 1% sample, Central Personnel Data File, 1980–2009.

Figures are average grade differences between veterans and nonveterans hired into the same grades in the same year, 1980–2008. Figures are regression coefficients on *veteran* from models with number of grades advanced since entry as the dependent variable. All models include dummy variables for entry years. The first two columns, with all entry grades combined, include dummy variables for entry grade.

All coefficients are significant at .001 level unless otherwise specified: [a]Not significant at .05 level. [b]Significant at .05 level. [c]Significant at .01 level.

Whether the federal service would be more productive in the absence of veterans' preference is less clear. It clearly leads to older, less educated people being hired, but this has both advantages and disadvantages. Veterans earn less than comparably educated and experienced nonveterans of the same race and sex and do not advance as quickly as nonveterans hired into similar positions for the first five years of their careers, but they get higher performance ratings thereafter. I tentatively conclude that nonveterans are more productive, on average, than veterans hired into the same entry grades.

Is veterans' preference worth its obvious costs to the diversity and less clear costs to the quality of the federal service? The nation clearly owes a debt of gratitude to veterans for their sacrifices for the nation. In addition to the physical and emotional costs they have paid, the time out of school and the civilian labor force depress their lifetime earnings. Especially a decade into the wars in Iraq and Afghanistan, with veterans experiencing high unemployment rates, any policy that increases their chances of finding jobs has its attractions. Veterans' preference is clearly an effective policy tool—it dramatically increases veterans' chance of federal employment—but it is also costly to those who do not get federal jobs because of it, to the representativeness of the federal bureaucracy, and perhaps to the quality of the federal service.

APPENDIX: DATA AND METHODS

I computed Tables 20.1 and 20.2 from the 5% Public Use Microdata Samples (PUMS) from the Census for 1980, 1990, and 2000 and the combined 2009–2011 American Community Surveys (ACS). I restricted the sample to full-time (36-plus hours per week), full-year (50-plus+ weeks) employees (dropping both the self-employed and part-time workers) between the ages of 21 and 65. I also dropped all noncitizens. I coded all respondents with military service as eligible to receive veterans' preference; although some military service does not qualify for preference, OPM (2011) reports that 90% of federally employed veterans receive preference, and any alternative coding appeared to create greater measurement error. The Census includes data on race/ethnicity, sex, age, educational attainment, and sector of employment.

In coding my race/ethnicity variable, I ignore the race of Hispanics so that the categories are mutually exclusive. The Census labels all individuals in a household based on their relationship to the "householder." Since 1990, people can be the "unmarried partner" of the householder, allowing me to identify people living with a same-sex or different-sex partner. Census data do not indicate whether people who do not live with a partner are gay or straight.

All the analyses of employee quality rely on a 1% random sample of the federal government's Central Personnel Data File (CPDF) for 1973–2009. OPM maintains files on federal employees in most federal agencies (the exceptions include the U.S. Postal Service and the CIA). For research purposes, OPM draws a 1% sample in April of each year, based on the final three digits of the social security number; employees in the sample one year appear in every year in which they are federal employees in March.

A major problem for this analysis, and all prior studies of veteran-nonveteran pay disparities that rely on the CPDF, is that the CPDF sample does not distinguish between military and civilian service; both count as federal service for seniority and retirement purposes. Work experience in the federal civil service has a much stronger positive impact on salaries than does nonfederal work experience. If military service has no more impact on pay than nonfederal work experience does, veterans could be earning less than "comparable" nonveterans in these previous analyses because the regression models treat their military service as equivalent to federal civilian service.

To try to get around that problem, I restrict the sample to employees who first appear in the CPDF in 1980 or later. I count them as having zero federal civilian experience in that first appearance, then add one year for each year of continuous federal service thereafter. I restrict the sample to full-time employees in the General Schedule and equivalent pay systems. In line with previous analyses, I regress the natural logarithm of salary on veteran status, race/ethnicity, sex, years of education, major field of study in college, age and age-squared, and a set of dummy variables for the recoded federal experience variable; I run the analyses separately for 1990 through 2009. I then run the model by each year of service, with the same control variables, but substituting dummy variables for year instead of years of service.

Finally, I compare veterans to nonveterans hired into the same positions, with no controls for education, age, race/ethnicity, or sex. I only have performance ratings through 2003. I run regressions for performance ratings (on a 5-point scale) and logit analyses for outstanding ratings. The independent variables are a dummy variable for veteran status, a set of dummy variables for entry grade, a set of dummy variables for agency (agencies vary enormously in their ratings patterns [Lewis 1997]), and a set of dummy variables for year of entry. I also run regressions for the number of grades advanced since entry on the same set of independent variables, minus the dummy variables for agency (promotion patterns vary less by agency); I have the advancement measures through 2009. I run separate models for each of the first 15 years of federal service for all new entrants, professional and administrative new hires, and (for the advancement analyses) professional and administrative new hires by entry grade.

Notes

1. The definition of who qualifies for veterans' preference has changed over time. The Veterans' Preference Act of 1944 covered nondisabled, honorably discharged members of the military who served on active duty in wartime or in peacetime campaigns for which campaign badges or service medals were authorized; veterans with service-related disabilities could also have served during peacetime (CSC 1955: 17). The 1944 Act also awarded five points to widows of veterans and wives of severely disabled veterans. In 1948, some mothers of deceased or severely disabled veterans were added. Congress has repeatedly changed which periods of military service qualify. Currently, 5-point preference requires service "during a war; or during the period April 28, 1952 through July 1, 1955; or for more than 180 consecutive days, other than for training, any part of which occurred after January 31, 1955, and before October 15, 1976; or during the Gulf War from August 2, 1990, through January 2, 1992; or for more than 180 consecutive days, other than for training, any part of which occurred

during the period beginning September 11, 2001, and ending on the date prescribed by Presidential proclamation or by law as the last day of Operation Iraqi Freedom; or in a campaign or expedition for which a campaign medal has been authorized. Any Armed Forces Expeditionary medal or campaign badge, including El Salvador, Lebanon, Grenada, Panama, Southwest Asia, Somalia, and Haiti, qualifies for preference. A campaign medal holder or Gulf War veteran who originally enlisted after September 7, 1980 (or began active duty on or after October 14, 1982, and has not previously completed 24 months of continuous active duty) must have served continuously for 24 months or the full period called or ordered to active duty. The 24-month service requirement does not apply to 10-point preference eligibles separated for disability incurred or aggravated in the line of duty" (OPM Vetguide).

2. OPM had previously approved category rating as a U.S. Department of Agriculture "demonstration project" (MSPB 1995). In 2002, Congress extended it as an option for all agencies.

3. I have shown elsewhere that veterans are three to four times as likely as nonveterans to work for the federal government, even after controlling for education, age, race, sex, citizenship status, English ability, and relationship status simultaneously (Lewis 2013).

4. Johnson (2012) analyzes the CPDF for 1974–1997, covering all white-collar new hires rather a 1% sample of professional and administrative new hires. He finds that, in 9 of 15 entry grades, nonveterans progress faster over the first 15 years of the federal career than do veterans hired into the same grades in the same year, but that veterans progress significantly faster in three other grades. When he looks at employees hired into the same grades in the same occupation in the same year, he finds few significant differences between preference recipients and nonrecipients. He is skeptical that conclusions can be drawn about whether veterans who receive preference differ in quality from the employees who would have been hired in the absence of veterans' preference.

References

Berube, Alan. 1990. *Coming Out under Fire: The History of Gay Men and Women in World War II*. New York: Free Press.

Blank, Rebecca M. 1985. An Analysis of Workers' Choice between Employment in the Public and Private Sectors. *Industrial & Labor Relations Review, 38*(2), 211–224.

Browne, Constance A. 1980. Absolute Veterans' Preference in Public Employment: Personnel Administrator of Massachusetts v. Feeney. *Boston College Law Review, 21*(5), 1110–1142.

Clemmitt, Marcia. 2009. Women in the Military: Should Combat Roles Be Fully Opened to Women? *CQ Researcher, 19*(40), 957–980.

Emmert, Mark A., and Gregory B. Lewis. 1982. Veterans Preference and the Merit System. In David H. Rosenbloom (Ed.), *Centenary Issues of the Pendleton Act of 1883.* New York: Marcel Dekker, pp. 45–61.

Gates, Gary J. 2004. *Gay Men and Lesbians in the US Military: Estimates from Census 2000.* Washington, DC: Urban Institute.

Grandjean, Burke D. 1981. History and Career in a Bureaucratic Labor Market. *American Journal of Sociology, 86*(5), 1057–1092.

Johnson, Ronald N., and Gary D. Libecap. 1989. Bureaucratic Rules, Supervisor Behavior, and the Effect on Salaries in the Federal Government. *Journal of Law, Economics, and Organization, 5*(1), 53–82.

Johnson, Tim. 2012. *Does Veterans' Preference Diminish the Quality of the U.S. Federal Service?* Salem, OR: Willamette University.

Kaufman, Herbert. 1969. Administrative Decentralization and Political Power. *Public Administration Review, 29*(1), 3–15.

Klingner, Donald E. 2009. Competing Perspectives on Public Personnel Administration: Civil Service, Patronage, and Privatization. In Steven W. Hays, Richard C. Kearney and Jerrell C. Coggburn (Eds.), *Public Human Resource Management: Problems and Prospects.* New York: Longman.

Lewis, Gregory B. 1988. Progress toward Racial and Sexual Equality in the Federal Civil Service? *Public Administration Review, 48*(3), 700–707.

Lewis, Gregory B. 1997. Race, Sex, and Performance Ratings in the Federal Service. *Public Administration Review, 57* (6), 479–489.

———. 2013. The Impact of Veterans' Preference on the Composition and Quality of the Federal Civil Service. *Journal of Public Administration Research and Theory.* 23(2):247-265.

Lewis, Gregory B., and Mark A. Emmert. 1984. Who Pays for Veterans' Preference? *Administration & Society, 16*(3), 328–345.

Lewis, Gregory B., and David W. Pitts. 2011. Representation of Lesbians and Gay Men in Federal, State, and Local Bureaucracies. *Journal of Public Administration Research and Theory, 21*(1), 159–180.

Losey, Stephen. 2010. Board Shuts Intern-Hiring Loophole. *Federal Times*, http://www.federaltimes.com/article/20101114/PERSONNEL01/11140302/1049/PERSONNEL

Lundquist, Jennifer Hicks. 2008. Ethnic and Gender Satisfaction in the Military: The Effect of a Meritocratic Institution. *American Sociological Review, 73*(3), 477–496.

Lutz, Amy. 2008. Who Joins the Military? A Look at Race, Class, and Immigration Status. *Journal of Political and Military Sociology, 36*(2), 167–188.

Manela, Stewart S. 1976. Veterans' Preference in Public Employment: The History, Constitutionality, and Effect on Federal Personnel Practices of Veterans' Preference Legislation. *George Washington Law Review, 44*(4), 623–641.

Newland, Chester A. 1993. The Politics of Civil Service Reform. In Patricia W. Ingraham and David H. Rosenbloom (Eds.), *The Promise and Paradox of Civil Service Reform.* Pittsburgh: University of Pittsburgh Press, pp. 63–89.

Rimmerman, Craig A. 1996. *Gay Rights, Military Wrongs: Political Perspectives on Lesbians and Gays in the Military.* New York: Garland.

Rosenberg, Alyssa. 2009. Court Rules Veterans' Preference Applies to Excepted Service Jobs. *Government Executive*, http://www.govexec.com/dailyfed/0109/010709ar1.htm.

Sanders, Jimy. 2007. Nativity, Human Capital, and Government Employment. *Social Science Research, 36*(1), 404–420.

Shilts, Randy. 1993. *Conduct Unbecoming: Gays and Lesbians in the U.S. Military.* New York: St. Martin's Press.

Taylor, Patricia A. 1979. Income Inequality in the Federal Civilian Government. *American Sociological Review, 44*(3), 468–479.

Tsugawa, James. 2011. PMF and Pathways Programs. In *PMF and Pathways Programs: Reinventing the Old and Implementing the New.* Washington, DC.

U.S. Civil Service Commission (CSC). 1918. *Annual Report.* Washington, DC: CSC.

———. 1955. *History of Veteran Preference in Federal Employment: 1865–1955.* Washington, DC: CSC.

U.S. General Accounting Office. 1977. *Conflicting Congressional Policies: Veterans' Preference and Apportionment vs. Equal Employment Opportunity.* Washington, DC: GAO.

———. 1992. *Federal Hiring: Does Veterans' Preference Need Updating?* Washington, DC: GAO.

U.S. Merit Systems Protection Board (MSNB). 1994. *Entering Professional Positions in the Federal Government.* Washington, DC: MSPB.

———. 1995. *The Rule of Three in Federal Hiring: Boon or Bane?* Washington, DC: MSPB.

———. 2008. *Federal Appointment Authorities: Cutting through the Confusion.* Washington, DC: MSPB.

U.S. Office of Personnel Management. *VetGuide.* Available from http://www.opm.gov/staffingportal/vetguide.asp#-2Types.

———. 2011. *Employment of Veterans in the Federal Executive Branch: Fiscal Year 2010.* Washington, DC: OPM.

Virelli, Louis J., III. 2004. Don't Ask, Don't Tell, Don't Work: The Discriminatory Effect of Veterans' Preferences on Homosexuals. *John Marshall Law Review, 38,* 1083–1119.

CHAPTER 21

THE AMERICANS WITH DISABILITIES ACT: CONTRADICTIONS IN PUBLIC POLICY

Bonnie G. Mani
East Carolina University

The Americans with Disabilities Act (ADA) was passed by Congress in 1990 (ADA 1990). Concerned that the judicial and executive branches' interpretation and implementation of the law were not consistent with legislative intent, in 2008 Congress passed the Americans with Disabilities Act Amendments Act (ADAAA 2008). Three years later the U.S. Equal Employment Opportunity Commission (EEOC) issued regulations for disability policy implementation that were consistent with legislative intent specified in the ADA Amendments Act of 2008 (EEOC 2011b). Simply stated, the goal of these policies was to eliminate discrimination against people with disabilities. Achieving the goal was complicated by vague terminology in the ADA of 1990, differences in application of the law to federal, state, and local government employees, and conflicts between the legislative, judicial, and executive branches of government.

To comply with the ADA, to take full advantage of available human resources, and to avoid costly litigation, employers need to know the provisions of this law. Thus this chapter discusses federal legislation and regulations, case law, and scholarly research analyzing the laws' effects on employment and wages of Americans with disabilities. Specific disabilities, such as human immunodeficiency virus (HIV) and acquired immunodeficiency syndrome (AIDS), alcohol and drug abuse, and mental health and emotional problems are discussed to a more limited extent.

Americans with Disabilities and Employment

Approximately 29.9 million people of the 250.1 million total U.S. population ages 16 and older have disabilities. Of the total population with disabilities, 17.5%, are employed. But 64.7% of those without disabilities are employed (U.S. Census Bureau 2011). While the purpose of the law was to improve their employment rates, DeLeire reported that employment rates of disabled men actually decreased 7.2 percentage points after the Americans with Disabilities Act of 1990 was passed (DeLeire 2000). See Table 21.1.

Unemployment rates for Americans with disabilities differ significantly based on disability status and gender. The 11.7% unemployment rate for Americans with disabilities is greater than the 5.3% unemployment rate for those without disabilities. Also, for the unemployed who have disabilities there are differences between the sexes. In March 2015, for those with disabilities

Table 21.1 Americans with Disabilities and Employment in 2013

	Total Population	With Disabilities	Without Disabilities
U.S. population ages 16 years and older	250.1 million	29.9 million	220.2 million
Employment status:			
Percentage employed	59.3%	17.5%	64.7%
Percentage not in the labor force	37.2%	80.2%	31.7%
Unemployment rates:			
Total	5.5%	11.7%	5.3%
Male	5.6%	13.8%	5.8%
Female	5.3%	11.2%	5.0%

Source: U. S. Bureau of Labor Statistics (2015b, 2015d).

the unemployment rate was 13.8% for men and 11.2% for women. For those without disabilities the unemployment rate was the slightly different for men and women—5.8% and 5.0%, respectively (U.S. Bureau of Labor Statistics [BLS] 2015a, 2015b).

With regard to income, since 1980 those with disabilities realized a slight increase then a decrease. See Table 21.2. That is, 10 years before the Americans with Disabilities Act of 1990 was signed into law, median household income for households including a man or woman with a disability was $32,700 per annum (in 2010 dollars). In 1990 and 2000 the statistic increased slightly. But two years after the Americans with Disabilities Act Amendment Act of 2008 was signed, the median household income decreased to $30,000 (Nazarov and Lee 2012). Furthermore, in 2013 28.8% of those with disabilities lived below the poverty level, compared with 12.3% of those without disabilities; the median income of those with disabilities was about 67.5% of the median income of those without disabilities; and those with disabilities were less likely to have higher but more likely to have lower per annum incomes than those without disabilities (U.S. Census Bureau 2013). Regardless of the disability-based wage gap, DeLeire argues that those with disabilities who remained employed still gained as

a result of the Americans with Disabilities Act because their employers likely provided greater accommodations for their disabilities (DeLeire 2000).

Employment, wages, and education generally are related. At each education level, those with disabilities are less likely to be employed than those without disabilities. For example, compared with the 50.6% of those without disabilities, 7.6% of those with disabilities who reported the highest level of education they completed was less than a high school (HS) diploma were employed in 2013. And 27.8% of those with disabilities but 75.9% of those without disabilities who reported they completed a bachelor's degree or higher were employed in 2013 (U.S. Bureau of Labor Statistics 2015a; 2015c).

Disability Policies

Before July 26, 1992—the effective date of the ADA of 1990—many people with disabilities experienced discrimination in employment but had no legal recourse. In the workplace, they faced intentional exclusions as a result of qualification standards and criteria along with structural barriers. As a result these employees had limited access to services, programs, activities, benefits, jobs, and other opportunities. In general, the 1990 law prohibits such discrimination against qualified

Table 21.2 Household Income, Poverty, and Education

	With or Without a Work Limitation or Disability	With a Work Limitation or Disability	Without a Work Limitation or Disability
Median Household income in 2010 dollars:			
1980	$50,400	$32,700	$52,100
1990	$53,700	$33,300	$56,600
2010	$54,900	$30,000	$59,500
Percentage living below the poverty line in 2013:			
	13.6%	28.8%	12.3%
Percentage employed by educational attainment in 2013:			
Less than a high school diploma	41.2%	7.6%	50.6%
High school graduate no college	54.2%	15.3%	61.8%
Some college or associate degree	64.4%	21.9%	69.3%
Bachelor's degree or higher	72.5%	27.8%	75.9%

Sources: Disability Statistics from the Current Population Survey (Nazarov and Lee 2012). Income and Poverty in the United States: 2013 (DeNavas-Walt and Proctor, 2014).

Bureau of Labor Statistics (2015a; 2015c).

US Census Bureau 2013.

individuals with disabilities. Employers must make reasonable accommodations so that qualified disabled employees can fulfill their job responsibilities. The law applies to "job application procedures, the hiring, advancement, or discharge of employees, employee compensation, job training, and other terms, conditions, and privileges of employment" (ADA 1990).

The Americans with Disabilities Act was not Congress's first policy affecting employment rights of those with disabilities. The Rehabilitation Act of 1973 prohibited employment discrimination in hiring, placement, and advancement decisions in the federal government and allowed remedies and attorney's fees when the law was violated (Pub. L. 93-112, 1973). The Rehabilitation Act was amended after the broader ADA was passed. Now, the law prohibits employment discrimination against qualified employees with disabilities by any employer with 15 or more workers.

All of the states have addressed the need to protect employees and prospective employees. Most of the states (39 of them) have adopted the definition of disability given in the federal law. Others developed statutes that give more or less protection, based on broader or narrower definitions of disabilities. For example, some states specifically protect those with the human immunodeficiency virus (HIV) or related conditions like the acquired immunodeficiency syndrome (AIDS), but other states have statutes that would allow some forms of discrimination. The ADA overrides state laws permitting such discrimination—such as North Carolina's older statute. Many local governments—especially those communities with large numbers of citizens with HIV/AIDS like New York, Los Angeles, and San Francisco—specifically protect those with HIV (Gostin, Feldblum, and Webber 1999).

Definitions

Many disputes to date have revolved around questions of coverage. The ADA gives a three-pronged definition of disability:

- an individual with physical or mental impairment that substantially limits one or more of the major life activities of such individual;
- a record of such an impairment; or
- being regarded as having such an impairment. (ADA 1990)

In the absence of more specific definitions and a clear understanding of congressional intent, in their decisions the federal courts developed case law based on their interpretation of disabilities and disabled individuals covered by the law, and the terms "substantially limits," "major life activities," the applicability of "mitigating measures," and "regarded as" disabled. Disagreeing with the courts—especially the way their decisions limited disabled individuals' coverage under the ADA of 1990—Congress passed the Americans with Disabilities Act Amendment Act of 2008 (ADAAA 2008). And in 2011 the EEOC issued new regulations (EEOC 2011b).

The 1990 law does not specifically define "physical or mental impairment." However, the 1996 EEOC regulations for implementation state that the definition given in the Rehabilitation Act of 1973 will apply in ADA cases. According to the 1973 law, a physical or mental impairment is "any physiological disorder or condition, cosmetic disfigurement, or anatomical loss affecting one or more of several body systems, or any mental or

psychological disorder" (EEOC 1996). For example, a physiological disorder might affect neurological, musculoskeletal, respiratory, cardiovascular, digestive, and endocrine systems. Mental or psychological disorders could include mental retardation, organic brain syndrome, emotional or mental illness, and specific learning disabilities (EEOC 1996).

Also having the effect of broadening coverage of the 1990 law, Congress clarified their meaning of the phrase "regarded as" in the third prong of the definition of disabilities in the ADAAA of 2008. If employees start a rumor that a coworker is HIV positive when he is not, then is the victim of the gossip covered by the Americans with Disabilities Act? Yes, an employee who is *regarded* as having an impairment is covered by the ADA. An employee or applicant who is HIV positive but asymptomatic is also covered (*Bragdon v. Abbott* 1998). Employees who are subject to actions prohibited by the law—for example, they were not hired or were terminated—no longer need to show that their employer perceived they were substantially limited in a major life activity due to an impairment that was not minor or temporary. But employees in this category—"regarded as disabled"—are not entitled to accommodation (ADAAA 2008).

In the 1990 law Congress did not specifically define the term "the major life activities of an individual." However, the EEOC—the federal agency with primary responsibility for implementation of the law—has given some guidelines. The EEOC refers to breathing, walking, standing, talking, learning, seeing, hearing, or other activities that the average person can perform with little or no problem, as major life activities (EEOC 1996). The ADAAA 2008 added the activities reading, bending, and communicating as well as the functions of the immune system, normal cell growth, digestive, bowel, bladder, neurological, brain, respiratory, circulatory, endocrine, and reproductive functions (ADAAA 2008). The EEOC warns prospective employers that interview questions about these activities could violate the ADA because they would very likely yield information about disabilities. Before a conditional offer of employment is made, the questions can be asked if and only if they specifically relate to the applicant's ability to perform the job (EEOC 1995).

The extent to which a major life activity is "substantially limited" must be determined on a case-by-case basis. At issue in *Toyota Motor Manufacturing, Kentucky, Inc. v. Williams* (2002) was the plaintiff's employer's denial of reasonable accommodation so she could perform her duties on an assembly line. Although she had carpal tunnel syndrome, the Supreme Court ruled that she was not covered by the Americans with Disabilities Act of 1990 because she was not substantially limited in performing major life activities—only one job task. In the Americans with Disabilities Act Amendment Act of 2008 Congress explained that their intent was not to set such a high standard for disabled individuals to be considered substantially limited in performing major life functions (ADAAA 2008). Subsequently the EEOC issued regulations more consistent with congressional intent, explaining the standard was lower than previously held by the courts. Yet the EEOC did not give a specific quantitative guideline that could be applied in every case (EEOC 2011b). One might have an impairment but not be disabled because the impairment presents no restriction on major life activities. To decide whether an impairment is a disability covered by the ADA, the court would ask how long the individual has been impaired, how severe the impairment is, and whether the problem is recurrent. As the 1990 law was interpreted by the courts, temporary impairments that will heal with treatment, such as a broken leg or a sprained wrist, would not substantially limit a major life activity (ADA 1990). But according to the ADAAA of 2008 individuals with impairments that are episodic or in remission are covered by the law if the impairment would substantially limit a major life activity when active (ADAAA 2008). Physical and personality characteristics and cultural and economic disadvantages are not impairments. To define this concept within the context of the workplace, "substantially limited" means that an individual is "significantly restricted in the ability to perform either a class of jobs or a broad range of jobs in various classes as compared to the average person having comparable training, skills, and abilities" (Naeve and Servino 1998).

Is a diabetic who is treated with insulin considered "substantially limited" and disabled? Initially, the EEOC said that an insulin-dependent diabetic is disabled and covered by the ADA. The First, Third, Seventh, Eighth, Ninth, and Eleventh Circuit courts agreed. However, the Fifth, Sixth, and Tenth Circuit courts *did* consider medications and other assistive devices when deciding whether an impairment substantially limits a major life activity. In these three circuits, if diabetes was treated the condition would not be considered "substantially limiting," and the diabetic would not be covered by the ADA (O'Neill 1998). These inconsistencies were resolved by the Supreme Court.

Is a visually impaired job applicant covered by the ADA? Although uncorrected vision might be an impairment, one's major life activities would not be limited if vision is corrected with lenses. Thus twin sisters who applied for positions as airline pilots were not covered by the ADA (*Sutton v. United Airlines, Inc.* 1999). After the Court issued decisions in the *Sutton* (1999) and *Murphy v. United Parcel Service, Inc.* (1999) cases, the EEOC revised its interpretive guidelines and stated that mitigating measures such as medications or assistive devices that eliminate or reduce the effects of an impairment *must* be considered in disability determinations. Congress disagreed with the Supreme Court's decision and the EEOC's earlier interpretive guidelines. The *Sutton* case was specifically referenced and rejected in the American with Disabilities Act Amendment Act of 2008 (ADAAA 2008). Congress did not intend for "ameliorative effects of mitigating measures" to eliminate those who are disabled from coverage under the ADA of 1990 (ADAAA 2008). The EEOC's 2011 regulations were more consistent with congressional intent. Ordinary glasses or contact lenses are mitigating factors that may be considered in determining whether someone is disabled and covered by the ADA—that is, vision is not impaired and a plaintiff is not covered by ADA if their vision is corrected by glasses or contact lenses. If, as United Airlines argued in the *Sutton* case, there is a business necessity for a higher standard for uncorrected vision, then the disability may not be accommodated. And other individuals may still be considered disabled under the ADA even though their disability is mitigated by medication—for example, a diabetic whose condition is controlled with insulin (EEOC 2011b).

An "employer," according to the ADA, is "a person engaged in an industry affecting commerce who has . . . employees for each working day in each of 20 or more calendar weeks in the current or preceding calendar year." As of July 26, 1992, employers with 25 or more employees were affected by the ADA. In 1994 smaller companies—those with 15 or more employees—were phased in. An "employee" is any individual employed by an employer.

Hiring

To reduce the likelihood that employers would discriminate during the hiring process, the ADA outlines procedures for screening job applicants. According to the ADA, employers cannot ask questions that would elicit information about physical or mental impairments before a job offer is made. Neither can prospective employers require medical examinations. Before the job offer, employers may ask applicants whether they would be able to meet the requirements of the job *with or without* accommodation. Applicants can answer questions phrased this way without revealing whether or not they are disabled.

Thus before a job is offered employers may require physical agility tests or physical fitness tests designed to measure whether an applicant could meet job requirements. However, the employer could not measure physiological or biological responses to exercise—heart rate or blood pressure—because these measurements would be considered medical examinations. Before a job is offered, an employer may ask applicants to take psychological tests that are related to job requirements as long as the tests do not identify mental disorders or impairments. For example, an employer may ask an applicant for a salesperson position to complete an instrument that measures extroversion, but not an instrument that

measures excessive anxiety, depression, or certain compulsive disorders. Instruments that assess mental impairments and disorders in the American Psychological Association's *Diagnostic and Statistical Manual of Mental Disorders (DSM)* are medical examinations (American Psychiatric Association 2000). Extroversion would not be among these, but anxiety, depression, and certain compulsive disorders would be. Vision tests that assess an applicant's ability to read material that they would have to read on the job or to distinguish between objects they would see on the job are not medical tests. But an examination by an optometrist or an ophthalmologist is a medical examination. The ADA permits tests to identify illegal drug users. These are not considered medical tests under the ADA. However, tests to measure alcohol consumption would not be permitted because these are medical tests and the ADA makes no exception for them (EEOC 1995).

After an employer has evaluated an applicant's qualifications and other nonmedical information and made an authentic conditional job offer, questions about disabilities and medical examinations are permitted. If the employer finds that the applicant has a disability that prevents the applicant from performing the duties of the job with reasonable accommodations, then the employer may withdraw the conditional job offer for legitimate, job-related reasons (EEOC 1995). With this sequence of events, it would be clear that the applicant was rejected based on information obtained in the medical examination.

Employers must protect all medical information obtained during the hiring process. However, there may be legitimate reasons to share the information with first aid personnel, a new employee's supervisor or manager, workers' compensation state offices or insurance carriers, or government officials investigating compliance with the ADA. These reasons are excluded from the confidentiality requirements of the Act (EEOC 1995).

Suppose a prospective employer makes a conditional job offer, then learns that an applicant is impaired and withdraws it. There are two significant issues: whether the applicant is otherwise qualified and whether the employer could provide a reasonable accommodation that would enable the applicant to perform the job. First, the ADA defines a qualified individual with a disability as someone who could perform the essential functions of the job with or without accommodations. Employers' job advertisements and job descriptions written before a job is advertised are evidence of employers' perceptions of essential functions. Second, according to the ADA reasonable accommodations may include job restructuring, part-time work schedules, reassignments to vacant positions, acquisition of equipment or devices, or changes in existing facilities so that employees with disabilities have access. Accommodations might include qualified readers for the blind, interpreters for the hearing impaired, job restructuring, or adjustments in policies related to administration of examinations.

Reasonable Accommodations

With regard to the ADA of 1990, the judicial branch found interpreting the legislature's "poorly-crafted statute" difficult (Issacharoff and Nelson 2001). Two concepts central to disputes under the law—reasonable accommodation and undue hardship—are ill defined (Issacharoff and Nelson 2001). As the law was originally written, employers were required to provide accommodations to disabled workers unless the costs would threaten the existence of the business (Tucker and Goldstein 1991). The law that was passed was more ambiguous and vague, saying that employers must make accommodations unless doing so would provide an "undue hardship." There are four criteria used to analyze the degree of hardship for an employer:

- Nature and cost of accommodation needed.
- The financial resources of the facility and the impact that accommodations would have on operations; also, the number of employees and the effect that providing the accommodations would have on expenses and resources.
- Overall financial resources of the employer, employment agency, labor organization, or joint labor-management committee (the covered entity); the

overall size of the business; and the number, type, and location of facilities.
- The composition, structure, and functions of the workforce; geographic autonomy of units; and relationship between the facility where the employee would work and the covered entity. (ADA 1990)

So, for instance, it would be very difficult for a university campus that is part of a state system to prove that providing accommodations would present an undue hardship when resources could be augmented by the legislature. On the other hand, a small private company might be unable to accommodate a hearing-impaired employee who would need an interpreter and special equipment to perform the essential functions of a job.

An employer would not want to spend time or money accommodating an employee when accommodation is not necessary. But failing to provide reasonable accommodation for an employee can lead to costly litigation. Moreover, employers who lose talented employees pay other costs that are more difficult to quantify—like knowledge, skills, and abilities that may be hard to find in others.

Care must be taken to avoid discrimination against those with disabilities as a way of avoiding costs of accommodations. Employers may ask applicants about their attendance records in prior jobs since there may be many reasons for absenteeism. However the interviewer must avoid any questions that might require the applicant to reveal any information about impairments or disabilities. For example, questions about an applicant's workers' compensation history would certainly reveal information about medical conditions. These questions can only be asked after a real, conditional offer of employment has been made.

Suppose a recruiter must decide whether to withdraw a conditional job offer extended to an individual after finding that the individual is disabled. First, the recruiter needs to determine whether the applicant would be able to perform essential job functions. Then there is a need to determine whether the accommodations that the applicant would require are reasonable. The ADA does *not* eliminate the need for the applicant to perform essential job functions. Job descriptions may include duties that are not truly *essential*. In these situations employers should consider restructuring the job to remove nonessential duties. Whether this is a reasonable accommodation would be decided on a case-by-case basis. Note that the ADA does not lower performance standards and requirements for disabled employees.

The choice of accommodations should be made by both the employer and the employee on a case-by-case basis. There should be an informal, interactive process to define the limitations of the disability and the accommodation options. For example, Patrick Jackan held a safety and health inspector (SHI) position that required driving, climbing ladders, and crawling through small spaces. He passed the physical examination and his performance was satisfactory for the first year. Then he underwent spinal surgery. After he recuperated his doctors cleared him for work at a desk job because he could no longer lift or crawl. He asked to be transferred to the job he held before he was transferred to the SHI position but his request was denied. One year later he was fired. The Second Circuit Court of Appeals dismissed his ADA claim. The Court agreed with the employer who said that civil service rules prohibited his transfer because preferred lists or reemployment rosters were used to fill the job that he wanted. There were no suitable vacancies. According to the Second Circuit, an employee who requests a transfer must show that a vacancy exists, and then the burden shifts to the employer to accommodate the request or prove that the request would pose an undue hardship (*Patrick C. Jackan v. New York State Department of Labor* 2000). Suppose the employer and disabled employee identify a reasonable accommodation. The employee can reject the accommodation. But the consequence of that rejection—if the employee is then unable to perform the essential functions of the job he or she holds—is that the employee will no longer be considered a qualified employee with a disability. So if there is an adverse personnel action—such as a reprimand, suspension, or firing—then the employee cannot claim discrimination under the ADA (EEOC 2011b).

Rulings on whether employees who are regarded as disabled have rights to accommodations varied in the federal courts until the ADAAA of 2008. Recall that the third prong of the ADA definition of an individual with a disability includes those who are regarded as disabled. Bonnie Cook's case serves as an example. In 1999, when Bonnie Cook reapplied for a job she held twice before and voluntarily left twice, she was not rehired. The Rhode Island hospital that refused to hire her predicted that she would not be able to perform the duties of the job because she was morbidly obese, even though the pre-hire physical revealed that she was physically able to perform the duties of the job for which she applied. The hospital claimed that she would be unable to quickly evacuate patients in an emergency and that she was more susceptible to infections that those who are not obese. The hospital claimed that if she was hired, Cook would be more likely to be absent and more likely to file workers' compensation claims than other employees. The EEOC supported her claim that she was covered by the ADA because she was regarded as disabled by her prospective employer. The First Circuit Court of Appeals ruled in Cook's favor (*Cook v. State of Rhode Island* 1993). If she had been hired, would she have been entitled to reasonable accommodation? Although she was perceived to be disabled, she claimed she was not. What accommodation could an employee who is *not* disabled request? None, according to the ADAAA of 2008. Note also, the courts decided Cook was covered by the ADA because she was regarded as disabled and ruled in her favor because her potential employer's determination that she was not qualified was deemed unreasonable. Other obese job applicants will not prevail, however, if they are not otherwise qualified (Bradbury 2007).

Discrimination and Prejudice

Cook's case is an example of *discrimination* based on *prejudice*. The terms are different. Prejudice is "an adverse or hostile attitude toward a person who belongs to a group, simply because he belongs to that group and is, therefore, presumed to have objectionable properties ascribed to that group" (Allport 1954). Prejudice may cause discrimination, that is, decisions about employment or wages that are not based on productivity (Phelps 1972). But—all else being equal—if wages are based on productivity and an employer pays a disabled employee a lower wage because he or she is less productive than a nondisabled employee, then the employer has not discriminated (Johnson and Lambrinos 1983).

Fears and stereotypes lead some people to perceive that others are disabled when there is no real impairment. The law gives some specific examples of such conditions and states that these are not covered by the ADA. For example, homosexuality and bisexuality; compulsive gambling, pyromania, and kleptomania; conditions resulting from the use of illegal drugs; and transvestism, and other sexual behavior disorders are among the conditions that are not considered disabilities according to the ADA. If individuals with these conditions experience discrimination they cannot file charges under the ADA.

Practical Application: HIV/AIDS

Employers and coworkers tend to fear and prejudge employees who have contracted the HIV virus. Meanwhile, the number of Americans with HIV infections and AIDS is increasing in the population and workforce. See Table 21.3. In the 50 states, the District of Columbia, and six dependent areas with confidential name-based reporting systems, there were 1,201,100 cumulative HIV infections reported in 2011, 914,826 individuals lived with HIV in 2012, and 160,300 cases had not yet been diagnosed at the end of 2011. The Centers for Disease Control also reports nearly 50,000 new HIV infections each year—with blacks about 150% as likely to be infected compared to whites. By the end of 2012, 13,712 persons with HIV infections died (Centers for Disease Control and Prevention [CDC] 2015).

At the end of 2012 in the same reporting areas, there were 1,194,039 cumulative AIDS diagnoses reported—26,688 diagnoses were reported in 2013 alone. At the end of 2012, in the same areas 508,845 individuals were living with AIDS, and 658,507 individuals with an AIDS diagnosis died (CDC 2015).

Table 21.3 Human Immunodeficiency Virus (HIV) and Acquired Immunodeficiency Syndrome (AIDS)

HIV:	
Cumulative HIV infections reported, 2011	1,201,100
Individuals living with HIV, 2012	914,826
HIV cases not yet diagnosed, 2011	160,300
New HIV infections each year, 2010	47,500
Deaths of those with HIV infections, 2012	13,712
AIDS:	
Cumulative AIDS infections reported, 2012	1,194,039
Individuals living with AIDS, 2012	508,845
AIDS cases diagnosed in 2013	26, 688
Cumulative deaths of those with AIDS diagnoses, 2012	658,507

Source: Centers for Disease Control, 2015. Data reported by 46 states and six dependent areas with confidential name-based reporting systems.

Prior to *Bragdon v. Abbott* (1998) many believed that the ADA did not cover those with asymptomatic HIV. But the 2008 ADAAA specified that "functions of the immune system . . . and reproductive functions" are major life activities covered by the law (ADAAA 2008). Bragdon told her dentist, Dr. Abbott, that she was HIV positive. He, therefore, refused to fill her cavity in his office. She filed suit and the Court ruled that she was indeed disabled according to the Americans with Disabilities Act. One of her major life activities, reproduction, was substantially limited because she was HIV positive. The major life activity that was impaired—reproduction—is not the most significant issue for employers. But the determination that HIV is a disability covered by the ADA *is very* significant to them. In an employment setting, Bragdon would be covered by each of the three prongs of the ADA definition of individuals with disabilities. First, the Supreme Court specified that Bragdon was substantially limited in a major life function. Also, those with HIV are more vulnerable to certain infections that are only *intermittent* physical impairments. An employee who learns that he or she is HIV positive will go through emotional adjustments such as depression, which, as a mental impairment, is covered by the ADA. Second, there would be a record of such an impairment, even after the HIV employee recovers from opportunistic infections or depression. Third, even though they are asymptomatic, HIV-positive employees may be regarded as being disabled. Thus public misconceptions about the disease may lead to prejudice and disparate treatment similar to Bragdon's treatment by her dentist (*Bragdon v. Abbott* 1998; Slack 1997).

In the EEOC complaints Priority Charge Handling Procedure (PCHP), HIV infection discrimination complaints are considered high priorities cases for investigations. Likely this is due to the high success rate in court because those with HIV infection are generally able to perform all the essential job tasks with or without accommodation (Moss et al. 2001).

James Slack (1997) gives public sector organizations several specific recommendations for dealing with HIV/AIDS employees and the Americans with Disabilities Act. First, analyze the agency's capacity to offer these employees reasonable accommodations. For example, analyze job descriptions and identify the essential functions of each job. Then consider job restructuring so that the employees will be able to remain in a job as long as they are able to perform essential functions. Employees with HIV/AIDS will want to conserve sick leave for later stages of the disease, so flex-time options in the earlier stages would be helpful. However, bear in mind that agencies may use discretion with flex-time options and sick or personal leave. Prepare to comply with the law's requirement for protecting employees' rights to confidentiality of medical information. Finally, provide employee assistance program (EAP) services. But be aware that asking employees about their problems and referring them to employee assistance programs are indications that the employer regards the employee as

disabled and this could come back to haunt an employer (*Holihan v. Lucky Stores, Inc.* 1997).

The costs of litigation associated with noncompliance with the ADA is high. For example, the ADA would be violated if an agency failed to hire an asymptomatic HIV-positive individual because he or she was HIV positive, when the applicant could perform the essential functions of the job. Thus it is important to develop policies, to develop and implement training programs to dispel employees' myths and misconceptions about HIV/AIDS, and to train anyone who plays a role in the hiring process (CDC 1998; Keeton 1993). The CDC can help agencies develop workplace policies and training programs and can provide information about health insurance options and costs (CDC 1998). Agencies' policies would have to comply with state statutes and, as previously mentioned, these differ.

Practical application: Alcoholism

Another costly problem for agencies is *alcoholism*. Alcoholism conforms to the ADA definition of a disability: "a physical . . . impairment that substantially limits one or more of the major life activities of such individual" (ADA 1990). Rates of alcohol use and substance dependence or abuse are associated with employment status, and employers pay high costs in the form of lower productivity, higher absenteeism rates, health care expenditures, crime, motor vehicle crashes, and fires (Harwood, Fountain, and Livermore 1998; Mani 1998).

In 2013 nearly 66% of full-time employed adults 18 years of age or older used alcohol and 30.5% of full-time employees reported binge drinking. See Table 21.4. In fact, over 76% of adult binge drinkers were employed full- or part-time in 2013. A subset of employed adults reported more serious problems of substance abuse or dependence: 9.5% of full-time employees and 9.3% of part-time employees (Substance Abuse and Mental Health Services Administration 2014).

According to the ADA of 1990 alcoholism is defined as a disability; but accommodations have generally been limited to time allowances for rehabilitation. The

Table 21.4 Alcoholism among Employed Adults over Age 18 in 2013

Percentage of full-time workers who used alcohol	65.8%
Percentage of full-time workers classified as binge drinkers	30.5%
Percentage of all binge drinkers and heavy drinkers employed full-time	76.1%
Percentage of full-time workers reporting substance abuse or substance dependence problems	9.5%
Percentage of part-time workers reporting substance abuse or substance dependence problems	9.3%

Source: Substance Abuse and Mental Health Services Administration (2014). Binge drinking is consumption of five or more drinks on one occasion on at least one of the 30 days prior to the National Survey on Drug Use and Health. Heavy drinking is binge drinking on at least five of the 30 days prior to the survey.

courts have not considered further accommodations reasonable. For example, alcoholics do not have a right to return to the job they held before treatment or the right to a work-release program after incarceration for driving under the influence of alcohol (*Bailey v. Georgia-Pacific Corp.* 2002; *Burch v. Coca-Cola Co.* 1997). Employers can legally hold alcoholics to the same performance standard as other employees (ADAAA 2008).

An employer that complies with the ADA unknowingly might hire a recovered alcoholic. During the pre-offer stage, employers may ask about drinking habits generally but may not ask any question that might elicit information about alcoholism specifically. The interviewer may ask applicants whether they drink alcohol or if they have been arrested for driving while intoxicated, but they may not ask how much applicants drink or whether they have participated in an alcohol rehabilitation program. There is no statutory exception for tests to measure alcohol consumption—these are medical tests and are not permitted during the pre-offer stage, even though there is a statutory exception for medical tests to identify illegal drug users (EEOC 1995). After a conditional job offer is made, employers may ask disability-related questions and may require a medical examination if those questions and the examination apply to all job applicants in that job category. If a disability is discovered, the offer may be withdrawn *only* if that disability is job related and based on a business necessity. That is, the employer must prove that the applicant could not,

with reasonable accommodations, perform the essential functions of the job (Naeve and Servino 1998).

Practical Application: Mental Retardation and Mental Health

Sometimes, fears and stereotypes lead people to discriminate against those with disabilities. Donald Perkl, a janitor with mental retardation working for Chuck E. Cheese's, was fired and his supervisor was criticized for hiring one of "those people" even though Perkl was fully qualified for his job and he received satisfactory performance ratings during his three weeks of employment. A jury awarded him $13,070,000 in punitive and compensatory damages. Although the award had to be reduced because the maximum allowable award is $300,000, the jury sent a strong message to corporations that discriminate against people with disabilities (*Perkl v. CEC Entertainment, Inc.* 2000).

Mr. Perkl represents a group of disabled Americans likely to be helped when employers comply with the law as Congress intended. A study that followed 1,100 individuals with mental retardation for three years after the law was passed showed increases in the average monthly income for all participants, substantial improvements in individuals' capabilities and qualifications, and levels of inclusion, accessibility, and empowerment in society. However 90% of individuals who were not employed at the beginning of the study were not employed at the end of the study (Blanck 1993).

As a final example, consider emotional and mental health problems. See Table 21.5. At the time the Americans with Disabilities Act was passed in 1990, 56% of companies surveyed reported that mental health and emotional problems were fairly pervasive in their companies. Thirty-six percent of them reported that stress, anxiety, and depression greatly affected employees' ability to function on the job. According to the Substance Abuse and Mental Health Services Administration (1999), 6% of full-time employees and 8% of part-time employees reported a major depressive episode in the year of the survey—one of four mental health diagnoses examined. In addition, 1%–3% of employees reported diagnoses in each of three other categories—general anxiety, agoraphobia, and panic attacks (Substance Abuse and Mental Health Services Administration 2000).

Twenty years after the law was passed mental illness was even more prevalent. In 2013 nearly 44 million Americans over 18 years of age—18.5% of all adults in this country—reported a mental illness. This includes about 15.4% of full-time and 20% of part-time employed persons. There is a higher probability of mental illness—about 26% of those living below the poverty level—among people at lower income levels who also are more likely dependent on public assistance. An estimated 10 million—4.2% of all adults—suffer from serious mental illness and 9.3 million adults—about 4% of individuals

Table 21.5 Percentage of Americans Reporting Mental Illness in 2013

All Americans over age 18	18.5%
Full-time workers	15.4%
Part-time workers	20.3%
Those living below the poverty level	26.1%
Serious mental illness	4.2%
Serious thoughts of suicide	3.9%

Source: Substance Abuse and Mental Health Services Administration (2014).

over age 18—reported having serious thoughts of suicide in the last year (Substance Abuse and Mental Health Services Administration 2014).

Absenteeism, death, lost productivity, crime and incarceration, social welfare administration, family caregiving, accidents, and expenses associated with property destruction contribute to mental illnesses' total costs to employers. The 2008 $700 billion bailout of Wall Street included mental health parity legislation that will affect employers' costs: health plans and self-insured employers must offer the same coverage for mental and physical health benefits (French and Goodman 2009).

Illnesses such as alcoholism, depression, paranoia, or post-traumatic stress disorder are covered by the Americans with Disabilities Act and the courts have made several decisions that favored employers of individuals with these impairments. These decisions likely were due to plaintiffs' difficulties substantiating their mental illness (Moss et al. 2001). Employers may discipline or terminate disabled employees for threatening behavior or misconduct as long as the personnel action imposed is the same action that would be imposed upon an employee who is not disabled—that is, it is no greater. In one case, a federal court of appeals upheld the termination of an employee who threatened to kill her supervisor. In another case, the court upheld the termination of a police officer who physically assaulted two people, one of whom was a fellow police officer (Bernert 1998). These decisions were supported by the ADA of 1990. First, the law defines a direct threat as "a significant risk to the health or safety of others that cannot be eliminated by reasonable accommodation" (ADA 1990). Second, the law allows employers to set qualifications standards that state that employees "shall not pose a direct threat to the health or safety of other individuals in the workplace" (ADA 1990).

Compliance

If a disabled individual believes they have experienced discrimination in violation of Title I of the ADA 1990 or the ADAAA 2008, to whom should they complain? The EEOC, the U.S. attorney general, and the U.S. secretary of transportation are empowered to enforce the ADAAA 2008. Many state and local government entities have fair employment practices agencies (FEPAs), and some FEPAs have agreements to share work with the EEOC in discrimination cases related to laws like the ADA (EEOC 2012).

In 2011 the EEOC reported receipt of 25,742 complaints of discrimination in violation of the Americans with Disabilities Act. About 15% of the cases were closed because the charging party could not be located, failed to respond to EEOC communications, failed to accept full relief, or requested withdrawal of the charges. Also included in this category are cases closed based on the outcome of related litigation or the determination that the EEOC has no jurisdiction in the case. Cases closed for these reasons are called administrative closures. In 2011 the EEOC resolved 27,873 cases—a number that exceeds the number of complaints since some cases routinely are carried over from the prior year. In almost 64% of those cases the EEOC found no reasonable cause but the cases that were resolved resulted in $103.4 million in monetary benefits. Note that sum does not include monetary benefits received through litigation (EEOC 2011a).

To address some problems related to their burgeoning case load, the EEOC developed Priority Charge Handling Procedures (PCHP) and began giving cases priorities based on initial data given to them—cases with the highest priority were given the most thorough investigations. Moss et al. (2001) criticized the PCHP system for failing to achieve its goals and eliminate unnecessary layers of review, change the data collection process, address perceptions of unfairness, and encourage utilization of alternative dispute resolution. The agency struggled with inadequate resources to handle the number of complaints filed, so a small percentage—12.4%—of those who filed complaints between 1992 and 2000 realized any benefits and the EEOC evolved into a place where cases go stale (Moss et al. 2001).

It pays to comply. The remedies for noncompliance cases are the same as the remedies for noncompliance under the Civil Rights Act of 1991: punitive and compensatory damages such as future pecuniary losses, emotional pain, suffering, inconvenience, mental anguish, loss of enjoyment of life, and other nonpecuniary losses (Civil Rights Act 1991). The previously mentioned Chuck E. Cheese case serves as an example (*Perkl v. CEC Entertainment, Inc.* 2000).

Employees who are dissatisfied with their employer's proposed resolution of their complaint or the length of time the EEOC takes to resolve their case may request a right to sue letter and proceed to federal district court—unless the complainant is a state government employee (French and Goodman 2009; Kuykendall and Lindquist 2001). For example, two employees of the University of Alabama took their case to the federal courts. One was a nurse who was transferred to a lower-paying position when she returned to work after taking extended leave to complete treatment for breast cancer. The second employee was a man with asthma who first asked to be reassigned to a job where he would have less exposure to cigarette smoke and carbon monoxide and then asked to be reassigned to a day shift because he had sleep apnea—both his requests were denied. In the *Board of Trustees of the University of Alabama v. Garrett* (2001) the Supreme Court ruled that Congress exceeded its power by abrogating states rights to sovereign immunity under the 11th Amendment to the U.S. Constitution—that is, according to the 11th Amendment private citizens cannot sue a state for monetary damages. Congress had included in the ADA a provision for abrogating a state's 11th Amendment rights when plaintiffs prove a pattern of discrimination against disabled persons that violates the 14th Amendment's due process and equal protection clauses. But the two plaintiffs in the *Garrett* case could not present sufficient evidence to prove a violation of the 14th Amendment (*Board of Trustees of the University of Alabama v. Garrett* 2001). A recourse for state government employees would be a suit by the EEOC (French and Goodman 2009; Kuykendall and Lindquist 2001; Riccucci 2003). Private and municipal corporations and individuals may sue and be sued in court—unlike states, local government entities do not have the same 11th Amendment sovereign immunity rights (*Lincoln County v. Luning* 1890).

The ADA Debate

The primary goal of the ADA is to reduce the 75% unemployment rate of Americans with disabilities. An impediment to accomplishing the policy goal is the prospective employers' cost-benefit analysis, but costs may be lower than employers expect. In 2011, the EEOC estimated the mean total cost of an employer's accommodation for one disabled employee to be $715. But since each accommodation is likely an initial cost that will last five years—for example, keyboards, software, chairs, carts, sound absorbing panels—the average cost per year is $143 (EEOC 2011b).

Employers tend to underestimate productivity of disabled workers because they have limited experience hiring people with particular disabling conditions. Disabling conditions may limit worker productivity but the costs of many accommodations that improve their productivity are small. So the cost-benefit analysis could still support hiring a disabled worker in many cases. If the disabled worker's productivity is lower than that of individuals without disabilities—even with accommodations—then there would be justifiable wage disparities (Johnson and Baldwin 1993).

Costs are not equitably distributed among those who might employ disabled workers, and benefits are not distributed equitably among all disabled potential workers. With regard to cost, companies with disabled patrons pay a one-time fixed cost for modifications to entrances, parking lots, and restrooms—a widely dispersed cost. But Congress failed to specify a cap on the additional costs—that is, reasonable costs that would not impose an undue hardship—that an employer would need to pay to accommodate an employee. Is it fair to say 10% of a company's budget is reasonable but 11% of its budget is an undue hardship? Is it fair that only a subset of all companies with 15 or more employees must pay these additional costs? Issacharoff and Nelson argue the intent of the ADA is nondiscrimination but that the law is, in fact, a redistributive public policy that discriminates against employers who hire disabled workers (Issacharoff and Nelson 2001).

Morin (1990) argues that the benefits of the ADA outweigh the costs. First, the ADA could reduce the $60 billion federal expenditures for disability benefits and programs as well as supplemental security income and disability, medical, and food stamp payments because employed disabled individuals could become self-sufficient. Second, disabled individuals include a great, untapped pool of labor and are among the most dedicated and conscientious employees. Third, studies show over half of disabled employees require accommodations that cost virtually nothing (EEOC 2011b).

Nevertheless, employers perceived that the costs of accommodations would be high, even though hiring of people with disabilities actually decreased after the law was passed. In lieu of requiring employers to pay for disabled workers' accommodations, DeLeire argues a better approach to the problem would be expansion of the Earned Income Tax Credit (EITC). As it currently exists the EITC has encouraged low-income workers to enter and stay in the workforce, has increased workforce participation, and has reduced the poverty status of families. Creating an EITC for people with disabilities could do the same for them, decrease the cost of hiring and accommodating disabled workers, and reduce the costs of enforcing, through prosecution and litigation, the current laws (DeLeire 2000).

A survey of personnel managers in states reflected more support for than opposition to the ADA (Kellough 2000). The majority of the respondents reported the ADA had little effect in their organizations because they were covered by and in compliance with Section 504 of the Rehabilitation Act of 1973. Over 66% of the managers responded the ADA would not force them to hire people who would not have been hired before the law was passed, over 84% stated they would not be forced to hire people who were not qualified to work in their organization, and less than 16% believe employees in their organization were concerned they would be exposed to communicable diseases as a result of the ADA (Kellough 2000).

CONCLUSION

One might argue that laws have neither narrowed the disability-based wage gap nor improved the unemployment rate for Americans with disabilities. However, Burgdorf argues, there is a compelling fiscal need for the law because a growing proportion—over one-third of working-age individuals with disabilities in 1990—are dependent on government benefits for their support (Burgdorf 1991). Between 1990 and 2003 the cost of Social Security disability benefits increased 93%, from less than $40 billion to $77 billion (U.S. Social Security Administration 2003). And the number of beneficiaries is expected to increase more than 40% between 2004 and 2030 (U.S. Social Security Administration 2006). The increasingly generous Social Security disability income and welfare reform laws are related to declining employment rates for disabled individuals, but laws improving access to education and employment could decrease dependence on government support (Burgdorf 1991; Hotchkiss 2004).

Additional research is needed to measure the effects of the ADAAA 2008 and the 2011 EEOC regulations on employment of Americans with disabilities. In future research effects of changes in the definitions of disabled Americans covered by the law should be controlled. Because—consistent with legislative intent—more recent public policies cast a wider net.

REFERENCES

Allport, G. 1954. *The Nature of Prejudice*. Garden City, NY: Doubleday.

Americans with Disabilities Act of 1990. Pub. L. No. 101-336, 104 Stat. 328 (codified as amended at 42 U.S.C. § 12101).

Americans with Disabilities Act Amendments Act of 2008 (ADAAA). Pub. L. 110-325, 122 Stat. 3553 (codified as amended at 42 U.S.C. § 12101).

American Psychiatric Association. 2000. *Diagnostic and Statistical Manual of Mental Disorders, Fourth Edition—Text Revision (DSM-IV-TR)*. Washington, DC: American Psychiatric Publishing.

Bailey v. Georgia-Pacific Corp., No. 02-1063 (1st Circuit Court of Appeals 2002).

Bernert, Kathryn A. 1998. Disability Decisions Tend to Favor Employers. *National Personnel Law Update* (The Council on Education in Management), June, 3.

Blanck, P. D. 1993. Employment Integration, Economic Opportunity, and the Americans with Disabilities Act: Empirical Study from 1990–1993 ADA Study and Commentary. *Iowa L. Rev.*, 79, 853–924.

Board of Trustees of the University of Alabama v. Garrett, 531 U.S. 356 (121 S. Ct. 955 2001).

Bradbury, M. D. 2007. The Legal and Managerial Challenge of Obesity as a Disability: Evidence from the Federal Courts. *Review of Public Personnel Administration, 27*(March), 79–90.

Bragdon v. Abbott, 526 U.S. 1131 (119 S. Ct. 1805 1998).

Burch v. Coca-Cola Co., 522 U.S. 1084 (5th Circuit Court of Appeals 1997).

Burgdorf, R. L., Jr. 1991. The Americans with Disabilities Act: Analysis and Implications of a Second-Generation Civil Rights Statute. *Harv. C.R.-C.L. L. Rev., 26*, 413–522.

Centers for Disease Control and Prevention. 1998. *Business Responds to AIDS: Manager's Kit*. Atlanta: U.S. Department of Health and Human Services.

Centers for Disease Control and Prevention. HIV Surveillance Report, 2013; vol. 25. http://www.cdc.gov/hiv/library/reports/surveillance/. Published February 2015. Accessed April 19, 2015.

Civil Rights Act of 1991, 42 U.S.C. § 1981(a), § 1977a (1991).

Cook v. State of Rhode Island, Department of Mental Health, Retardation, and Hospitals, 10 F.3d 17 (First Circuit Court of Appeals 1993).

DeLeire, T. 2000. The Wage and Employment Effects of the Americans with Disabilities Act. *The Journal of Human Resources, 35*(4), 693–715.

DeNavas-Walt, C., & Proctor, B. D. (2014). *Income and Poverty in the United States: 2013*. (P60-249). Washington, DC: U.S. Government Printing Office, Retrieved from http://www.census.gov/content/dam/Census/library/publications/2014/demo/p60-249.pdf.

French, P. E., and Goodman, D. 2009. The New Mental Health Parity Law: Issues and Concerns for Public and Private Sector Employers. *Review of Public Personnel Administration, 29*(March), 189–196.

Gostin, Lawrence O., Chai Feldblum, and David W. Webber. 1999. Disability Discrimination in America: HIV/AIDS and Other Health Conditions. *The Journal of the American Medical Association, 281*, 745–752.

Harwood, H., D. Fountain, and G. Livermore. 1998. *The Economic Costs of Alcohol and Drug Abuse in the United States 1992*. Bethesda, MD: National Institute on Drug Abuse. http://archives.drugabuse.gov/EconomicCosts/Index .html.

Holihan v. Lucky Stores, Inc., 87 F.3d 362 (Ninth Circuit Court of Appeals 1997).

Hotchkiss, J. L. 2004. A Closer Look at the Employment Impact of the Americans with Disabilities Act. *The Journal of Human Resources, 39*(4), 887–911.

Issacharoff, S., and Nelson, J. 2001. Discrimination with a Difference: Can Employment Discrimination Law Accommodate the Americans with Disabilities Act. *N.C. L. Rev., 79*, 307–358.

Johnson, William G., and Marjorie Baldwin. 1993. The Americans with Disabilities Act: Will It Make a Difference? *Policy Studies Journal, 21*(4), 775–788.

Johnson, W. G., and J. Lambrinos. 1983. Employment Discrimination against the Handicapped. *Society, 20*(3), 47–50.

Keeton, K. B. 1993. Aids Related Attitudes among Government Employees: Implications for Training Programs. *Review of Public Personnel Administration, 13*(2), 65–81.

Kellough, J. E. 2000. The Americans with Disabilities Act: A Note on Personnel Policy Impacts in State Government. *Public Personnel Management, 29*(2), 211–224.

Kuykendall, C. L., and S. A. Lindquist. 2001. Board of Trustees of the University of Alabama v. Garrett: Implications for Public Personnel Management. *Review of Public Personnel Administration, 21*(1), 65–69.

Lincoln County v. Luning, 133 U.S. 529 (10 S. Ct. 363 1890).

Mani, B. G. (Ed.). 1998. *International Encyclopedia of Public Policy and Administration* (Vols. 1). Boulder, CO: Westview Press.

Morin, E. C. 1990. Americans with Disabilities Act of 1990: Social Integration through Employment Note. *Cath. U. L. Rev., 40*, 189–214.

Moss, K. S. Burris, M. Ullman, and M. Johnson. 2001. Unfunded Mandate: An Empirical Study of the Implementation of the Americans with Disabilities Act by the Equal Employment Opportunity Commission. *U. Kan. L. Rev., 50*, 1–110.

Murphy v. United Parcel Service, Inc., 527 U.S. 516 (119 S. Ct. 2133 1999).

Naeve, Robert A., and Mark D. Servino 1998. ADA and the Non-Disabled Employee: Why Regarding an Employee as Disabled Can Cost You Millions. In *Personnel Law Update.* Walnut Creek, CA: Council on Education in Management.

Nazarov, Z., and C. G. Lee. 2012. Disability Statistics from the Current Population Survey. Cornell University Rehabilitation Research and Training Center on Disability Demographics and Statistics (StatsRRTC). http:// disabilitystatistics.org/reports/cps.cfm?statistic=houseinc. Accessed November 10, 2012.

O'Neill, Maureen. 1998. Corrective or Mitigating Measures Under the ADA. *National Personnel Law Update* (The Council on Education in Management), May, 4.

Patrick C. Jackan v. New York State Department of Labor, 205 F.3d 562 (Second Circuit Court of Appeals 2000).

Perkl v. CEC Entertainment, Inc., No. 98-C-698-X (Western District of Wisconsin 2000).

Phelps, E. S. 1972. The Statistical Theory of Racism and Sexism. *American Economic Review, 62*, 659–661.

Rehabilitation Act of 1973. Pub. L. No. 93-112, 87 Stat. 355 (codified as amended at 29 U.S.C. § 701).

Riccucci, N. M. 2003. The U.S. Supreme Court's New Federalism and Its Impact on Antidiscrimination Legislation. *Review of Public Personnel Administration, 23*, March, 3–22.

Slack, James D. 1997. AIDS and Disability Policy: How Can the Public Sector Prepare Itself? In Carolyn Ban and Norma M. Riccucci (Eds.), *Public Personnel Management: Current Concerns, Future Challenges* (2nd ed.). White Plains, NY: Longman.

Substance Abuse and Mental Health Services Administration. 1999. *Substance Use and Mental Health Characteristics by Employment Status*. http://www.samhsa.gov/data/NHSDA/ A10.pdf. Accessed November 28, 2012.

———. 2000. *Mental Illness: Costs by Disorder*. http:// www.samhsa.gov/OAS/srcbk/costs-05.htm. Accessed September 12, 2000.

Substance Abuse and Mental Health Services Administration, Results from the 2013 National Survey on Drug Use and Health: Summary of National Findings, NSDUH Series H-48, HHS Publication No. (SMA) 14-4863. Rockville, MD: Substance Abuse and Mental Health Services Administration, 2014. http://www.samhsa.gov/data/sites/ default/files/NSDUHresultsPDFWHTML2013/Web/ NSDUHresults2013.pdf . Accessed April 19, 2015.

Substance Abuse and Mental Health Services Administration, Results from the 2013 National Survey on Drug Use and Health: Mental Health Findings, NSDUH Series H-49, HHS Publication No. (SMA) 14-4887. Rockville, MD: Substance Abuse and Mental Health Services Administration, 2014. http://www.samhsa.gov/data/sites/default/files/

NSDUHmhfr2013/NSDUHmhfr2013.pdf. Accessed April 19, 2015.

Sutton v. United Airlines, Inc., 527 U.S. 471 (119 S. Ct. 2139 1999).

Toyota Motor Manufacturing, Kentucky, Inc. v. Williams, 534 U.S. 184 (122 S. Ct. 681 2002).

Tucker, B. P., and B. Goldstein 1991. *Legal Rights of Persons with Disabilities*. Hursham, PA: LRP Publications.

U.S. Bureau of Labor Statistics, Division of Labor Force Statistics. (2014). *Persons with a Disability: Labor Force Characteristics 2013*. (USDL-14-1076). Washington, DC: Retrieved from http://www.bls.gov/news.release/disabl .nr0.htm. Accessed April 13, 2015.

———. (2015a). *Economic News Release Table 1. Employment status of the civilian noninstitutional population by disability status and selected characteristics, 2013 annual averages*. Washington D.C.: http://www.bls.gov/news.release/dis abl.t01.htm. Accessed April 18, 2015.

———. (2015b). *Table A-1. Employment status of the civilian population by sex and age*. http://www.bls.gov/news.release/ empsit.t01.htm. Accessed April 18, 2015.

———. (2015c). *Economic News Release Table A-4. Employment status of the civilian population 25 years and over by educational attainment*. Washington, DC: Division of Current Employment Statistics Retrieved from http://www.bls.gov/ news.release/empsit.t04.htm. Accessed April 18, 2015.

———. 2015d. *Economic News Release Table A-6. Employment status of the civilian population by sex, age, and disability status, not seasonally adjusted*. Washington, DC: Division of Current Employment Statistics. http://www.bls.gov/ news.release/empsit.t06.htm. Accessed April 13, 2015.

U.S. Census Bureau. (2013). *Selected Economic Characteristics for the Civilian Noninstitutionalized Population by Disability Status. American Community Survey 1-Year Estimates. 2013* http://factfinder.census.gov/faces/tableservices/jsf/

pages/productview.xhtml?src=bkmk. Accessed May 12, 2015.

U.S. Equal Employment Opportunity Commission (EEOC). 1995. *ADA Enforcement Guidance: Preemployment Disability-Related Questions and Medical Examinations*. Washington, DC: ADA Division, Office of Legal Counsel, October 10.

———. 1996. Regulations to Implement the Equal Employment Provisions of the Americans with Disabilities Act. 29 C.F.R. §1630.2(H)(1) & (2).

———. 2011a. *Americans with Disabilities Act of 1990 (ADA) Charges (includes concurrent charges with Title VII, ADEA, and EPA) FY 1997– FY 2011*. http://www.eeoc.gov/eeoc/statistics/ enforcement/ada-charges.cfm. Accessed November 24, 2012.

———. 2011b. Regulations to Implement the Equal Employment Provisions of the Americans With Disabilities Act, as Amended, 29 C.F.R. § 1630. https://www .federalregister.gov/articles/2011/03/25/2011-6056/ regulations-to-implement-the-equal-employment-provisions-of-the-americans-with-disabilities-act-as. Accessed November 5, 2012.

———. 2012. *Fair Employment Practices Agencies (FEPAs) and Dual Filing*. http://www.eeoc.gov/employees/fepa.cfm. Accessed November 26, 2012.

U.S. Social Security Administration. 2003. *Trends in the Social Security and Supplemental Security Income Disability Programs—Program Cost and Size*. Re http://www.ssa.gov/ policy/docs/chartbooks/disability_trends/sect01.html. Accessed November 22, 2012.

———. 2006. *Trends in the Social Security and Supplemental Security Income Disability Program—Projected Future Course for SSA Disability Programs*. http://www.ssa.gov/policy/ docs/chartbooks/disability_trends/sect06.html. Accessed November 22, 2012.

CHAPTER 22

ETHICS AND HUMAN RESOURCE MANAGEMENT

Jonathan P. West
University of Miami

INTRODUCTION

The institutionalization of ethics is a major challenge for public institutions. HR managers can help address this challenge by assuming a leadership role in identifying the need for ethics programs and implementing them. They are well positioned as the primary employee-focused leaders in most organizations to positively influence practices shaping workplace environments, to reduce fiscal risks and liabilities, to ensure worker compliance with ethics directives, to apply ethical standards more consistently, and to enhance the reputation of government among its stakeholders. In many organizations the HR department is a pivotal unit for formulating and implementing ethics policies.[1] However, HR manages are often frustrated, feeling that they are not truly integrated into the ethics infrastructure of their organization and are nevertheless frequently asked to "clean up the messes" (Society for Human Resource Management/Ethics Resource Center [SHRM/ERC] 2008: 16–18).

This pattern of frustration is especially evident among respondents from government, suggesting that there is some ambivalence among public HR professionals regarding the extent of their participation in the development of ethics policy. Nonetheless, it is clear that HR professionals are often required to deal with ethical issues and to ensure that the right programs and policies are in place, so it is important for them to stay abreast of these ethics issues (Vickers 2005; Kolodinsky 2006; Hoekstra, Belling and van der Heide 2008; West, Beh, and Sabharwal 2013).

Several government organizations have a designated ethics officer appointed to oversee policy implementation. Public sector studies of the Federal Designated Agency Ethics Officials (DAEOs) indicate heavy reliance on those housed in agency legal offices (Gibson 2007), but other DAEOs have an HR background. Weaver and Trevino (2001) conclude that "an ethics program is more likely to be perceived as fairly administered when HR clearly is associated with it" (p. 11), in contrast to the legal staff that might be seen as favoring employer over employee concerns. The organizational location and orientation of the DAEO can clearly influence the selection of legal, code-based (compliance) strategies or behavioral principle-and-relationship (values) strategies. Best results are likely achieved when there is a balancing of these approaches. In any event, the role of the ethics officer has gained prominence, reflected in the establishment of a professional society, the Ethics Officer Association, with 1,200 members in more than 30 countries.

This chapter briefly reviews the responses that organizations are taking to the ethics challenge and some of the strategies that have been employed to build integrity in the public sector. The particular ethical challenges facing the HR manager are reviewed by briefly examining specific components of public HR systems and processes that are vital in building and maintaining an ethical organization. Leverage points for strategic responses to these ethical challenges by the HR professional are considered. Throughout the chapter the problems and prospects for public integrity and HRM are discussed.

GENERAL ORGANIZATIONAL RESPONSES

Responses to the ethics challenge have been multifaceted, but typically they have taken two complementary tracks: legal and behavioral.[2] Legal action seeks to curb wrongdoing by raising employees' awareness of legal prohibitions and unethical activities (e.g., sexual harassment, discrimination, nepotism) and mandates regarding such matters as financial disclosure and postservice employment (Cozzetto et al. 2009; West and Berman 2006; Bowman, West, and Beck 2010). Legal responses have their limitations: They are quite narrow in scope, and they may help in defining the black and white areas of permissible and impermissible behaviors, but they provide insufficient guidance in dealing with the gray areas.

The behavioral response, by contrast, emphasizes training and information dissemination to help managers and employees recognize and cope with ethical problems and conflicts. Such guidance seeks to better inform ethical decision making, to minimize ethical missteps by altering attitudes and promoting ethical awareness, and to provide resources for consultation to aid in thinking through tough ethical issues. Mission, vision, values, and pledge statements have been adopted by some jurisdictions; ethics codes and standards of conduct are used as well. These topics are typically reviewed in training sessions. Increasingly, however, training has gone beyond this, using case studies, role plays, scenarios, games, and other techniques to more closely approximate the real world conditions confronting managers and employees and to foster ethical responsibility.

SPECIFIC ORGANIZATION RESPONSES AND STRATEGIES

Code-Based Strategies

Organizational strategies can be further examined by distinguishing between code-based strategies and approaches that stress principles and relationships. Code-based strategies can be categorized as aspirational, prohibitive, and hybrid. Aspirational codes go beyond the letter of the law and are characterized by norms of desired behavior and provisions ranging from general to specific statements (e.g., stressing trust, integrity). Prohibitive codes, by contrast, focus on illegal and unethical conduct, hearings, investigations, and sanctions for violations. Finally, hybrid codes contain a blend of both aspirational and prohibitive provisions. In general, ethical competency is supported best by codes that combine aspirational goals and operational guidelines with enforcement provisions (Meine and Dunn 2013).

Principle and Relationship Strategies

Principled approaches to ethical decision making can be categorized as deductive, inductive, or a combination of the two. Use of the deductive approach entails a top-down process where decision makers are guided by abstract ethical principles (e.g., honesty, justice) when confronting situations involving moral choice. By contrast, use of the inductive approach is a bottom-up process that focuses on the stakeholders who are most affected by the decision and the relationships among them. Obviously, a training session could be designed that would combine both of these approaches.

A jurisdiction's decision to pursue a law-based or behavior-oriented approach to institutionalizing ethics or a code-based or principle-oriented strategy should be preceded by examining the organization's values, visualizing the ethical environment, and surveying the ethical climate.

Fostering Ethics in the Organization

What else do we know about shaping and maintaining ethical behavior in organizations? While answers to this question are still evolving, some key system components can be identified: First, executive and managerial leaders set the moral tone for the organization; second, codes of ethics capture core values and norms; third, HR managers use traditional administrative mechanisms (e.g., hiring, promotion, training) to implement these values and norms; fourth, line managers sharpen ethical insight by giving priority to ethical dialogue and timely feedback on job-related behavior; finally, managerial actions can convert ethical insight into ethical action by assisting individuals to internalize ethics and hone their ethical reasoning skills.

The interconnectedness of the system requires specific attention. For example, many jurisdictions go beyond merely adopting an ethics code; their leaders provide sterling examples of ethical conduct and stimulate discussion of ethical issues. They might also offer training covering vexing ethical issues, make ethics a criterion in both hiring and promotion, and consider the range of benefit offerings from an ethical perspective. Such actions are most effective when they are tightly integrated and used in combination with other components in an ethics system and when they are balanced between a values and a compliance orientation (Bowman and West 2015).

Up to now we have considered strategies available to those operating in the broader organizational environment. Next we shift and narrow the focus to those factors that relate more closely to the responsibilities of the HR manager. These factors are especially important because both explicit and implicit aspects of ethics programs are subject to the influence of HR managers. Explicit factors are specifically created programs designed to promote ethics (e.g., employee orientation and training programs). Implicit aspects are inherent in the culture, systems, and processes of the organization (e.g., incentive systems and performance evaluation). Both factors are vital in creating and maintaining an ethical organization. The analysis that follows considers the HR systems and processes that reinforce this effort.

HUMAN RESOURCES IMPLEMENTATION STRATEGIES

Hiring

Ethical considerations are important in the recruitment and selection process. Subtle and not so subtle messages about organizational ethics are communicated in job announcements, screening procedures, and communications with applicants. At each stage of this process the mission, vision, and values of the organizations can be emphasized and reinforced as employers seek to attract and select employees who share their values. For example, job announcements might highlight "ethical sensitivity" or "meeting customer needs" as a crucial qualification. Similarly, the selection interview presents an opportunity for employers to discuss organizational values and clearly communicate the importance of ethics to job prospects, including examples of acceptable and unacceptable conduct. Bogus job requirements, unrealistic job previews, invalid selection tests, inconsistent interviewing procedures, and invasion of applicant privacy should be avoided.

It is important to make sure that interview questions and selection criteria are job-related and that candidates are given adequate interview time to make a case for themselves (Johnson 2012). Interview questions could include situation-specific questions (e.g., "What would you do if your spouse and children had colds and would be alone at home if you left for work?") with responses scored high ("I'd go to work, a cold is not serious") or low ("I'd remain home") (cited in Brumback 1998). Hirt (2003) describes one possible interview question. The interviewer would ask a job applicant to imagine that they are an assistant town manager who has just been told by the city council that they intend to fire the existing town manager shortly. The interviewer then asks the job applicant, "If you were the assistant town manager, what would you do? "Would you be interested in the manager's position? How would you respond? Should you inform the manager that he or she is going to be fired?" Svara (2007) and Kellar (2004) provide additional scenarios in this vein. Obviously, there are questions to be avoided in interviews as well (e.g., "Do you plan to have more children?" "Would child care issues keep you from getting to work?") (Pomeroy 2006; Berman et al. 2016).

Job applicants can likewise ask questions that probe employers' ethical stances by raising questions about things mentioned in the organizations' values statement or code of conduct book. More general questions might give clues as well: "What is the profile of a successful person in your jurisdiction?" "Are there any unusual demands in this job that I should be aware of?" Some jurisdictions require a signed pledge from new hires to adhere to ethical principles. Steiner and Gilliland (1996) report that applicants are more positive about the organization and the selection procedures in situations where screening tests are perceived to be fair and to have face validity. Integrity tests, prohibited in certain states and legal in others, are used to assess applicant attitudes on wrongdoing in the workplace or to identify the propensity for irresponsible behavior. For example, Valmores (2005, cited in Menzel 2012: 215) mentions that the Philippines Civil Service Commission is developing an ethics-based personality test believing it will aid in "recruitment of the right people in all aspects and dimensions." However, caution should be used in employing such screening devices due to increasing legal complexities and litigious job applicants. Integrity tests can raise validity issues and possible decision errors due, in part, to faking (applicants misrepresenting their past history or beliefs), coaching, and test retaking (see Karren and Zacharias 2007). They also raise fairness and privacy concerns.

Employers can demonstrate their commitment to values like fairness and respect in their courteous acknowledgment of receipt of job applications, frequent updates on the status of the search, and tactful letters of rejection (Johnson 2012). Privacy concerns can be addressed by safeguarding personal information, exercising discretion in conducting background investigations, and the prudent use of potentially invasive techniques. In general, prospects for ethical hiring are improved when procedures allow for meaningful two-way communication, transparency wherever appropriate, absence of bias, and

consistent screening across applicants (Alder and Gilbert 2006). Risk can be minimized by investigating the character of job applicants, verifying that candidates have demonstrated high moral standards in the past through careful background investigations and reference checks (Sauser 2010). In short, the recruitment and selection process presents an opportunity to ensure a good fit between person-organization values (Schwepker 2013).

Orientation

New employee orientation sessions afford an opportunity to increase ethical awareness by explicit discussion of the oath of office, the goals and values of the organization, and the policies and procedures that managers and employees are expected to use as guides for behavior and decision making. Among the topics that might be included in new employee orientation are clear statements by top officials of expectations regarding ethical behavior of all employees and a review of relevant laws, ethics codes, rules/regulations, and procedures and the penalties for noncompliance. Other key topics could involve discussion of management's philosophy regarding the organization's mission, values, rules, and the processes for enforcement, safeguards against unfairness, and channels for appeal. More specific orientation subjects might include discussion of behaviors promoting organizational values (e.g., promise keeping, honest dealings) and unethical practices (e.g., conflict of interest, use of public resources for private gain). Also, consideration of frequently encountered dilemmas (e.g., outside employment, gifts) and resources available to aid ethical decision making (e.g., ombudspersons, ethics officers and committees, ethics hotlines, ethics newsletters) is useful. Further, private sector research has found that providing an overview of the organization's ethics code in orientation is linked to "an individual's perception of the importance of incorruptibility [in the hiring decision]" (Valentine and Johnson 2005:49).

Compensation

"Equal pay for equal work" was a reform theme in the late 1880s and has been a core value espoused by merit system advocates since that time. However, implementing this principle has proven difficult, and complaints about pay inequities continue to this day. Monetary incentives to do things right and to do the right thing are absent if organizations are rewarding unproductive and unethical behavior or failing to reward productive and ethical behavior. When pay is not linked to performance but based more on the personal views and prejudices of managers, the potential increases for misuse of discretion and unfairness to employees. Failing to reward top performers and moral exemplars for their efforts sends a powerful message. The key is designing a pay policy with incentives for employee performance in sync with ethical expectations (Sauser and Sims 2007). Often the reward system communicates to employees the "real story" regarding the employer's commitment to ethical behavior. For example, excessive executive compensation can breed resentment. Actions by HR managers can help to ensure employee perceptions of equitable treatment, fair reward systems, compliance with legal mandates for pay fairness, and minimization of wage compression.

Training

HR managers who decide to deliver ethics training have various tools and resources available.[3] Numerous books or manuals serve as useful instructional and training materials (e.g., West and Berman 2006; Bowman, West and Beck 2010; Bowman and West 2015; Frederickson and Ghere 2012 Menzel 2010, 2012; Svara 2007; Lewis and Gilman 2012; Richter and Burke 2007; Cooper 2001; Cox 2009; Gueras and Garofalo 2010; Kellar 2004; O'Leary 2005). Also *Public Integrity* is the journal of the American Society for Public Administration Ethics Section and a valuable resource on public service ethics. It is Taylor & Francis published by Routledge. These resource materials contain case studies, commentaries, scenarios, exercises, "brainteasers," role plays, "ethics moments," self-assessment instruments, problem-solving guides, field reports, individual and group projects, profiles of moral exemplars, analytic frameworks, sample ethics codes, and essays that help reinforce public

service values like fairness, honesty, integrity, and belief in democratic processes.

The objectives of ethics training are multiple as well as varied. Training may be designed to increase ethical awareness; ensure familiarity with key legal, code, and policy requirements; explain and discuss ethical standards and expectations; foster insight from situation-specific examples; provide tools and frameworks for resolving ethical conflicts; stimulate ethical reflection; and support practical ways to approach ethical decision making. Such training is needed not just for newly hired employees, but for all employees who periodically need a "booster shot" to inoculate against wrongdoing (West et al. 1998; West and Berman 2004; Berman et al. 2016).

One important focus of ethics training deals with managerial work habits (good and bad) because ethical leadership at the top sets the tone for those throughout the organization. A recent national study surveyed senior managers in city governments with populations over 50,000 concerned the workplace habits of their subordinate managers (West and Berman 2011). While findings show nearly 90% of senior administrators report that their subordinates "regularly demonstrate civility, courtesy and decency" as well as "take a stand where issues of ethics are at stake" (69), the authors nonetheless stress the need for sustained vigilance because of two unexpected findings. First, 45% of those surveyed reported that one or more negative managerial habits (such as being overly judgmental, aggressive, passive, or defensive) were present alongside good habits (71). And, second, although poor management habits can crowd out good habits, the converse relationship does not hold, such that "managers cannot rely on the presence of good management work habits in order to reduce the presence of bad management work habits" (77). Human resource leaders need to work with top managers to heighten awareness of the presence of bad habits in order for training and incentives to be effective. Nevertheless, the results also indicate that top managers are least likely to concentrate attention on work habits when there are high levels of good managerial work habits (and thus high organizational performance). This contributes to a vicious cycle whereby "when things are going well, the possibility exists of giving insufficient attention to bad management work habits which, however minimal, sow the seeds of subsequent performance problems" and, it should be added, ethical problems, when ethical habits are at stake (79). This makes ethics training even more crucial.

Ethics training takes many forms. Ponemon and Felo (1996) offer a concise summary of 12 key features or ingredients of successful ethics training programs: live instruction, small class sizes, a decision-based focus, the use of a professional trainer, a powerful message from the manager, realistic case materials, significant group interaction, a minimum of four hours of training, comprehensive involvement of employees, separate courses for compliance areas, follow-up communications, and new-employee programs. Providing "what if" cases or ethics moments for discussion and resolution can be very effective (Menzel 2010; Sauser 2010). The potential benefits resulting from ethics training include increased legal protection, an improved ethical climate, and enhanced trust linked to more open communication channels. It also helps to assess multiple ethical perspectives, clarify values, and guide ethical action. While two of every three cities currently offer ethics training, the depth of such training is modest at best (West and Berman 2004). Furthermore, there is some evidence that ethics training may be effective in the short run but ineffective in the long term (van Montfort, Beck and Twijnstra 2013). Larger jurisdictions such as Chicago, Tampa, King County in Washington, and Salt Lake County in Utah offer ethics training as merely one part of their ethics management program (see Menzel 2012).

West and Berman's (2004) empirical study of ethics training in U.S. cities finds a link between ethics training, other ethics activities, leadership, and important organizational outcomes. Specifically, "moral leadership of senior managers affects the use of ethics training, as well as the monitoring of employee adherence to the code of ethics, and using ethics as a criterion in hiring and promotion" (202). Targeted training is also related to positive labor-management relations and a positive organizational culture, which is linked to heightened employee productivity, which in turn is related to citizen trust. This research highlights the important role of ethics in improving organizational performance. The absence of such training can bring negative results. Kolodinsky (2006: 60) provides two examples of the negative consequences that can result from inadequate supervisory training. First, lack of awareness regarding policies on nepotism could lead a supervisor to hire a less qualified applicant who happens to be a relative of a top official over a job candidate who is much better qualified. Second, a highly productive male supervisor who lacked sufficient training in sexual harassment could make a quid pro quo mistake in approaching a female subordinate ("Date me and I'll give you a better performance review"). Supervisory training on subjects like nepotism and sexual harassment is necessary.

Performance Appraisal

Merit is the stated basis for appraising employee performance in public personnel systems. When questionable appraisal practices occur, it undermines established principles and systems and promotes cynicism (Bowman 1999). Issues of justice can arise when workers are not given adequate notice of review, not involved in setting performance standards, and not afforded hearings where "evidence" of worker performance is provided (Johnson 2012). The gap between theory and practice can be reduced when top officials model appropriate behavior; sound policies and procedures are supported by managers and employees; appropriate tools are selected; raters are trained; and continuous, positive, or corrective feedback is provided (Cardy and Selvarajan 2006). Performance appraisal can be viewed as an "accountability episode" that more explicitly includes ethics as a dimension of evaluation. For example, Bowman, West, and Beck (2010) suggest that administrators' performance be evaluated on the general conduct and ethics factor together with the more customary managerial or professional/technical factors.

Menzel (2012: 110–111) suggests inserting a check box on the appraisal form next to the statement: "Employee treats others with respect and dignity." Building an ethically sound government requires that managers and employees recognize that ethical concerns are inherent in their job responsibilities.

Using ethics as a factor in evaluations, clarifying issues of criteria definition and measurement, addressing ethical violations consistently and fairly, and publicly acknowledging examples of positive ethical conduct can demonstrate a unit's commitment to ethical behavior. Relevant questions to consider are: Is the employee performing in compliance with relevant laws, rules, and regulations? Does he/she set a positive example in circumstances where discretion is exercised? Does he/she demonstrate commitment to the organization's mission, goals and values? Are self-appraisals truthful? Considering answers to these questions brings ethics into the performance appraisal process. However, a caution should be noted: The existing appraisal process itself might inadequately address ethical issues. For example, does the system provide a clear avenue of recourse for an employee who doesn't concur with a job evaluation and fails to resolve the issue with their manager?

Managers can use an ethics code, as appropriate, when providing performance-related feedback to subordinates. For example, Berman and West (2003b: 36) reported interview data where one manager observed,

> We had an incident whereby a manager hung some of her colleagues out to dry by blaming them for a problem and thereby deflecting her responsibility for a mistake. In counseling with her, I used the GFOA Code of Ethics to explain why her conduct violated a provision of the professional code. She recognized the problem, and there has been no recurrence of unethical behavior.

When more serious breaches of the organizational or professional ethics code occur, the employees must be punished, often following the steps of "progressive discipline."

Employee Assistance Programs

Employee assistance programs (EAPs) seek to help people resolve problems that impede workplace performance, including difficulties stemming from health or work and family conflict.[4] Problems addressed might include substance abuse, personal debt, domestic violence, or other issues, and EAPs provide educational, treatment, and referral services to help employees cope with such matters. Service quality issues can arise, especially given the trend toward outsourcing EAP services. Sharer and White (2001, n.d.) discuss compromised service quality from EAP venders resulting from underpricing ("low balling"), overpromising, and underresourcing of services. They express concern about the knowledge, experience, and technical skills of national subcontractors who may lack a contextual understanding of local conditions. They also cite instances of deceptive marketing practices by vendors and outsourced services that in some cases are EAPs in name only. The EAPs providing services need to deal with ethical issues and, given widespread outsourcing, to carefully monitor services to assure individual well-being and organizational productivity.

Adverse Actions

Fairness and due process considerations are crucial in discipline or employee discharge cases. Nonprobationary public sector employees have traditionally enjoyed job protection and appeals procedures designed to shield workers from arbitrary or capricious punishment and wrongful discharge. While there has been some movement in the direction of employment-at-will (e.g., Georgia and Florida; see Bowman and West 2007; Condrey and West 2011; Kellough and Nigro 2006), civil service procedures typically create a "property interest" or expectation of continued employment assuming satisfactory performance for such employees (Coggburn et al. 2010; Goodman, French, and Neaves 2014; Kim and Kellough 2014). Where these protections exist, employees may be terminated only for cause. Managers must be aware of legal strictures and use the ethical principles of fairness, rights, and proportionality as guidance in taking adverse actions against employees. Several HR strategies other than discharge can be used when seeking to reduce personnel costs (see West and Condrey 2011).

Are people who violate ethical norms appropriately disciplined? If not, it sends an implied message that misbehavior is tolerated. Also, HR managers must employ sensitivity when implementing reorganizations, mergers, and cutback operations, more prevalent in recent years, which can be perceived as violating the psychological contract (Berman and West 2003a; West 2012) existing between individual and organization. Giacalone, Jurkiewicz, and Knouse (2003) suggest the use of an ethics exit survey at the time of termination as a way to diagnose ethical problems in work environments and a tool to improve managerial efficiency, responsiveness, and accountability.

Diversity

Public sector ethics codes often have equal opportunity or nondiscrimination clauses. For example, the ICMA code stresses merit-based personnel actions based on fairness and impartiality. ICMA's implementing guidelines go further to support equal employment opportunities for all persons, prohibit discrimination against those in protected categories, and promote diversity. Similarly, the American Society for Public Administration's code, in the section on Serve the Public Interest, states, "Oppose all forms of discrimination, and harassment, and promote affirmative action." The International Personnel Management Association's Statement of Principles and Values contains similar language. As "keepers of the policies," HR managers clearly need to be vigilant in ensuring a workplace free of discrimination, where personnel actions are merit based, fair, and impartial. While reasonable people can disagree on the contentious issue of affirmative action (e.g., Wardlaw 2000), it continues to be supported in ethics codes of visible national and international professional associations. Cultural diversity is a core value that with proper supporting initiatives can become integral to the cultural fabric of the organization (Buckley et al. 2001).

Union-Management Relations

Union organizing is one area where ethical challenges exist. Greater attention is needed on the ethics of union avoidance behavior. Employers who follow a union suppression approach sometimes skirt the law and rely on intimidation, implied threats, fear, manipulation, distorted information, and other aggressive tactics to prevail in union certification elections. Similarly, antiunion campaign tactics can involve legal delays or harassment along with illegal discharge of employees who support the union. Also, hiring practices are sometimes designed to screen out applicants perceived to be favorably disposed to unions or surveillance might be used to detect union organizing activity. In contrast, more acceptable best practices for avoiding unionization involve establishing high productivity work systems and HR policies that engender enhanced loyalty and commitment of employees (see Beck and West 2012), thereby making the union alternative less attractive.

Historically, union-management relations in the United States have been adversarial. This adversarial approach, when taken to an extreme, can lead to instances of unethical behavior. Wooten (2001: 170) has identified five examples of unethical behavior in labor-management relations, including (1) when one side deliberately misrepresents the organizational position of the other in an effort to win an agreement, (2) when facts are distorted in a grievance case to garner bargaining power, (3) when one side uses bargaining tactics that force the other side to compromise on known needs, (4) when due to technical ineptness one side resists a settlement because of inadequate understanding or unwillingness to solve problems, and (5) when ambiguous demands are made with the intent of polarizing the other party's position.

Increasing fiscal pressures have led many government and union leaders to change the way they look at union-management relations. Competing models emphasizing partnership and cooperation have been proposed and tried in various jurisdictions (see Berman et al. 2016: Chapter 12). The adversarial model of union-management relations is based on conflicting interests and is not likely to change in the near term. Nonetheless, public sector efforts to create labor-management partnerships based on common interests are promising (see Beck and West 2012), and one way to emphasize the value to be derived from fair play and trust between parties is to insert an ethics standards clause into the labor-management contract.

Health Insurance

Health care coverage is a crucial benefit for most people. However, employees can no longer be confident that employers will absorb the full cost of individual health insurance and family health premiums. Costs are increasingly transferred to employees through higher premiums, copays, and deductibles (Hacker 2006:139). Further load shedding occurs with the increased use of part-time and temporary employees as organizations economize and downsize (Thompson and Mastracci 2005; Klingner and Lynn 2005) with benefits primarily available in the first tier (West 2012). These trends have led Richardson (1998: 14) to ask: "Ethically, which carries more weight? Holding down costs or keeping your employees satisfied and healthy?" She further asks: "Is it legitimate for employers to require employees to assume an increasing burden of economic risk 'simply because it is advantageous,'" or "Should organizations, frequently large and well-resourced, accept responsibility for the promotion of employee well being?" As organizations evaluate their responsibilities regarding health insurance, key principles come into play, as noted by West and Bowman (2008: 36: "rights (individual, property), justice (distributive, procedural), utilitarianism (ratio of benefits to costs) and beneficence (serving the good)" in an effort to promote the greatest good and avoid the greatest harm. In doing so, HR managers must carefully weigh both ethical and economic concerns in their search for best practices.

Human Resource Information Systems

Human resource information systems (HRIS) contain personal data about each employee. The creation and use of such data should be guided by both legal and ethical considerations. Privacy-related issues such as the types of information placed on the system (e.g., pay and health information) and determinations of who has access to such data will confront HR managers. Under the 5th and 14th Amendments to the U.S. Constitution, an individual's rights to life, liberty, and property cannot be denied without due process of law. Applying these statements to HRIS raises issues of property and liberty interest in HR records management. Those controlling personnel records need to be aware of privacy concerns and to determine what is and what is not confidential, what may or may not stigmatize an employee, and what information deserves restricted access (Hubbard, Forcht, and Thomas 1998). Along with legal concerns, moral rights of employees—fair treatment, respect, and privacy—should be respected (Velasquez 2001). Kolodinsky (2006) provides numerous examples of ethical issues involved in decisions regarding use of HRIS. These legal and moral issues should be kept in mind when employers are responding to requests for job references.

Electronic Surveillance

In an effort to detect and correct unproductive and unethical work behavior, organizations might use monitoring software and videotaping. Such strategies can yield positive results (e.g., cost-effective service, a decrease in "cyberlollygagging" or wasted time on nonwork-related websites), but also negative consequences by downplaying privacy concerns (see West, Bowman, and Gertz 2014). To minimize ethical problems with electronic surveillance, HR managers need to keep abreast of pertinent legal provisions regarding notification (federal and state constitutional protections and statutes, common law [intrusion upon seclusion] and case law), and use surveillance techniques involving minimal invasiveness and maximal enterprise protection (e.g., security of proprietary information). It is important to disclose surveillance policies in advance, solicit employee input on productivity problems prior to adopting electronic surveillance and be wary of employee backlash (e.g., resistance, sabotage) (see West and Bowman 2014).

Health, Safety, and Accessibility Issues

Government agencies face ethical challenges in keeping the workplace healthy, safe, and accessible. Fiscal constraints have prompted cost cutting that, in some cases, has resulted in compromised health and safety conditions at work (e.g., accidents, contaminated food, fires resulting from outdated electrical wiring). Deregulation and privatization may increase the potential risks to health and safety where proper safeguards, monitoring mechanisms, information disclosure, and sanctions are lacking. Health and safety issues can be partially addressed through orientation and training programs, well-conceived contingency plans, and emergency response capabilities. Accessibility issues have emerged in response to the Americans with Disabilities Act and its requirements for reasonable accommodations.

Pension Plans

As we noted with health care, individuals are assuming greater responsibility as organizations, facing economic pressures, shift retirement investment risks to workers (Hacker 2006). The trend is away from defined benefit plans (like traditional pensions) in favor of defined contribution plans (like 401ks). Furthermore, pension deficits at the state and local government levels are increasing; several states have overall pension deficits larger than their total yearly budget (Greenblat 2007). A pension scandal in San Diego led to the resignation of the mayor and other officials who were charged with conspiracy and fraud for using pension funds to pay expenses and using unfunded pension liability to hide municipal debt (Berman et al. 2016). Prudent pension decision making requires efforts to both preserve security and contain costs. Problems of risk shifting, underfunding, and wrongdoing have led to increased insecurity for many workers. Public officials need to balance both the ethical and economic sides of this problem as they seek to achieve best practice.

Family/Work Relations

Work/family initiatives are attractive benefits provided by many public and private employers. These might include (but are not restricted to) child care, elder care, flextime and telecommuting, leave sharing and pooling, domestic partner benefits, and adoption assistance (see West 2012). From an ethical perspective, caring for the needs of members of the "organizational family" is fundamental to ensuring a high-quality work environment.

Productivity and Quality

The dueling pressures to improve government performance while simultaneously cutting costs have intensified in the past decade. Calls for diffusing the quality paradigm and businesslike approaches to the public sector have continued along with admonitions to reengineer, reinvent, partner, reorganize, and employ market models to improve government service delivery (Kamarck 2007). Francis Burke (1999) refers to the "three Es" of efficiency, effectiveness, and economy as vital and enduring values with deep historical roots and contemporary applications in our culture. Paul Light's (1998) analysis of reform tides highlights the importance of these values to the heritage of the public service. Burke outlines a new "three E" paradigm—empathy, evaluation, and ethics—that builds upon the earlier values and provides management tools for the future. She sees benefits in stronger networking (empathy), enhanced accountability (evaluation), and strengthened leadership (ethics). Both sets of "three E" values serve as powerful guides to behavior. Empirical research findings in recent years have confirmed a link between ethics and organizational performance (see Menzel 2012; Berman and West 1997; West and Berman 2004). HR managers are encouraged to follow Burke's advice to employ the tools of efficiency, effectiveness, and economy together with those of empathy, evaluation, and ethics. Such leadership by HR managers can help to enhance the integrity as well as the productivity of the organization, enabling managers to make "right good" decisions (Bowman and West 2015). Cohen and Eimicke (2002: 233–235) offer five useful guidelines to public servants in this regard: seek justice under the law, serve the public interest, ensure thorough analysis, act with compassion and empathy, and take personal responsibility for decisions (see also Kolthoff, Huberts, and van den Heuvel 2007).

Privatization

Ethical issues surrounding the move to privatization have been addressed repeatedly in the public administration literature (e.g., Bowman, West, and Beck 2010; Frederickson 1999; Kettl 1993; Kolbrack 1998; Lawther 2004). Timmons (1990) notes five adverse impacts that privatization can have on career employees: "career disruption and dislocation; morale and productivity; relocation and reciprocity; erosion of civil service and merit systems; and undermining trust and credibility" (106). He suggests that employers have an ethical obligation to provide workers with retraining, reciprocity provisions, and advance notice. The other authors cited earlier, though writing separately, point to additional adverse consequences of privatization and contracting out for services: kickbacks, skimming, fraud, cozy politics (contractors winning or keeping a contract via politics), conflicts of interest, and monitoring problems. Coggburn (2007) and Crowell and Guy (2010) have examined the outsourcing of all HR activities in the state governments of Texas and Florida, respectively; however, preliminary assessments are mixed at best. HR managers may support or oppose efforts to privatize, but two crucial parts of their role are to serve as advocates for the public sector employee and for the public interest. As advocates, they should exercise due diligence, insisting that the pros and cons of privatization initiatives are carefully considered and that harm done to public employees or the public interest is avoided or minimized.

CONCLUSION

Building public organizations of integrity is the business of all public servants. Top-level officials have a wide range of explicit or implicit strategies to choose from in "managing ethics." HR managers have special opportunities and obligations to ensure that priority is given to ethics. Those with HR responsibilities must recognize the relative importance of government ethics as a precondition for good government. Ethical leadership is required to signal that adherence to ethics standards is expected and that avoiding even the appearance of impropriety is also important. The personnel system contains numerous leverage points where ethical leadership can be exercised.

The prospects for achieving and maintaining organizational integrity are enhanced when the top officials' model exemplary moral leadership, adopt an organizational credo that promotes aspirational values, conduct an ethics audit, and develop and enforce an ethics code. Using ethics as a criterion in hiring and promotion, factoring ethics into performance appraisal, and including ethics in management and employee training programs further increase the prospects of institutionalizing ethical behavior. In addition, orientation programs highlighting ethical concerns, pay policies that reward productive and ethical behavior, and fairness in handling discipline and adverse actions enhance the ethical climate.

Prospects for institutionalizing integrity also increase as HR professionals seek ethical resolutions to employee grievances and problems; keep the workplace healthy, safe, and accessible; and act as strong advocates for employees and the public interest in privatization initiatives. A willingness to engage in risk sharing with employees via economically sound and ethically defensible health insurance and pension plans demonstrates appropriate attention to both taxpayer and employee interests. Continuing efforts to ensure a diverse workforce, protect the legitimate privacy interest of employee records, enable employees and managers to balance work and family responsibilities, and improve quality service delivery helps to create the ethical environment. In short, building organizational integrity and advancing a strong sense of public service ethics is one of the major HR challenges in the 21st century. Leadership by those with HR responsibility is critical to meeting this challenge.

NOTES

1. Based on a randomly selected sample of 3,452 from the Society for Human Resource Management's membership database, which includes 225,000 members (SHRM/ERC 2008).

2. This subsection and the next one are adapted from West and Berman (2006).

3. Some material in the subsection on training comes from Bowman and West (2015) and West and Berman (2011).

4. The material in the subsections on EAPs, health coverage, pensions, and work/family policies are adapted from West and Bowman (2008) and West (2012).

REFERENCES

Alder, Stoney G., and Joseph Gilbert. 2006. Achieving Ethics and Fairness in Hiring: Going Beyond the Law. *Journal of Business Ethics*, 68, 449–464.

Beck, Marcia A., and Jonathan P. West. 2012. Millennials in the Workforce: Unions and Management Battle for the Soul of a Generation. In R. Sims and W. Sauser, eds. *Managing Human Resources from the Millennial Generation.* Greenwich, CT: Information Age Publishing, pp. 355–398.

Bell, Fleming A. 1997. *Ethics, Conflicts, and Offices: A Guide for Local Officials*. Chapel Hill, NC: Institute of Government.

Berman, Evan M., James S. Bowman, Jonathan P. West, and Montgomery Van Wart. 2016. *Human Resource Management in Public Service*. 5th edition. Thousand Oaks, CA: Sage.

Berman, Evan M., and Jonathan P. West. 1997. Managing Ethics to Improve Performance and Build Trust. *Public Integrity Annual*, 2, 23–32.

———. 2003a. Psychological Contracts in Local Government: A Preliminary Survey. *Review of Public Personnel Administration*, 23(4), 30–52.

———. 2003b. Solutions to the Problem of Managerial Mediocrity. *Public Performance & Management Review*, 27(December), 30–52.

Bowman, James S. 1999. Performance Appraisal: Verisimilitude Trumps Veracity. *Public Personnel Management*, 28(4), 557–576.

Bowman, James S., and Jonathan P. West. 2007. *American Public Service: Radical Reform and the Merit System*. New York: Taylor & Francis Group.

———. 2013. Conscious Deliberation and Subconscious Action: The Dishonesty of Honest People. In H. G. Frederickson and R. Ghere, eds., *Ethics and Public Management*. Armonk, NY: M.E. Sharpe, pp. 155–171.

———. 2015. *Public Service Ethics: Individual and Institutional Responsibilities*. Washington, DC: CQ Press.

Bowman, James S., Jonathan P. West, and Marcia A. Beck. 2010. *Achieving Competencies in Public Service: The Professional Edge*. Armonk, NY: M.E. Sharpe.

Brumback, Gary B. 1998. Institutionalizing Ethics in Government. In E. Berman, J. West, and S. Bonczek, eds., *The Ethics Edge*. Washington, DC: ICMA, pp. 61–71.

Buckley, M. Ronald, Danielle S. Beu, Dwight D. Frink, Jack L. Howard, Howard Berkson, Tommie A. Mobbs, and Gerald R. Ferris. 2001. Ethical Issues in Human Resource Management. *Human Resource Management Review*, 11, 11–29.

Burke, Francis. 1999. Ethical Decision-Making: Global Concerns, Frameworks and Approaches. *Public Personnel Management*, 28(4), 529–540.

Cardy, Robert, and T. T. Selvarajan. 2006. Beyond Rhetoric and Bureaucracy: Using HRM to Add Ethical Value. In J. R. Deckop, ed., *Human Resource Management Ethics*. Greenwich, CT: Information Age Publishing, pp. 71–86.

Coggburn, Jerrell. 2007. Outsourcing Human Resources: The Case of the Texas Health and Human Services Commission. *Review of Public Personnel Administration*, 27(4), 315–335.

Coggburn, Jerrell, R. Paul Battaglio, James S. Bowman, Stephen E. Condrey, Doug Goodman, and Jonathan P. West. 2010. State Government Human Resource Professionals' Commitment to Employment at Will. *American Review of Public Administration*, 40(2), 189–208.

Cohen, Stephen, and William Eimicke. 2002. *The Effective Public Manager: Achieving Success in a Changing Government*. San Francisco: Jossey-Bass.

Condrey, Stephen E., and Jonathan P. West. 2011. Civil Service Reform: Past as Prologue? In D. Menzel and H. White, eds. *The State of Public Administration: Issues, Challenges, and Opportunities*. Armonk, NY: M.E. Sharpe, pp. 351–367.

Cooper, Terry. 2001. *Handbook of Administrative Ethics*. San Francisco: Marcel Dekker.

Cox, Raymond, ed. 2009. *Ethics and Integrity in Public Administration: Concepts and Cases*. Armonk, NY: M.E. Sharpe.

Cozzeto, Don A., Theodore Pedeliski, Jonathan Tompkins, and Jonathan P. West. 2009. Employee Responsibilities: Setting Expectations. In S. Fox Freyss, ed., *Human Resource Management in Local Government*. Washington, DC: International City/County Management Association, pp. 213–238.

Crowell, E., and Mary Ellen Guy. 2010. Florida's HR Reforms: Service First, Service Worst, and Something in Between. *Public Personnel Management*, 39(1), 15–46.

Frederickson, H. George. 1999. Public Ethics and the New Managerialism. *Public Integrity*, 1(3), 265–278.

Frederickson, H. George, and Richard K. Ghere, eds. 2013. *Ethics in Public Management*. Armonk, NY: M.E. Sharpe.

Giacalone, Robert A., Carole L. Jurkiewicz, and Stephen B. Knouse. 2003. Exit Surveys as Assessments of Organizational Ethicality. *Public Personnel Management*, 32(3), 397–410.

Gibson, Pamela S. 2007. *Examining the Moral Reasoning of the Ethics Advisor and Counselor: The Case of the Federal Designated Agency Ethics Official*. Unpublished paper presented at the Transatlantic Ethics Conference in College Park, MD. March 21, 22.

Goodman, Doug, P. Edward French, and Tonya Neaves. 2014. *Review of Public Personnel Administration*, 34(3), 199–217.

Greenblat, A. 2007. Pension Crisis. In CQ Researcher, ed., *Issues for Debate in American Public Policy*. Washington, DC: CQ Press, pp. 261–283.

Gueras, Dean, and Charles Garofalo. 2010. *Practical Ethics in Public Administration*. 3rd edition. New York: Management Concepts.

Hacker, Jacob. 2006. *The Great Risk Shift*. New York: Oxford University Press.

Hirt, M. J. 2003. Assessing the Ethical Judgment of a Potential Employee. *Public Administration Times*, July.

Hoekstra, A., A. F. Belling, and E. van der Heide. 2008. A Paradigmatic Shift in Ethics and Integrity Management within the Dutch Public Sector: Beyond Compliance. In L. W. J. C. Hubert, C. L. Jurkiewics, and J. Maesschalck, eds., *Ethics and Integrity of Governance: Perspectives across Frontiers*. Cheltenham, UK: Edward Elgar.

Hubbard, Joan C., Karen A. Forcht, and Daphyne S. Thomas. 1998. Human Resource Information Systems: An Overview of Current Ethical and Legal Issues. *Journal of Business Ethics*, 17(12), 1319–1323.

Johnson, Craig E. 2012. *Organizational Ethics: A Practical Approach*. Thousand Oaks, CA: Sage.

Kamarck, Elaine C. 2007. *The End of Government as We Know It: Making Public Policy Work*. Boulder, CO: Lynne Reiner.

Karren, Ronald J., and Larry Zacharias. 2007. Integrity Tests: Critical Issues. *Human Resource Management Review*, 17, 221–234.

Kellar, Elizabeth. 2004. Helping Employees Make Sound Ethical Decisions. *Public Management*, 86(8), 4–6.

Kellough, Edward J., and Lloyd G. Nigro. 2006. *Civil Service Reform in the States*. Albany, NY: SUNY Press.

Kettl, Donald. 1993. *Sharing Power: Public Governance and Private Markets*. Washington, DC: Brookings.

Kim, Jungin, and J. Edward Kellough. 2014. At-Will Employment in the States: Examining the Perceptions of Agency Personnel Directors. *Review of Public Personnel Administration*, 34(3), 218–236.

Klingner, Donald, and D. Lynn. 2005. Beyond Civil Service: The Politics of the Emergent Paradigms. In S. Condrey, ed., *Handbook of Human Resource Management in Government*. San Francisco: Jossey-Bass, pp. 37–57.

Kolbrack, Peter. 1998. Privatization and Cozy Politics. In E. Berman, J. West, and S. Bonczek, eds., *The Ethics Edge*. Washington, DC: ICMA, pp. 178–193.

Kolodinsky, Robert. 2006. Wisdom, Ethics and Human Resources Management. In John Deckop, ed., *Human Resource Management Ethics*. Greenwich, CT: Information Age Publishing, 47–70.

Kolthoff, E., L. Huberts, and H. van den Heuvel. 2007. The Ethics of New Public Management: Is Integrity at Stake? *Public Administration Quarterly*, 30(4), 399–439.

Lawther, Wendell C. 2004. Ethical Challenges in Privatizing Government Services. *Public Integrity*, 6(2), 141–153.

Lewis, Carol W., and Stuart C. Gilman. 2012. *The Ethics Challenge in Public Service*. San Francisco: Wiley.

Light, Paul. 1998. *The Tides of Reform*. Washington, DC: Brookings.

Meine, Manfred, and Thomas Dunn. 2013. The Search for Ethical Competency: Do Ethics Codes Matter? *Public Integrity*, 15(2), 149–166.

Menzel, Donald C. 2006. Ethics Management in Cities and Counties. In J. West and E. Berman, eds., *The Ethics Edge*, 2nd ed. Washington, DC: ICMA, pp. 108–115.

———. 2010. *Ethics Moments in Government: Cases and Controversies*. Boca Raton, FL: CRC Press.

———. 2012. *Ethics Management for Public Administrators: Building Organizations of Integrity*. Armonk, NY: M.E. Sharpe.

O'Leary, Rosemary. 2005. *The Ethics of Dissent*. Washington, DC: CQ Press.

Pomeroy, Ann. 2006. The Ethics Squeeze. *HR Magazine*, March, pp. 48–54.

Ponemon, Larry, and Andrew J. Felo. 1996. Key Features of an Effective Ethics Training Program. *Management Accounting*, October, 66–67.

Richardson, Catherine M. 1998. Ethics and Employee Benefits. *Benefits Quarterly*, 14(1), 9–16.

Richter, William L., and Frances Burke, eds. 2007. *Combating Corruption, Encouraging Ethics*, 2nd ed. Lanham, MD: Rowman & Littlefield.

Riddick, Christopher G., and Jerrell D. Coggburn, eds. 2008. *Handbook of Employee Benefits and Administration*. New York: Auerbach.

Sauser, William I. 2010. Creating an Ethical Culture in Local Government. In R. Sims, ed., *Change (Transformation) in Government Organizations*. Greeenwich, CT: Information Age Publishing, pp. 53–70.

Sauser, William I., and Ronald R. Sims. 2007. Fostering an Ethical Culture for Business. In R. Sims, ed., *Human Resource Management: Contemporary Issues, Challenges, and Opportunities*. Greenwich, CT: Information Age Publishing, pp. 253–285.

Schwepker, Charles H. 2013. Ethical Climate: Causes, Consequences, and Implications for Improving Well-Being. In R. Giacalone and M. Promisio, eds., *Handbook of Unethical Work Behavior*. Armonk, NY: M.E. Sharpe, pp. 271–286.

Sharer, David A., and William White. 2001. EAP Ethics and Quality: Does National vs. Local Service Delivery Make a Difference. *Performance Resource Press* (Fall). http://www.prponline.net/Work/EAP/Articles/eap_ethics_and_quality.htm. Accessed September 5, 2008.

———. n.d. The Pricing of EAPs. http://www.eapage.com/The%20Pricing%20of%20EAPs.doc. Accessed September 5, 2008.

SHRM/ERC. 2008. *The Ethics Landscape in American Business*. Alexandria, VA: Society for Human Resource Management/Ethics Resource Center.

Steiner, D. D., and S. W. Gilliland. 1996. Fairness Reactions to Personnel Selection Techniques in France and the United States. *Journal of Applied Psychology*, 81(2), 134–141.

Svara, James. 2007. *The Ethics Primer for Public Administrators in Government and Nonprofit Organizations*. Sudbury, MA: Jones and Bartlett Publishers.

Thompson, James, and Susan Mastracci. 2005. Toward a More Flexible Public Workforce: Issues and Applications. In S. Condrey, ed., *Handbook of Human Resource Management in Government*. San Francisco: Jossey-Bass, pp. 125–142.

Timmons, William M. 1990. *A Casebook of Public Ethics and Issues*. Pacific Grove, CA: Brooks Cole.

Valentine, Sean, and Anthony Johnson. 2005. Codes of Ethics, Orientation Programs, and the Perceived Importance of Employee Corruptibility. *Journal of Business Ethics*, 61, 45–53.

Valmores, D. J. 2005. Presentation on Fighting and Preventing Corruption. ASEAN+3 Senior Officials Consultative Meeting on Creative Management for Government, September 30–October 1, Bangkok, Thailand.

Van Montfort, Andre, Laura Beck, and Anneke Twijnstra. 2013. Can Integrity Be Taught in Public Organizations? The Effectiveness of Integrity-Training Programs for Municipal Officials. *Public Integrity*, 15(2), 117–132.

Velasquez, Manuel G. 2001. *Business Ethics: Concepts and Cases*. Upper Saddle River, NJ: Pearson Prentice Hall.

Vickers, Mark R. 2005. Business Ethics and the HR Role: Past, Present, and Future. *Human Resource Planning*, 28(1), 26–33.

Wardlaw, J. Lew. 2000. Strong Disagreement with ASPA Code of Ethics. *PA Times*, 23(5), 10.

Weaver, Gary R., and Linda K. Trevino. 2001. The Role of Human Resources in Ethics/Compliance Management: A Fairness Perspective. *Human Resource Management Review*, 11(1–2), 113–134.

West, Jonathan P. 2012. Employee Friendly Policies and Developmental Benefits for Millennials. In R. Sims and W. Sauser, eds., *Managing Human Resources for the Millennial Generation*. Greenwich, CT: Information Age Publishing, 201–228.

West, Jonathan P., Lucy Beh, and Meghna Sabharwal. 2013. Charting Ethics in Asia-Pacific HRM: Does East Meet West, Ethically? *Review of Public Personnel Administration*, 33(2), 185–204.

West, Jonathan P., and Evan M. Berman. 2004. Ethics Training in U.S. Cities. *Public Integrity*, 6(3), 189–206.

———, eds. 2006. *The Ethics Edge*. Washington, DC: International City/County Management Association.

———. 2011. The Impact of Management Work Habits on Public Sector Performance: A Study of Local Government Managers. *Public Personnel Management*, 40(1), 63–86.

West, Jonathan P., Evan M. Berman, Stephen Bonczek, and Elizabeth Kellar. 1998. Frontiers of Ethics Training. *Public Management* 80 (6): 4-9.

West, Jonathan P., and James S. Bowman. 2008. Employee Benefits: Weighing Ethical Principles and Economic Imperatives. In C. Riddick and J. Coggburn, eds., *Handbook of Employee Benefits and Administration*. New York: Auerbach, pp. 29–53.

———. 2014. Electronic Surveillance at Work: An Ethical Analysis. *Administration & Society,* published online DOI:10.117/0095399714556502.

West, Jonathan P., James S. Bowman, and Sally Gertz. 2014. Electronic Surveillance in the Workplace: Legal, Ethical and Management Issues. In R. Sims and W. Sauser, eds. *Legal and Regulatory Issues in Human Resources Management.* Charlotte, NC: Information Age Publishing, pp. 285–314.

West, Jonathan P., and Stephen Condrey. 2011. Local Government Strategies for Controlling Personnel Costs. *Journal of Public Budgeting, Accounting and Financial Management,* 23(3), 423–454.

Wooten, K. 2001. Ethical Dilemmas in Human Resource Management: An Application of a Multidimensional Framework, a Unifying Taxonomy, and Applicable Codes. *Human Resource Management Review,* 11, 159–175.

PUBLIC SECTOR LABOR ISSUES: RIGHTS, RETRENCHMENT, AND DEMOCRACY

Patrice Mareschal
Rutgers University–Camden

Patricia Ciorici
Rutgers University–Camden

INTRODUCTION

Public sector unions operate in politically challenging environments. The susceptibility of unions to political forces stems in part from the legal environment in which they operate and in part from the nature of their employers (Slater 2012). State law governs collective bargaining for public sector employees. The employers, who are also elected officials, can change the law depending on their preferences. Elected officials' attitudes toward collective bargaining rights and unions more broadly depend on various factors ranging from party ideology, legitimacy concerns, and power relations among political actors to changes in local fiscal conditions and shifts in public opinion. The election of public officials unsympathetic to unions in several states and the pressure created by recent budget crises even on sympathetic elected officials resulted in what some scholars called a "war on public sector collective bargaining" and "the most widespread and substantive attack on collective bargaining in the US since the 1930s' battles in the private sector" (Freeman and Han 2012: 387).

This chapter discusses recent developments in public sector labor relations at the state and local levels. The

chapter begins with an overview of union representation, the roles unions play in society, and compensation differentials between public and private sector workers. Next, it examines the influence of the political and economic environments on public sector unions, and selected cases in which collective bargaining rights for public employees were rescinded or severely restricted. The chapter further discusses forms, causes, and implications of restrictions on collective bargaining for public sector employees. Finally, concluding remarks focus on some of the lessons learned from recent developments in public sector labor relations.

UNION REPRESENTATION AND THE ROLES OF UNIONS IN THE PUBLIC SECTOR

Public sector workers are much more likely than private sector workers to be represented by unions. Over the past 30 years union representation remained relatively stable in the public sector. During the same period, union representation in the private sector declined continuously (Figure 23.1). To illustrate, in the public sector 45.5% of workers were covered by collective bargaining agreements in 1983. The level of representation has

Figure 23.1 Percentage of Public and Private Sector Workers Covered by Collective Bargaining Agreements, 1983–2011

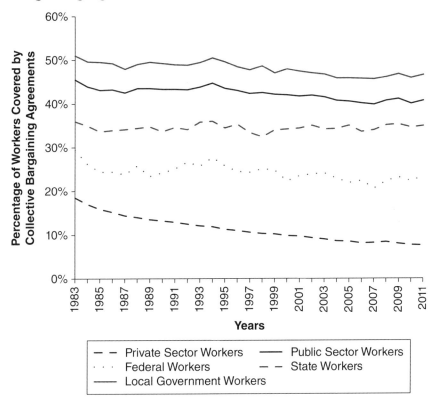

Source: Hirsch, Barry T., and David A. Macpherson. 2012. "Union Membership and Coverage Database from the Current Population Survey." http://www.unionstats.com.

hovered around 40% since then. In contrast, the percentage of workers covered by collective bargaining agreements in the private sector was 18.5% in 1983 and steadily declined to 7.6% in 2011.

Local government employees are the most unionized workers in the public sector, followed by state workers. In comparison, federal employees are the least unionized. In 2011, collective bargaining agreements covered 46.6% of local government employees, 34.9% of state employees, and 23.4% of federal employees.

Union representation in the public and private sectors looks somewhat different if absolute values are considered (Figure 23.2). Workers represented by unions in the private sector historically outnumbered union represented

workers in the public sector. Yet in 2009 a significant change occurred. Union representation among private sector workers continued a downward trend and for the first time in history public sector employees covered by collective bargaining agreements outnumbered their counterparts in the private sector (U.S. Bureau of Labor Statistics [BLS] 2010). In 2011, unions represented about 8.3 million workers in the public sector and slightly less than 8 million workers in the private sector (BLS 2012).

The relative strength of public sector unions elicits conflicting views among researchers. While some celebrate the role that unions play in the workplace and in policy making, others lament the perceived negative effects that unions have on state and local budgets,

Figure 23.2 Public and Private Sector Workers Covered by Collective Bargaining Agreements, 1983–2011

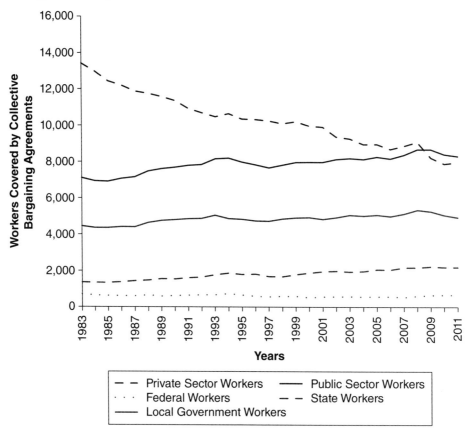

Source: Hirsch, Barry T., and David A. Macpherson. 2012. "Union Membership and Coverage Database from the Current Population Survey." http://www.unionstats.com.

size of government, and government efficiency. Freeman and Medoff (1979) identified two faces of unionism that lead to different views of the institution. If analyzed from an economic perspective, unions may appear to be monopolies, driving up the costs of compensation and benefits. From a sociopolitical perspective, unions may be viewed as agents of collective voice. These two views of unionism trigger distinct and often contrary responses: monopoly viewholders generally perceive unions as "undesirable impediments to the social good," whereas the collective voice/institutional viewholders take an opposite perspective and see

unions as important "contributors to the functioning of the economy" (Freeman and Medoff 1979: 74).

In the public sector context, the responses to the monopoly and collective voice views of unionism are more nuanced and are set even further apart. McGinnis and Schanzenbach (2010), for example, argue that, by exerting their influence on public policy, unions distort spending priorities, inhibit innovation, and lower government efficiency. They further contend that, compared with private sector unions, government worker unions can exert greater influence over their employers whom they often help elect through significant campaign contributions. DiSalvo (2010) advances similar arguments and groups the effects of public sector unionism into three categories: compensation, size of government, and efficiency. Overall, DiSalvo (2010: 17) argues that public sector unions "distort the labor market, weaken public finances, and diminish the responsiveness of government and the quality of public services."

Others focus on the collective voice/institutional view of unions. Gapasin (2012), for example, argues that it is only through collective action that employees gain a voice at the workplace. In addition to giving workers voice, unions may help governments solve budget crises by using union mechanisms to motivate employees to manage work more efficiently (Fisk and Olney 2011). In Olson's (2011) view, unions may also motivate workers to be responsible health care consumers and, therefore, help control health care costs. Lewin et al. (2011: 28) provides what can be considered a summary of the response to the collective voice/institutional view of unions, arguing that as institutions unions retain a fundamental role in civil society by "providing checks and balances in the workplace and society, increasing consumer-purchasing power, reducing economic inequality, providing worker voice (including on matters of productivity, public service and consideration for the disadvantaged in society), and advancing basic constitutional rights."

COMPENSATION DIFFERENTIALS BETWEEN PUBLIC AND PRIVATE SECTOR WORKERS

Pay differentials between public and private employees are a highly contested subject. The debate primarily focuses on whether public sector employees are over-compensated compared with their private sector counterparts. Researchers have come to different conclusions on the subject, depending on the employed methodologies and measurements of compensation (Bender and Heywood 2010). From the more recent studies, Edwards (2010), for example, after examining the raw BLS data on compensation, including wages and benefits for state, local government, and private sector employees, concluded that the average compensation per hour in the public sector was 45% higher compared to the private

sector. Similarly, Gittleman and Pierce (2012), using the Employer Costs for Employee Compensation data from the 2009 National Compensation Survey, found that hourly compensation in the public sector at the state level is 3.7% higher compared to compensation in the private sector, controlling for work level, Census division interaction with metropolitan area, and full-time jobs. They found an even larger compensation differential, 12.9%, between local government workers and private sector employees.

In contrast, Keefe (2012) found that, on average, state and local employees are slightly undercompensated, experiencing a 3.7% penalty in total compensation compared with private sector workers, controlling for education, experience, hours of work, organizational size, gender, race, ethnicity, and disability. Several other recent studies found similar results. For example, after controlling for education, work experience, occupation, location, race, and gender, Lewis and Galloway (2011) estimated that state and local government employees earned between 4% and 6% less than comparable workers in the private sector in 1990, 2000, and 2005–2006. Bender and Heywood (2010) found a slightly larger compensation penalty in the public sector where, on average, state and local employees earn, respectively, 6.8% and 7.4% less than comparable private sector workers.

BARGAINING RIGHTS IN THE CROSSHAIRS: THE ROLE OF ECONOMICS AND POLITICS

The scholarly debate on compensation differentials between private and public sector employees reflects the political debate surrounding the limitations on collective bargaining rights and union activity. Governors who led the efforts to limit collective bargaining rights in their states argued that public sector employees received higher compensation compared with their private sector counterparts and identified union-negotiated salaries for public workers as one of the reasons for state budget crises. Furthermore, unions were portrayed as an obstacle to efforts to balance state budgets. Some of the arguments advanced in the political debate find support in current research, while others, such as the compensation differentials between public and private employees, are highly disputed.

Studies on the effects of collective bargaining suggest that unions raise wages and benefits for represented workers in both the public and private sectors. These findings are consistent with the goals of labor unions to improve work conditions for the organized employees. It is also accurate that states and local governments experienced a sharp decline in their revenues during the recession. State revenues fell by 8.5% from 2008 to 2009 (Freeman and Han 2012). Moreover, 44 states projected budget deficits for fiscal year 2012, and 31 states, a smaller but considerable number, projected budget deficits for fiscal year 2013 (McNichol, Oliff, and Johnson 2011; Oliff, Mai, and Palacios 2012). Local governments experienced similar budgetary issues. According to a survey conducted in 2009 among the 150 largest cities and 150 largest counties, 95% of local governments that responded to the survey reported experiencing budgetary shortfalls (Reilly and Reed 2011). Therefore, fiscal problems represent a real and immediate concern for state and local governments.

Given that worker compensation represents a large portion of state and local expenditures, it is not unusual that elected officials would link the fiscal crises in their states with worker compensation and would seek to balance budgets by cutting compensation costs (Levine and Scorsone 2011). Nevertheless, the direct relationship between union-negotiated employment conditions and fiscal problems is disputed. Marlow (2013), for example, found a positive relationship between public sector unionism and several measures of state and local government size, including real per capita spending, spending as percentage share of gross state product, and population per government employee. On the other hand, Fisk and Olney (2011) and Allegretto, Jacobs, and Lucia (2011) found no significant relationship between the extent of public sector unionism and state deficit levels, identifying the economic recession as the main cause of state and local budget crises.

The cyclical nature of economic recessions makes consequent budgetary shortfalls largely unavoidable (Befort 2012). Therefore, states and local governments will continue to experience similar budgetary constraints that will pressure public officials to make political decisions to balance budgets in ways that most effectively reconcile political ideology, group interests, and constituent attitudes toward alternatives to address fiscal crises. The recent developments in public sector labor relations showed that in the current environment "riling the unions in the name of protecting the public treasury became the right thing to do politically" (Chaison 2012: 46).

A range of factors contributed to a political environment favorable to fundamental reforms in public sector labor relations. The state and local fiscal crises resulting from the recent recession and the election of a group of Republican governors adverse to public sector unions represent the immediate triggers of the limitations on unions and collective bargaining rights in the public sector (Lewin, Kochan, and Keefe 2012). The political rationale behind the limitations appears, nevertheless, greater than the economic reasons. Several arguments advanced in the literature support this view. First, the existence of a conflicting body of evidence on compensation differentials between private and public sector workers suggests that elected officials had to make decisions based primarily on principled convictions to balance state and local budgets rather than on economic considerations only. The mixed evidence on the relationship between the extent of public sector unionism and deficit levels points to the same conclusion.

Second, the underfunded pension systems, which had been given as examples of collective bargaining outcomes by critics of public sector unions, are set through regulation rather than collective bargaining in most states (Freeman and Han 2012; Slater 2012). Furthermore, Slater (2012) argued that the problem of underfunded pension systems may have been exaggerated. Slater (2012) based his argument on the conclusion, provided at the beginning of 2011 by a coalition of 10 organizations representing states and local government employers, which stated that overall pension systems at local and state levels were not in crisis.

Third, alternative measures, such as taxation, could have been implemented to reduce overall budget deficits rather than limiting collective bargaining rights and imposing prohibitive conditions on union activity. Zweig (2012) argued, for example, that, in Wisconsin, the anticipated savings from the restrictions imposed on public sector unions and collective bargaining closely matched the $140 million in tax cuts to businesses approved by Governor Walker a few weeks earlier. Moreover, many of the implemented restrictions on public sector unions lacked fiscal relevance (Collins 2012). Governor Walker also declined to accept the union's wage and benefit concessions as a means to address the budget deficit in the state.

Zweig (2012) and others view the Wisconsin example as illustrative of the political rather than budgetary nature of motives to limit collective bargaining rights for public sector workers and impose restrictions on public sector unions. The arguments based on the cyclical nature of recessions, the conflicting findings on compensation differentials, the mixed evidence on the relationship between the extent of public sector unionism and deficit level, the availability of alternative measures to balance state and local budgets, and other factors led some researchers to conclude that the economic crisis was primarily used by conservative elected officials as an opportunity and excuse to limit collective bargaining rights for public sector employees and diminish the power of public sector unions (Fraser and Freeman 2011; Boris and Klein 2012; Olson 2011). McGinnis and Schanzenbach (2010: 4) emphasized that the recession opened political opportunities for both conservative and liberal elected officials, explaining that "for conservatives, taking on public employee unions provides a way to eliminate inefficient spending and create a policy of low taxes and lean government [and for] liberals, it provides a way to redirect spending to effective public goods."

In addition to the economic recession, public opinion facilitated the enactment of limitations on public sector unions. Elected officials seeking to impose limitations on public sector unions found reinforcement for their policies in the declining support for labor unions among the general public (Chaison 2012; Cooper and Greenhouse 2011). Based on data from the Gallup Poll Social Series (Gallup 2012), overall union approval dropped to 48% in 2009, representing an 11-point decline compared with the previous year. Despite the all-time low in union approval, in 2009 more people approved than disapproved of labor unions.

Recent developments of economic and political nature, as described in this section, have led to the limitation or elimination of collective bargaining rights and weakening of public sector unions in a number of states. Specific measures included the elimination of collective bargaining rights for entire groups of employees, restricting the scope of collective bargaining to cover a limited number of issues, enacting bureaucratic barriers to union activity, and prohibiting automatic extensions of collective bargaining agreements beyond the expiration of their term in the event of an impasse, among others. The next section will discuss the cases of Wisconsin, Ohio, Indiana, and Michigan that are illustrative of the types of measures aimed at weakening collective bargaining rights and public sector unions.

CASE STUDIES IN RESTRICTING COLLECTIVE BARGAINING RIGHTS

Wisconsin

Wisconsin was the first state to grant collective bargaining rights to public sector employees. A 1959 statute granted local and county government workers the right to union representation in negotiations with their employers. Nevertheless, in early 2011, Governor Walker, with the support of the state legislature, attempted to reverse the course of public sector unionism in Wisconsin by signing into law the Budget Repair Bill that greatly reduced the rights of public employees and their unions. The new legislation only exempted police, firefighters, and state troopers from the limitations. Political considerations, such as the support received by Governor Walker from some public safety unions during his election campaign, may explain the exemptions for the three categories of public workers (Saltzman 2012).

For the remaining public employees, Governor Walker's legislation included several important limitations. First, the legislation eliminated all collective bargaining rights for the University of Wisconsin system employees and certain home care and child care workers, among others. The faculty and academic staff in the University of Wisconsin system as well as home care and child care workers gained collective bargaining rights only recently. Second, the legislation restricted the scope of collective bargaining to base wages and capped negotiated wage increases to inflation as measured by the percent changes in the consumer price index. Third, the law effectively increased the required employee contributions for pension and health insurance and eliminated collective bargaining over these issues.

In addition to limitations on collective bargaining rights, the 2011 legislation created several bureaucratic barriers to union activity. The law prohibited the automatic collection of union dues directly from the employee paychecks. The law limited the term of collective bargaining agreements to one year, requiring unions to negotiate a new agreement every year. More important, the legislation mandated the recertification of unions on a yearly basis under considerably different conditions compared with the previously mandated process. Under the previous system, the decertification process could be initiated by 30% of the bargaining unit every three years. The majority of those voting decided the outcome of the decertification election. In contrast, for the yearly recertification, the new law required a majority of the employees in the collective bargaining unit to vote in favor of continued union representation. This new system penalizes unions for the failure of its members to participate in union elections.

Ohio

Ohio enacted a public sector labor law in 1983. The law was relatively favorable to collective bargaining and even allowed most public workers to strike. In 2011, nevertheless, Governor Kasich signed into law Senate Bill No. 5 that was designed to change significantly public sector labor relations in Ohio. Although the bill was later repealed through a popular referendum, its provisions are illustrative of the limitations on collective bargaining rights and restrictions on union activity imposed to various degrees across the United States.

Similar to Wisconsin, the Ohio bill limited collective bargaining rights for state employees, including workers in the state institutions of higher education. It prohibited "collective bargaining for 42,000 state workers and 19,500 college system workers" (Wisniewski 2011). The new legislation prohibited all public employees from striking, establishing penalties for violations of the prohibition. Measures against employees in violation of the prohibition on striking included the potential removal of the employee or assessment of deductions from the employee's compensation. Furthermore, the legislation prohibited bargaining over pensions, limited bargaining over health care benefits, and capped the public employer contributions toward health care benefits at 85% of the total cost. The bill also banned fair share agreements, prohibiting provisions in collective bargaining agreements that would require employees that are not union members to pay fair share fees to the union.

The bill included limitations that in some cases were even broader in scope than the restrictions on collective bargaining rights in Wisconsin. While the Wisconsin law exempted police and firefighters from the limitations, the Ohio bill aimed to limit the collective bargaining rights for these categories of workers along with the rest of public employees. In addition, the new legislation substantially modified the dispute resolution procedures to allow the legislative body of the public employer to unilaterally impose its last best offer as the agreement between parties.

Indiana

Indiana eliminated collective bargaining rights for state employees in 2005 when Mitch Daniels, a Republican, first took office as governor of the state. On his first day in office, Governor Daniels revoked an executive order that had established collective bargaining rights for state employees 16 years earlier under his Democratic predecessor (Freeman and Han 2012;

Wilson and Early 2012). The elimination of collective bargaining rights led to pay freezes for state employees in some of the subsequent years, higher health insurance payments, and the weakening of seniority preferences through the implementation of a merit-based pay system (Wilson and Early 2012; Greenhouse 2011a). The end of collective bargaining for state employees also facilitated the consolidation of state operations and the outsourcing of government services (Erickson 2011).

Teachers were unaffected by the 2005 measures since their collective bargaining rights were established by statute. However, more recently Indiana enacted legislation to limit the collective bargaining rights of this group of employees. In 2011, with the support of the legislature, Governor Daniels signed into law Senate Bill 575 that included prohibitions on bargaining over school restructuring options, teacher dismissal procedures and criteria, and any other subjects except those expressly listed in the new legislation. The bill restricted the subjects of collective bargaining to salary, wages, and related fringe benefits. It further limited the rights of state employees in the workplace by replacing binding arbitration as a dispute resolution method in the event of an impasse in negotiations with fact-finding procedures.

Michigan

Michigan is another state where public sector workers and unions experienced a limitation in their collective bargaining rights with the election of a Republican governor. In 2011, Governor Snyder, with support from the legislature, signed into law several bills that impacted public sector labor relations. For example, the *Local Government and School District Fiscal Accountability Act* provided broad powers to emergency managers appointed by the state to manage fiscal crises of cities and school districts experiencing financial emergencies. The law allowed emergency managers to renegotiate, alter, or terminate collective bargaining agreements and even remove from office public officials that failed to comply with the terms imposed by the legislation. The law also allowed emergency managers to consolidate schools, townships, cities, and counties without the

approval of the electorate (Dau-Schmidt and Lin 2012). Emergency managers were appointed to several cities and school districts in Michigan after enactment of the legislation. The first emergency manager was appointed for the city of Benton Harbor in April 2011, followed by Ecorse, Flint, and Pontiac. Emergency managers were also appointed to several school districts including Detroit, Highland Park, and Muskegon Heights.

Michigan also enacted legislation that limited the collective bargaining rights of teachers by expanding the list of prohibited subjects for bargaining between public school employers and employees. The new legislation prohibited bargaining over decisions on teacher placement, staffing, performance evaluation systems, disciplinary sanctions, method of employee compensation, determination of performance-based compensation, classroom observation procedures, and notification procedures of parents and legal guardians of students assigned to teachers rated as ineffective. Additional legislative changes that affect collective bargaining and public employee rights include, among others, the amendments to the Public Employment Relations Act and the enactment of the Public Employee Domestic Partner Benefit Restriction Act. The amendments to the Public Employment Relations Act limited public employee wages and benefits during the negotiation of new collective bargaining agreements to the levels and amounts not exceeding those in effect on the expiration date of the preceding agreement. The Public Employee Domestic Partner Benefit Restriction Act eliminated the right of employees to extend their medical benefits to their domestic partners.

More recently, at the end of 2012, Michigan became the 24th state to pass right-to-work legislation. Governor Snyder, who had previously thought of right-to-work legislation as overly divisive and had avoided the issue (Davey 2012), signed the legislation into law. The legislation prohibits requiring individuals to pay dues and any other fees to labor organizations and bargaining representatives as a condition of obtaining or continuing public employment. The legislation excludes police officers and firefighters from the right-to-work provisions, allowing fair share agreements between public employers and labor organizations representing the excluded groups of employees. The attachment of the right-to-work provisions to an appropriations bill excludes the possibility of overturning them through a referendum (Fletcher and Sullivan 2012), limiting the union options for reversing the new legislation.

PUBLIC SECTOR LABOR'S RESPONSE: CONCESSIONS AND RESISTANCE

The threat of limitations on collective bargaining rights led unions to make substantial wage and benefits concessions in the bargaining process in exchange for the protection of past gains. Collective bargaining in the public sector, therefore, took the form of concession bargaining in recent years. In both Wisconsin and Ohio unions agreed to large cuts in wages and benefits. The governors of both states, nevertheless, declined to accept the union concessions. In other states, such as New York, Connecticut, Vermont, Iowa, Minnesota, and Wyoming, unions negotiated reductions in wages and benefits to help address deficits and avoid more drastic measures (DiSalvo 2010; Freeman and Han 2012; Wallsten and Dennis 2011).

In the public sector, instead of limiting collective bargaining rights, some governors and municipal officials engaged in ultra-concession bargaining, using public pressure and the threat of limitations to obtain significant concessions from unions (Greenhouse 2011b; Reilly and Reed 2011). Although agreements reached through concession bargaining maintained the collective bargaining rights of public employees, at least temporarily, they affected employee wages and benefits, and in some case were insufficient to prevent layoffs and later limitations. Concession bargaining is a challenging process since on the one hand governments are constrained to balance budgets and on the other unions attempt to protect the wages and benefits of current employees, being reluctant to make concessions. The nature of the concession bargaining process and political expediency, therefore, guided the decision of some elected officials to limit collective bargaining rights for public employees.

The limitations on public employee bargaining rights triggered various responses among workers, unions, and supporters of public sector collective bargaining including protests, election recalls, ballot initiatives, and court challenges. In Wisconsin, for example, unions supported and organized massive demonstrations of tens of thousands in February and March of 2011 to oppose the Budget Repair Bill. University of Wisconsin students, professors, and staff members, firefighters, health care workers, correction officers, and private sector union members, among others, joined the protests to oppose the bill (Buhle 2011).

Despite these efforts, the movement failed to prevent the enactment of the new legislation. Deficiencies in historical capacity characterized by a "lack of working-class organization, historic memory, and collective experience" (Sernatinger 2012: 57), explain the ineffectiveness of the movement (Donegan 2012). Unions, nevertheless, were able to collect sufficient signatures for the state to hold recall elections for eligible Republican state senators supporting the limitations. The unions accomplished five recalls. Moreover, the unions collected sufficient signatures for the state to organize a recall election for Governor Walker when he became eligible for a recall during his second year in office. This latter effort was, nevertheless, unsuccessful, with Governor Walker winning 53% of the vote in the 2012 recall election.

Like in Wisconsin, several protests against limitations on public employee collective bargaining rights occurred in Ohio. The extent of the Ohio protests was smaller compared with Wisconsin (Greenhouse 2011c; Saltzman 2012). The unions in Ohio primarily focused on overturning the senate bill that, if enforced, would have limited collective bargaining rights in the public sector. A union-supported coalition gathered nearly 1.3 million signatures, a number far exceeding the requirement, to place the law on the ballot for repeal (Berg 2012). A majority of Ohio voters, 61%, supported the repeal of the legislation, proving the union strategy to regain collective bargaining rights in the public sector successful.

Challenging in court the recently imposed legal limitations on collective bargaining and government actions that attempted to prevent unions from pursuing strengthened legal protections for collective bargaining proved marginally successful in Michigan and Wisconsin. For example, in *Wisconsin Education Association Council v. Walker* (824 F.Supp.2d 856 [W.D.Wis. 2012]), the federal district court struck down, in part, the Wisconsin legislation by ruling that "so long as the State of Wisconsin continues to afford ordinary certification and dues deductions to mandatory public safety unions with sweeping bargaining rights, there is no rational basis to deny those rights to voluntary general unions with severely restricted bargaining rights." Nevertheless, in January 2013, the Seventh Circuit Court of Appeals upheld the constitutionality of the law in its entirety, reversing the previous ruling (Horowitz 2013).

At the state level, although a challenge of unconstitutionality on procedural grounds to the same legislation was unsuccessful, in September 2012, a state circuit court found the legislation unconstitutional on substantive grounds. The state court decision reinstated the collective bargaining rights for city, county, and school employees but did not affect state employees. Subsequently, the circuit court decision was appealed to the Supreme Court of Wisconsin. In July 2014, the Wisconsin Supreme Court upheld Act 10 in its entirety (*Madison Teachers, Inc. v. Scott Walker*, 2014, WI 99, ¶ 164, —— Wis.2d ——, 851 N.W.2d 337).

In Michigan, a coalition of unions collected nearly 700,000 signatures for a ballot initiative to grant public and private employees a constitutional right to organize in unions and bargain collectively (McCune, Wisniewski, and Bailey 2012). Opponents of the law feared that the amendment would limit government control over employment and budget decisions. According to Governor Snyder, the constitutional amendment could have affected up to 170 laws, resulting in confusion and disorganization (Greenhouse 2012). Governor Snyder and Attorney General Schuette attempted to block the initiative in court. Although the attempt to block the initiative from appearing on the ballot proved unsuccessful, Michigan voters rejected the constitutional amendment at the polls, opening a political path for the right-to-work

legislation. Nevertheless, the voters repealed the controversial emergency manager law at the same time.

OUTCOMES, LESSONS LEARNED, AND PROSPECTS

The limitations on unions and collective bargaining rights directly affect the security and stability of wages, benefits, and work of public employees but also have broader institutional, economic, and social implications. These limitations have already depressed union membership in several states. The power of labor unions lies in the number and commitment of its members. Therefore, declines in membership negatively affect the capacity of labor organizations to effectively engage in collective bargaining and political initiatives. Declining membership may also demoralize remaining members, further contributing to worker withdrawal from unions. Similar to legal limitations on collective bargaining, ultra-concession bargaining may have demoralizing effects on unionized and nonunionized workers. Chaison (2012: 66) explained that "concession bargaining sullies the reputation of unions as bargaining agents, making bargaining seem like a losing deal in the eyes of nonunion workers." The perception of unions as powerless and ineffective limits their capacity to attract new members while retaining their existing membership.

In addition to the effects on union membership and organizing capacity, limitations on collective bargaining may have broader social and economic implications. Levine and Scorsone (2011), for example, suggested that changes in wages and benefits may alter purchasing behavior of public employees, reduce their consumption, and lead to early withdrawals from retirement savings. They further explained that the restrictions on collective bargaining rights and unions may impact the cost of government, the types of workers attracted to employment in the public sector, and the quality of public services.

Several scholars argue that the restructuring of public sector labor relations and other austerity measures will especially impact women and minorities. A number of arguments support their claim. First, since women and blacks are overrepresented in the public sector, budget cuts affect them disproportionately (Cooper, Gable, and Austin 2012). Second, since public sector employment "has been an especially important upward-mobility strategy" for women and blacks (Collins 2012: 10), budget cuts may leave both groups with a more difficult path toward wage equity and especially vulnerable to economic hardships. Third, in contrast to the unionized men who are overrepresented in the private sector, the majority of unionized women work in the public sector (Abramovitz 2012). Consequently, women will disproportionately bear the effects of the recently implemented limitations on public sector unions and collective bargaining rights.

Moreover, a large number of job cuts as well as limitations on collective bargaining rights have been implemented in traditional female occupations (Abramovitz 2012). The limitations on collective bargaining rights for home care workers, for example, heavily impact women both as providers and receivers of care (Boris and Klein 2012). Similarly, limitations on collective bargaining rights that affect teachers, nurses, and child care workers also have a disproportionate impact on women since these are predominantly female occupations (National Women's Law Center 2012). In contrast, workers and unions in some predominantly male occupations—police officers, firefighters, and state patrol officers—were unaffected by the limitations as was the case in Wisconsin (Abramovitz 2012; Freeman and Han 2012; National Women's Law Center 2012).

The limitations on unions and collective bargaining rights may also have important implications for civil society and American democracy more broadly (Lewin et al. 2011). Unions play an internal role of representing the voice of their members at the workplace. In addition, unions have an external role of representing the voice of their members and supporters in the political and policy-making processes. Restrictions on union activity diminish the capacity of unions to perform their internal and external roles, weakening the voice of workers at the workplace and limiting their opportunities for collective action.

Conditions that facilitated the weakening of unions and worker bargaining power in the public sector continue to exist. The political-economic environment and public opinion remain unfavorable to unions. The recovery of the economy may gradually moderate the aggressive measures that elected officials across the country took against public sector unions and collective bargaining rights either to address state and local fiscal imbalances, as argued by some, or pursue their political ends, as argued by others. The lack of historical capacity and the structural dependence of public sector unions on their private counterparts, nevertheless, will continue to affect union chances to withstand future threats to their role in public sector labor relations.

Given the institutional and political challenges that unions face, labor will have to develop new approaches to advance their agenda. The lessons from previous union efforts provide important insights that can help shape new union strategies. The Wisconsin protests, for example, brought multiple stakeholders together, nevertheless the movement lacked internal coordination and appropriate channels for workers and community members to work together (Sernatinger 2012). Therefore, unions will have to continue building broad alliances with other institutions and with the communities within which they are embedded, emphasizing coordination efforts. Since the membership size largely determines the power of labor organizations, unions will have to increase worker mobilization and engagement in union activities. Overall, unions will need to strengthen their relationships internally with their existing and potential members and externally with institutional partners and communities.

Unions will require an improved technical capacity and intellectual resources to develop organized and coordinated efforts to mobilize workers and maintain broad coalitions. Expanding the union discourse beyond collective bargaining and union rights as human rights may help attract new coalition members and improve the public perception of unions. Unions will have to make the broader argument that a democratic society needs unions, "including unions of government workers, not only because workers should have the right to associate to advance their collective interests, but also because a democratic society requires them to associate if economic life and work are to serve the common good in ways that are truly sustainable" (McCartin 2012: 403). The broadening of the union discourse to focus on democracy, equity, and the quality of public services may help replace the current politics of resentment, in which private sector employees are set against public sector employees by union opponents, with the politics of solidarity, in which unions can bring employees from the public and private sectors to work together toward common goals.

REFERENCES

Abramovitz, Mimi. 2012. The Feminization of Austerity. *New Labor Forum, 21*(1), 30–39. doi: 10.4179/NLF.211.0000006.

Allegretto, Sylvia A., Ken Jacobs, and Laurel Lucia. 2011. The Wrong Target: Public Sector Unions and State Budget Deficits. Policy Brief, Institute for Research on Labor and Employment, University of California, Berkeley, CA. http://www.irle.berkeley.edu/research/state_budget_deficits_oct2011.pdf.

Befort, Stephen F. 2012. Public-Sector Employment under Siege. *Indiana Law Journal, 87*(1), 231–238. http://www.repository.law.indiana.edu/ilj/vol87/iss1/14.

Bender, Keith A., and John S. Heywood. 2010. Out of Balance? Comparing Public and Private Sector Compensation over Twenty Years. Center for State and Local Government Excellence / National Institute on Retirement Security, Washington, DC. http://www.nirsonline.org/storage/nirs/documents/final_out_of_balance_report_april_2010.pdf.

Berg, John C. 2012. Does Changing the Story Change Voting Behavior? The Occupy Movement and the Crisis of the American Party System. APSA 2012 Annual Meeting Paper. http://papers.ssrn.com/sol3/papers.cfm?abstract_id=2108707.

Boris, Eileen, and Jennifer Klein. 2012. *Caring for America: Home Health Workers in the Shadow of the Welfare State*. New York: Oxford University Press.

Buhle, Mari Jo. 2011. The Wisconsin Idea. In *It Started in Wisconsin: Dispatches of the New Labor Protest*, edited by Mari Jo Buhle and Paul Buhle, 11–26. Brooklyn, NY: Verso.

Chaison, Gary. 2012. *The New Collective Bargaining*. New York: Springer.

Collins, Jane. 2012. Theorizing Wisconsin's 2011 Protests: Community-Based Unionism Confronts Accumulation by Dispossession. *American Ethnologist, 39*(1), 6–20. doi: 10.1111/j.1548-1425.2011.01340.x.

Cooper, David, Mary Gable, and Algernon Austin. 2012. The Public-Sector Jobs Crisis: Women and African Americans Hit Hardest by Job Losses in State and Local Governments. EPI Briefing Paper 339, Economic Policy Institute, Washington, DC. http://www.epi.org/files/2012/bp339-public-sector-jobs-crisis.pdf.

Cooper, Michael, and Steven Greenhouse. 2011. Unions Debate What to Give to Save Bargaining. *New York Times*, February 27. http://www.nytimes.com/2011/02/28/us/28unions.html?pagewanted=all&_r=0.

Dau-Schmidt, Kenneth Glenn, and Winston Lin. 2012. The Great Recession, the Resulting Budget Shortfalls, the 2010 Elections and the Attack on Public Sector Collective Bargaining in the United States. *Hofstra Labor and Employment Law Journal, 29*(2), 407–432. http://lawarchive.hofstra.edu/pdf/academics/journals/laborandemploymentlawjournal/labor_vol29no2_dauschmidt_format.pdf.

Davey, Monica. 2012. Michigan Labor Fight Cleaves a Union Bulwark. *New York Times*, December 10. http://www.nytimes.com/2012/12/11/us/battle-over-labor-unions-cleaves-michigan.html.

DiSalvo, Daniel. 2010. The Trouble with Public Sector Unions. *National Affairs*, 5, 3–19. http://www.nationalaffairs.com/doclib/20100918_DiSalvo_pdf%5B1%5D.pdf.

Donegan, Connor. 2012. Disciplining Labor, Dismantling Democracy: Rebellion and Control in Wisconsin. In *Wisconsin Uprising: Labor Fights Back*, edited by Michael D. Yates, 29–44. New York: Monthly Review Press.

Edwards, Chris. 2010. Public Sector Unions and the Rising Costs of Employee Compensation. *Cato Journal, 30*(1), 87–115. http://www.cato.org/pubs/journal/cj30n1/cj30n1-5.pdf.

Erickson, Doug. 2011. In Indiana, a Case Study in Ending Collective Bargaining. *Wisconsin State Journal*, March 10. http://host.madison.com/wsj/news/local/govt-and-politics/article_badb25e6-4b71-11e0-97c4-001cc4c002e0.html.

Fisk, Catherine, and Brian Olney. 2011. Collective Bargaining Is Not the Cause of State Budget Problems. Legal Studies

Research Paper Series 2011-48, School of Law, University of California, Irvine, CA. http://papers.ssrn.com/sol3/papers.cfm?abstract_id=1920424.

Fletcher, Michael A., and Sean Sullivan. 2012. Michigan Enacts Right-to-Work Law, Dealing Blow to Unions. *Washington Post*, December 11. http://www.washingtonpost.com/business /economy/michigan-enacts-right-to-work-law-dealing-blow-to-unions/2012/12/11/bb9f8e5a-43ad-11e2-9648-a2c323a991d6_story.html.

Fraser, Steve, and Joshua B. Freeman. 2011. In the Rearview Mirror: A Brief History of Opposition to Public Sector Unionism. *New Labor Forum, 20*(3), 93–96. doi: 10.4179/NLF.203.0000013.

Freeman, Richard B., and Eunice Han. 2012. The War against Public Sector Collective Bargaining in the US. *Journal of Industrial Relations, 54*(3), 386–408. doi: 10.1177/0022185612442279.

Freeman, Richard B., and James L. Medoff. 1979. The Two Faces of Unionism. *Public Interest, 57*(Fall), 69–93. http://www.nationalaffairs.com/public_interest/detail/the-two-faces-of-unionism.

Gallup. 2012. Gallup Poll Social Series: Work and Education. Gallup. www.gallup.com/file/poll/142010/Confidence_Unions_100812.pdf.

Gapasin, Fernando. 2012. Building Communities of Solidarity from Madison to Bend. In *Wisconsin Uprising: Labor Fights Back*, edited by Michael D. Yates, 251–266. New York: Monthly Review Press.

Gittleman, Maury, and Brooks Pierce. 2012. Compensation for State and Local Government Workers. *Journal of Economic Perspectives, 26*(1), 217–242. doi: 10.1257/jep.26.1.217.

Greenhouse, Steven. 2011a. In Indiana, Clues to Future of Wisconsin Labor. *New York Times*, February 26. http://www.nytimes.com/2011/02/27/business/27collective-bargain.html?pagewanted=all.

———. 2011b. A Watershed Moment for Public-Sector Unions. *New York Times*, February 18. http://www.nytimes.com/2011/02/19/us/19union.html.

———. 2011c. Ohio's Anti-Union Law Is Tougher Than Wisconsin's. *New York Times*, March 31. http://www.nytimes.com/2011/04/01/us/01ohio.html.

———. 2012. Michigan Vote a Test Case on Enshrining the Rights of Unions. *New York Times*, October 25. http://www.nytimes.com/2012/10/26/business/in-midwest-labor-presses-for-a-vote-to-lock-in-union-rights.html?pagewanted=all.

Hirsch, Barry T., and David A. Macpherson. 2012. Union Membership and Coverage Database from the Current Population Survey. http://www.unionstats.com.

Horowitz, Carl. 2013. Federal Appeals Court Upholds Curbs on Wisconsin Public-Sector Unions; Reverses Lower Court. National Legal and Policy Center, Falls Church, VA. http://nlpc.org/stories/2013/01/24/federal-appeals-court-upholds-curbs-wisconsin-public-sector-unions-reverses-lower.

Keefe, Jeffrey. 2012. Are Public Employees Overpaid? *Labor Studies Journal, 37*(1), 104–126. doi: 10.1177/0160449X11429263.

Levine, Helisse, and Eric Scorsone. 2011. The Great Recession's Institutional Change in the Public Employment Relationship: Implications for State and Local Governments. *State and Local Government Review, 43*(3), 208–214. doi: 10.1177/0160323X11428811.

Lewin, David, Thomas Kochan, Joel Cutcher-Gershenfeld, Teresa Ghilarducci, Harry Katz, Jeffrey Keefe, Daniel J. B. Mitchell, Craig Olson, Saul Rubinstein, and Christian Weller. 2011. *Getting It Right: Empirical Evidence and Policy Implications from Research on Public-Sector Unionism and Collective Bargaining*. Employment Policy Research Network / Labor and Employment Relations Association, Champaign, IL. http://ssrn.com/abstract=1792942.

Lewin, David, Thomas Kochan, and Jeffrey Keefe. 2012. *Toward a New Generation of Empirical Evidence and Policy Research on Public Sector Unionism and Collective Bargaining*. Employment Policy Research Network, Champaign, IL. http://www.employmentpolicy.org/topic/402/research/toward-new-generation-empirical-evidence-and-policy-research.

Lewis, Gregory B., and Chester S. Galloway. 2011. *A National Analysis of Public/Private Wage Differentials at the State and Local Levels by Race and Gender*. Research Paper Series, Working Paper 11-10, Andrew Young School of Policy Studies, Georgia State University, Atlanta. http://papers.ssrn.com/sol3/papers.cfm?abstract_id=1768190##.

Marlow, Michael L. 2013. Public Sector Unions and Government Size. *Applied Economics Letters, 20*(5), 466–470. doi: 10.1080/13504851.2012.714058.

McCartin, Joseph A. 2011. Convenient Scapegoats: Public Workers under Assault. *Dissent, 58*(2), 45–50. http://www.dissentmagazine.org/article/convenient-scapegoat-public-workers-under-assault.

———. 2012. Beyond Human Rights: Understanding and Addressing the Attack on Public Sector Unions. *Human*

Rights Review, 13(3), 399–403. doi: 10.1007/s12142-012-0234-2.

McCune, Greg, Mary Wisniewski, and David Bailey. 2012. Michigan High Court Allows Pro-Union Measures on November Ballot. *Reuters*, September 5. http://www.reuters.com/article/2012/09/05/us-usa-campaign-michigan-idUSBRE8841DS20120905.

McGinnis, John O., and Max Schanzenbach. 2010. The Case against Public Sector Unions. *Policy Review, 162*, 3–12. http://www.hoover.org/publications/policy-review/article/43266.

McNichol, Elizabeth, Phil Oliff, and Nicholas Johnson. 2011. States Continue to Feel Recession's Impact. Center on Budget and Policy Priorities, Washington, DC. http://faculty.cbpp.uaa.alaska.edu/afgjp/PADM628%20Spring%202011/State%20shortfalls%20continue.pdf.

National Women's Law Center. 2011. Women's Stake in the Battle over Public Employees' Collective Bargaining Rights. Fact Sheet, National Women's Law Center, Washington, DC. http://www.nwlc.org/sites/default/files/pdfs/women_and_unions_final_fact_sheet_march_2011_final.pdf.

———. 2012. Women's Stake in the Battle over Collective Bargaining Rights. Fact Sheet, National Women's Law Center, Washington, DC. http://www.nwlc.org/sites/default/files /pdfs/unions_fact_sheet_6.5.12_final.pdf.

Oliff, Phil, Chris Mai, and Vincent Palacios. 2012. States Continue to Feel Recession's Impact. Center on Budget and Policy Priorities, Washington, DC. http://www.cbpp.org/files/2–8–08sfp.pdf.

Olson, Craig. 2011. *The Battle over Public Sector Collective Bargaining in Wisconsin and Elsewhere.* Employment Policy Research Network, Champaign, IL. http://www.employmentpolicy.org/topic/402/op-ed/battle-over-public-sector-collective-bargaining-wisconsin-and-elsewhere.

Reilly, Thom, and Mark B. Reed. 2011. Budget Shortfalls, Employee Compensation, and Collective Bargaining in Local Governments. *State and Local Government Review,* 43(3), 215–223. doi: 10.1177/0160323X11428621.

Saltzman, Gregory M. 2012. An Anti-Union Tide: The 2011 Attacks on Public-Employees' Bargaining Rights. *The NEA 2012 Almanac of Higher Education,* 39–50. http://www.nea.org/assets/docs/_2012_Almanac_Saltzman_final.pdf.

Sernatinger, Andrew. 2012. Capitalist Crisis and the Wisconsin Uprising. In *Wisconsin Uprising: Labor Fights Back,* edited by Michael D. Yates, 45–58. New York: Monthly Review Press.

Slater, Joseph E. 2012. Public-Sector Labor in the Age of Obama. *Indiana Law Journal, 87*(1), 189–229. http://www.repository.law.indiana.edu/ilj/vol87/iss1/13.

U.S. Bureau of Labor Statistics (BLS). 2010. Union Members—2009. News Release, U.S. Bureau of Labor Statistics. http://www.bls.gov/news.release/archives/union2_01222010.pdf.

———. 2012. Union Members—2011. News Release, U.S. Bureau of Labor Statistics. http://www.bls.gov/news.release/pdf/union2.pdf.

Wallsten, Peter, and Brady Dennis. 2011. Democratic Governors Try to Enlist Labor's Help in Dealing with Budget Crises. *Washington Post,* February 25. http://www.washingtonpost.com/wp-dyn/content/article/2011/02/25 /AR2011022501888.html.

Wilson, Rand, and Early, Steve. 2012. Back to the Future: Union Survival Strategies in Open Shop America. In *Wisconsin Uprising: Labor Fights Back,* edited by Michael D. Yates, 125–137. New York: Monthly Review Press.

Wisniewski, Mary. 2011. Factbox: Several States Beyond Wisconsin Mull Union Limits. *Reuters*, March 10. http://www.reuters.com/article/2011/03/11/us-usa-unions-states-idUSTRE7295QI20110311.

Zweig, Michael. 2012. Beyond Wisconsin: Seeking New Priorities as Labor Challenges War. In *Wisconsin Uprising: Labor Fights Back*, edited by Michael D. Yates, 235–249. New York: Monthly Review Press.

CHAPTER 24

HUMAN RESOURCES MANAGEMENT AND GOVERNMENT CONTRACTING

Sergio Fernandez
Indiana University Bloomington

Deanna Malatesta
Indiana University–Purdue University, Indianapolis

Craig Smith
University of Arizona

Government's increasing reliance on alternative service delivery arrangements is one of the most striking developments in public administration over the past three decades. We see no signs of the trend abating anytime soon. On the contrary, the fiscal challenges brought about by the recent recession appear to have exacerbated government's reliance on businesses and nonprofit organizations. Faced with financial and demographic challenges, politicians and public managers are pressured to do more with less. To accomplish their goals they seek to harness the power of the private sector. The allure of cost savings and efficiency gains linked to privatization is difficult for managers to ignore, even though the empirical evidence suggests that it is no panacea (Boyne 1998; Jang 2006). Indeed, privatization of government programs—particularly in its most common form, government contracting—encompasses nearly every aspect of contemporary public administration, including human resources management (HRM). This chapter describes the direct and indirect effects of public sector contracting on HRM, including how recent trends in contracting have altered the role of the public manager.

The most direct effect occurs when an organization chooses to contract out all or part of its HRM function. Contracting HRM to the private sector provides several potential benefits, including gains in efficiency, improvements in service quality, and the ability to provide more targeted HR services (Coggburn 2009). While contracting out individual HRM services such as payroll and benefits administration is somewhat common (Lawther 2003; Fernandez, Rainey, and Lowman 2006), more wholesale contracting of HRM is a relatively new phenomenon and less widespread (Coggburn 2009). Like any contracted service, the potential benefits of contracting out HRM must be weighed against its inherent challenges.

Contracting results in other, more indirect HRM challenges as well. For instance, it frequently provokes opposition from both inside and outside the organization. Public employees oppose contracting initiatives out of fear that it may adversely affect wages and benefits or result in job losses (Jackson 1997; Fernandez and Smith 2006). Public sector unions oppose contracting because they perceive it as a direct assault on public employment and the civil service (Chandler and Feuille 1991; Becker, Silverstein, and Chaykin 1995). In both cases, opposition constitutes a potential barrier to effective contracting and thus requires a managerial response.

Contracting presents a number of other challenges (and potential opportunities) for public managers. The expanded scale and scope of public sector contracting creates additional space between the public manager and the street-level workers in direct contact with the public. Multiorganizational arrangements have become central to the delivery of public services. The extra layers make communication more difficult. As Agranoff explains in his recent book *Collaborating to Manage* (2012), public managers must develop and maintain essential conduits of communication with a network of partners if they are to be effective in this new environment. At the same time, public managers must continue to adhere to public sector values. How do managers maintain equity, transparency, and responsiveness while simultaneously shifting more responsibility to the private sector? How is accountability achieved in networks of service providers? If public managers are to take these values seriously, they must find ways to ensure that traditionally disadvantaged groups, such as minorities and women, have equitable access to the procurement process. On the upside, contracting may be an effective instrument for achieving some forms of social equity. For example, relying on the theory of representative bureaucracy, some scholars argue that demographic diversity among decision makers, along with rules requiring the consideration of race and gender in contracting decisions, can lead to more equitable contracting (Fernandez et al. 2013; Smith and Fernandez 2010).

We begin the chapter with a discussion of the impact of government contracting on wages, benefits, and jobs and of strategies for managing opposition to contracting from public employees and unions. We then describe government contracting of HRM and the rationales and challenges associated with contracting out all or part of an organization's HRM function. We briefly discuss a few recent trends that we observe, in particular the upsurge in large-scale public-private partnerships (PPPs) in the delivery of social services and for infrastructure. We provide examples of how these forms of extensive contracting have affected workers and have reshaped the role of public managers in contemporary governance. Last, we discuss how efficiency and cost savings are not the only goals when contracting for services. Maintaining equity and transparency in the procurement process can result in positive benefits for society, since historically disadvantaged groups gain access to economic benefits offered by government.

EFFECTS OF GOVERNMENT CONTRACTING ON PUBLIC SECTOR EMPLOYMENT

The prevailing view among researchers, policy makers, and public employees is that government contracting results in the loss of public sector jobs. Few empirical studies have explored this important policy question, and up until recently, most of the evidence suggested that contracting had little if any effect on the size of the public workforce. One of the earliest studies conducted by the National Commission for Employment Policy (NCEP 1988) concluded that federal employee job displacement from contracting was very low, with only about 5% of federal workers having been displaced. Moreover, the NCEP also concluded that at the local level, very few employees were laid off because of contracting, and most of those were given opportunities for other jobs within government or were hired by contractors. Stein (1990) found that complete and partial contracting with for-profit providers often resulted in significant reductions in public employment within specific municipal departments. Complete and partial contracting with nonprofit providers, however, appeared to have no effect on the size of a department's workforce, nor did other alternative forms of service delivery like franchises/concessions, vouchers, and volunteers (see also Greene 2002, for a similar conclusion). Donahue (2002) examined trends in the size of the public workforce and in government contracting and concluded that the relationship between the two was quite weak. As he explained, "a greater readiness to rely on private delivery almost surely has had a smaller influence on the size of the public workforce than have shifts in the size and composition of government's mission, productivity growth, and simple austerity. Far from cutting to the heart of public employment, privatization seems to have been (at least so far) nibbling around its edges" (275).

More recently, Fernandez, Smith, and Wenger (2007) took an innovative approach to analyzing the relationship between government contracting and public employment. The authors used local government data from multiple sources and points in time to model the joint effects of contracting on full-time and part-time employment under the assumption that decisions about hiring part-time and full-time employees are interrelated. Their results showed that contracting has a sizeable negative effect on full-time public employment, but that the negative effect was offset in part by a positive effect on part-time public employment. The failure of previous studies to account for the part-time/full-time shift in the composition of the public workforce as a result of contracting may explain why those studies suggested the loss of few public sector jobs when public officials privatize service delivery.

PUBLIC EMPLOYEES, PUBLIC SECTOR UNIONS, AND OPPOSITION TO GOVERNMENT CONTRACTING

The threat to job security posed by government contracting has made public employees and public sector unions fervid and vigorous opponents of privatization throughout the United States and abroad (Fernandez et al. 2006; Fernandez and Smith 2006; Becker et al. 1995; Chandler and Feuille 1991; NCEP 1988). Evidence from various sources demonstrates the capacity of public employees and their unions to successfully oppose contracting initiatives, making them formidable opponents in the privatization debates that occur in many jurisdictions. Ferris and Graddy (1986) found that the extent of public sector unionization had a significant negative effect on the likelihood that a city contracts

out. In addition, a large survey of sanitation collection services in U.S. municipalities with populations over 10,000 revealed that unionized cities were less likely to consider contracting than nonunionized ones. The survey also found that opposition to contracting was significantly higher in unionized cities than in nonunionized cities, and cities that considered contracting but never did so reported significantly higher levels of opposition from both city employees and residents than cities that ultimately contracted out (Chandler and Feuille 1991). Hefetz and Warner (2004) found that union opposition to privatization was negatively related to the amount of contracting out and positively related with the amount of contracting back in. Even in right-to-work states, public opinion survey data shows that rank-and-file public employees are more opposed to privatization than their counterparts in the private sector (Fernandez and Smith 2006). Fernandez, Ryu, and Brudney (2008) found that even when controlling for the presence of a collective bargaining agreement, public employee opposition to privatization had a larger negative effect on the amount of contracting in larger local governments than in smaller ones.

Public employees and public sector unions have employed various methods to influence policy making and obstruct contracting initiatives. In many instances, public unions have mounted legal challenges, claiming that the decision was not taken to improve efficiency or effectiveness; that the decision was driven by political favoritism; that the agency or unit of government failed to bargain in good faith with unionized employees; or that the agency or unit of government acted in an unlawful, unilateral manner that caused it to violate its duty to bargain (Elam 1997). Though success in the courts has been mixed for unions (Naff 1991), the mere threat of a lawsuit may convince policy makers to reconsider plans to contract out.

Efforts to block privatization reach beyond the courtroom. Lobbying activity to influence policy making and legislation has produced some success for public unions. In California, the Service Employees International Union, the largest public sector union in the state, was a driving force behind a proposed bill to ensure that any outsourcing of public library administration would safeguard against dislocation of public employees (Duffy 2011). In Pennsylvania, a coalition of public and private sector unions joined forces to successfully lobby the state legislature to stop initiatives aimed at privatizing state liquor stores and nursing services at state prison health facilities (Vail 2012). The American Federation of State, County and Municipal Employees (AFSCME), the National Education Association (NEA), and the American Federation of Teachers (AFT) all provide a variety of published reports and other written materials, including talking points, draft media releases, and lobbying advice, to public employees to enable them to successfully mount a public relations campaign aimed at generating opposition to privatization.

Political opposition from public unions can pose a significant barrier to privatization at the local level. Public employees tend to vote more frequently than the average citizen, and their collective voting power can influence the results of local elections significantly. In Hallandale Beach, Florida, and Miami-Dade County, recent public relations campaign by AFSCME succeeded in dissuading local elected officials from outsourcing building safety inspections and the entire Miami-Dade Jackson Health System (Lawrence 2012), respectively. In what appears to be the most comprehensive study of public sector union responses to privatization, Jalette and Hebdon (2012) found that among Canadian local governments, unionized jurisdictions were more likely to attract new privatization proposals—due to the potential for labor cost savings—but they were also more likely to have such proposals rejected. The authors found that less adversarial responses, like proposing alternatives to privatization, were more successful tactics at stopping privatization from occurring than labor strikes, which created an adversarial climate and appeared to embolden advocates for privatization.

Given public employee attitudes toward privatization, it is crucial for public officials to plan for and execute steps to reduce resistance to privatization when such an approach is being considered. Fernandez et al.

(2006) and Fernandez and Smith (2006) describe a range of options available for reducing such resistance (see also NCEP 1988; Eggers and O'Leary 1994; Jackson 1997; Rainey 2005; Elam 1997). First, public officials can try to reduce the number of employees affected by contracting by establishing a "no lay-off" policy when contracting out existing services; transferring employees to other positions within the agency; offering early retirement incentives to persuade employees to leave voluntarily; and contracting for new services or the expansion of existing ones. Second, for employees who will become displaced, measures can be taken to ease the burden of separation. These include providing displaced employees with employee assistance programs and services like retraining, job placement, counseling, and reimbursement for lost pension and other benefits; offering hiring preference for new positions within an agency; and requiring contractors to offer the right of first refusal. Third, resistance to contracting may be reduced by promoting the creation of employee-owned private enterprises and providing them with assistance such as capital asset transfers, subsidized or free use of public facilities and materials, low-interest loans and seed grants, and legal start-up assistance. Finally, there are various steps public officials can take to minimize the legal risks involved with contracting. These include clearly stating purposes, goals, and technical specifications; providing evidence of anticipated gains from contracting out; employing competitive bidding procedures; and if required, bargaining in good faith with public employees by allowing ample time for bargaining, notifying unions of the intent to contract out in a timely fashion, avoiding unnecessary and burdensome deadlines and other time constraints, and granting concessions to maintain an atmosphere of good faith during the negotiations.

GOVERNMENT CONTRACTING OF HUMAN RESOURCES MANAGEMENT SERVICES

State and local government have witnessed drastic cuts in revenues and collections since 2008 (National Governors Association 2012). In an effort to get their fiscal houses in order, states have been forced to reduce funding to local governments, who are already in a perilous position given decreases in property taxes. Making matters worse, the General Accounting Office (GAO 2011) predicted that state and local governments can anticipate declines in fiscal resources for the next 50 years. Demographic trends have exasperated the problem. The aging population and the continued influx of immigrants have brought a steady increase in the demand for many social services. States have witnessed an increase in the demand for many services that serve these populations, including Medicaid, Medicare, mental health services, migrant worker services, and health services for children not covered by private insurance, to name a few. Public officials seeking to harness the power of the market are lured by the possibilities that the private sector can help them do more with less, or in some cases that they can do it all for less.

As the extent of government contracting has spread, agencies have turned to contracting for the delivery of support functions and internal processes, including HRM services. Private firms frequently turn to external providers to perform human resources activities in an effort to reduce costs and gain access to specialized knowledge and skills (Sunno and Laabs 1994; and Csoko 1995, as cited in Klaas, McClendon, and Gainey 1999; Dell 2004; Nelson Staffing 2009). A comprehensive survey of HRM contracting by private firms showed that approximately three-quarters of the respondents contract out at least one HRM service (Dell 2004). Another survey found that 58% of respondents engaged in contracting HRM services, with for-profit firms being used at a higher rate (63%) than nonprofit organizations (just 37%) (Society for Human Resource Management 2004). The most commonly contracted HRM services included background checks, employee counseling, flexible spending account administration and Consolidated Omnibus Budget Reconciliation Act (COBRA) account management; the least contracted HRM services included strategic business planning, HRM policy development, training and development programs, performance management, and risk management.

Evidence from various sources also points to growing HRM contracting in the public sector in the United States and other countries, including the United Kingdom, Australia, and Canada. A study of 22 federal agencies conducted by the National Academy of Public Administration (1996) found that more than half contract out one or more HRM services, most often with franchise programs, which are administrative offices within federal agencies that operate on a self-sustaining reimbursable basis by offering services to other federal agencies. A survey of the 100 largest cities in America found that approximately 24% of the respondents contracted out for employment and training activities (Dilger, Moffett, and Struyk 1997: 22). A more recent study of American local governments indicated that in 2007, approximately 11% of respondents relied at least in part on an external provider to deliver HRM services, with the service provider usually being a for-profit firm (see Warner and Hefetz 2009); this number was up from approximately 8% in 1988 (International City/County Management Association 1989).

A report by The Conference Board (Koch 2004) cited several notable examples of successful HRM outsourcing initiatives in American government. Soon after its founding in 2001, the U.S. Transportation Security Administration began hiring contractors to provide a wide range of HRM services, including recruitment, assessment, and selection of new hires, training and development, and administration of health insurance and employee assistance programs. In Florida, the Department of Management Services opted not to modernize its antiquated in-house computerized personnel system and instead hired a private contractor to design and implement a new comprehensive system that includes recruitment, payroll, benefits management, and employee database management. In Australia, the state of Victoria awarded a contract to provide its Department of Premier and Cabinet, Department of Treasury and Finance, and Department of Victorian Communities with a wide range of HRM services, including payroll, employee database management, HRM policy development, and self-service kiosks for public employees. Finally, the city of Copenhagen, Denmark, when faced with the need to modernize its aging personnel system, hired a vendor to develop an integrated system to process payroll, collect and manage employee data, and enable employees to manage their own benefits plans.

Why would a public agency consider contracting out all or part of its HRM function? HRM contracting offers public agencies several potential advantages over in-house provision (Koch 2004; GAO 2004). By contracting with larger firms that specialize in particular services, a public agency may be able to take advantage of economies of scale to reduce the cost of service provision. Cost savings can also emerge from being able to avoid large up-front investments required to modernize existing systems that may be quite outdated. Contracting for HRM services can free up existing HRM staff to focus on core competencies and strategic management issues. It can also enable an agency to leverage the expertise of others and benefit from the latest innovations in HRM technologies and processes that may not be available in-house, including 24/7 access to services. Dilger et al.'s (1997) survey of America's largest cities found that among the 16 cities in their sample that contracted for one or more HRM services, more than half reported satisfaction with services received from external providers.

Some governments take the additional step of turning over staffing to contractors. Consider recent decisions in Indiana and Texas to privatize social services. In 2005, the state of Texas signed an $899 million, five-year contract with a group headed by Accenture LLP to develop, operate, and staff call centers and to upgrade and run their eligibility and enrollment system for critical health and social services. In 2006, Indiana Family and Social Services Administration (FSSA) signed a 10-year $4 billion contract with IBM and its affiliated subcontractors (a consortium referred to as "ACS") to process applications for public benefits eligibility. The nonprofit watch dog, In the Public Interest (www.inthepublicinterest .org), has reported extensively on the personnel issues associated with these contracts. In short, both states encountered numerous problems introducing the new systems and in implementing the contract. Clients complained that the contract staff was inadequately trained. In Indiana, the American Federation of State, County, and Municipal Employees (AFSCME) aggressively opposed the staffing plans for the new system (AFSCME 2005). However, in each state many government workers became employees of the contractors. When both states decided to cancel their contracts, workers were transferred back to the agencies as government workers. Both states continue to report problems associated with the loss of workers and the need to rebuild agency capacity that was diminished as a result of these initiatives.

COPING WITH THE MANAGERIAL CHALLENGES OF GOVERNMENT CONTRACTING

Contracting for HRM services is no panacea or magic bullet (National Academy of Public Administration [NAPA] 1997; Siegel 1999; Dell 2004; Fernandez, Rainey, and Lowman 2006; Coggburn 2007). It requires careful and diligent design and implementation of the acquisition process, an effectively structured agreement that discourages opportunistic behavior and enables task performance, and ongoing management of the contractual relationship. Several factors are crucial to ensure success in contracting for HRM services. First, the decision must be made as to which specific HRM services to assign to contractors. No single criterion can be used to make this decision. Coggburn (2007) offers a useful framework for assessing the appropriateness of outsourcing an HRM service or activity. His framework takes into account criteria that include the extent to which the service contributes to public value; the degree to which outsourcing a service would threaten the public interest; the cost-effectiveness of outsourcing the service; the degree to which the service is routine and easy to specify; the level of competition among potential providers of the service; and the extent to which outsourcing the service would compromise public sector HRM values like merit, fairness and equity. Second, ample time must be allocated for planning the acquisition, and input and advice should be sought from a range of internal and external stakeholders, including potential vendors.

Third, the legal complexities and potential constraints on HRM outsourcing must be understood and addressed early in the process. Constitutional, statutory, and regulatory law impose requirements that can significantly influence the manner in which an HRM contractor provides services to an agency (Battaglio and Ledvinka 2007). For example, a contractor may be deemed a "state actor" and held liable for violating a citizen's individual and due process rights, it may be compelled to disclose information relating to the work it is performing for an agency, and the right of first refusal may have to be offered to public employees displaced as a result of outsourcing. Fourth, as with most other acquisitions, the agency should clearly specify its goals, requirements, and performance standards and develop a scope of work that strikes a balance among the needs for specificity, accountability, flexibility, and learning. Fifth, competition should be promoted during the solicitation and screening stage of the acquisition. Evaluations of vendors should be rigorous, taking into account various sources of information regarding past vendor performance and current capabilities.

Sixth, to the extent possible, contract awards should be based on best value, that is, on a combination of criteria that include cost, effectiveness, timeliness, service coverage, and customer satisfaction, and not just lowest bid. Seventh, the agency should establish clear and challenging performance benchmarks and monitor vendor performance using a range of sources of performance feedback in an iterative and dynamic process, where learning, change, and innovation can occur, and with payments tied to performance (see Coggburn 2007; Lawther et al. 2004). Eighth, the ongoing relationship must be managed effectively, with performance problems and contract disputes handled in a constructive and collaborative manner and with effort by the contracting parties to build mutual trust. Finally, a transition plan should be in place to minimize service disruptions at the end of a contract.

Most forms of government contracting, not just contracting for HRM services, pose difficult challenges for public managers operating in an era of new governance.

Indeed, managing the web of relationships associated with the multiparty governance demands more in terms of communication and collaboration than in the past. Moreover, contracts have become increasingly larger in scale and scope. The recent initiatives of the outsourcing of social services in Texas and Indiana underscore this trend and the shift toward the preference for contracting with large consortiums rather than single partners. These contracts also go beyond the usual nonservices procurement and administrative support services. For-profit consortiums become part of the service delivery and operations function that was once the exclusive province of government or nonprofit contractors. This outsourcing trend is of interest to many states (Goldsmith and Eggers 2004: 21; Cohen and Eimicke 2008; Van Slyke 2007). The public managers involved in negotiating these contracts find themselves interacting with a broad array of actors, including elected and appointed officials, multiple agencies, contractors, subcontractors, advisory boards, and a mix of for-profit and nonprofit groups. In Texas the contract involved several private and nonprofit organizations working together for an umbrella group, Accenture LLP. Consortiums are also typical of government contracts for infrastructure (e.g., parking meters, toll roads, and skyways), which are also increasing in popularity. For example, the recent contract with the city of Indianapolis to privatize its parking meters involves a team of organizations, comprised of the Xerox-affiliated subsidiary Affiliated Computer Services (ACS) and several local organizations, including Denison Global Parking, ParkIndy, and Evens Time.

Agranoff (2012) discusses how the multiorganizational arrangements that have become central to the delivery of public services have changed the nature of public management. Shared authority and mutual adjustment are at the core of successful collaboration. The public manager that develops and maintains essential conduits of communication with a network of partners can encourage mutual understanding, flexibility, and innovation. This is the essence of what Agranoff calls a "conductive" agency, and by extension the key to a conductive (and effective) public manager.

Certainly public managers can draw important lessons from these experiences. Why did they fail? Should these programs have been privatized in the first place? Could they have been saved? Such lessons go to the heart of contract decision making, contract design, and implementation. Newspaper accounts and post mortem analyses point to many contracting mistakes. The contracting literature also includes lessons relevant to scoping contracts to attract more competition, improving vendor selection, and recognizing potential implementation problems as early as possible and before they spell disaster, among others (Johnston and Romzek 2010; Cohen and Eimicke 2008; Kelman 2002; Brown, Potoski, and Van Slyke 2006; Hodge and Greve 2004; Fernandez 2009; Malatesta and Smith 2011, 2012a, 2012b). Yet the experiences in these cases also point to the practical importance of engaging the many stakeholders, including the federal government and the public.

Consider the importance of communicating with the federal government in the social service cases. The federal government has an important role in health care services; as partial funders of TANF and Medicare they are partners with the states in delivering many social services. The federal government also rewards and penalizes states for poor performance. Yet records show that the federal government was engaged little or not at all in the early stages of consideration. Indiana had actually received high performance awards from the U.S. Department of Health and Human Services for program performances in previous years. However, there is nothing on the record to suggest that officials budgeted for possible differences in awards (or fines) when considering the privatization plan. When the contract was cancelled the federal government was considering sanctioning the FSSA for poor performance. Likewise, in Texas, officials did not attempt to obtain the approval of the USDA before proceeding with the contract, although there were questions as to the statutory requirements for approval. When Texas cancelled the contract with Accenture, the state was facing fines of $3.96 million dollars from the federal government for claims processing errors. These examples underscore

the importance of interagency communication, whether or not their approval is required. What Bardach (1998) calls "interagency collaborative capacity" is at a premium in a contracted and networked state. The lesson here is that upward channels of communication are not optional but an imperative. In a contracted and networked state it is essential to maintain communication channels with partner agencies that encourage cooperation, mutual understanding and friendly dispositions (Agranoff 2012). The public manager who consistently engages other agencies has a better chance of sharing ownership of successes and failures.

In a contracted state, public managers can be the main connection to the community. Conductive managers also connect outward to the public (Agranoff 2012). This being the case, public managers must develop the capacity to engage the public at every stage of the contracting process. As Goss (2001) notes, conductive agencies think about their roles and responsibilities to the wider community. This means public managers have an important role in engaging the public, for example by way of town meetings and opportunities to provide comment on agency websites, but also in carefully assessing the implications for the public when these initiatives are being considered. In Indiana once the contract was cancelled, lawmakers were criticized for not engaging the public at length or early enough in the process. The experience in both Indiana and Texas suggest that the consequences of poor program management on the public welfare were not fully understood or considered. In both states, mismanagement of the privatized system resulted in the loss of an important safety net for many; eligible claims were delayed or denied and there were even deaths reportedly connected to the mismanagement. The voices of mid-level public managers, those who had a direct role in overseeing these programs before they were privatized, would have been especially valuable when privatization was being considered. These managers were in the best position to understand the advantages and disadvantages of privatizing the system. They were in the best position to assess the contracts and the potential shortfalls; they could likely foresee potential glitches in the implementation, the possibilities of staff turnover, diminished employee morale, and even what it would take to transition the programs back to government if they failed.

As the programs are rolled out, managers work with a web of contractors, subcontractors, other government agencies, and nonprofits. Contracting with a web of partners also means that training cannot be directed to a single party, even if a primary contractor is named. For example, reports in Texas indicate that subcontractors lacked training and did not fully understand federal and state welfare laws, which contributed to errors in claims processing and ultimately to contract failure. These examples and others make clear that a public manager must develop the skills to successfully navigate many relationships. Communication with diverse groups many who have competing interests is no small task. In addition, training must extend to the entire web of partners.

The involvement of a diverse array of nonprofit groups further complicates the management. First, from the public's viewpoint the separation between government and nonprofits are increasingly difficult to distinguish. In social service delivery systems, nonprofits are a primary vehicle for delivery and the point of contact for citizens. Nonprofits and government share aspects of daily operations of these programs. The interdependencies created in these contracts put the public manager and the delivery agency in a position of interacting regularly over day-to-day operations and such issues as rate reimbursement, program regulations, and reimbursement as well as employee hiring and training, which affect both organizations.

As Agranoff (2012: 66) so aptly points out, the contemporary public manager is a "conductive manager." The planning, organizing, staffing, directing, coordinating, reporting, and budgeting skills we affectionately refer to as "POSDCORB" have been replaced by a more complicated, iterative, and creative set of processes. Hunter et al. (2008), for example, emphasizes several characteristics of the process that are relevant to the role of the networked manager: enlisting different partners;

gathering and synthesizing information; framing (visioning and creating principles); and mobilizing into action. Honing theses skills comes with the new territory.

GOVERNMENT CONTRACTING AS AN INSTRUMENT FOR PROMOTING SOCIAL EQUITY

To this point we have discussed trends in government contracting and some of the challenges it brings, for government personnel in general and for the public manager. It seems fitting to conclude with the possibility that government contracting may also provide a means to achieve social equity. While this is rarely the primary rationale or stated goal of any contracting initiative, it has been institutionalized as an important secondary consideration. Recent research proposes that demographic representation within the bureaucracy as well as rules and regulations can lead to more equitable decision making, which in turn benefits historically disadvantaged groups. That is, more minority representation in public agencies, along with formal rules institutionalizing equity as an identifiable goal, will stimulate contract awards to minority-owned businesses. From a societal perspective, contracting acts as a mechanism for leveling decades-old barriers that have limited the economic vitality of historically disadvantaged groups. Equitable contracting, particularly when coupled with the more traditional rationales described above, can lead to positive externalities for society. For example, contracting with small minority-owned businesses bolsters economic activity in minority communities in need of economic development. Equitable contracting also highlights another reason for public managers to take diversity in the workplace seriously. In this section we describe how diversity in hiring can affect procurement decisions, particularly when such decisions are guided by formal rules mandating equity in the process. We begin by providing a brief overview of the theory of representative bureaucracy.

Representative bureaucracy is a theory of bureaucratic politics (Frederickson et al. 2012). It seeks to reconcile the seemingly undemocratic nature of public bureaucracies within democratic systems of governance. Unlike bureaucratic control theories that rely on overhead control mechanisms (see Meier and Bohte 2006) or codes of professionalism (Friedrich 1941), representative bureaucracy posits that when public organizations mirror the constituents they serve, they will act in ways that are beneficial to the constituents and thus will be more responsive and democratic. Theorists initially considered how class differences in Britain might affect bureaucratic outcomes (Kingsley 1944), whereas recent research focuses on race and gender diversity as predictors of policy outputs. The goal is to identify when demographic representation—otherwise known as passive representation—leads to actual policy outputs that benefit citizens who are passively represented. Such "active representation" ensues when bureaucrats have considerable discretion in decision making and when the policy issue is salient to the demographic group in question (Keiser et al. 2002: 556).

In the empirical research, hypotheses regarding racial representation and policy outputs have witnessed consistent support in the literature (Meier 1993; Selden 1997; Wilkins and Williams 2008). Explicitly, racial representation within public agencies appears to lead to policy outputs favoring racial subgroups within the population. The empirical support for hypotheses regarding gender representation is less convincing (Keiser et al. 2002; Meier and Nicholson-Crotty 2006). Recent research suggests gender may have a more nuanced effect than race; it's more a question of *when* gender representation matters and not *if* gender representation matters (see Keiser et al. 2002).

These empirical findings generally hold in the contracting domain. Research on federal procurement has found that an increase in minority representation in the Senior Executive Service results in more contracting with small disadvantaged businesses, which are minority-owned firms (Smith and Fernandez 2010). However, similar to other policy domains, gender representation does not always lead to increases in contracting with women-owned businesses (Fernandez, Malatesta, and Smith 2013). Despite the mixed findings, there does appear to be enough evidence to suggest that public managers should take diversity seriously, given that it affords a pathway for maintaining democratic accountability. Demographic diversity without formal preference policies in place to mandate transparent and equitable procurement, however, may result in suboptimal outcomes.

Both federal and state governments have formal policies in place to ensure that historical patterns of discrimination do not persist. The federal government has instituted the Small Disadvantaged Business (SDB) and the Women Owned Small Business (WOSB) programs to ensure the historically disadvantaged businesses have access to the procurement process. The SDB Program targets small businesses owned by members of racial minority groups. In the past, the program has offered two benefits to qualifying firms: the price evaluation adjustment (PEA), and the evaluation factor or subfactor. However, the PEA, which provided a 10% price benefit given to qualifying firms bidding as prime contractors was suspended in 2004. The second benefit, the evaluation factor or subfactor, grants qualified prime contractors a credit when planning to use small disadvantaged businesses as subcontractors (FAR Subpart 19.12). Similar to the SDB program, the WOSB program is intended to improve women-owned firms' ability to compete for federal contracts. The WOSB program permits procurement officials to set aside acquisitions for certified women-owned small businesses, given that they meet the program's criteria. The set asides are only to be used in industries where women-owned small businesses have been underrepresented (see Fernandez et al. 2013 for a more detailed overview of the programs).

Some state governments have instituted similar policies for equitable contracting. In fact, the trend for including preference policies at the state level appears to be on the rise. According to the National Association of State Procurement Official's (NASPO) 2009 Survey of State Government Purchasing Practices, policies for providing preference for minority- and women-owned firms has increased considerably between 2007 and 2009. In 2009, 13 states followed vendor-based price preferences for minorities (compared to 5 states in 2007) and 11 states allowed vendor-based price preferences for women-owned firms in 2009 (compared with four states in 2007). Also, 21 states included women-owned firms in their definition of minority-owned firms, suggesting that states view women and minorities as similarly disadvantaged in public sector contracting (NASPO 2009).

To summarize, contracting out goods and services provides governments with more than potential cost savings; it can also act as an instrument for achieving social equity. Given the increase in contracting in recent years, it is important that HRM managers continue to maintain diversity both inside public agencies and within its supply of potential contractors, as increasing diversity can help promote equity in the government procurement arena.

CONCLUSION

In this chapter, we reviewed several of the main issues and challenges relating to human resources management that are encountered in the government contracting arena. We reviewed evidence pertaining to the effects of government outsourcing on public sector employment. Contracting out does appear to negatively impact full-time employment in the public sector, although this is partly offset by increases in part-time employment. Not surprisingly, public sector employees and unions are ardent opponents of outsourcing initiatives and have been found to successfully employ a variety of tactics to block such initiatives from going forward. In our discussion, we recommended various steps public managers and elected officials can take to reduce such resistance and make the contracting process less adversarial and more collaborative. We also reviewed the growing practice of outsourcing human resources management services, the challenges involved in undertaking this form of contracting, and its advantages.

In the chapter we also discussed how contracting out has helped redefine the role of the public manager in terms of the knowledge, skills, and abilities needed to be an effective manager in an era where governments increasingly rely on external actors and networks of service providers and partners to conduct the public's business. Finally, we explored how different forms of passive bureaucratic representation can promote equity in the government procurement arena. Space limitations preclude examining other important HRM issues associated with government outsourcing, including the practice and consequences of competitive sourcing and public-private competitions, managing reductions in force (RIF) that are initiated in response to government outsourcing, and the courts' evolving thought on the state actor doctrine and its implications.

The importance of understanding and managing these issues is likely to grow in the future, as the practice of government contracting is unlikely to diminish. In the early part of this century, we saw the growth in government contracting taper off, particularly contracting with for-profit and nonprofit firms, although the frequency of intergovernmental contracting continued to rise (Warner and Hefetz, 2009). The practice of contracting back in, or insourcing, due to contract failure and organizational learning has now become nearly as common as that of contracting out. However, in recent years, we have witnessed a renewed interest in government outsourcing for larger-scale infrastructure development projects, like toll roads and parking meters, and public services, like welfare enrollment and corrections. In the aftermath of the Great Recession but in an ongoing period of fiscal austerity, public officials in many jurisdictions will continue to consider outsourcing initiatives to ease their fiscal distress.

REFERENCES

Agranoff, R. 2012. *Collaborating to Manage: A Primer for the Public Sector.* Washington, DC: Georgetown University Press.

American Federation of State, County, and Municipal Services. 2005. *Report on Proposal to Restructure/ Privatize the Indiana Family Social Services Administration.* October 2005. http://www.inthepublicinterest.org/sites/default/files/AFSCME_Report_on_FSSA.pdf.

Bardach, E. 1998. *Getting Agencies to Work Together.* Washington, DC: Brookings Institution Press.

Battaglio, R. P., and C. B. Ledvinka. 2007. Privatizing Human Resources in the Public Sector: Legal Challenges to

Outsourcing the Human Resource Functions. *Review of Public Personnel Administration*, 27, 293–307.

Becker, F. W., G. Silverstein, and L. Chaykin. 1995. Public Employee Job Security and Benefits: A Barrier to Privatization of Mental Health Services. *Public Productivity and Management Review*, 19, 25–33.

Boyne, G. A. 1998. Bureaucratic Theory Meets Reality: Public Choice and Service Contracting in U.S. Local Government. *Public Administration Review*, 58, 474.

Bradford, R. 2004. Outsourcing HR for State and Local Government: A Review of the Business Case and Challenges of Outsourcing State Functions. https://www.fasttrackabm.com/fasttrackpublic/SampleArticles/HR%20Outsourcing%20-%20Florida.pdf.

Brown, T., M. Potoski, and D. Van Slyke. 2006. Managing Public Service Contracts, Aligning Values, Institutions, and Markets. *Public Administration Review*, 66, 323–331.

Center for Public Policy Priorities. 2006. *Updating and Outsourcing Enrollment in Public Benefits: The Texas Experience.* http:www.cppp.org.

Chandler, T., and P. Feuille. 1991. Municipal Unions and privatization. *Public Administration Review*, 51, 15–22.

Coggburn, J. D. 2007. Outsourcing Human Resources: The Case of the Texas Health and Human Services Commission. *Review of Public Personnel Administration*, 27, 315–335.

———. 2009. Outsourcing Human Resources: Problems and Prospects for the Public Sector. In S. W. Hays, Kearney, R. C. and J. D. Coggburn (Eds.), *Public Personnel Administration* (5th ed.). Upper Saddle River, NJ: Prentice Hall.

Cohen, S., and W. Eimicke. 2008. *The Responsible Contract Manager*. Washington, DC: Georgetown University Press.

Csoko, L. S. 1995. *Rethinking Human Resources: A Research Report*. The Conference Board, Report No: 1124-95-RR.

Dell, D. 2004. *HR Outsourcing: Benefits, Challenges, and Trends*. The Conference Board, R-1347-04-RR.

Dilger, R. J., R. R. Moffett, and L. Struyk. 1997. Privatization of Municipal Services in America's Largest Cities. *Public Administration Review*, 57, 21–26.

Donahue, J. D. 2002. The Problem of Public Jobs. In J. Nye and D. Donahue (Eds.), *Market-Based Governance: Supply Side, Demand Side, Upside, and Downside*. Washington, DC: Brookings Institution Press.

Duffy, P. 2011. Privatizing Public Libraries in California, Unions Opposed. *HULIQ*, August 16.

Eggers, W. D., and J. O'Leary. 1994. Overcoming Public Employee Opposition to Privatization. *Business Forum*, 19, 16–20.

Elam, L. B. 1997. Reinventing Government Privatization Style: Avoiding the Pitfalls of Replacing Civil Servants with Contract Providers. *Public Personnel Management*, 26, 15–29.

Fernandez, Sergio. 2009. Understanding Contracting Performance: An Empirical Analysis. *Administration and Society*, 41, 67–100.

Fernandez, S., H. G. Rainey, and C. E. Lowman. 2006. Privatization and Its Implications for Human Resource Management. In Riccucci, Norma M. (Ed.), *Public Personnel Management: Current Concerns, Future Challenges*, 4th edition. New York: Longman, 204–224.

Fernandez, Sergio, D. Malatesta, and C. Smith. 2013. Race, Gender, and Government Contracting: Different Explanations or New Prospects for Theory? *Public Administration Review*, 73, 109–120.

Fernandez, S., J. E. Ryu, and J. L. Brudney. 2008. Exploring Variations in Contracting for Services among American Local Governments: Do Politics Still Matter? *American Review of Public Administration*, 38, 439–462.

Fernandez, S., and C. R. Smith. 2006. Looking for Evidence of Public Employee Opposition to Privatization: An Empirical Study with Implications for Practice. *Review of Public Personnel Administration*, 26, 356–381.

Fernandez, S., C. R. Smith, and J. B. Wenger. 2007. Employment, Privatization, and Managerial Choice: Does Contracting Out Reduce Public Sector Employment? *Journal of Policy Analysis and Management*, 26, 57–77.

Ferris, J., and E. Graddy. 1986. Contracting Out: For What? With Whom? *Public Administration Review*, 46, 332–344.

Frederickson, H. G., K. B. Smith, C. W. Larimer, and M. Licari. 2012. *The Public Administration Theory Primer*. Boulder, CO: Westview Press.

Friedrich, C. 1941. *The Nature of Administrative Responsibility*. Cambridge, MA: Harvard University Press.

GAO (General Accounting Office). (2004). *Human capital: Selected agencies' use of alternative service delivery options for human capital activities* (GAO-04-679). Washington, DC: GAO. http://www.gao.gov/assets/250/243108.pdf

GAO (Government Accountability Office). 2011. *State and Local Governments. Knowledge of Past Recessions Can Inform Future Federal Fiscal Assistance*. Report GAO-11-401. March 2011. Washington, DC: GAO.

Goldsmith, S., and W. D. Eggers. 2004. *Governing by Network*. Washington, DC: Brookings Institution Press.

Goss, S. 2001. *Managing Local Governance Work. Networks, Relationships, and the Managements of Change*. Basingstoke, UK: Palgrave.

Greene, J. D. 2002. *Cities and Privatization: Prospects for the New Century*. Upper Saddle River, NJ: Prentice Hall.

Hefetz, A., and M. Warner. 2004. Privatization and Its Reverse: Explaining the Dynamics of the Government Contracting Process. *Journal of Public Administration Research and Theory*, 14, 171–190.

Hodge, G. A. 2000, *Privatization: An International Review of Performance*, Boulder, CO: Westview Press.

Hodge, G., and C. Greve. 2004. Public-Private Partnerships: An International Performance Review. *Public Administration Review*, 67, 545–558.

Hunter, M. R., M. Agranoff, J. McGuire, J. Greenbaum, M. Morrison, M. Cohen, and J. Liu. 2008. *Metro High School: An Emerging STEM Community. Report for Grant 420038AC-07*. Columbus: PAST Foundation/Battelle Center for Mathematics and Science Education Policy.

International City/County Management Association (ICMA). 1989. *Service Delivery in the 90s: Alternative Approaches for Local Government*. Washington, DC: ICMA.

Jackson, C. Y. 1997. Strategies for Managing Tensions Between Public Employment and Private Service Delivery. *Public Productivity and Management Review*, 21, 119–136.

Jalette, P., and R. Hebdon. 2012. Unions and Privatization: Opening the "Black Box." *Industrial and Labor Relations Review*, 65, 17–35.

Jang, H. 2006. Contracting Out Local Government Services to Nonprofit Organizations. *International Journal of Public Administration*, 29, 799–818.

Johnston, J., and B. Romzek. 2010. *The Promises, Performance and Pitfalls of Government Contracting*. The Oxford Handbook of American Bureaucracy, edited by Robert F. Durant. New York: Oxford University Press.

Keiser, L. R., V. M. Wilkins, K. J. Meier, and C. A. Holland. 2002. Lipstick and Logarithms: Gender, Institutional Context, and Representative Bureaucracy. *American Political Science Review*, 96, 553–564.

Kelman, S. 2002. Contracting, In *The Tools of Government*, edited by Lester M. Salamon. New York: Oxford University Press.

Kenny, H., and A. Summers. 2011. *Annual Privatization Report. 2011: Local Government Privatization*. Reason Foundation. http://reason.org/apr2011.

Kingsley, D. 1944. *Representative Bureaucracy: An Interpretation of the British Civil Service*. Yellow Springs, OH: Antioch Press.

Klaas, B. S., J. McClendon, and T. W. Gainey. 1999. HR Outsourcing and Its Impact: The Role of Transaction Costs. *Personnel Psychology*, 52, 113–136.

Koch, J. 2004. *HR Outsourcing in Government Organizations: Emerging Trends, Early Lessons*. The Conference Board, E-0007-04-RR.

Lawrence, J. 2012. Florida Local Stops Privatization Scheme. American Federation of State, County and Municipal Employees, *Blog*, March 27, 2012.

Lawther, E. E., D. Ulrich, J. Fitz-Enz, and J. C. Madden. 2004. *Human Resources Business Process Outsourcing: How HR Gets Its Work Done*. San Francisco: Jossey-Bass.

Lawther, W. C. 2003. Privatizing Personnel: Outsourcing Public Sector Functions. In S. W. Hays and R. C. Kearney (Eds.), *Public Personnel Administration* (4th ed., pp. 196–208). Upper Saddle River, NJ: Prentice Hall.

Malatesta, Deanna, and Craig R. Smith. 2011. Resource Dependence, Alternative Supply Sources and the Design of Formal Contracts. *Public Administration Review*, 71, 608–617.

———. 2012a. Balancing Hazards and the Design of Local Franchise Contracts. *Urban Affairs Review*, 48, 615–641.

———. 2012b. Government Contracts for Legal Services. Does a Previous Contracting Relationship Alter Accountability? *State & Local Government Review*, 44, 113–126.

Meier, K. J. 1993. Latinos and Representative Bureaucracy: Testing the Thompson and Henderson Hypotheses. *Journal of Public Administration Research and Theory*, 3, 393–414.

Meier, K. J., and J. Bohte. 2006. *Politics and the Bureaucracy: Policy Making in the Fourth Branch of Government*. 5th ed. Belmont, CA: Thompson Wadsworth.

Meier, K. J., and J. Nicholson-Crotty. 2006. Gender, Representative Bureaucracy, and Law Enforcement: The Case of Sexual Assault. *Public Administration Review*, 66, 850–860.

Meier, K. J., and J. Stewart. 1992. The Impact of Representative Bureaucracies: Educational Systems and Public Policies. *American Review of Public Administration*, 22, 157–171.

Naff, K. C. 1991. Labor-Management Relations and Privatization: A Federal Perspective. *Public Administration Review*, 51, 23–30.

National Academy of Public Administration. 1996. *Alternative Administrative Service Delivery: Improving the Efficiency and Effectiveness of Human Resources Services. Implementing Real Change in Human Resources Management, Phase II: Practical Applications*. Washington, DC: NAPA.

———. 1997. *Alternative Service Delivery: A Viable Strategy for Federal Government Human Resources Management.* Implementing Real Change in Human Resources Management, Phase III: Practical Tools. Washington, DC: NAPA.

National Association of State Procurement Officials. 2009. *Survey of State Government Purchasing Practices.* Lexington, KY: NASPO.

National Commission for Employment Policy. 1988. *Privatization and Public Employees: The Impact of City and County Contracting Out on Government Workers.* Washington, DC: Dudek and Company for NCEP.

National Governors Association. 2012. *The Fiscal Survey of the States. An Update of State Fiscal Conditions.* http://www.nga.org/files/ive/sites/nga/files/pdf/FSS1212.pdf.

Nelson Staffing. 2004. Outsourcing Your Human Resources Functions. http://www.nelsonstaffing.com/files/2010/02/NFC_Outsourcing_WP_07.pdf

Pack, J. R. 1987. Privatization of Public-Sector Services in Theory, Practice. *Journal of Policy Analysis and Management,* 6, 523–540.

Privatization Watch. 2012. http://www.privatization.org. Accessed October 5, 2012.

Rainey, H. G. 2005. Human Resource Consultants and Outsourcing: Focusing on Local Government. In S. E. Condrey (Ed.). *Handbook of Human Resource Management in Government.* 2nd ed. San Francisco: Jossey-Bass, 701–734.

Selden, S. C. 1997. *The Promise of Representative Bureaucracy: Diversity and Responsiveness in a Government Agency.* Armonk, NY: M.E. Sharpe.

Siegel, G. B. 1999. Where Are We on Local Government Service Contracting? *Public Productivity and Management Review,* 22, 365–388.

Smith, C. R., and S. Fernandez. 2010. Equity in Federal Contracting: Examining the Link between Minority Representation and Federal Procurement Decisions. *Public Administration Review,* 70, 87–96.

Society for Human Resource Management (SHRM). 2004. *Human Resource Outsourcing: Is It Here to Stay?* Alexandria, VA: SHRM.

Stein, R. M. 1990. *Urban Alternatives: Public and Private Markets in the Provision of Local Services.* Pittsburgh: University of Pittsburgh Press.

Sunno, B. P., and Laabs, J. J. 1994. Winning Strategies for Outsourcing Contracts. *Personnel Journal,* 73, 69–76.

Vail, B. 2012. Pennsylvania Politicians Push Broad Privatization Agenda, But Unions Are Pushing Back—Hard. *In These Times,* June 26.

Van Slyke, D. 2007. Agents or Stewards: Government Nonprofit Service Contracting Relationship. *Journal of Public Administration Research and Theory,* 17, 157–187.

Warner, M. E., and Hefetz, A. 2009. Cooperative Competition: Alternative Service Delivery, 2002–2007. In ICMA (Ed.), *The Municipal Year Book 2009.* Washington, DC: International City County Management Association, 11–20.

Wilkins, V., and Williams, B. 2008. Black or Blue: Racial Profiling and Representative Bureaucracy. *Public Administration Review,* 68, 654–664.

CHAPTER 25

HUMAN RESOURCE MANAGEMENT ISSUES WITH SOCIAL MEDIA

Shannon H. Tufts
University of North Carolina at Chapel Hill

Willow S. Jacobson
University of North Carolina at Chapel Hill

INTRODUCTION

Due to the massive proliferation of social media, its use by both individuals and organizations for personal and professional reasons has come to the forefront as a critical issue at the intersection of human resources and information technology. Social media has been defined as "a group of Internet-based applications that build on the ideological and technological foundations of Web 2.0, and that allow the creation and exchange of user-generated content" (Kaplan and Haenlein 2010). The hallmark applications found in the social media landscape include Facebook, Twitter, LinkedIn, Flickr, FourSquare, MySpace, Pinterest, and hundreds of others.

Facebook is consistently viewed as the leader among social media tools, and recent metrics solidify its utility and importance in the lives of individual and organizational users. Current estimates place the number of Facebook users at over 900 million people, with over 51% of all Internet-using people 12 years and older in the United States having a Facebook account (Facebook 2012). With over half of the American population participating on Facebook, the platform offers governments a unique opportunity to efficiently engage and inform citizens in lean economic times (Grossman 2010). Governments have been capitalizing on the opportunity for citizen communication and connection offered by the social media outlets. In fact, a recent study conducted by Stateline.org indicates that 47 of the 50 U.S. governors have a social media presence for official governmental communications, with Facebook pages and Twitter accounts being the most frequently used tools (Mahling 2011).

The proliferation of social media forms and use has been unprecedented (Lenhart et al. 2010). At the same time, the recruitment, development, and management of human capital in organizations are more important than ever. To effectively address these challenges, HR professionals must balance the legal, cultural, and value considerations in helping the organization achieve its strategic objectives (Pynes 2009). Social media tools, practices, and abuses create additional challenges within all workplaces. This new medium does not fundamentally alter the nature of the human resources department's work, but it does change the medium, reach, speed, and permanency of employee actions, from pre-employment through transition out of the organization, thereby impacting HR efforts for managing employee performance.

Many organizations are still trying to determine how they will leverage social media for HR functions for employee management as well as how they will address employee social media usage and conduct, on and off duty, in HR policies. Much of the previous research has focused on leveraging social media for pre-employment recruitment or screening, and creating policies that protect the employer (Cohen and Cohen 2007). However, there is limited research on HR management of employee performance throughout the employment lifecycle with respect to this new form of communication and engagement, and there are many unanswered questions for government organizations around how to manage both social media and employees (Jacobson and Tufts 2013).

This chapter focuses specifically on the human resources function in social media and does not take into consideration issues related to social media use for e-government purposes or civic engagement. (For information on using social media for these purposes, see Mergel 2010). Additionally, this chapter is not focused on employees whose job description includes management of organizational social media sites; rather it is focused on the issues related to employee performance management as an HR function throughout the employment lifecycle for all types of employees.

Social Media and the Human Resources Function

As the chapter progresses, the following employment lifecycle framework will be used to think about social media as a tool for human resources but also to highlight challenges and opportunities related to social media at each stage (see Figure 25.1). The HR function touches employees from the point that a position need is identified (human capital planning) to when an employee leaves the organization either voluntarily or involuntarily (separation).

Currently, social media is having the largest impact on three of the stages of the employee lifecycle. This

Figure 25.1 Employment Lifecycle

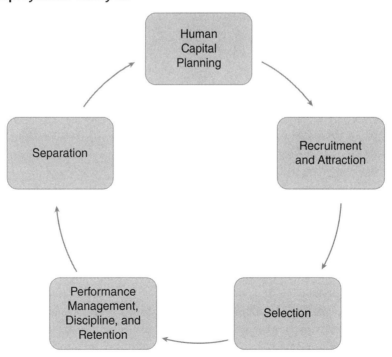

chapter will focus on those stages, namely recruitment and attraction; selection; and performance management, discipline, and retention.

RECRUITMENT AND ATTRACTION: APPLICANT IDENTIFICATION AND INTEREST MANAGEMENT

At the beginning of the 21st century, many governments moved to posting employment opportunities on their organizational website as well as online job boards like Monster.com (Llorens and Kellough 2007). The explosion of social media in the past five years has opened additional platforms for attracting and recruiting talent as well as posting employment opportunities. Many social media platforms, as well as private consultants, are hosting webinars or workshops to train recruiters in the use of social media (e.g., sessions of GovLoop's popular webinar series DigitalGov University; Nelson 2012). This shift has not negated the need for posting employment opportunities on the organization's website, but rather it adds another medium for reaching diverse audiences. As more people leverage social media sites like Facebook, LinkedIn, Twitter, and Pinterest on a daily, if not hourly basis, HR professionals and recruiters are turning to those sites to identify and attract talented applicants for their organization.

According to a 2011 survey by the Society for Human Resource Management (SHRM), 56% of HR professionals said they use social networking sites to recruit candidates, up from 34% in 2008 (SHRM 2011). Ninety-five percent of HR professionals polled in 2011 said they use LinkedIn, 58% use Facebook, and 42% indicate they use Twitter. Facebook is the leading social media platform, in terms of sheer number of subscribers, hence many HR professionals utilize it for advertising open positions as well as actively recruiting targeted individuals. LinkedIn is a more traditional choice for applicant identification and recruitment, as the site is designed as a professional networking tool, with the ability to list skills, offer endorsements and recommendations on individual's abilities, and provide both reference points and connections between various LinkedIn members to allow for

a more detailed analysis of possible matches for positions. Recent proliferation of Twitter usage, particularly among younger professionals, has also led to an increase in job announcements and targeted recruitment from its members. The use of social media platforms for applicant identification, attraction, and recruitment allows organizations to tap into new applicant pools that may have been previously missed. Additionally, there is clear evidence that these new platforms allow the organization to reach newer generations of applicants, who may participate more actively on these sites.

Organizations are consistently leveraging more social media platforms to recruit qualified applicants for open positions. As previously noted, LinkedIn, Facebook, and Twitter are the most common platforms for recruiting potential applicants and job posting. However, as social media platforms emerge, new opportunities for talent identification emerge. In fact, the technology company VMWare Inc. has over a dozen social media recruiters whose sole function is to identify and recruit talented applicants from a host of social media platforms, including LinkedIn, Facebook, Google+, and Twitter (Azevedo 2012). These employees are in addition to the company's traditional recruiting staff. Furthermore, many organizations—including governmental entities—are using social media platforms as a way to showcase their work environment and the work being performed by their employees, particularly through video blogs and image sharing. This provides potential applicants a feel for the organization, its community, and its employees and creates a level of familiarity and attraction for the organization.

As with the use of any new recruitment and attraction vehicles, social media platforms also offer some unique challenges for HR professionals. As noted in the VMWare example, there is a substantial level of management required to fully leverage social media for applicant identification and attraction. To effectively manage these efforts, the HR professionals need to develop new skills to operate in this new digital framework. For example, writing an attractive job posting announcement in 140 characters or less to feed to

Twitter is quite difficult but required given the amount of tweets that such a posting would compete with in any given timeframe. One solution to this problem is to create channels for social media engagement of potential applicants, such as a Twitter account established solely for posting job opportunities, instead of feeding such job postings through the normal government Twitter account, which will also be featuring information about upcoming events, board meetings, and more. Another potential challenge associated with leveraging these social media platforms is the movement toward fee-based services on many social media sites. For example, LinkedIn offers premium services to its subscribers for a monthly fee. If the government is not willing to fund those additional costs, it may limit the applicant pool available for active, targeted recruitment. Additionally, the challenges associated with integrating and revising recruitment plans designed to effectively target various qualified applicants with diverse backgrounds can be complex when leveraging a social media platform that may not be used by some potential candidates. Many of these issues related to recruitment and attraction are not fundamentally altered by the use of social media; rather this new medium offers another vehicle for hiring authorities to consider and manage.

One of the most commonly expressed concerns or challenges associated with using social media for attracting and identifying potential job applicants is the limited number of metrics (see Ammons' chapter in this volume) organizations track related to the impact of these methods. HR departments and professionals should be using standard metrics to determine if these platforms lead to greater numbers of qualified applicants. Additionally, they should be assessing if employee recruitment, selection, and retention is positively impacted by the use of social media tools. In some cases, organizations that have traditionally used search firms for targeted applicant identification and recruitment have noted that social media platforms, like LinkedIn and Facebook, are offering better results with substantially lower costs to the organization than the use of search firms. For example, the head of global brand and

talent attraction at Expedia, Jeremy Langhans, notes, "When I looked at the ROI (return on investment) from our different channels such as LinkedIn, our own website and agencies, I realized we were hiring more people through social media than through agencies" (Azevedo 2012). Governmental entities need to assess the benefits and impact of leveraging social media platforms in order to determine where to most effectively target their attraction and recruitment efforts. In addition, special attention should be paid by HR professionals to ensuring a diverse recruitment effort, and the social media platforms should be only one of multiple attraction and recruitment strategies in order to avoid potential bias and limited audience reach. Managers want to be sure the use of social media, or any recruitment effort, is appropriate for the position, targeted candidates, and broader recruitment plan. Using social media is an additional, not a replacement, activity.

SELECTION: USING SOCIAL MEDIA TO SCREEN AND ACCESS CANDIDATES

The purpose of the selection process is to predict the performance of candidates and choose the best performer. This process involves designing assessment tools and processes that will provide decision makers with the needed data to determine who will be the best performer. Gathering relevant and focused information about candidates is critical to this process. More and more employers are turning to social media outlets to gather this information. While these resources can be important sources they are not without managerial risk—both legally and ethically. Reppler, a social media monitoring service, conducted a survey in 2011 of 300 hiring professionals exploring if, when, and how they are using social media to screen job applicants. Results indicate that 91% of the recruiters and hiring managers stated they have used social networking sites to screen prospective employees. Moreover, 69% disclosed that they did not hire a job applicant due to the content on the applicant's social media site (Wu 2012).

The Reppler study reports figures were on the high end of other studies; still, the use of social media for screening (and decision-making purposes) continues to be on the rise. A 2012 resurvey of members of the International Public Management Association for Human Resources found that 61% of respondents indicated that they do not use social media/Google searches to investigate job applicants. A CareerBuilder survey discovered that over a third of hiring managers researched job candidates using social media, and two-thirds of the hiring mangers used Facebook as a primary source. Furthermore, "34 % of hiring managers said they had come across something that caused them not to hire a candidate. In nearly half of these cases, the person posted a provocative photo or had made reference to drinking or drug use" (CareerBuilder 2012).

Social media outlets may provide a wealth of information about candidates and assist in the important decision of person-organization fit, potential benefits need to be carefully considered in light of the risks, namely discrimination concerns, associated with these practices.

Discrimination Claims (Issues with Title VII)

Issues of merit hiring are at the core of public service practices and laws. From the Pendleton Act through the ADA legislation issues related to fair, equitable and nonbias hiring are central to public personnel management, laws, and regulations. As new opportunities are made available to employers for gaining information on candidates, employers need to pay close attention to privacy and antidiscrimination laws. Employers will need to ensure that they do not make hiring decisions based on protected characteristics of applicants. Many of these characteristics can be quickly identified on social media profiles: "with so many employers conducting pre-employment research on a job applicant's social profile, employers are opening themselves up to discrimination claims under federal, state, and even local laws" (Wu 2012). Wu states the challenge aptly:

By reviewing social networking profiles and information, employers are learning about job applicants' religious beliefs, marital status, family relation-ships, race, ethnicity, medical conditions, and other information that cannot be used to make an employment-based decision—information that is considered "taboo." As a result, employers must take care when performing such research. Ultimately, should a discrimination claim arise, the employer will have the burden of proof to demonstrate that the decision to reject a job applicant was based on a legitimate non-discriminatory reason, rather than the fact that the employer learned of the job applicant's sexual orientation, the projected due date of the job applicant's baby, or any other protected characteristic.

If it is determined that the additional information gained from conducting a social media background check is desired, one recommendation is to have someone not involved in the hiring of the specific position conduct the search; that person can filter out information that may be in a protected class and only provide the search committee with relevant, legal information relevant to the search (Michale 2012).

Requests for Login/Password Information

A specific practice that is gaining attention and concern relates to requesting login/password information from candidates. Numerous news articles have covered the issue of employers who are requiring applicants and employees to provide passwords to their private social media accounts (Kravets 2013). Requiring social media access or passwords is not a wise practice. Maryland passed the first law prohibiting employers from asking for employees' social media passwords and other states have followed suit (Deschenaux 2012). As of May 2013, seven states have outlawed asking for login information, including California, Michigan, Maryland, Arkansas, New Mexico, Utah, and Illinois (Jacobson and Tufts 2013). In addition to legislation on the issue, many potential employers are protesting the practice (CareerBuilder 2012).

In general, employers should think twice, and consult an employment attorney, before establishing a practice of requiring employees and applicants to turn over login information. And, though the law is evolving in this specific area, employers should understand that such a practice might have many "nonlegal" ramifications, like the company losing talented employees or potential employees who refuse to give access to social media login credentials. Furthermore, such policies may lead to lower employee morale, distrust, and other issues. Employers will want to keep track of emerging state and national laws and policies. The National Labor Relations Board (NLRB) cautioned that it believes that numerous common clauses in social media policies violate the National Labor Relations Act (NLRA). Acting General Counsel Lafe Solomon's report outlined six cases where it found clauses in employers' social media policies to violate Section 7 of the NLRA, and it found only one social media policy that was deemed lawful in its entirety.

Having more information available to make informed hiring decisions is a noble objective for any hiring authority; yet the challenge remains that in gaining additional information, especially through social media outlets, can be fraught with problems. "While employers can continue to use social media for recruiting purposes, they should take care not to violate existing laws in the hiring process (and be mindful of the various laws developing in this area as well)" (Michale 2012). Managers need to carefully weigh the need and efficacy of additional information against the legal and ethical issues related to obtaining it.

PERFORMANCE: MANAGING ORGANIZATIONAL CULTURE, EMPLOYEE BEHAVIOR, AND DISCIPLINE

Issues of employee conduct and performance management related to social media sites are filling the courts, media articles, and water cooler conversations. The issue of employee conduct on and off-duty is not a new concern, but this new medium is offering new twists on old challenges. Recent news stories about employee rights and social media use include tales of misconduct coupled with concerns about legal rights.

For example, in Savannah, Georgia, a female firefighter was terminated due to personal photographs placed on her private MySpace page. The chief contended that the firefighter was using her role as a Savannah firefighter to "promote herself as a model for other personal publicity reasons," which violated departmental policy (Skutch 2009). The court upheld the termination and denied the firefighter's claims of discrimination and First Amendment protection. In another case, a Staten Island HR manager was fired due to falsely claiming to be serving jury duty, while her Facebook status indicated she was on vacation in Baltimore (Slattery 2010). Beyond losing her job, she was arrested, charged with jury duty summons forgery, and faces up to 14 years in prison for her crime.

The aforementioned examples speak to a range of issues, including First Amendment rights, Fourth Amendment rights, conduct policies, and discipline and termination practices. At the same time, the use of social media for employers of all kinds is being promoted and greatly lauded. HR departments and professionals face many challenges as they seek to advise, manage, and discipline employees for both professional work-related use of social media and personal off-duty use of social media. Policy, legal, and management concerns are plentiful and add another layer of complexity to the traditional e-government literature by moving the focus from the citizen to the employee.

Policy Issues

The 2011 SHRM survey of employers indicates that only 40% of respondents said their organization has implemented formal social media policies (SHRM 2011). A 2012 study found similar results for state governments, indicating that 23 U.S. states had specific social media policies to govern employee and employer conduct on social media platforms (Jacobson and Tufts 2013). It is imperative that HR departments and professionals work in a collaborative manner with senior management, legal, and IT to develop appropriate policies to govern both organizational and individual use of social media for performance management, retention and discipline. The Center for Technology in Government identified eight essential elements for governmental social media policies (Hrdinová, Helbig, and Peters 2010). The elements it identified provide a solid framework for developing public sector-specific social media policies. They include (1) employee access to social media accounts, (2) account management for organizational or professional social media accounts, (3) acceptable use policies related to employee use of government resources for social media access and posting, (4) employee conduct and behavior clauses, (5) content guidelines, (6) security requirements, (7) legal issues, and (8) citizen conduct policies related to posting content on governmental social media accounts. While policies may act to restrict the specific behaviors and conduct of employees, they also provide clarity of what is permitted, what consequences can be expected, and what protections are in place. Rosenbloom and Bailey (2003) underscore the importance of understanding the legal rights of employees due to the personal liability a state or local government manager may take on for infringing on the constitutional rights of an employee. Substantial research into proper policy formulation has been conducted, and high-quality sample policies can be found in many governmental organizations for replication and refinement.

Legal Issues

While the legal rights of public sector employees do not vary based on form of media, the permanence and prevalence of social media usage has certainly created interesting intersections and challenges between the law and the shifting technological sands. This chapter will briefly cover legal issues related to employee constitutional rights and conduct rules. (For a detailed discussion of constitutional rights of employees, see Rosenbloom and Chanin's chapter in this volume).

First Amendment Issues

In the public sector, employees have a different expectation of free speech. General First Amendment protection in the public sector applies for speech at work, away from work, spoken speech, and speech that is disseminated in other forms of communication; the form of speech is not legally relevant. There is a three-prong test for determining if a public employee's speech is protected under the First Amendment (McLaughlin 2010). First, the speech must touch on a matter of public concern, called the Pickering test, as it arose from *Pickering v. Board of Education* (1968), where the Supreme Court extended protections to public employees' speech when certain conditions were met because of the employees' ability to add substantive contribution to the "free and open debate" of the citizenry (Rosenbloom and Bailey 2003). Second, the speech must fall outside of the employee's job duties, per *Garcetti v. Ceballos* (2006). Third, the employee's interest in free speech must outweigh the government's interest in efficient/effective provision of services.

For the third prong, the courts will consider if the First Amendment interest of the employee outweighs that of the efficient and effective provision of services by the government. In recent cases related to social media and public employees, there have been two significant trends related to this balancing test. If an employee is posting on a personal Facebook account while at work about matters of public concern, then it is likely that the courts would find such speech more disruptive (and likely unprotected) than an employee posting from home during nonwork hours (Nolo 2011). Additionally, the more involved in policy issues an employee is, the more the government's interest will override the employee's First Amendment rights. Finally, while the balance is different, the structure of the law is the same regardless of on-duty or off-duty status. Heaton's (2011) examination of a contentious policy implemented in Kent County, Delaware, that limited employees' off-duty options on social media sites underscores the challenge many governments are facing regarding writing and implementing appropriate social media policies that do not infringe on First Amendment rights. In this situation, a local law professor determined that the ban on speech proposed by this new policy would limit employees' free speech rights and would inappropriately apply the *Garcetti* case.

While social media does not fundamentally change any part of what constitutes protected employee speech, it does allow for more rapid and lasting record of an employee's behavior. In fact, the courts are not in agreement about protected public employee speech via social media, as evidenced by a recent ruling upholding an employee's freedom of expression rights in a situation that, heretofore, was not protected. In *Mattingly v. Milligan* (2011), an employee in a county clerk's office posted negative commentary on her Facebook page about a newly elected county clerk who had laid off some staff. Her commentary resulted in her termination; subsequently, she sued for violation of her First Amendment rights. Historically, complaints about a boss' actions, assuming the actions are legal, would not be protected speech. But the court upheld her rights, using the reasoning that the speech was made in the public domain, citizens who were Facebook friends of the plaintiff offered commentary about the lay-offs, and the posting led to complaints from six citizens to the Clerk's Office and media coverage (Brown 2011). This case highlights the emergent nature of intersection between the law and social media and demonstrates how the definition of "matters of public concern" may be altered by this new medium for communication.

First Amendment rights are an interesting area within public sector employment, as these rights have moved from essentially no right of free speech in the pre-1950s to a slightly more expansive legal assessment of employee rights in both the *Pickering* and *Garcetti* cases. The courts do not consider organizational policies when assessing First Amendment rights, so the primary goal of many policies is to influence employee behavior, understanding, and beliefs (i.e., portray the organization in a favorable light through direct speech about the government or through employee conduct restrictions). The most common types of First Amendment policy-based restrictions are related to authority and disclaimers, which are designed to indicate who can speak on behalf of an organization and also to indicate that personal speech is not reflective of organizational viewpoints.

BOX 25.1

SAMPLE FIRST AMENDMENT POLICY LANGUAGE

"Individual, originating from a State employee clearly representing themselves as a State employee publishing content to any social media site outside of a Maryland domain and not conducting state business, must use a disclaimer such as this: 'The postings on this site are my own and don't necessarily represent Maryland's positions, strategies, or opinions."

State of Maryland Social Media Policy

Fourth Amendment Issues

Public employees also have an expectation of protection under the Fourth Amendment that is distinct from private sector employee protections. Government employees have a protection against intrusion, when there is a legitimate expectation of privacy, and against unreasonable searches and seizures. An expectation of privacy can extend to computers, electronic devices, stored communication, and so on by virtue of allowing password protections and the like. However, employers can remove an expectation of privacy by creating and consistently applying policies on the issue of privacy. Essentially, Fourth Amendment restrictions or protections deal with the ability of the government to monitor employee use of either government-owned resources for work or personal purposes or, less frequently, to monitor employee use of personal resources for personal purposes when there might be an impact on the government's reputation. For example, employers can routinely remind employees that their use of email or other electronic forms of communication are subject to monitoring and no expectation of privacy exists (Tabak and Smith 2005). *City of Ontario v. Quon* (2010) further strengthened the government employer's right to limit or remove expectations of privacy with the use of disclaimers, policies indicating monitoring or no right to privacy. Again, the courts employ a balancing test that looks at the employees' privacy rights compared with the importance of government interests, particularly the reasonableness of a search with respect to work-related purposes for said search or seizure. The issue of privacy is a central concern when it comes to employees' use and conduct on social media. Most governmental social media policies are quite broad and varied in their treatment of Fourth Amendment (privacy) rights. The main purpose of these policies, whether intentional or consequential, is to restrict expectations of privacy in a clear and consistent manner, which the courts may weigh in favor of the government in the event of legal action.

BOX 25.2

SAMPLE FOURTH AMENDMENT POLICY LANGUAGE

"Privacy—Employees should have no expectation of privacy in information stored on state computers or devices. Furthermore, there should be no expectation of privacy when employee conduct concerns the agency or its clients."

State of Washington Social Media Policy

Employee Rights: On- and Off- Duty Conduct

When considering the rights of employees, the expectation is that employees have rights beyond those constitutionally mandated to citizens. Employees should be able to expect that they will work in a safe and harassment-free work environment (Daley 2002). Employers are expected to create working environments that are safe and nonhostile (U.S. Equal Employment Opportunity Commission [EEOC] 2011). In order to achieve this environment, there is a need for appropriate policies, reporting mechanisms, and enforcement actions (Eberhardt, Moser, and McFadden 1999). There is still a long way to go in creating workplaces in which sexual harassment, discrimination, and violence are no

longer issues. Managers are finding that increased use of electronic communication is associated with increased electronic harassment (Tyler 2008; McMullen 2011). Managers, HR departments, and organizations broadly are continuing to work to create policies, reporting mechanisms, appropriate investigation practices, discipline procedures, and training methods that will ensure a safe and harassment-free work environment. While policies alone are not a solution to these issues, they serve as a key and foundational element necessary to begin to safeguard employees.

Public employees are seen as having greater rights than their private sector counterparts in relationship to their personal conduct (Wise et al. 2004). Still, actions undertaken during off-duty time can have a direct impact on the employment relationship (Wise et al. 2004; Allred 1999). In particular, when there is a nexus of conduct (Allred 1999), or the connection between the behavior and the "efficiency of the public service" is called into question, the off-duty conduct becomes subject to regulation and inspection. For example, if a police officer were arrested for DUI or a financial analyst were caught embezzling funds from their church, the behavior would cast dispersion upon the public trust of that employee in their official capacity and raise questions about their ability to perform their job. In arguing that public employees have greater personal rights than before, Wise et al. give the example that "gone are the days when a public school teacher could be terminated for cohabitating with another person out of wedlock" (2004: 208–209). While this is true, the realm of social media has created an intersection of mass dispersion of private actions. While public school teachers may have no worries about cohabitating they may need to be careful of what they do online, as a Boston biology teacher found out when a post she made on Facebook insulting the residents of the community resulted in a quick termination (H.S. Teacher Loses Job 2010). Through the establishment of codes of conduct, organizations are articulating expectations for employees' behaviors, on and off duty, as well as disciplinary and termination consequences.

BOX 25.3

SAMPLE EMPLOYEE CONDUCT POLICY LANGUAGE

"Expectation of appropriate and ethical conduct of a State representative including cautions against posting offensive, profane, scandalous, libelous, defamatory, pornographic, or otherwise offensive language or materials"

State of Georgia Social Media Policy

"All agency-related communication through social media outlets should remain professional in nature and should always be conducted in accordance with the agency's communications policy, practices and expectations."

State of North Carolina Social Media Policy

Training

As HR professionals work with employees throughout their employment lifecycle, it is imperative that the HR department offers training on social media issues as they relate to employee policies and procedures. Training is critical for all employees, particularly in the event that discipline issues arise. Likewise, managers and supervisors should be trained on how to enforce policies consistently and fairly for all personnel.

PARTNERS AND ADDITIONAL ISSUES TO CONSIDER

HR professionals serve a multitude of roles, including administrative, organization development/consulting, contract management and coordination, and strategic human resource management roles (Ban and Gossett 2010). They must serve as partners to every department and employee within the organization as well as provide direction for other departments and the enterprise at large. As HR professionals become more strategic, it is important for them to consider how issues link to the goals and mission of the organization. Considering the

linkages should be part of the social media policy and usage conversations, and the HR department is likely to be looked at to take the lead on partnering with other departments (such as IT and communications) as well as linking with other organization usage and conduct policies.

Often social media policies are seen as technological issues; for example, HR managers often ask, "Can we block Facebook from company computers?" This is a technical question that overlooks broader policy concerns related to managing employee performance. Too often, the IT department is being tasked with managing employee access and participation in social media endeavors through technical solutions without management involvement or consideration of human resources issues and challenges. It is imperative that the HR department be heavily involved in policy discussions instead of relying on technical solutions to limit access, as those solutions will not appropriately address employee performance management. The decision to utilize technology to mediate a nontechnical HR issue is problematic at best and creates the potential for a multitude of legal challenges. Social media policies should be linked to and take direction from the values of the organization around communication and conduct. Communicating on a social media platform is just another means of communication; it just happens to be one that tends to have more immediate and far reaching impact. While social media can be a powerful tool for HR professionals it is fraught with problems and challenges that need to be carefully considered and responded to. For example, using social media to screen applicants can expose an organization to discrimination claims if not carefully managed.

It is important to recognize that using social media is part of the expectations of the new workforce. HR professionals will need to think carefully about policies that govern both their own and employees' use of social media. Technology is evolving and as such policies and practices should be grounded in the values of the organization and written in an inclusive manner and not directed simply at the most recent technological change.

NOTE

1. According to the 2012 annual technology market survey conducted by Eurocom Worldwide, "Almost one in five technology industry executives say that a candidate's social media profile has caused them not to hire that person." Previous Eurocom Worldwide surveys had found almost 40% of the survey respondents from technology companies review job candidate's profiles on social media sites. While we've all heard about the increase in companies checking the social media profiles of job candidates, this survey provides the first evidence that prospective job candidates are actually being rejected because of their profiles." Source: http://www.forbes.com/sites/lisaquast/2012/04/23/your-social-media-profile-could-make-or-break-your-next-job-opportunity/.

REFERENCES

Allred, S. 1999. *Employment law: A guide for North Carolina public employers.* Chapel Hill, NC: The Institute of Government Press.

Azevedo, M. A. 2012. Going Social: Digital Age Ushers New Era of Recruiting. August 20. http://newsroom.cisco.com/feature/996343/Going-Social-Digital-Age-Ushers-New-Era-Of-Recruiting.

Ban, C., and Gossett, C. 2010. The Changing Roles of the Human Resources Office. In Steve Condrey, ed., *Handbook of Human Resource Management in Government* (3rd ed.). San Francisco: Jossey-Bass.

Brown, E. 2011. Employee's Facebook status update was protected by the First Amendment. November 9. http://blog.internetcases.com/2011/11/09/employee%e2%80%99s-facebook-status-update-was-protected-by-the-first-amendment/.

CareerBuilder. 2012, April 18. Thirty-seven percent of companies use social networks to research potential job candidates. http://www.careerbuilder.com/share/aboutus/pressreleasesdetail.aspx?id=pr691&sd=4%2F18%2F2012&ed=4%2F18%2F2099.

City of Ontario v. Quon. 130 U.S. 2619 (2010).

Cohen, C. F., and Cohen, M. E. 2007. On-duty and off-duty: Employee right to privacy and employer's right to control in the private sector. *Employee Responsibilities and Rights Journal,* 19, 235–246.

Daley, D. M. 2002. *Strategic human resource management: People and performance management in the public sector.* Englewood Cliffs, NJ: Prentice Hall.

Deschenaux, J. 2012. Maryland enacts country's first social media password law. Society for Human Resource Management. May 3. www.shrm.org/legalissues/stateandlocalresources/pages/marylandenactscountrysfirst.aspx.

Eberhardt, B. J., Moser, S. B., and McFadden, D. 1999. Sexual harassment in small government units: An investigation of policies and attitudes. *Public Personnel Management,* 28(3), 351–365.

Facebook. 2012. September 10. Facebook statistics. https://www.facebook.com/press/info.php?statistics.

Garcetti v. Ceballos. 547 U.S. 410 (2006).

Grossman, L. 2010. 2010 Person of the Year Mark Zuckerberg. *Time Magazine,* January 3, 44–74.

Heaton, B. 2011. Social media usage becoming a free speech question for governments. May 17. http://www.govtech.com/policy-management/Social-Media-Free-Speech-Question.html.

Hrdinová, J., Helbig, N., and Peters, C.S. 2010. Designing social media policy for governments: Eight essential elements. Center for Technology in Government, May. http://dev3.bremerhaven.de/generaldocuments/pdf/center_for_technology_in_government_-_social_media_policy_in_government.pdf.

H.S. teacher loses job over Facebook posting. 2010, August 18. WCVB TV Boston, August 18. http://www.thebostonchannel.com/r/24670937/detail.html.

Jacobson, W., and Tufts, S. 2013. To post or not to post: Employee rights and social media. *Review of Public Personnel Administration,* 33(1), 84–107.

Jamieson, D. 2011. Facebook firings: Feds, managers navigate 'new territory' in employment. Huffington Post, August 2. http://www.huffingtonpost.com/2011/08/02/facebook-firings-new-territory_n_915520.html.

Kaplan, A.M., and Haenlein, M. 2010. Users of the world, unite! The challenges and opportunities of social media. *Business Horizons,* 53(1), 59–68.

Kravets, D. 2013. *Six states bar employers from demanding Facebook passwords.* http://www.wired.com/threatlevel/2013/01/password-protected-states/.

Lenhart, A., Purcell, K., Smith, A., and Zickuhr, K. 2010. Social Media and Mobile Internet Use Among Teens and Young Adults. Pew Internet and American Like Project. Pew Research Center. http://pewinternet.org/Reports/2010/Social-Media-and-Young-Adults.aspx.

Llorens, J., and Kellough, J. E. 2007. A revolution in public personnel administration: The growth of web-based recruitment and selection processes in the federal service. *Public Personnel Management, 36(3), 207–221.*

Mahling, M. 2011. How many governors are using social media? July 22. http://www.stateline.org/live/details/story?contentId=589178.

Mattingly v. Milligan, No. 4: 11CV00215 JLH (E.D. Ark. Nov. 1, 2011).

McLaughlin, C. 2010. The First Amendment and government employees. October 14. http://sogweb.sog.unc.edu/blogs/localgovt/?p=3319.

McMullen, J. 2011. Balancing the right to manage with dignity at work. *Perspectives: Policy and Practice in Higher Education, 15(1),* 3–6.

Mergel, I. A. 2010. Government 2.0 revisited: Social media strategies in the public sector. *PA Times, American Society for Public Administration, 33(3).*

Michale, R. 2012. Using Facebook to Screen Potential Hires Can Get You Sued. July 19. http://www.fastcompany.com/1843142/using-facebook-screen-potential-hires-can-get-you-sued.

Nelson, L. 2012. Using social media for recruiting for government employees. GovLoop, November. http://www.govloop.com/profiles/blogs/using-social-media-for-recruiting-for-government-employees.

Nolo. 2011. Monitoring employees' off-duty conduct: Should you keep track of what employees do when they're not on the job?: http://www.nolo.com/legal-encyclopedia/monitoring-employees-off-duty-conduct-29994.html.

Pickering v. Board of Education. 391 U.S. 563 (1968).

Pynes, J. 2009. *Human resources management for public and nonprofit organizations: A strategic approach.* San Francisco: Jossey-Bass.

Rosenbloom, D. H., and Bailey, M. 2003. What every public personnel manager should know about the Constitution. In S. W. Hays and R. C. Kearney (Eds.), *Public personnel administration: Problems and prospects* (4th ed.). Upper Saddle River, NJ: Prentice Hall, pp. 20–36.

Skutch, J. 2009. Judge: Firefighter not victim of discrimination. *Savannah Morning News,* June 13. http://savannahnow.com/intown/2009-06-13/judge-firefighter-not-victim-discrimination#.TshTzIBW7wE.

Slattery, J. 2010. S.I. woman allegedly faked jury duty to take vacation. CBS New York. October 28. http://newyork.cbslocal.com/2010/10/28/s-i-woman-allegedly-faked-jury-duty-to-take-vacation/.

Society for Human Resource Management (SHRM). 2011. Social Media in the Workplace Survey Findings. November 10. http://www.shrm.org/research/surveyfindings/articles/pages/socialmediaintheworkplace.aspx.

Tabak, F., and Smith, W. P. 2005. Privacy and electronic monitoring in the workplace: A model of managerial cognition and relational trust. *Employee Responsibilities and Rights Journal,* 17, 173–189.

Tyler, K. 2008. Millennials may be out of touch with the basics of workplace behavior. *HR Magazine,* 53(1).

U.S. Equal Employment Opportunity Commission. 2011. http://www.eeoc.gov/.

U.S. Office of Special Counsel. 2010. Frequently asked questions regarding social media and the Hatch Act. August 10. http://www.osc.gov/documents/hatchact/federal/2010-08-10%20FAQs%20Re%20Social%20Media.pdf.

Wise, C. R., Clemow, B., Murray, S. P., and Bingham, L. B. 2004. When things go wrong. In S. F. Freyss (Ed.), *Human Resource Management: An Essential Guide* (2nd ed.). Washington, DC: ICMA Press, 201–224.

Wu, J. 2012. Employers Be Cautious Using Social Media To Screen Job Applicants. April 6. http://windmillnetworking.com/2012/04/06/employers-be-cautious-using-social-media-to-screen-job-applicants/.

PART IV
PROSPECTS

CHAPTER 26

PUBLIC SECTOR WORKPLACE DESIGN: NEW CHALLENGES AND FUTURE DYNAMICS[1]

Katherine C. Naff
San Francisco State University

It's tough to make predictions, particularly about the future.

—Yogi Berra

M ore than 25 years ago the Hudson Institute's *Workforce 2000* (Johnston and Packer 1987) and *Civil Service 2000* (Johnston et al. 1988) sent shock waves through the human resource management community. They foretold that the prototypical skilled, white, male workforce was being replaced by one that was older, with more women and people of color facing jobs that demanded higher skills than they, on average, would have. So popular were these publications, that the Institute produced an update called *Workforce 2020* (Judy and D'Amico 1997) a decade later. As the latter book noted, its predecessors created a "diversity craze" as employers sought to prepare themselves for a new kind of labor force. But what these studies missed were changes occurring in the nature of where and how work is performed. That is the purpose of this chapter.

In their study for RAND, Karoly and Panis (2004) focused on three forces that would shape the future workforce and workplace in the U.S.: demographic trends, technological advances, and economic globalization. "Formulation of sound labor policy will require an understanding of how those trends will evolve" (2004: xiii). That is because existing labor policy was written to address the distinguishing features of an earlier era, and the laws that govern employment today will not fit the workplace of the future.

As does the RAND study, this chapter sees demographic change as just one of several independent variables that are breaking down traditional organizational structures like waves crashing on a sandcastle. While the RAND study is primarily focused on the private sector, public sector human resource management is buffeted by the same forces. Public human resource managers must understand what these forces are, what they mean for how work is done, and how traditional personnel functions must evolve. This chapter is based on a review of literature, largely focused on private sector enterprises, which is extrapolated to the public sector and supplemented with data from the Office of Personnel Management's Central Personnel Data File and the Bureau of Labor Statistics. It concludes with the implications for human resource management in the public sector.

THE TRADITIONAL ORGANIZATION

Classical organizational theorists described work as divided and assigned according to each worker's specialized skill within a structure of authority with a limited span of control. Work was homogenous; for example, public welfare and police administration would be two distinct departments with fixed organizational boundaries governed by rules and based on written documents. Office holding within these hierarchical organizations was a vocation and officials would move through a hierarchy from lower to higher offices with each receiving regular, fixed salaries (see, e.g., Gulick 1937; Weber 1946). Despite later critiques (e.g., Merton 1940), this classic notion of bureaucracy is still reflected in many of today's organizations (Meier and Hill 2005). In this organization, "repressive, at the same time integrative of its work force" (Binde 2005: 32), what matters is vertical relationships, not lateral ones (Jerald 2009). So why isn't this method of organizing work enduring?

FORCES IMPACTING WORK AND THE WORKFORCE

The traditional organization is being buffeted by several forces that are making its structure obsolete, including technology, demographic change, and globalization. By the end of 2013, more than 2 billion people were using the Internet, according to Internet World Statistics. Jobs are disappearing into what W. Brian Arthur (2011) calls the second (digital) economy as work becomes automated. Package tracking, revolutionized by FedEx and UPS in the 1990s, no longer requires human intervention; neither do freight forwarding or airline check-in. Customers still wait in line to talk to someone if they have a problem, but few are working where many once did. The start-up Cue employs two engineers rather than the 60 that would be needed without Amazon Web Services (AWS). AWS also enables GoodData to get by with 80 workers rather than 3,000 (Hardy 2012). The number of jobs requiring expert thinking and complex communications is rising steadily while routine work is tumbling. Moreover, technology and social networking tools are facilitating collaborative work by people around the world (Morello and Burton 2006).

The demographic change impacting work is comprised of growing numbers of women and people of color, but there are now multiple generational cohorts in the workplace. These are people who share the same values and expectations because of similarities in economic conditions and historical events during their formative years (Hamidullah 2012; Gratton 2011; Crumpacker and Crumpacker 2007; Benson and Brown 2011).

For example, the traditionalists, while now retiring, share values that have left an imprint on the organizational architecture that fit well in the hierarchical, career-based notions of classical organizational theorists. Newer cohorts don't share the organizational loyalty that characterized traditionalists and the 77 million baby boomers. Moreover, they are much more disposed toward the use of social media than previous cohorts. Those from Gen X grew up in a time of uncertainty (from the Vietnam War to the dotcom bubble) and so have less expectation of a long-term relationship with their employer (Gratton 2011). It is Generation Y, also known as the Millennials or Net generation, that is on the ascendency in the workplace. They grew up alongside digital media and are well suited to what Bennet and Bennet (2010) call the CUCA (changing, uncertain, complex, and anxious) environment that faces us. This generation values face-to-face interaction, so they work well in collaborative teams. They are looking for a good balance between work and personal lives (Ascente 2010). They prefer low-structure, improvisational work settings (Bollier 2011), expect to be using Web 2.0 social networking tools at work (Charles et al. 2009), and are more project-based than job-based. Nearly three-quarters expect an overseas assignment during their career. Nearly 90% think it is important to be consistently learning on the job (Cornerstone on Demand 2013). This cohort will comprise 75% of the workforce by 2025 (Kerrigan 2012a).

In addition to their values, the numbers that comprise each cohort are significant. The annual rate of growth of the workforce between 2000 and 2010 was about 1.1%; over the subsequent decade it is projected to be just 0.4%, and to decline further to 0.3% between 2020 and 2030 (Karoly and Panis 2004). That means there will be great competition for fewer workers, which will have to be compensated for by increasing the participation of older workers, allowing greater immigration, or doing a better job of accommodating people with disabilities (Karoly and Panis 2004). The third force affecting the future of work is globalization. This has, in part, been driven by technology, which has reduced the cost and increased the speed of transmitting information across national borders. Trade agreements further shrink barriers to trade, while globalization is also facilitated by flexible exchange rates and increased capital mobility. A global economy means a global marketplace for talent. Organizations can contract with anyone from anywhere in the world, virtually linking managers, designers, and producers (Bollier 2011; Jerald 2009). Similarly, organizations can provide services anywhere in the word. Globalization has produced "wise crowds" whose collective knowledge can be shared to come up with better solutions to complex problems (Gratton 2011).

Finally, climate change and energy depletion are forces driving change in how work is performed. According to the U.S. Energy Information Agency statistics as of 2003, buildings accounted for about 40% of primary energy use, 70% of electricity consumption, 30% of raw materials used, and 30% of greenhouse gas emissions (cited in Charles et al. 2009). Employers cannot continue to use scarce resources so inefficiently. Enabled by technology, work is being driven out of the traditional building sites. Employers are recognizing the need to reduce their own carbon footprint and that of their suppliers while also educating their "public" about the importance of environmental stewardship (Gratton 2011).

What Organizations Are Becoming

The synergistic effect of these forces is that no longer can we expect people to work from 9:00 to 5:00, for a single, hierarchical employer, in prescribed job roles. Work is too enigmatic and evolving for that. That model is being replaced by less-structured arrangements of small, spatially and organizationally distributed units (Binde 2005). Work is being outsourced, moved to lower-cost locations with decision making pushed wider and lower. The traditional, rigid framework obstructs collaboration and co-creation. New generations of workers respect professional norms more than organizational ones and use reciprocity and knowledge sharing as exchange currency. In 1977 only 32% of workers agreed with the statement, "It is basically my responsibility to decide how my job gets done." By 2002, that number had risen to 55% (Jerald 2009: 14).

With fewer supervisors, and with access to knowledge through information technology, workers are free to be creative and take the initiative (Jerald 2009). In the emerging, uncertain world where the number of unknown exceeds our capacity to plan for contingencies, the strategic plan as the main catalyst for action is no longer viable. A problem arises and a key leader or expert is sought to assemble the team of specialists to address it. The leader and teams do not come from an existing workforce but skill banks and social networks. Once the issue is resolved, the team is dissolved. Distance among team members, where they live, and the hours they work become irrelevant. "Global virtual teams are the norm, not the exceptions (Ibarra and Hansen 2011: 70). The gains in energy efficiency and worker productivity will be enormous. Instead of stable hierarchies, organizations are flattening as work is performed through social networking technology (Bollier 2011).

The number of square feet per person in the workplace has dropped from 350–500 in the 1990s to 150–250 or less today. Growing numbers of employers are giving their staff laptops, smartphones, and network connections in exchange for giving up their own office space. Workers rely instead on "hotelling" (i.e., using shared, reservable desks when they are in the office). By 2016, 43% of the U.S. workforce is expected to be telecommuting rather than working in a traditional office space. This is at least in part because a survey of CFOs found that nearly half find telecommuting to be second only to salary as the way to recruit talent (Asure 2013).

Much of work is being accomplished through crowd-sourcing where people can contribute to a project without even necessarily being paid for their time (Jerald 2009). Also called co-creation, customers, suppliers, specialists, and independent contractors produce new products and services. Wikipedia is a commonly known example. In South Korea OhmyNews is an online newspaper written by 60,000 "citizen reporters" (Manyika, Roberts, and Sprague 2007). Administrative costs are significantly lowered (Bollier 2011; Manyika et al. 2007). Another example is TopCoders, an organization of software developers tapped by those who need software. Whoever comes up with the best product gets a prize (Manyika et al. 2007). At Google, innovation is fostered through employees submitting ideas and other employees deciding if the idea is worth pursuing or worth their own expenditure of effort (Manyika et al. 2007). Similarly, Innocentive posts problems on its website and awards a fee to anyone who can solve them (Jerald 2009).

TopCoders presents an example of another recent phenomenon—hyperspecialization. There is not a single "software developer" who is creating a TopCoders product. Rather, there may be as many as dozens of individuals contributing to design, coding, testing, and doing all other minuscule aspects of the software development process (Malone, Laubacher, and Johns 2011). A software developer who is particularly good at one part of the process, for example designing interfaces, can devote herself to that full-time on dozens of projects. Similarly, a project manager today may spend time putting together slide decks. In the future, he may access a network of "PowerPoint jockeys" comprised of chart producers, proofreaders, context experts, graphic designers, and so on. Quality improves, cost is reduced, and speed of delivery is increased through such hyperspecialization. There are even specialists who dedicate themselves to coordinating the work of others (Malone et al. 2011).

Work is disaggregating. Rather than working for one employer at a centralized workplace today, 2.23 million contractors are registered with oDesk in Silicon Valley, working for over 1 million businesses, according to the company's website (www.odesk.com). This is an example of the world becoming a single market for labor as employers develop contracts with individuals all over the world (The Great Mismatch 2011).

While the federal workforce at the Centers for Disease Control increased only 3.5% between 2000 and 2006, its contractor workforce increased by 139% (U.S. General Accountability Office [GAO] 2008). This was because talent has been needed in new fields where skills are constantly changing. Overall, between 1999 and 2005, the number of grantees and contractors working for the federal government grew by more than 50% (Copeland 2011). Since Barack Obama took office in 2009, however, federal outsourcing has declined, at least in part for budgetary reasons (*Bracing for Change* 2012).

Managers can exploit increasing amounts of data to foster smarter decisions. Toll road operators have the data to segment drivers and charge them according to congestion pricing while the City of San Francisco is doing the same with parking meters. Technology is used to ensure not just compliance but efficiency and participation (Bollier 2011).

THE WORKFORCE OF THE FUTURE

Today's work can be categorized by three types: (1) transformational, involving physical activity (such as construction), which has long been in decline in most rich countries; (2) transactional or routine jobs such as in call centers or banks, which is currently done by people but can be automated and so has the potential to decline; and (3) interactional, relying on expertise and collaboration (such as investment banking or management consulting). Interactional jobs are difficult to standardize with technology and so will continued to be valued (Winners and Losers 2011). Wymbs (2011) envisions three categories of workers in the emerging economy: (1) "finders, or the experts who are the interface between the firm and customer, or perhaps citizen and agency; (2) "minders," or the team members who work with clients and projects the finders bring in; and (3) "grinders," who don't interact with the client but have the knowledge required to complete the task. The trend toward outsourcing and project-based employment means their job security and bargaining is constrained.

Despite the increases in productivity, the shrinking labor force and retirement of the baby boomers means employers have to be creative in their strategies for retention and meeting demands for greater work/life balance (Morello and Burton 2006). These demands and the dispersion of work across time zones require employers to accommodate flexible schedules. "The traditional concept of owning information and being limited by employment levels is fading away" (Charles et al. 2009: 5). Rather, employees will be replaced by a collective network of volunteers, concerned citizens, contractors, and experts from various levels of government and nonprofits who work toward achieving an objective.

Tomorrow's world belongs to those with specialized skills, who can sort out information, identify buoyant trends, and decode information (Binde 2005). Professionals will need skills in collaboration, teamwork, negotiation, conflict management, entrepreneurship, and the ability to solve complex problems (Bollier 2011; Burke and Koelbl 2008; Jerald 2009; Karoly and Panis 2004). By 2015, 44% of U.S. employment will be involved in work requiring interactions (Manyika et al. 2007; Burke and Koelbl 2008). By the same year workers will spend more than 80% of their time working collaboratively with few working at the same time in the same space (Charles et al 2009). "Easy, efficient interaction among multiple participants on a network is the most powerful innovator today" (Taipale in Bollier 2011: 20). The percentage of workers in Fortune 1,000 companies using self-managed work teams rose from 28% in 1998 to 65% in 2005 (Jerald 2009: 14).

Figure 26.1, taken from the oft-cited Gartner Report (Morello and Burton 2006), projects the decreasing amount of time people are spending working alone, and the increasing time they are spending doing work that depends on group input. It also projects the growing proportion of time people will spend working in different times and places.

This is a world in which people need to acquire new expertise every few years—that is, they must gain "serial mastery" (Gratton 2011). Capitalizing on their knowledge and skills requires a culture of trust, empowerment, innovation, creativity, self-direction, knowledge sharing, and teamwork (Ascente 2010). This shift in work is brought about by innovative technology and global competition and requires higher-level cognitive skills (Karoly and Panis 2004). The workforce will have multiple jobs, much of it "swarm work," where many people jump in to try to solve a problem (Morello and Burton 2006). Many will be what the *Wall Street Journal* called "nanobots" (nearly autonomous, not in the office, doing business in their own time, cited in Fox and Lawson 2009b: 11). Critical competencies require working effectively with strangers, balancing remote face-to-face and personal work, becoming fluent in collaborative languages and tools, and being resourceful in finding and interpreting information.

The average tenure in a job will be 18 months (Morello and Burton 2006). Already the median tenure in a job for a U.S. employee is 4.4 years, with workers holding an average of about 11 jobs during their lifetime (Kamenetz 2012). Declines are being seen in the tenure of federal employees where the proportion of those with less than five years of service doubled from 16% in 1998 to 30% in 2010 (Copeland 2011). Employees will see their managers on average three times during their 18 months with the organization. These changes are putting more pressure on individuals to provide for their own health care, support themselves with savings between jobs, manage their own retirements, and keep their skills up to date (Kamenetz 2012). Telecommuting will be seen as a management strategy and taxpayer benefit rather than employee benefit program (Charles et al. 2009).

The traditional line between manager and worker is blurring (Karoly and Panis 2004). Management's role will change from direct supervision to resource management, priority setting, and negotiation. They will need to provide communication platforms that adapt quickly to change, such as video conferencing. Those in charge also need to create workplace strategies that cater to multigenerational needs and offer work-life balance and flexible work arrangements (Burke and Koelbl 2008).

Interestingly, and in summary, today's workforce is already beginning to look much like that hypothesized in the popular Gartner Future Worker 2015 scenario

Figure 26.1 Proportion of Time Spent Collaborating, Working Alone, in Same and Different Times and Places

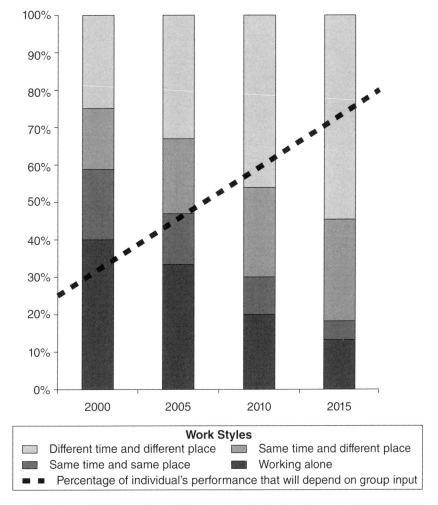

Source: Morello, Diana, and Betsy Burton. 2006. "Future Worker 2015: Extreme Individualization," *Gartner*, Inc. ID # G00138172: 17.

(Morello and Burton 2006). That scenario suggested that with the amplification of globalization and technology, the work environment will be characterized by a disappearance of the expectation of physical proximity and the typical office environment, the advent of "truly personal computing," and the replacement of physical work products by ethereal services and information. People will choose where they work based on peer networks rather than employer brands (2006: 4).

IMPLICATIONS FOR THE PUBLIC SECTOR

The challenges faced in the public sector for achieving the work environment that responds to issues described here are great. First, governments at all levels in the U.S. face increasing fiscal challenges. Although the effects of the Great Recession of 2008–2009 have been receding, most estimates of government's fiscal condition project major gaps between revenues and required expenditures. No matter what fiscal scenario is used for the federal government, Congressional Budget Office projections show negative federal operating deficits for the next decade with entitlement programs continuing to crowd out discretionary programs (CBO 2012). Annual state and local fiscal outlook forecasts are even more dire, showing declining operating balances far into the future (see Figure 26.2) (GAO 2012). This will impact these jurisdictions' ability to compete with the private sector for scarce talent and to invest in the technology needed to meet the demands of the Millennials (see also Charles et al. 2009). It is probably also the reason that state and local governments are choosing to replace laid-off full-time workers with part-time employees. March 2011 census data showed that state governments lost nearly 25,000 full-time workers in the previous year while gaining nearly 13,000 part-time employees. Localities reduced their full-time workforce by 185,000 employees while adding 10,000 part-time positions (Maciaq 2012).

Second, the public sector workforce tends to be older than the private sector (Franzel 2009). For example, 60% of the federal workforce is over 45 years of age,

compared with 31% of the private sector. Only 3% of the federal workforce is under 25 years old (Eggers 2007). Over the next years, it will become even older. In 2010, 26% of the federal workforce was 55 or older, compared with 16% in 1998 (Copeland 2011). This means it faces the loss of the experienced baby boomers at a faster rate than the private sector.

The composition of federal jobs is changing in other ways as well. The number of blue collar jobs decreased 15.3% between 1998 and 2010, and the number of clerical positions declined by 27.6%. During the same time period, the number of professional and administrative jobs increased 21.7% and 45%, respectively (Copeland 2011). Federal jobs are also shifting from lower-grade to higher-grade ones. Fifty years ago less than 25% of the federal workforce was in grades GS 11 and above (U.S. Civil Service Commission 1962); now almost 60% is (U.S. Office of Personnel Management 2012). Table 26.1 shows the 20 federal occupations with the greatest number of net new hires in mid- to upper grade levels (i.e., where

Figure 26.2 State and Local Government Balance Measure, as a Percentage of Gross Domestic Product (GDP)

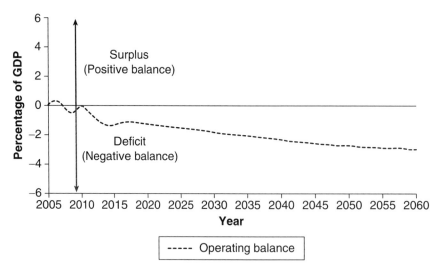

Source: U.S. General Accountability Office. 2012. State and Local Government's Fiscal Outlook, April 2012 Update. Washington, DC: U.S. Government Accountability Office (April): 1.

Table 26.1 Top 20 Occupations with the Greatest Number of Net New Hires Where Hiring Salary Was at Least $50,000/Year (2007–2011)

Occupation	Net New Hires
Nurse	17,302
Information technology management	11,499
Medical officer	7,575
Social work	5,994
Medical support assistance	5,455
Intelligence	5,427
Practical nurse	5,305
Nursing assistant	4,245
Health aide and technician	3,739
General health science	3,208
Psychologist	3,049
Pharmacist	2,696
Mechanical engineering	2,616
Pharmacy technician	1,991
Medical and health student trainee	1,955
Dental trainee	1,579
Civil engineer	1,539
Social science	1,474
Computer science	1,387
Engineer and architecture student trainee	1,384

Source: Central Personnel Data File.

Note: Net new hires means total hires minus separations in each occupation at grade levels where majority of entrants earn $50,000 or more at entry.

the majority earn $50,000) between the years 2007 and 2011. These numbers reflect new positions; that is, they do not include those who merely replaced employees who left. Not surprisingly, many of the occupations showing the greatest numerical growth are in either health care or information technology. Fifteen percent of the just over 114,000 new employees brought in during that time period (over and above replacements) were nurses while another 10% worked in information technology.

A third challenge facing the public sector is that citizens' expectations for quick service and response times are increasing (Charles et al. 2009). As technology continues to get better and faster, citizens' demands for the accessibility and convenience of the ATM will grow. The aging of the workforce is a reflection of the aging of the citizenry, and that means there will be increased demands on services provided by the public sector, whether directly or through contracting out. Those public sector entities responding to a 2006 survey admitted the need to change their practices in order to better serve an increasingly bilingual and older population and citizens with higher expectations for service (Davidson, Lepeak, and Newman 2007). Yet public sector organizations do not appear to be adopting proactive techniques in preparation for such demands.

A 2011 survey of information technology officials revealed that federal managers were readying themselves for the post-PC era, driven by a need to reduce costs and increase employee productivity. Cloud computing is expected to rise from a $41 billion enterprise to a $241 enterprise by 2020 (Deloitte and Bersin 2014). However, there are significant risks and challenges in moving to this reality, including security, acquiring the staffing to support multiple and diverse devices, and budget restrictions (Kash 2012).

Another challenge faced by government agencies will be Gen X and Gen Y employees' benefit expectations. Most local governments lack the finances to offer child care, an increasing concern for families (Franzel 2009). Gen Xers are looking for mortgage assistance, infertility and adoption assistance, career planning, stock options, and alternative work schedules. Gen Y workers want career coaching, continuing education, and a link between work and their social lives. They are looking for a fast-moving, technologically savvy employer, which contradicts the commonly held image of government. (Eggers 2007; *Bracing for Change* 2012). It is no wonder that only 6% of college students indicated they planned to work for government at any level (*Federal Leaders Face Challenges* 2012).

The good news for the public sector is that its workforce tends to be more educated than the private sector. In state and local government, workers have, on average, five to seven more years of education than their private sector counterparts (Kellar 2010). In that sense, they are better prepared to take on the knowledge work required in the future. About 70% of the state and local workforce is engaged in knowledge work, compared with 30% of the private sector (Franzel 2009). The Bureau of Labor Statistics reports that two-thirds of jobs created between 2006 and 2016 will require post-secondary education or training (cited in Jerald 2009: 24). Yet, overall, educational attainment has not kept up with skill demands, which contributes to massive income inequality. While in the U.S. there is now nearly universal access to high school, the same is not true for college (Jerald 2009).

This does not mean that all future jobs will require high levels of education. The third and fourth fastest growing occupations between 2008 and 2018 will be home health aides and personal and home care aides, growing 53% and 50%, respectively (U.S. Census 2012: 398). These are among the least educated and lowest-paid service occupations, which grew by 30% between 1980 and 2005. In fact, increasing wage polarization between those with low skills and little education and those with high levels of education leaves less opportunity for those with middle amounts of education such as high school diplomas. The declining cost of computer technology along with consumer preferences for variety over specialization has driven low-skilled workers performing now-automated routine tasks into service occupations that are difficult to automate (Autor and Dorn 2012).

Table 26.2 shows projections for the occupations with the largest numerical growth in employment at the local, state, and federal levels projected from 2010 to 2020.

Table 26.2 Numeric Change in Employment in Local, State, and Federal Occupations, 2010–2020 projected

Occupation / Title	Projected 2020		Employment change, 2010–2020	
	Employment (in thousands)	Percent of Industry	Number (in thousands)	Percent
All Local Occupations*	6,164.50	100.00	456.9	8.0
Police and sheriff's patrol officers	609.9	9.90	49.4	8.8
Firefighters	307.1	5.00	25.9	9.2
Office clerks, general	215.5	3.50	18.2	9.2
Emergency medical technicians and paramedics	79.8	1.30	13.1	19.6
Maintenance and repair workers, general	119.8	1.90	10.1	9.2
Highway maintenance workers	114.1	1.90	9.6	9.2

Occupation / Title	Projected 2020		Employment change, 2010–2020	
	Employment (in thousands)	Percent of Industry	Number (in thousands)	Percent
Recreation workers	113	1.80	9.5	9.2
Bus drivers, transit and intercity	100.8	1.60	8.5	9.2
Court, municipal, and license clerks	97.1	1.60	8.2	9.2
Water and wastewater treatment plant and system operators	94.5	1.50	8	9.2
All State Occupations*	**2,502.50**	**100.00**	**95.1**	**4.0**
Correctional officers and jailers	282.4	11.30	14.1	5.3
Probation officers and correctional treatment specialists	60	2.40	8.2	15.8
Compliance officers	35.2	1.40	4.8	15.8
Management analysts	30.1	1.20	3.8	14.4
Office clerks, general	91.8	3.70	3.6	4.0
Police and sheriff's patrol officers	69.7	2.80	3.5	5.3
Home health aides	21.7	0.90	2.8	14.9
Child, family, and school social workers	66	2.60	2.6	4.0
Registered nurses	45.2	1.80	2.3	5.3
Business operations specialists, all other	56.6	2.30	2.2	4.0
All Federal Occupations**	**2,121.30**	**100.00**	**−190.3**	**−8.2**
Lawyers	44.2	2.10	6.9	18.5
Transportation security screeners (federal only)	52.3	2.50	4.6	9.6
Tax examiners and collectors, and revenue agents	39.7	1.90	3.2	8.7
Financial examiners	8	0.40	1	14.1
Statisticians	5.8	0.30	0.7	13.2
Industrial machinery mechanics	6.5	0.30	0.5	8.7
Psychologists, all other	6.9	0.30	0.3	4.1

(Continued)

Table 26.2 (Continued)

Occupation / Title	Projected 2020		Employment change, 2010–2020	
	Employment (in thousands)	Percent of Industry	Number (in thousands)	Percent
Microbiologists	3.2	0.20	0.3	8.8
Computer and information systems managers	5.5	0.30	0.3	5.5
Geographers	1	0.00	0.2	18.5

Source: Bureau of Labor Statistics.

*Excluding education and hospital industry.

**Excluding Postal Service.

As expected, the largest growing occupations are in the service industry. At the local level these include fire fighters and police officers, clerks, and emergency medical personnel; at the state level those working in criminal justice and compliance. Overall, federal employment (not including the postal service) is expected to decline by 190,000 jobs. However, certain service industry occupations such as lawyers, transportation security screeners, and tax examiners are expected to grow.

Despite the growth occurring and projected to occur in some public sector occupations, government continues to face challenges in hiring. It is still largely the case that the time it takes from accepting an application from a job seeker to the job offer is longer in the public than private sector (Franzel 2009). Moreover, government offices are often located in dense areas (such as state capitals) where there are long commutes as well as competition from the private sector. While public sector employers have often had an advantage over the private sector in terms of the health and pension benefits they offer, about one-quarter of state and local government employers indicated they increased employee contributions to their pension plans for current employees and new hires. Another 20% have increased age and service requirements for normal retirement. Over half have shifted more health care costs from employers to employees (Survey Findings 2012). Because of fiscal challenges, the public sector can no longer afford many of the benefits that made it the employer of choice for decades.

IMPLICATIONS FOR HUMAN RESOURCE MANAGEMENT

How is the human resource profession responding to technology, globalization, demographic change, and the other forces described here?

Deloitte and Bersin (2014) found in response to their 2014 global survey that respondents were most concerned about these issues, in order of urgency (see Figure 26.3):

- Leadership, arising from globalization and the speed and breadth of technological change.
- Retention and engagement, issues that everyone owns within the organization.
- The reskilling of HR, meanings its skills, reorganization, and changing relationships with organizational leaders and issues.
- Talent acquisition and access, also undergoing meaningful disruption as a result of globalization, technology, social media, changing worker expectations, and shrinking skills and knowledge relative to emerging technology. Employers must be able to attract highly skilled people to survive.

Yet, at the same time, survey respondents reported

Figure 26.3 Urgency of Twelve Global Trends

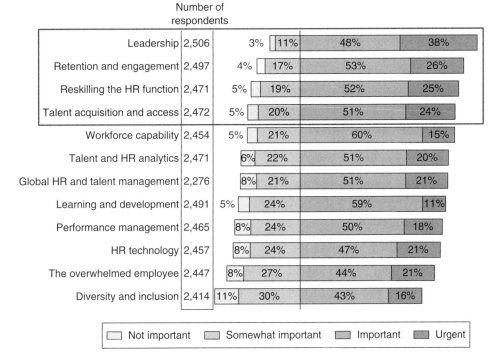

Source: Deloitte Consulting LLP and Bersin by Deloitte. 2014. *Global Human Capital Trends 2014: Engaging the 21st-Century Workforce.* http://www2
.deloitte.com/global/en/pages/human-capital/articles/human-capital-trends-2014.html. Accessed December 1, 2014, p. 8.

being ill-prepared to respond to these global trends. For example, only 15% reported ready to respond to leadership and 17% ready to respond to retention and engagement (Deloitte and Bersin 2014).

In response to a recent Towers Watson survey, nearly half of organizations indicated they would undertake structural change of their HR function (Towers Watson 2012a). For most companies (80%), the primary anticipated change was moving to a shared services model or bringing additional services into their existing shared services model. A shared service model generally means relying on a semiautonomous business unit to provide service to internal customers. It is a means for centralizing human resources management responsibilities to avoid duplication, achieve economies of scale, and thus secure greater efficiency. These HR centers can also make use of technology to offer employees self-service systems

for obtaining information, submitting claims, or managing their retirement accounts. Nonadministrative "professional services" such as sourcing candidates, career planning, and compensation programs that require greater expertise are then left to the shared service center (Selden and Wooters 2011). State governments are also moving to a shared services model. In response to a 2007 survey administered by the Government Performance Project, 16 of 42 states (38%) indicated they had adopted a shared services model in the past two years while another 26% were considering it.

Another 26% of companies report that they will consider outsourcing some or more functions. Most likely to be outsourced are pension, payroll, health and savings plan administration, and other transactional activities (Towers Watson 2012a). This is also a trend in the public sector where jurisdictions at all levels are relying on the private sector for payroll and benefits administration, wage and salary surveys, and job analysis. The rationale again is to achieve efficiency through economies of scale or the ability of in-house HR personnel to pursue other core functions (Battaglio 2009).

However, in neither the case of shared services or outsourcing are principle HR functions being rethought to meet the challenges of changing organizations and a shifting workforce. Technology is a principal driver of the shift to shared services, because it enables such a change (Towers Watson 2012a). Few employers are responding to the way technology and other driving forces are affecting the way work is performed, and therefore the applicability of traditional HR functions. Those core functions require rethought.

Rethinking Core Functions

It should be remembered that the core functions of human resources management were developed during a very different era—a time when organizations resembled the machine model envisioned by classical organizational theorists. It was a time when individuals worked on their own in a centralized, hierarchical organization rather than a dispersed, collaborative environment. Many of the core functions that continue to be taught in human resource management courses today have no place in a rapidly evolving, technologically-driven, globally-impacted organizational structure with a diverse workforce embracing divergent values.

For example, most current classification and compensation systems assume an individual begins work with an organization at the entry level and moves up through the hierarchy to supervisor and management positions in order to receive a pay increase. As organizations flatten, supervisory positions are disappearing and therefore promotional opportunities are as well. Ascente (2010) and Fox and Lawson (2009a) promote the development of a dual career ladder where professionals can avoid the traditional management path while still earning similar status and salary. They would retain their professional autonomy, recognition, and resources parallel to those on the managerial path. Another possible career path begins with the grinder at the entry level, who is elevated to the

minder—that is, from the worker who performs the tasks to the one who interacts with clients and customers (Wymbs 2011). Even supervision will have to change. It is a much different era when supervising requires overseeing a workforce that is not seen or heard throughout the work day and is located in multiple locations.

It used to be the practice that employers would develop a new job classification every time a change occurred in a job. This no longer makes sense when new technology can make an existing classification outdated in a matter of months. While broadbanding was designed to provide additional flexibility in classification, it never caught on in the federal government except in limited agencies. Federal human capital officers in paybanding systems don't believe these systems go far enough in solving the compensation issues they face today (*Bracing for Change* 2012). Just 12 states have adopted broadbanding, four in a limited way. Eighteen states considered it and rejected it for a variety of reasons, including union opposition, a concern that employees would lose the motivation that comes from the potential for promotion to a higher classification, or because the costs seemed prohibitive (Whalen and Guy 2008).

Recently some organizations have moved to a competency-based approach to classification. One southeastern state, which previously had 6,000 job titles, created just ten occupational groups with three levels (basic, journey-level, and advanced) defined by skills and competencies (Fox and Lawson 2009a). According to Fox and Lawson, "This is the flexibility that we believe is needed for the future—multiple skills, multiple ways for employees to apply those skills to achieve the outcomes desired, and to fulfill the role needed. It is a far more flexible definition of the job; it is more appealing to the younger workers and simplifies administration." The city of Los Angeles has recently adopted competency-based job analysis, incorporating the newly identified competencies into competency models and then dividing them into "needed at entry" and "related to job performance" for examination and training purposes. The city also plans to expand their use to classification, performance evaluation, and workforce planning (Lynes et al. 2012). However, as work becomes more project-based, with individuals frequently assuming new tasks and responsibilities each time a new issue presents itself, even this system of competency-based classification may become outmoded. Companies are now abandoning formal job evaluation systems and using market-based strategies to assign jobs and salary ranges (Risher 2012). As things stand, public sector jurisdictions lack that kind of flexibility. In the federal government, for example, the General Schedule pay levels are written into law. Many federal human capital officers believe the pay system is "out-of-date, fragmented, and inefficient" (*Bracing for Change* 2012: 4). However, cultural transformation would be required for change, not just statutory change.

Position descriptions and their corresponding vacancy announcements similarly need to be adjusted to attract people with the necessary skill sets (Eggers 2007). Too often position announcements and crediting plans reward years of education and experience. These are no longer what necessarily make someone better qualified. More important are creativity, flexibility, and one's potential to learn (Binde 2005; Burke and Koelbl 2008; Jerald 2009). In examining applicants for jobs (or projects) what they know is less important than their capacity to learn, whether they can embrace realignment, comprehend diversity, and engage tacit knowledge (Bennet and Bennet 2010). Rather than valuing long experience, employers will value the diversity of experiences that job-changing brings (Bollier 2011). Instead of using traditional job descriptions, organizations are beginning to use more flexible work assignment descriptions that include simply the project title and its end goal (Jerald 2009).

Public human resource offices are already joining their private sector counterparts in using social media technology in their recruitment practices and as a means for keeping in touch with current employees (Didawick 2014). This is necessary because 74% of workers are either actively looking for a new job at any given time or open to the prospect of one (Cornerstone on Demand 2013). Just two examples are the National Institutes of Health (NIH) and the National Security Agency (NSA). The NIH uses Twitter to alert people to available jobs and to keep them informed of relevant HR news, benefits, upcoming career fairs, and their loan repayment program. They use the free bit.ly application to manage the links and the Hootsuite application to schedule and track tweets (MSPB 2011). The NSA relies on Facebook and Twitter and also has developed an iPhone application listing all of its job openings. The agency has further developed an iPhone game called CryptoChallenge, encouraging people to decipher encrypted quotes and historical events in order to interest them in national security work (Ziegler 2012). John Sullivan (2012) predicts the mobile platform will dominate recruitment in the future with the leading organizations allowing applicants to apply for jobs using only their mobile phone. It is important to note, however, that people of color are underrepresented among social media users (Didawick 2014).

Public sector jurisdictions abroad are updating their recruitment efforts. An example is the Australian Department of Finance whose 11-month Graduate Recruitment Program provides graduates with financial skills as well as knowledge of government processes and issues. It further encourages networking and provides a supportive working environment. Intake went from 15 in 2002 to 56 in 2005, with a retention rate of 72%. The report further cites a "fast stream" program in the British Civil Service that is designed to prepare new recruits for senior management roles. It attracted nearly 14,000 applicants from universities across the country. New Zealand is vigorously working to recruit mid-career workers from outside government while Japan has developed exchange programs between the public and private sectors (Eggers 2007). The U.S. Office of Personnel Management has made hiring reform a priority. The number of days required to fill a job has been reduced and the quality of those hired has increased (*Bracing for Change* 2012).

The City of Albuquerque, New Mexico, is already piloting a test, called WorkKeys, that measures a worker's potential to learn and perform well a specific job rather than relying on traditional education and experience requirements. Those who don't pass the first time are given online training and a chance to reapply. The city is expecting this to result in shorter hiring times for hard-to-fill jobs as well as lower turnover (Kerrigan 2012b). The city of Riverside, California, has developed a web-based employee on-boarding process that has reduced costs and paperwork and shortened the time for employees to get to work (Suleman 2014). Nevertheless, these reforms are only small increments toward the radical re-envisioning of the personnel system that will be required over the next decade. While seeking more creative ways to locate recruits for jobs, organizations must also ensure they foster continuous skill development rather than just use up the skills and talent of those they hire (Deloitte and Bersin 2014).

Public sector organizations continue to emphasize that pay should be based on performance, as opposed to the more traditional system of basing pay on job classification with pay raises awarded nearly automatically on an annual basis. While this would seem to make sense in this results-driven environment, pay systems are not principal motivators in collaborative organizations (Adler, Heckscher, and Prusak 2011). While people will be ultimately disgruntled if they are not paid according to their contributions, their day-to-day work is not driven by an effort to maximize pay. Instead, the issue is what Tracy Kidder calls "the 'pinball' theory of management: If you win, you get to play again—to take on a new challenge, to move to a new level" (cited in Adler et al. 2011: 101). Those who excel develop a reputation for their achievements and so are offered new projects to work on. That's where multisource performance appraisals (discussed below) play an important role. Moreover, workers should be offered incentives to use technology to engage in interactions that create value (Manyika et al. 2007).

Much more emphasis must be put on developing workers, because new skills are needed to address increasingly complex problems and rapidly evolving technology. Moreover, development is a priority for tomorrow's workforce. College students who were asked to rate 15 first-job characteristics in terms of their importance to them selected the opportunity for personal growth more than any other, including job security (although that came in second) and a high salary (*Federal Leaders Face Challenges* 2012). In 2007, organizations in the U.S. spent nearly $140 billion on employee learning and development (Morello and Burton 2007),

a number we can expect to rise dramatically. According to Deloitte and Bersin (2014), training is moving from a push to a pull model; that is, one from where employees passively listen to a series of lectures to one where training is incorporated into the everyday work of employees so that they can continuously update their skills at their own speed. Workers must take responsibility for educating themselves and sharing their knowledge with others.

Traditional performance appraisals in which employees are judged positively based on showing up for work are clearly outmoded. Also outmoded are those processes in which employees compete with one another for higher rankings, with those at the top earning rewards and those in the middle becoming demoralized and spurred to look for work elsewhere. Instead performance management should be focused on coaching and development (Deloitte and Bersin 2014).

Moreover, workers in the emerging environment need to be measured on competencies such as relationship management skills, leadership, degree of connectedness, and influence in the network (Bollier 2011). A focus on how they interact in communities of practice is even more important than outcomes. What's critical is the ability to experiment and follow up. Morello and Burton (2006) argue that organizations must reward workers for participation and collaborative outcomes. Some jurisdictions are developing competency-based performance measures for use instead of, or in addition to, outcome-based ones. Competency-based models are particularly useful where events are not under an individual's control, the work environment is rapidly changing, results are not objectively measurable, or potential contribution to the organization is more important than what workers accomplish at the present time. In its effort to move from a reactive hospital system to a proactive health care organization, the Veterans Administration developed a competency called "systems thinking," defined as making calculated decisions that take into account impact on other activities, units, and individuals (Sanchez and Levine 2009). Table 26.3 provides an example of a "problem solving" competency from Washington state.

A second trend affecting the performance appraisal

process is the diminished role the direct supervisor is taking in an employee's workday as the sole judge of the worker's performance. Burke and Koelbl (2008) predict the percentage of individual performance that is dependent on group input will grow from about 30% in 2000 to 75% in 2015. Michael Chui proposes a 720-degree appraisal where people outside the organization evaluate the employee in addition to those inside (cited in Bollier 2011). One private sector company, wishing to expand the scope of evaluation of managers, adopted a concept called "Happy Feet" whereby any employee whom a manager may affect in any way may contribute to the manager's evaluation, regardless of their reporting relationship (Ibarra and Hansen 2011).

Even unions may take on some new roles. Growing quickly is America's Freelancers' Union, with 165,000 members across the U.S. It offers freelancers some things public sector unions have always demanded such as pensions and benefits. But it offers these to the self-employed. According to the *Economist*, it also runs fitness centers and has developed a crowdsourced system for rating employers on how promptly they pay freelancers (My Big Fat Career 2011). Where traditional unions do exist, they are necessarily becoming part of the collaborative community. An example is the Labor

Management Partnership at Kaiser Permanente where unions worked with management and physicians to re-engineer operating room practices to make them more efficient (Adler et al. 2011).

The job security that civil service systems provide appears to be on the demise. Recall that work of the future is project-based with the worker's prospects for being asked to do the next project based strictly on her performance on the last one. Moreover, Gen Y doesn't have the interest in a career that baby boomers did. By the late 1990s, only 6% of corporate managers agreed with the statement "employees who are loyal to the company and further its business goals deserve an assurance of continued employment" (cited in Jerald 2009: 17). Today the overwhelming majority of companies say that continued employment is based on performance (Jerald 2009: 18). The short tenure of the average worker requires employers to redesign work, as well as hiring, benefit, and reward packages (Morello and Burton 2006).

Pension and benefit packages are already undergoing change because public sector jurisdictions have not been able to keep up with their cost. The movement from defined benefit pension plans to defined contribution approaches is driven by the fiscal reality that state and local governments can no longer afford

Table 26.3 Example of a Competency with Performance Statements

Problem Solving

Definition: Resolves difficult or complicated challenges.

Performance Statement Examples

- Frames problems before trying to solve them. Breaks down problems and identifies all of their facets, including hidden or tricky aspects.
- Shows insight into the root causes of problems. Generates a range of solutions and courses of action with benefits, costs, and risks associated with each.
- Probes all fruitful sources for answers and thinks "outside the box" to find options. Uses the good ideas of others to help develop solutions. Seeks advice from those who've solved similar problems.
- Tests proposed solutions against the reality of likely effects before going forward; looks beyond the obvious and does not stop at the first answers.
- Evaluates the chosen course of action after it has been implemented to determine its worth and impacts.

Source: Washington State Department of Human Resources. www.dop.wa.gov/SiteCollectionDocuments/Strategic%20HR/. Accessed July 17, 2012.

these arrangements. At least 10 states have proposed reducing pensions or eliminating them all together (Cuda 2014). Employees are increasingly responsible for their own pension plans and are being forced to make larger contributions to their health care. At the same time, with the need to promote labor force participation by older workers and those with disabilities who may prefer nonstandard work arrangements, benefit policies must be oriented to these segments of the workforce. In particular, there is increasing pressure to make such benefits portable across jobs or even independent of jobs (Karoly and Panis 2004). The plurality (47%) of public HR professionals have changed their system of providing benefits (Equaterra 2006). It just so happens that this model also fits with the greater portability of the incoming workforce and the nature of the work. The generational shift in the workforce is also having an impact on the importance of benefits. Benefits play a stronger role in influencing employment decisions for Gens X and Y than they do for baby boomers. As the least financially stable generation, Gen Y places a lot of weight on a strong benefits package (Shutan 2012).

HR needs to become much more data-driven and to develop the capacity for the mobile delivery of human capital metrics. In part, the capability to engage in succession planning must be in place, including the ability to transfer knowledge from those retiring workers to new entrants. Public sector organizations tend to lag behind their private sector counterparts in this regard (Eggers 2007). But beyond that, organizations of the future will rely on a host of cloud-based applications to provide decision makers with real time information about workforce skills, retention, levels of employee engagement, performance, demographics and other analytics (Towers Watson 2012b). Historical metrics will be replaced by predictive analytics so that employers can be prepared for challenges around the bend (Johnson 2012). Big data can also be leveraged from vendors such as Work4, TalentBin, Gild, and LinkedIn to find high-quality candidates and determine how well they would fit the organization (Deloitte and Bersin 2014).

Impediments to Reform

Standing in the way of this new fluid and flexible human resource management system are the laws that public sector jurisdictions operate under, which are not easy to amend. In some cases, such as Colorado, a practice as simple as allowing supervisors to select from the top six qualified candidates rather than the top three had to be approved by the voters because these requirements were written into the state's constitution. Some states, most notoriously Georgia, Texas, and Florida, have already replaced their civil service protections with at-will employment. More recently, this wave of reform has picked up speed, with Indiana reducing the number of classified employees and weakening seniority. The state further amended rules to place less emphasis on education and years of experience and more on the knowledge, skills, and abilities to do a job (Kerrigan 2012c). Arizona eliminated civil service protections for all employees hired after September 28, 2012, and Tennessee for its senior level employees. Tennessee further changed the way raises are awarded to base them mainly on performance, and it now allows new employees to be selected from a list of all qualified applicants (Cuda 2012). Mississippi is taking a more incremental approach, temporarily moving portions of its workforce into an at-will employment status for purposes of reorganization (Goodman and French 2011). In many cases, the rationale is to be able to remove ineffective employees from the payroll. Regardless of the reason, all of this took legislative change, which is not as simple and straightforward to realize as the stroke of a CEO's pen.

Also impeding the transformation of human resource management in the public sector are factors internal to organizations themselves. About 69% of HR professionals indicated funding was a key barrier to transformation, while 32% cited lack of management support, and 32% pointed to poor information technology systems (Equaterra 2006). Federal human capital officers also said that declining budgets are a key concern. They further expressed concerns about how they are perceived by agency leadership; only 42% reported that HR staff are viewed by leadership as a trusted advisor to a great or very great extent (*Bracing for Change* 2012). "The health of the federal HR profession remains fragile," noted the report (2012: 23), ". . . but prospects for continued rehabilitation remain."

CONCLUSION

The traditional, vertical organization where employees spent their careers on fixed schedules in permanent workplaces is meeting its demise. Rapid advancements in technology, globalization, and energy depletion mean that employers can and must meet the demands of the emergent workforce for flexibility, agility, and compensation and benefits that cater to their generation. In its place is project-based work that is being handed to high-performing specialists who are ready to work in largely self-directed, cross-functional teams on a short-term basis and then move with little if any opportunity for promotion or job security. In the public sector, transformation is occurring, albeit at a much slower pace due to legal restrictions, budgetary shortfalls, and an older, less resilient workforce. Standing in the way of change are also outmoded personnel functions such as classification and compensation systems, performance appraisal, and slow hiring processes. Some jurisdictions are taking steps to push their systems into the 21st century, but the steps are incremental. Those human resource professionals who wish to stay ahead of the curve must prepare themselves for deep organizational transformation and to look for new ways to manage the workforce that is consistent with the requirements of a changing world.

NOTES

1. I would like to thank Albert C. Hyde and Geetanpreet Virdi from SFSU for extracting the CPDF data and Chris Roseland and Jacqueline Midkiff from the BLS for providing the BLS data used in this chapter.

REFERENCES

Adler, Paul, Charles Heckscher, and Laurence Prusak. 2011. Building a Collaborative Enterprise. *Harvard Business Review* (July-August): 95–101.

Arthur, W. Brian. 2011. The Second Economy. *The McKinsey Quarterly.* http://www.mckinseyquarterly.com/The_second_economy_2853. Accessed August 8, 2012.

Ascente, Diana. 2010. Literature Review: A Representation of How a Future Knowledge Worker is Shaping the Twenty-First Century Workplace. *On the Horizon* 18: 279–287.

Asure. 2013. Five Strategies Revolutionizing Your Workplace. Executive Briefing. http://www.asuresoftware.com/resources/executive-briefings/five-strategies-revolutionizing-workplace/. Accessed November 13, 2014.

Autor, David H., and David Dorn. 2012. The Growth of Low Skilled Service Jobs and the Polarization of the U.S. Labor Market. Unpublished manuscript, April.

Battaglio, R. Paul, Jr. 2009. Privatization and Its Challenges for Human Resource Management in the Public Sector. *Review of Public Personnel Administration* 29: 203–206.

Bennet, Alex, and David Bennet. 2010. Multidimensionality: Building the Mind/Brain Infrastructure for the Next Generation Knowledge Worker. *On the Horizon* 10: 240–254.

Benson, John, and Michelle Brown. 2011. Generations and Work: Are There Differences and Do They Matter? *The International Journal of Human Resources Management* 22 (May): 1843–1865.

Binde, Jerome. 2005. What Future Is There for Work? *Foresight* 7: 31–38.

Bollier, David. 2011. *The Future of Work.* Washington, DC: The Aspen Institute.

Bracing for Change: Chief Human Capital Officers Rethink Business as Usual. 2012. Partnership for Public Service and Grant Thornton, August. http://ourpublicservice.org/publications/viewcontentdetails.php?id=47. Accessed April 6, 2015.

Burke, Jim, and Lee Koelbl. 2008. The Workforce of Tomorrow. Nortel. http://media.govtech.net/GOVTECH_WEBSITE/EVENTS/PRESENTATION_DOCS/2008/Ohio_DGS/1230WorkforceofTomorrowBURKEKOELBL.ppt. Accessed August 8, 2012.

Charles Jr., Gerald, Philip Grone, Patrick Spencer, J. D. Stanley, and Fred Thompson. 2009. *Workforce and Workspace Sustainability: Integrating a Dynamic Workforce, Work Environments, and Technology.* Cisco Internet Business Solutions (September). http://www.cisco.com/web/about/ac79/docs/pov/WWS_POV_FINAL.pdf. Accessed August 10, 2012.

Copeland, Curtis. 2011. *The Federal Workforce: Characteristics and Trends.* Washington, DC: Congressional Research Service, April 19. http://digitalcommons.ilr.cornell.edu/cgi/viewcontent.cgi?article=1560&context=key_workplace.

Accessed August 16, 2012.

Cornerstone on Demand. 2013. *Reimagine Work*. http://www.cornerstoneondemand.com/sites/default/files/insight/csod-in-reimagine-work.pdf. Accessed November 13, 2014.

Crescimano, Laura. 2012. The Not-So-Corporate Campus. *The Urbanist* (San Francisco Planning and Urban Research Assoc.) 509 (January): 16–19.

Crumpacker, Martha, and Jill M. Crumpacker. 2007. Succession Planning and Generational Stereotypes. *Public Personnel Management* 4 (Winter): 349–369.

Cuda, Amanda. 2012. Civil Service Reform a Concern for Many. *HR News* (International Public Management Association–Human Resources) August: 10–11.

———. 2014. Building Bulwarks against the Breakdown of Retirement Benefits for Public Sector Employees. *HR News* November: 6–7.

Davidson, Glenn, Stan Lepeak, and Elizabeth Newman. 2007. *The Impact of the Aging Workforce on Public Sector Organizations and Mission*. February. Alexandria, VA: International Public Management Association–Human Resources.

Deloitte Consulting LLP and Bersin by Deloitte. 2014. *Global Human Capital Trends 2014: Engaging the 21st-Century Workforce*. http://www2.deloitte.com/global/en/pages/human-capital/articles/human-capital-trends-2014.html. Accessed December 1, 2014.

Didawick, Josh. 2014. Social Media Highs and Lows for Human Resources. *HR News* September: 8–9.

Eggers, William. 2007. The Graying Government Workforce. Deloitte Touche. http://www.deloitte.com/assets/Dcom-Shared%20Assets/Documents/dtt_publicsector_snapshot_greygovt_113007.pdf. Accessed August 9, 2012.

Equaterra. 2006. Human Resources Transformation in Public Sector Organizations. June. Alexandria, VA: International Public Management Association–Human Resources.

Federal Leaders Face Challenges Attracting College Graduates to Government Service. 2012. Partnership for Public Service and the National Association of Colleges and Employers. February. http://ourpublicservice.org/publications/viewcontentdetails.php?id=82. Accessed April 6, 2015.

Fox, Jim and Bruce Lawson. 2009a. Designing Classification and Compensations Systems for the Change That Is Coming. *HR News Magazine* January: 8–9, 12–13. http://www.ipma-hr.org/sites/default/files/pdf/News/IPMANews0109.pdf. Accessed April 5, 2012.

———. 2009b. Multi-Generational Workforces: Challenges and Opportunities. *HR News* June: 10–11, 13.

Franzel, Joshua M. 2009. The Public Sector Workforce: Past, Present and Future. Paper presented to the Labor and Employment Relations Association Meeting, January 5. http://lera.press.illinois.edu/proceedings2009/franzel.html. Accessed August 8, 2012.

Goodman, Doug, and P. Edward French. 2011. Assessing the Use of At-Will Employment for Reorganization and Workforce Reduction in Mississippi State Government. *Review of Public Personnel Administration* May 31: 270–290.

Gratton, Lynda. 2011. *The Shift: The Future of Work Is Already Here*. London: HarperCollins.

Gulick, Luther. 1937. Notes on the Theory of Organization. In *Classics of Public Administration*, ed. Jay M. Shafritz and Albert C. Hyde, 81–89. Originally in *Papers on the Science of Administration*, edited by Luther Gulick and Lyndall Urwick. New York, Institute of Public Administration, 1937.

Hamidullah, Madinhal F. 2012. Generational Differences and the Public Sector Workforce. In *Public Personnel Management: Current Concerns, Future Challenges*, ed. Norma M. Riccucci. 28–38. Boston: Longman.

Hardy, Quentin. 2012. Active in Cloud, Amazon Reshapes Computing. *The New York Times*, August 27. http://www.nytimes.com/2012/08/28/technology/active-in-cloud-amazon-reshapes-computing.html.

Ibarra, Herminia, and Morten T. Hansen. 2011. Are You a Collaborative Leader? *Harvard Business Review* July-August: 69–75.

Internet World Statistics. 2012. Miniwatts Marketing Group. http://www.internetworldstats.com/top20.htm. Accessed August 15, 2012.

Jerald, Craig D. 2009. *Defining a 21st Century Education*. The Center for Public Education. http://www.centerforpubliceducation.org/Learn-About/21st-Century/Defining-a-21st-Century-Education-Full-Report-PDF.pdf. Accessed August 13, 2012.

Johnson, John. 2012. Next Year's Recruiting Headlines, Trends, and Next Practices. November 5. http://www.ere.net/2012/11/05/next-year. Accessed November 14, 2012.

Johnston, William B., and Arnold E. Packer. 1987. *Workforce 2000: Work and Workers for the 21st Century*. Indianapolis: Hudson Institute.

Johnston, William B., et al. 1988. *Civil Service 2000*. Washington, DC: U.S. Office of Personnel Management.

Judy, Richard W., and Carol D'Amico. 1997. *Workforce 2020:*

Work and Workers in the 21st Century. Indianapolis: Hudson Institute.

Kamenetz, Anya. 2012. The Four Year Career. *Fast Company,* January 12. http://www.fastcompany.com/1802731/four-year-career. Accessed October 1, 2012.

Karoly, Lynn A., and Constantijn A. Panis. 2004. *The 21st Century at Work: Forces Shaping the Future Workforce and Workplace in the United States.* Santa Monica, CA: RAND Corporation.

Kash, Wyatt. 2012. Agencies Prepare for Post-PC Era, New Study Finds. February 27. http://gov.aol.com/2012/02/27/agencies-prepare-for-post-pc-era-new-study-finds. Accessed October 1, 2012.

Kellar, Elizabeth. 2010. Keeping a Strategic Focus in a Tough Economy. *HR News* (International Public Management Association–Human Resources) September. http://slge.org/wp-content/uploads/2011/12/Keeping-a-Strategic-Focus_IPMANews_0910.pdf. Accessed August 9, 2012.

Kelly Services, Inc. 2012. Business or Pleasure? Social Media in the Workplace. http://www.kellyocg.com/Knowledge/Infographics/Business_or_Pleasure_-_Social_Media_in_the_Workplace/. Accessed September 13, 2012.

Kerrigan, Heather. 2012a. Government Unprepared for Boomers' Mass Exodus. *Governing,* December. http://www.governing.com/templates/gov_print_article?id=181390611. Accessed November 19, 2014.

———. 2012b. Testing Employees to Find the Best. *Governing,* July 11. http://www.governing.com/columns/col-testing-employees-to-find-best.html. Accessed August 9, 2012.

———. 2012c. Civil Service Reform: Lessons from Georgia and Indiana. *Governing.* http://www.governing.com/topics/public-workforce/col-civil-service-reform-lessons-from-georgia-indiana.html. Accessed August 14, 2012.

Lynes, Phyllis, Michael Gold, Vincent Cordero, and Steve Rivera. 2012. City of Los Angeles: A Competency Model. *HR News* (International Public Management Association–Human Resources) March: 14–15, 18–19.

Maciaq, Mike. 2012. Full-time Government Jobs Down, Part-Time Employment Up. *Governing,* August 23. http://www.governing.com/blogs/by-the-numbers/state-local-full-time-part-time-jobs-data.html. Accessed September 13, 2012.

Malone, Thomas W., Robert J. Laubacher, and Tammy Johns. 2011. The Age of Hyperspecialization. *Harvard Business Review* July-August: 56–65.

Manyika, James M., Roger P. Roberts, and Kara L. Sprague.

2007. Eight Business Technology Trends to Watch. *The McKinsey Quarterly* December. http://www.mckinsey-quarterly.com/Eight_business_technology_trends_to_watch_2080. Accessed August 9, 2012.

Meier, Kenneth, and Gregory C. Hill. 2005. Bureaucracy in the 21st Century. In *The Oxford Handbook of Public Administration,* edited by Ewan Ferle, Laurence E. Lynn and Christopher Pollitt, 51–71. Oxford: Oxford University Press.

Merton, Robert K. 1940. Bureaucratic Structure and Personality. *Social Forces, 18,* 560–568.

Morello, Diana, and Betsy Burton. 2006. Future Worker 2015: Extreme Individualization. *Gartner,* Inc. ID # G00138172.

My Big Fat Career. 2011. *The Economist,* September 10, 8–11.

Ouye, Joe Aki. 2011. Five Trends That Are Dramatically Changing Work and the Workplace. Knoll Research. http://www.knoll.com/research/downloads/WP_FiveTrends.pdf. Accessed August 8, 2012.

Risher, Howard. 2012. Time to Move in a New Direction. *HR News* (International Public Management Association–Human Resources) August: 16–17, 23.

Sanchez, Juan I., and Edward L. Levine. 2009. What Is (or Should Be) the Difference Between Competency Modeling and Traditional Job Analysis. *Human Resource Management Review* 19: 53–63.

Selden, Sally C., and Robert Wooters. 2011. Structures in Public Human Resources Management: Shared Services in State Governments. *Review of Public Personnel Administration* 39: 349–368.

Shutan, Bruce. 2012. Multigenerational Employee Engagement Imperative. *Employee Benefit News,* August 14. http://ebn.benefitnews.com/news/multigenerational-engagement-recruitment-retention-2726836-1.html. Accessed August 17, 2012.

Suleman, Razor. 2014. City of Riverside Streamlines Hiring Process and Saves Thousands Annually. *HR News* September: 11.

Survey Findings: State and Local Government Workforce 2012 Trends. 2012. Center for State and Local Government Excellence, April. http://slge.org/wp-content/uploads/2012/04/S-L-Govt-Workforce-2012_12–195_web.pdf. Accessed August 9, 2012.

Terplan, Egon. 2012. The Urban Future of Work. *The Urbanist* (San Francisco Planning and Urban Research Assoc.) 509 (January): 8–14.

The Great Mismatch. 2011. *The Economist,* September 1.

http://www.economist.com/node/21528433/. Accessed February 6, 2012.

Towers Watson. 2012a. *Emerging Choices, Enduring Changes: Creating Service Delivery Success in a New Era of Opportunity.* http://www.towerswatson.com/assets/pdf/7805/TWH RSD-Survey2012-NA%281%29.pdf. Accessed September 13, 2012.

———. 2012b. *Perspectives. To Drive Strategic Alignment and Workforce Agility.* www.towerswatson.com. Accessed October 2, 2012.

U.S. Congressional Budget Office (CBO). 2012. *An Update to the Budget and Economic Outlook: Fiscal Years 2012–2022.* August. Washington, DC: CBO.

U.S. Census Bureau. 2012. *Statistical Abstract of the United States.* Washington, DC: U.S. Census Bureau.

U.S. Civil Service Commission. 1962. *Federal Workforce Statistics: Pay Structure of the Federal Civil Service.* March. Washington, DC: CSC.

U.S. General Accountability Office (GAO). 2008. *Centers for Disease Control and Prevention: Human Capital Planning Has Improved but Strategic View of Contractor Workforce Is Needed.* May. Washington, DC: GAO.

———. 2012. *State and Local Government's Fiscal Outlook, April 2012 Update.* April. Washington, DC: GAO.

U.S. Merit Systems Protection Board. 2011. Agency Corner: Lessons in Tweeting from NIH. *Issues of Merit,* February. http://www.mspb.gov/netsearch/viewdocs.aspx?docnu mber=578061&version=579783&application=ACROBAT. Accessed May 14, 2012.

U.S. Office of Personnel Management. 2012. Central Personnel Data File, September. www.fedscope.opm.gov.

Walker, Richard W. 2012. What Army Learned Moving to New Email System. *AOL Government,* August 21.

Weber, Max. 1946. Bureaucracy. In *Classics of Public Administration,* edited by Jay M. Shafritz and Albert C. Hyde, 44–49. Originally published in *Essays in Sociology,* edited and translated by H. H. Gerth. Oxford University Press, 1946.

Whalen, Cortney, and Mary E. Guy. 2008. Broadbanding Trends in the States. *Review of Public Personnel Administration* 4 (December): 349–366.

Winners and Losers. 2011. *The Economist,* September 10, 6–8.

Wymbs, Clifford. 2011. 21st Century Workers: How Will They Be Organized? *Technological Forecasting and Social Change* 79: 1–9.

Ziegler, Julia. 2012. NSA Hiring Reforms Serve as Model for Government. FederalNewsRadio.com, June 6. http://www.federalnewsradio.com/?nid=411&sid=2890348. Accessed June 26, 2012.

CHAPTER 27

THE CIVIL SERVICE UNDER SIEGE

Richard C. Kearney
North Carolina State University

Jerrell D. Coggburn
North Carolina State University

Taken together, the contributors to the sixth edition of *Problems and Prospects* present a rich mosaic of public human resource management's current challenges. Seven chapters set out the fundamentals and the most critical challenges of human resource management (HRM) in federal, state, and local government and in the nonprofit sector and discuss the values and constitutional principles underpinning public HRM. Traditional HRM techniques, including performance appraisal, motivation, and grievance administration, are reexamined along with newer ones including benchmarking, volunteer management, and the contracting out of HRM functions. And new as well as enduring issues are addressed including the constitutional rights of public workers, pay and benefits, emotional labor invested in their jobs by public servants, gender, diversity, and disability, the attack on public employee unions and collective bargaining, and HRM concerns with the use of social media. Two chapters are devoted to nonprofit HRM issues.

In this concluding chapter, we attempt to build on our contributors' work and take a critical look at what the changes and forces buffeting the public sector portend for the future of merit-based civil service in general and public HRM in particular.

Almost 20 years ago, Kearney and Hays (1998) wrote a controversial essay in the *Review of Public Personnel Administration* attacking the negative aspects of what had become known as "reinventing government" in the United States and the "new public management" in Europe and elsewhere, while defending the virtues of a traditional merit-based civil service. New public management (NPM) represents a global paradigm shift in public administration with important implications for HRM. Arguing that "the reinventing government movement represents a pervasive and potentially pernicious attack on bureaucracy that may ultimately undermine the professional service," Kearney and Hays (1998: 39) lamented the scapegoating of government and its workers by "those espousing anti-bureaucratic, non-statist ideologies" at the expense of professionalism and neutral competence. Hays and Kearney's article was greeted with both praise and criticism (see Van Wart 1999). We expect that this essay will receive similar mixed responses as we unburden ourselves of some gnawing concerns about the future of the public service. (A great thing about editing this book is having an opportunity to write what we really think.)

NPM's prevalent themes of decentralizing administrative authority (debureaucratization), increasing managerial flexibility (politicization), and embracing of market-based approaches to providing public services (privatization) were widely celebrated as leading components of a new wave of long-needed administrative reforms (e.g., Barzelay 1992, 2001; Kettl 2000; Light 1997; Osborne and Gaebler 1992). As Kathy Naff (Chapter 26) points out, some NPM-style reforms have been appropriate and are needed, particularly customer service improvements, productivity measurement, greater concern for outcomes, improving techniques for facilitating recruitment and hiring new workers to replace the rapidly retiring baby boom generation, and revising antiquated position classification systems to reflect the needs of the contemporary public workplace. But taken to an extreme, NPM in the U.S. puts reformist lipstick on the pig of "new-conservative efforts to eviscerate public employee unions, shrink government, and punish public servants" (Kearney and Hays 1998: 46; see also Hood 1991). Such ideological attacks on government and public service continue today.

Reinventing government and NPM have lost some currency in today's broader discussion and debate on administrative reform. However, their principal elements of debureaucratization, politicization, and privatization endure, and some concerns raised by Kearney and Hays have, if anything, become even more salient during the intervening years. One cannot deny the powerful changes occurring in the nature of work and their implications for the public workforce. The public sector must evolve, just as the private sector has, but in what direction? What sort of civil service best serves the nation and its people? One staffed by competent, qualified professionals hired based on objective criteria and granted strong job rights, one staffed by politically loyal, contracted, at-will employees, or a civil service that combines the best qualities of the two polar approaches? We elaborate on several of these concerns below.

CIVIL SERVICE DYNAMICS

Civil service systems exist to meet several purposes, including recruiting qualified workers for government jobs, rewarding and developing the public workforce, and providing rules for the public workforce to meet public objectives (Ingraham 1995). As these purposes suggest, civil service systems are directly linked to government performance (Kellough and Nigro 2005; Kellough and Selden 2003; Ingraham, 1995). Typically, civil service systems embody merit principles designed, in part, to insulate public servants from political interference and abuses and to capitalize on their professional expertise and competence (Brewer and Walker 2013; Selden 2006; Kellough and Nigro 2005). In other words, "merit" has long represented the ideal for public employment, and civil service systems have been the means to that end (Moynihan and Ingraham 2012). Since merit has been the hallmark of public HRM, we would do well to remind readers what merit means in practice. Perhaps the clearest statement of merit principles is found in Title V of the Civil Service Reform Act of 1978 (see Table 27.1).[1] In practice, merit-based civil service systems have provided public servants protection from political interference and helped facilitate the professionalization of the public sector, something that has served governments and the people quite well (Coggburn et al. 2010). As Bowman (2012: 50) puts it, "The establishment of a unified, permanent, merit-based, apolitical civil service has certainly been one of the distinctive accomplishments in United States history."

Despite their accomplishments, civil service systems have been frequently targeted for reform (Light 2006). The centralized and rule-based systems that have evolved reflect an underlying bureaucratic paradigm (Moynihan and Ingraham 2012), and bureaucracy is an easy target; after all, it has few defenders (but see Goodsell 2004). It is the nature of civil service systems to be bureaucratic, with all of the Weberian bureaucracy's virtues and problems (see Tompkins 2005: 54–57). This, in turn, has led to a familiar list of criticisms of civil service systems, including that they are inflexible, inefficient, unresponsive to political direction and citizens, and— by making it difficult both to remove poor performers and reward superior ones (Brewer and Walker 2013)— performance hindering. Reformers trumpeting NPM-inspired themes (e.g., achieving results, injecting market competition, ensuring responsiveness, and streamlining management) advocate for radical civil service reforms

Table 27.1 Merit System Principles (5 USC § 2301)

1. Recruitment should be from qualified individuals from appropriate sources in an endeavor to achieve a workforce from all segments of society, and selection and advancement should be determined solely on the basis of relative ability, knowledge and skills, after fair and open competition which assures that all receive equal opportunity.

2. All employees and applicants for employment should receive fair and equitable treatment in all aspects of personnel management without regard to political affiliation, race, color, religion, national origin, sex, marital status, age, or handicapping condition, and with proper regard for their privacy and constitutional rights.

3. Equal pay should be provided for work of equal value, with appropriate consideration of both national and local rates paid by employers in the private sector, and appropriate incentives and recognition should be provided for excellence in performance.

4. All employees should maintain high standards of integrity, conduct, and concern for the public interest.

5. The Federal workforce should be used efficiently and effectively.

6. Employees should be retained on the basis of adequacy of their performance, inadequate performance should be corrected, and employees should be separated who cannot or will not improve their performance to meet required standards.

7. Employees should be provided effective education and training in cases in which such education and training would result in better organizational and individual performance.

8. Employees should be—

    A. protected against arbitrary action, personal favoritism, or coercion for partisan political purposes, and

    B. prohibited from using their official authority or influence for the purpose of interfering with or affecting the result of an election or a nomination for election.

9. Employees should be protected against reprisal for the lawful disclosure of information which the employees reasonably believe evidences—

    A. a violation of any law, rule, or regulation, or

    B. mismanagement, a gross waste of funds, an absence of authority, or a substantial and specific danger to public health or safety.

Source: http://www.gpo.gov/fdsys/pkg/USCODE-2011-title5/html/USCODE-2011-title5-partIII-subpartA-chap23-sec2301.htm.

that debureaucratize, decentralize, and deregulate HRM decision-making authority and reflect market-based tools like pay-for-performance and outsourcing (Kellough and Nigro 2005; Kellough and Selden 2003; Selden, Ingraham, and Jacobson 2001; Condrey and Battaglio 2007). In effect, such reforms propose to improve government performance by providing greater political and managerial control over public employees and making government operations "more businesslike."

The dynamism of civil service, as witnessed by reforms either proposed or adopted, reflects the presence of competing values (Kaufman 1956, 1969; Rosenbloom 2010; Kellough and Nigro 2006; Kellough 1998). Long ago, Kaufman (1956, 1969) described how fluctuating emphasis on three sets of values—neutral competence, executive control, and representativeness—explains the content of various reforms. Scholars have since identified additional important values, including managerial, political, and legal (see Chapter 2 by Rosenbloom and Chanin); accountability and procedural fairness (Kellough 1998); and management flexibility (Kellough and Nigro 2006). As Donald Klingner (Chapter 1) points out, these shifting values have aligned with various waves of reform and eras in American civil service. Klingner's analysis describes the current era as one in which the "emergent paradigms" are privatization and partnerships.

OUTSOURCING AND PRIVATIZATION

Privatization—whether clothed in the dress of contracting out, outsourcing, vouchers, or other such attire—is designed to move traditionally public work and workers to private provider organizations. Like all such reforms, it produces winners and losers. The chief beneficiary is the business community, reaping profits from government contracts and deregulation (though nonprofit organizations win a substantial number of contracts). The political class also comes out ahead by gaining influence with private sector patrons and, in all too many instances, steering government contracts to cronies and political supporters.

Public employees and public employee unions are the direct losers. Public sector jobs are eliminated and replaced by jobs carrying less security, less compensation (both pay and benefits), and less status. Indirectly, the values of professionalism, bureaucratic accountability, neutral competence, and the merit principle itself suffer (Coggburn 2007). As Fernandez, Malatesta, and Smith (Chapter 24) point out, there are some things that employers can do to mitigate the effects on employees, thereby reducing worker resistance to outsourcing and, from an ethical perspective, demonstrating a modicum of fairness to employees (Lawther 1997). Still, public employee (individual and collective) resistance to outsourcing is indicative of the stakes facing men and women who have dedicated their careers to the service of others.

In some cases, the general public also loses, as a decentralized, downsized, politicized, and privatized public administration results in confusion over who or what is responsible for delivering "public" services and presents new opportunities for waste, fraud, and abuse by contractors (Kearney and Hays 1998: 48–49). Ironically, privatization and other elements of NPM done badly can engender some of the very same dysfunctions usually attributed to bureaucracy. Quality and levels of service delivery sometimes decline, and promised monetary savings often prove to be illusory. Privatization has become highly controversial in prisons and schools. There are several recent cases of states canceling contracts for "private prisons" and resuming public control after determining that promised cost savings were not realized and prison conditions had deteriorated. Indiana's decision to cancel a $1.34 billion IBM contract to privatize welfare services and the 2014 bankruptcy filing of the company that won a 75-year concession for operating a toll road present other instructive examples of failed privatization (Schneider and Ruthhart 2009).

Lurking beneath the surface of the privatization and outsourcing tide are important and enduring public values. With outsourcing and privatization, a premium is being placed on cost-effectiveness but at the expense of other salient values like merit, equity, and accountability. In the public sector, the means matter—or at least they have historically. We are not arguing that cost-effectiveness is not important (indeed, it is), but we are pointing out that accepting a little less efficiency and economy in preserving merit while ensuring accountability is a bargain that the public has been willing to strike (Romzek 1998).

THE ATTACK ON PUBLIC EMPLOYEES AND THEIR UNIONS

Public workers throughout the United States were major victims of the Great Recession as hard-pressed governments laid off teachers, office workers, and even police and firefighters. The ranks of public employees declined precipitously across all levels of government. According the U.S. Bureau of Labor Statistics (2013), state government employment (excluding education) in 2011 had fallen by 173,000 from its peak in August 2008 and local government employment had declined by 581,000 from its June 2008 peak. Moreover, the long-awaited baby boom exodus is fully underway, threatening to leave some public organizations without senior leadership and institutional memory.

The Great Recession brought dramatic—and decidedly negative— changes in the political and economic environments of public employee unions. They have suffered membership losses from the aforementioned layoffs and, even more damaging, frontal attacks from their enemies in business and conservative political circles. As Mareschal and Ciorici explain (Chapter 23), conservatives argue that public employees enjoy higher pay and better benefits than their private sector counterparts, thereby commanding a larger portion of public budgets than they should. However, as shown by Llorens (Chapter 11) and Calabrese and Marlowe (Chapter 13), empirical data cast significant doubt on these assertions. Nonetheless, unions and nonrepresented employees as well have been forced to accept substantial pay and benefits reductions in many state and local jurisdictions.

The conservative narrative of overpaid and underworked public employees has enabled opponents of unions and collective bargaining to win important victories in states such as Wisconsin and Michigan, where Republican governors effectively declared war on public employee collective bargaining, eventually garnering hard-fought victories that curtailed collective bargaining and clipped union-negotiated pay and benefits. Not surprisingly, the number of dues-paying union members in these and other states has declined precipitously. Unions have responded by taking up their case in ballot initiatives, litigation, and public demonstrations, but with only modest success to date. For the first time in some 50 years, public sector unions are confronting today an existential threat to their relevance and continued existence (Kearney and Mareshal 2014).

Public employees working under collective bargaining agreements have rights and responsibilities contractually delineated and enforced in the courts. For millions more who are not represented by unions, merit protections and employee rights are embodied in civil service system regulations, employment law, and constitutional safeguards. Such protections were developed and have evolved in association with the goal of insulating the public service from politicization. But union bashing has been accompanied by new employment-at-will laws, which effectively remove job protections for career public servants and replace them with at-will arrangements or fixed-term contracts (Coggburn et al. 2010; Hays and Sowa 2006).

From an HRM perspective, massive employee layoffs resulting from the ravages of the Great Recession, along with declining unions and potent threats to collective bargaining, create new problems and worsen old ones. Recruiting, motivating, and retaining a workforce in demographic and technological transition, under constant and sometimes withering criticism, present daunting challenges, including low employee morale, high rates of employee grievances and absenteeism, and increases in litigation. Forever caught in the middle between organizational leadership and rank-and-file workers, HR managers confront dilemmas and crises not of their own making. Yet their ability to serve as public sector linking pins between top management and employees has never been of greater importance.

THE SUBVERSION OF THE PUBLIC SERVICE

For more than a century, people have been attracted to government service by the promise of a secure job with good benefits and reasonable pay. For many, public service has served as a calling, providing deep meaning and engagement from their work in service of the people (Bowman 2012). Employees were encouraged to believe in their employer's mission and purpose and to aspire to "making a difference" (Crum 2012). Professional public employees were respected and frequently consulted by elected officials for their expertise and independence (Lee and Whitford 2012). Though it may seem quaint today, there was considerable support for holding government to account as a "model employer." These features helped make a government job desirable for intrinsic, and well as extrinsic, reasons (Moynihan 2010) and gave birth to the notion of a public service "ethos."

At the time of this writing, the attractions of public work appear to be dissipating from efforts to debureaucratize, politicize, and privatize government work. In the asserted interests of enhancing government performance and responsiveness to political leadership, NPM reforms have put merit systems in jeopardy of being supplanted by increased numbers of political appointees, short-term at-will employment contracts, and noncompetitive pay and reduced benefits for civil service workers. The Great Recession was a convenient excuse to cut total public employment to its lowest level in some 30 years (Greenstone and Looney 2012) and to reduce pension and health care benefits nationwide while implementing strategies to outsource work to private providers.

As noted above, political assaults on public employee unions have exacted a membership and economic toll in a growing number of collective bargaining jurisdictions. The effects of virulent and sometimes mean-spirited attacks by public officials and organized interests against public employees can be seen in recent public opinion polls on trust and confidence in government. For instance, a 2013 Pew Research Center poll found that only 28% of the people trust government in Washington "to do the right thing" (Pew 2013). Citizens indicate a much higher level of trust in their state (57%) and especially their local (63%) governments, though even here there has been a decline since 1999 (Jones, 2012; Pew 2013).

In these and other respects, public service is becoming less attractive to new labor market entrants. Take compensation, for example. In Chapter 11 of this book, Jared Llorens addresses the issue of pay comparability between the public and private sectors and its importance for recruiting and retaining a qualified public labor force. As he points out, ideological agendas have politicized the issue, with those aligned against government and public employees asserting that public workers are paid excessively generous wages and awarded retirement, health care, vacation, and other benefits far superior to those available to most private sector workers. Careful research, however, that accounts for levels of employee education as well as differences in professions and job categories, finds that the alleged pay and benefit disparities are at best overstated and at worst misleading. When workers doing comparable work are compared through a human capital approach, results show that though some public workers do enjoy pay premiums, most suffer a pay disadvantage, a disadvantage that has gotten worse, particularly in management and administrative positions (Center for State and Local Government Excellence 2011). More specifically, lower-level clerical and blue collar workers in government, and particularly in the federal sector, enjoy compensation advantages over their private sector counterparts; higher-level managers and executives in government tend to be significantly underpaid relative to private counterparts (see Kearney 2009: 164–168). Moreover, in recent years average public employee pay appears to have grown at a rate below that of average private sector pay, as the shortfalls of the Great Recession are gradually worked out of public budgets through reduced appropriations and concessionary collective bargaining settlements.

There is truth to the assertion that public employees have traditionally had retirement and health care *benefits* superior to those prevailing in the private sector. And, as pointed out by Mareschal and Ciorici (Chapter 23) and Calabrese and Marlowe (Chapter 13), unsustainable unfunded liabilities in retiree pensions and health care programs have driven many state and local governments into a condition of serious long-term financial distress. As a consequence, a growing number of legislative bodies have imposed defined contribution retirement plans on new and future employees, phasing out longstanding defined benefit plans. Legislatures have also begun to take steps to reduce employee and retiree health insurance costs by hiking premiums and copays, extending vesting periods, and implementing related dollar-saving actions. In collective bargaining jurisdictions, management pressures have resulted in significant union benefits givebacks.

If somewhat modest pay but superior benefits have acted as important inducements for high-quality employees to join the public workforce in the past, any recruitment and retention advantage is being substantially weakened. The implications for recruiting, retaining, and motivating a high-performing public workforce in the years ahead should be obvious. As a consequence, the staffing demands on HR professionals will need to adapt to what Kathy Naff (Chapter 26) terms powerful demographic forces and the subsequent "deep organizational transformation" buffeting the public sector, while searching for new tools to recruit, retain, and motivate the future public workforce.

Increased employee probationary periods, indefinite provisional and temporary appointments, reductions in force, contracting out, and the spread of employment at will are all developments that threaten public sector job security and erode the public service ethos. But there is more to the story. Limits on public employees' workplace speech following the U.S. Supreme Court's 2006 *Garcetti v. Ceballos* decision, in conjunction with the developments outlined above, mean that the current environment for many public employees is not one that encourages the internal voicing of dissent (O'Leary 2006). Even where managers and organizations embrace constructive conflict management and ostensibly encourage dissent, the incentive for public employees to speak truth to power, take creative risks, or otherwise engage in organizational controversies may be lacking. If employee-drones and downtrodden cynics come to dominate the public labor force, the potential ramifications for government performance should be obvious. The prospects would be in place for a self-fulfilling prophesy of government underperformance leading to further declines in public trust and confidence in government and diminished interest in government service (Moynihan 2010).

Should fundamental public service values be rejected like unwanted jetsam? Are merit, neutral competence, and professionalism no longer important? Will a reinvented public service be "more servile, more specialized, more responsive to political direction, yet lacking in continuity, competence, and fortitude of its predecessors" (Kearney and Hays 1998: 51)? Should positive and still-relevant public service values and methods of conducting the public's business be rejected in the name of efficiency, markets, and political control? Other questions arise: Is "the problem" an outdated, nonresponsive merit-based civil service system and poor public service provision? Is it poorly designed or outdated government employment policies and approaches to service delivery problems? Or is it politics?

PROSPECTS

Despite the rather grim patterns and trends outlined above, there are seeds of hope for reversing course and preserving the most important elements of a competent, merit-based public service. For one, evidence indicates that the public service ethos survives (Bowman 2012). Perhaps the innate desire to serve the people and "do good" will be sufficient to overcome the declining extrinsic rewards of public employment. In Chapter 26, Naff finds reason for hope in Gen Y, the so-called Millennial Generation born after 1982. Surveys indicate that Gen Y desires to make the world a better place and, in general, has a much more positive assessment of government than older generations (Pew 2013; Molyneux and Teixeira 2010). The Millennials, however, join their elders in wanting to eliminate government inefficiencies and improve performance.

More broadly, perhaps a Hegelian dialectic will bring about a "value oscillation" as described by Kaufman (1969) or a counter "tide of reform" written about by Light (2006), which will manifest in a resistance to and rejection of some of the excesses of NPM and the negative rhetoric and actions of those ideologically opposed to government. Perry and Buckwalter (2010), among others, discern signs of a revaluing of public service through a broader understanding of the legitimate role government plays in our lives and well-being, ranging from trash collection to national security.

Scholars and other researchers in public administration generally and HRM specifically can contribute much of value through studying the efficacy of NPM reforms and, through evidence-based research, determining what is worth keeping and what should be tossed into the waste bin with past fads and reforms. An important consideration for public HRM's prospects concerns the field's knowledge base. If the practice of HRM is to avoid being grounded in a rejection of traditional merit system values and practices, then a solid evidentiary base is needed (Light 2006). Too often, the rhetoric of reform drowns out careful analysis, with the result being the adoption of the wrong "solutions" to ill-defined "problems" (e.g., Colley, McCourt, and Waterhouse 2012; Light 2006). Writing in the 30th anniversary edition of the field's most prestigious journal, *Review of Public Personnel Administration,* James Perry (2010) sketches out a strategic research agenda for public HRM. His list of topics includes compensation, motivation, cultural and political context, efficacy and effectiveness, and training and development. With more time devoted to exploring what does and does not work in these topical areas, public sector HRM may be able to break free of the reform spiral where "Yesterday's reform is swept aside by today's, which will be quickly forgotten by tomorrow" (Light 2006: 17).

An example of HRM research that contradicts a key NPM principle has to do with the value of merit pay, or pay-for-performance. Research clearly demonstrates that pay-for-performance plans have a dismal track record in the public sector (Brewer and Walker 2013; Bowman's Chapter 10 in this volume) because of such problems as flawed performance appraisal systems, supervisory bias, poor performance indicators, and political unwillingness to provide a merit increase or bonus sufficient to effectively motivate would-be recipients.

For a specific example of a "keeper" NPM principle, research by Brewer and Walker (2013) is instructive. In examining both the carrot (rewards) and stick (punishment) techniques in public HRM, the authors' findings show that the inability to remove poor performers hinders performance and creates morale problems. In any organization, public, nonprofit, or private, in schools or sanitation departments, poor performers should be counseled then rooted out if they fail to bloom. So long as basic due process is ensured and relevant laws and regulations are followed, very few individuals would disagree. Yet government, as viewed through vivid but unrepresentative anecdotes, is notorious for tolerating and even protecting underperforming, incompetent, and misbehaving workers. Those who caution about the abuses of employment at will and union representation are usually not apologists for poor performers; to

the contrary, there is explicit appreciation for the fact that pruning the ranks of underperformers is important.

The focus should be on recruiting, retaining, and motivating high performers with an appropriate mix of intrinsic and extrinsic incentives (see Moynihan 2010; Crum 2012), and at the same time facilitating removal (while protecting due process rights) of chronic underperformers. But to attract the right individuals to government service, those who seek to be productive and do something worthwhile, HRM systems must be better aligned with public service values. Otherwise, there is a risk of attracting and retaining the wrong sort of worker, one motivated to pursue narrow self-interest and nonaltruistic ends.

The public service ethos will surely endure in some context—if not in government, then perhaps in segments of the nonprofit sector. Indeed, in many respects, a transformation is occurring now with the growth of nonprofit organizations charged with direct and indirect service delivery responsibilities (Moynihan and Ingraham 2012; Mesch 2010). Recent research by Park and Perry (2013) finds that whereas government and private employee attitudes about government size, spending, and scope are trending similarly, nonprofit workers tend to favor a larger and more expansive role for government. Should the patterns we lament continue, the nonprofit sector may become the primary reservoir for those who subscribe to the public service ethos.

We conclude by returning to the theme of continual reform. Similar to Newton's laws of motion, every administrative action seems to generate an equal and opposite reaction. And so, contemporary reformers are unwittingly planting the seeds for the next round of reform. The arguments made in support of this inevitable next wave will very likely have a familiar ring to students of public administration and public HRM. We can well imagine that discussion will turn, in the not-too-distant future, to the need to restore the professional public service, root out political influence (e.g., inexperienced appointees, overresponsiveness to political control), and again embrace the notion that governments should be model employers. A public service staffed by committed professionals, responsive to the needs and wishes of the public (both directly and through their elected representatives), possessed of technical and substantive expertise, and pursuing the public interest will be a welcome reaction to the current fixation on debureaucratization, politicization, and privatization.

NOTE

1. Title V also includes a statement of "prohibited personnel practices," which applies to any federal employee with human resources decision-making authority. A summary of these prohibited practices can be found on the U.S. Merit Systems Protection Board's webpage (http://www.osc.gov/pppwhatare.htm).

REFERENCES

Barzelay, M. 2001. *The new public management.* Berkeley: University of California Press.

Barzelay, M., with Armajani, B. J. 1992. *Breaking through bureaucracy.* Berkeley: University of California Press.

Bowman, J. S. 2012. Public service as a calling: Reflections, retreat, revival, resolve. *Journal of Workplace Rights, 16*(1), 47–61.

Brewer, G. A., and Walker, R. M. 2013. Personnel constraints in public organizations: The impact of reward and punishment on organizational performance. *Public Administration Review, 73*(1), 121–131.

Center for State and Local Government Excellence. 2011. *Comparing compensation: State-local versus private sector workers.* www.slge.org.

Coggburn, J. D. 2007. Outsourcing human resources: The case of the Texas Health and Human Services Commission. *Review of Public Personnel Administration, 27*(4), 315–335.

Coggburn, J. D., Battaglio, R. P., Jr., Bowman, J. S., Condrey, S. E., Goodman, D., and West, J. P. 2010. State government human resource professionals' commitment to employment at will. *American Review of Public Administration, 40*(2), 189–208.

Colley, L., McCourt, W., and Waterhouse, J. 2012. Hybrids and contradictions: Human resource management in the contemporary public sector. *International Journal of Public Administration, 35*(8), 507–512.

Condrey, S. E., and Battaglio, R. P., Jr. 2007. A return to spoils? Revisiting radical civil service reform in the United States. *Public Administration Review, 67*(3), 424–436.

Crum, J. 2012. A look back to look forward. *Issues of Merit, 17*(3), 2–3. Office of Policy and Evaluation, U.S. Merit Systems Protection Board, Washington, DC.

Goodsell, C. T. 2004. *The case for bureaucracy,* 4th ed. Washington, DC: CQ Press.

Greenstone, M., and Looney, A. 2012. *A record decline in government jobs: Implications for the economy and America's workforce.* Brookings, August 12. www.brookings.edu.

Hays, S. W., and Sowa, J. E. 2006. A broader look at the 'accountability' movement: Some grim realities. *Review of Public Personnel Administration, 26*(2), 102–117.

Hood, C. 1991. A public management for all seasons? *Public Administration, 69*(1), 3–19.

Ingraham, P. W. 1995. *The foundation of merit: Public service in American democracy.* Baltimore: The Johns Hopkins University Press.

Jones, J. M. 2012. In U.S., trust in state, local government up. www.gallup.com/poll/1157700/trust-state-local-government.

Kaufman, H. 1956. Emerging conflicts in the doctrines of public administration. *American Political Science Review, 50*(4), 1057–1073.

———. 1969. Administrative decentralization and political power. *Public Administration Review, 29*(1), 3–15.

Kearney, R. C. 2009. *Labor relations in the public sector,* 4th ed. New York: CRC Press.

Kearney, R. C., and S. W. Hays. 1998. Reinventing government, the new public management and civil service systems in international perspective. *Review of Public Personnel Administration, 18*(4), 38–54.

Kearney, R. C., and Mareshal, P. M. 2014. *Labor relations in the public sector,* 5th ed. New York: CRC Press.

Kellough, J. E. 1998. The reinventing government movement: A review and critique. *Public Administration Quarterly, 22*(1), 6–20.

Kellough, J. E., and Nigro, L. G. 2005. Dramatic reform in the public service: At-will employment and the creation of a new public workforce. *Journal of Public Administration Research and Theory, 16*(3), 447–466.

Kellough, J. E., and Nigro, L. G. (Eds.). 2006. *Civil service reform in the states: Personnel policy and politics at the subnational level.* Albany, NY: SUNY Press.

Kellough, J. E., and Selden, S. C. 2003. The reinvention of public personnel administration: An analysis of the diffusion of personnel management reforms in the states. *Public Administration Review, 63*(2), 165–176.

Kettl, D. F. 2000. *The global management revolution.* Washington, DC: Brookings.

Kim, J. 2010. Strategic human resource practices: Introducing alternatives for organizational performance improvement in the public sector. *Public Administration Review, 70*(1), 38–49.

Lawther, W. C. 1997. The role of public employees in the privatization process: Personnel and transition issues. *Review of Public Personnel Administration, 19*(1), 28–40.

Lee, S., and Whitford, A. B. 2012. Assessing the effects of organizational resources on public agency performance: Evidence from the US federal government. *Journal of Public Administration Research and Theory, 18*(4), 647–671.

Light, P. 1997. *The tides of reform: Making government work, 1945–1995*. New Haven, CT: Yale University Press.

———. 2006. The tides of reform revisited: Patterns in making government work, 1945–2002. *Public Administration Review, 66*(1), 6–19.

Mahler, J. 2012. The telework divide: Managerial and personnel challenges of telework. *Review of Public Personnel Administration, 32*(4), 407–418.

Mesch, D. J. 2010. Management of human resources in 2020: The outlook for nonprofit organizations. *Public Administration Review, 70*(s1), 173–174.

Molyneux, G., and Teixeira, R 2010. *The generation gap on government*. Center for American Progress. www.americanprogress.org.

Moynihan, D. P. 2010. A workforce of cynics? The effects of contemporary reforms on public service motivation. *International Public Management Journal, 13*(1), 24–34.

Moynihan, D. P, and Ingraham, P. W. 2012. The suspect handmaiden: The evolution of politics and administration in the American state. *Public Administration Review, 70*(s1), 229–237.

O'Leary, R. 2006. *The ethics of dissent*. Washington, DC: CQ Press.

Osborne, D., and Gaebler, T. 1992. *Reinventing government*. Reading, MA: Addison-Wesley.

Park, H. M, and Perry, J. L. 2013. The transformation of governance: Who are the new public servants and what difference does it make for democratic governance? *American Review of Public Administration, 43*(1), 26–49.

Perry, J. L. 2010. A strategic agenda for public human resource management research. *Review of Public Personnel Management, 30*(1), 20–43.

Perry, J. L., and Buckwalter, N. D. 2010. The public service of the future. *Public Administration Review, 70*(s1), 238–245.

Pew Research Center. 2013. *Majority says the federal government threatens their personal rights*. Washington, DC: Brookings.

Price, B. E. *Merchandising prisoners: Who really pays for prison privatization?* Westport, CT: Praeger.

Romzek, B. S. 1998. Where the buck stops: Accountability in reformed public organizations. In P. W. Ingraham, J. R. Thompson, and R. P. Sanders (Eds.), *Transforming government: Lessons from the reinvention laboratories*. San Francisco: Jossey-Bass.

Rosenbloom, D. H. 2010. Public sector human resource management in 2020. *Public Administration Review, 70*(s1), 175–176.

Schneider, M. B., and B. Ruthhart. 2009. Indiana axes welfare contract with IBM. *Indianapolis Star*, October 16. http://www.indystar.com/article/20091016/NEWS05/910160379/Indiana+axes+welfare+contract+with+IBM.

Selden, S. C. 2006. The impact of discipline on the use and rapidity of dismissal in state governments. *Review of Public Personnel Administration, 26*(4), 335–355.

Selden, S. C., Ingraham, P. W., and Jacobson, W. 2001. Human resource practices in state government: Findings from a national survey. *Public Administration Review, 61*(5), 598–607.

Tompkins, J. R. 2005. *Organization theory and public management*. Belmont, CA: Wadsworth, 53–57.

U.S. Bureau of Labor Statistics. 2013. Current Employment Statistics Highlights: February 2013. www.bls.gov/web/empsit/ceshighlights.pdf.

Van Wart, M. 1999. Is making any fundamental change in the civil service dangerous? *Review of Public Personnel Administration, 19*(1), 71–76.

INDEX

ABOUT THE EDITORS

RICHARD C. KEARNEY is professor (retired) of public administration in the School of Public and International Affairs at North Carolina State University. He has also served in faculty and administrative roles at East Carolina University, the University of Connecticut, and the University of South Carolina. His published research embraces public human resource management and labor relations, state and local politics and policy, and US federalism. He is the coauthor of *Labor Relations in the Public Sector*, 5th ed. (CRC Press, 2014) and coauthor of *State and Local Government*, 9th ed. (Cengage, 2014). rick_kearney@ncsu.edu

JERRELL D. COGGBURN is professor, chair, and director of graduate programs of public administration in North Carolina State University's School of Public and International Affairs (SPIA). His main research interests are in public human resource management, civil service reform, and public management. His research has been recognized with the 2010 Best Article Award from the *American Review of Public Administration* and the 1998 William E. and Frederick C. Mosher Award for the best *Public Administration Review* article written by an academician. His research has appeared in *Public Administration Review, Journal of Public Administration Research and Theory, Review of Public Personnel Administration, American Review of Public Administration, Public Performance & Management Review*, and other scholarly outlets. He received a BA in political science from Oklahoma State University and the MPA and PhD degrees from the University of South Carolina. jcoggburn@ncsu.edu

ABOUT THE AUTHORS

DAVID N. AMMONS is Albert Coates Professor of Public Administration and Government at the University of North Carolina at Chapel Hill. He writes and teaches about performance measurement, benchmarking, and productivity improvement in local government. His books on local government management include *Municipal Benchmarks* (M.E. Sharpe, 2012), *Tools for Decision Making: A Practical Guide for Local Government* (CQ Press, 2009), and *Leading Performance Management in Local Government* (ICMA, 2008). He was elected as a fellow of the National Academy of Public Administration in 2006 and served on the National Performance Management Advisory Commission. Ammons earned a PhD from the University of Oklahoma. ammons@sog.unc.edu

JAMES S. BOWMAN is professor of public administration at the Askew School of Public Administration and Policy, Florida State University. Noted for his work in ethics and human resource management, he has also published in quality management and environmental administration literatures. Dr. Bowman is author of over 100 journal articles and book chapters. He is coauthor of the prize-winning *Human Resource Management in Public Service: Paradoxes, Processes and Problems,* 5th ed. (Sage, 2015) and *The Professional Edge: Competencies in Public Service,* 2nd ed. (M.E. Sharpe, 2010). His most recent book, with Jonathan P. West, is *Public Service Ethics: Individual and Institutional Responsibilities* (CQ Press, 2015). He has also edited six anthologies.

Bowman served as the inaugural editor-in-chief of *Public Integrity* (1995–2014), an American Society for Public Administration journal cosponsored by three other professional associations. A past National Association of Schools of Public Affairs and Administration Fellow, as well as a Kellogg Foundation Fellow, he has experience in the military, civil service, and business. jbowman@fsu.edu

LAUREN BOWMAN is a PhD candidate in the Department of Public Administration at the University of Illinois at Chicago. Her dissertation is entitled *Work-Life Balance Policies in the Federal Government: What Factors Are Related to Use?* Her research focuses on gender and administration as well as public organizations and public management. lbowma3@uic.edu

JEFFREY L. BRUDNEY is the Betty and Dan Cameron Family Distinguished Professor of Innovation in the Nonprofit Sector at the University of North Carolina, Wilmington. Dr. Brudney is the faculty director of Quality Enhancement for Nonprofit Organizations (QENO), a university-community partnership to build the capacity of nonprofit organizations and increase philanthropy in southeastern North Carolina. The Urban Institute calls him "the foremost research expert on volunteer management programs and community volunteer centers in the United States." Dr. Brudney is the editor-in-chief of *Nonprofit and Voluntary Sector Quarterly*, the premier journal in nonprofit sector studies. He is the author of *Fostering*

Volunteer Programs in the Public Sector: Planning, Initiating, and Managing Voluntary Activities, which received the John Grenzebach Award for Outstanding Research in Philanthropy for Education, and many other publications. Dr. Brudney serves on the United Nations Volunteers Programme Technical Advisory Board on the *State of the World's Volunteerism Report*. brudneyj@uncw.edu

THAD CALABRESE is assistant professor of public and nonprofit financial management at the Robert F. Wagner Graduate School of Public Service at New York University. His research focuses on public pensions, nonprofit debt management, government contracting with nonprofit organizations, and evaluating and sustaining nonprofit financial conditions. He has also coauthored two textbooks, *Financial Management for Public, Health, and Not-for-Profit Organizations*, 4th ed. (Prentice Hall, 2013) and *Accounting Fundamentals for Health Care Management*, 2nd ed. (Jones & Bartlett, 2011). Thad. Calabrese@baruch.cuny.edu

JOSHUA CHANIN is assistant professor in the School of Public Affairs at San Diego State University. His scholarly interests lie at the intersection of law, criminal justice, and governance. Current research examines the US Department of Justice's "pattern or practice" initiative, with a focus on the implementation and sustainability of federal efforts to remedy systematic misconduct among state and local police departments. Trained as a lawyer, Josh has also written about the effects of constitutional law on government agencies and the administration of public programs. He coauthored the 2010 volume *Public Administration and Law*, 3rd ed. (with David Rosenbloom and Rosemary O'Leary) and has been published recently in *Administration & Society* and *Public Administration Review*. He received his JD from Indiana University in 2005 and his PhD from American University in 2011. jchanin@mail.sdsu.edu

PATRICIA CIORICI is a PhD candidate in the Department of Public Policy and Administration at Rutgers University. Her dissertation research focuses on municipal international relations and development cooperation. Her other research interests include public sector labor relations, labor unions, and conflict resolution in labor relations. She served as a legal and policy specialist on the USAID-funded Moldova Local Government Reform Project, developed and implemented the Community and Economic Development through Education and Action Project to support youth engagement in community development in Moldova. She also conducted research for several community development organizations in the US. Patricia holds an MPP degree from the Humphrey School of Public Affairs, University of Minnesota, and a law degree from Moldova State University.

TRENTON J. DAVIS is associate professor and director of the Institute for Public and Nonprofit Studies at Georgia Southern University. His research focuses on employee motivation, organizational change, compensation systems, and small group behavior. His work has appeared in the *Review of Public Personnel Administration*, *State and Local Government Review*, and *Nonprofit Management and Leadership* and a variety of other journals. tjdavis@georgiasouthern.edu

REX L. FACER II received his PhD at the University of Georgia. He is associate professor of public finance and management in the Romney Institute of Public Management at Brigham Young University's Marriott School of Management where he teaches in the Master of Public Administration program. Professor Facer recently completed a three-year term on the Commission on Peer Review and Accreditation, including serving as chair for the last year. The commission is the accrediting body for master's degree programs in public administration. Facer has served as a member of the United States Federal Salary Council since October 2010. He regularly lectures and consults nationally and internationally on human resource management and local public finance issues. His published research has appeared in leading peer-reviewed journals. This research has addressed municipal annexation, budget and personnel reform, public service motivation, infrastructure financing, and alternative work schedules. His current research focuses on public sector compensation practices, alternative work schedules, and local government finance. rfacer@byu.edu

SERGIO FERNANDEZ is associate professor in Indiana University's School of Public and Environmental Affairs (IU SPEA). His research focuses on government outsourcing and procurement, leadership, organizational change, and employee empowerment. He serves as IU SPEA's director of the PhD in public affairs and joint PhD in public policy programs. sefernan@indiana.edu

GERALD T. GABRIS is a Distinguished Teaching Professor with the Department of Public Administration and also a senior research scholar with the Center for Governmental Studies, Northern Illinois University. Dr. Gabris is a former managing editor of *Public Administration Review* and has published broadly on various topics in public human resources management. His most recent research and publications focus on the topic of governing board effectiveness. ggabris@niu.edu

BETH GAZLEY is associate professor in the School of Public and Environmental Affairs at Indiana University–Bloomington. Her research addresses volunteerism, governance, management capacity, and organizational collaboration in nonprofit and governmental settings. She has earned teaching and research awards from the Academy of Management, the Indiana University Board of Trustees, and ARNOVA, and she serves on the board of editors of *Nonprofit and Voluntary Sector Quarterly, Public Administration Review,* and *Nonprofit Management and Leadership*. Before entering academia, she had a sixteen-year fundraising and consulting career in the public and private sectors. For publication detail, go to http://www.iu.edu/~speaweb/faculty/gazley.php.bgazley @indiana.edu

HEATHER GETHA-TAYLOR is assistant professor in the School of Public Affairs and Administration at the University of Kansas. Her research and teaching interests include human resource management, collaborative governance, and public service leadership. Her work has appeared in edited volumes and journals, including *Review of Public Personnel Administration* and *Public Performance and Management Review.* In 2012, her training evaluation project with the City of Olathe received the Best Practices Award from the American Society of Training and Development (Kansas City Chapter). She is a graduate of the Maxwell School of Citizenship and Public Affairs, Syracuse University (PhD) and the University of Georgia (MPA). hgtaylor@ku.edu

MARY E. GUY is professor of public administration in the School of Public Affairs at the University of Colorado, Denver. Her teaching and research focus on the human processes involved in public service delivery. Her recent work focuses on the emotive aspects of the service relationship between public officials and citizens. She is a fellow of the National Academy of Public Administration and past president of the American Society for Public Administration. Mary.Guy@ucdenver.edu

ALBERT HYDE is currently a lecturer and adjunct faculty at San Francisco State University's Public Administration Program with the School of Public Affairs and Civic Engagement. He was a senior consultant at the Brookings Institution in Washington, DC, from 1992 to 2008 where he directed strategy and innovation consulting projects with federal agencies. He is coeditor of *Classics of Public Administration,* now in its 7th edition (Cengage, 2011). Achyde@aol.com

WILLOW S. JACOBSON is associate professor of public administration and government at the School of Government at the University of North Carolina at Chapel Hill. Her research interests include strategic human resource management, leadership, and organizational performance. Her work has appeared in the *Journal of Public Administration Research and Theory, Public Administration Review,* and the *Review of Public Personnel Administration*. She holds a PhD from the Maxwell School at Syracuse University. jacobson@sog.unc.edu

J. EDWARD KELLOUGH is professor in the Department of Public Administration and Policy at the University of Georgia. Dr. Kellough specializes in public personnel management, public administration, and program evaluation. Recent books include *The New Public Personnel Administration*, 7th ed., with Lloyd G. Nigro (Wadsworth, Cengage Learning, 2014); *Understanding Affirmative Action: Politics, Discrimination, and the Search for Justice* (Georgetown University Press, 2007); and *Civil Service Reform in the States: Personnel Policy and Politics at the Sub-National Level*, edited with Lloyd G. Nigro (State University of New York Press, 2006). His research has appeared also in numerous academic journals. kellough@uga.edu

DONALD KLINGNER is a University of Colorado Distinguished Professor in the School of Public Affairs and MPA program director at the University of Colorado Colorado Springs. He is an elected fellow of the National Academy of Public Administration (NAPA) and a past president of the American Society for Public Administration (ASPA). He is coauthor of *Public Personnel Management*, 6th ed. (Pearson, 2010), also published in Spanish and Chinese. He has been a Fulbright Senior Scholar (Central America 1994), a visiting professor at UNAM, Mexico (1999–2003), and a consultant to the United Nations, the World Bank, and the Interamerican Development Bank on public management capacity building. He was a faculty member at IUPUI (1974–1980) and Florida International University (1980–2001). Prior to earning a PhD in public administration from the University of Southern California in 1974, he worked for the US government's central personnel agency (US Civil Service Commission, 1968–1973). dklingne@uccs.edu

GREGORY B. LEWIS is professor and chair of the Department of Public Management and Policy in the Andrew Young School of Policy Studies at Georgia State University. A fellow of the National Academy of Public Administration, he has recently received awards from the American Society for Public Administration and the Network of Schools of Public Policy, Affairs, and Administration for his contributions to research on public administration. His research focuses on career patterns in the public service and on diversity issues more broadly. glewis@gsu.edu

JARED J. LLORENS is associate professor in the Public Administration Institute at Louisiana State University. His research interests include public human resources management, compensation, and civil service reform. He received his PhD in public administration from the University of Georgia in 2007 and is a former human resources specialist with the US federal government. jared1@lsu.edu

DEANNA MALATESTA is associate professor in the School of Public and Environmental Affairs at Indiana University–Purdue University, Indianapolis. She has published numerous works on contracting, public management, and governance. dmalates@iupui.edu

BONNIE G. MANI earned both master of public administration and PhD at Virginia Commonwealth University. She worked for the Internal Revenue Service from 1973 to 1993. There she served in various administrative positions including training and development branch chief, customer service coordinator, and internal management development consultant. She joined the East Carolina University faculty in 1992. Since then she has published articles in *Public Administration Review, American Review of Public Administration, Public Personnel Management, Southeastern Political Review, Gender Issues*, and *Sage Open*. Also, several of her articles were published in the *International Encyclopedia of Public Policy and Administration*. She has published two books: *Women, Power, and Political Change* and *Women, Men, and Human Capital Development in the Public Sector: Return on Investments*. Her teaching and research interests include American national government, women and public policy, and human resources management. manib@ecu.edu

PATRICE M. MARESCHAL is associate professor in the Department of Public Policy and Administration, Rutgers University. Her research and teaching interests include: conflict resolution, personnel/labor relations, labor unions/organizing, and public policy. In addition to her academic training, Dr. Mareschal has extensive professional work experience in organizational consulting, human resource management, training and development, and labor-management relations. She has worked for both public and private sector employers including the National Labor Relations Board, Ford Motor Company, and Andersen Consulting. marescha@camden.rutgers.edu

JUSTIN MARLOWE is Endowed Professor of Public Finance and Civic Engagement at the Daniel J. Evans School of Public Affairs at the University of Washington. He is also a senior fellow at the *GOVERNING* Institute. His research and teaching are focused on public financial management, with particular interests in public capital markets, financial reporting, pensions and OPEB, and public-private partnerships. He is author or editor of three books and more than fifty scholarly articles, book chapters, and technical reports. He also writes an occasional column for *Governing* magazine. Prior to academia, Marlowe worked in local government in Michigan. He holds a PhD and MA from the University of Wisconsin–Milwaukee and BS and MPA degrees from Northern Michigan University. jmarlowe@u.washington.edu

SHARON H. MASTRACCI is associate professor at the University of Utah. In 2014-15 she was in residence at the University of Birmingham (UK) as a Fulbright Scholar to the United Kingdom. There, she continued her research on emotional labor in public service, expanding that work to incorporate a comparative approach. She has written on emotional labor in public service, gender, and images of public service in popular culture.

KATHERINE C. NAFF is professor emerita of public administration at San Francisco State University. Prior to joining the faculty at SFSU, she was a senior research analyst with the US Merit Systems Protection Board in Washington, DC. Her teaching specialties include human resource management, public law, and diversity issues in public administration. Her research interests include the impact of the Supreme Court on public policy and the theory of representative bureaucracy as implemented in the US and South Africa. Dr. Naff is lead author of *Personnel Management in Government: Politics and Process,* 7th ed. (CRC Press, 2014). kcnaff@sfsu.edu

MEREDITH A. NEWMAN is vice provost for faculty and global affairs and professor of public administration at Florida International University. Dr. Newman joined FIU as director of the School of Public Administration in 2006, after serving three years as chair of the Department of Public Administration, University of Illinois at Springfield, and nine years as a member of the public affairs faculty at Washington State University, Vancouver. Prior to her career in academia, Newman served with the Australian Foreign Service (in France and Vietnam), the US Department of State (in Senegal, Malaysia, and Singapore), and the World Bank. She is widely published in the areas of public management, human resources, and the emotive aspects of work. Dr. Newman is past chair of the Commission on Peer Review and Accreditation, Network of Schools of Public Policy, Affairs, and Administration; past vice-president for North America, the International Association of Schools and Institutes of Administration; past president of the American Society for Public Administration; and a fellow of the National Academy of Public Administration. newmanm@fiu.edu

JOAN E. PYNES is professor of public administration at the University of South Florida. She is the author or coauthor of four books including, most recently, *Human Resources Management for Public and Nonprofit Organizations*: *A Strategic Approach*, 4th ed. (Jossey-Bass, 2013), coauthor of *Human Resources Management for Health Care Organizations*: *A Strategic Approach* (Jossey-Bass, 2012), and *Effective Nonprofit Management: Context and Environment* (M.E. Sharpe, 2012). She is the author or coauthor of more than fifty academic articles, book chapters, technical reports, and encyclopedia entries about public and nonprofit human resources management. pynes@cas.usf.edu

DAVID H. ROSENBLOOM, Distinguished Professor of Public Administration at American University in Washington, DC, researches public administration and democratic-constitutionalism. He received the 2012 Leslie Whittington Award for Excellence in Teaching, 2001 Gaus Award for Exemplary Scholarship in the Joint Tradition of Political Science and Public Administration, and 1999 Waldo Award for Outstanding Contributions to the Literature and Leadership of Public Administration through an Extended Career. He is author or coauthor of more than 300 professional publications, including *Public Administration: Understanding Management, Politics, and Law in the Public Sector*, which was voted the fifth most influential book in public administration published from 1990 to 2010. Rosenbloom is known for his three perspectives model that views public administration through the lenses of management, politics/policy, and law. His public service includes appointment to the Clinton-Gore Presidential Transition Team for the Office of Personnel Management in 1992 and expert testimony on public administrative matters at Senate committee hearings. rbloom@american.edu

ROB SEIDNER is on the career staff in the Executive Office of the President of the United States' Office of Management and Budget where he specializes in human capital policy. He completed his Presidential Management Fellowship at the US Office of Personnel Management and has served in a variety of federal human capital policy positions. He earned his MBA from Brandeis University's Heller School for Social Policy and Management as well as his BA from Brandeis University. Rob published more than a half-dozen articles and chapters while he was working on a PhD. rbseidner@juno.com

SALLY SELDEN is associate dean of academic affairs and professor of management and educational leadership at Lynchburg College. She holds the Senior Professional in Human Resources (SPHR) certification, and her primary teaching interests are in the areas of public and nonprofit management, human resource management, and leadership. Dr. Selden is a fellow in the National Academy of Public Administration and author of *Human Capital: Tools and Strategies for the Public Sector* (CQ Press, 2009), which was named the 2010 best book by the Personnel and Labor Relations section of the American Society of Public Administration. Her work has appeared in publications such as *Personnel Review, Human Resource Development Quarterly, American Journal of Political Science, Administration and Society, Review of Public Personnel Administration, Public Administration Review,* and *Journal of Public Administration Research and Theory.* Professor Selden serves on the editorial boards of *Journal of Public Administration Research, Administration and Society and Theory,* and *Journal of Public Affairs Education.* selden@lynchburg.edu

CRAIG R. SMITH is associate professor of public administration and policy in the School of Government and Public Policy at the University of Arizona. His research focuses on urban affairs, public sector contracting, and interorganizational collaboration. He studies the emergence and evolution of cooperation and collaboration between organizations across sectoral boundaries, particularly under conditions of uncertainty. He has published in the *Journal of Public Administration Research and Theory,* the *Journal of Policy Analysis and Management, Public Administration Review, Urban Affairs Review,* and the *Review of Public Personnel Administration.* crsmith@email.arizona.edu

JESSICA E. SOWA is associate professor of public administration at the School of Public Affairs at the University of Colorado, Denver. Her research and teaching focuses on public and nonprofit management, including human resource management, leadership, organizational effectiveness, and interagency collaboration. Her current research focuses on high-performance work systems in nonprofit organizations. Her research has appeared in such journals as *Review of Public*

Personnel Administration, Public Personnel Management, Public Administration Review, and the *Journal of Public Administration Research and Theory.* jessica.sowa@ucdenver.edu

JAMES R. THOMPSON is associate professor of public administration at the University of Illinois at Chicago. He is interested in issues of organizational change and reform in the public sector. He also does research on the civil service, civil service reform, and human resource management. Recent publications include "Toward 'Flexible Uniformity'? Civil Service Reform, 'Big Government Conservatism,' and the Promise of the Intelligence Community Model" (*Review of Public Personnel Administration,* 2010) and "Personnel Demonstration Projects and Human Resource Management Innovation" (*Review of Public Personnel Administration,* 2008). Professor Thompson has written several human resource management–related reports for the IBM Center for the Business of Government including "Federated Human Resource Management" in the *Federal Government: The Intelligence Community Model* (2009) and *Designing and Implementing Performance-Oriented Payband Systems* (2007). In 2007, the Partnership for Public Service published Professor Thompson's report on *Training Supervisors to Be Leaders: The Missing Element in Efforts to Improve Federal Performance.* jthomp@uic.edu

SHANNON TUFTS is assistant professor and director of the Center of Public Technology at the School of Government at the University of North Carolina at Chapel Hill. She designed and implemented the first local government Chief Information Officers Certification program in the nation and continues to run CIO certification programs for local and state government IT professionals. She created a National Certified Government Chief Information Officer program in 2007 in order to serve the growing needs of public sector IT professionals across the nation. Tufts has taught numerous courses on public sector information systems across the US, including IT investment strategies, embracing technology, project management, and stakeholder engagement in technology-enabled government. She serves on several federal, state, and local government committees to promote the effective use of technology in the public sector. Her scholarly interests include information technology planning, electronic government, survey methodology, wireless technologies, and business process reengineering. Her publications in the area of e-government and public sector information technology include *Humanizing IT: Advice from the Experts* with G. David Garson, numerous book chapters, and articles in *Social Sciences Computer Review and Popular Government.* Tufts holds a BA from UNC-Chapel Hill, an MPA from UNC-Charlotte, and a PhD in public administration with a concentration in public sector information systems from North Carolina State University. tufts@sog.unc.edu

FREDERIK UYS is professor at the School of Public Leadership at the University of Stellenbosch in South Africa. He is the author of numerous articles on public management innovation and performance theory including the recent "Architectural Management: An Alternative Approach to Public Management," published in *Administratio Publica,* December 2011. frederik.uys@spl.sun.ac.za

LORI L. WADSWORTH is associate professor in the Romney Institute of Public Management at Brigham Young University. Her research focuses on work-family interaction, particularly how organizations can assist employees in balancing their work and family life. Within this general theme, her research includes flexible benefits, alternative work schedules, social support, mentoring, and ethical behavior in the workplace. Her research has been published in *Public Administration Review, Review of Public Personnel Administration, Connecticut Law Review, Journal of Family and Economic Issues,* and *Journal of Managerial Issues.* She teaches human resource management and ethics in management. She received her PhD from the University of Utah. lori_wadsworth@byu.edu

JONATHAN P. WEST is professor and chair of political science and director of the Graduate Public Administration Program at the University of Miami. His research interests include human resource management, productivity, local government, and ethics. He has published nine books and more than 100 scholarly articles and book chapters. *Public Service Ethics: Individual and Institutional Responsibility* (2014), *Achieving Competencies in Public Service: The Professional Edge* (2010, 2nd ed.), *American Public Service: Radical Reform of the Merit System* (2007), and *The Ethics Edge* (2006, 2nd ed.) are his most recent coauthored or coedited books. His coauthored book titled *American Politics and the Environment* will be published in 2015 (2nd ed.). He served for sixteen years as managing editor of Public Integrity and is a member of the editorial board of three other professional journals. He has experience as a management analyst working for the Office of the Surgeon General, Department of the Army. jwest@miami.edu

CQ Press, an imprint of SAGE, is the leading publisher of books, periodicals, and electronic products on American government and international affairs. CQ Press consistently ranks among the top commercial publishers in terms of quality, as evidenced by the numerous awards its products have won over the years. CQ Press owes its existence to Nelson Poynter, former publisher of the *St. Petersburg Times*, and his wife Henrietta, with whom he founded *Congressional Quarterly* in 1945. Poynter established CQ with the mission of promoting democracy through education and in 1975 founded the Modern Media Institute, renamed The Poynter Institute for Media Studies after his death. The Poynter Institute (*www.poynter.org*) is a nonprofit organization dedicated to training journalists and media leaders.

In 2008, CQ Press was acquired by SAGE, a leading international publisher of journals, books, and electronic media for academic, educational, and professional markets. Since 1965, SAGE has helped inform and educate a global community of scholars, practitioners, researchers, and students spanning a wide range of subject areas, including business, humanities, social sciences, and science, technology, and medicine. A privately owned corporation, SAGE has offices in Los Angeles, London, New Delhi, and Singapore, in addition to the Washington DC office of CQ Press.